WALDEN

GARLAND REFERENCE LIBRARY
OF THE HUMANITIES
(VOL. 557)

WALDEN
A Concordance

Marlene A. Ogden
Clifton Keller

GARLAND PUBLISHING, INC. · NEW YORK & LONDON
1985

Library of Congress Cataloging in Publication Data

Ogden, Marlene A.
Walden, a concordance.

(Garland reference library of the humanities ;
vol.557)
1. Thoreau, Henry David, 1817–1862. Walden—Con-
cordances. I. Keller, Clifton. II. Thoreau, Henry
David, 1817–1862. Walden. III. Title. IV. Series:
Garland reference library of the humanities ; v. 557.
PS3048.035   1985   818'.303   84-48402
ISBN 0-8240-8786-0-(alk. paper)

Printed on acid-free, 250-year-life paper
Manufactured in the United States of America

CONTENTS

PREFACE

Thoreau, while actively trying to work out the full significance of his Walden experience, wrote:

> But why I changed? why I left the woods? I do not think that I can tell. I have often wished myself back. I do not know any better how I ever came to go there. Perhaps it is none of my business, even if it is yours. Perhaps I wanted a change. There was a little stagnation, it may be. . . . Perhaps if I lived there much longer, I might live there forever. One would think twice before he accepted heaven on such terms. . . . I must say that I do not know what made me leave the pond. I left it as unaccountably as I went to it. To speak sincerely, I went there because I had got ready to go; I left it for the same reason.

In a similar way, we felt the time was right for making public a complete word concordance of the Princeton version of Thoreau's *Walden*. We asked ourselves, "Why should we create another word concordance if our efforts will be made insignificant by computers in the near future?" Soon a high school student will be able to duplicate our efforts with a touch of a few keys on his home computer's keyboard. In addition to making the work of others more efficient, it is our desire that publication of this work will widen the "circle" of events to bring about profitable interactions to an increased number of participants. We look forward to the day when computer availability and protection schemes are adequate to provide "touch of a button" access. While the day of instant access may call to a halt publication of works of this type, it will initiate new "circles" of interaction to enrich mankind.

As with most such insignificant events of life, it has been a very important, worthwhile, and happy experience. Our lives are far richer because we have worked together with Steve Young, Scott Moncrieff, Marion Jones, and Rusty Gregston. Steve Young and Scott Moncrieff copied *Walden* into Andrews University's Xerox Sigma Six. Marion Jones and Rusty Gregston painstakingly compared computer printout to the Princeton edition and corrected typographical errors. Steve Timm made major changes to our computer programs and to him we are particularly indebted. We greatly appreciated suggestions made by Michael Preston, Gary Kuris, and Elizabeth Witherell. To trace the "circles" of interaction becomes too complex to follow. To all who have had a direct part, we express our gratitude. To those who have been our students and teachers, we are indebted.

If for some reason this publication does not meet your needs, we will be happy to assist you in any way we can.

FOREWORD

Henry David Thoreau holds a place among the few authors of the world who never go out of style. His works and his philosophy continue to impress and affect new generations in much the same way that they did previous ones. Of all his works, the one that people return to most is the book *Walden*. *Walden* has something for everyone.

English majors study it for its literary value as part of the Transcendentalist movement. Biologists enjoy it for its descriptions of New England plant and animal life. Countless political scientists have found in it a philosophy for political action, while historians find a record of a previous political and social context. Most readers, however, are enthralled by the sheer pleasure involved in obtaining a glimpse of the life and thought of a man as interesting and individualistic as Thoreau.

Having loved the writing of Thoreau, and *Walden* in particular, for several years, I was excited about the production of this word concordance. Despite the time and manpower saved by using the computer, its production was still a large undertaking. First, workers entered the entire Princeton edition of *Walden* into the computer line for line, shifting all hyphenated words so that the full word fell on the line where it began. Next, the book was painstakingly proofread and run through a series of programs. The initial program made a sequential list of all the words with their page and line numbers. Another program sorted the words alphabetically, and a third counted the number of times the word appeared in the text. Two final programs arranged the words in the form for printing.

The result is the first of its kind—a complete alphabetical listing of all the words in *Walden* including high frequency words like articles and pronouns as well as separate entries for each form of a given verb. Following the word index are several appendices. The first lists words appearing in the text one hundred or more times. The words are arranged alphabetically and sorted according to frequency. The second contains histograms for each chapter of *Walden* summarizing word lengths for that chapter. The third gives the listings of a simple word search program that might be useful to students of stylistic analysis or others attempting to find words in a text using a microcomputer.

The concordance is easy to use. Word counts, the number of times the word occurs in the text, appear in parentheses on the first line of each word entry, at the top of the fourth column. References are given by page and line number (the number before the period indicates the page, and the one after, the line) and are arranged to be read sequentially across the four columns and then down to the next line.

A reference tool like this is notable not primarily for its manner of production or arrangement of content but for its myriad uses. Most obvious is its value in locating quotations through key words or phrases or in discovering the frequency with which the author uses certain words. This particular concordance has the advantage of containing not only a complete listing, that is, of including references to *all* the words in the text, but also of listing all words that occur less than a set number of times or fall into certain categories.

The inclusion of high frequency words makes possible more technical types of literary research. Those interested in stylistic analysis might use its entries of pronouns, articles, etc. to evaluate the author's use of persona, inflectional forms, deictic devices, etc. in part or all of the text. Discourse analysts might do similar examinations of evaluation devices as seen through the author's use of repetition, negation or the use of marked and unmarked cases, and auxiliary constructions. Traditional literary analysts might use it to study imagery and metaphor as they compare the author's use of a word or words in different contexts. Biologists and scientists might find it a useful tool in quickly locating references to specific species of animals or plants. Whatever the type of study done on *Walden*, this concordance aims to help make the study faster and easier.

The compilers of this concordance realize that it is not perfect; it possesses a couple of idiosyncrasies. The text was entered into the computer as capital and lower-case letters but was converted to all capitals so that words that begin sentences would not be differentiated from the same words used elsewhere in the text. Thus, our entries appear in all capitals. As a result, the concordance does not distinguish between lower case and capitalized forms of words, e.g., "god" and "God." Second, the program for sorting words does not recognize possessives, contractions, and other words that contain apostrophes. These words appear in the concordance in their unmarked form without the apostrophe and the letter or letters that follow it. Instead, what follows the apostrophe appears in a separate listing. A reference to a word such as "we're" would appear twice, once under "we" and again under "re." For words ending in "'s," no distinction is made between the contraction and the possessive form. In Appendix B, values on the Y-axis vary from graph to graph. Care should be taken to examine each histogram carefully as a casual glance may be misleading.

Despite these idiosyncracies, the serious Thoreau scholar, the student, or the lover of words and word play will find this concordance a valuable tool and a great time saver in his/her analysis of where, how, and why Thoreau used the words he did.

Janice Watson
Andrews University

```
003.04  003.05  003.09  003.32  003.35        047.22  047.31  047.33  048.05  048.06
004.01  004.15  004.18  004.26  004.36        048.10  048.14  048.16  048.18  048.23
005.07  005.13  005.15  005.17  005.22        048.27  048.28  048.30  048.30  048.30
005.24  005.26  005.29  006.04  006.06        048.31  049.19  049.26  049.28  049.32
006.06  006.15  006.18  006.38  007.07        049.33  050.01  050.04  050.05  050.06
007.13  007.14  007.21  007.22  007.24        050.10  050.15  050.18  050.26  050.26
007.29  007.33  007.34  007.35  008.11        050.28  050.29  050.30  050.31  051.10
008.14  008.28  008.33  008.33  008.34        051.17  051.22  051.22  051.27  051.29
008.35  009.15  009.21  010.13  010.15        051.31  051.36  052.11  052.13  052.21
010.24  010.35  011.03  011.07  011.19        052.23  052.25  052.34  052.34  053.01
011.19  011.23  011.24  011.29  011.32        053.10  053.11  053.16  053.25  053.31
012.15  012.23  012.27  012.36  013.03        053.34  053.35  054.05  054.07  054.09
013.08  013.11  013.29  013.31  013.33        054.10  054.12  054.21  054.22  054.29
013.34  014.05  014.05  014.06  014.06        054.32  055.02  055.02  055.20  055.22
014.07  014.08  014.16  014.21  014.23        055.28  055.36  055.38  056.09  056.10
014.31  014.35  014.36  015.02  015.05        056.23  056.25  056.27  056.29  056.29
015.09  015.16  015.16  015.18  017.11        057.04  057.07  057.21  057.22  057.24
017.11  017.11  017.17  018.06  018.06        057.31  057.33  057.34  057.35  058.03
018.19  018.19  018.23  018.28  018.32        058.08  058.18  058.23  059.04  059.33
018.32  019.01  019.02  019.10  019.18        059.34  059.36  059.38  059.39  059.40
019.18  020.02  020.02  020.10  020.19        060.23  060.32  060.36  060.39  060.40
020.21  020.22  020.32  020.33  021.03        061.01  061.03  061.12  061.13  061.16
021.03  021.06  021.07  021.10  021.11        061.17  061.18  061.19  061.23  061.24
021.13  021.13  021.24  021.25  021.31        061.27  061.28  061.30  061.34  061.36
021.33  022.04  022.07  022.11  022.14        062.03  062.03  062.05  062.06  062.11
022.15  022.16  022.17  022.20  022.21        062.12  062.14  063.03  063.06  063.07
022.23  022.24  022.24  022.25  022.27        063.24  063.24  063.24  063.27  063.33
022.29  022.32  023.01  023.03  023.09        064.01  064.05  064.08  064.09  064.18
023.11  023.12  023.13  023.14  023.16        064.18  064.23  064.29  064.30  064.36
023.17  023.18  023.26  023.30  023.31        065.07  065.07  065.11  065.18  065.18
023.35  024.04  024.22  024.30  024.32        065.18  065.19  065.19  065.20  065.20
024.32  024.32  024.33  024.33  024.33        065.20  065.21  065.21  065.22  065.22
024.33  024.34  024.34  024.35  024.36        065.23  065.24  065.25  065.28  065.28
025.02  025.02  025.09  025.20  025.23        065.30  065.31  065.33  065.34  065.34
025.27  025.30  025.35  026.05  026.12        066.02  066.03  066.07  066.10  066.13
026.15  026.17  026.25  026.25  026.28        066.14  066.14  066.15  066.20  066.21
027.08  027.08  027.12  027.14  027.20        066.27  066.31  066.36  067.01  067.03
027.26  027.28  027.28  027.29  027.29        067.08  067.08  067.16  067.18  067.19
027.30  027.33  028.03  028.05  028.05        067.20  067.25  067.30  067.32  067.33
028.08  028.10  028.10  028.15  028.23        067.34  068.03  068.09  068.11  068.23
028.27  028.30  028.31  028.32  028.33        068.34  069.01  069.11  069.20  069.20
028.33  028.33  028.34  028.34  028.35        069.24  069.26  070.14  070.25  070.27
029.02  029.06  029.08  029.12  029.12        070.35  070.35  071.02  071.16  071.19
029.12  029.17  029.20  029.21  029.22        071.22  071.22  071.23  071.30  071.31
029.23  029.25  029.25  029.36  030.02        071.35  072.01  072.09  072.16  072.23
030.09  030.10  030.10  030.11  030.12        073.02  073.10  073.17  073.18  073.21
030.15  030.21  030.23  030.23  030.26        073.31  073.32  073.32  074.03  074.12
030.35  031.01  031.05  031.08  031.09        074.14  074.17  074.17  074.25  074.25
031.10  031.14  031.20  031.21  031.25        074.27  074.28  074.33  074.36  075.11
031.25  031.27  031.29  031.32  031.36        075.33  075.33  075.34  075.34  076.05
032.01  032.03  032.26  032.29  032.36        076.08  076.11  076.18  076.19  076.22
033.01  033.03  033.10  033.19  033.19        076.23  076.28  076.35  076.36  077.03
033.22  033.24  033.25  033.36  034.01        077.07  077.08  077.10  077.10  077.20
034.07  034.20  034.31  034.32  034.32        077.21  077.23  077.24  077.27  077.32
034.33  034.34  035.13  035.27  035.29        077.35  078.04  078.12  078.21  078.25
035.32  036.01  036.02  036.08  036.17        078.35  079.04  080.06  081.04  081.06
036.21  036.30  036.36  037.06  037.07        081.07  081.13  081.14  081.18  081.21
037.12  037.13  037.14  037.16  037.19        081.21  081.21  081.22  081.22  081.23
037.21  037.26  037.27  037.27  037.28        081.26  081.27  082.02  082.11  002.12
037.31  037.32  038.01  038.03  038.04        082.13  082.18  082.22  082.22  082.24
038.04  038.04  038.05  038.12  038.30        082.25  082.27  082.33  082.34  082.35
038.30  039.02  039.07  039.13  039.19        082.37  083.06  083.07  083.17  083.34
039.19  039.36  040.15  040.15  040.18        083.34  084.06  084.10  084.30  084.35
040.25  040.27  040.28  041.05  041.08        085.04  085.04  085.06  085.07  085.16
041.23  041.23  041.23  041.24  041.25        085.16  085.22  085.24  085.27  085.29
041.28  041.30  041.33  042.03  042.14        085.36  086.03  086.03  086.04  086.09
042.30  042.33  043.07  043.09  043.10        086.12  086.12  086.22  086.23  086.27
043.12  043.15  043.16  043.17  043.18        086.28  086.31  086.32  086.33  086.34
043.21  043.23  043.25  043.25  043.26        087.01  087.02  087.06  087.19  087.20
043.27  044.03  044.04  044.05  044.10        087.20  087.21  087.31  088.01  088.07
044.11  044.18  044.22  044.23  044.26        088.12  088.17  088.25  088.27  088.29
045.01  045.02  045.13  045.16  045.22        088.36  089.05  089.06  089.18  089.18
045.33  045.33  045.33  045.33  045.35        089.24  089.24  089.29  089.36  090.02
046.02  046.03  046.15  046.18  046.26        090.09  090.10  090.11  090.12  090.20
046.27  046.27  046.28  046.29  046.30        090.21  090.21  090.22  091.04  091.05
046.32  047.06  047.07  047.08  047.19        091.10  091.11  091.20  091.25  091.26
                                              091.26  091.26  091.30  091.33  091.35
```

091.35	092.01	092.03	092.10	092.11
092.12	092.15	092.16	092.18	092.27
092.27	092.31	092.32	092.34	092.34
093.01	093.02	093.04	093.08	093.09
093.12	093.13	093.14	093.17	093.17
093.23	093.24	093.25	093.30	093.33
093.34	094.09	094.12	094.19	094.20
094.22	094.23	094.28	094.28	094.33
094.34	095.07	095.10	095.13	095.20
095.20	095.25	095.26	095.33	095.35
096.13	096.13	096.15	096.20	096.28
096.32	096.33	096.33	096.33	096.34
096.35	097.14	097.22	097.24	098.03
098.05	098.06	098.06	098.07	098.07
098.07	098.08	098.08	098.09	098.11
098.13	098.19	098.26	099.03	099.08
099.08	099.11	099.11	099.21	099.30
100.12	100.14	101.01	101.01	101.04
101.09	101.12	101.12	101.01	101.16
101.27	101.35	101.35	102.11	102.19
102.19	102.27	102.30	103.04	103.17
103.20	103.24	104.06	104.12	104.15
104.16	104.17	104.23	104.29	104.31
105.07	105.20	105.21	105.30	105.31
105.35	106.03	106.13	106.14	106.16
106.24	106.31	106.35	106.36	107.01
107.09	107.27	107.34	107.35	107.36
107.36	108.09	108.28	108.28	108.31
109.06	109.19	109.22	109.23	110.04
110.05	110.05	110.05	110.07	110.07
110.17	111.13	111.17	111.17	111.18
111.24	111.25	111.27	112.14	112.22
112.29	112.34	112.35	113.04	113.09
113.10	113.19	113.26	113.27	113.28
113.29	114.14	114.15	114.16	114.28
114.28	114.30	114.30	114.31	114.35
115.02	115.04	115.07	115.09	115.13
115.20	115.23	116.01	116.08	116.11
116.12	116.13	116.23	116.36	117.01
117.09	117.11	117.22	117.30	117.36
118.08	118.14	118.16	119.08	119.24
120.04	120.12	120.17	120.23	120.24
120.27	120.28	120.29	120.33	120.36
121.03	121.04	121.09	121.31	121.37
122.03	122.04	122.07	122.14	122.22
122.24	122.25	122.27	122.36	123.03
123.04	123.05	123.07	123.11	123.13
123.19	123.21	124.01	124.03	124.04
124.05	124.08	124.11	124.11	124.13
124.13	124.21	124.34	125.07	125.10
125.14	125.16	125.20	125.26	125.28
125.35	125.36	126.04	126.07	126.10
126.20	126.21	126.22	126.36	127.03
127.04	127.14	127.14	127.31	128.02
128.03	128.03	128.04	128.05	128.05
128.05	128.06	128.07	128.10	128.15
128.15	128.16	129.03	129.05	129.06
129.26	129.27	129.28	129.28	129.28
129.32	129.32	130.02	130.02	130.04
130.05	130.06	130.16	130.17	130.19
130.25	130.26	130.36	131.09	131.10
131.11	131.11	131.13	131.25	131.29
131.30	131.32	131.34	131.36	132.13
132.13	132.25	132.33	132.34	132.37
133.03	133.09	133.15	133.27	133.29
133.30	133.31	134.03	134.28	134.29
134.33	134.34	135.01	135.04	135.07
135.09	135.12	135.13	135.16	135.17
135.26	135.28	135.31	135.35	136.09
136.13	136.13	136.15	136.23	136.25
136.26	136.28	136.29	136.34	137.01
137.03	137.10	137.12	137.13	137.14
137.14	137.14	137.14	137.15	137.16
137.17	137.18	137.25	137.27	137.34
138.03	138.14	138.23	138.27	139.02
139.03	140.04	140.14	140.27	140.31
140.31	140.34	141.08	141.09	141.10

141.19	141.28	141.36	142.05	142.06
142.10	142.15	142.16	142.24	142.27
142.31	142.31	143.02	143.02	143.09
143.10	143.15	143.16	143.17	143.18
143.33	144.13	144.15	144.16	144.16
144.17	144.18	144.27	144.34	144.35
144.37	145.01	145.02	145.04	145.07
145.08	145.10	145.11	145.13	145.14
145.15	145.16	145.17	145.19	145.19
145.20	145.23	145.26	145.26	145.27
145.36	146.01	146.04	146.06	146.07
146.10	146.14	146.14	146.18	146.19
146.27	146.29	146.30	146.30	147.03
147.11	147.11	147.11	147.12	147.15
147.18	147.26	147.33	147.35	148.09
148.11	148.14	148.15	148.17	148.19
148.20	148.21	148.24	148.27	148.29
149.04	149.16	149.16	149.17	149.23
149.24	149.31	150.03	150.10	150.13
150.17	150.20	150.29	150.31	150.33
151.15	151.17	151.27	151.28	151.32
151.33	152.08	152.19	152.26	152.26
152.27	152.28	152.29	152.32	152.33
152.35	153.08	153.11	153.12	153.25
153.27	153.28	153.28	153.30	153.30
153.31	153.34	154.15	154.15	155.21
155.26	156.03	156.11	156.28	156.33
156.35	157.12	157.14	157.14	157.21
157.32	157.34	157.35	158.10	158.15
158.15	158.19	158.30	158.32	159.13
159.14	159.15	159.15	159.17	159.26
159.31	159.33	159.33	159.35	160.01
160.08	160.09	160.10	160.18	160.31
160.33	160.35	160.35	161.02	161.02
161.03	161.04	161.06	161.07	161.12
161.30	161.31	161.32	161.35	162.01
162.01	162.09	162.13	162.14	162.16
162.23	163.01	163.24	163.37	163.38
164.15	164.17	164.24	164.25	164.30
165.06	165.07	165.07	165.07	165.08
165.23	165.29	165.33	166.01	166.05
166.11	166.13	166.15	167.05	167.18
167.20	167.23	167.25	167.28	168.02
168.03	168.06	168.07	168.14	168.15
168.15	168.16	168.20	168.27	168.34
169.09	169.09	169.20	169.23	169.26
170.02	170.06	170.10	170.11	170.18
170.19	170.27	170.29	170.30	170.31
170.33	170.35	170.36	171.02	171.03
171.04	171.11	171.21	171.23	171.27
172.03	172.06	172.08	172.13	172.16
172.18	172.34	172.35	173.03	173.09
173.15	173.16	173.27	173.27	173.33
173.35	174.04	174.10	174.12	174.13
174.21	174.21	174.23	174.24	174.27
174.28	174.31	174.33	174.34	175.06
175.10	175.25	175.29	175.30	175.31
175.31	175.32	175.33	176.04	176.04
176.04	176.06	176.10	176.10	176.12
176.19	176.23	176.25	176.26	176.27
176.28	176.28	177.02	177.07	177.07
177.08	177.10	177.15	177.18	177.20
177.20	177.22	177.23	177.24	177.25
177.27	177.31	177.32	178.03	178.11
178.19	178.21	178.23	178.26	178.30
178.34	178.34	178.34	178.35	178.35
178.36	179.01	179.03	179.06	179.08
179.11	179.13	179.14	179.20	179.21
179.27	179.31	179.36	180.01	180.09
180.09	180.11	180.11	180.11	180.24
180.26	180.30	180.31	180.33	181.02
181.10	181.10	181.12	181.21	181.26
181.28	181.30	181.30	181.33	182.02
182.13	182.13	182.27	182.29	183.01
183.25	183.28	183.28	183.30	183.31
183.31	183.32	183.36	184.04	184.05
184.06	184.08	184.09	184.10	184.15

```
184.17  184.21  184.22  184.32  184.33
184.34  184.36  185.07  185.07  185.08
185.12  185.15  185.16  185.17  185.25
185.32  185.33  185.36  186.03  186.04
186.07  186.11  186.12  186.19  186.19
186.22  186.23  187.02  187.03  187.04
187.09  187.13  187.16  187.16  187.17
187.23  187.25  187.25  187.26  187.33
187.35  187.35  188.05  188.07  188.16
188.17  188.19  188.20  188.22  188.25
188.28  188.34  189.06  189.10  189.12
189.21  189.23  189.24  189.27  189.30
189.35  189.36  190.01  190.07  190.07
190.09  190.10  190.14  190.21  190.25
190.30  190.34  191.01  191.03  191.11
191.13  191.20  191.24  191.32  191.36
192.07  192.18  192.20  192.20  192.25
193.05  193.10  193.14  193.23  193.35
194.06  194.08  194.10  194.12  194.20
194.24  194.27  194.32  195.01  195.02
195.03  195.16  195.18  195.20  195.24
195.32  195.32  196.03  196.10  196.31
196.31  196.32  196.34  196.35  197.02
197.07  197.11  197.12  197.13  197.20
197.23  197.30  198.02  198.03  198.08
198.13  198.27  198.33  198.34  199.03
199.12  199.13  199.28  201.23  201.26
201.27  201.31  202.05  202.05  202.05
202.06  202.11  202.14  202.15  202.15
202.24  202.25  202.32  203.04  203.08
203.10  203.12  203.21  203.23  203.24
203.26  203.29  203.32  203.34  204.01
204.03  204.15  204.34  204.34  204.35
205.02  205.05  205.05  205.06  205.08
205.09  205.10  205.14  205.22  205.25
205.30  205.32  205.34  206.01  206.06
206.08  206.10  206.12  206.13  206.14
206.16  206.23  206.27  206.33  206.34
206.35  206.36  207.08  207.34  208.07
208.34  208.34  209.01  210.05  210.05
210.06  210.11  210.11  210.16  210.17
210.29  210.29  210.30  210.34  211.01
211.01  211.02  211.06  211.15  211.19
211.20  211.36  212.03  212.20  212.23
212.26  212.33  213.01  213.02  213.03
213.03  213.06  213.07  213.07  213.12
213.16  213.18  213.21  213.23  213.25
213.30  213.34  213.36  214.03  214.07
214.09  214.10  214.14  214.25  214.25
215.03  215.07  215.10  215.11  215.11
215.15  215.20  215.29  215.36  215.36
216.01  216.02  216.05  216.06  216.08
216.23  216.25  217.01  217.02  217.04
217.09  217.10  217.11  217.11  217.12
217.34  218.03  218.06  218.11  218.12
218.15  218.18  218.21  218.22  218.23
219.04  219.05  219.06  219.07  219.15
219.17  219.22  219.26  219.27  220.24
220.27  220.29  220.30  220.35  220.40
221.01  221.02  221.05  221.27  221.28
221.32  221.35  222.01  222.03  222.04
222.12  222.16  222.17  223.03  223.06
223.08  223.10  223.16  223.19  223.21
223.23  223.24  223.34  224.02  224.06
224.07  224.25  224.35  225.01  225.03
225.08  225.09  225.15  225.16  225.19
225.23  225.24  225.30  225.33  226.04
226.07  226.08  226.08  226.09  226.11
226.13  226.15  226.16  226.18  226.19
226.24  226.24  226.27  226.28  226.30
226.32  227.08  227.11  227.12  227.13
227.14  227.17  227.25  227.27  227.31
227.31  227.32  227.32  227.33  227.34
227.36  228.01  228.02  228.02  228.04
228.05  228.08  228.09  228.25  228.34
228.34  228.34  229.10  229.11  229.15
229.25  230.05  230.15  230.21  230.24
```

```
230.25  230.32  230.33  231.13  231.25
231.31  231.33  231.34  232.02  232.06
232.12  232.12  232.13  232.17  232.19
232.24  232.27  232.31  232.33  232.34
233.01  233.03  233.05  233.05  233.07
233.08  233.09  233.09  233.11  233.12
233.15  233.16  233.22  234.05  234.07
234.09  234.10  234.14  234.15  234.19
234.21  234.22  234.30  235.05  235.06
235.06  235.15  235.25  236.01  236.09
236.11  236.11  236.12  236.13  236.25
236.36  237.04  237.05  237.05  237.05
238.03  238.10  238.17  238.20  238.23
238.24  238.32  239.03  239.07  239.13
239.14  239.16  239.23  240.03  240.04
240.18  240.30  240.34  241.07  241.09
241.14  241.24  241.24  241.26  241.27
241.28  241.35  242.10  242.26  242.32
242.33  243.02  243.03  243.09  243.11
243.11  243.12  243.13  243.14  243.16
243.18  243.23  243.24  243.24  243.26
243.29  243.32  243.33  243.34  244.01
244.03  244.04  244.04  244.04  244.04
244.13  244.14  244.16  244.19  244.25
244.26  244.29  244.30  244.32  245.05
245.07  245.11  245.13  245.14  245.18
245.19  245.23  245.26  245.30  245.31
245.32  246.01  246.06  246.06  246.10
246.21  246.23  246.23  247.07  247.11
247.21  247.34  247.34  248.04  248.05
248.08  248.09  248.14  248.18  248.28
248.28  248.34  248.35  249.11  249.15
249.17  249.28  249.34  249.35  250.01
250.02  250.02  250.05  250.08  250.21
250.25  250.27  250.33  250.34  251.01
251.15  251.23  251.26  252.02  252.05
252.05  252.09  252.14  252.18  252.23
252.23  252.23  252.26  253.03  253.03
253.04  253.07  253.14  253.15  253.17
253.21  253.27  253.28  253.30  253.33
253.35  253.35  253.36  254.02  254.09
254.11  254.12  254.13  254.16  254.17
254.21  254.22  254.26  255.04  255.05
256.10  256.15  256.25  256.28  256.29
256.33  256.34  257.06  257.09  257.09
257.11  257.16  257.21  257.24  257.28
257.34  258.03  258.07  258.13  258.19
258.20  258.24  258.25  258.29  258.35
259.03  259.09  259.10  259.12  259.18
259.34  260.02  260.10  260.19  260.32
261.05  261.09  261.20  261.23  261.23
261.26  262.02  262.04  262.06  262.09
262.13  262.18  262.27  262.32  262.33
263.01  263.06  263.08  263.10  263.12
263.23  264.01  264.10  264.15  264.17
264.20  264.24  264.25  264.33  264.35
265.19  265.20  265.23  265.25  265.30
265.35  266.03  266.05  266.06  266.12
266.13  266.14  266.16  266.26  266.29
266.32  267.01  267.08  267.09  267.10
267.18  267.20  267.22  267.24  267.26
267.26  267.28  267.32  268.01  268.01
268.01  268.01  268.01  268.02  268.03
268.13  268.13  268.29  269.01  269.09
269.13  269.22  269.36  270.03  270.20
270.21  270.23  271.10  271.20  271.26
271.30  271.34  272.01  272.02  272.06
272.12  272.13  272.17  272.22  272.23
272.28  272.30  272.31  273.02  273.13
273.04  273.04  273.04  273.07  273.13
273.17  273.23  273.28  273.32  273.35
273.35  274.01  274.01  274.02  274.02
274.04  274.06  274.10  274.16  274.20
274.26  274.28  274.29  274.32  274.35
274.35  275.02  275.02  275.04  275.06
275.12  275.12  275.15  275.16  275.30
```

A   (CONTINUED)
```
275.31  275.34  276.02  276.03  276.03
276.22  276.26  276.31  277.03  277.04
277.07  277.12  277.14  277.15  277.19
277.22  277.24  277.24  277.26  277.27
277.28  277.31  277.32  277.33  278.01
278.03  278.15  278.16  278.19  278.21
278.23  278.24  279.04  279.06  279.08
279.13  279.19  279.20  279.23  279.28
279.28  279.29  279.36  280.01  280.02
280.05  280.13  280.15  280.18  280.21
280.21  281.01  281.02  281.05  281.10
281.17  281.23  281.24  281.24  281.25
281.31  281.32  282.02  282.17  282.22
282.23  282.23  282.27  282.27  282.28
282.34  283.01  283.01  283.02  283.04
283.04  283.06  283.25  283.31  283.35
284.11  284.13  284.13  284.14  284.15
284.20  284.24  284.25  285.04  285.06
285.16  285.20  285.25  285.28  285.29
285.34  285.35  286.01  287.01  287.01
287.02  287.02  287.08  287.12  287.15
287.22  287.23  287.24  287.29  287.34
288.03  288.08  288.08  288.11  288.13
288.17  288.21  288.32  289.04  289.12
289.15  289.24  289.26  289.29  289.32
290.05  290.07  290.09  290.15  290.15
290.20  290.26  290.31  290.35  291.05
291.08  291.17  291.17  291.19  291.20
291.21  291.22  291.28  291.31  291.34
291.34  291.36  292.03  292.10  292.10
292.18  292.21  292.22  292.22  292.23
292.24  292.26  292.27  292.31  292.35
292.36  293.02  293.03  293.10  293.11
293.12  293.14  293.21  293.21  293.22
293.23  293.23  293.25  293.28  293.29
294.03  294.13  294.16  294.21  294.24
294.28  294.30  294.33  294.36  295.02
295.04  295.05  295.07  295.08  295.10
295.12  295.13  295.16  295.18  295.19
295.19  295.20  295.22  295.28  295.32
295.32  296.02  296.06  296.09  296.12
296.15  296.18  296.19  296.26  296.32
296.32  296.34  296.35  297.01  297.01
297.03  297.06  297.14  297.18  297.21
297.29  297.30  297.31  297.32  297.33
298.07  298.13  299.04  299.08  299.13
299.14  299.15  299.21  299.21  299.24
299.28  299.29  299.30  299.32  300.03
300.06  300.10  300.17  300.19  300.20
300.22  300.23  300.26  300.30  300.32
300.33  300.34  301.04  301.04  301.12
301.13  301.16  301.17  301.21  301.21
301.23  301.25  301.30  302.02  302.24
302.28  302.32  303.07  303.10  303.12
303.14  303.17  303.24  303.29  303.30
303.31  303.36  304.01  304.04  304.07
304.08  304.09  304.17  304.18  304.22
304.25  304.30  304.32  304.33  305.01
305.02  305.07  305.11  305.16  305.17
305.21  305.22  306.02  306.03  306.09
306.15  306.23  306.23  306.25  306.27
306.28  306.30  307.10  307.13  307.14
307.20  307.21  307.31  307.32  307.35
307.36  308.01  308.05  308.06  308.07
308.10  308.17  308.19  308.34  309.01
309.02  309.04  309.05  309.05  309.18
309.24  310.10  310.11  310.14  310.22
310.28  310.35  311.04  311.16  311.18
311.19  311.26  311.32  311.33  312.04
312.12  312.12  312.15  312.16  312.17
312.19  313.09  313.12  313.14  313.17
313.20  314.12  314.18  314.26  314.28
314.28  314.28  314.32  314.32  314.32
315.01  315.03  315.03  315.14  315.17
315.20  316.08  316.22  316.25  316.25
316.26  316.26  316.29  316.34  316.38
317.09  317.10  317.14  317.15  317.17
```

A   (CONTINUED)
```
317.20  317.24  318.12  318.26  318.29
318.33  319.01  319.13  320.03  320.07
320.08  320.09  320.12  320.28  320.33
321.05  321.14  321.16  321.18  321.19
321.20  321.24  321.32  322.19  322.25
322.26  322.32  322.34  322.35  322.37
323.04  323.08  323.10  323.14  323.15
323.16  323.16  323.25  323.32  324.01
324.02  324.09  324.28  324.28  324.31
324.31  325.12  325.13  325.19  325.19
325.36  326.01  326.01  326.02  326.07
326.09  326.16  326.16  326.22  326.24
326.31  326.36  327.01  327.02  327.15
327.16  327.16  327.23  327.24  327.27
327.29  327.31  328.02  328.10  328.14
328.16  328.28  328.28  328.29  329.13
329.13  329.14  329.17  329.18  329.20
329.27  329.27  329.33  330.02  330.03
330.08  330.12  330.13  330.15  330.18
330.22  330.24  330.25  330.25  330.27
330.29  330.35  331.06  331.06  331.11
331.12  331.12  331.19  331.22  331.35
332.03  332.23  332.23  332.27  332.28
332.29  333.07  333.09  333.15  333.33
```

ABANDON   (1)
  075.16
ABANDONED   (3)
  130.15 134.32 267.33
ABANDONMENT   (1)
  210.12
ABANDONS   (1)
  011.01
ABDOMEN   (1)
  215.12
ABDOMENS   (1)
  215.18
ABEELARD   (1)
  109.08
ABETTED   (1)
  256.10
ABILITY   (3)
  090.19 108.07 235.16
ABJECT   (2)
  080.20 328.33
ABLE   (8)
  034.09 034.11 048.36 090.21 091.10
  101.08 170.06 245.22
ABOARD   (1)
  053.32
ABODE   (6)
  030.35 084.26 085.29 085.30 296.13
  328.13
ABORIGINAL   (1)
  180.05
ABORIGINES   (2)
  147.08 239.07
ABOUNDED   (1)
  127.15
ABOUT   (154)
```
003.28  004.11  008.03  009.18  011.30
014.25  016.33  017.09  017.22  017.22
042.04  043.05  048.01  048.03  051.17
052.04  052.12  054.20  055.28  058.28
061.01  063.15  063.24  069.11  069.25
073.28  073.30  073.32  074.02  074.05
077.23  078.19  083.05  085.20  086.03
086.06  089.05  091.12  093.01  098.18
105.02  106.19  106.23  106.27  113.22
113.36  114.05  114.25  115.13  118.26
124.16  130.08  136.18  142.08  142.26
143.05  143.14  143.31  145.01  145.05
146.34  150.35  152.12  156.11  156.12
157.01  158.32  161.20  162.26  163.27
164.23  164.24  165.05  168.35  169.09
170.18  170.20  175.09  175.11  175.32
176.03  177.02  179.11  180.27  181.23
182.06  184.34  189.30  190.30  194.20
```

```
ABOUT                    (CONTINUED)      ACCESSIBLE                 (   1)
197.12  198.01  198.33  202.21  203.15    106.10
204.29  211.31  212.10  213.29  214.12   ACCIDENT                   (  13)
221.17  224.25  224.36  227.36  233.16    022.15  022.17  053.36  062.34  084.28
241.18  241.21  241.28  242.21  243.10    094.13  099.10  101.21  124.08  153.23
244.25  245.27  246.26  247.09  249.06    250.21  314.21  318.25
249.06  251.31  253.32  259.04  260.14   ACCIDENTAL                 (   4)
260.18  261.02  263.20  265.08  265.18    012.25  023.05  060.38  062.21
266.21  267.30  271.07  271.13  272.11   ACCIDENTALLY               (   2)
274.16  274.21  275.08  276.12  280.06    129.31  226.36
285.13  287.02  287.30  290.10  295.33   ACCOMPANIED                (   2)
297.05  299.15  300.03  300.34  301.18    089.16  179.21
302.28  303.04  304.03  306.13  312.22   ACCOMPANIMENT              (   1)
313.11  315.01  328.30  329.26            159.07
ABOVE                            (  40)  ACCOMPANY                  (   1)
013.16  015.32  034.23  058.31  060.42    116.29
072.13  076.28  080.20  083.15  086.13   ACCOMPLISH                 (   4)
086.29  102.03  106.15  112.01  119.10    034.09  095.19  097.15  242.09
125.34  134.25  141.22  156.22  162.02   ACCOMPLISHED               (   5)
163.37  169.31  188.32  188.36  190.15    021.29  035.12  057.01  112.06  231.16
198.04  206.33  228.09  241.25  247.11   ACCOMPLISHING              (   1)
252.32  259.24  270.07  271.21  284.13    020.01
300.14  326.19  328.19  328.21  332.05   ACCOMPLISHMENT             (   1)
ABROAD                           (   5)   181.09
029.19  112.26  135.25  265.27  271.22   ACCORDING                  (  13)
ABRUPT                           (   1)   009.33  013.08  015.01  028.04  039.12
183.01                                    063.14  108.07  110.08  112.31  160.18
ABRUPTLY                         (   1)   166.03  207.29  233.18
176.01                                   ACCORDINGLY                (   4)
ABS                              (   1)   013.26  069.17  081.21  108.16
104.23                                   ACCOUNT                    (  25)
ABSENCE                          (   2)   003.33  003.34  021.01  021.08  060.41
079.11  129.34                            061.22  065.18  065.32  071.07  090.04
ABSENT                           (   4)   091.10  096.31  096.36  161.22  182.25
170.04  172.05  204.27  265.05            183.24  211.06  220.08  231.32  250.09
ABSOLUTE                         (   4)   273.12  278.08  279.08  299.10  318.25
009.03  096.02  263.17  299.19           ACCOUNTED                  (   1)
ABSOLUTELY                       (   5)   182.31
020.35  167.08  189.11  260.32  291.01   ACCOUNTS                   (   7)
ABSORB                           (   1)   018.33  020.14  061.19  091.27  104.14
166.10                                    149.05  261.21
ABSORBED                         (   3)  ACCUMULATE                 (   1)
013.23  025.09  032.02                    067.31
ABSORBING                        (   1)  ACCUMULATED                (   5)
256.13                                    016.24  066.32  104.02  133.29  254.24
ABSTAIN                          (   2)  ACCURACY                   (   2)
068.22  215.02                            094.29  288.27
ABSTEMIOUSNESS                   (   1)  ACCURATELY                 (   2)
061.35                                    012.19  287.02
ABSTINENCE                       (   1)  ACCURSED                   (   1)
142.11                                    264.27
ABSTRACT                         (   2)  ACCUSTOMED                 (   8)
057.17  148.28                            065.02  081.04  111.25  132.11  169.16
ABSTRACTION                      (   1)   180.30  288.37  310.09
171.16                                   ACHERON                    (   1)
ABUNDANCE                        (   3)   138.24
048.17  166.28  330.36                   ACHILLEAN                  (   1)
ABUNDANT                         (   4)   291.15
015.22  083.30  182.08  184.13           ACHILLES                   (   3)
ABUTMENT                         (   1)   080.29  144.25  229.31
202.10                                   ACID                       (   1)
ABUTS                            (   1)   063.13
186.04                                   ACKNOWLEDGE                (   1)
ABUTTED                          (   1)   295.17
195.29                                   ACORNS                     (   1)
ACANTHUS                         (   1)   009.36
305.19                                   ACQUAINTANCE               (  10)
ACCENT                           (   3)   053.22  071.04  106.08  115.18  161.12
105.28  148.02  148.12                    161.21  210.24  210.27  265.30  287.17
ACCENTED                         (   1)  ACQUAINTANCES              (   4)
272.08                                    022.10  045.04  069.33  159.11
ACCEPT                           (   3)  ACQUAINTED                 (  11)
004.04  040.16  315.12                    016.31  032.27  040.23  042.33  094.18
ACCEPTED                         (   1)   106.12  107.11  124.06  179.12  268.30
018.35                                    332.03
ACCESS                           (   2)  ACQUIRE                    (   5)
014.07  300.28                            019.32  020.04  070.16  136.11  303.19
```

5

```
ACQUIRED                    (  8)     ADELAIDE                    (  1)
005.05  050.14  070.17  089.15  101.29     052.33
193.03  194.13  195.25              ADEQUATE                    (  1)
ACQUIRES                    (  2)     324.21
077.35  123.05                      ADHERE                      (  1)
ACQUIRING                   (  4)     241.06
012.28  040.03  099.08  165.35      ADJACENT                    (  1)
ACRE                        (  8)     291.13
054.26  055.28  064.31  155.26  179.11     ADJOINING                   (  1)
204.36  295.34  316.20              049.26
ACRES                       ( 13)     ADJUNCT                     (  1)
005.10  005.19  054.21  054.24  071.05     203.07
156.11  157.34  175.33  194.22  197.11     ADMETUS                     (  1)
197.12  288.30  290.10              070.02
ACROSS                      ( 23)     ADMINISTRATOR               (  1)
018.15  046.15  086.34  087.17  132.33     262.24
141.09  156.22  167.05  186.23  189.03     ADMIRABLE                   (  7)
191.31  210.06  240.01  249.34  250.03     014.34  014.35  057.18  083.01  111.15
257.04  260.17  277.17  289.05  289.29     287.26  294.35
291.21  293.12  302.34              ADMIRABLY                   (  1)
ACT                         (  4)     125.26
077.08  110.08  118.13  263.12      ADMIRATION                  (  1)
ACTAEON                     (  1)     282.15
277.02                              ADMIRE                      (  3)
ACTED                       (  1)     058.27  102.01  195.06
258.25                              ADMIRED                     (  4)
ACTION                      (  3)     179.15  238.06  240.06  245.34
182.31  195.20  231.34              ADMIRING                    (  2)
ACTIONS                     (  2)     038.09  269.27
089.32  134.35                      ADMIT                       (  8)
ACTIVE                      (  3)     018.31  029.13  036.03  080.23  244.21
080.14  080.20  311.34              253.34  284.20  325.20
ACTIVITY                    (  2)     ADMITS                      (  1)
053.29  077.33                      029.24
ACTON                       (  1)     ADMITTANCE                  (  1)
123.02                              017.10
ACTOR                       (  1)     ADMITTED                    (  1)
144.30                              103.09
ACTS                        (  3)     ADO                         (  1)
080.24  219.28  306.07              047.36
ACTUAL                      (  5)     ADOPT                       (  1)
016.32  082.07  082.08  135.06  290.24     071.07
ACTUALLY                    ( 15)     ADOPTED                     (  2)
006.14  006.31  023.24  032.32  035.30     037.29  284.07
037.36  050.32  069.23  088.06  102.24     ADORN                       (  4)
107.17  152.08  211.26  222.20  259.35     038.14  038.27  199.25  201.15
ACTUATED                    (  1)     ADORNED                     (  2)
268.03                              113.34  327.10
AD                          (  3)     ADORNS                      (  1)
250.14  250.15  314.01              310.12
ADAM                        (  7)     ADULT                       (  1)
010.07  028.03  052.09  097.02  179.18     227.05
209.03  331.29                      ADVANCE                     (  5)
ADAPT                       (  1)     015.13  031.10  052.13  080.22  108.26
063.11                              ADVANCED                    (  4)
ADAPTED                     (  4)     028.18  030.08  051.30  112.04
011.06  039.24  039.32  040.05      ADVANCES                    (  1)
ADD                         (  6)     323.30
063.22  067.18  091.23  106.18  161.16     ADVANTAGE                   ( 15)
211.26                              011.32  020.26  031.29  032.04  032.05
ADDED                       (  3)     037.18  050.07  056.18  071.28  082.01
127.12  155.04  287.06              099.29  112.25  243.08  300.30  314.21
ADDING                      (  3)     ADVANTAGES                  (  8)
021.30  269.08  302.17              021.09  031.12  040.16  083.24  109.26
ADDITION                    (  3)     132.06  264.07  268.14
013.21  024.13  061.26              ADVENT                      (  1)
ADDITIONAL                  (  1)     291.35
047.20                              ADVENTURE                   (  2)
ADDITO                      (  1)     015.26  210.20
063.18                              ADVENTURERS                 (  1)
ADDRESS                     (  1)     020.36
060.22                              ADVENTURES                  (  5)
ADDRESSED                   (  2)     072.13  164.20  207.26  208.29  329.22
004.03  107.31                      ADVENTUROUS                 (  4)
ADDS                        (  6)     022.34  100.29  115.26  119.15
027.17  030.05  162.22  198.12  231.34     ADVENTUROUSLY               (  2)
306.31                              174.20  187.31
```

ADVERSARY (2)
229.15 235.07
ADVERTISED (3)
118.16 121.18 187.20
ADVERTISEMENT (1)
089.05
ADVICE (5)
009.05 009.12 160.18 245.28 268.35
ADVISE (4)
067.01 070.22 156.24 224.15
ADVISED (1)
251.36
AEACUS (1)
144.31
AENEAS (1)
231.31
AEOLIAN (1)
131.09
AERIAL (1)
159.23
AES (1)
007.01
AESCHYLUS (2)
100.07 103.25
AESCULAPIUS (1)
139.01
AFAR (1)
229.33
AFFAIR (1)
025.14
AFFAIRS (5)
003.10 016.05 091.25 161.20 172.32
AFFECT (5)
049.37 061.12 090.25 121.14 181.05
AFFECTED (9)
088.35 118.30 135.04 135.05 138.10
211.34 262.09 299.20 306.09
AFFECTING (1)
167.35
AFFECTION (1)
251.27
AFFECTIONS (3)
028.07 135.08 297.16
AFFECTS (1)
025.14
AFFIRMED (1)
259.23
AFFLICTED (2)
010.11 277.22
AFFORD (16)
006.16 030.32 030.33 036.01 036.04
075.29 082.04 083.31 111.22 138.08
141.16 148.36 253.18 281.29 313.25
320.29
AFFORDED (5)
045.27 059.37 271.02 273.29 318.19
AFFORDING (1)
087.29
AFFORDS (6)
020.09 079.18 246.08 246.18 307.26
330.10
AFOOT (1)
053.07
AFORETHOUGHT (2)
073.28 331.20
AFRAID (5)
003.17 069.23 130.36 210.33 280.08
AFRICA (3)
130.23 320.26 321.01
AFRICAN (1)
074.20
AFRICANUS (1)
258.06
AFTER (98)
003.27 008.14 018.18 018.31 024.12
026.27 027.14 028.32 044.35 045.16
047.31 049.27 052.33 061.02 063.05
064.21 067.28 067.32 068.19 075.11

AFTER (CONTINUED)
076.24 079.16 085.18 089.24 093.25
093.30 094.22 097.02 101.34 104.34
121.04 123.35 124.09 131.30 144.37
145.28 147.02 167.03 169.12 170.01
170.19 173.24 173.27 174.31 180.09
190.25 193.03 197.04 198.11 199.04
199.27 202.23 206.19 207.05 207.12
221.28 221.35 223.27 227.30 231.15
231.31 235.32 236.03 242.01 242.16
246.34 248.27 248.29 249.31 250.36
251.16 253.22 254.19 262.12 263.23
264.02 266.12 271.06 275.18 277.27
280.19 282.02 282.23 287.32 288.21
301.07 301.13 301.19 302.23 302.32
304.03 315.23 318.28 320.27 324.26
326.21 326.29 332.33
AFTERNOON (21)
081.31 086.25 114.24 122.35 132.23
167.08 171.20 183.13 186.19 188.15
189.12 190.25 198.25 203.04 234.17
253.04 266.02 267.21 278.01 278.09
331.19
AFTERNOONS (3)
159.13 203.19 276.30
AFTERWARD (9)
044.04 143.01 146.04 226.06 227.02
247.18 253.05 259.31 333.10
AFTERWARDS (2)
268.24 275.07
AGAIN (89)
003.09 018.04 025.29 028.11 037.21
038.20 044.09 054.30 061.09 068.03
088.33 088.33 088.34 089.27 093.05
095.07 101.18 105.06 105.11 113.07
114.20 115.03 124.15 126.06 126.33
126.33 132.15 132.37 140.28 141.04
142.28 152.12 160.21 160.29 163.34
165.13 167.04 169.16 171.15 174.29
175.19 178.22 181.01 181.07 181.11
181.25 187.10 188.07 188.13 193.06
194.11 205.13 205.18 207.13 208.27
213.35 213.35 214.10 224.34 225.01
226.29 226.36 227.20 231.07 234.12
234.24 234.27 235.09 235.27 235.29
235.30 251.34 259.02 262.03 264.20
266.11 274.29 276.11 276.35 278.08
279.05 307.10 308.25 311.07 311.35
313.21 315.21 316.36 316.37
AGAINST (35)
007.13 008.04 031.30 033.36 039.02
078.11 078.14 084.30 102.33 115.35
120.22 128.13 142.12 156.24 159.05
168.06 171.32 171.33 176.31 186.24
186.32 211.28 222.08 226.09 228.35
235.06 236.22 246.36 248.03 248.16
261.24 264.17 273.02 280.30 322.19
AGE (19)
008.36 015.13 083.30 102.16 103.34
106.13 107.04 130.01 153.22 179.31
210.26 212.31 241.06 243.14 250.34
303.20 313.35 315.34 331.04
AGENT (1)
259.28
AGES (15)
010.26 010.27 012.04 037.18 088.35
097.06 098.09 101.20 101.35 105.20
211.15 221.20 268.31 273.12 333.18
AGGREGATE (1)
291.08
AGITATED (4)
176.10 177.04 187.29 299.05
AGO (18)
017.11 091.17 094.07 108.14 133.04
164.14 178.04 181.01 186.11 190.27
193.09 198.02 198.08 251.04 259.03
261.26 277.36 282.14

AGREE (3)
073.06 127.24 136.14
AGREEABLE (8)
045.20 047.30 054.19 062.07 186.01
214.30 242.22 305.24
AGRI (1)
037.30
AGRICOLA (1)
157.14
AGRICULTURAL (2)
033.16 158.04
AGRICULTURE (3)
014.31 039.33 166.02
AGUISH (1)
043.16
AH (5)
217.12 240.04 270.04 284.18 317.16
AHEAD (1)
053.20
AID (6)
056.35 065.28 075.13 157.07 198.25
236.25
AIDS (1)
090.16
AIL (2)
077.20 078.07
AILED (1)
165.19
AILMENT (1)
108.34
AILS (1)
013.33
AIM (3)
027.04 027.05 092.10
AIMING (1)
073.27
AIMS (1)
329.05
AIR (62)
015.34 028.21 029.13 030.18 033.31
036.31 085.25 086.24 086.29 089.04
089.18 114.16 114.28 118.21 121.32
121.35 123.13 138.28 138.28 159.18
159.24 162.32 164.29 174.25 175.15
175.21 177.19 183.10 187.05 188.34
189.06 189.14 189.35 190.18 207.20
217.17 236.21 236.27 247.15 247.26
248.20 253.29 270.01 278.32 285.06
294.08 294.10 296.02 296.05 296.22
297.09 300.09 300.14 300.21 300.27
301.28 316.36 317.07 318.15 319.09
320.04 324.06
AIRS (1)
230.10
AIRY (4)
084.35 085.06 242.13 306.35
AISLES (3)
192.08 278.17 278.29
AKIN (1)
123.31
ALABASTER (1)
177.29
ALARM (2)
227.18 259.32
ALARMED (2)
065.13 190.08
ALARMING (1)
272.25
ALAS (10)
040.12 046.08 109.08 152.35 164.06
205.35 206.25 207.01 259.36 264.18
ALBURNUM (1)
333.20
ALDEBARAN (1)
088.09
ALDER (5)
129.13 201.17 250.02 284.08 284.13

ALDERMAN (1)
218.14
ALDERMANIC (1)
126.20
ALDERS (3)
181.24 182.01 284.15
ALERT (9)
008.21 011.13 104.19 106.32 111.13
119.15 127.19 233.28 302.18
ALEXANDER (2)
102.18 298.23
ALGONQUINS (1)
212.25
ALIENUM (1)
007.01
ALIGHT (3)
146.32 248.30 276.02
ALIGHTED (2)
165.10 275.36
ALIKE (4)
099.06 166.11 176.11 197.24
ALIMENT (2)
108.33 108.34
ALIVE (12)
058.05 090.12 098.18 153.31 153.34
190.29 253.05 268.28 280.17 302.05
311.35 312.25
ALKALI (1)
063.13
ALL (447)
003.14 003.27 005.13 006.27 006.30
007.23 007.31 009.23 009.32 010.26
010.26 011.01 011.12 011.18 011.25
012.09 014.08 016.23 017.09 017.31
018.15 018.16 018.31 020.12 020.20
020.26 020.27 020.35 021.05 023.29
023.33 024.20 024.24 025.04 025.24
026.11 028.32 030.25 032.05 032.12
033.16 033.25 033.31 034.12 035.05
035.10 035.30 036.03 036.28 037.12
037.16 039.16 040.07 041.11 042.07
042.16 043.09 043.22 043.28 044.02
044.02 044.31 046.14 046.28 048.34
049.22 049.24 051.28 052.33 053.26
053.29 053.32 054.11 054.30 055.21
055.27 056.01 056.22 057.04 057.19
058.14 059.14 059.29 060.07 060.10
060.10 060.20 060.29 063.11 063.28
064.22 065.09 066.06 066.15 066.17
066.24 067.04 067.06 067.06 067.37
068.14 068.17 068.20 068.24 069.11
069.36 071.19 072.12 072.13 072.20
072.25 072.31 072.34 073.11 073.29
075.12 076.28 076.35 078.27 078.29
080.25 081.08 081.09 082.06 082.18
082.30 083.02 083.15 083.27 083.29
083.33 084.04 086.25 087.20 087.30
089.11 089.28 089.30 089.32 091.03
091.04 091.32 092.04 092.06 093.18
094.20 096.35 097.03 097.06 097.07
098.29 099.04 099.06 100.17 102.16
102.24 102.32 103.13 104.04 104.25
104.34 105.10 105.12 105.16 105.22
105.22 105.32 106.05 106.11 106.26
107.09 107.23 107.30 108.05 108.20
109.33 110.11 110.14 111.07 112.36
115.05 115.36 116.01 116.02 116.23
117.11 117.13 118.08 118.21 119.20
120.02 120.06 120.11 120.33 120.35
121.33 122.32 123.07 125.18 125.31
125.31 126.07 127.23 127.24 129.09
130.18 130.25 131.01 132.04 132.31
133.23 134.04 134.06 134.09 134.21
134.26 134.35 135.32 136.03 136.22
138.04 138.04 138.10 140.12 140.27
141.19 142.35 145.17 145.33 145.35
146.27 147.02 147.28 149.21 149.35
150.25 151.05 151.30 152.29 152.33

```
153.10  153.13  153.19  154.01  154.17
155.14  155.25  156.03  156.23  156.24
158.09  158.21  159.10  160.10  160.24
160.34  161.16  162.17  162.25  162.26
163.11  163.22  163.37  164.24  164.27
104.35  165.04  166.10  166.13  166.26
166.34  168.10  168.28  169.22  170.04
172.19  173.04  173.31  174.32  176.05
176.11  178.31  179.01  181.26  182.03
182.10  183.07  183.09  184.24  184.26
185.06  185.10  185.17  187.34  188.06
188.29  190.02  190.25  190.28  192.23
192.30  193.02  193.03  196.13  196.33
197.19  199.16  201.32  203.02  205.31
206.12  209.01  211.29  213.18  213.21
214.08  214.12  214.16  215.07  216.27
217.16  217.32  218.35  220.21  220.26
220.27  221.04  221.30  222.20  223.09
224.14  225.19  226.13  227.06  228.23
229.01  229.16  230.06  231.01  232.27
232.32  233.27  234.04  236.07  236.22
242.33  243.02  243.34  243.36  244.32
244.35  246.03  248.13  249.23  250.36
252.13  254.35  257.27  257.31  258.17
259.22  259.25  259.31  260.26  260.29
261.05  262.05  262.32  263.15  263.18
264.10  267.03  268.05  269.08  269.11
272.16  273.28  274.03  274.04  274.12
274.13  275.01  276.32  277.29  278.13
278.29  280.26  282.06  283.10  284.03
284.32  284.33  285.04  287.10  287.26
289.02  289.12  289.28  290.05  290.23
290.25  293.24  293.28  295.05  297.02
297.20  297.25  301.07  302.05  302.33
303.15  303.26  304.09  305.16  308.16
309.06  310.18  310.29  310.33  311.26
311.34  312.04  313.27  314.27  314.39
315.13  317.05  317.23  317.34  317.35
318.28  320.05  321.26  322.13  322.16
322.17  322.18  322.18  326.25  327.01
327.14  328.28  328.36  329.30  330.02
333.02  333.28
```
ALLEY   (1)
```
244.23
```
ALLIED   (3)
```
220.09  220.11  281.21
```
ALLIGATOR   (1)
```
303.12
```
ALLOW   (5)
```
036.16  095.31  113.07  134.07  209.01
```
ALLOWANCE   (3)
```
018.33  036.17  112.01
```
ALLOWED   (3)
```
091.30  153.33  280.21
```
ALLOWING   (1)
```
181.13
```
ALLOY   (2)
```
146.12  329.18
```
ALLURE   (1)
```
168.29
```
ALLUVION   (1)
```
097.35
```
ALMANAC   (3)
```
148.25  296.14  297.22
```
ALMOND   (1)
```
046.34
```
ALMONDS   (1)
```
046.35
```
ALMOST   (51)
```
007.18  009.02  020.17  023.07  027.27
029.27  031.28  044.31  053.09  076.15
093.18  095.03  101.05  101.13  103.27
105.34  108.33  113.08  120.34  124.02
126.04  126.12  129.13  140.19  152.14
156.05  163.33  176.16  187.16  189.21
193.07  193.19  211.13  215.07  228.06
238.31  239.27  250.04  251.11  252.11
```

```
253.19  261.08  281.09  288.31  290.04
293.11  295.16  299.24  305.31  311.09
313.27
```
ALMS   (2)
```
257.02  328.12
```
ALMSHOUSE   (3)
```
028.34  034.27  151.03
```
ALOFT   (2)
```
039.01  243.28
```
ALONE   (39)
```
003.04  023.07  038.16  046.17  051.06
061.01  065.01  072.14  082.04  083.31
111.08  122.34  131.33  135.20  135.22
135.27  135.32  135.35  136.03  136.24
136.36  137.09  137.11  137.12  144.29
166.06  197.05  200.04  211.06  224.07
224.23  256.27  260.22  290.09  317.03
321.35  324.18  325.04  327.28
```
ALONG   (32)
```
009.25  044.10  066.28  095.36  115.15
121.34  122.37  124.26  127.23  129.06
130.06  145.21  146.17  164.33  168.05
175.11  178.21  185.05  194.30  198.28
224.03  226.01  229.25  232.24  233.10
234.16  274.36  304.02  304.17  308.34
311.17  319.12
```
ALOOF   (1)
```
134.35
```
ALOUD   (1)
```
158.02
```
ALPHABET   (1)
```
098.24
```
ALREADY   (33)
```
006.32  019.33  041.17  042.38  048.24
050.14  052.19  056.11  064.23  155.04
179.20  190.10  195.25  203.22  211.05
211.20  228.14  229.02  229.18  229.20
239.36  242.07  247.07  249.08  270.11
288.08  294.31  306.20  310.05  310.31
312.11  314.26  319.05
```
ALSO   (67)
```
008.03  013.22  015.30  016.22  024.06
029.36  032.13  042.07  043.19  046.21
049.26  054.22  060.40  062.06  068.34
070.02  071.31  072.24  087.09  125.07
132.12  136.33  141.04  143.20  159.03
163.40  166.28  166.36  176.35  177.01
180.23  181.15  183.27  184.08  184.26
104.32  185.14  195.12  202.31  204.28
217.20  236.02  238.30  241.19  247.07
249.26  258.08  266.36  272.33  275.24
276.06  276.23  279.23  279.31  289.25
289.35  291.20  292.20  293.28  300.02
300.12  300.35  301.28  306.26  306.34
307.19  320.29
```
ALTAIR   (1)
```
088.10
```
ALTER   (1)
```
322.01
```
ALTERED   (1)
```
208.32
```
ALTERNATELY   (5)
```
159.27  160.34  180.02  280.35  316.26
```
ALTERNATING   (1)
```
177.13
```
ALTERNATIVE   (2)
```
015.25  029.17
```
ALTHOUGH   (1)
```
198.15
```
ALTO   (1)
```
180.14
```
ALTOGETHER   (3)
```
053.22  064.19  174.05
```
ALWAYS   (49)
```
003.27  006.36  007.03  018.22  020.04
020.10  032.07  036.04  052.13  061.08
063.25  065.35  079.13  083.34  088.23
```

9

```
096.04 098.25 100.12 100.29 111.16
112.30 129.33 130.11 134.05 135.26
138.21 141.33 149.30 150.17 150.24
151.23 153.32 161.03 165.16 165.17
212.34 213.05 214.01 217.08 228.35
238.25 246.24 254.22 260.29 268.28
284.21 314.21 325.08 333.03
```
AM   (91)
```
003.09 003.30 009.17 017.12 022.05
025.08 025.09 025.15 029.07 029.23
032.28 038.21 040.04 049.40 050.02
053.06 056.14 056.25 061.33 063.06
063.06 065.02 065.06 067.13 070.33
073.06 073.17 082.30 090.02 093.02
094.11 110.09 115.15 115.20 117.14
118.30 119.18 122.34 127.01 131.24
133.07 135.08 135.11 137.04 137.13
137.15 138.15 138.35 140.04 140.06
140.24 144.15 151.25 162.09 164.08
172.19 179.12 184.06 193.26 206.28
207.10 211.32 212.02 212.07 212.17
214.07 214.08 215.35 217.05 217.13
217.23 217.23 217.28 224.05 224.07
233.02 244.27 244.28 244.33 264.23
272.26 276.27 284.20 287.11 302.18
306.09 309.35 324.29 329.24 329.31
332.15
```
AMATEUR   (1)
```
158.27
```
AMAZEMENT   (1)
```
278.34
```
AMBASSADORS   (1)
```
164.33
```
AMBER   (1)
```
283.07
```
AMBITION   (2)
```
057.27 245.24
```
AMBITIOUS   (2)
```
058.08 332.09
```
AMBROSIAL   (1)
```
173.19
```
AMENDS   (1)
```
268.08
```
AMERICA   (8)
```
025.24 062.29 204.21 205.22 205.24
217.16 230.15 324.09
```
AMERICAN   (3)
```
035.19 052.32 120.10
```
AMERICANS   (1)
```
325.33
```
AMERICANUS   (1)
```
280.25
```
AMID   (17)
```
042.27 113.12 117.04 125.34 185.34
188.02 194.34 229.12 235.22 238.25
257.32 266.26 278.21 280.08 282.34
323.27 332.10
```
AMIDST   (3)
```
111.27 318.32 333.25
```
AMMIRAL   (1)
```
121.28
```
AMNESTY   (1)
```
068.23
```
AMOK   (2)
```
171.32 171.33
```
AMONG   (27)
```
055.31 067.31 072.23 105.14 108.18
120.05 121.11 135.25 144.31 151.02
152.02 152.03 152.24 167.17 211.14
224.16 224.19 230.03 257.10 259.19
259.27 265.30 273.13 281.18 294.14
310.03 313.28
```
AMOST   (1)
```
269.01
```
AMOUNT   (12)
```
031.14 046.13 055.20 057.28 076.01
106.03 149.11 153.31 164.32 181.04
```

AMOUNT   (CONTINUED)
```
288.21 293.11
```
AMOUNTED   (3)
```
060.02 150.15 294.30
```
AMOUNTS   (2)
```
205.09 263.19
```
AMPHITHEATRE   (1)
```
191.27
```
AMPLE   (3)
```
087.29 186.04 199.26
```
AMUSE   (1)
```
172.10
```
AMUSED   (7)
```
026.09 146.26 249.33 256.30 266.03
273.25 284.06
```
AMUSEMENT   (6)
```
062.08 112.27 112.28 162.15 206.13
313.07
```
AMUSEMENTS   (3)
```
008.13 211.09 211.12
```
AN   (356)
```
004.33 005.27 006.34 007.08 007.14
008.05 009.01 009.14 010.25 010.26
010.36 011.33 012.31 012.32 014.05
014.28 018.20 022.15 022.29 023.15
024.07 024.25 025.05 025.14 025.31
026.03 028.13 028.33 030.24 030.35
030.36 031.16 031.33 031.36 033.07
035.05 037.14 037.15 037.30 040.32
041.02 041.28 043.01 043.03 043.25
043.28 044.12 044.32 045.05 046.16
046.34 047.36 048.17 048.20 049.33
050.15 050.22 051.04 052.12 052.18
052.18 052.35 053.28 054.26 055.28
055.34 056.03 057.27 057.35 058.14
061.34 062.10 063.05 063.10 064.30
065.18 066.30 067.02 067.04 067.35
068.36 069.03 072.30 074.31 077.12
079.01 079.19 081.26 081.31 083.12
084.22 085.05 085.29 086.05 088.10
089.03 089.09 089.22 089.32 090.04
090.16 091.21 092.06 092.16 092.27
093.01 094.02 094.08 094.36 095.06
095.24 096.30 098.31 100.22 102.27
103.05 106.20 112.30 113.15 114.12
115.18 115.19 115.35 118.15 118.31
119.13 120.29 121.23 123.17 123.36
125.12 127.34 128.07 131.31 132.03
132.05 132.25 134.24 134.27 134.31
135.05 137.04 137.17 137.21 137.31
142.11 143.25 143.26 145.29 146.20
147.06 148.25 148.25 148.28 149.07
149.18 150.04 150.30 151.13 155.20
155.26 156.16 157.36 159.06 159.07
160.30 163.32 164.16 165.16 169.10
173.31 177.19 177.29 178.01 178.17
179.17 181.25 182.07 187.05 187.14
187.17 188.07 188.16 188.16 188.17
190.05 190.06 190.26 190.31 191.02
191.04 191.09 191.27 191.29 192.28
193.05 195.14 195.22 195.26 197.10
199.01 202.34 203.07 203.24 204.07
204.21 204.36 205.36 205.36 206.07
206.24 207.16 210.16 211.17 211.21
211.22 214.19 214.32 215.25 217.07
217.12 218.01 218.13 218.14 218.29
219.06 219.09 219.18 220.40 224.26
224.31 227.09 227.30 228.28 229.16
229.36 230.18 231.06 231.15 231.36
236.03 238.09 239.20 240.28 241.07
241.35 242.31 243.06 243.22 246.20
247.03 247.04 247.04 247.09 247.19
247.22 248.05 248.09 248.11 248.11
249.16 249.19 250.29 251.29 257.13
258.09 258.33 259.11 261.32 261.35
262.15 265.05 265.29 265.30 266.12
267.04 269.02 269.02 271.12 272.17
272.27 273.04 274.31 275.12 275.19
```

11

AND				(CONTINUED)
053.31	053.32	053.33	053.35	053.35
054.03	054.08	054.19	054.21	054.21
054.23	054.24	054.24	054.25	054.29
054.30	054.32	054.35	054.36	055.02
055.08	055.09	055.09	055.18	055.23
055.29	055.32	055.33	055.33	055.35
055.36	055.38	056.01	056.03	056.05
056.07	056.16	056.21	056.24	056.27
056.30	056.32	056.35	056.36	057.03
057.13	057.13	057.20	057.21	057.30
058.01	058.01	058.09	058.10	058.12
058.13	058.17	058.17	058.19	058.20
058.23	058.25	058.26	058.29	058.33
059.04	059.17	059.32	059.34	059.36
059.43	060.05	060.08	060.09	060.10
060.10	060.23	060.33	060.34	060.35
060.35	060.38	061.02	061.04	061.04
061.09	061.17	061.18	061.21	061.23
061.27	061.30	061.35	062.01	062.05
062.06	062.07	062.09	062.12	062.15
062.17	062.18	062.19	062.20	062.22
062.29	062.31	062.33	062.36	063.02
063.03	063.05	063.06	063.08	063.10
063.12	063.21	063.22	063.23	063.29
063.30	063.30	063.31	063.32	063.33
063.33	063.35	063.36	064.03	064.04
064.05	064.05	064.06	064.06	064.09
064.10	064.15	064.15	064.22	064.23
064.24	064.28	064.29	064.33	065.01
065.09	065.16	065.20	065.20	065.21
065.23	065.27	065.30	065.31	066.02
066.06	066.07	066.16	066.17	066.18
066.18	066.19	066.24	066.34	067.01
067.01	067.02	067.08	067.13	067.13
067.16	067.32	067.33	067.37	068.01
068.13	068.14	068.15	068.16	068.16
068.18	068.19	068.20	068.23	068.28
068.29	068.29	068.30	068.30	068.31
068.33	069.02	069.03	069.03	069.10
069.13	069.14	069.17	069.17	069.18
069.22	069.28	069.30	070.01	070.07
070.10	070.11	070.16	070.18	070.24
070.29	070.33	070.35	071.12	071.12
071.24	071.29	071.30	071.31	071.33
071.34	072.08	072.16	072.23	072.26
072.30	072.32	072.34	072.35	073.01
073.05	073.07	073.10	073.13	073.13
073.14	073.14	073.24	073.26	073.27
073.32	073.34	073.34	073.36	074.02
074.02	074.07	074.09	074.10	074.10
074.12	074.19	074.21	074.21	074.21
074.31	074.32	075.08	075.11	075.16
075.18	075.18	075.18	075.19	075.22
075.23	075.26	075.27	075.28	075.29
075.32	075.36	076.01	076.10	076.17
076.21	076.22	076.23	076.25	076.26
076.30	076.30	076.32	076.35	077.01
077.01	077.04	077.05	077.06	077.07
077.09	077.13	077.14	077.14	077.15
077.15	077.19	077.24	077.25	077.29
077.30	077.31	077.31	077.32	078.01
078.01	078.02	078.04	078.09	078.18
078.19	078.22	078.23	078.26	078.27
078.28	078.29	078.30	078.33	078.35
079.06	079.09	079.09	079.11	079.11
079.13	080.10	080.13	080.14	080.26
080.30	081.02	081.09	081.15	081.16
081.20	081.26	081.27	081.28	081.32
081.33	081.34	082.01	082.09	082.10
082.14	082.14	082.16	082.19	082.21
082.23	082.23	082.23	082.26	083.02
083.03	083.07	083.10	083.11	083.11
083.12	083.13	083.21	083.26	083.28
084.01	084.01	084.04	084.08	084.11
084.14	084.15	084.34	084.34	084.35
085.06	085.07	085.17	085.23	085.34
085.35	086.02	086.04	086.04	086.06

AND				(CONTINUED)
086.06	086.14	086.15	086.15	086.24
086.26	086.26	086.28	086.29	086.30
087.03	087.04	087.06	087.08	087.13
087.21	087.22	087.29	087.33	087.34
087.34	087.35	088.02	088.03	088.05
088.07	088.12	088.13	088.18	088.26
088.28	088.29	088.33	088.33	088.36
089.01	089.03	089.04	089.06	089.09
089.11	089.15	089.17	089.19	089.20
089.22	089.23	089.24	089.26	089.29
089.31	089.31	089.31	089.33	089.34
089.35	090.01	090.02	090.15	090.22
090.23	090.24	090.28	090.34	090.34
091.02	091.03	091.05	091.06	091.06
091.07	091.08	091.10	091.13	091.14
091.19	091.19	091.20	091.23	091.25
091.27	091.29	091.29	091.29	091.30
091.31	091.32	091.33	091.36	092.06
092.07	092.08	092.09	092.10	092.11
092.12	092.13	092.15	092.15	092.16
092.19	092.19	092.20	092.22	092.23
092.28	092.29	092.30	092.31	092.33
092.35	092.36	093.01	093.03	093.06
093.08	093.11	093.18	093.21	093.22
093.26	093.29	093.33	093.34	094.01
094.11	094.20	094.21	094.21	094.31
094.31	094.31	094.32	094.34	094.36
095.01	095.02	095.05	095.15	095.24
095.24	095.29	095.31	095.33	095.35
095.35	096.01	096.01	096.02	096.03
096.05	096.05	096.06	096.07	096.07
096.10	096.15	096.19	096.20	096.24
096.29	096.34	096.35	097.02	097.03
097.04	097.04	097.04	097.05	097.07
097.08	097.08	097.10	097.13	097.16
097.17	097.19	097.19	097.20	097.21
097.22	097.23	097.24	097.26	097.32
097.32	097.33	097.34	097.34	097.34
097.34	097.36	097.36	098.01	098.01
098.02	098.02	098.03	098.04	098.04
098.04	098.05	098.06	098.09	098.11
098.13	098.14	098.14	098.17	098.20
098.27	098.29	098.32	098.32	098.33
098.35	098.36	099.05	099.06	099.10
099.12	099.13	099.15	099.22	099.26
099.34	099.35	100.05	100.10	100.13
100.14	100.16	100.16	100.17	100.19
100.20	100.21	100.24	100.26	100.28
100.31	100.33	100.35	101.02	101.06
101.10	101.11	101.13	101.15	101.16
101.19	101.25	101.27	101.32	101.34
101.35	102.05	102.07	102.08	102.11
102.13	102.14	102.15	102.21	102.23
102.30	102.31	102.34	102.35	102.35
102.36	103.02	103.04	103.05	103.06
103.07	103.08	103.08	103.09	103.11
103.11	103.12	103.13	103.13	103.16
103.26	103.29	103.29	103.30	103.33
103.34	103.35	103.36	104.03	104.03
104.04	104.04	104.04	104.14	104.17
104.19	104.19	104.22	104.23	104.24
104.26	104.27	104.28	104.33	104.35
105.02	105.03	105.04	105.05	105.06
105.06	105.08	105.11	105.15	105.16
105.23	105.23	105.24	105.31	105.31
105.33	105.34	105.34	106.06	106.06
106.07	106.09	106.10	106.16	106.18
106.20	106.30	106.31	106.32	106.32
107.03	107.04	107.05	107.06	107.07
107.07	107.08	107.08	107.10	107.14
107.15	107.15	107.19	107.20	107.20
107.20	107.23	107.24	107.27	107.32
107.34	108.02	108.02	108.04	108.04
108.06	108.08	108.11	108.11	108.12
108.14	108.16	108.17	108.17	108.19
108.21	108.23	108.31	108.36	109.01
109.06	109.09	109.10	109.14	109.15

AND   (CONTINUED)

109.23	109.30	109.34	109.35	110.03
110.05	110.09	110.12	110.12	110.13
110.17	111.04	111.04	111.06	111.07
111.08	111.19	111.27	111.28	111.28
111.34	112.01	112.03	112.05	112.06
112.13	112.16	112.16	112.18	112.20
112.24	112.27	112.28	112.29	112.31
112.31	112.34	112.36	113.01	113.03
113.04	113.04	113.05	113.07	113.10
113.11	113.11	113.12	113.13	113.15
113.17	113.20	113.22	113.24	113.28
113.28	113.31	113.31	113.32	113.32
114.01	114.06	114.11	114.12	114.14
114.14	114.20	114.20	114.26	114.29
114.31	114.32	114.33	114.34	115.03
115.04	115.05	115.10	115.15	115.19
115.20	115.23	115.32	115.35	115.36
115.37	116.10	116.13	116.19	116.20
116.24	116.28	116.30	116.34	116.34
116.36	117.05	117.07	117.09	117.12
117.14	117.15	117.17	117.17	117.22
117.22	117.24	117.24	117.31	117.32
117.33	117.34	117.34	117.35	118.03
118.10	118.11	118.17	118.19	118.25
118.25	118.27	118.28	118.32	119.04
119.08	119.09	119.11	119.14	119.15
119.17	119.17	119.18	119.19	119.22
119.23	119.23	119.27	119.28	119.29
119.30	120.02	120.03	120.03	120.06
120.07	120.12	120.14	120.14	120.16
120.17	120.19	120.21	120.21	120.22
120.23	120.23	120.27	120.28	120.28
120.31	120.34	120.34	121.03	121.03
121.04	121.08	121.09	121.12	121.13
121.21	121.23	121.24	121.30	121.31
121.32	121.36	121.36	122.02	122.12
122.14	122.14	122.15	122.16	122.16
122.23	122.25	122.28	122.29	122.29
122.32	122.33	123.03	123.06	123.13
123.14	123.16	123.16	123.17	123.18
123.21	123.23	123.24	123.26	123.28
123.32	124.08	124.12	124.15	124.16
124.20	124.23	124.27	124.27	124.28
124.29	124.31	124.35	125.01	125.05
125.09	125.12	125.15	125.18	125.19
125.19	125.21	125.26	125.27	125.28
125.30	125.33	125.34	125.35	125.35
125.36	125.36	126.05	126.09	126.15
126.15	126.16	126.17	126.19	126.19
126.23	126.24	126.27	126.28	126.30
126.32	126.32	126.33	126.34	126.36
127.02	127.06	127.09	127.10	127.13
127.15	127.16	127.19	127.20	127.21
127.27	128.02	128.06	128.11	128.12
128.13	128.19	129.04	129.05	129.08
129.08	129.10	129.13	129.18	129.19
129.21	129.22	129.22	129.26	129.32
129.35	130.03	130.11	130.12	130.12
130.13	130.16	130.20	130.24	130.24
130.25	130.31	130.33	130.33	130.33
131.01	131.01	131.04	131.04	131.06
131.08	131.10	131.11	131.14	131.15
131.19	131.20	131.25	131.26	131.26
131.29	131.32	131.35	132.01	132.02
132.03	132.04	132.07	132.08	132.09
132.12	132.12	132.13	132.24	132.26
132.29	132.31	132.34	132.35	132.36
133.01	133.01	133.03	133.06	133.06
133.07	133.16	133.25	133.35	133.35
133.36	134.04	134.05	134.07	134.15
134.16	134.17	134.18	134.21	134.22
134.23	134.35	134.35	135.01	135.08
135.08	135.12	135.14	135.19	135.22
135.29	135.33	135.36	136.01	136.02
136.03	136.06	136.06	136.07	136.08
136.13	136.15	136.16	136.18	136.18
136.19	136.20	136.20	136.22	136.28

AND   (CONTINUED)

136.29	136.32	136.33	136.33	136.35
136.35	137.07	137.20	137.21	137.23
137.23	137.24	137.24	137.26	137.27
137.29	137.34	137.35	137.36	138.01
138.03	138.04	138.04	138.06	138.07
138.07	138.07	138.09	138.10	138.11
138.12	138.12	138.13	138.16	138.21
138.24	138.30	138.34	139.01	139.02
139.05	139.05	139.06	139.08	139.09
140.04	140.11	140.14	140.16	140.19
140.20	140.21	140.23	140.34	141.01
141.02	141.02	141.05	141.07	141.15
141.17	141.18	141.19	141.28	141.31
141.36	142.01	142.01	142.04	142.06
142.07	142.11	142.12	142.13	142.15
142.17	142.21	142.27	142.35	143.04
143.04	143.08	143.08	143.10	143.11
143.31	143.18	143.20	143.22	143.29
144.24	144.31	145.02	145.03	145.06
145.06	145.08	145.12	145.14	145.18
145.20	145.26	145.27	145.27	146.01
146.02	146.03	146.04	146.05	146.09
146.10	146.10	146.13	146.14	146.17
146.18	146.19	146.20	146.21	146.23
146.30	146.32	146.32	146.33	146.36
147.01	147.03	147.03	147.05	147.07
147.10	147.11	147.13	147.13	147.14
147.15	147.16	147.20	147.21	147.22
147.29	147.31	148.02	148.04	148.07
148.09	148.18	148.23	148.25	148.30
148.31	148.34	148.35	149.01	149.01
149.05	149.06	149.08	149.08	149.09
149.14	149.17	149.18	149.32	149.34
149.36	150.05	150.09	150.11	150.12
150.14	150.16	150.19	150.24	150.27
150.30	150.30	150.32	151.01	151.03
151.05	151.07	151.09	151.10	151.12
151.16	151.17	151.18	151.26	151.29
151.29	151.30	151.33	152.05	152.13
152.19	152.26	152.27	152.30	152.31
153.02	153.02	153.04	153.04	153.06
153.06	153.07	153.15	153.17	153.21
153.22	153.23	153.23	153.25	153.29
153.34	154.16	154.17	154.18	155.08
155.12	155.16	155.17	155.19	155.20
155.22	155.22	155.24	155.25	155.27
155.27	155.29	155.33	155.35	156.03
156.06	156.08	156.09	156.10	156.11
156.12	156.13	156.17	156.17	156.18
156.27	156.29	156.31	157.02	157.04
157.05	157.05	157.09	157.13	157.13
157.15	157.17	157.20	157.20	157.22
157.24	157.29	157.32	157.34	157.34
157.35	157.36	157.36	158.05	158.08
158.09	158.10	158.10	158.11	158.12
158.13	158.17	158.18	158.18	158.25
158.29	158.34	158.35	159.03	159.03
159.03	159.06	159.06	159.08	159.09
159.15	159.16	159.17	159.18	159.20
159.24	159.28	159.20	159.32	159.34
159.35	159.36	160.01	160.05	160.09
160.11	160.15	160.17	160.17	160.21
160.22	160.24	160.28	160.29	160.30
160.33	160.34	160.35	160.36	161.01
161.03	161.06	161.07	161.11	161.14
161.14	161.14	161.14	161.15	161.19
161.20	161.24	161.26	161.31	161.33
161.33	161.35	162.03	162.05	162.06
162.11	162.13	162.17	162.18	162.21
162.25	162.26	162.27	162.29	163.02
163.08	163.09	163.16	163.29	163.30
163.34	163.35	163.36	163.38	163.38
163.41	164.03	164.03	164.04	164.04
164.07	164.07	164.07	164.11	164.13
164.15	164.18	164.20	164.21	164.21
164.23	164.25	164.29	164.30	164.30

164.34	165.01	165.01	165.03	165.10	193.34	193.34	193.34	193.35	193.38
165.12	165.12	165.18	165.18	165.21	194.01	194.04	194.07	194.07	194.10
165.22	165.24	165.25	165.27	165.30	194.12	194.20	194.22	194.22	194.23
165.31	165.33	165.33	165.37	166.03	194.26	194.27	194.29	194.30	194.33
166.04	166.05	166.06	166.06	166.09	195.03	195.04	195.05	195.08	195.09
166.09	166.10	166.11	166.15	166.15	195.15	195.16	195.17	195.22	195.28
166.17	166.20	166.33	166.35	167.03	195.35	196.13	196.17	196.17	196.19
167.05	167.08	167.12	167.14	167.15	196.29	196.33	196.33	196.35	197.01
167.16	167.20	167.25	167.27	167.28	197.04	197.12	197.13	197.15	197.15
167.28	167.30	167.31	167.32	167.34	197.17	197.17	197.26	197.33	198.06
168.04	168.05	168.12	168.14	168.14	198.12	198.17	198.23	198.24	198.27
168.16	168.16	168.18	168.19	168.20	198.28	198.28	198.31	198.33	199.01
168.22	168.22	168.24	168.26	168.27	199.04	199.06	199.06	199.18	199.19
168.30	168.31	168.31	168.35	169.02	199.19	199.21	199.23	199.26	199.26
169.06	169.07	169.09	169.11	169.12	199.26	199.27	200.01	201.05	201.05
169.13	169.14	169.16	169.19	169.19	201.06	201.09	201.10	201.13	201.14
169.22	169.31	170.02	170.04	170.07	201.17	201.18	201.19	201.21	201.21
170.11	170.13	170.14	170.18	170.21	201.31	202.07	202.09	202.12	202.13
170.24	170.30	170.30	170.32	170.33	202.17	202.19	202.27	202.28	202.32
170.36	171.08	171.08	171.10	171.13	202.33	203.14	203.18	203.19	203.25
171.18	171.19	171.22	171.24	171.25	203.26	203.29	203.35	204.01	204.07
171.28	171.29	171.35	172.07	172.09	204.07	204.09	204.12	204.13	204.16
172.12	172.15	172.17	172.20	172.33	204.16	204.19	204.23	204.25	204.27
173.04	173.04	173.07	173.08	173.09	204.31	204.36	204.37	205.04	205.05
173.19	173.21	173.26	173.27	173.31	205.07	205.09	205.12	205.12	205.15
173.34	174.01	174.11	174.14	174.16	205.15	205.16	205.17	205.18	205.20
174.17	174.21	174.24	174.27	174.33	205.21	205.23	205.23	205.26	205.27
174.35	174.35	175.02	175.03	175.05	205.28	206.03	206.04	206.04	206.07
175.06	175.10	175.13	175.15	175.17	206.11	206.13	206.14	206.18	206.20
175.19	175.25	175.29	175.30	175.31	206.22	206.25	206.28	206.30	206.32
175.31	175.32	175.32	175.33	175.35	206.33	207.02	207.02	207.03	207.05
176.02	176.03	176.03	176.04	176.07	207.05	207.08	207.15	207.15	207.17
176.08	176.10	176.13	176.16	176.21	207.19	207.21	207.22	207.22	207.22
176.22	176.31	176.32	177.01	177.02	207.23	207.25	207.26	207.30	207.34
177.08	177.08	177.10	177.11	177.26	208.01	208.02	208.02	208.18	208.20
177.31	177.36	178.02	178.10	178.12	208.21	208.26	208.27	208.29	208.29
178.13	178.14	178.14	178.17	178.20	208.30	208.35	209.03	210.06	210.07
178.21	178.22	178.25	178.27	178.30	210.07	210.13	210.15	210.17	210.18
178.32	178.36	178.36	179.02	179.02	210.18	210.20	210.22	210.23	210.25
179.04	179.08	179.11	179.14	179.16	210.28	210.29	210.35	211.01	211.03
179.16	179.16	179.17	179.19	179.20	211.03	211.10	211.10	211.12	211.16
179.21	179.22	179.22	179.25	179.25	211.16	211.16	211.29	211.31	212.01
179.26	179.26	179.28	180.03	180.03	212.09	212.37	213.01	213.04	213.04
180.05	180.10	180.11	180.17	180.18	213.05	213.20	213.22	213.24	213.25
180.20	180.21	180.22	180.28	180.34	213.35	213.35	214.10	214.12	214.12
181.01	181.03	181.04	181.10	181.10	214.13	214.14	214.16	214.16	214.17
181.14	181.14	181.15	181.19	181.22	214.17	214.21	214.22	214.22	214.22
181.24	181.24	181.26	181.29	181.30	214.24	214.24	214.26	214.33	214.34
181.31	181.33	181.34	182.02	182.04	215.02	215.04	215.06	215.10	215.16
182.05	182.15	182.17	182.18	182.18	215.19	215.19	215.26	215.31	215.32
182.19	182.21	182.23	182.24	182.28	215.32	215.35	216.01	216.04	216.06
182.29	182.35	183.08	183.10	183.21	216.16	216.16	216.19	216.24	216.25
183.26	183.29	184.02	184.05	184.07	216.26	216.28	216.29	216.33	216.35
184.10	184.16	184.18	184.19	184.19	217.08	217.10	217.15	217.15	217.16
184.25	184.26	184.26	184.27	184.28	217.19	217.25	217.33	218.08	218.09
184.29	184.32	184.32	184.33	184.34	218.09	218.21	218.24	218.26	218.26
185.02	185.02	185.04	185.14	185.19	218.29	218.34	219.03	219.11	219.11
185.21	185.29	185.31	186.01	186.05	219.12	219.17	219.17	219.19	219.21
186.07	186.12	186.16	186.16	186.24	219.27	219.28	219.31	219.31	219.32
186.27	186.30	186.33	187.05	187.06	219.33	219.35	219.36	220.01	220.02
187.08	187.10	187.11	187.12	187.13	220.05	220.07	220.09	220.11	220.12
187.21	187.31	187.36	188.03	188.04	220.16	220.20	220.21	220.24	220.29
188.06	188.11	188.14	188.14	188.14	220.38	220.39	221.04	221.11	221.17
188.17	188.22	188.24	188.29	188.33	221.21	221.24	221.24	221.25	221.30
188.35	189.01	189.01	189.06	189.08	221.30	221.31	221.31	222.02	222.05
189.10	189.10	189.14	189.21	189.23	222.07	222.08	222.13	222.15	222.15
189.31	189.32	189.33	189.35	190.08	222.16	222.20	222.22	222.23	223.05
190.09	190.11	190.12	190.13	190.17	223.13	223.13	223.17	223.18	223.20
190.19	190.21	190.24	190.29	190.29	223.20	223.23	223.28	224.01	224.14
190.31	190.33	190.35	190.35	191.05	224.33	225.25	225.27	225.28	225.29
191.08	191.12	191.21	191.21	191.22	225.30	225.31	225.32	226.01	226.01
191.23	191.25	191.31	191.33	191.35	226.02	226.03	226.03	226.04	226.05
192.03	192.03	192.07	192.13	192.14	226.05	226.06	226.07	226.07	226.08
192.15	192.23	192.27	192.31	192.34	226.13	226.13	226.17	226.18	226.19
192.34	192.35	192.36	193.04	193.05	226.20	226.21	226.23	226.26	226.27
193.13	193.13	193.14	193.16	193.17	226.29	226.32	226.33	226.36	227.04
193.19	193.24	193.27	193.29	193.30	227.05	227.14	227.18	227.20	227.21

227.22	227.28	227.31	227.31	227.32
228.01	228.03	228.05	228.11	228.11
228.12	228.13	228.14	228.21	228.29
228.31	228.31	228.36	229.01	229.02
229.03	229.03	229.07	229.09	229.15
229.20	229.32	230.02	230.04	230.06
230.09	230.10	230.13	230.17	230.18
230.20	230.22	230.23	230.25	230.26
230.27	230.32	231.04	231.07	231.09
231.11	231.13	231.13	231.16	231.18
231.24	231.25	231.27	231.28	231.33
232.03	232.14	232.15	232.17	232.28
232.28	232.31	232.32	233.03	233.06
233.08	233.08	233.10	233.11	233.12
233.13	233.20	233.25	233.28	233.28
233.29	233.30	233.36	234.02	234.04
234.05	234.06	234.06	234.11	234.22
234.23	234.25	234.27	234.28	234.28
234.32	234.32	234.33	234.35	234.36
235.02	235.08	235.12	235.16	235.24
235.26	235.28	235.30	236.02	236.04
236.10	236.14	236.16	236.21	236.25
236.26	236.26	236.27	236.28	236.29
236.32	236.32	236.36	236.36	237.02
237.03	238.04	238.05	238.08	238.11
238.11	238.12	238.15	238.18	238.24
238.26	238.26	238.28	238.31	238.33
238.35	239.02	239.09	239.09	239.14
239.17	239.18	239.22	239.22	239.24
239.28	239.29	239.30	239.30	239.32
239.33	239.34	240.04	240.06	240.12
240.13	240.19	240.21	240.25	240.26
241.01	241.02	241.05	241.06	241.10
241.11	241.17	241.17	241.19	241.30
241.33	241.33	241.36	242.02	242.03
242.13	242.15	242.22	242.27	242.29
242.29	242.31	242.32	242.35	242.35
243.06	243.08	243.09	243.11	243.12
243.12	243.13	243.15	243.18	243.20
243.20	243.26	243.27	243.30	243.31
243.31	243.32	243.35	243.36	244.03
244.05	244.05	244.06	244.07	244.07
244.09	244.12	244.14	244.14	244.15
244.18	244.19	244.23	244.26	244.30
244.35	245.04	245.01	245.04	245.04
245.06	245.11	245.17	245.24	245.25
245.30	245.33	245.35	245.36	246.01
246.05	246.11	246.15	246.17	246.18
246.18	246.22	246.24	246.20	246.27
246.30	246.36	247.02	247.05	247.05
247.15	247.16	247.24	247.25	247.25
247.27	247.28	247.31	247.35	248.01
248.03	248.06	248.10	248.11	248.13
248.17	248.19	248.21	248.25	248.28
248.30	248.36	249.03	249.04	249.06
249.09	249.12	249.12	249.22	249.23
249.25	249.31	249.36	250.01	250.04
250.11	250.11	250.13	250.16	250.18
250.19	250.20	250.22	250.30	250.32
250.34	250.35	250.36	251.02	251.05
251.06	251.11	251.11	251.13	251.15
251.16	251.19	251.20	251.20	251.21
251.22	251.22	251.24	251.28	251.34
252.02	252.10	252.16	252.17	252.31
252.33	252.35	252.36	252.38	253.04
253.06	253.08	253.08	253.11	253.14
253.14	253.15	253.17	253.17	253.21
253.22	253.23	253.24	253.30	253.34
253.34	253.36	254.04	254.10	254.20
254.21	254.24	254.25	254.26	254.34
254.35	255.03	255.06	255.08	255.10
256.01	256.04	256.06	256.09	256.13
256.14	256.20	256.20	256.21	256.21
256.22	256.26	256.26	256.27	256.28
256.31	257.07	257.11	257.12	257.17
257.24	257.26	257.27	257.27	257.28
257.36	258.01	258.12	258.26	258.27

258.29	258.30	258.33	258.34	258.36
259.01	259.01	259.02	259.07	259.11
259.13	259.17	259.19	259.19	259.24
259.25	259.27	259.29	259.29	259.30
259.31	259.32	259.35	259.36	260.03
260.08	260.10	260.11	260.13	260.18
260.20	260.21	260.23	260.26	260.28
260.29	260.33	260.35	261.02	261.04
261.07	261.10	261.12	261.15	261.16
261.18	261.19	261.24	261.26	261.28
261.31	262.07	262.10	262.21	262.22
262.25	262.31	263.02	263.04	263.06
263.09	263.16	263.16	263.17	263.20
263.24	263.24	263.26	263.28	263.32
263.33	263.34	263.34	263.35	263.35
264.02	264.03	264.08	264.09	264.13
264.15	264.21	264.27	264.27	264.29
264.36	265.05	265.07	265.11	265.12
265.13	265.22	265.22	265.23	265.31
265.32	265.35	265.36	266.01	266.07
266.09	266.10	266.11	266.17	266.21
266.22	266.23	266.33	266.34	267.04
267.05	267.09	267.12	267.12	267.14
267.18	267.19	267.27	267.29	267.31
267.36	268.04	268.07	268.09	268.19
268.20	268.21	268.25	268.28	268.30
268.34	268.34	269.03	269.05	269.07
269.07	269.09	269.11	269.13	269.15
269.16	269.17	269.17	269.21	269.27
269.27	269.29	269.32	269.33	269.34
269.36	269.36	270.04	270.05	270.06
270.15	271.03	271.07	271.08	271.11
271.15	271.18	271.19	271.21	271.24
271.26	271.28	271.29	271.31	271.33
272.04	272.07	272.12	272.18	272.21
272.23	272.23	272.27	272.28	272.30
272.35	272.36	273.03	273.04	273.08
273.11	273.11	273.18	273.20	273.20
273.25	273.27	273.27	273.29	273.29
273.32	273.34	273.36	274.01	274.02
274.07	274.09	274.11	274.12	274.15
274.19	274.21	274.22	274.24	274.25
274.32	274.33	274.36	275.01	275.03
275.04	275.05	275.07	275.12	275.13
275.14	275.14	275.17	275.18	275.18
275.21	275.26	276.01	276.04	276.07
276.10	276.12	276.14	276.16	276.20
276.28	276.32	276.33	276.35	277.02
277.09	277.10	277.12	277.13	277.17
277.20	277.21	277.21	277.27	277.35
278.01	278.02	278.03	278.04	278.05
278.07	278.08	278.12	278.13	278.15
278.20	278.21	278.22	278.24	278.26
278.27	278.28	278.31	278.32	278.35
278.35	278.35	278.36	279.02	279.02
279.05	279.07	279.10	279.11	279.13
279.18	279.24	279.26	279.30	279.31
279.33	279.36	280.02	280.03	280.08
280.10	280.15	280.15	280.17	280.18
280.22	280.27	280.32	280.35	281.02
281.05	281.06	281.06	281.09	281.10
281.12	281.12	281.13	281.14	281.17
281.18	281.19	281.20	281.21	281.22
281.26	281.29	281.30	281.32	281.34
282.07	282.08	282.09	282.10	282.13
282.15	282.16	282.21	282.22	282.23
282.24	282.26	282.26	283.01	283.08
282.30	282.32	283.01	283.01	283.08
283.11	283.12	283.13	283.14	283.15
283.16	283.17	283.21	283.21	283.28
283.32	283.34	283.34	283.34	283.36
284.02	284.03	284.10	284.10	284.13
284.24	284.26	284.30	284.33	284.35
284.36	285.01	285.02	285.11	285.11
285.23	285.27	285.29	287.01	287.02
287.02	287.06	287.08	287.12	287.19
287.27	287.30	288.03	288.14	288.18

```
ANIMALS                          (CONTINUED)
  253.23  271.01  273.26
ANIMATE                                ( 1)
  321.24
ANIMATED                               ( 1)
  129.24
ANNIHILATION                           ( 1)
  073.10
ANNOUNCES                              ( 1)
  119.06
ANNUAL                                 ( 6)
  030.24  030.36  150.34  185.09  205.08
  333.13
ANNUALLY                               ( 6)
  033.16  049.34  068.06  082.26  109.23
  251.08
ANON                                   ( 3)
  259.29  307.23  311.06
ANOTHER                                ( 78)
  006.26  007.01  010.23  010.28  011.02
  015.25  034.25  041.18  046.21  048.12
  056.32  066.05  071.09  071.28  072.15
  094.17  097.28  121.24  124.08  125.04
  133.18  135.10  136.20  136.21  140.18
  143.32  149.15  149.34  151.23  156.04
  156.36  158.22  159.29  161.27  164.01
  164.06  164.07  164.07  165.01  168.18
  176.07  176.13  176.21  178.16  183.35
  184.19  186.26  187.06  193.10  196.34
  210.17  220.33  221.17  224.27  227.11
  228.30  235.21  243.27  247.11  247.29
  247.29  259.01  259.24  260.05  260.11
  265.35  268.18  279.34  280.19  281.22
  292.20  294.32  305.07  307.23  315.06
  318.20  324.24  330.32
ANSWER                                 ( 8)
  003.23  025.15  038.24  054.12  065.03
  212.28  277.30  282.04
ANSWERED                               ( 13)
  017.14  045.28  095.17  108.07  133.33
  147.03  148.11  150.07  212.11  236.28
  255.02  282.08  330.19
ANSWERING                              ( 3)
  152.13  159.25  311.23
ANSWERS                                ( 5)
  030.34  097.10  100.34  125.20  282.13
ANT                                    ( 3)
  229.25  230.21  230.34
ANTAEUS                                ( 1)
  155.12
ANTE                                   ( 1)
  172.27
ANTHROPIC                              ( 1)
  212.35
ANTICIPATE                             ( 3)
  017.19  020.25  043.33
ANTICIPATED                            ( 2)
  081.31  190.21
ANTICIPATION                           ( 1)
  300.17
ANTIQUARIES                            ( 1)
  309.03
ANTIQUE                                ( 1)
  310.06
ANTIQUITY                              ( 6)
  080.27  100.19  101.33  107.02  107.26
  281.20
ANTS                                   ( 5)
  091.16  228.27  228.35  231.27  232.03
ANXIETY                                ( 7)
  011.07  011.30  022.05  024.27  145.22
  166.31  273.10
ANXIOUS                                ( 4)
  017.02  017.17  226.20  253.13
ANXIOUSLY                              ( 2)
  212.10  328.34
ANY                                    ( 227)
  003.05  003.29  004.34  004.35  006.18

ANY                              (CONTINUED)
  007.26  008.20  009.03  009.14  009.16
  010.09  010.31  012.11  016.09  016.21
  017.01  017.01  017.21  018.01  019.03
  019.04  019.19  019.25  019.28  019.28
  019.29  021.29  022.32  023.32  025.16
  025.25  026.02  026.15  027.15  028.15
  028.25  029.17  029.19  030.33  032.06
  032.11  035.06  035.19  035.33  036.15
  036.15  038.01  042.16  044.27  045.05
  047.26  048.08  049.01  049.29  049.41
  051.03  051.20  055.06  055.10  055.26
  056.08  056.28  057.22  057.23  057.26
  063.11  063.12  063.34  066.28  070.15
  070.26  071.07  071.07  073.03  073.12
  075.01  075.07  076.33  077.20  078.02
  078.15  078.26  081.12  082.25  083.23
  089.02  092.04  093.10  093.32  093.33
  094.11  096.02  098.28  101.03  102.16
  102.21  103.22  105.05  105.27  105.28
  106.12  106.31  106.35  106.36  107.21
  108.23  108.33  109.24  109.28  109.34
  111.23  111.34  112.12  115.31  118.12
  126.05  127.06  130.17  130.35  131.05
  131.24  134.03  136.11  138.13  140.05
  141.24  142.17  142.25  143.35  144.01
  144.03  145.05  146.22  147.20  147.27
  148.36  149.12  149.15  149.29  150.01
  150.06  150.07  150.14  150.21  151.19
  152.03  153.25  156.14  156.21  157.33
  160.01  165.19  165.20  169.27  170.35
  171.16  172.01  172.16  175.34  176.14
  182.22  182.24  183.08  183.19  185.19
  187.16  196.22  203.34  206.21  212.16
  212.31  213.12  214.29  215.03  216.03
  220.29  221.33  224.30  227.26  229.09
  233.22  236.13  250.20  253.02  253.19
  254.09  258.12  258.27  260.12  261.13
  264.23  268.28  269.16  269.31  272.19
  275.04  276.06  276.27  280.04  282.30
  285.03  285.26  285.30  288.31  288.36
  290.11  290.27  292.09  292.28  299.18
  303.21  303.32  304.06  305.19  312.27
  312.28  313.25  315.35  318.28  323.12
  324.33  325.21  326.14  327.35  328.01
  328.17  331.16
ANYWHERE                               ( 1)
  204.28
APACE                                  ( 3)
  223.28  310.34  311.16
APART                                  ( 9)
  133.09  141.18  141.23  141.30  163.29
  169.36  229.32  234.26  284.09
APARTMENT                              ( 7)
  030.13  088.37  242.14  242.18  242.32
  253.30  262.26
APARTMENTS                             ( 3)
  031.03  071.25  140.19
APEX                                   ( 1)
  247.09
APEXES                                 ( 1)
  010.18
APIOS                                  ( 1)
  239.06
APOLOGIES                              ( 1)
  143.29
APOLOGY                                ( 1)
  078.10
APOTHEOSIZED                           ( 1)
  036.13
APPARENT                               ( 1)
  242.03
APPARENTLY                             ( 14)
  041.26  115.19  187.30  190.04  193.05
  195.13  217.14  231.03  231.11  234.33
  235.11  280.17  289.14  297.20
APPEAL                                 ( 2)
  152.04  152.06
```

```
APPEAR                    (  17)      APPROVING                 (   1)
003.14  029.16  035.29  060.39  066.18   006.04
070.18  078.28  105.21  137.10  140.21  APPROXIMATION             (   1)
176.09  176.11  235.09  288.09  297.04   219.30
297.29  324.04                          APPUI                     (   1)
APPEARANCE                (   9)       098.05
047.20  097.34  163.35  189.22  190.06  APRIL                     (  12)
191.27  214.15  233.16  300.20          042.01  042.36  137.17  150.35  233.06
APPEARANCES               (   1)      299.15  303.01  303.02  303.03  303.04
098.10                                 313.21  316.19
APPEARED                  (  25)      AQUAE                     (   1)
004.17  017.35  020.03  041.30  087.21   063.18
148.16  150.03  151.31  156.15  167.25  ARAB                      (   2)
177.14  202.26  206.14  207.15  214.32   036.11  036.18
235.23  246.35  265.15  278.17  281.09  ARABIA                    (   1)
287.35  293.04  313.07  317.01  333.12   284.23
APPEARING                 (   1)      ARABIAN                   (   1)
180.09                                 095.33
APPEARS                   (  18)      ARABS                     (   1)
008.18  013.16  015.28  060.42  091.11   038.17
096.28  135.06  177.06  177.29  181.08  ARBITARILY                (   1)
198.14  231.30  232.27  252.14  277.13   288.32
287.22  288.08  297.35                  ARC                       (   2)
APPENDAGES                (   1)      187.05  187.08
233.14                                 ARCADIA                   (   1)
APPETITE                  (  12)      057.25
061.27  068.22  152.09  167.29  168.29  ARCH                      (   3)
218.02  218.14  218.16  220.12  220.29   110.17  202.11  330.11
224.13  318.16                          ARCHING                   (   1)
APPETITES                 (   1)      310.01
215.24                                 ARCHITECT                 (   1)
APPLE                     (   9)      058.18
041.04  059.22  077.27  083.14  083.21  ARCHITECTS                (   3)
257.36  276.24  326.12  333.08          046.24  048.02  048.03
APPLES                    (   7)      ARCHITECTURAL             (   5)
059.21  077.26  081.11  082.36  137.27   040.07  046.26  047.15  047.32  305.18
203.18  238.18                          ARCHITECTURE              (   7)
APPLIANCES                (   2)      046.13  046.30  047.08  047.35  048.11
022.02  042.14                          048.21  057.16
APPLICABLE                (   1)      ARCTIC                    (   1)
306.23                                 295.11
APPLICATIONS              (   1)      ARDOR                     (   1)
094.20                                 260.02
APPLY                     (   3)      ARE                       ( 594)
004.04  184.23  288.07                  004.02  004.10  004.29  005.05  005.12
APPLYING                  (   1)      005.26  006.04  006.10  006.13  006.27
032.27                                 006.28  006.30  006.31  006.32  007.20
APPOINTED                 (   2)      007.23  008.12  008.17  008.34  009.09
018.12  079.09                          009.26  009.28  009.28  010.07  010.08
APPOINTMENT               (   1)      010.18  010.20  010.22  011.08  011.11
265.29                                 011.15  011.17  011.34  012.03  012.06
APPRECIATE                (   4)      012.22  013.04  013.27  014.01  014.03
103.34  150.04  171.13  325.13          014.14  014.15  014.18  014.32  015.08
APPRECIATED               (   4)      015.12  015.24  015.33  015.34  015.36
076.16  133.11  187.35  216.30          016.09  016.15  016.16  016.17  016.20
APPRECIATES               (   1)      016.21  016.31  017.06  017.12  020.05
199.35                                 021.23  021.33  023.03  023.09  023.09
APPRECIATION              (   1)      023.18  023.22  024.08  024.14  024.17
123.30                                 024.18  025.12  026.09  026.18  027.09
APPREHEND                 (   1)      027.17  028.22  029.31  029.35  029.35
097.07                                 029.36  031.01  032.09  032.12  032.16
APPREHENDING              (   1)      032.32  032.34  033.01  033.04  033.10
222.02                                 033.12  033.25  034.03  034.03  034.11
APPROACH                  (  11)      034.14  034.17  034.26  035.07  035.12
028.15  043.15  175.26  210.32  226.15   035.22  035.26  035.28  035.30  036.19
226.28  227.34  266.20  273.30  275.12   036.20  037.03  037.08  037.32  038.05
310.13                                 038.17  038.22  039.23  039.24  040.01
APPROACHED                (   5)      040.05  040.13  040.14  040.19  040.26
022.27  146.16  190.08  235.25  290.13   045.08  046.08  046.24  046.35  047.24
APPROACHES                (   2)      047.26  047.32  048.04  048.06  048.07
261.14  315.17                          048.36  049.24  050.21  050.33  050.33
APPROACHING               (   5)      052.16  052.17  052.20  052.29  053.16
159.23  180.03  245.12  270.24  278.03   053.34  053.35  054.14  055.16  056.14
APPROPRIATE               (   1)      056.15  056.16  056.31  057.14  057.20
079.09                                 057.27  058.01  058.28  060.10  063.31
APPROPRIATED              (   1)      063.34  065.11  066.01  066.09  066.14
130.11                                 068.02  070.15  070.18  070.36  071.16
                                       072.24  072.35  073.04  073.26  073.26
```

AS

195.03				
196.30				
197.23				
198.21				
204.06				
205.19				
206.02				
207.12				
210.16				
212.16				
213.03				
215.07				
216.10				
217.27				
219.06				
223.06				
224.28				
226.20				
230.05				
230.28				
233.02				
235.23				
236.04				
239.03				
240.18				
242.25				
244.14				
244.34				
247.13				
248.24				
250.06				
250.19				
252.13				
253.10				
253.26				
258.13				
259.25				
260.30				
262.13				
263.20				
264.36				
266.21				
267.?3				
27?				

ARE (CONTINUED)

074.22	074.33	074.35	075.34	076.21
076.35	077.01	077.04	078.13	079.13
081.04	084.05	085.12	087.30	088.02
089.13	089.14	089.26	089.33	090.06
090.08	091.11	091.29	092.06	092.22
092.26	092.28	092.28	092.30	093.07
093.07	094.04	094.18	094.21	094.22
095.07	095.29	095.36	096.03	096.11
097.04	097.07	097.26	097.31	098.16
098.18	099.06	099.09	099.09	099.26
100.20	100.23	100.31	100.33	100.33
100.34	101.09	101.36	102.03	102.05
102.07	102.33	103.04	104.25	104.33
104.36	105.01	105.16	106.01	106.01
106.10	106.11	106.25	107.01	107.07
107.09	107.12	107.19	107.27	107.30
107.31	108.23	108.28	109.03	109.09
110.10	110.10	111.03	111.05	111.06
113.22	114.25	115.25	116.02	116.03
116.35	117.32	118.16	118.21	119.02
119.06	119.33	120.08	120.34	122.06
122.07	122.12	122.32	122.36	124.17
124.29	125.25	126.12	126.12	127.26
129.09	129.16	129.23	130.35	131.01
132.11	132.18	134.08	134.11	134.14
134.25	134.27	135.01	135.24	136.14
136.19	136.36	140.23	141.15	141.26
141.26	144.27	145.32	149.33	150.25
152.03	152.06	152.10	152.28	154.09
155.21	155.24	157.31	158.13	158.23
159.21	162.10	164.28	165.05	166.02
166.08	166.21	166.29	168.09	171.06
171.10	171.17	171.19	172.34	172.35
176.05	176.12	176.19	176.32	177.30
179.02	181.26	181.35	182.30	182.33
182.36	183.11	184.07	184.13	184.24
184.27	184.32	185.10	185.20	185.22
185.23	185.25	186.09	186.15	186.17
186.30	186.31	186.33	187.11	187.23
187.29	188.01	188.11	191.25	192.12
192.14	192.17	193.29	193.36	195.17
195.18	195.21	195.22	196.27	196.27
196.29	196.30	197.03	197.14	197.24
197.26	197.29	197.30	198.15	199.19
199.21	199.28	199.31	200.01	201.09
201.24	202.36	203.01	203.02	205.24
207.02	207.11	207.28	208.01	208.02
210.20	210.30	211.04	212.08	212.24
213.05	213.24	214.04	215.16	215.31
215.32	216.14	216.24	216.30	216.32
216.33	217.08	217.26	218.24	219.01
219.01	219.09	219.29	219.34	219.35
220.01	220.02	220.10	220.28	221.07
221.07	221.09	221.14	221.17	221.18
221.30	223.09	223.12	223.22	224.09
225.05	225.08	225.18	225.22	227.02
227.18	232.04	233.28	241.04	241.08
242.03	242.22	244.08	244.10	245.01
246.25	246.30	246.36	246.36	247.03
247.07	247.12	248.19	249.22	249.22
251.14	252.11	253.25	254.37	255.03
257.09	257.31	258.16	260.15	260.16
261.10	203.15	263.24	264.25	265.01
267.25	267.34	268.29	269.05	279.26
280.24	281.18	281.26	283.10	283.22
284.04	284.22	284.27	284.32	284.33
284.35	287.18	287.21	288.30	288.37
290.30	290.34	291.16	291.23	291.24
291.25	292.01	292.03	293.34	294.04
294.13	297.25	300.21	301.10	302.14
302.17	304.26	304.27	305.14	305.24
305.30	305.34	305.35	306.20	306.28
306.33	307.05	307.06	307.12	307.27
308.07	308.11	309.12	310.08	310.09
310.28	311.11	311.11	313.28	314.27
314.39	315.31	316.31	317.34	318.09
318.28	320.14	320.15	320.16	321.06

ARE (CONTINUED)

321.28	322.21	323.01	324.23	325.05
325.05	325.11	325.12	325.33	325.34
327.29	327.29	327.32	328.07	328.07
328.17	328.19	328.20	329.03	329.06
329.08	329.10	329.12	329.26	330.01
330.02	331.27	331.33	331.34	332.03
332.06	332.06	332.09	332.09	332.20
332.21	332.22	332.27	333.32	

AREA (3)
287.09 287.19 287.22

ARGUMENTS (3)
019.08 216.19 310.21

ARISES (1)
074.15

ARISTOCRACY (1)
103.04

ARITHMETIC (4)
082.16 148.25 206.16 206.25

ARM (4)
144.35 146.32 249.16 278.24

ARMED (2)
161.35 294.21

ARMFUL (1)
275.36

ARMS (2)
045.15 206.14

ARMY (1)
328.31

AROSE (4)
012.27 086.14 087.28 191.33

AROUND (30)
029.02 043.09 043.23 051.28 085.23
086.26 111.29 132.03 144.09 156.04
174.17 185.17 186.17 190.03 196.13
199.17 202.13 202.18 248.01 248.26
271.05 271.10 280.11 281.33 284.05
301.17 318.33 321.05 323.35 329.02

AROUSED (2)
170.05 191.33

AROUSING (1)
041.33

ARRANGE (1)
173.35

ARRANGED (2)
113.35 168.17

ARRANGEMENTS (3)
056.07 061.10 330.02

ARRIVAL (4)
018.01 094.25 233.27 270.21

ARRIVALS (2)
117.32 121.14

ARRIVE (4)
052.19 053.14 071.19 275.10

ARRIVED (6)
142.33 143.04 143.06 173.29 277.18
278.36

ARRIVING (2)
115.25 302.19

ARROW (1)
121.23

ARROWHEADS (1)
156.15

ARROWY (1)
040.35

ART (23)
014.32 026.03 037.32 037.34 038.01
051.21 058.13 062.15 089.31 102.22
102.22 146.02 165.23 208.13 239.35
244.23 250.31 254.34 254.35 261.32
310.04 327.25 331.26

ARTERY (1)
307.20

ARTHUR (1)
055.31

ARTICLE (1)
108.33

ARTICLES
020.08
ARTICULAT'
123.32
ARTIFICER
314.11
ARTIFICIA
071.01
ARTILLERY
303.10
ARTIST
097.13
ARTISTIC
057.03
ARTS
038.14
090.26
AS
003.29
004.14
005.01
005.27
008.05
009.02
010.22
011.06
013.29
015.07
017.18
020.03
022.03
023.21
024.28
025.05
026.18
028.12
029.27
030.15
031.29
032.16
033.23
034.35
035.32
036.19
039.14
041.03
042.04
044.18
045.28
047.09
048.02
049.30
050.18
051.3?
052.2?
056.0?
056.1?
058.0?
058.3?
060.3?
061.1?
062.1?
064.2?
065.2?
066.3?
069.1?
070.1?
070.3?
071.2
072.1
073.0
073.2
074.2
076.2
078.?
081.1
084.1
084.?

ASSIGNED
220.15   (1)
ASSIMILATED
021.35   (1)
ASSIST
045.08 321.33   (2)
ASSISTANCE
057.04 170.09   (2)
ASSISTED
017.26 058.16 204.08   (3)
ASSOCIATED
027.24 316.31   (2)
ASSOCIATING
050.24   (1)
ASSOCIATIONS
125.23   (1)
ASSUAGE
258.33   (1)
ASSUAGED
188.05   (1)
ASSUME
141.28 300.19 304.29   (3)
ASSUMED
114.19   (1)
ASSURANCE
318.16   (1)
ASSURE
092.30 285.33   (2)
ASSURED
043.35 063.02 107.04 216.17 220.06   (5)
ASSYRIA
331.33   (1)
ASTABAT
172.27   (1)
ASTONISH
016.33   (1)
ASTONISHED
118.05 327.14 333.23   (3)
ASTONISHING
004.30   (1)
ASTONISHMENT
052.01 164.17   (2)
ASTOR
140.26   (1)
ASTOUNDING
216.33 258.26   (2)
ASTRAY
170.25   (1)
ASTROLOGICALLY
104.11   (1)
ASTRONOMERS
088.02 102.06   (2)
ASTRONOMICALLY
104.11   (1)
ASTRONOMY
310.06   (1)
AT   (607)
003.09 003.14 004.21 004.26 007.24
010.15 010.21 011.13 011.25 011.32
012.02 012.27 013.03 013.30 014.04
014.08 014.13 015.33 016.01 016.34
017.01 017.28 017.36 018.02 018.16
019.02 019.15 019.25 019.32 020.12
020.17 021.22 022.06 022.27 023.12
023.13 024.10 024.21 024.29 024.35
024.35 025.04 025.11 025.23 026.03
026.05 026.06 026.07 026.09 026.35
027.04 027.05 027.28 027.34 028.14
028.21 029.10 029.13 029.14 029.32
030.12 031.21 032.03 032.04 032.16
032.29 032.31 034.06 034.11 034.31
035.11 036.15 036.20 036.35 037.18
038.13 038.25 039.02 039.12 039.36
042.27 043.04 043.05 043.31 043.32
043.36 044.05 044.17 045.02 045.03
045.08 045.14 046.25 046.31 046.31
048.14 048.31 049.33 050.04 050.17
051.12 051.14 051.30 051.35 052.19

AT   (CONTINUED)
053.13 053.30 053.36 054.09 055.18
056.02 056.04 057.21 058.06 058.22
059.06 062.01 062.06 062.32 063.25
064.01 064.01 064.01 064.31 065.01
065.02 066.04 066.13 066.20 066.35
067.25 068.05 068.35 070.20 071.19
072.12 072.12 072.28 073.01 073.19
073.29 073.33 074.11 074.13 075.04
075.35 075.36 081.04 081.12 081.12
084.02 084.11 084.16 084.20 084.33
086.19 086.28 088.10 088.37 089.10
089.34 091.32 092.04 092.23 093.13
094.24 095.22 096.32 097.07 097.14
098.19 099.33 099.35 100.01 100.28
102.20 103.10 104.07 104.11 105.05
105.16 106.26 107.23 108.02 109.30
110.04 110.13 110.17 111.17 111.30
112.08 112.25 114.13 114.24 115.03
117.15 117.20 117.29 118.06 118.16
118.31 119.24 120.25 122.01 122.11
123.04 123.08 123.22 123.24 123.32
123.34 124.07 124.14 125.07 126.05
126.15 130.09 130.10 130.25 130.27
130.28 131.25 131.34 132.04 135.34
135.35 136.06 136.10 136.12 136.17
136.18 136.29 138.28 140.16 142.19
142.20 142.35 143.04 143.08 143.08
143.13 143.15 143.36 145.08 146.08
146.11 146.12 146.22 146.26 146.28
146.29 146.32 147.02 148.08 148.31
149.08 149.15 150.25 150.32 151.32
152.03 152.19 152.34 153.04 153.07
153.27 156.06 157.16 158.19 159.10
159.16 160.07 160.13 161.28 164.18
164.24 165.04 165.22 166.18 166.28
167.22 167.26 168.16 168.20 168.23
168.34 169.01 169.09 169.24 169.30
171.22 174.01 174.01 175.01 175.13
176.06 176.06 176.07 176.10 176.10
176.20 176.21 176.24 177.05 177.07
177.08 177.34 178.31 179.15 180.13
180.23 181.02 181.16 181.19 181.20
181.20 182.01 182.22 183.07 184.01
184.14 184.15 185.09 185.18 186.18
186.35 187.10 188.04 188.15 188.
189.06 189.12 189.23 190.11 190.
190.19 190.33 191.05 191.17 192.
192.27 193.33 193.37 193.38 195.
195.19 195.22 196.18 197.06 197.
198.17 198.33 201.04 202.18 202
202.32 203.02 203.26 204.09 204
204.35 205.01 205.24 206.02 206
206.24 207.27 208.14 208.24 210
210.26 211.01 211.02 211.25 212
212.14 213.01 213.01 213.12 212
213.35 214.08 214.08 215.22 216
217.20 218.36 220.03 220.32 220
221.05 221.32 221.34 224.25 22
226.32 227.13 227.29 227.30 22
229.12 229.17 230.14 230.28 23
231.10 231.15 232.15 232.28 23
233.27 233.31 234.35 235.01 2
236.22 236.36 238.21 239.17 2
241.23 241.25 242.10 242.21 2
243.27 243.36 244.01 244.15 2
244.20 244.24 244.36 244.20 2
246.35 248.13 248.24 248.33
249.25 250.03 251.26 252.03
252.12 253.11 254.07 254.23
257.12 257.13 257.24 259.34
260.19 260.23 260.33 262.02
262.18 264.10 264.17 264.33
265.09 265.36 266.19 266.22
267.21 268.05 268.10 268.17
270.14 270.19 271.10 271.12
272.04 272.20 272.25 272.27

```
AT                              (CONTINUED)        ATTITUDES                        ( 1)
273.30  274.01  274.13  274.15  274.20               090.01
274.22  274.26  274.32  275.04  275.10             ATTORNEY                         ( 1)
275.22  275.27  275.31  275.36  276.01               050.03
276.07  276.23  276.27  276.34  277.02             ATTRACT                          ( 3)
277.35  278.30  279.05  279.13  280.05               129.09  226.21  228.13
280.17  280.31  281.02  281.04  282.07             ATTRACTED                        ( 8)
283.26  284.16  285.35  285.35  287.17               042.34  087.36  114.18  159.30  162.31
287.27  288.29  289.18  289.27  289.35               174.22  273.17  310.01
290.07  290.25  291.30  291.34  292.13             ATTRACTION                       ( 2)
293.01  294.34  296.08  296.31  296.32               230.05  302.10
297.12  297.19  298.01  298.13  299.26             ATTRACTIONS                      ( 2)
299.26  299.27  299.28  299.29  299.35               083.04  242.33
300.13  300.17  300.21  300.26  301.23             ATTRACTIVE                       ( 3)
302.12  303.09  303.21  304.09  304.15               191.35  197.18  228.23
304.16  304.19  305.26  305.33  306.12             ATTRACTS                         ( 2)
307.16  308.19  308.24  309.35  310.13               162.24  330.06
310.14  310.28  311.12  311.18  312.05             AUCTION                          ( 3)
312.07  312.19  312.21  312.28  312.28               067.25  067.35  251.15
312.32  312.34  313.08  313.09  313.13             AUDITED                          ( 1)
313.14  314.36  317.33  319.06  322.11               018.34
322.11  322.24  322.28  323.29  326.18             AUGEAN                           ( 1)
326.36  327.05  327.20  327.28  327.32               005.18
329.23  330.12  330.22  330.29  330.35             AUGER                            ( 1)
333.20  333.27                                       029.13
ATE                                       ( 4)    AUGUST                           ( 2)
055.33  143.16  227.31  295.36                       086.23  114.17
ATHLETES                                  ( 1)    AUNTS                            ( 1)
101.04                                               076.21
ATHWART                                   ( 1)    AURORA                           ( 5)
114.26                                               036.24  088.28  089.34  138.35  314.04
ATLANTIC                                  ( 3)    AURORAL                          ( 2)
052.29  127.27  321.34                               085.03  089.22
ATLANTIS                                  ( 1)    AURORAM                          ( 1)
298.19                                               314.01
ATLAS                                     ( 1)    AUSTERE                          ( 1)
083.25                                               194.12
ATMOSPHERE                               ( 15)    AUSTERITY                        ( 1)
007.08  041.10  077.12  085.25  089.29               222.21
090.23  102.32  118.05  123.10  132.05             AUSTERLITZ                       ( 1)
176.14  186.25  202.12  254.03  314.40               230.19
ATMOSPHERIC                               ( 2)    AUSTRALIANS                      ( 1)
270.08  302.06                                       322.05
ATOMS                                     ( 1)    AUTHOR                           ( 3)
306.20                                               105.20  198.11  231.30
ATUNING                                   ( 1)    AUTHORITIES                      ( 3)
314.24                                               023.02  062.16  283.15
ATROPOS                                   ( 1)    AUTHORITY                        ( 5)
118.15                                               025.05  025.13  025.22  171.24  211.03
ATTACHED                                  ( 4)    AUTHORS                          ( 1)
155.11  178.19  261.19  293.05                       103.03
ATTACHES                                  ( 1)    AUTUMN                           ( 2)
070.08                                               017.29  233.31
ATTACKED                                  ( 1)    AUTUMNAL                         ( 1)
220.32                                               102.30
ATTAIN                                    ( 1)    AUXILIARIES                      ( 1)
176.02                                               155.21
ATTAINED                                  ( 4)    AVAIL                            ( 1)
181.15  219.25  304.19  325.24                       009.15
ATTAINING                                 ( 1)    AVAILABLE                        ( 1)
037.05                                               053.26
ATTEMPT                                   ( 6)    AVAILS                           ( 1)
012.12  016.29  197.07  259.14  275.16               221.06
285.32                                             AVARICE                          ( 1)
ATTEMPTED                                 ( 1)      165.33
277.30                                             AVAST                            ( 1)
ATTEND                                    ( 6)      095.27
007.18  095.06  103.34  159.11  251.15             AVENGE                           ( 1)
262.08                                               229.32
ATTENDANCE                                ( 1)    AVENGER                          ( 2)
330.36                                               315.35  316.06
ATTENDED                                  ( 4)    AVENGING                         ( 1)
051.34  107.16  148.07  222.03                       192.28
ATTENTION                                 ( 5)    AVENUES                          ( 2)
038.14  052.17  212.04  226.22  228.13               167.31  169.16
ATTITUDE                                  ( 3)    AVERAGE                          ( 3)
268.28  323.05  323.06                               031.16  035.22  095.06
```

23

```
AVERAGES                              (  1)
  291.05
AVERSION                              (  1)
  157.36
AVOID                                 (  6)
  011.12  019.23  064.22  067.23  221.04
  230.25
AVOIDED                               (  3)
  034.02  034.05  262.14
AVOIDING                              (  1)
  240.21
AWAIT                                 (  4)
  266.29  270.21  277.11  303.34
AWAITED                               (  1)
  267.14
AWAITING                              (  2)
  262.25  273.15
AWAITS                                (  1)
  320.12
AWAKE                                 ( 12)
  089.30  090.02  090.08  090.09  090.11
  090.13  090.16  191.32  252.27  259.13
  330.25  333.32
AWAKENED                              (  5)
  089.13  089.15  117.06  117.15  127.28
AWAKENING                             (  2)
  089.08  134.03
AWAKENS                               (  1)
  219.09
AWAKES                                (  4)
  089.10  126.01  171.15  310.32
AWARE                                 (  6)
  132.10  140.17  244.27  244.28  264.23
  274.14
AWAY                                  ( 54)
  007.13  010.36  033.23  041.15  053.33
  065.26  066.35  079.19  087.28  091.21
  098.21  114.34  115.03  122.15  129.13
  130.03  142.17  144.24  146.07  158.01
  160.07  160.21  161.05  166.19  169.27
  179.16  185.04  188.04  191.36  201.25
  222.14  226.07  226.17  231.01  236.30
  245.08  257.26  275.27  276.15  277.07
  281.10  281.24  293.17  295.06  299.06
  299.12  302.26  302.34  322.23  326.11
  327.18  328.32  328.34  331.01
AWE                                   (  2)
  133.01  250.26
AWED                                  (  1)
  055.30
AWFUL                                 (  2)
  077.28  125.14
AWNING                                (  1)
  113.15
AWOKE                                 (  3)
  282.02  282.08  327.11
AXE                                   ( 17)
  014.06  040.32  041.03  041.22  042.08
  042.34  178.06  178.11  178.22  186.03
  199.01  251.29  251.36  252.16  282.21
  283.34  301.16
AXES                                  (  1)
  291.26
AXILS                                 (  1)
  307.07
AY                                    (  9)
  010.26  017.29  066.15  153.21  188.14
  193.14  264.08  294.32  312.28
AZAD                                  (  2)
  079.07  079.19
AZADS                                 (  1)
  079.14
AZURE                                 (  6)
  123.12  137.08  258.33  294.11  296.13
  325.32
```

```
B                                    (  5)        BANDS                                (  2)
  104.23  153.27  306.28  306.29  306.30           160.32  230.08
BABOONS                              (  1)        BANISH                               (  1)
  092.18                                            165.01
BABY                                 (  1)        BANISHED                             (  1)
  308.31                                            254.34
BABYLON                              (  1)        BANK                                 ( 15)
  241.10                                            007.15  032.31  058.15  119.05  168.14
BACK                                 ( 26)          176.31  191.11  228.09  269.32  305.27
  031.04  044.09  044.15  049.20  058.19            306.01  306.07  306.12  308.34  316.20
  062.16  080.29  088.34  122.13  137.35        BANKRUPT                             (  1)
  145.26  149.36  152.22  178.07  184.10            033.10
  191.07  191.31  195.16  224.30  239.25        BANKRUPTCY                           (  1)
  242.28  244.15  262.33  278.22  303.32            033.11
  310.02                                        BANKS                                (  7)
BACKING                              (  1)          120.17  122.23  304.21  304.33  305.34
  244.31                                            309.16  333.04
BACKS                                (  1)        BANNER                               (  1)
  232.32                                            116.12
BACKWARD                             (  2)        BAR                                  ( 13)
  112.17  156.31                                    124.08  133.20  140.08  168.13  180.24
BACON                                (  1)          289.07  289.29  289.34  289.35  290.01
  076.25                                            291.21  291.27  291.36
BAD                                  ( 11)        BARB                                 (  1)
  004.14  010.31  034.01  034.04  071.31            117.02
  074.15  084.01  135.01  158.15  272.36        BARBARIC                             (  1)
  328.06                                            058.01
BADGE                                (  1)        BARBAROUS                            (  5)
  122.06                                            014.10  026.30  096.17  143.21  158.14
BAFFIN                               (  1)        BARBER                               (  1)
  271.09                                            168.32
BAG                                  (  3)        BARBERRY                             (  1)
  027.12  169.20  238.23                            238.16
BAGDAD                               (  1)        BARE                                 ( 13)
  079.16                                            023.18  027.34  159.19  185.17  192.34
BAGGAGE                              (  1)          195.30  204.25  243.18  252.09  271.23
  066.32                                            309.23  310.25  311.30
BAGS                                 (  1)        BAREFOOTED                           (  1)
  119.28                                            156.28
BAIT                                 (  8)        BARGAIN                              (  6)
  206.29  206.30  208.40  213.30  224.09            017.32  043.28  069.18  205.02  205.21
  224.12  224.21  283.24                            285.22
BAITED                               (  4)        BARK                                 ( 21)
  128.01  130.31  202.01  273.26                    024.19  027.30  028.18  039.16  039.20
BAKE                                 (  2)          040.21  042.20  083.19  099.25  128.06
  062.08  063.23                                    144.35  146.19  191.02  242.15  249.29
BAKED                                (  3)          252.14  275.28  280.16  283.32  283.34
  045.21  062.02  105.33                            322.14
BAKER                                (  6)        BARKED                               (  2)
  201.01  203.07  208.04  232.30  259.22            022.27  273.17
  278.14                                        BARKING                              (  5)
BAKES                                (  1)          122.09  223.17  232.19  273.08  283.35
  244.07                                        BARKS                                (  1)
BAKING                               (  1)          029.32
  063.24                                        BARN                                 (  9)
BALANCE                              (  1)          005.17  057.11  066.30  083.11  126.07
  060.32                                            168.07  259.21  259.23  267.28
BALANCED                             (  1)        BARNS                                (  2)
  274.24                                            005.04  166.31
BALANCING                            (  2)        BARRED                               (  1)
  055.20  274.34                                    266.03
BALCOM                               (  1)        BARREL                               (  2)
  058.17                                            244.04  319.13
BALDEST                              (  1)        BARRELS                              (  1)
  308.33                                            295.29
BALES                                (  1)        BARROW                               (  1)
  120.06                                            117.11
BALKED                               (  2)        BARROWS                              (  1)
  075.03  236.10                                    294.19
BALL                                 (  5)        BARS                                 (  1)
  026.17  146.19  160.08  307.15  307.31            178.02
BALLOON                              (  1)        BARTER                               (  1)
  189.35                                            064.22
BALLS                                (  2)        BARTRAM                              (  1)
  195.13  233.29                                    068.10
BANDBOX                              (  1)        BASCOM                               (  1)
  066.34                                            260.08
```

BASE   (1)
295.31
BASIN   (3)
087.20 289.32 290.02
BASIS   (3)
011.26 151.33 202.35
BASKET   (2)
019.18 264.12
BASKETS   (6)
019.01 019.03 019.10 019.11 019.22
130.32
BASS   (1)
202.03
BATH   (1)
111.26
BATHE   (4)
192.16 233.25 277.34 298.02
BATHED   (5)
088.29 167.04 196.02 221.36 317.20
EATHER   (2)
177.29 179.01
BATHING   (2)
088.31 177.27
BATTERING   (1)
115.34
BATTLE   (11)
086.08 229.04 229.05 229.05 229.24
229.28 230.26 230.28 231.25 232.01
232.08
BATTLES   (2)
231.27 262.03
BAWBLES   (1)
038.25
BAY   (5)
017.11 271.09 272.22 287.29 289.30
BAYING   (2)
126.05 152.19
BAYOU   (1)
320.10
BAYOUS   (1)
236.34
BAYS   (4)
185.29 197.28 290.14 292.04
BE   (647)
003.25 004.13 004.14 004.17 006.12
006.17 006.18 006.24 007.13 007.17
008.24 008.26 009.08 010.10 010.29
010.31 010.32 011.18 011.24 011.31
011.32 012.06 012.20 012.33 013.02
013.15 013.18 014.08 014.28 014.35
015.16 015.36 017.28 019.13 019.17
020.01 020.08 020.11 020.12 020.16
020.18 020.19 020.28 020.29 020.31
020.34 021.02 021.07 021.10 021.11
021.18 021.19 021.20 021.21 021.29
022.13 022.14 022.16 023.27 023.31
023.34 024.02 024.04 024.09 024.10
024.16 024.19 024.22 024.29 024.30
024.35 025.01 025.27 025.30 026.01
026.15 026.26 026.35 027.01 027.03
027.22 028.24 029.03 029.16 029.25
031.12 031.15 031.24 031.28 033.34
033.34 034.01 034.02 034.05 034.22
034.28 034.29 034.33 035.28 036.05
036.11 036.17 036.18 036.25 036.27
036.36 037.02 037.11 037.13 037.36
038.28 038.29 038.30 040.08 040.09
043.08 043.33 044.33 045.31 046.07
047.09 047.21 047.21 047.28 047.29
050.13 050.29 050.33 050.33 050.36
051.01 051.27 051.33 052.01 052.16
052.22 052.24 052.32 053.17 053.34
053.35 053.35 055.36 056.03 056.18
056.25 056.26 056.30 056.33 057.16
057.31 058.07 058.14 060.01 060.34
063.03 063.04 064.18 065.13 065.26
065.29 066.06 066.11 066.13 066.19
067.08 067.09 068.05 068.08 069.22

BE   (CONTINUED)
069.24 070.04 071.10 071.11 071.14
071.27 071.30 071.30 072.11 072.16
073.21 073.24 074.26 074.27 074.35
075.08 075.13 075.14 075.33 075.36
076.07 077.05 077.07 077.36 078.07
078.08 078.15 078.33 079.01 079.17
079.19 081.09 081.18 081.23 081.30
081.34 082.01 082.20 083.28 084.02
084.02 084.15 088.13 089.02 089.11
089.18 089.20 090.11 090.12 090.20
090.31 091.07 091.10 091.25 091.30
091.33 091.35 092.33 093.07 093.21
093.28 094.35 095.15 095.32 095.33
095.35 096.06 096.20 096.24 096.28
097.06 097.17 097.23 098.15 098.28
099.29 100.12 100.24 100.30 100.31
101.06 101.08 101.17 101.18 102.10
102.14 102.23 102.24 102.25 102.26
103.23 103.32 103.34 104.02 104.14
104.22 104.35 107.11 107.25 107.33
108.16 108.26 108.27 108.36 109.04
109.06 109.13 109.18 109.28 109.31
110.13 111.10 111.17 111.17 112.29
112.32 113.14 113.23 114.10 115.20
116.30 117.34 118.11 118.15 118.17
118.21 119.30 120.09 120.13 120.26
120.27 120.28 121.03 121.27 122.11
123.26 123.29 124.29 126.32 127.03
127.06 127.19 131.05 131.07 131.20
131.21 131.27 131.33 132.14 133.06
133.11 133.14 134.19 134.33 135.02
135.04 135.05 135.15 135.20 135.21
135.22 135.27 135.36 136.09 136.24
136.32 136.34 137.10 137.30 138.10
140.23 141.12 141.18 141.22 142.05
142.09 142.11 142.27 142.29 143.20
145.03 146.04 147.23 147.29 148.07
148.10 149.09 149.26 149.27 149.35
150.11 150.21 150.22 150.26 150.27
151.08 152.02 152.05 152.08 153.03
153.17 153.27 153.33 153.33 155.05
155.07 155.29 157.33 161.31 162.33
164.12 164.23 164.25 164.33 165.15
166.24 167.35 168.22 170.14 170.34
171.12 171.13 172.05 172.20 172.34
173.22 176.13 176.17 176.19 176.32
177.22 177.23 177.34 178.03 178.28
178.28 179.27 180.15 181.05 181.11
182.31 183.32 184.24 184.29 185.24
185.27 186.10 187.04 188.33 189.25
189.34 191.15 192.07 192.10 192.17
193.14 194.02 194.11 194.15 196.05
197.04 197.04 197.25 197.35 198.13
198.35 199.09 199.23 199.24 202.35
203.31 205.31 205.31 205.36 206.14
207.29 207.34 209.02 213.04 213.21
213.28 214.10 215.21 215.23 215.33
215.34 215.34 216.04 216.07 216.22
217.14 217.17 217.18 217.24 217.34
218.11 218.12 219.11 219.16 219.29
220.33 220.34 221.05 221.06 221.06
221.12 221.23 223.27 224.05 224.08
224.08 224.10 224.21 224.22 224.27
225.10 225.11 227.25 230.27 231.21
233.22 233.33 234.01 234.11 235.02
235.15 235.21 235.31 238.12 239.05
239.12 239.34 240.27 240.28 240.34
241.03 241.12 241.29 242.19 243.07
243.08 243.33 244.16 244.17 244.18
244.32 245.22 246.35 247.06 250.31
251.12 252.12 253.05 254.07 254.08
254.17 254.29 257.11 258.07 261.02
263.10 263.12 263.25 264.21 264.28
267.10 267.21 268.02 268.27 268.30
268.30 269.12 270.09 270.14 271.22
273.11 273.13 273.14 274.10 274.29
274.34 275.35 276.07 276.19 277.06

BE (CONTINUED)
```
280.21  280.33  281.25  281.31  281.33
282.22  282.30  283.17  283.23  285.03
285.25  287.06  287.09  287.13  287.14
287.16  288.24  288.24  289.06  289.30
290.17  291.11  292.11  292.12  292.27
292.29  292.36  294.05  295.07  295.20
296.18  297.06  298.07  300.21  300.33
301.06  302.02  302.13  302.21  304.02
305.06  308.01  309.02  314.20  316.32
317.35  317.36  318.03  318.19  318.19
318.21  318.26  318.29  318.30  320.27
320.30  320.34  321.08  321.10  321.13
321.16  321.20  322.18  323.08  323.23
323.36  324.05  324.07  324.08  324.19
324.21  325.25  326.03  326.04  326.06
326.15  326.18  326.25  326.28  327.26
328.17  328.22  328.29  328.34  328.36
329.05  330.23  330.30  330.32  331.36
332.14  333.01
```
BEACH   (2)
```
026.05  186.18
```
BEACHES   (1)
```
178.25
```
BEACON   (1)
```
133.21
```
BEACONS   (1)
```
171.08
```
BEADS   (1)
```
247.12
```
BEAM   (1)
```
330.07
```
BEAN   (12)
```
059.35  137.14  145.21  155.01  156.09
156.26  157.01  157.04  160.07  163.27
251.32  257.04
```
BEANS   (35)
```
010.15  054.22  054.34  055.08  100.01
111.20  131.14  155.03  155.10  155.18
155.18  155.29  156.18  156.31  157.06
157.10  157.25  158.16  159.08  159.09
161.13  161.17  161.34  162.09  162.10
162.32  163.03  163.16  163.26  163.41
164.13  164.23  165.05  166.17  166.21
```
BEAR   (11)
```
015.33  043.17  089.19  120.03  153.13
161.22  166.33  182.07  196.24  230.15
318.30
```
BEARD   (1)
```
181.36
```
BEARERS   (1)
```
036.14
```
BEARING   (8)
```
085.10  112.12  121.30  166.26  171.09
259.27  268.26  304.27
```
BEARINGS   (1)
```
329.32
```
BEARS   (3)
```
079.07  166.27  279.17
```
BEAST   (4)
```
220.20  227.15  236.13  269.13
```
BEASTLY   (1)
```
218.26
```
BEASTS   (5)
```
174.13  219.22  220.11  220.16  225.19
```
BEAT   (4)
```
114.35  234.05  245.12  272.17
```
BEATEN   (4)
```
022.26  074.07  153.18  323.15
```
BEAUTIFUL   (21)
```
038.26  038.27  038.28  038.29  038.31
090.22  103.26  132.19  175.26  185.33
186.12  187.12  197.19  199.30  201.15
214.33  247.05  309.10  316.38  333.07
333.17
```
BEAUTIFULLY   (5)
```
185.29  201.31  293.24  296.32  305.31
```

BEAUTY   (18)
```
040.09  046.27  047.15  047.20  047.22
103.29  188.09  196.26  200.03  201.21
238.05  247.31  264.19  269.22  284.21
284.25  309.26  309.30
```
BEAUX   (1)
```
048.04
```
BECAME   (14)
```
018.30  039.32  044.03  044.05  045.17
127.21  157.09  182.09  182.22  183.26
190.35  225.31  295.15  296.11
```
BECAUSE   (51)
```
008.20  014.34  016.21  025.07  026.31
030.30  030.32  033.05  035.31  035.35
041.28  048.35  050.13  055.24  061.31
067.06  067.06  070.19  074.26  076.19
080.07  090.32  096.26  100.36  110.06
113.25  119.36  135.33  146.09  149.13
171.22  177.06  184.01  184.06  208.26
211.09  214.29  214.30  217.23  217.24
221.13  221.15  242.11  253.24  296.20
315.11  318.01  325.13  326.02  326.09
326.36
```
BECOME   (36)
```
012.10  021.35  029.07  030.25  032.18
037.05  037.24  037.26  040.26  042.32
050.03  056.29  057.06  073.27  079.02
080.22  099.04  106.12  112.28  115.09
120.12  124.06  126.16  127.07  152.30
162.16  173.21  199.04  207.31  210.14
214.10  215.11  252.13  261.27  281.30
305.20
```
BECOMES   (15)
```
004.22  026.28  032.25  086.30  102.27
103.17  183.23  264.27  282.27  282.32
289.07  291.31  291.34  297.14  306.36
```
BECOMING   (4)
```
026.18  026.34  049.35  305.29
```
BED   (20)
```
013.30  043.20  043.25  044.02  065.18
066.36  067.02  113.01  133.35  143.07
153.15  253.14  253.21  253.27  253.31
256.15  262.17  272.34  272.35  288.04
```
BEDDED   (1)
```
240.19
```
BEDFORD   (1)
```
123.02
```
BEDS   (2)
```
013.27  093.04
```
BEDSTEAD   (1)
```
113.01
```
BEDSTEADS   (1)
```
113.25
```
BEE   (1)
```
137.15
```
BEECH   (3)
```
201.30  202.01  265.29
```
BEECHEN   (1)
```
172.30
```
BEEF   (3)
```
205.16  223.13  252.17
```
BEEN   (159)
```
003.12  003.18  004.01  005.06  006.36
009.06  009.06  009.31  009.32  010.08
010.09  010.10  011.10  011.35  012.10
014.24  016.10  017.02  017.22  025.35
031.26  032.17  032.35  034.07  034.09
034.13  034.22  034.24  040.12  050.14
056.12  056.13  056.34  058.09  060.09
067.26  068.10  069.31  077.26  078.20
081.31  082.25  085.15  086.33  088.27
090.05  090.06  098.25  103.22  103.24
104.08  104.10  104.26  104.32  108.06
111.35  112.22  118.05  124.36  125.03
129.26  131.02  147.06  148.13  151.23
159.02  164.05  167.22  170.06  170.17
170.23  170.29  172.08  173.17  173.25
174.07  178.05  179.07  179.30  179.35
```

27

```
BEEN                    (CONTINUED)        BEGINNINGS                              (  1)
180.01 180.28 181.29 182.09 182.20        067.24
182.34 183.15 183.34 191.11 191.16        BEGINS                                  (  6)
192.32 198.24 199.03 199.12 201.35        028.10 221.32 300.19 302.12 305.03
203.35 207.16 210.13 212.06 212.27        307.01
213.09 214.02 214.17 214.36 215.01        BEGUN                                   (  6)
218.03 218.05 225.22 230.05 230.12        067.31 082.10 157.26 181.06 239.08
231.28 233.19 233.20 235.18 239.32        242.07
241.14 244.26 244.27 244.28 245.21        BEHAVE                                  (  1)
247.22 249.04 249.20 250.19 253.13        022.12
254.01 258.04 260.25 261.05 262.02        BEHAVED                                 (  1)
262.19 262.28 264.17 265.19 267.07        010.33
268.11 276.05 277.28 279.08 279.14        BEHAVIOR                                (  3)
280.13 282.03 282.04 285.12 288.18        010.32 226.14 232.29
289.28 300.01 300.25 301.30 303.14        BEHAVIORS                               (  1)
303.16 304.34 315.18 315.23 317.21        291.09
324.22 327.21 333.18 333.21               BEHELD                                  (  2)
BEES                                (  2)  096.31 193.38
114.18 160.17                             BEHIND                                  ( 50)
BEETS                               (  1)  005.32 006.07 007.14 009.23 017.16
064.09                                     054.36 066.16 067.17 072.09 075.15
BEFELL                              (  1)  083.17 085.27 088.04 088.11 097.01
314.22                                     102.03 102.05 114.28 116.13 116.34
BEFORE                              ( 125) 120.23 122.09 124.08 125.12 128.05
005.14 005.17 005.30 006.22 014.15         128.17 132.30 141.34 150.18 154.19
017.21 023.32 028.04 031.24 035.20         195.11 213.04 227.28 232.18 235.32
036.10 038.26 038.27 042.30 045.13         238.30 246.23 248.35 249.35 253.08
045.16 045.21 048.23 053.12 054.18         259.30 269.18 277.09 278.06 278.21
056.13 062.02 063.15 067.23 071.08         294.29 295.13 306.30 323.33 332.28
072.08 072.16 077.29 081.34 082.12        BEHINDHAND                              (  1)
083.19 085.05 085.15 093.07 096.35        057.13
097.02 102.12 105.04 111.18 112.09        BEHOLD                                  (  6)
114.30 120.05 121.16 124.16 127.35        032.12 119.08 196.19 204.03 225.14
140.25 140.35 141.02 145.07 148.13        311.29
148.18 148.32 155.06 155.16 156.21        BEHOLDER                                (  3)
162.02 168.11 176.32 177.17 190.04        116.09 186.14 201.20
190.14 190.35 191.03 198.20 198.29        BEHOLDING                               (  3)
199.33 201.10 202.21 203.17 203.20        026.09 133.02 297.32
204.20 207.25 208.31 211.32 213.19        BEHOLDS                                 (  2)
225.27 225.30 226.23 231.26 232.10        121.25 166.12
232.33 233.06 233.26 234.24 234.29        BEHOOVES                                (  1)
239.01 239.23 240.22 241.14 242.10        028.31
246.04 246.16 247.26 251.27 252.21        BEING                                   ( 99)
258.14 259.21 261.34 262.13 264.27        007.31 029.24 032.26 038.14 039.22
265.13 271.11 272.10 274.09 274.18        043.08 044.17 054.28 055.30 056.11
275.11 285.06 285.10 287.04 287.33        060.32 061.11 065.06 069.27 071.35
295.15 302.35 304.18 305.06 319.05        073.30 075.04 075.05 077.23 079.12
323.16 323.25 327.01 327.03 327.13        083.05 084.31 086.24 086.29 095.19
328.03 328.13 330.11 330.14 333.05        096.13 099.28 106.16 108.15 111.12
BEFOREHAND                          (  2)  125.11 127.07 131.21 134.10 134.11
094.29 288.36                              137.11 140.17 141.22 143.09 143.15
BEFRIENDED                          (  1)  143.32 157.36 162.19 162.27 162.29
132.09                                     163.29 165.25 168.08 171.33 176.15
BEGAN                               ( 29)  176.36 177.08 189.26 190.18 194.21
040.34 041.21 045.09 046.31 075.32         196.36 199.26 210.04 212.30 213.08
084.27 140.32 141.28 156.25 168.25         216.30 217.31 218.07 220.07 221.03
190.13 203.29 205.15 214.12 242.09         224.28 227.26 231.12 232.04 240.33
242.24 242.25 248.25 254.02 266.11         241.13 242.32 246.17 247.32 250.07
280.28 293.12 293.15 295.03 296.10         257.15 260.15 260.33 261.21 262.09
299.18 301.18 315.21 333.05                271.23 275.03 284.03 284.12 284.14
BEGGAR                              (  1)  292.16 295.25 299.20 301.05 301.07
262.31                                     301.27 301.28 314.14 321.35 323.07
BEGGARLY                            (  1)  326.27 328.19 329.13 331.23
065.31                                     BEINGS                                  (  4)
BEGGARS                             (  1)  010.19 035.04 087.31 324.02
269.07                                     BELFRY                                  (  1)
BEGIN                               ( 17)  105.08
005.12 012.33 040.36 057.02 058.21        BELIEF                                  (  1)
058.22 073.26 098.05 098.36 108.36        068.35
124.02 141.11 153.34 171.18 206.15        BELIES                                  (  1)
323.35 331.17                             009.09
BEGINNERS                           (  1)  BELIEVE                                 ( 21)
107.07                                     009.09 010.31 024.20 025.07 026.32
BEGINNING                           ( 12)  055.25 069.17 073.10 078.05 089.21
039.26 045.03 051.13 077.36 095.24         121.07 130.35 214.35 217.09 217.27
108.31 125.15 203.08 205.33 272.10         250.28 285.15 287.13 327.36 332.24
299.16 310.23                              332.28
```

28

BELIEVED			(4)	
022.12	136.32	150.08	285.18	
BELIEVES			(1)	
108.12				
BELL			(15)	
093.13	093.14	097.30	105.10	105.18
118.09	119.05	122.01	122.02	122.16
123.02	123.19	168.15	259.30	329.18
BELLA			(1)	
172.26				
BELLES			(1)	
048.04				
BELLIED			(1)	
185.03				
BELLOWING			(1)	
126.35				
BELLOWS			(1)	
160.33				
BELLS			(5)	
089.17	097.21	123.01	259.17	271.29
BELLUM			(1)	
228.34				
BELLY			(3)	
149.36	192.25	317.33		
BELONG			(5)	
046.17	096.16	108.22	171.29	178.33
BELONGED			(4)	
022.33	065.34	173.29	191.01	
BELONGING			(1)	
094.26				
BELONGS			(3)	
010.01	214.05	326.02		
BELOVED			(1)	
254.35				
BELOW			(8)	
034.24	098.05	122.12	175.08	186.29
198.15	311.08	323.28		
BELT			(3)	
066.07	145.20	178.23		
BELTS			(1)	
143.31				
BEN			(2)	
124.19	212.21			
BENCH			(1)	
225.35				
BENCHER			(1)	
105.26				
BENDED			(1)	
129.34				
BENDERS			(1)	
330.12				
BENDING			(3)	
114.31	207.13	232.21		
BENDS			(1)	
172.37				
BENE			(2)	
063.17	063.18			
BENEATH			(19)	
125.35	128.03	177.35	190.01	228.10
235.07	235.14	235.18	236.08	240.02
244.13	247.13	247.17	248.19	260.24
284.36	301.02	317.05	332.05	
BENEFACTOR			(3)	
216.05	332.14	332.16		
BENEFACTORS			(2)	
014.27	036.12			
BENEFICENCE			(3)	
073.36	074.06	138.06		
BENEFICENT			(3)	
116.27	132.01	315.15		
BENEFICIENT			(1)	
315.25				
BENEFIT			(3)	
031.35	138.30	166.14		
BENEFITED			(1)	
051.01				
BENEFITS			(1)	
031.02				

BENEVOLENCE			(1)	
077.01				
BENT			(7)	
056.10	114.20	149.19	160.25	212.29
271.31	294.36			
BENUMBETH			(1)	
080.13				
BENVENUTO			(1)	
202.23				
BEQUEATHED			(1)	
193.17				
BERRIES			(7)	
069.36	114.17	156.35	201.09	201.20
218.06	263.03			
BERRY			(1)	
201.17				
BERRYING			(2)	
154.15	232.30			
BESEECHINGLY			(1)	
152.19				
BESET			(1)	
281.34				
BESIDE			(22)	
023.10	033.08	055.08	055.18	056.11
060.35	064.11	071.08	106.18	117.01
134.33	144.10	148.36	183.21	202.35
214.11	225.05	237.06	255.04	317.14
321.18	332.06			
BESIDES			(2)	
168.33	214.21			
BEST			(46)	
026.32	029.30	030.05	030.16	036.35
037.32	054.04	064.05	065.25	067.23
074.34	076.31	076.32	082.01	088.30
091.19	098.30	102.35	104.22	106.01
106.04	106.17	106.22	109.30	111.15
112.32	135.21	141.32	142.36	152.09
183.09	185.36	192.31	192.31	205.35
212.12	212.24	215.01	225.18	246.18
249.17	251.07	307.26	313.33	323.26
324.17				
BESTOW			(3)	
011.05	023.26	075.33		
BESTOWED			(3)	
023.27	121.05	329.04		
BESTOWER			(1)	
239.33				
BESTOWS			(1)	
076.01				
BETIMES			(1)	
311.13				
BETRAY			(6)	
008.05	215.18	226.29	235.33	235.35
325.02				
BETRAYED			(5)	
022.09	078.15	189.27	234.22	289.05
BETRAYING			(1)	
221.15				
BETRAYS			(1)	
188.34				
BETTER			(61)	
005.06	005.24	008.36	015.17	019.31
021.33	024.34	027.05	030.33	031.13
034.20	037.06	040.16	042.33	045.35
046.29	047.14	048.18	050.36	051.14
054.15	055.26	055.27	056.11	057.32
059.32	067.17	081.22	105.07	105.12
109.24	111.21	111.34	118.29	121.01
136.24	142.21	143.28	146.25	149.02
149.12	151.35	193.36	195.31	206.31
213.02	214.02	223.19	239.15	250.06
251.28	253.02	266.36	268.29	299.18
314.12	314.20	322.10	326.01	327.35
331.14				
BETWEEN			(47)	
028.25	031.34	073.12	083.12	084.01
086.06	087.03	101.10	107.22	135.28
137.25	141.08	151.12	156.32	158.12

```
BETWEEN                    (CONTINUED)      BIT                              (  1)
165.07  169.30  169.35  174.02  176.22        215.14
185.31  186.33  188.36  192.28  211.15      BITE                             (  1)
218.29  226.05  228.34  232.02  241.18        284.15
242.12  248.02  248.10  260.08  260.31      BITING                           (  1)
265.20  266.15  267.03  271.19  275.02        301.32
281.13  287.21  296.04  297.16  299.30      BITS                             (  2)
303.22  311.34                                159.03  218.22
BEVERAGE                           (  2)    BITTER                           (  1)
148.36  258.36                                075.24
BEWARE                             (  1)    BITTERN                          (  1)
023.29                                        317.29
BEY                                (  1)    BLACK                            ( 25)
329.32                                        018.26  130.34  131.07  138.25  157.29
BEYOND                             ( 16)      177.25  184.21  190.14  201.13  201.27
038.20  087.10  087.20  099.22  123.23        228.29  228.35  228.36  229.03  229.07
131.24  171.08  197.13  201.08  223.11        229.19  230.01  231.02  231.07  237.02
252.25  253.36  311.28  324.20  325.32        258.12  262.23  262.24  263.06  321.02
333.13                                      BLACKBERRIES                     (  2)
BHAGVAT                            (  2)      122.25  155.16
057.19  298.03                              BLACKBERRY                       (  5)
BIBBERS                            (  1)      044.24  113.21  113.31  128.12  156.35
126.09                                      BLACKER                          (  1)
BIBLE                              (  1)      258.12
104.27                                      BLACKS                           (  1)
BIBLES                             (  4)      229.34
048.02  104.03  106.10  106.33             BLACKSMITH                        (  1)
BIBLICAL                           (  1)      252.01
069.06                                      BLADE                            (  2)
BICOLOR                            (  1)      311.04  311.15
185.03                                      BLADES                           (  4)
BIDDING                            (  1)      156.10  177.12  199.18  311.11
057.22                                      BLAKE                            (  1)
BIENNIALS                          (  1)      251.21
015.36                                      BLANCHARD                        (  1)
BIG                                (  9)      230.20
140.33  140.33  143.15  160.08  168.15      BLANCHED                         (  1)
198.33  227.25  253.16  275.17                264.26
BIGGER                             (  1)    BLAST                            (  2)
274.33                                        254.09  308.35
BIGGEST                            (  1)    BLASTED                          (  1)
326.03                                        082.01
BIGHTS                             (  1)    BLASTS                           (  2)
292.04                                        254.02  316.16
BILL                               (  3)    BLEACH                           (  1)
050.23  072.09  232.11                        044.09
BILLOWS                            (  1)    BLEAK                            (  1)
062.31                                        110.07
BILLS                              (  3)    BLEATING                         (  1)
060.09  275.20  275.28                        121.36
BIOGRAPHY                          (  1)    BLESS                            (  2)
258.28                                        216.29  314.38
BIPED                              (  1)    BLESSED                          (  2)
149.17                                        220.05  314.20
BIRCH                              (  9)    BLESSING                         (  4)
158.19  178.18  178.22  201.27  201.29        039.04  040.27  076.35  217.22
250.01  250.02  263.06  265.30             BLEW                             (  1)
BIRCHES                            (  2)      256.12
083.22  181.24                              BLIND                            (  3)
BIRD                               ( 24)      006.06  128.15  268.37
046.03  113.19  127.04  127.06  127.12      BLINDLY                          (  3)
127.22  175.01  226.11  226.20  227.09        050.28  307.16  315.02
227.15  228.18  233.33  234.09  236.13      BLINDS                           (  1)
244.14  252.29  267.14  272.05  276.18        031.05
276.28  302.20  310.26  320.06             BLISTERED                         (  1)
BIRDS                              ( 35)      156.30
008.35  013.28  028.28  030.18  041.17      BLOATED                          (  1)
046.07  046.10  085.29  085.31  111.29        192.29
112.07  112.20  114.32  124.17  124.27      BLOCK                            (  1)
127.14  127.18  128.07  166.29  167.15        295.27
190.01  192.11  199.18  199.35  212.02      BLOCKS                           (  1)
212.05  227.03  232.06  295.11  305.14        074.08
306.33  309.34  313.29  319.04  324.15      BLOOD                            (  9)
BIRTH                              (  4)      074.24  119.04  132.12  140.04  184.22
074.06  101.21  106.16  108.10                221.31  304.26  307.11  318.24
BISON                              (  3)    BLOODED                          (  1)
012.14  238.14  320.10                        140.05
```

30

BLOODS				(1)
281.08				
BLOOM				(4)
006.24	111.22	173.20	313.30	
BLOOMING				(2)
079.11	080.12			
BLOSSOM				(2)
239.11	264.14			
BLOSSOMING				(1)
264.02				
BLOSSOMS				(1)
157.04				
BLOTTING				(1)
252.36				
BLOW				(7)
113.17	168.23	194.26	245.23	301.30
304.20	313.31			
BLOWING				(4)
117.20	122.24	194.31	242.08	
BLOWN				(7)
053.33	094.15	121.34	128.16	191.16
199.04	273.32			
BLOWS				(7)
042.15	085.11	129.18	140.25	241.07
241.13	275.20			
BLUE				(27)
087.05	087.08	128.03	137.07	137.08
145.12	176.09	176.13	176.17	176.20
176.33	177.07	177.11	177.15	199.15
201.09	265.26	269.22	284.28	296.09
296.32	297.05	297.08	297.08	310.26
325.28	326.17			
BLUEBERRIES				(1)
173.09				
BLUEBERRY				(2)
113.32	182.06			
BLUEBIRD				(1)
302.23				
BLUER				(1)
087.06				
BLUES				(1)
136.04				
BLUEST				(1)
297.10				
BLUISH				(2)
197.30	199.18			
BLUNDER				(1)
056.23				
BLUNDERING				(2)
006.06	175.12			
BLUNT				(1)
124.20				
BLUSH				(3)
048.20	077.35	120.20		
BLUSHES				(1)
036.24				
BLUSTERING				(1)
266.33				
BOARD				(17)
043.13	043.16	043.17	043.19	056.28
065.03	108.21	110.13	119.10	145.24
229.18	235.08	241.27	245.25	245.30
331.02	333.24			
BOARDED				(3)
045.10	109.06	145.28		
BOARDING				(1)
045.13				
BOARDS				(15)
028.20	033.12	040.19	043.02	043.22
043.22	044.08	045.11	045.22	049.04
049.05	084.32	242.12	242.14	296.25
BOAST				(5)
049.35	076.08	108.22	184.14	254.06
BOASTING				(1)
018.29				
BOAT				(25)
085.16	085.18	174.01	174.10	174.15
174.34	176.19	184.35	185.01	185.12

			(CONTINUED)	
BOAT				
189.20	191.20	191.24	191.30	191.33
194.32	199.12	208.36	234.10	234.35
235.11	245.19	297.32	303.24	303.32
BODIES				(15)
004.26	006.04	013.21	013.24	022.03
028.26	029.32	041.36	140.16	168.04
219.13	231.09	232.05	269.04	291.19
BODILY				(5)
108.33	136.31	136.33	141.23	216.21
BODY				(34)
003.29	008.25	013.08	034.34	042.16
058.10	129.04	145.10	147.13	150.35
170.07	176.27	177.21	177.23	177.27
177.29	215.21	219.28	219.32	221.28
222.22	223.16	253.28	254.02	281.11
285.26	303.31	304.09	304.12	306.16
306.23	307.34	307.34	311.19	
BOG				(7)
204.10	204.35	206.01	207.15	209.05
295.08	330.18			
BOCCING				(3)
204.34	206.02	208.33		
BOGGY				(1)
209.04				
BOGS				(1)
330.20				
BOIL				(2)
180.26	244.05			
BOILED				(6)
061.21	061.25	120.28	143.15	223.12
239.15				
BOILING				(2)
183.18	192.22			
BOISTEROUS				(2)
268.06	310.11			
BOLD				(6)
066.13	099.15	245.11	245.32	255.02
291.19				
BOLDER				(1)
185.29				
BOLDLY				(1)
169.02				
BOLE				(1)
201.31				
BOLSTERS				(1)
038.22				
BOLT				(2)
133.03	172.02			
BOLTED				(1)
169.07				
BOLTS				(2)
118.17	118.22			
BOMBAY				(1)
297.36				
BONAPARTE				(1)
118.35				
BONE				(1)
329.12				
BONES				(7)
009.20	009.23	009.24	221.31	257.31
257.32	308.09			
BONFIRE				(1)
067.34				
BONNET				(1)
157.29				
BONY				(2)
281.05	307.29			
BOO				(4)
272.23	272.28	272.28	272.29	
BOOBY				(1)
058.08				
BOOK				(15)
003.23	005.27	006.29	096.13	104.27
107.14	107.36	108.01	121.21	144.25
152.33	172.16	279.22	298.09	309.02
BOOKS				(29)
003.24	014.07	078.21	099.24	099.29

BOOKS   (CONTINUED)
100.04 100.11 101.01 101.06 102.33
102.35 106.01 106.05 106.22 107.05
107.06 107.07 107.30 110.02 111.03
111.20 113.11 116.05 119.31 144.19
148.25 172.11 283.21 329.08
BOOM   (2)
187.15 301.18
BOOMED   (1)
301.23
BOOMING   (2)
301.11 317.30
BOOTS   (3)
024.32 145.15 206.03
BOPEEP   (1)
226.03
BOR   (3)
125.01 125.04 125.05
BORDER   (3)
035.02 192.36 256.21
BORDERERS   (1)
250.09
BORDERS   (1)
250.11
BORE   (2)
159.02 241.13
BORED   (2)
029.12 291.02
BORES   (1)
154.01
BORN   (11)
005.06 005.13 043.26 098.26 101.18
209.02 223.22 227.09 314.11 315.03
316.16
BORNE   (2)
129.11 207.19
BORROW   (2)
245.07 279.22
BORROWED   (4)
006.33 040.32 042.23 047.34
BORROWING   (1)
041.01
BOSE   (2)
223.17 232.12
BOSOM   (5)
188.33 245.34 277.06 291.16 312.13
BOSTON   (12)
017.25 052.20 098.01 109.29 114.36
116.35 118.08 155.32 162.05 173.17
238.12 331.24
BOTANIC   (2)
078.32 138.19
BOTH   (33)
007.21 009.31 035.07 040.24 050.01
050.19 055.29 059.17 070.33 077.36
086.24 087.34 098.12 120.11 140.18
163.36 176.16 176.23 182.35 186.31
199.18 202.08 206.14 210.19 215.22
229.03 249.12 256.25 260.21 281.32
299.10 300.28 306.04
BOTHER   (1)
105.16
BOTTLE   (4)
062.28 063.07 138.30 145.19
BOTTLES   (2)
024.03 138.27
BOTTOM   (55)
041.26 086.13 091.32 098.03 098.20
098.23 132.35 174.18 177.01 177.33
178.28 179.04 185.20 185.26 189.27
190.36 191.05 191.16 192.13 194.34
195.07 195.17 196.18 197.29 198.32
199.09 199.12 206.36 213.20 235.16
246.19 246.22 247.01 247.24 247.32
247.35 285.09 285.13 285.13 285.30
285.34 287.03 288.03 288.27 289.02
291.14 293.21 300.07 300.11 300.29
304.01 305.36 330.13 330.15 330.18

BOTTOMLESS   (5)
150.25 178.30 189.33 285.17 287.14
BOTTOMLESSNESS   (1)
285.15
BOTTOMS   (1)
020.11
BOUGH   (7)
113.20 114.15 190.11 228.19 228.19
228.21 275.16
BOUGHS   (7)
028.19 042.28 114.12 114.27 201.05
203.25 266.26
BOUGHT   (11)
012.02 024.30 032.20 040.17 043.01
067.37 081.08 081.09 082.09 143.18
261.26
BOUNCE   (1)
281.02
BOUND   (7)
020.21 080.26 121.03 157.15 217.32
248.31 259.29
BOUNDARIES   (1)
141.07
BOUNDARY   (3)
092.02 186.02 323.34
BOUNDED   (3)
092.04 130.18 187.27
BOUNDING   (1)
083.08
BOUNDLESS   (2)
211.18 238.21
BOUNDS   (4)
030.17 057.34 320.15 324.28
BOUNTEOUS   (1)
080.24
BOUQUET   (1)
238.32
BOUT   (1)
156.36
BOW   (1)
115.17
BOWELS   (5)
077.22 252.07 305.15 308.23 308.25
BOWER   (1)
028.04
BOWERS   (1)
191.23
BOWL   (3)
065.21 126.33 262.18
BOWLDERS   (1)
119.12
BOWLS   (1)
172.30
BOWS   (1)
251.03
BOX   (5)
029.08 029.21 029.22 047.29 048.07
BOXES   (2)
065.32 253.29
BOY   (21)
023.26 051.17 051.31 051.34 056.21
056.32 093.17 115.01 157.27 163.08
173.14 204.08 211.14 212.26 227.26
281.35 303.17 330.14 330.15 330.17
330.21
BOYHOOD   (1)
212.31
BOYS   (12)
107.07 121.33 153.02 157.08 167.16
211.10 212.10 213.24 259.06 259.19
316.23 321.33
BRACING   (1)
267.30
BRAG   (2)
049.36 084.23
BRAHMA   (4)
298.11 327.10 327.15 327.23

BRAHME (1)
096.24
BRAHMIN (1)
298.10
BRAHMINS (1)
004.19
BRAIN (6)
117.22 235.04 268.26 325.22 327.23
327.24
BRAINS (3)
197.01 268.24 305.15
BRAKEMEN (1)
193.34
BRAKES (1)
207.30
BRAN (1)
268.13
BRANCH (3)
186.06 307.10 307.10
BRANCHES (5)
075.35 109.32 198.31 284.08 307.23
BRANDS (1)
174.25
BRANDY (1)
121.10
BRASS (4)
007.01 007.02 007.03 316.03
BRAT (1)
204.17
BRAVE (11)
080.24 095.24 127.24 131.11 164.12
164.12 193.15 197.07 204.23 276.18
295.15
BRAVELY (1)
206.19
BRAVERY (2)
008.10 118.25
BRAZEN (1)
195.33
BREAD (27)
039.05 039.06 040.06 042.26 042.28
045.21 051.24 058.17 062.01 062.15
062.24 062.25 063.02 063.13 063.20
142.06 142.09 165.16 214.25 218.13
223.13 223.24 224.04 239.04 243.15
244.07 249.22
BREADSTUFFS (1)
063.29
BREADTH (13)
004.27 025.19 133.11 266.24 269.09
287.30 288.25 289.18 289.21 290.02
290.12 290.13 291.08
BREADTHWISE (1)
269.16
BREAK (10)
005.29 097.19 114.16 141.14 146.08
155.27 160.12 299.04 299.33 313.13
BREAKFAST (1)
093.31
BREAKING (6)
044.30 086.19 128.12 179.20 303.05
318.35
BREAKS (4)
033.07 299.09 309.22 320.08
BREAM (1)
143.15
BREAMS (1)
184.04
BREAST (8)
188.11 204.25 231.01 231.03 235.35
236.06 236.21 249.12
BREASTS (2)
013.28 285.24
BREATH (14)
006.28 017.32 102.08 102.26 119.06
129.14 141.17 188.31 208.26 265.07
282.26 315.15 315.25 315.26

BREATHE (2)
037.16 049.41
BREATHED (2)
102.24 188.31
BREATHES (2)
208.26 217.17
BREATHING (1)
116.19
BRED (2)
106.06 106.19
BREECHES (1)
022.21
BREED (3)
258.22 259.03 281.07
BREEDER (1)
076.04
BREEZE (4)
175.10 189.03 190.07 193.27
BREEZES (1)
160.22
BRIARS (1)
223.28
BRICK (4)
007.15 048.31 049.11 057.09
BRICKS (11)
040.19 240.33 241.01 241.09 241.14
241.17 241.18 241.24 246.03 257.32
260.32
BRIDGE (2)
110.16 316.20
BRIDGED (1)
018.16
BRIDGES (1)
126.04
BRIGHT (23)
114.19 117.27 134.01 169.19 179.02
179.08 184.17 186.33 187.06 189.17
195.32 223.18 223.19 249.11 254.29
254.31 255.01 283.05 312.03 314.34
317.15 317.20 324.16
BRIGHTEN (1)
314.19
BRIGHTER (1)
312.24
BRIGHTLY (1)
328.12
BRIGHTNESS (3)
074.01 138.11 318.33
BRIGHTON (1)
134.01
BRILLIANT (3)
117.29 238.16 240.09
BRING (7)
008.03 052.29 100.18 133.17 133.32
192.17 224.26
BRINGING (2)
045.14 249.14
BRINGS (3)
088.34 114.29 310.02
BRISTER (12)
227.33 257.03 257.33 257.34 257.36
258.06 258.18 262.11 262.21 263.20
264.08 267.01
BRISTLING (1)
271.32
BRITAIN (1)
332.33
BRITISH (3)
258.04 332.25 332.29
BRITTLE (1)
043.11
BROAD (22)
030.03 039.14 052.32 053.25 083.07
091.05 107.21 111.24 114.07 141.07
155.21 166.18 190.05 204.08 204.37
205.19 246.30 266.05 267.02 282.07
288.03 305.29

BROADCAST   (1)
  164.29
BROADER   (1)
  205.19
BROADEST   (1)
  074.30
BROADWAY   (2)
  047.06 268.09
BROKE   (6)
  114.20 236.20 247.15 247.34 285.11
  312.01
BROKEN   (14)
  022.14 022.15 036.32 056.27 085.10
  094.27 113.05 114.16 198.16 207.02
  228.13 262.17 262.18 302.26
BROKER   (1)
  081.19
BRONZE   (2)
  189.30 305.17
BROOD   (4)
  080.20 226.11 226.19 228.08
BROOK   (5)
  137.16 203.12 203.18 227.33 259.20
BROOKS   (2)
  207.23 310.29
BROOM   (2)
  113.04 264.12
BROTHER   (3)
  054.14 159.23 266.14
BROTHERS   (1)
  109.35
BROUGHT   (15)
  039.04 039.30 062.28 096.15 113.14
  143.14 155.32 158.36 159.04 160.15
  179.08 208.32 239.27 241.29 245.17
BROW   (3)
  071.03 291.19 308.33
BROWN   (10)
  158.20 177.25 184.21 218.13 223.23
  224.04 242.14 253.22 305.25 319.03
BROWNISH   (1)
  233.07
BROWS   (3)
  078.35 186.17 308.07
BROWSED   (1)
  192.23
BROWSING   (1)
  109.32
BRUSH   (3)
  188.30 277.03 279.04
BRUSHY   (1)
  190.10
BRUTAL   (1)
  077.19
BRUTE   (5)
  012.17 219.21 223.01 315.29 315.30
BRUTES   (2)
  101.14 273.13
BRUTISH   (2)
  101.13 220.09
BUBBLE   (3)
  248.01 248.07 248.10
BUBBLES   (14)
  189.32 246.35 247.03 247.08 247.11
  247.17 247.19 247.26 247.33 248.12
  248.14 248.16 300.15 301.01
BUCK   (1)
  320.05
BUCKET   (2)
  207.03 297.14
BUCKETS   (2)
  296.01 298.15
BUCKLED   (1)
  066.07
BUD   (2)
  028.02 276.24
BUDDING   (1)
  225.02

BUDGET   (1)
  113.02
BUDS   (4)
  114.09 163.36 276.28 302.04
BUENA   (1)
  118.31
BUFFALO   (2)
  274.35 324.23
BUFFET   (1)
  081.28
BUG   (3)
  152.29 187.24 333.07
BUGINE   (1)
  279.21
BUGS   (2)
  187.30 189.08
BUILD   (15)
  016.06 021.12 039.12 040.34 045.31
  046.36 049.28 058.02 058.31 071.14
  071.27 092.21 205.10 240.32 244.22
BUILDED   (1)
  204.01
BUILDER   (4)
  047.18 085.23 221.27 329.34
BUILDERS   (1)
  058.13
BUILDING   (11)
  039.28 046.02 046.03 046.16 049.27
  050.08 058.14 062.04 173.33 225.26
  269.36
BUILDINGS   (2)
  057.14 160.34
BUILDS   (1)
  317.32
BUILT   (28)
  003.05 034.28 037.31 038.06 039.33
  045.15 046.10 048.23 054.12 058.29
  092.22 096.08 154.04 154.05 154.10
  180.15 192.35 204.21 226.08 227.28
  241.08 242.29 249.30 257.06 264.23
  264.24 296.13 324.06
BULK   (3)
  003.04 018.08 121.13
BULL   (4)
  056.27 094.34 229.22 232.19
BULLET   (2)
  140.35 278.05
BULLFROGS   (2)
  126.08 129.10
BULRUSH   (2)
  029.36 178.34
BUNCH   (3)
  129.26 130.02 174.23
BUNDLE   (4)
  044.01 066.34 067.03 144.34
BUNKER   (1)
  230.28
BUOYANCY   (1)
  087.12
BUOYANT   (1)
  165.18
BUOYS   (1)
  020.29
BURDEN   (5)
  131.13 222.06 225.19 261.05 332.22
BURGOYNE   (1)
  279.20
BURIED   (8)
  007.02 034.30 084.15 137.31 232.05
  263.02 265.02 333.18
BURIES   (1)
  058.04
BURN   (8)
  004.36 066.18 066.33 093.21 093.21
  105.19 260.03 314.29
BURNED   (18)
  056.12 066.06 067.34 074.08 075.04
  082.07 094.14 159.02 242.02 246.11

```
BURNED                          (CONTINUED)      BUT                             (CONTINUED)
  250.05  250.06  250.07  250.20  250.21           050.14  050.30  051.04  051.06  051.09
  253.15  257.27  261.02                           051.13  051.21  052.18  052.19  052.22
BURNING                                            052.25  052.30  053.05  053.31  053.34
  174.25  246.07  248.18  260.22  (   5)           054.02  054.13  054.22  054.27  054.28
                                  301.02           056.09  056.17  057.03  057.07  057.14
BURROW                           (   8)            057.16  058.02  058.12  058.26  058.32
  013.30  038.35  044.23  045.02  098.33           059.29  059.37  061.11  061.29  062.04
  167.23  220.33  309.19                           062.06  062.36  063.25  064.33  065.28
BURROWING                        (   2)            066.04  066.22  066.25  067.06  067.09
  098.31  273.14                                   067.12  067.20  069.19  069.21  069.31
BURROWS                          (   2)            070.05  070.30  070.35  071.11  071.18
  232.15  263.15                                   071.20  071.25  072.15  072.20  073.10
BURRS                            (   3)            073.12  073.22  074.07  074.32  076.34
  238.24  238.28  238.35                           077.03  077.08  078.06  079.01  079.18
EURS                             (   1)            080.22  080.28  080.31  081.14  081.21
  113.22                                           081.24  082.07  082.12  082.15  082.26
BURST                            (   5)            083.15  083.28  083.31  084.03  084.05
  160.08  248.12  277.15  278.31  315.05           084.14  084.23  084.30  085.12  085.13
BURSTING                         (   1)            085.18  085.32  085.34  086.08  086.24
  305.04                                           087.02  087.09  087.15  087.23  087.31
BURSTS                           (   4)            088.07  089.13  090.09  090.16  090.22
  102.02  276.15  276.35  281.24                   091.35  092.17  092.20  092.23  093.18
BURY                             (   2)            093.20  093.25  094.01  095.18  095.27
  031.33  183.31                                   096.04  096.11  097.03  097.14  098.08
BURYING                          (   1)            098.19  098.20  098.22  099.09  099.21
  258.03                                           100.29  100.32  101.23  101.25  101.28
BUSH                             (   1)            102.12  102.24  102.26  103.02  103.10
  163.27                                           103.36  104.14  104.18  106.15  106.27
BUSHEL                           (   5)            106.35  107.01  107.17  107.26  107.27
  064.02  151.15  238.11  238.20  273.23           108.13  108.15  108.24  108.30  109.16
BUSHELS                          (   4)            109.20  111.03  111.05  111.09  112.01
  055.07  055.08  162.32  163.16                   112.20  113.02  115.02  116.05  117.02
BUSHES                           (   9)            118.22  118.36  121.33  122.05  122.06
  145.25  182.06  232.21  261.11  263.03           122.16  122.27  123.20  123.26  123.29
  280.08  281.29  303.34  311.20                   124.10  124.21  125.19  125.35  126.18
BUSHY                            (   2)            126.35  127.28  128.09  129.14  129.21
  145.11  233.09                                   130.10  130.17  130.21  130.32  131.09
BUSINESS                         (  27)            131.15  131.27  131.29  131.33  133.09
  006.37  017.22  018.24  018.29  019.10           133.22  133.26  134.13  135.13  135.14
  019.32  019.36  020.03  020.04  021.08           135.34  135.36  136.04  136.25  136.35
  021.18  062.29  069.25  070.09  092.24           137.07  137.10  137.11  138.18  138.32
  098.18  118.19  118.27  120.25  140.08           138.33  139.04  140.06  140.12  140.12
  144.04  152.12  153.05  213.11  264.13           141.17  141.23  141.26  142.07  142.10
  268.04  326.04                                   142.12  143.05  143.24  143.26  144.03
BUSK                             (   2)            144.13  145.10  147.04  147.10  147.11
  068.09  068.12                                   147.21  147.28  148.05  148.11  151.04
BUST                             (   1)            151.32  152.02  152.04  152.35  153.01
  038.04                                           154.07  154.13  155.12  155.26  156.14
BUSTLE                           (   1)            156.29  157.10  157.19  157.34  158.09
  263.16                                           158.25  160.35  161.32  162.12  162.27
BUSTLING                         (   1)            162.33  163.37  164.01  164.06  164.19
  329.36                                           164.28  165.08  165.17  165.23  165.32
BUSY                             (   5)            166.01  166.11  166.19  166.36  171.03
  098.28  165.05  167.21  267.07  297.19           171.27  171.32  172.01  172.02  172.16
BUT                              ( 715)            173.12  174.02  174.03  174.30  176.18
  003.14  004.24  004.33  005.01  005.24           176.24  176.30  177.14  177.22  177.28
  006.18  007.18  007.22  007.32  008.11           178.07  178.35  179.12  180.17  180.34
  008.14  008.21  009.15  010.07  011.17           182.32  184.20  185.07  185.20  185.22
  011.19  012.04  012.14  012.24  012.31           185.36  187.18  187.27  187.30  188.04
  013.15  013.27  014.14  014.18  014.29           188.08  188.32  189.01  189.18  189.22
  014.33  015.01  015.04  015.09  015.31           190.22  190.34  191.06  191.10  191.18
  016.16  016.23  016.24  017.08  017.20           192.05  192.32  193.39  194.04  194.23
  017.27  019.18  019.24  019.29  019.35           196.26  197.29  198.29  198.34  199.02
  021.31  022.08  022.17  022.19  022.20           199.03  199.05  199.25  200.02  201.33
  022.28  023.08  023.21  023.34  024.08           202.04  202.31  202.36  203.34  204.06
  024.18  025.17  025.19  025.21  026.08           204.23  204.22  205.14  205.15  205.23
  027.02  027.18  027.32  027.34  029.24           205.35  206.04  206.08  206.24  206.32
  030.01  030.17  030.27  030.30  030.34           207.01  207.17  207.35  207.35  208.33
  031.06  031.25  031.32  032.03  032.22           208.35  211.12  211.18  211.20  211.22
  033.04  033.07  033.10  033.13  033.34           211.33  212.02  212.25  213.08  213.20
  034.09  034.15  034.21  035.27  036.26           213.24  213.28  214.01  214.09  214.32
  037.19  037.24  037.28  037.34  038.11           215.20  215.25  216.02  216.13  217.20
  040.01  040.09  040.12  040.14  040.28           217.23  218.16  218.17  218.20  219.01
  041.01  041.05  041.13  041.31  042.12           219.05  219.14  220.02  220.08  220.23
  042.37  043.11  043.34  044.02  044.28           220.28  220.36  221.06  221.13  221.15
  044.29  045.01  045.13  045.25  045.25           222.06  222.11  222.19  224.05  224.08
  046.04  046.08  046.22  046.29  047.07           225.02  225.06  225.16  225.23  227.03
  048.09  048.12  048.33  049.40  050.11
```

35

36

(CONTINUED)

201.21	201.34	201.35	202.01	202.32
203.13	203.23	204.09	206.17	206.28
207.08	207.22	207.23	207.26	208.38
208.38	211.03	212.32	215.03	215.27
215.30	216.01	216.34	217.13	217.17
219.20	219.29	220.04	220.07	221.02
221.21	221.26	221.29	225.33	227.08
227.17	227.24	227.31	228.24	229.18
230.07	231.24	231.33	232.03	232.16
232.28	233.11	233.19	233.28	233.29
235.31	235.34	236.18	237.04	237.07
238.10	239.11	239.21	239.36	240.08
240.11	240.17	240.27	240.28	240.29
241.12	241.30	241.33	242.14	246.07
247.20	248.05	248.35	249.29	250.07
250.13	250.21	250.24	251.01	251.10
251.30	252.14	252.26	252.35	252.35
253.34	254.32	254.35	255.07	255.10
256.05	256.13	256.23	256.31	257.15
257.20	257.25	258.19	259.05	259.09
259.18	260.10	260.29	260.34	261.04
261.08	261.11	261.18	262.16	263.18
263.25	263.26	263.28	264.10	265.04
265.06	265.19	266.03	266.15	266.26
266.27	266.36	267.22	268.03	268.33
271.31	272.11	272.16	272.22	272.25
273.01	273.01	273.17	273.24	273.25
273.26	273.30	273.32	273.32	274.25
274.35	275.19	276.05	276.06	276.19
276.19	277.15	277.19	277.22	277.28
277.31	278.19	278.36	279.01	279.25
279.28	280.02	280.13	280.27	280.28
281.03	283.04	283.15	283.35	284.06
284.21	284.25	285.23	285.31	287.03
287.09	287.31	288.21	289.06	289.10
289.21	290.07	290.27	290.28	291.14
291.25	291.27	292.15	292.16	292.29
292.33	293.02	293.25	293.27	293.27
294.09	295.02	295.24	295.27	295.28
295.30	295.35	298.20	299.03	299.05
299.20	300.24	300.35	301.30	302.26
302.31	302.32	304.14	304.24	306.21
308.08	309.03	310.01	311.06	312.26
312.27	312.30	317.08	318.01	318.03
318.13	319.09	320.13	321.20	321.30
322.11	323.21	323.29	325.11	326.31
327.07	327.19	328.19	328.21	329.07
329.14	330.01	330.07	333.12	333.14
333.16	333.23			

C (9)
014.06 043.13 055.05 060.17 060.18
120.11 214.28 250.15 250.32
CABBAGE (1)
267.13
CABIN (5)
085.06 142.29 169.26 204.03 323.25
CABINS (1)
271.21
CABLE (1)
191.01
CACKLE (1)
128.09
CACKLING (2)
042.04 127.10
CADAVEROUS (1)
284.26
CADIS (1)
246.27
CAGED (1)
085.32
CAKE (4)
247.21 247.34 292.23 300.19
CAKES (6)
062.02 292.14 295.24 296.01 296.02
296.36
CALCULABLE (1)
071.20
CALCULATE (2)
235.29 288.35
CALCULATED (3)
158.08 241.34 296.16
CALCULATION (2)
092.09 290.29
CALCULATOR (2)
020.31 091.33
CALCULATORS (1)
090.06
CALCUTTA (1)
298.01
CALF (2)
218.23 324.26
CALIDAS (1)
319.14
CALIFORNIA (1)
329.28
CALIPHS (1)
079.17
CALKED (1)
270.09
CALL (23)
003.13 010.30 014.30 023.11 031.15
050.30 058.03 073.15 079.06 098.04
103.35 132.11 158.21 160.20 162.24
168.34 170.31 197.34 227.19 260.27
293.26 314.25 328.06
CALLED (51)
005.09 005.26 006.38 007.19 008.08
008.12 014.17 026.30 036.35 038.12
043.04 046.24 053.35 065.34 069.24
074.20 089.12 092.05 094.21 097.24
102.09 104.29 106.02 106.06 106.26
129.34 133.29 136.15 140.08 147.05
147.23 149.18 151.09 151.19 152.14
165.28 166.04 183.05 194.02 197.35
198.03 212.25 220.01 221.27 232.34
232.36 258.07 262.01 316.32 331.09
331.14
CALLING (7)
073.08 150.31 165.29 201.23 221.26
226.13 236.24
CALLOUS (1)
029.08
CALLOW (1)
227.02
CALLS (6)
017.14 077.13 137.02 223.20 226.20
268.05

CALM (11)
112.23 117.22 141.13 160.31 185.12
186.19 187.30 189.10 189.12 234.17
312.11
CALVES (1)
121.36
CAMAR (1)
099.27
CAMBRIDGE (6)
050.04 050.17 135.30 295.23 300.26
325.29
CAME (93)
041.14 043.13 044.15 046.15 062.23
070.01 075.12 075.25 082.08 090.35
113.23 115.03 123.12 130.29 131.30
133.03 139.09 140.11 141.36 142.03
142.07 144.03 145.20 146.04 150.29
151.04 153.15 154.18 155.10 156.18
158.03 172.14 175.18 179.34 182.27
186.21 190.30 194.32 203.23 204.09
205.05 210.03 214.25 216.11 222.11
223.04 226.05 229.25 233.05 233.24
234.23 234.26 234.31 235.34 236.02
236.06 236.25 240.05 240.11 240.32
246.09 247.17 248.27 250.27 252.21
256.08 259.32 261.19 262.05 262.12
267.01 267.35 268.19 269.32 273.16
273.27 273.29 275.24 275.30 276.13
277.26 278.06 278.12 278.28 279.02
279.06 294.16 295.08 295.23 304.18
313.02 313.27 333.08
CAMP (4)
037.28 172.18 183.32 252.23
CAMPED (1)
027.31
CAMPS (1)
183.30
CAN (156)
004.24 005.15 006.19 006.24 007.17
008.24 008.30 010.09 010.34 011.12
011.18 014.08 014.28 015.16 018.33
019.11 022.16 023.19 023.31 024.23
024.25 024.29 024.30 026.04 026.05
030.33 032.34 038.27 039.21 047.35
049.33 051.06 053.23 053.36 060.01
061.23 063.11 064.14 064.37 065.03
065.27 065.27 066.20 072.14 074.01
074.28 082.03 088.34 089.12 089.27
090.25 098.04 102.06 102.12 102.16
104.09 104.33 105.27 106.05 106.17
106.23 106.34 109.07 109.14 110.11
111.12 115.32 117.34 119.31 120.19
131.07 131.10 131.13 133.17 134.28
134.34 135.09 135.31 135.36 136.03
137.30 137.36 141.15 144.17 146.24
147.23 150.21 166.27 167.30 171.29
173.22 175.27 176.25 177.33 180.22
184.29 187.16 187.23 188.07 188.25
188.28 189.04 192.11 193.19 194.11
214.19 216.01 216.22 218.11 218.26
219.30 220.20 220.31 221.29 223.16
234.01 240.27 243.35 244.03 245.07
246.20 253.31 254.22 263.18 268.02
268.04 269.24 278.25 283.21 285.33
287.09 292.25 296.33 302.13 303.18
305.32 309.10 318.02 318.19 318.21
321.20 322.10 324.10 324.16 326.03
326.15 327.27 328.31 329.15 330.09
330.10 330.28 331.31 332.25 332.29
333.30
CANADA (3)
145.06 313.12 320.08
CANADIAN (4)
106.16 144.16 146.15 148.12
CANAL (2)
177.02 311.16
CANDAHARS (1)
327.05

CANDLES (1)
131.01
CANINE (1)
232.19
CANKER (1)
160.13
CANNIBAL (1)
026.11
CANNIBALS (1)
321.32
CANNON (1)
026.17
CANNOT (57)
004.14 006.12 006.16 008.29 009.13
009.19 021.32 024.19 025.07 026.01
026.32 026.35 029.24 030.32 032.29
038.11 050.11 065.04 065.04 066.22
066.22 092.03 093.11 095.18 098.23
107.22 109.05 120.26 133.11 134.19
135.34 141.23 141.27 144.15 171.03
181.34 193.24 212.25 213.33 218.12
219.04 219.11 221.15 221.18 224.04
224.33 226.24 233.33 244.15 268.37
269.25 292.36 301.33 320.17 324.30
328.33 329.07
CANOE (3)
190.31 191.09 192.14
CANS (1)
321.14
CANT (2)
049.38 076.31
CANTERING (1)
232.21
CANVAS (1)
102.25
CAP (6)
024.34 025.23 035.34 145.14 148.23
262.34
CAPABLE (1)
262.07
CAPACIOUS (2)
284.35 288.04
CAPACITIES (1)
010.07
CAPACITY (3)
124.35 285.33 306.32
CAPE (2)
171.10 289.07
CAPES (3)
185.30 289.33 290.13
CAPITAL (7)
017.32 019.33 021.19 069.31 073.21
206.15 251.07
CAPTAIN (2)
020.13 279.23
CAPTURED (1)
004.34
CAR (7)
036.15 037.03 037.15 119.28 120.15
122.03 294.18
CARAVANSARY (1)
269.10
CARAWAY (1)
046.34
CARBUNCLES (1)
231.04
CARD (1)
142.31
CARDS (2)
129.26 262.22
CARE (13)
006.03 011.04 047.02 067.08 075.10
077.15 094.19 145.24 207.25 221.14
226.32 239.24 316.32
CARED (3)
009.33 151.22 246.11
CAREER (1)
098.15

CAREERING (1)
120.32
CAREFUL (4)
011.32 071.11 163.29 253.25
CAREFULLY (10)
042.22 045.11 062.10 067.37 153.26
158.08 178.20 219.24 244.18 285.10
CARELESS (1)
274.25
CARELESSLY (2)
070.01 190.08
CARES (1)
006.11
CAREW (1)
080.32
CARIBOU (1)
120.03
CARITATEM (1)
243.05
CARLOS (1)
094.31
CARMINE (1)
262.11
CARNAGE (2)
230.18 231.25
CARNIVOROUS (1)
215.36
CAROLS (1)
310.30
CARPENTER (2)
046.13 048.12
CARPENTRY (1)
058.33
CARPET (2)
067.16 141.33
CARPETED (1)
030.06
CARPETS (1)
070.13
CARRIAGE (3)
007.11 122.37 266.36
CARRIED (19)
042.25 049.19 053.01 082.05 082.20
082.27 102.18 102.31 145.11 174.07
183.36 199.24 211.36 230.31 242.11
247.15 283.36 292.32 296.27
CARRIER (1)
159.32
CARRION (2)
074.16 318.11
CARRY (18)
017.31 052.34 067.07 070.03 081.17
082.11 083.24 138.26 171.09 178.26
196.21 196.22 197.16 206.16 217.22
225.19 239.24 275.06
CARRYING (6)
063.07 072.09 145.16 261.23 276.01
330.33
CARS (15)
053.04 092.29 092.36 114.34 116.07
116.31 116.35 117.02 117.11 117.32
119.06 122.17 122.32 193.33 296.18
CART (11)
037.14 038.26 065.30 070.05 122.27
157.35 163.09 169.32 170.12 173.20
197.32
CARTING (1)
044.13
CARTLOADS (2)
044.08 045.14
CARTS (4)
157.36 167.17 207.34 294.08
CARVE (2)
090.21 090.23
CARVED (1)
102.26
CARYATIDES (1)
168.07

CASE				(23)
018.10	019.20	022.32	039.15	057.02
071.21	073.17	074.24	118.14	123.13
141.24	142.15	174.08	185.36	202.34
206.07	214.20	217.33	315.10	327.31
327.34	330.08	330.09		

CASES (7)
091.23 151.06 207.11 246.27 246.30
290.05 327.32

CASHIERED (1)
024.10

CASINGS (1)
084.34

CASKET (1)
102.19

CASKS (2)
049.12 243.07

CASSIOPEIA (1)
088.05

CAST (11)
066.09 068.18 077.12 145.03 145.09
169.27 175.20 195.17 203.27 247.14
309.09

CASTALIAN (1)
179.30

CASTING (2)
039.01 068.06

CASTLE (2)
202.25 262.15

CASTLES (2)
269.36 324.06

CASTS (3)
024.06 116.36 220.05

CASUAL (1)
178.30

CASUALTIES (1)
246.01

CAT (18)
043.24 044.03 044.03 044.05 127.29
128.05 232.24 232.26 232.31 232.35
233.20 233.21 233.22 257.26 266.14
266.14 279.28 309.31

CATCH (15)
018.03 033.22 087.05 126.10 168.29
178.06 206.09 206.27 206.29 206.29
207.14 208.40 262.24 280.01 292.32

CATCHING (4)
208.34 223.05 224.13 285.23

CATECHISM (1)
008.17

CATERPILLAR (2)
024.06 215.09

CATERPILLARS (1)
004.27

CATHOLIC (1)
147.08

CATO (8)
063.15 084.07 166.01 243.02 257.04
257.07 257.14 263.20

CATOWL (1)
272.17

CATS (2)
012.28 322.09

CATT (1)
279.28

CATTLE (14)
005.04 033.15 033.21 063.35 109.09
121.30 121.31 133.31 151.16 157.07
165.27 171.25 239.18 264.36

CAUGHT (20)
018.03 059.33 144.18 145.26 159.21
174.23 175.22 183.34 184.16 210.05
214.21 215.28 217.01 235.18 244.33
253.14 272.26 283.29 284.35 317.12

CAUSE (11)
056.33 103.01 131.18 134.09 134.21
138.14 216.28 220.08 231.22 266.31
322.19

CAUSED (4)
095.14 229.18 241.28 308.14

CAUSES (4)
181.05 217.14 299.04 315.15

CAUSEWAY (2)
115.15 202.17

CAUSING (2)
265.31 300.14

CAVE (5)
028.15 028.17 040.15 094.01 305.22

CAVERN (1)
319.07

CAVERNOUS (2)
243.23 308.04

CAVES (2)
028.28 040.20

CAVILLERS (1)
061.07

CAVING (1)
039.17

CAVITIES (1)
296.07

CAVITY (1)
292.24

CEASE (1)
166.31

CEASED (6)
112.28 153.17 160.22 190.22 229.17
278.33

CEASELESS (1)
132.24

CEASELESSLY (1)
187.24

CEASES (1)
307.08

CEDAR (2)
120.01 201.07

CEILING (2)
039.19 243.17

CELEBRATE (1)
068.09

CELEBRATED (5)
055.30 079.05 105.20 127.22 231.28

CELEBRATES (1)
068.11

CELEBRATING (1)
330.02

CELESTIAL (9)
020.06 028.26 037.10 085.10 088.03
089.17 102.31 117.01 179.28

CELL (2)
080.29 244.19

CELLAM (1)
243.04

CELLAR (27)
031.05 038.10 039.13 039.18 043.20
044.22 044.34 045.33 047.36 071.24
128.13 133.27 138.33 145.27 168.30
183.26 232.13 243.07 243.09 244.12
253.20 257.14 259.12 260.23 260.28
263.02 263.14

CELLARS (3)
039.23 140.20 294.10

CELLINI (2)
202.23 202.34

CELLS (1)
300.21

CELLULAR (3)
024.17 062.26 307.30

CELT (1)
251.20

CELTIS (1)
202.03

CEMENT (1)
241.10

CEMENTS (1)
230.06

```
CEMETERIES                        (  1)
264.26
CENT                              (  4)
105.26  195.32  296.16  296.18
CENTIPEDE                         (  1)
152.32
CENTRAL                           (  1)
309.06
CENTRE                            (  5)
011.18  179.13  287.23  289.14  293.28
CENTS                             ( 11)
024.34  043.30  050.27  053.09  053.11
054.26  061.01  064.33  082.16  082.17
082.23
CENTURIES                         (  5)
031.03  058.21  063.15  104.05  164.14
CENTURY                           (  6)
067.33  108.22  109.26  109.27  264.01
329.36
CERASUS                           (  1)
113.34
CERBERUS                          (  1)
142.25
CEREAL                            (  1)
062.11
CEREALIAN                         (  1)
062.30
CEREMONIES                        (  1)
126.29
CEREMONY                          (  4)
143.03  164.36  165.27  243.30
CERES                             (  3)
165.31  166.05  239.32
CERTAIN                           ( 26)
036.08  038.17  043.34  056.26  056.31
060.39  060.40  064.36  072.31  081.04
085.04  118.17  123.06  123.25  125.14
135.09  136.15  150.10  162.23  171.07
182.22  202.24  213.36  219.15  222.13
330.22
CERTAINLY                         ( 12)
016.32  035.10  040.16  056.21  067.01
099.05  127.05  136.21  215.33  216.14
230.13  285.14
CERTAINTY                         (  1)
074.17
CERULEAN                          (  1)
177.12
CESSATION                         (  1)
089.25
CHAFF                             (  1)
049.39
CHAIN                             (  3)
194.06  194.08  285.11
CHAINED                           (  1)
004.25
CHAINS                            (  1)
294.09
CHAIR                             (  3)
088.05  116.01  140.12
CHAIRS                            (  6)
065.19  065.25  113.24  115.35  140.09
141.29
CHAISE                            (  1)
256.25
CHAISES                           (  1)
284.36
CHALK                             (  1)
049.18
CHALMERS                          (  1)
259.14
CHAMBER                           (  2)
242.35  244.02
CHAMBERS                          (  3)
036.10  135.26  196.32
CHAMPION                          (  2)
192.26  229.14

CHAMPLAIN                         (  1)
119.21
CHAMPOLLION                       (  1)
308.17
CHANCE                            (  4)
141.19  269.16  302.19  323.09
CHANCED                           (  6)
075.06  170.10  202.10  260.17  267.21
285.03
CHANGE                            ( 15)
011.16  011.18  023.21  099.10  176.14
193.02  211.20  215.33  219.14  301.12
312.02  320.04  328.26  328.26  332.25
CHANGEABLE                        (  1)
177.11
CHANGED                           (  8)
082.13  087.34  091.17  094.33  148.10
208.36  208.36  265.32
CHANGES                           (  4)
023.21  291.33  299.20  302.06
CHANGING                          (  1)
121.01
CHANNEL                           (  5)
198.27  220.04  289.09  307.20  307.27
CHANNELS                          (  3)
293.27  311.11  321.17
CHANTED                           (  1)
123.36
CHANTICLEER                       (  2)
084.23  127.24
CHAOS                             (  1)
313.35
CHAPMAN                           (  1)
033.27
CHAPS                             (  2)
126.21  181.36
CHAR                              (  1)
311.21
CHARACTER                         ( 22)
021.36  025.19  033.06  045.07  047.17
055.25  085.03  095.08  096.19  096.23
100.11  179.14  184.11  208.30  228.25
240.05  258.27  290.03  290.08  291.11
308.22  333.29
CHARACTERISTIC                    (  1)
008.15
CHARACTERS                        (  4)
088.31  192.30  199.31  312.24
CHARGE                            (  2)
050.25  152.28
CHARGED                           (  1)
229.29
CHARIOT                           (  1)
074.07
CHARITABLE                        (  1)
003.19
CHARITY                           (  7)
023.26  073.03  075.33  076.09  077.10
152.10  331.20
CHARLESTON                        (  1)
297.36
CHARM                             (  1)
123.18
CHARMED                           (  1)
174.17
CHARMING                          (  1)
219.05
CHART                             (  1)
321.02
CHARTS                            (  1)
020.28
CHASE                             (  3)
223.26  276.33  320.26
CHASM                             (  3)
287.34  288.10  288.13
CHASTE                            (  2)
220.34  220.35
```

CHASTITY   (2)
  219.36 220.34
CHATTED   (1)
  042.35
CHATTERING   (1)
  046.11
CHAUCER   (1)
  212.18
CHE   (2)
  311.21 311.21
CHEAP   (7)
  024.28 080.09 100.17 101.27 123.28
  136.10 158.30
CHEAPER   (6)
  040.20 055.37 059.11 071.27 071.30
  191.18
CHEAPEST   (1)
  059.09
CHEAPLY   (1)
  019.35
CHEAT   (1)
  165.01
CHEATED   (1)
  104.14
CHECKED   (2)
  035.10 311.06
CHECKER   (1)
  235.07
CHECKERED   (1)
  304.22
CHEEK   (5)
  141.16 190.21 194.26 266.35 308.09
CHEEKS   (2)
  077.36 308.07
CHEEPING   (1)
  054.27
CHEER   (4)
  046.10 134.30 138.08 230.10
CHEERED   (4)
  136.34 164.25 304.24 318.10
CHEERFUL   (8)
  088.25 118.32 137.25 242.13 253.07
  256.05 264.04 265.10
CHEERFULLY   (4)
  116.29 158.16 160.31 205.01
CHEERING   (3)
  154.14 328.15 332.15
CHEERS   (1)
  255.05
CHEESE   (2)
  136.14 226.05
CHEMIC   (1)
  254.17
CHEMISTRY   (1)
  051.23
CHERISH   (4)
  016.12 028.29 155.19 332.13
CHERISHED   (2)
  016.34 315.36
CHERRIES   (1)
  114.01
CHERRY   (3)
  018.25 113.32 113.33
CHEST   (3)
  007.14 153.31 191.05
CHESTNUT   (3)
  113.21 238.21 239.03
CHESTNUTS   (2)
  166.33 238.19
CHESTNUTTING   (1)
  194.27
CHEW   (1)
  146.19
CHEWED   (2)
  078.12 078.14
CHEWERS   (1)
  078.12

CHEWINK   (1)
  319.04
CHICADEE   (1)
  125.34
CHICADEES   (2)
  146.31 275.24
CHICCORY   (1)
  305.19
CHICKAREE   (2)
  310.20 310.20
CHICKEN   (2)
  152.26 262.23
CHICKENS   (5)
  152.29 154.12 204.28 227.04 227.20
CHIDING   (1)
  274.11
CHIEF   (5)
  008.17 091.14 143.10 184.14 244.08
CHIEFLY   (12)
  027.25 049.26 054.22 076.36 146.35
  162.34 165.35 184.11 213.27 309.03
  324.18 329.26
CHILD   (10)
  010.11 028.10 147.11 147.12 147.15
  148.19 168.20 196.08 212.33 243.01
CHILDERS   (1)
  053.01
CHILDHOOD   (2)
  151.24 239.09
CHILDISH   (1)
  026.19
CHILDREN   (24)
  003.20 032.09 077.28 089.33 096.09
  097.21 103.15 107.24 118.19 127.33
  138.05 151.25 154.14 171.25 204.08
  208.19 213.13 239.16 250.32 256.26
  258.13 263.27 263.30 269.06
CHILLED   (1)
  119.06
CHILLING   (1)
  119.04
CHIMNEY   (12)
  045.14 045.16 048.23 084.31 240.32
  241.14 241.35 242.11 242.28 252.27
  263.06 265.06
CHIN   (3)
  126.20 233.12 308.06
CHINA   (3)
  058.24 322.26 331.21
CHINESE   (4)
  004.09 014.22 058.26 077.31
CHINKS   (3)
  084.32 242.12 284.03
CHIP   (10)
  129.28 157.32 158.01 230.09 230.30
  261.20 311.20 311.21 311.21 332.29
CHIPS   (6)
  042.35 064.15 228.31 228.33 229.12
  251.28
CHIRP   (1)
  302.20
CHIRRUPED   (1)
  310.18
CHIRRUPING   (1)
  310.16
CHISEL   (1)
  178.17
CHIVALRY   (1)
  161.04
CHIVIN   (1)
  185.25
CHIVINS   (1)
  184.03
CHOICE   (3)
  008.21 031.25 099.03
CHOICEST   (1)
  102.20

42

CHOIR (1)
125.10
CHOKES (1)
275.17
CHOOSE (3)
060.37 224.20 243.28
CHOP (1)
161.29
CHOPPED (1)
145.17
CHOPPER (3)
144.16 146.01 251.16
CHOPPERS (1)
250.18
CHOPPING (5)
091.28 135.33 136.06 146.25 213.10
CHOSE (2)
205.09 234.33
CHOSEN (4)
008.19 070.30 288.33 320.16
CHOWDER (1)
180.26
CHRIST (2)
063.16 108.20
CHRISTEN (1)
246.05
CHRISTIAN (4)
076.26 152.22 221.07 331.19
CHRISTIANITY (3)
037.29 058.03 131.01
CHRISTIERN (1)
232.08
CHRONOLOGIES (1)
310.28
CHUCKLE (3)
112.10 148.11 316.37
CHUCKLING (1)
310.15
CHURCH (6)
047.07 093.24 098.01 108.21 197.02
267.27
CHURCHES (1)
048.03
CHURN (1)
127.32
CIDER (2)
137.27 223.13
CIDERISH (1)
258.01
CIGAR (1)
130.05
CIMETER (1)
098.13
CINDERELLA (1)
105.26
CINDERS (1)
260.24
CINQUEFOIL (1)
155.15
CIPHER (1)
104.13
CIRCLE (7)
115.26 124.12 228.11 236.35 277.20
277.23 320.24
CIRCLED (2)
159.12 313.10
CIRCLES (9)
009.26 054.33 103.09 103.11 115.29
125.02 188.01 188.06 277.10
CIRCLING (7)
114.25 159.27 174.11 187.22 188.08
252.32 313.17
CIRCUIT (2)
126.28 130.14
CIRCULAR (2)
185.15 270.08
CIRCULATE (2)
099.24 125.33

CIRCULATED (1)
300.27
CIRCULATING (3)
099.23 104.30 167.10
CIRCULATION (2)
018.07 037.14
CIRCULATIONS (1)
105.31
CIRCUMFERENCE (1)
175.31
CIRCUMSPECTION (2)
050.30 274.07
CIRCUMSTANCE (2)
198.01 276.05
CIRCUMSTANCES (16)
003.15 004.12 016.15 034.23 035.28
063.12 096.22 110.09 134.07 134.29
144.02 182.08 289.01 291.13 291.15
305.20
CIRCUMSTANTIAL (1)
231.31
CITADEL (1)
272.25
CITIES (3)
030.22 307.06 327.17
CITIZEN (4)
036.06 047.28 119.24 283.20
CITIZENS (3)
019.27 198.10 213.13
CITY (14)
008.09 044.33 070.05 096.14 115.25
115.35 116.01 116.03 117.30 159.11
264.24 264.25 326.20 327.02
CIVIL (2)
262.08 264.04
CIVILITY (2)
007.08 116.01
CIVILIZATION (13)
011.34 020.26 030.22 031.09 033.13
034.13 034.33 035.03 035.24 040.27
058.01 103.23 273.13
CIVILIZED (21)
003.09 013.07 022.32 023.03 030.20
030.31 030.35 031.08 031.34 031.36
034.17 035.21 035.22 040.27 091.28
120.19 158.13 158.14 213.31 215.31
216.12
CLAD (4)
024.22 024.36 027.02 085.22
CLAIM (2)
080.06 166.34
CLAIMED (2)
049.25 251.30
CLAIMS (1)
043.34
CLAMMY (1)
043.16
CLAMOR (1)
313.01
CLANGOR (3)
127.09 248.28 313.17
CLARIFIED (3)
179.25 193.16 227.08
CLARIFYING (1)
213.21
CLARIONS (1)
127.11
CLARKE (1)
321.10
CLASP (1)
118.25
CLASS (9)
014.23 016.23 022.33 034.25 035.11
064.36 107.05 172.14 325.12
CLASSES (2)
032.16 104.24
CLASSIC (4)
103.36 106.25 111.04 157.14

CLASSICS (7)
100.27 100.30 100.32 103.19 103.35
106.09 106.10
CLAWS (1)
275.27
CLAY (7)
040.22 261.28 304.29 305.01 307.31
309.13 321.24
CLEAN (17)
021.34 022.06 031.03 084.35 113.04
153.16 154.16 155.26 163.33 179.02
184.32 199.34 205.07 215.19 228.02
241.07 295.04
CLEANED (3)
214.22 226.06 240.34
CLEANER (2)
184.27 245.17
CLEANEST (1)
181.27
CLEANING (1)
221.05
CLEANSE (1)
068.16
CLEANSED (4)
005.18 196.33 207.20 312.26
CLEAR (18)
008.22 032.30 039.19 069.13 086.28
127.16 156.18 175.30 176.09 177.04
180.09 180.14 228.04 247.05 252.38
267.30 268.15 269.28
CLEARED (3)
038.18 156.13 186.03
CLEARER (1)
005.08
CLEARING (7)
114.25 121.12 127.02 128.08 130.11
161.10 313.23
CLEARLY (3)
096.10 123.31 206.18
CLEAVAGES (1)
247.30
CLEAVER (1)
098.26
CLEFT (1)
291.02
CLERK (1)
320.16
CLEW (1)
028.33
CLIFF (1)
018.01
CLIFFS (1)
186.16
CLIFFY (1)
317.13
CLIMATE (3)
012.19 027.27 303.07
CLIMATES (4)
013.34 027.23 063.12 127.24
CLIMBED (1)
238.29
CLIMBING (1)
037.23
CLIMES (4)
119.23 309.20 313.27 322.18
CLINCH (1)
330.27
CLINCHED (1)
319.08
CLING (1)
261.06
CLINGING (1)
122.05
CLOCK (9)
112.14 118.34 124.03 143.13 161.18
183.13 248.33 272.11 274.11
CLOCKS (2)
090.01 117.35

CLOSE (18)
012.36 022.24 091.05 146.03 148.23
165.13 170.21 174.22 175.01 176.07
180.13 226.03 248.03 254.30 266.05
300.05 303.14 317.33
CLOSED (1)
120.15
CLOSELY (3)
112.33 246.33 307.12
CLOSER (2)
178.34 212.04
CLOSES (1)
282.32
CLOSEST (1)
210.24
CLOSET (2)
048.30 172.12
CLOSING (1)
096.05
CLOTH (3)
029.01 116.04 145.13
CLOTHE (5)
006.21 028.03 134.22 147.21 156.07
CLOTHED (2)
012.36 015.15
CLOTHES (31)
012.25 013.05 013.28 021.34 022.05
022.07 022.28 022.31 023.04 023.10
023.24 023.29 023.30 023.31 023.33
024.08 024.14 028.05 068.13 068.15
075.23 225.32 226.01 244.29 245.27
262.16 262.32 308.31 328.24 328.26
332.25
CLOTHING (18)
012.21 012.30 013.22 013.26 014.03
015.22 021.21 021.26 024.28 026.33
027.16 059.43 060.17 064.24 086.15
206.03 206.04 253.32
CLOTHS (1)
062.14
CLOUD (12)
008.28 017.17 116.12 116.14 116.16
116.25 177.17 203.29 207.33 317.10
317.13 318.06
CLOUDS (15)
078.34 086.30 091.29 102.05 116.33
138.12 175.35 188.32 189.34 223.31
269.33 295.31 297.27 309.20 312.07
CLOUDY (2)
129.08 318.34
CLOUT (1)
091.19 091.19
CLUCK (1)
124.09
CLUCKING (1)
226.12
CLUMSY (3)
006.14 075.21 190.34
CLUSTERS (1)
238.04
CLUTCHED (2)
199.23 217.02
CLUTTERED (2)
036.20 092.07
CO (2)
109.35 225.18
COARSE (5)
006.11 195.21 217.18 217.25 296.10
COARSELY (1)
217.20
COARSER (2)
030.16 063.34
COARSEST (2)
145.10 168.10
COAST (10)
020.07 020.17 121.14 223.34 289.34
292.03 318.04 321.03 322.12 322.13

COASTWISE
020.21   (1)
COAT
004.06 007.11 022.24 023.24 024.07   (13)
024.30 025.20 035.33 042.30 157.29
262.09 294.03 294.32
COATS
006.31 022.20 023.20 023.20   (4)
COBBLER
171.21   (1)
COBS
274.21 275.08   (2)
COBWEB
187.15 188.14   (2)
COCK
127.01 149.17 192.20 228.07   (4)
COCKEREL
127.03   (1)
COCKERELS
127.16 128.08   (2)
COCKS
320.29   (1)
COCOA
119.27   (1)
COD
284.26 287.01   (2)
CODDLING
238.18   (1)
CODMAN
259.23   (1)
COENOBITES
173.30   (1)
COEVAL
227.10   (1)
COFFEE
043.27 044.02 093.34 145.18 146.30   (11)
148.35 205.11 205.15 205.23 214.28
217.12
COFFIN
048.11 048.12   (2)
COGNATE
314.16   (1)
COHABIT
220.28 221.24   (2)
COIL
024.09 261.36   (2)
COIN
087.20   (1)
COINCIDE
149.05   (1)
COINCIDENCE
289.13 330.22   (2)
COINCIDENT
263.13   (1)
COINS
007.01 087.08   (2)
COL
262.01   (1)
COLD
013.10 013.32 013.32 027.14 028.12   (32)
035.09 062.07 075.18 075.25 098.17
110.07 145.18 145.18 183.07 240.15
240.21 245.36 254.10 267.30 282.23
285.24 293.34 296.06 299.05 299.21
300.27 301.13 302.01 311.26 312.10
321.31 331.03
COLDER
027.10 183.10 183.17 254.11   (4)
COLDEST
183.17 183.20 292.12   (3)
COLIC
026.16   (1)
COLLAPSED
160.34   (1)
COLLECT
068.14 197.32 249.13 261.19   (4)
COLLECTED
067.36 082.10 189.25 238.17 319.12   (5)

COLLECTION
259.14   (1)
COLLECTIONS
198.10   (1)
COLLECTIVELY
110.08   (1)
COLLEGE
050.05 050.26 052.02 106.06 106.19   (7)
135.30 207.17
COLLEGES
052.08 052.11 106.28   (3)
COLLINS
043.01 043.03   (2)
COLLOQUIES
102.08   (1)
COLMAN
158.05 162.34   (2)
COLONIES
039.26   (1)
COLONY
029.30 143.02 167.18 271.20   (4)
COLOR
026.26 047.10 048.15 083.10 120.12   (24)
176.12 176.17 176.23 176.24 176.34
189.30 197.22 197.31 199.18 233.07
240.04 247.24 258.07 262.10 280.33
297.08 305.17 311.03 325.28
COLORADO
320.11   (1)
COLORED
041.11 145.14 179.26 184.16 184.19   (8)
202.13 257.21 292.29
COLORING
240.09   (1)
COLORLESS
177.19 177.22   (2)
COLORS
024.10 048.07 176.06 176.20 189.18   (9)
264.04 284.29 305.01 305.25
COLUMBIA
210.35   (1)
COLUMBUS
321.16   (1)
COLUMNS
107.28 141.06 206.21   (3)
COLYMBUS
233.24   (1)
COM
153.28   (1)
COMB
300.19 300.20   (2)
COMBAT
229.08 229.33 231.18   (3)
COMBATANTS
228.33 229.36 230.11   (3)
COMBED
300.16 302.13 302.29   (3)
COMBINE
013.06   (1)
COMBINED
268.14   (1)
COMBUSTION
013.09 013.11   (2)
COME
006.32 021.22 025.11 038.01 038.19   (89)
040.10 041.18 041.22 041.29 052.36
055.10 061.28 068.36 078.08 081.29
097.20 098.03 099.23 104.05 105.10
105.16 105.22 106.21 109.33 110.12
115.27 115.30 116.05 117.33 120.29
121.19 129.05 129.28 136.17 136.35
138.25 140.17 140.26 144.13 146.32
154.15 161.34 164.11 170.28 170.36
174.19 188.24 189.10 191.06 193.24
199.34 208.17 208.24 208.28 216.31
220.38 222.19 224.03 224.30 225.28
229.32 233.30 233.34 234.34 235.10
236.11 236.23 248.36 251.14 258.22

```
COME                  (CONTINUED)        COMMONLY              (CONTINUED)
261.30  268.35  276.23  276.24  277.09   085.33  094.08  101.12  102.03  102.09
277.34  280.31  283.11  294.23  298.14   130.08  136.10  141.23  141.31  152.01
302.12  303.08  303.18  306.11  319.05   161.19  164.11  168.08  173.29  174.08
326.21  329.32  332.31  333.25           180.19  182.07  184.07  202.33  205.08
COMES                      ( 24)         213.14  218.04  227.29  234.14  236.01
008.14  047.12  058.16  077.17  106.24   245.05  252.19  253.08  267.34  269.08
116.03  116.04  121.30  125.05  126.18   290.30  297.15  299.04  299.14  305.01
126.25  135.34  140.06  164.30  223.28   COMMONNESS                 ( 1)
258.29  268.33  270.18  276.17  282.18   197.21
293.35  303.13  305.02  309.17           COMMUNE                    ( 2)
COMET                      ( 1)          108.18  174.09
116.09                                   COMMUNICABLE               ( 1)
COMFORT                    ( 5)          042.08
021.33  028.06  033.22  127.34  253.23   COMMUNICATE                ( 1)
COMFORTABLE                ( 4)          052.23
029.25  037.35  060.36  242.18           COMMUNICATED               ( 1)
COMFORTABLY                ( 3)          216.33
014.12  014.14  072.32                   COMMUNICATING              ( 1)
COMFORTS                   ( 7)          175.06
014.18  014.20  027.20  033.26  033.31   COMMUNICATION              ( 2)
034.19  133.33                           078.20  154.21
COMING                     ( 17)         COMMUNICATIONS             ( 2)
074.17  119.07  134.03  147.26  170.02   094.04  136.23
174.26  194.06  205.22  223.12  238.34   COMMUNITIES                ( 2)
253.26  265.22  268.12  302.10  304.10   172.21  213.31
308.26  313.34                           COMMUNITY                  ( 2)
COMINGS                    ( 2)          046.17  051.12
268.04  283.16                           COMPACT                    ( 3)
COMMAND                    ( 1)          066.23  190.01  255.07
219.27                                   COMPACTLY                  ( 1)
COMMANDER                  ( 1)          024.24
313.10                                   COMPANION                  ( 10)
COMMANDING                 ( 1)          135.23  141.10  143.02  173.25  174.21
117.24                                   223.03  254.21  313.19  317.02  328.04
COMMEMORATE                ( 1)          COMPANIONABLE              ( 1)
057.18                                   135.23
COMMENCE                   ( 2)          COMPANIONS                 ( 3)
041.18  330.11                           072.11  078.10  326.08
COMMENCED                  ( 5)          COMPANY                    ( 15)
015.27  039.26  179.24  230.02  241.23   022.32  025.30  072.03  097.20  097.20
COMMENCES                  ( 3)          135.21  137.01  137.06  137.12  141.33
120.25  214.13  239.33                   144.05  167.26  168.35  218.33  259.28
COMMENT                    ( 2)          COMPARABLE                 ( 1)
102.06  157.24                           162.20
COMMENTATOR                ( 1)          COMPARATIVE                ( 1)
217.34                                   061.13
COMMERCE                   ( 4)          COMPARATIVELY              ( 11)
014.32  092.14  118.24  119.14           006.09  026.29  054.12  074.33  108.28
COMMERCIAL                 ( 1)          166.30  194.14  194.23  247.02  268.32
120.16                                   299.32
COMMIT                     ( 2)          COMPARE                    ( 3)
011.14  056.23                           095.32  131.22  309.25
COMMITTED                  ( 3)          COMPARED                   ( 11)
078.03  084.06  153.10                   007.28  007.34  030.29  030.35  111.16
COMMITTEE                  ( 1)          158.02  288.25  289.36  290.01  309.06
330.02                                   325.34
COMMODIOUS                 ( 1)          COMPARISON                 ( 6)
031.05                                   004.31  126.11  177.15  230.16  268.09
COMMODITIES                ( 1)          298.04
020.22                                   COMPARISONS                ( 1)
COMMODITY                  ( 1)          137.03
167.29                                   COMPASS                    ( 4)
COMMODORE                  ( 1)          118.18  171.15  272.23  285.11
272.16                                   COMPASSION                 ( 3)
COMMON                     ( 27)         066.23  278.23  318.28
008.19  018.09  020.02  046.29  051.18   COMPEL                     ( 2)
068.19  071.28  071.29  073.23  100.15   131.11  205.27
103.03  108.29  124.35  163.27  169.29   COMPELLED                  ( 8)
172.35  184.18  199.14  211.20  219.23   011.15  203.24  212.07  217.19  236.35
225.22  233.03  254.37  261.07  304.32   256.26  318.14  329.10
323.33  325.09                           COMPELLER                  ( 1)
COMMONEST                  ( 1)          116.16
325.09                                   COMPENSATED                ( 1)
COMMONLY                   ( 50)         151.07
003.26  005.26  012.02  015.05  022.06   COMPENSATION               ( 2)
030.05  030.32  031.07  031.23  032.19   083.26  318.17
032.22  047.25  050.26  071.26  071.33
```

COMPLACENCY (1)
331.21
COMPLACENT (1)
245.31
COMPLAIN (3)
013.31 016.20 035.35
COMPLAINED (1)
162.33
COMPLAINING (1)
016.18
COMPLAINT (3)
259.10 312.33 325.19
COMPLEMENTAL (1)
080.01
COMPLETE (5)
083.05 129.20 207.01 214.19 245.33
COMPLETED (2)
204.02 319.18
COMPLETELY (14)
037.02 088.32 171.10 187.32 189.14
191.21 234.12 250.03 265.04 280.19
300.16 301.28 302.27 303.01
COMPLETENESS (1)
060.40
COMPLEX (2)
036.18 324.04
COMPLEXION (1)
048.19
COMPLICATED (2)
033.19 290.22
COMPLIMENT (1)
114.03
COMPLIMENTED (1)
240.17
COMPOSE (1)
049.02
COMPOSED (3)
178.23 195.13 239.02
COMPOSITION (2)
298.03 329.18
COMPOST (3)
005.25 043.09 162.19
COMPOUND (1)
052.14
COMPREHENDED (1)
291.02
COMPROMISE (1)
326.34
COMRADES (2)
162.02 262.14
CON (1)
224.36
CONCEAL (2)
288.19 332.11
CONCEALED (10)
008.12 083.17 252.07 254.21 257.15
260.31 276.21 278.18 291.14 303.33
CONCEALMENT (1)
281.29
CONCEALS (1)
116.35
CONCEITED (1)
245.26
CONCEIVE (2)
147.25 150.03
CONCEIVING (1)
097.12
CONCENTRATED (3)
064.06 098.30 242.34
CONCENTRIC (1)
333.18
CONCEPTIONS (2)
097.11 298.08
CONCERN (5)
135.06 164.22 166.32 175.27 321.07
CONCERNED (14)
017.33 031.31 058.28 064.23 135.18
143.27 144.08 149.13 162.10 164.23

CONCERNED (CONTINUED)
207.11 211.29 222.09 265.08
CONCERNING (4)
003.12 004.08 017.13 261.25
CONCERNS (2)
048.05 230.28
CONCLUDE (1)
098.15
CONCLUDED (7)
043.29 091.13 153.18 173.28 182.29
236.16 260.03
CONCLUDING (1)
224.06
CONCLUSION (2)
095.23 320.01
CONCLUSIONS (2)
263.19 285.23
CONCORD (43)
003.06 004.15 032.15 032.35 049.29
055.26 056.08 063.32 076.18 086.04
086.08 093.15 098.01 106.02 107.12
108.10 109.07 115.11 120.23 123.02
176.05 179.32 193.18 194.07 197.10
197.14 198.09 225.11 230.14 230.19
257.06 258.05 258.14 259.25 264.06
272.24 272.31 272.34 279.06 279.09
279.18 284.23 332.02
CONCORDIENSIS (1)
257.08
CONCUR (1)
292.07
CONCURRING (1)
290.33
CONDEMNED (1)
005.11
CONDENSED (2)
053.33 136.09
CONDIMENT (1)
215.25
CONDITION (18)
004.11 004.12 016.11 026.33 031.10
034.34 035.13 035.18 035.23 037.34
041.31 107.31 120.06 204.26 215.01
215.16 222.20 326.13
CONDITIONED (1)
139.07
CONDITIONS (1)
291.33
CONDUCES (1)
110.01
CONDUCT (3)
170.12 289.23 322.25
CONDUCTED (3)
023.36 117.36 331.10
CONDUCTOR (1)
053.32
CONE (1)
204.11
CONES (2)
113.21 247.09
CONFEDERACY (1)
092.01
CONFESS (7)
072.21 093.20 107.21 120.35 212.02
217.24 242.17
CONFESSED (1)
262.20
CONFESSES (1)
314.22
CONFESSIONS (1)
151.06
CONFIDENCE (2)
015.30 160.30
CONFIDENT (3)
110.09 119.14 236.17
CONFIDENTLY (1)
323.30

47

CONFINE   (2)
035.27 216.06
CONFINED   (10)
003.30 087.25 109.04 111.03 132.22
250.07 271.27 290.30 328.28 329.08
CONFINEMENT   (2)
202.25 244.20
CONFINES   (1)
117.25
CONFIRM   (1)
096.07
CONFIRMED   (2)
008.08 078.24
CONFLAGRATIONS   (1)
260.07
CONFLICT   (1)
182.25
CONFLICTING   (1)
290.32
CONFLUENT   (1)
308.06
CONFORM   (1)
322.16
CONFORMABLY   (1)
220.37
CONFORMING   (1)
069.27
CONFORMITY   (4)
015.07 216.23 289.03 323.24
CONFOUND   (1)
108.05
CONFOUNDED   (1)
013.15
CONFUCIUS   (2)
011.20 134.31
CONFUSED   (1)
329.20
CONFUSION   (1)
290.27
CONGEALED   (4)
187.11 199.23 307.32 308.05
CONGENIAL   (2)
129.09 255.02
CONGRATULATE   (1)
331.23
CONGRATULATION   (1)
216.28
CONGREGATE   (1)
133.22
CONGREGATION   (1)
315.11
CONGRESS   (1)
164.34
CONICAL   (1)
233.29
CONJECTURE   (1)
021.19
CONJECTURED   (1)
182.20
CONJECTURING   (1)
100.14
CONJURE   (2)
211.28 256.17
CONLUCARE   (1)
250.28
CONNECT   (1)
129.23
CONNECTED   (2)
197.25 303.05
CONNECTICUT   (3)
121.23 268.22 333.10
CONNECTING   (1)
158.12
CONNECTION   (1)
292.28
CONQUER   (1)
229.24

CONSANGUINITY   (1)
025.12
CONSCIENCE   (1)
022.07
CONSCIOUS   (9)
004.29 074.18 090.20 131.24 131.34
134.34 135.11 203.01 219.09
CONSCIOUSLY   (2)
073.07 118.29
CONSCIOUSNESS   (3)
147.10 148.20 168.01
CONSECRATE   (2)
026.14 100.10
CONSECRATED   (2)
250.27 272.25
CONSENTING   (1)
096.06
CONSEQUENCE   (6)
052.08 093.10 152.31 185.10 205.33
259.14
CONSEQUENCES   (2)
134.35 216.22
CONSEQUENT   (2)
012.26 270.10
CONSIDER   (14)
008.16 011.29 028.35 032.15 038.05
056.17 081.05 097.31 108.24 136.23
161.20 176.17 213.09 331.21
CONSIDERABLE   (5)
141.08 148.29 195.12 236.36 304.17
CONSIDERABLY   (6)
106.36 147.33 148.26 155.06 187.29
274.33
CONSIDERATE   (1)
142.13
CONSIDERED   (8)
035.29 043.03 055.21 064.34 250.12
322.35 325.19 326.22
CONSIDERING   (4)
003.14 045.32 055.22 059.05
CONSIDERS   (2)
022.18 106.17
CONSIST   (2)
035.24 243.16
CONSISTED   (1)
065.18
CONSISTENCY   (1)
195.25
CONSISTING   (1)
185.16
CONSOLATION   (2)
075.07 312.33
CONSOLATIONS   (1)
124.22
CONSOLE   (1)
008.10
CONSOLED   (1)
078.24
CONSPICUOUS   (5)
132.34 187.26 202.28 247.16 329.34
CONSPIRACIES   (1)
208.21
CONSPIRES   (1)
200.02
CONSTANT   (6)
061.12 077.08 157.12 188.09 202.32
216.13
CONSTANTLY   (5)
024.17 097.10 171.06 189.31 222.10
CONSTELLATION   (1)
088.04
CONSTELLATIONS   (1)
105.15
CONSTITUTION   (1)
073.07
CONSTITUTIONAL   (1)
120.35

48

CONSTITUTIONS (1)
 010.22
CONSTRAIN (1)
 171.29
CONSTRUCT (3)
 028.30 052.21 195.24
CONSTRUCTED (4)
 030.11 046.04 056.34 118.14
CONSTRUCTING (2)
 048.10 058.08
CONSTRUCTION (2)
 046.12 191.10
CONSULTATION (1)
 207.05
CONSULTED (1)
 283.20
CONSULTING (1)
 062.15
CONSUME (1)
 068.19
CONSUMED (2)
 055.18 238.27
CONSUMER (1)
 145.15
CONSUMES (1)
 132.17
CONSUMMATE (1)
 033.21
CONTACT (3)
 035.20 040.10 216.11
CONTAGION (1)
 077.16
CONTAIN (9)
 107.18 140.15 148.28 194.21 197.11
 199.29 238.29 296.24 297.09
CONTAINED (4)
 066.01 067.03 281.07 313.24
CONTAINING (3)
 243.34 247.34 296.21
CONTAINS (5)
 054.23 089.21 175.32 290.10 300.15
CONTEMPLATE (2)
 011.19 282.15
CONTEMPLATED (2)
 037.20 069.35
CONTEMPLATING (3)
 010.20 051.29 331.29
CONTEMPLATION (4)
 090.27 112.02 162.06 297.11
CONTEMPORARIES (6)
 015.15 050.25 162.04 211.14 214.27
 329.21
CONTEMPORARY (3)
 038.35 101.27 159.35
CONTENDING (1)
 228.29
CONTENT (3)
 036.06 118.27 215.11
CONTENTED (1)
 138.18
CONTENTEDLY (1)
 328.15
CONTENTMENT (4)
 142.36 146.11 146.36 147.13
CONTENTS (5)
 063.09 066.01 245.34 267.02 329.25
CONTESTED (1)
 231.32
CONTIGUOUS (1)
 196.33
CONTINALLY (1)
 247.01
CONTINENT (3)
 087.15 219.35 321.05
CONTINENTS (3)
 144.11 321.16 321.28
CONTINUAL (1)
 162.20

CONTINUALLY (6)
 134.11 136.34 188.27 188.35 306.35
 325.01
CONTINUANCE (1)
 079.10
CONTINUE (3)
 072.02 079.16 131.18
CONTINUED (5)
 157.25 162.15 197.33 217.19 293.16
CONTINUES (1)
 096.21
CONTRACT (1)
 047.06
CONTRACTED (2)
 035.08 087.24
CONTRACTING (1)
 007.07
CONTRACTOR (1)
 050.30
CONTRAST (2)
 035.17 311.34
CONTRIBUTE (1)
 248.20
CONTRIBUTED (1)
 293.18
CONTRIBUTIONS (1)
 018.08
CONTRIVING (1)
 222.08
CONTROL (1)
 219.31
CONVENIENCE (8)
 027.19 037.04 084.20 104.12 141.25
 149.04 173.33 245.35
CONVENIENCES (1)
 050.16
CONVENIENT (5)
 036.02 045.20 062.07 168.16 244.04
CONVENTICLE (1)
 086.19
CONVERSANT (1)
 292.03
CONVERSATION (5)
 107.08 141.28 142.04 151.07 329.26
CONVERSATIONS (1)
 332.34
CONVERSE (4)
 106.23 243.32 255.01 270.02
CONVERSED (1)
 123.14
CONVERSING (1)
 165.15
CONVERTED (2)
 180.33 333.21
CONVEY (1)
 137.03
CONVEYANCE (2)
 118.09 245.19
CONVEYING (2)
 114.35 292.29
CONVICTED (1)
 104.26
CONVINCE (3)
 071.28 261.06 288.15
CONVINCED (4)
 070.33 172.19 324.22 324.29
CONVINCES (1)
 308.30
CONVIVIALITY (1)
 268.15
CONVULSION (1)
 287.33
CONVULSIVE (1)
 285.04
COOK (7)
 013.35 204.23 214.17 215.19 244.11
 249.22 251.24

COOKED (5)
012.25 014.01 014.15 156.02 214.22
COOKERY (3)
012.33 070.13 215.27
COOKING (5)
045.17 241.32 244.25 254.13 254.15
COOKS (1)
244.06
COOL (14)
084.33 087.16 117.22 129.07 155.24
183.26 207.06 222.01 242.07 242.13
264.08 283.08 294.01 294.06
COOLED (3)
187.11 260.01 301.07
COOLEST (1)
138.33
COOLLY (1)
234.32
COOPERATE (3)
072.01 072.04 072.11
COOPERATION (2)
071.32 071.34
COPE (1)
159.17
COPIED (1)
099.26
COPIOUS (1)
111.08
COPPER (2)
031.05 048.16
COPSE (2)
156.34 257.32
COPY (1)
310.04
COQUITOQUE (1)
063.19
CORAL (2)
119.22 305.14
CORDED (2)
146.06 294.09
CORDIALS (1)
006.22
CORDS (3)
054.31 156.14 251.09
CORE (4)
046.26 046.32 252.12 283.33
CORMORANTS (1)
104.33
CORN (26)
053.02 054.23 055.05 055.09 055.09
059.04 061.25 063.29 063.33 064.03
065.08 068.29 111.33 156.10 156.17
157.27 157.28 158.25 163.41 164.13
239.25 239.25 264.13 273.23 274.15
274.30
CORNER (7)
088.04 091.05 099.11 179.11 257.20
316.20 328.28
CORNERS (2)
018.21 141.30
CORNFIELD (2)
022.23 061.21
CORNFIELDS (1)
288.12
CORNICE (3)
034.30 046.31 047.13
CORNICES (1)
048.03
CORONET (1)
179.33
CORPORATION (1)
050.07
CORPORATIONS (1)
027.02
CORRECT (2)
287.27 313.31
CORRECTED (1)
020.31

CORRECTION (1)
119.33
CORRESPONDENT (1)
320.23
CORRESPONDING (6)
166.15 180.21 195.10 283.07 291.17
291.20
CORROSION (1)
102.33
CORRUGATIONS (1)
105.24
CORRUPT (1)
005.28
CORRUPTED (1)
078.20
CORTEX (1)
024.18
COSMICAL (1)
089.05
COSMOGONAL (2)
175.17 298.02
COSMOGRAPHY (1)
320.35
COSMOPOLITE (1)
320.07
COSMOS (1)
313.34
COST (19)
014.09 024.35 030.31 031.14 032.22
048.32 048.36 049.01 049.30 050.17
061.01 061.15 064.01 065.17 205.07
205.14 206.05 214.14 214.24
COSTLY (2)
031.13 100.21
COSTS (6)
031.17 055.06 058.15 059.16 067.11
077.08
COSTUME (4)
026.09 026.11 026.14 329.26
COTTAGE (7)
043.07 048.21 073.33 080.07 103.01
265.04 279.07
COTTAGES (1)
047.24
COTTON (4)
029.01 116.04 120.07 309.31
COUCH (1)
078.09
COUGH (1)
052.33
COULD (168)
004.34 008.06 010.24 022.10 022.31
023.28 029.17 035.15 036.01 036.04
036.30 051.14 054.14 056.01 056.09
056.36 058.07 064.02 064.07 064.11
064.22 065.33 066.08 069.11 069.26
069.29 070.11 072.11 075.08 075.29
078.14 081.27 082.01 083.31 083.33
087.05 087.10 089.02 090.13 090.34
094.03 097.14 101.34 107.32 111.22
118.29 125.08 127.06 129.33 132.14
133.32 141.11 141.12 142.16 143.28
143.30 144.03 144.22 145.29 145.33
145.35 146.08 147.25 147.34 148.05
148.06 148.06 148.33 148.35 149.03
149.11 149.21 150.01 153.01 153.13
156.34 161.01 168.22 168.26 169.08
170.03 170.27 172.09 178.18 185.18
185.24 186.26 189.21 191.24 195.02
195.32 196.09 196.22 198.02 198.21
199.07 202.07 203.30 205.22 206.08
207.10 210.13 217.04 219.26 222.21
225.17 225.32 228.04 228.17 229.09
231.06 234.29 235.02 236.01 236.19
237.01 241.17 242.31 247.20 251.25
251.35 253.18 254.25 260.10 260.27
261.01 261.06 261.21 262.08 262.19
262.24 265.11 266.06 266.08 266.25

COULD			(CONTINUED)	
271.08	271.22	271.25	274.10	274.14
276.06	277.08	277.23	279.16	280.33
287.02	287.16	287.31	288.26	288.34
289.06	290.06	295.32	301.30	302.30
312.20	312.34	313.20	313.24	319.12
320.28	323.12	323.26	324.13	324.14
326.36	327.26	331.07		

COULDN (1)
115.06

COUNCIL (1)
213.22

COUNT (4)
091.22 091.26 098.23 322.09

COUNTENANCE (1)
144.26

COUNTERBALANCED (2)
034.25 300.29

COUNTING (4)
020.07 048.34 059.04 333.12

COUNTRIES (5)
027.11 127.23 213.06 221.20 332.21

COUNTRY (43)
006.09	008.10	014.04	020.09	023.03
026.02	031.01	034.33	035.26	039.32
040.04	046.24	047.23	053.05	053.20
057.15	064.29	065.30	066.08	081.06
081.22	109.11	114.36	115.26	115.30
116.01	117.12	117.13	118.01	145.09
148.36	160.02	173.23	192.26	197.13
205.24	208.39	208.39	225.23	250.34
281.17	281.31	291.13		

COUNTRYMAN (1)
115.33

COUNTRYMEN (1)
115.31

COUNTY (1)
084.06

COUPLE (5)
145.16 184.05 208.34 229.10 242.26

COURAGE (6)
066.33 077.14 118.27 118.35 118.36
322.34

COURAGEOUS (1)
125.18

COURSE (33)
013.14	014.16	039.31	039.35	041.01
051.19	071.21	105.04	111.13	140.34
141.02	142.13	156.15	166.12	168.20
171.05	171.09	178.15	206.16	232.12
234.33	235.23	241.24	249.27	271.17
273.22	274.36	279.28	284.32	289.34
290.20	290.27	299.13		

COURSING (3)
228.20 273.20 278.18

COURT (4)
019.28 096.33 270.20 329.31

COURTIER (1)
015.06

COUSIN (2)
146.36 201.29

COUSINS (1)
313.16

COVE (6)
126.26 180.31 234.09 289.36 290.03
291.21

COVER (11)
021.28 039.20 063.24 071.24 119.25
158.24 158.24 187.33 201.14 225.07
294.31

COVERED (32)
029.31	029.35	041.06	042.30	083.13
086.10	092.28	105.26	119.09	176.15
179.22	188.15	201.08	228.33	229.01
248.29	249.08	258.17	261.01	263.09
265.04	271.06	276.10	276.19	277.16
282.33	293.29	296.11	296.25	302.05
303.29	319.11			

COVERING (2)
027.28 263.12

COVERS (3)
097.35 201.11 282.29

COVERTED (1)
305.34

COVES (8)
167.05 185.04 185.31 191.22 246.15
289.22 289.28 291.10

COVETED (2)
051.02 103.08

COW (13)
056.04 094.15 123.22 123.29 123.32
126.06 127.30 168.27 173.14 270.20
281.35 324.25 324.26

COWARDS (1)
322.23

COWBIRDS (1)
046.09

COWERS (1)
007.30

COWHIDE (2)
024.32 145.14

COWS (2)
057.12 270.23

COWYARDS (1)
121.31

CR (1)
279.25

CRACK (8)
188.26 248.20 267.24 273.03 275.19
295.13 303.09 311.22

CRACKED (2)
168.11 311.18

CRACKING (2)
273.01 301.11

CRACKLING (1)
259.35

CRACKS (1)
301.27

CRADLE (1)
295.34

CRAFT (1)
320.21

CRAG (1)
317.09

CRANBERRIES (1)
238.07

CRANBERRY (2)
116.02 196.15

CRANES (2)
091.18 161.32

CRASH (1)
287.32

CRAVE (1)
098.16

CRAWL (1)
152.33

CRAWLING (1)
332.10

CRAWLS (1)
317.33

CRAZY (1)
058.23

CREAKING (2)
128.13 174.36

CREAM (1)
083.03

CREASED (1)
246.29

CREATE (2)
034.16 242.19

CREATED (5)
005.31 034.15 079.06 300.35 315.34

CREATING (1)
314.35

CREATION (8)
012.18 085.12 088.14 214.06 282.18

CREATION   (CONTINUED)
  306.09   313.34   329.03
CREATIONS   (1)
  327.15
CREATOR   (1)
  207.24
CREATURE   (6)
  149.11   212.31   219.20   226.25   246.26
  281.24
CREATURES   (8)
  012.13   098.32   126.01   129.19   220.12
  227.21   271.15   282.06
CREDIT   (3)
  279.27   279.30   279.31
CREDITORS   (1)
  006.34
CREEPING   (5)
  005.16   140.26   201.10   265.36   324.16
CREPT   (2)
  028.09   194.30
CREST   (1)
  162.01
CREVICE   (2)
  225.17   317.09
CREVICES   (2)
  240.20   296.11
CREW   (2)
  169.23   279.36
CRIED   (2)
  120.08   259.23
CRIES   (2)
  158.23   212.33
CRIMPLED   (1)
  239.10
CRIMSON   (1)
  114.19
CRIPPLED   (1)
  231.17
CRISIS   (4)
  024.04   072.13   245.12   312.04
CRISP   (1)
  283.10
CRITICAL   (1)
  090.28
CRITICALLY   (2)
  094.05   186.34
CRITICISM   (1)
  135.12
CROAKING   (1)
  262.25
CROESUS   (1)
  329.05
CROMWELL   (1)
  076.25
CRONCHED   (1)
  266.07
CRONCHING   (1)
  267.22
CROOKED   (2)
  056.10   195.35
CROP   (13)
  039.05   055.32   083.30   156.20   158.06
  158.07   158.11   159.08   163.09   163.39
  164.21   182.08   294.24
CROPPING   (1)
  320.11
CROPS   (7)
  056.12   095.05   164.06   164.22   165.25
  196.25   207.32
CROSS   (1)
  122.27
CROSSED   (4)
  267.17   271.05   271.22   279.13
CROSSING   (2)
  037.23   145.21
CROTCHETS   (1)
  269.15

CROW   (4)
  127.16   128.08   163.07   239.24
CROWD   (4)
  053.31   102.14   117.30   316.03
CROWDED   (3)
  037.13   087.25   135.30
CROWDING   (1)
  162.02
CROWDS   (1)
  101.19
CROWING   (1)
  127.01
CROWN   (1)
  036.01
CRUDITY   (1)
  078.01
CRUISE   (1)
  278.01
CRUMBLED   (1)
  304.16
CRUMBLING   (1)
  156.29
CRUMBS   (3)
  225.29   275.25   275.31
CRUSADERS   (1)
  161.06
CRUSHED   (2)
  005.01   005.16
CRUSHES   (1)
  201.18
CRUSHING   (1)
  259.27
CRUST   (9)
  087.21   218.13   265.14   273.07   273.24
  273.32   281.11   293.08   298.13
CRUSTY   (1)
  082.35
CRY   (7)
  093.01   097.21   229.24   276.32   278.02
  278.12   278.30
CRYING   (1)
  127.34
CRYSTAL   (2)
  202.14   307.02
CRYSTALLINE   (1)
  177.28
CRYSTALLIZATION   (1)
  085.22
CRYSTALS   (2)
  199.21   284.31
CUBIC   (1)
  005.22
CUCKOOS   (1)
  046.09
CUFFS   (1)
  245.29
CULINARY   (1)
  207.03
CULMINATES   (1)
  097.05
CULTIVATE   (4)
  005.22   054.29   055.35   328.22
CULTIVATED   (17)
  015.36   038.31   050.24   064.32   081.15
  083.34   109.36   157.21   158.13   158.15
  158.17   161.13   166.05   166.09   166.13
  186.04   251.10
CULTIVATING   (1)
  161.27
CULTIVATION   (2)
  196.36   239.12
CULTIVATOR   (4)
  084.07   163.08   166.19   294.22
CULTIVATORS   (1)
  159.04
CULTURE   (9)
  037.30   040.05   103.12   103.15   106.02
  108.25   110.02   205.35   205.36

52

CUMBROUS				(1)
253.32				
CUMMINGS				(1)
257.35				
CUNNING				(1)
235.33				
CUNNINGLY				(2)
234.29	236.31			
CUP				(4)
065.22	126.23	139.03	217.11	
CUPBEARER				(1)
139.04				
CUPBOARD				(2)
153.15	244.04			
CUPREOUS				(1)
317.15				
CUPS				(1)
287.21				
CUR				(2)
121.03	232.16			
CURACY				(1)
019.28				
CURE				(4)
092.11	121.06	325.21	325.22	
CURED				(1)
120.18				
CURES				(1)
077.34				
CURIOSITY				(2)
105.23	178.10			
CURIOUS				(11)
003.18	075.17	100.20	151.02	155.14
161.21	167.21	172.11	195.13	247.32
320.21				
CURLED				(1)
262.16				
CURLS				(1)
308.32				
CURRENT				(3)
098.21	207.09	292.33		
CURRENTS				(3)
291.28	292.07	305.08		
CURRY				(1)
007.05				
CURSE				(2)
070.08	273.18			
CURSED				(1)
196.12				
CURSES				(1)
070.06				
CURSING				(1)
078.22				
CURTAIN				(1)
067.18				
CURTAINS				(1)
067.12				
CURVE				(1)
116.12				
CURVES				(1)
311.23				
CUSHION				(1)
037.13				
CUSHIONS				(1)
008.04				
CUSTOM				(3)
007.05	026.30	068.10		
CUSTOMER				(1)
120.26				
CUSTOMERS				(3)
024.29	121.15	325.27		
CUSTOMS				(5)
068.04	101.03	142.21	216.19	322.17
CUT				(38)
010.03	016.01	027.30	035.33	039.06
040.06	040.35	041.23	042.28	042.32
052.01	053.21	075.22	086.33	091.04
146.02	170.27	180.01	182.35	190.33
192.12	192.27	193.10	250.24	250.25

CUT			(CONTINUED)	
253.01	254.08	256.09	261.03	265.12
265.14	281.28	282.34	291.32	293.13
295.20	304.30	305.21		
CUTICLE				(1)
024.08				
CUTS				(3)
025.22	284.19	294.07		
CUTTERS				(3)
292.17	294.12	299.03		
CUTTING				(8)
042.06	083.20	178.05	178.17	191.17
213.10	293.21	295.07		
CUTTINGSVILLE				(2)
121.10	121.18			
CYCLOPAEDIA				(1)
148.27				
CYLINDRICAL				(1)
305.28				
CYLINDRICALLY				(1)
113.35				
CYNOSURE				(2)
204.16	285.04			
CYPRESS				(3)
079.07	079.12	079.19		
CZAR				(1)
321.19				

```
D
080.18  080.29  098.05  206.30      (  4)
DABBLING                            (  1)
 156.28
DACE                                (  1)
 184.10
DAILY                               ( 22)
 004.30  035.04  036.27  096.07  102.08
 105.33  107.29  157.06  161.11  161.34
 166.12  181.26  193.07  208.28  216.34
 261.08  263.33  275.30  279.32  291.09
 324.21  329.25
DAINTY                              (  1)
 274.22
DAISIES                             (  1)
 119.11
DALE                                (  1)
 123.26
DAM                                 (  2)
 096.30  233.27
DAMAGE                              (  1)
 082.25
DAME                                (  2)
 137.31  138.03
DAMODARA                            (  1)
 087.32
DAMS                                (  1)
 287.17
DAMUS                               (  1)
 005.35
DANCE                               (  2)
 068.30  093.11
DANCING                             (  1)
 274.06
DANDELION                           (  1)
 137.13
DANGER                              (  8)
 077.28  097.25  100.08  111.06  153.24
 153.24  153.32  169.07
DANGEROUS                           (  1)
 288.37
DANGERS                             (  1)
 169.01
DANGLED                             (  1)
 145.19
DANK                                (  1)
 043.16
DANTES                              (  1)
 104.04
DAPES                               (  1)
 172.27
DARE                                (  1)
 270.07
DARK                                ( 36)
 024.23  041.11  043.15  093.36  124.27
 125.13  129.17  130.36  145.11  150.27
 169.18  170.02  170.11  170.16  174.20
 175.16  176.12  176.27  177.13  177.25
 184.21  190.27  192.14  210.05  231.04
 232.07  246.17  247.02  247.23  248.28
 256.16  260.20  276.30  293.25  300.32
 312.03
DARKENED                            (  1)
 086.29
DARKENING                           (  2)
 089.24  252.36
DARKER                              (  5)
 110.18  169.28  177.07  187.13  312.29
DARKEST                             (  2)
 117.27  170.01
DARKNESS                            ( 12)
 073.35  089.19  124.32  130.31  130.33
 133.36  170.26  174.28  260.36  268.20
 328.36  333.31
DART                                (  3)
 117.27  185.04  187.10
DARTING                             (  1)
 203.15

DARWIN                              (  1)
 012.33
DASH                                (  3)
 129.18  234.04  322.19
DASHED                              (  2)
 113.02  229.19
DASHES                              (  1)
 189.03
DASHING                             (  1)
 217.11
DATE                                (  5)
 059.06  079.18  089.32  231.28  241.27
DATED                               (  1)
 107.36
DATES                               (  1)
 060.01
DATING                              (  1)
 254.10
DAUBED                              (  2)
 048.07  048.09
DAUGHTER                            (  3)
 132.19  138.36  139.05
DAUNTED                             (  1)
 268.02
DAVENANT                            (  1)
 259.08
DAVIS                               (  1)
 230.22
DAWN                                ( 10)
 017.19  088.37  090.03  090.17  124.16
 207.25  252.31  273.20  333.30  333.33
DAWNING                             (  2)
 266.30  282.06
DAWNS                               (  2)
 125.36  333.32
DAY                                 (203)
 006.15  006.16  007.04  007.13  007.25
 007.31  008.04  008.26  009.21  011.12
 014.04  017.01  018.23  020.16  021.01
 021.35  022.24  026.34  027.29  030.11
 031.21  041.22  042.03  044.16  045.09
 053.05  053.10  053.11  053.18  055.23
 058.33  060.27  066.30  067.31  070.25
 070.28  074.07  075.25  076.18  084.28
 085.03  086.21  088.33  089.08  089.11
 089.12  089.12  089.21  089.26  089.36
 090.05  090.25  091.35  093.09  094.24
 095.22  097.16  097.22  098.26  101.03
 112.04  112.15  112.19  112.23  117.13
 117.21  117.27  117.33  118.26  125.23
 125.28  125.31  125.36  127.20  131.15
 133.01  135.32  136.02  136.04  136.13
 138.21  138.29  138.33  143.06  143.13
 143.18  144.17  144.37  145.32  145.36
 146.27  147.02  148.30  149.21  149.29
 149.35  150.14  151.13  155.20  156.29
 158.36  159.13  160.11  161.20  162.14
 164.16  166.34  167.08  170.19  170.35
 171.34  172.05  173.24  174.33  176.13
 180.15  183.14  183.19  183.27  183.29
 188.19  189.11  192.02  193.39  194.30
 197.15  197.27  204.26  205.23  207.22
 207.22  208.30  210.22  213.12  214.15
 215.30  216.24  219.16  220.07  220.07
 221.35  223.19  223.30  223.32  224.01
 224.35  225.35  228.06  228.26  229.12
 231.23  234.13  239.05  245.28  247.17
 249.33  252.35  253.09  253.19  253.35
 254.25  258.28  260.26  261.22  263.10
 266.30  268.33  273.28  275.34  275.34
 275.34  276.22  277.26  279.12  282.18
 292.15  295.08  295.23  295.32  297.07
 299.27  301.03  301.08  301.14  301.27
 302.31  303.23  303.30  305.03  306.05
 312.19  314.28  314.38  315.14  315.20
 317.17  322.27  326.21  329.19  330.04
 331.17  333.32  333.33
```

```
DAYBOOKS                            (  1)    DECIDED                             (  2)
 011.36                                        009.35  320.16
DAYLIGHT                            (  3)    DECIPHER                            (  1)
 027.36  266.06  282.09                        308.18
DAYS                                ( 66)    DECK                                (  1)
 017.29  028.25  041.13  041.19  042.06        323.26
 042.24  045.24  058.30  062.17  068.20    DECLARED                            (  3)
 068.30  068.31  070.27  084.27  092.20        202.20  219.29  322.32
 100.21  112.11  112.12  129.24  132.18    DECLARES                            (  1)
 133.07  141.35  144.20  155.25  160.04        268.24
 161.09  161.32  162.04  172.05  173.10    DECLINE                             (  1)
 187.30  187.34  189.13  190.28  191.34        073.14
 192.03  194.28  206.10  207.24  231.19    DECLINED                            (  2)
 232.27  234.17  236.31  239.18  246.15        067.22  279.11
 247.22  249.05  249.17  251.30  254.18    DEDUCTING                           (  1)
 261.30  271.34  275.34  293.17  297.18        055.14
 297.25  299.15  299.21  302.15  302.35    DEED                                (  6)
 303.08  303.12  309.24  311.10  318.34        023.26  081.14  081.15  082.12  196.10
 328.28                                         330.25
DAZZLED                             (  1)    DEEDS                               (  8)
 201.21                                         007.33  008.30  008.31  059.32  116.26
DAZZLING                            (  2)       124.32  245.29  331.30
 202.13  284.24                             DEEM                                (  1)
DE                                  (  2)       062.25
 084.07  158.18                             DEEMED                              (  1)
DEACON                              (  1)       323.01
 067.26                                     DEEP                                ( 57)
DEAD                                ( 29)       026.31  029.02  039.14  043.06  043.21
 044.05  054.35  066.13  066.14  066.20        044.26  091.02  098.09  117.08  126.22
 091.32  100.12  114.10  134.04  137.30        132.36  175.30  178.09  180.25  181.06
 138.24  153.34  161.36  199.03  206.17        182.14  183.32  184.18  185.14  185.29
 229.03  249.13  249.15  266.04  278.26        191.07  192.27  197.29  198.04  198.23
 278.33  280.20  291.34  309.01  311.35        235.14  242.09  246.30  248.05  252.19
 317.21  318.13  326.01  333.19                263.09  264.08  265.24  265.34  267.17
DEADLY                              (  2)       271.26  280.15  282.10  284.35  287.12
 095.27  229.08                                287.18  287.22  287.29  288.03  288.37
DEAF                                (  3)       289.08  293.14  293.17  294.27  295.34
 052.25  174.05  310.24                        299.31  300.06  300.07  301.06  304.30
DEAL                                ( 11)       323.23  332.09
 004.15  011.03  018.19  043.10  051.10    DEEPENED                            (  2)
 066.31  137.01  137.12  165.06  206.23        156.35  193.16
 329.10                                     DEEPENS                             (  1)
DEALING                             (  1)       176.26
 099.09                                     DEEPER                              (  9)
DEALINGS                            (  1)       029.03  098.22  235.20  283.29  287.23
 148.15                                         288.23  289.30  290.01  290.19
DEAR                                (  3)    DEEPEST                             ( 14)
 090.36  105.11  254.30                        179.05  193.30  235.17  256.11  264.34
DEARLY                              (  3)       265.17  265.29  267.36  287.18  288.30
 019.35  040.17  081.15                        289.23  290.07  290.16  290.17
DEARTH                              (  1)    DEER                                (  2)
 044.18                                         279.31  279.33
DEATH                               ( 10)    DEFACED                             (  1)
 013.12  029.20  029.22  034.10  074.13        269.05
 098.15  122.11  153.23  262.20  317.24    DEFEATED                            (  1)
DEBATE                              (  1)       322.22
 208.12                                     DEFECT                              (  1)
DEBAUCHED                           (  1)       013.13
 314.37                                     DEFENCE                             (  4)
DEBT                                (  2)       073.19  084.30  153.29  273.15
 006.38  052.10                             DEFEND                              (  2)
DECAY                               (  3)       149.11  186.32
 063.04  142.13  179.06                     DEFENDED                            (  1)
DECAYED                             (  2)       329.12
 100.33  195.01                             DEFIANT                             (  1)
DECAYING                            (  3)       117.15
 138.22  227.16  318.05                     DEFICIENCY                          (  2)
DECEIVED                            (  1)       127.31  143.33
 096.06                                     DEFICIENT                           (  1)
DECEMBER                            (  4)       151.20
 190.16  249.03  249.06  249.08            DEFILED                             (  1)
DECENT                              (  2)       036.21
 108.29  309.34                             DEFILETH                            (  1)
DECENTLY                            (  1)       218.15
 034.29                                     DEFILING                            (  1)
DECIDE                              (  1)       188.25
 081.33                                     DEFINED                             (  1)
                                               195.01
```

DEFINES 069.02				(1)
DEFINGITO 063.19				(1)
DEFINITE 325.05				(1)
DEFINITION 149.16				(1)
DEFORMED 165.36				(1)
DEFRAUDING 051.05				(1)
DEFRAYING 031.31				(1)
DEFYING 310.19				(1)
DEGENERACY 264.17				(1)

DEGENERATE (4)
015.09 040.14 100.13 244.35

DEGRADED (8)
034.24 034.35 034.36 035.01 035.20
058.07 165.36 221.18

DEGRADETH 080.13 (1)

DEGREE (10)
025.12 027.14 057.11 147.09 147.10
152.14 183.16 248.18 304.36 322.30

DEGREES (6)
086.15 183.15 183.16 217.08 241.33
299.30

DEITY 112.13 (1)

DEJECTION 084.23 (1)

DEL (2)
012.34 320.17

DELAY (4)
022.02 119.07 207.05 274.07

DELAYED 224.08 (1)

DELECTABLE 088.02 (1)

DELIBERATELY (9)
008.19 045.31 073.08 090.32 097.16
101.06 236.14 241.23 265.23

DELIBERATING 145.28 (1)

DELIBERATION (2)
099.03 169.02

DELICACY 310.09 (1)

DELICATE (9)
006.25 019.18 070.13 113.35 161.24
168.12 266.26 293.06 307.01

DELICIOUS 129.03 (1)

DELIGHT (4)
129.04 210.07 304.28 329.32

DELIGHTS (2)
124.23 138.03

DELIQUIUM 105.31 (1)

DELIRIUM 262.10 (1)

DELIVER 264.24 (1)

DELLS (2)
158.09 310.33

DELPHI 100.35 (1)

DELUDED 095.32 (1)

DELUGE 132.30 (1)

DELUSION 097.34 (1)

DELUSIONS 095.29 (1)

DELVED 332.04 (1)

DEMAND (3)
021.05 076.34 324.09

DEMANDED (2)
050.20 322.21

DEMANDS (2)
061.27 073.09

DEMIGOD 116.16 (1)

DEMIGODS (2)
147.25 220.10

DEMOCRATIC 023.04 (1)

DEMON (2)
010.33 258.24

DEMONIAC (2)
236.08 278.30

DEMONIACALLY 273.08 (1)

DEMURRED 206.32 (1)

DENIED 254.29 (1)

DENIZENS 232.18 (1)

DENOMINATION 035.14 (1)

DENSE (2)
083.17 175.22

DENSELY 280.24 (1)

DENT (3)
045.01 263.01 263.08

DENTS 263.14 (1)

DENY (2)
027.08 221.08

DENYING 011.16 (1)

DEPARTED (5)
048.09 143.23 240.30 263.11 279.11

DEPARTING 252.33 (1)

DEPARTURE (3)
206.35 279.15 280.28

DEPEND (4)
017.34 063.30 142.19 330.27

DEPENDS (2)
176.08 324.22

DEPOSITED (5)
025.31 104.05 144.09 333.11 333.20

DEPOSITING 267.08 (1)

DEPOSITS 307.28 (1)

DEPOT (3)
053.32 118.03 133.20

DEPRECIATED 006.17 (1)

DEPSTICIUM 063.16 (1)

DEPTH (20)
175.29 177.34 183.24 186.14 282.27
282.30 285.35 287.05 287.08 287.15
288.24 288.33 289.14 289.18 291.11
291.13 291.17 291.20 299.11 305.11

DEPTHS (4)
190.11 190.24 191.14 201.26

DER 272.09 (1)

DERISION 236.17 (1)

DERIVATION 149.07 (1)

DERIVATIVE (1)
208.38
DERIVE (1)
243.01
DERIVED (3)
183.03 197.21 218.01
DERVISH (1)
135.31
DES (1)
231.19
DESCEND (3)
120.07 222.22 244.11
DESCENDANTS (1)
261.16
DESCENDED (1)
316.07
DESCENDING (3)
089.24 159.28 227.35
DESCENT (1)
331.25
DESCRIBE (1)
084.20
DESCRIBED (5)
015.19 230.31 244.31 294.22 310.10
DESCRIBES (3)
068.10 187.04 287.28
DESCRIBING (2)
017.13 149.13
DESCRIPTION (5)
096.32 175.30 198.09 290.24 295.25
DESERT (2)
074.11 135.31
DESERTED (3)
263.14 268.09 326.30
DESERTERS (1)
322.22
DESERTS (2)
074.20 131.24
DESERVE (1)
192.33
DESERVES (1)
258.27
DESIGN (4)
074.18 097.14 244.25 296.15
DESIGNED (1)
295.31
DESIGNS (4)
028.30 031.35 058.18 306.13
DESIRABLE (4)
024.22 046.22 056.26 240.18
DESIRE (7)
050.36 054.03 056.04 061.23 071.09
244.33 324.27
DESIRED (2)
016.29 205.31
DESIRES (1)
095.17
DESIROUS (1)
285.09
DESK (4)
036.26 065.18 172.03 192.05
DESPAIR (5)
008.12 025.25 048.13 077.14 125.02
DESPAIRED (2)
089.23 314.34
DESPATCH (1)
020.21
DESPATCHED (1)
229.27
DESPERATE (8)
008.09 008.09 008.15 171.30 171.33
322.37 326.06 326.07
DESPERATION (2)
008.07 008.08
DESPICABLE (2)
029.17 068.15
DESPISED (1)
314.33

DESSERT (1)
267.31
DESTINATION (1)
296.17
DESTINED (4)
045.08 047.21 238.12 305.20
DESTINY (4)
007.27 099.06 216.08 296.19
DESTROY (2)
131.19 217.15
DESTROYED (3)
217.15 254.08 264.28
DESTROYING (1)
024.20
DESTROYS (2)
015.11 315.22
DESTRUCTION (2)
067.35 204.04
DETAIL (2)
091.21 206.22
DETAILS (5)
020.12 048.35 067.19 090.27 201.32
DETAIN (1)
210.25
DETAINED (2)
213.12 291.23
DETECT (12)
051.26 098.20 178.34 179.36 183.02
187.13 187.24 226.25 274.14 288.16
290.31 293.07
DETECTED (3)
150.11 236.03 290.33
DETER (1)
268.03
DETERMINE (1)
288.26
DETERMINED (9)
011.11 019.31 093.07 097.21 161.17
272.21 275.03 289.06 291.25
DETERMINES (1)
007.36
DETERRED (3)
040.04 142.24 272.15
DETERRING (1)
240.14
DETRIMENT (2)
061.10 250.16
DEUCALION (1)
005.31
DEVASTATION (1)
044.17
DEVELOPED (5)
046.07 114.10 146.35 227.03 328.35
DEVELOPING (2)
315.21 315.24
DEVELOPMENT (2)
035.09 213.32
DEVIL (7)
050.03 052.13 069.23 072.27 091.12
137.11 223.18
DEVILISH (1)
192.21
DEVILS (2)
137.07 220.23
DEVISED (1)
118.29
DEVOTE (4)
014.11 070.29 092.19 104.19
DEVOTED (4)
003.19 072.35 162.05 162.08
DEVOTES (1)
009.21
DEVOTING (1)
076.04
DEVOTION (2)
218.17 219.33
DEVOUR (3)
059.36 210.07 210.13

DEVOURED				(1)
051.28				

DEW				(8)
084.36	086.20	152.30	156.23	156.25
188.15	202.29	314.23		

DEWS			(3)
155.22	161.33	179.28	

DEWY	(1)
156.29	

DI	(1)
153.33	

DIAGONAL	(1)
275.02	

DIALECT	(2)
101.12	263.17

DIALECTS	(2)
101.25	111.05

DIALOGUES	(1)
107.17	

DIAMETER				(13)
065.19	114.12	185.15	187.23	195.15
198.17	198.33	201.29	247.04	248.06
248.14	280.12	288.06		

DIAMETERS	(1)
291.06	

DIAMOND	(1)
199.28	

DIAMONDS	(1)
262.22	

DICTATES	(1)
015.02	

DICTIONARY	(1)
069.02	

DID				(125)
003.16	008.31	015.08	018.13	018.22
019.20	025.17	027.18	028.26	029.16
039.03	040.07	045.32	054.30	055.21
055.26	055.27	057.26	058.31	059.29
059.30	062.29	063.12	063.25	064.19
069.18	070.12	071.06	074.13	075.10
075.12	081.26	085.24	087.25	088.17
088.20	088.30	090.36	091.01	092.25
093.22	099.14	105.04	105.05	105.11
108.35	111.20	111.21	113.11	114.13
114.36	118.03	119.35	119.36	120.24
124.31	137.29	145.02	147.19	147.27
148.10	148.18	148.35	151.17	151.31
152.11	153.09	154.07	154.12	156.14
161.16	162.17	164.11	164.14	169.08
170.21	171.23	172.20	172.29	184.02
186.11	190.36	192.04	196.18	205.11
205.12	205.13	205.13	211.19	211.28
211.33	211.34	213.15	211.34	220.23
222.14	234.12	235.33	235.34	236.20
238.06	238.24	240.16	241.15	241.26
242.27	245.16	250.26	254.14	254.14
255.01	256.27	263.30	264.06	270.23
271.11	271.15	279.11	283.27	288.33
294.23	314.24	316.03	316.34	323.24

DIDN	(1)
145.23	

DIE				(7)
014.13	032.14	090.35	153.32	229.24
269.25	331.31			

DIED				(7)
127.35	144.32	160.21	258.09	262.11
264.02	326.31			

DIES			(3)
036.10	068.03	311.14	

DIET				(8)
061.17	062.19	214.12	215.20	216.07
239.31	276.29	280.16		

DIETETIC	(1)
061.34	

DIFFER			(3)
026.24	219.21	315.28	

DIFFERENCE				(11)
003.26	084.05	149.19	151.12	161.11

DIFFERENCE			(CONTINUED)	
181.02	230.13	293.11	297.16	299.29
301.35				

DIFFERENT				(12)
010.19	071.10	124.07	125.36	133.26
176.20	184.15	222.12	296.19	305.24
325.16	326.09			

DIFFERENTLY	(1)
211.31	

DIFFICULT				(6)
025.06	040.36	049.39	181.21	189.16
327.33				

DIFFICULTIES	(2)
106.29	106.30

DIFFICULTY	(1)
140.31	

DIFFUSED	(1)
308.08	

DIG				(5)
039.13	044.31	058.24	133.27	182.26

DIGBY	(1)
162.31	

DIGEST	(1)
104.33	

DIGESTED	(1)
168.11	

DIGESTIVE	(1)
167.30	

DIGGING				(6)
005.12	054.15	194.10	224.09	224.12
239.05				

DIGNIFIED	(1)
213.24	

DIGNITARY	(1)
095.13	

DIGNITY			(3)
026.03	239.31	281.14	

DIJLAH	(1)
079.15	

DILAPIDATED	(1)
083.11	

DILATING		(2)
007.08	174.11	

DILETTANTISM	(1)
046.30	

DILIGENT	(1)
135.29	

DILIGENTLY	(1)
036.34	

DILUTE	(1)
264.10	

DILUVIAN	(1)
287.32	

DIM				(5)
188.28	255.04	255.09	262.27	324.35

DIMENSIONS	(1)
043.07	

DIMINISH	(1)
095.18	

DIMLY	(1)
190.24	

DIMPLE	(1)
187.10	

DIMPLES			(4)
114.29	188.08	190.16	190.22

DIMPLING		(3)
175.05	188.01	189.32

DIN	(1)
160.35	

DINED	(1)
061.08	

DINGY	(1)
145.14	

DINING		(2)
061.11	142.26	

DINNER				(25)
042.25	059.34	061.18	093.25	097.24
104.34	120.29	142.08	145.16	145.25

DINNER (CONTINUED)
146.31 171.36 172.12 174.33 215.29
223.05 223.20 226.02 244.06 245.04
245.05 275.31 280.22 329.23 332.33
DINNERS   (3)
006.30 142.23 204.24
DINNING   (1)
325.33
DIP   (2)
193.05 228.04
DIPPED   (2)
138.24 183.29
DIPPER   (2)
065.21 150.33
DIRECT   (3)
320.32 322.15 322.26
DIRECTED   (7)
121.10 170.16 178.08 207.09 228.16
293.02 293.10
DIRECTION   (14)
086.18 087.01 116.10 133.26 167.18
170.13 186.06 234.25 288.36 289.06
289.33 290.18 291.25 323.30
DIRECTIONS   (6)
010.02 087.09 093.28 226.27 275.09
308.12
DIRECTLY   (16)
013.33 069.04 176.18 177.26 178.08
178.16 194.07 205.28 227.18 235.11
247.11 247.29 248.06 278.32 300.13
310.14
DIRT   (7)
005.11 043.08 043.15 048.18 054.15
157.32 158.01
DIRTY   (5)
023.36 075.18 075.28 112.36 171.28
DISADVANTAGE   (3)
030.29 032.06 206.24
DISAFORESTED   (1)
220.16
DISAPPEAR   (4)
017.16 189.08 191.08 239.23
DISAPPEARED   (6)
044.35 191.19 240.20 278.08 302.33
302.35
DISAPPEARING   (2)
190.25 236.29
DISAPPEARS   (2)
235.07 300.17
DISAPPOINTED   (4)
084.03 123.27 142.17 268.31
DISCERN   (3)
096.09 101.32 314.30
DISCERNED   (2)
177.10 177.34
DISCERNS   (1)
098.26
DISCHARGE   (2)
020.16 063.08
DISCHARGED   (1)
020.18
DISCHARGES   (1)
234.03
DISCIPLINE   (2)
111.12 111.16
DISCOLORED   (1)
258.07
DISCOMFITURE   (2)
063.09 245.33
DISCONSOLATE   (1)
126.06
DISCONTENT   (1)
041.20
DISCONTENTED   (2)
016.17 205.20
DISCORDANT   (1)
275.10

DISCORDS   (1)
272.29
DISCOURAGE   (1)
039.30
DISCOURSE   (2)
221.16 270.04
DISCOURSED   (1)
081.11
DISCOVER   (4)
026.21 051.25 090.35 234.12
DISCOVERED   (15)
019.13 062.34 074.04 081.22 088.06
096.18 193.09 239.06 249.28 253.29
260.20 263.10 292.08 292.17 321.03
DISCOVERERS   (1)
020.35
DISCOVERIES   (3)
062.35 208.29 250.36
DISCOVERING   (2)
027.19 226.31
DISCOVERS   (2)
036.35 077.24
DISCOVERY   (2)
012.26 077.24
DISCRIMINATES   (1)
084.01
DISCRIMINATING   (1)
272.30
DISCUSSED   (1)
263.18
DISEASE   (6)
011.08 013.12 077.15 078.29 145.03
160.11
DISEASED   (2)
009.27 136.31
DISEASES   (1)
320.25
DISGORGE   (1)
275.18
DISGRACE   (4)
122.13 200.05 220.13 272.21
DISGRACING   (1)
268.25
DISGUISE   (1)
148.24
DISGUST   (1)
036.29
DISGUSTS   (1)
318.11
DISH   (4)
061.20 215.26 217.12 268.14
DISHABILLE   (1)
226.24
DISHEARTENS   (1)
318.11
DISHES   (3)
091.36 192.19 214.18
DISHONEST   (1)
328.21
DISK   (1)
133.11
DISMAL   (4)
117.31 124.19 125.36 267.36
DISMISS   (2)
315.09 315.10
DISORDER   (1)
328.32
DISOWN   (1)
066.16
DISPEL   (1)
078.34
DISPENSE   (1)
148.35
DISPENSING   (1)
119.20
DISPERSE   (2)
226.15 227.18

DISPERSES				(1)
126.34				
DISPERSING				(1)
304.21				
DISPLAYED				(1)
230.17				
DISPLAYING				(1)
235.32				
DISPOSE				(1)
070.01				
DISPOSED				(2)
029.25	326.21			
DISPOSITION				(2)
120.36	229.23			
DISPUTE				(1)
082.31				
DISPUTED				(1)
280.10				
DISREGARD				(1)
199.27				
DISREGARDED				(1)
268.32				
DISREPUTABLE				(1)
328.22				
DISSIPATE				(1)
104.28				
DISSIPATED				(1)
036.33				
DISSIPATES				(1)
219.34				
DISSIPATING				(1)
135.22				
DISSIPATION				(3)
100.08	162.16	328.36		
DISSOLVE				(2)
018.04	269.35			
DISSOLVED				(2)
041.10	300.24			
DISSOLVES				(1)
310.33				
DISTANCE				(30)
026.06	028.23	038.20	053.08	123.05
123.08	125.21	140.32	144.05	153.06
157.21	176.07	176.10	176.11	177.07
187.04	189.24	226.28	234.35	244.24
251.09	256.28	271.12	274.08	284.10
290.15	296.32	300.06	312.15	326.36
DISTANCES				(2)
009.34	224.22			
DISTANT				(32)
003.35	004.01	010.19	020.22	063.30
086.10	087.04	087.07	111.32	116.36
122.37	123.11	123.22	124.13	126.03
126.07	126.25	130.04	130.16	130.19
133.10	160.16	186.24	187.21	237.05
239.02	246.23	252.15	275.07	276.26
289.04	304.04			
DISTANTLY				(1)
194.04				
DISTEND				(1)
126.17				
DISTENDED				(1)
126.31				
DISTENTION				(1)
126.19				
DISTILLED				(1)
207.04				
DISTILLER				(1)
179.28				
DISTINCT				(7)
101.29	133.02	147.24	180.07	198.03
219.19	323.18			
DISTINCTION				(3)
031.34	107.21	166.10		
DISTINCTIONS				(2)
161.25	212.35			
DISTINCTLY				(6)
090.30	132.09	150.17	185.32	247.20

DISTINCTLY			(CONTINUED)
258.25			
DISTINGUISH			(3)
035.12	187.22	189.16	
DISTINGUISHABLE			(2)
054.33	180.12		
DISTINGUISHED			(15)
012.06	052.25	087.18	124.09	141.35
148.09	178.01	184.30	202.22	203.01
225.25	240.08	276.04	280.33	282.30
DISTINGUISHES			(2)
213.03	218.10		
DISTORTED			(1)
177.31			
DISTRACT			(1)
052.17			
DISTRACTED			(1)
102.14			
DISTRACTION			(2)
069.32	134.09		
DISTRESS			(2)
078.06	217.36		
DISTRESSED			(1)
169.27			
DISTRIBUTE			(1)
164.35			
DISTRIBUTED			(2)
012.20	172.24		
DISTURB			(1)
108.04			
DISTURBANCE			(3)
088.05	181.13	188.03	
DISTURBED			(6)
158.33	178.16	184.36	185.06	208.33
266.22			
DISTURBING			(1)
161.23			
DISTURBS			(1)
187.18			
DITCH			(1)
074.28			
DITCHER			(1)
262.04			
DITTY			(1)
124.22			
DIVANS			(1)
037.07			
DIVE			(3)
186.29	233.34	234.11	
DIVED			(4)
234.23	234.24	235.27	236.04
DIVERGED			(1)
240.02			
DIVERGING			(1)
187.27			
DIVERT			(1)
277.23			
DIVES			(2)
288.22	297.31		
DIVEST			(1)
231.14			
DIVESTED			(3)
022.31	229.21	253.32	
DIVIDED			(2)
177.09	295.24		
DIVIDERS			(1)
265.24			
DIVIDING			(1)
098.13			
DIVINE			(11)
007.32	036.14	074.16	090.11	097.06
220.07	220.11	235.04	235.14	314.13
331.30			
DIVINING			(3)
098.35	182.27	282.24	
DIVINITY			(4)
007.24	007.26	099.12	099.17

DIVISION   (2)
046.20 050.28
DIVISIONS   (1)
328.31
DIVULGE   (1)
021.10
DO   (184)
003.14 003.26 004.06 006.25 008.15
008.29 010.09 011.04 011.09 011.21
011.22 012.13 014.26 015.09 016.04
016.14 019.03 019.04 019.05 019.11
021.25 022.13 023.13 023.14 023.15
023.19 023.23 023.28 023.33 023.34
025.01 025.03 025.17 025.24 028.28
028.28 030.28 034.21 036.14 038.13
046.09 046.22 047.07 047.35 048.04
048.18 049.37 051.07 051.09 053.03
056.01 056.28 057.02 057.04 061.09
064.05 064.20 066.03 066.13 066.26
067.08 067.28 069.05 069.26 069.30
070.21 070.23 071.03 071.16 072.27
073.08 073.20 073.23 074.29 074.34
075.01 075.08 075.16 076.36 078.16
079.01 083.27 084.11 084.22 088.33
090.25 092.17 092.19 092.24 094.03
094.19 096.26 098.27 106.17 106.20
106.20 106.34 107.21 108.25 110.04
116.32 118.02 118.09 122.02 123.29
125.25 129.20 131.27 133.18 134.17
134.18 134.28 143.27 144.20 148.33
149.03 149.24 149.25 150.25 152.16
153.24 156.24 158.28 161.30 164.15
165.04 166.22 171.13 171.18 173.10
178.33 179.13 180.28 192.03 195.23
203.30 205.26 206.27 210.17 210.22
211.10 211.11 212.34 214.03 220.29
222.16 223.29 224.30 225.06 225.07
225.14 227.10 231.20 237.07 237.09
240.20 246.11 248.27 251.25 252.03
259.06 269.24 272.09 272.24 272.26
277.31 277.31 288.28 315.11 322.09
322.10 323.27 325.24 326.26 327.11
328.05 328.14 328.23 328.25 328.27
328.34 330.26 332.27 333.28
DOBBIN   (1)
157.30
DOBSON   (1)
058.20
DOCKS   (1)
292.05
DOCTOR   (1)
138.36
DOCTORS   (4)
153.14 268.05 320.03 320.24
DOCTRINE   (1)
325.17
DOCTRINES   (1)
099.32
DOCUMENTA   (1)
005.35
DODGED   (1)
226.03
DODONA   (1)
100.35
DOES   (82)
007.26 007.28 009.15 015.19 025.18
028.13 029.07 038.08 046.13 046.20
052.34 052.36 056.19 056.36 057.21
058.03 061.12 064.04 073.06 073.13
077.15 077.20 078.17 078.27 078.30
082.36 089.21 090.17 095.09 096.26
106.02 108.24 116.11 118.25 118.36
134.31 136.04 136.08 148.29 149.24
157.28 165.17 175.26 178.34 182.24
193.36 193.37 205.26 208.37 212.33
216.01 217.16 218.08 218.09 218.10
218.12 219.04 221.25 223.14 227.11
244.21 255.06 264.18 281.31 301.33

DOES   (CONTINUED)
301.35 315.08 315.09 315.10 315.19
315.25 315.27 315.28 320.05 321.01
321.01 321.09 322.24 322.33 326.08
326.24 333.15
DOG   (12)
022.27 074.29 083.18 094.16 127.29
144.18 145.25 197.27 213.08 257.27
277.32 325.36
DOGGING   (1)
029.19
DOGS   (10)
012.28 058.11 122.06 126.05 167.22
229.22 242.26 271.13 273.09 273.11
DOGWOOD   (1)
201.17
DOING   (22)
004.17 008.24 016.21 045.17 055.25
056.31 069.24 071.15 073.03 073.16
073.19 073.28 074.03 074.18 076.02
095.16 118.28 157.31 223.07 236.07
260.12 314.25
DOLEFUL   (1)
124.25
DOLIA   (1)
243.04
DOLLAR   (7)
024.32 024.33 029.12 031.21 107.01
195.32 238.11
DOLLARS   (21)
024.30 024.32 031.01 031.17 043.30
050.07 050.27 054.19 054.25 064.33
082.14 082.18 082.19 082.22 109.19
109.23 119.36 196.26 196.28 204.36
294.31
DOLPHIN   (1)
202.15
DOMESTIC   (8)
027.20 028.22 061.10 127.31 141.36
160.19 232.26 233.20
DOMESTICATED   (1)
127.07
DON   (8)
024.12 094.31 094.31 105.22 116.22
153.25 161.30 310.20
DONE   (34)
011.10 019.12 023.12 025.26 027.10
042.30 048.34 054.13 060.08 061.08
071.29 074.23 075.08 075.10 076.10
090.31 093.23 100.18 103.26 119.33
121.08 143.28 173.24 174.24 214.02
214.26 215.21 243.22 283.22 294.27
326.17 330.22 331.14 331.30
DONNED   (1)
267.26
DOOR   (47)
035.05 043.11 043.12 043.13 045.33
048.31 067.23 081.34 084.34 085.27
087.24 089.01 112.10 114.30 120.24
124.01 130.10 130.27 132.30 171.26
172.04 172.12 199.33 221.34 223.18
231.26 243.30 244.11 244.15 263.07
263.24 267.18 272.06 272.12 273.03
273.24 275.32 277.20 280.31 281.01
281.03 312.34 313.02 313.04 319.06
323.16 328.13
DOORS   (15)
027.34 028.12 029.26 038.31 045.18
048.31 062.03 085.25 085.27 113.01
113.19 168.09 168.12 249.13 315.09
DOORWAY   (2)
111.26 173.34
DORMANT   (2)
262.32 309.18
DOSES   (1)
167.12
DOST   (1)
080.05

```
DOTS                              (   1)    DRAGGLE                              (   1)
265.20                                       095.25
DOTTED                            (   3)    DRAGON                               (   1)
256.21  265.19  282.10                       116.21
DOUBLE                            (   5)    DRAIN                                (   1)
125.32  293.29  294.21  294.29  306.30       305.26
DOUBLED                           (   1)    DRAINED                              (   2)
246.26                                       196.17  287.20
DOUBLENESS                        (   2)    DRAMA                                (   2)
135.09  135.18                               112.29  319.14
DOUBLY                            (   1)    DRANK                                (   5)
327.33                                       149.01  150.32  179.15  207.09  246.03
DOUBT                             (  31)    DRASTIC                              (   1)
006.29  009.02  017.23  017.27  031.35       077.29
032.34  035.21  046.21  053.01  053.36    DRAUGHT                              (   4)
069.04  073.18  074.31  077.34  083.36       013.14  126.22  138.27  207.10
092.16  112.20  115.06  142.21  143.26    DRAUGHTS                             (   1)
185.08  212.08  213.20  216.08  216.31       264.09
230.24  239.08  282.17  288.11  298.06    DRAW                                 (   4)
322.15                                       157.35  190.05  291.07  298.14
DOUBTED                           (   1)    DRAWING                              (   3)
131.31                                       037.06  044.06  192.20
DOUBTFUL                          (   1)    DRAWN                                (   4)
031.25                                       011.18  183.18  236.11  294.12
DOUBTLESS                         (   2)    DRAWS                                (   1)
093.29  257.01                               311.13
DOUGH                             (   1)    DREAM                                (   5)
062.21                                       193.22  202.24  243.13  252.33  282.23
DOVE                              (   2)    DREAMED                              (   5)
017.16  208.19                               016.10  070.03  078.02  093.30  239.10
DOVECOTS                          (   1)    DREAMING                             (   3)
028.29                                       093.36  170.04  191.32
DOVERS                            (   1)    DREAMS                               (   7)
122.03                                       136.24  156.08  175.19  266.17  266.22
DOVES                             (   2)    272.36  323.31
028.28  228.18                            DREAR                                (   1)
DOWN                              ( 112)      131.15
005.17  016.01  021.01  025.35  029.14    DREARY                               (   1)
030.12  033.07  037.28  038.01  040.33       132.12
040.35  042.32  044.06  044.24  052.04    DRENCHED                             (   1)
058.21  062.20  067.02  070.28  075.28       170.24
083.20  085.19  092.31  093.03  097.26    DRENCHING                            (   1)
105.11  105.16  105.19  113.30  114.01       097.09
114.20  115.03  116.04  116.05  116.05    DRESDEN                              (   1)
119.11  121.19  126.27  126.31  133.03       230.19
133.06  135.04  135.35  146.21  160.20    DRESS                                (  10)
164.19  171.26  174.26  176.19  177.26       021.32  022.21  023.01  023.06  023.12
178.10  178.17  178.20  180.01  182.21       027.12  069.17  120.08  145.27  329.27
184.01  187.09  189.04  189.05  191.26    DRESSED                              (   3)
192.12  193.10  195.24  197.28  198.31       059.41  206.06  208.15
207.17  215.07  215.22  220.05  221.36    DRESSING                             (   2)
224.15  228.09  228.20  229.13  234.18       026.02  158.30
237.04  245.21  250.24  250.25  255.08    DREW                                 (   5)
257.33  258.15  260.30  261.30  262.14       143.31  158.32  178.21  229.35  260.19
265.13  265.35  271.31  273.21  276.17    DRIED                                (   8)
280.23  283.03  283.12  284.14  285.21       059.22  067.32  074.10  113.06  226.17
285.28  288.03  289.11  294.17  295.04    269.26  306.28  309.24
295.14  296.08  298.09  303.27  304.30    DRIER                                (   1)
305.03  305.12  311.14  320.14  322.28       306.33
322.28  322.28                            DRIFT                                (   3)
DOWNWARD                          (  10)      135.03  249.27  265.07
004.21  015.29  097.33  175.21  182.29    DRIFTED                              (   3)
248.13  300.16  306.25  307.16  325.08       175.09  199.06  304.13
DOWNY                             (   1)    DRIFTS                               (   4)
116.14                                       265.02  267.06  271.24  276.20
DOZEN                             (  14)    DRIFTWOOD                            (   1)
032.29  066.02  066.03  081.07  091.27       054.36
113.28  145.07  179.13  181.11  185.15    DRILL                                (   2)
187.23  234.30  259.03  299.28               117.11  294.19
DR                                (   1)    DRINK                                (  21)
153.27                                       012.16  061.04  064.20  098.19  098.20
DRAG                              (   1)    098.22  138.28  145.20  192.16  206.36
067.07                                       217.09  217.19  220.28  221.24  264.09
DRAGGED                           (   1)    276.29  283.03  294.01  294.06  298.01
250.03                                       311.12
DRAGGING                          (   3)    DRINKING                             (   2)
066.09  066.09  175.08                       061.32  218.27
```

DRINKS   (1)
139.04
DRIPPING   (1)
312.08
DRIPPINGS   (1)
308.06
DRIVABLE   (1)
044.14
DRIVE   (6)
007.29 091.05 138.34 285.26 330.24
330.27
DRIVEN   (8)
043.14 108.11 179.19 235.02 273.02
285.23 285.25 330.31
DRIVER   (2)
007.23 251.32
DRIVING   (6)
021.13 041.23 132.27 133.31 312.35
318.11
DRONE   (1)
160.23
DROOLING   (1)
126.21
DROOP   (1)
265.32
DROOPING   (1)
238.15
DROP   (11)
051.29 158.23 158.24 194.02 215.11
307.14 307.32 308.03 308.05 308.06
308.10
DROPPED   (8)
129.32 130.02 233.14 275.15 275.26
295.01 303.27 312.23
DROPPING   (1)
194.29
DROPS   (2)
132.02 190.07
DROPSICAL   (1)
281.09
DROSS   (2)
016.24 254.24
DROVE   (2)
044.10 074.07
DROVERS   (1)
121.32
DROVES   (1)
122.04
DROWN   (2)
126.18 333.02
DROWNED   (2)
058.10 169.06
DROWNING   (2)
078.18 127.17
DROWSINESS   (1)
090.07
DROWSY   (1)
095.22
DRUDGERY   (1)
157.11
DRUIDS   (1)
201.06
DRUM   (1)
301.18
DRUMMER   (1)
326.09
DRUMSTICKS   (1)
127.13
DRUNK   (2)
099.31 217.05
DRUNKARD   (1)
314.32
DRUNKENNESS   (1)
217.08
DRY   (29)
008.33 018.27 039.21 068.26 074.19
079.11 087.23 114.10 155.22 168.31
186.27 190.25 195.26 199.05 248.34

DRY   (CONTINUED)
252.20 256.15 263.09 276.16 277.33
283.18 284.14 292.05 293.19 306.27
311.11 333.03 333.08 333.19
DRYING   (1)
249.33
DRYNESS   (1)
180.21
DUBIOUS   (1)
258.34
DUCK   (2)
173.27 187.02
DUCKING   (1)
075.31
DUCKLING   (1)
152.26
DUCKS   (12)
179.22 185.02 190.29 195.34 199.33
199.34 236.31 248.34 303.25 303.32
304.01 313.14
DUE   (5)
038.16 076.34 220.15 297.09 313.22
DUELLUM   (1)
228.34
DUG   (8)
044.22 044.23 051.32 137.22 183.06
190.32 228.03 239.09
DULL   (7)
080.15 107.30 115.04 145.12 175.12
252.03 254.37
DULLEST   (1)
325.08
DULNESS   (3)
105.30 270.10 332.19
DUM   (1)
172.27
DUMB   (2)
245.02 278.34
DUMPS   (1)
225.01
DUN   (1)
120.29
DUNCAN   (1)
257.05
DUNGINGS   (1)
162.26
DURATION   (2)
189.13 299.21
DURING   (13)
041.12 054.05 068.21 079.10 079.11
132.21 183.27 193.39 202.24 211.35
254.25 268.17 319.01
DURUM   (1)
005.34
DUSK   (1)
280.31
DUSKY   (2)
258.13 263.30
DUST   (14)
036.22 036.31 067.33 068.01 068.03
074.21 099.16 156.27 162.03 167.06
188.28 217.01 276.18 319.15
DUSTCLOTH   (1)
188.30
DUSTED   (3)
036.27 142.01 188.30
DUSTY   (4)
023.15 043.21 257.01 323.22
DUTCH   (1)
039.08
DUTY   (6)
007.26 016.22 018.13 072.23 270.22
314.25
DWARFS   (1)
325.34
DWELL   (9)
028.27 115.14 115.37 133.10 133.19
145.30 173.06 303.09 333.03

```
DWELLING                              (  14)
  004.25   028.30   034.20   039.27   044.06
  047.31   071.26   085.08   096.34   124.36
  175.08   242.30   248.35   259.22
DWELLINGS                             (   6)
  031.13   040.03   046.04   047.23   256.22
  263.02
DWELLLING                             (   1)
  257.25
DWELLS                                (   4)
  137.31   242.19   245.08   298.13
DWELT                                 (  10)
  037.21   087.23   087.34   153.07   156.17
  204.06   245.06   258.10   271.21   313.26
DWINDLED                              (   1)
  088.12
DYED                                  (   1)
  319.15
DYING                                 (   9)
  007.02   007.04   098.16   114.34   125.10
  136.28   220.06   229.03   230.11
DYNASTIES                             (   1)
  327.17
DYNASTY                               (   2)
  243.23   327.04
DYSPEPSIA                             (   1)
  077.35
```

				(1)
EDIT				(1)
094.21				
EDITION				(1)
105.26				
EDITOR				(1)
018.07				
EDUCATED				(3)
106.07	118.21	147.09		
EDUCATION				(8)
050.13	050.15	050.23	108.36	109.06
109.10	212.13	212.27		
EELS				(2)
184.05	184.08			
EFFECT				(12)
030.09	037.34	047.31	059.35	088.32
123.09	171.31	177.32	214.31	268.34
289.01	299.07			
EFFECTIVE				(1)
090.10				
EFFECTS				(4)
067.26	113.09	204.27	214.29	
EFFECTUAL				(1)
121.06				
EFFECTUALLY				(4)
142.24	245.36	269.18	312.25	
EFFEMINATE				(1)
037.10				
EFFETE				(1)
155.24				
EFFORT				(4)
090.03	134.34	182.05	307.18	
EFFORTS				(2)
106.12	236.17			
EGG				(5)
025.31	185.17	317.08	333.11	333.18
EGGS				(5)
046.09	062.11	124.14	127.13	159.18
EGOTISM				(1)
003.25				
EGYPT				(1)
159.35				
EGYPTIAN				(5)
025.34	058.14	062.10	099.11	310.07
EH				(1)
223.29				
EIGHT				(16)
031.17	048.29	054.25	054.26	059.01
060.16	060.17	060.18	064.33	064.33
133.04	145.06	184.01	185.13	247.18
265.28				
EIGHTEEN				(3)
055.08	163.28	169.36		
EIGHTH				(3)
247.04	248.11	275.12		
EIGHTHS				(1)
244.19				
EIGHTIETH				(1)
247.04				
EIGHTS				(1)
248.09				
EIGHTY				(3)
176.01	199.07	235.18		
EITHER				(23)
017.33	034.11	037.22	052.23	064.08
108.27	129.26	129.31	129.34	135.02
144.32	157.21	160.12	162.24	167.11
168.03	169.01	191.16	195.18	229.27
231.10	281.22	296.20		
EJACULATES				(1)
126.29				
EJACULATION				(1)
126.24				
EKE				(1)
203.05				
ELABORATE				(1)
103.29				
ELABORATENESS				(1)
187.20				

ELAPSED				(4)
099.17	181.32	298.04	327.22	
ELASTIC				(5)
089.35	216.26	281.10	301.28	312.04
ELASTICITY				(2)
054.03	066.12			
ELBOW				(1)
225.35				
ELBOWS				(2)
130.09	157.17			
ELDER				(1)
109.02				
ELDERLY				(2)
063.03	137.31			
ELECT				(1)
202.19				
ELECTION				(1)
259.06				
ELECTRIFYING				(1)
118.04				
ELEGANCE				(1)
269.09				
ELEMENT				(5)
061.12	175.21	179.03	208.06	294.08
ELEMENTAL				(1)
159.25				
ELEMENTS				(10)
023.25	116.24	116.28	117.17	123.15
129.09	256.10	272.31	290.04	290.28
ELEVATE				(1)
090.19				
ELEVATED				(5)
076.28	087.18	090.28	194.05	326.33
ELEVATING				(1)
221.25				
ELEVATION				(5)
014.19	092.13	120.31	288.18	291.26
ELEVEN				(2)
054.23	248.33			
ELICITED				(1)
174.13				
ELIZABETH				(1)
026.10				
ELIZABETHAN				(1)
325.35				
ELM				(2)
161.08	202.04			
ELMS				(1)
167.20				
ELOQUENCE				(2)
102.02	102.09			
ELSE				(21)
003.29	018.27	019.16	019.29	032.20
039.17	043.08	043.32	050.18	073.03
141.03	144.03	168.06	220.22	248.34
252.33	261.21	275.33	277.25	283.17
326.26				
ELSEWHERE				(10)
011.05	050.17	073.11	106.07	151.04
162.22	163.24	171.23	271.26	292.19
ELYSIAN				(1)
013.35				
EMACEM				(1)
163.14				
EMANCIPATION				(1)
008.01				
EMASCULATED				(1)
037.02				
EMBANKMENT				(1)
114.06				
EMBERS				(1)
240.29				
EMBRACES				(3)
077.31	229.11	269.06		
EMBRACING				(1)
305.24				
EMBROIDERED				(1)
030.07				

ENGLISHMEN (2)
  154.20 154.20
ENGRAVEN (2)
  088.31 269.04
ENHANCE (1)
  264.19
ENHANCED (2)
  064.34 269.21
ENJOY (14)
  031.07 054.05 070.22 083.24 087.31
  091.15 109.26 131.12 141.20 146.24
  162.30 207.35 219.15 333.26
ENJOYED (5)
  081.17 082.33 132.31 153.12 243.02
ENJOYMENT (2)
  038.13 059.38
ENJOYS (1)
  196.28
ENLIGHTEN (1)
  103.02
ENLIGHTENED (3)
  035.17 080.30 332.21
ENLIST (1)
  322.23
ENNUI (4)
  010.05 112.33 127.35 136.04
ENORMITY (1)
  078.03
ENORMOUS (1)
  067.04
ENOUGH (66)
  005.22 008.32 012.20 020.08 027.18
  027.35 046.06 053.16 053.29 055.07
  058.07 075.29 078.13 081.17 082.20
  084.12 087.26 090.08 090.09 094.18
  101.07 103.32 109.13 109.15 112.34
  115.36 140.04 141.12 141.31 142.09
  146.25 148.14 149.35 151.30 172.23
  174.04 185.27 199.23 202.35 206.10
  206.15 206.16 212.15 214.34 228.22
  235.35 242.19 245.06 245.11 249.23
  261.36 270.11 270.23 290.04 292.16
  293.07 294.28 318.02 319.02 322.38
  324.12 324.19 324.20 324.30 325.15
  328.18
ENRICHED (1)
  027.03
ENSLAVE (1)
  007.20
ENTANGLED (1)
  066.27
ENTER (2)
  269.13 326.24
ENTERED (2)
  021.18 315.07
ENTERETH (1)
  218.15
ENTERING (3)
  125.13 206.22 240.14
ENTERPRISE (11)
  017.24 020.02 023.32 041.03 048.20
  103.07 117.07 117.23 118.24 205.36
  208.01
ENTERPRISED (1)
  024.01
ENTERPRISES (6)
  011.01 016.34 023.29 072.22 119.17
  326.07
ENTERPRISING (1)
  028.09
ENTERTAIN (5)
  012.22 085.06 142.16 242.31 309.34
ENTERTAINED (4)
  143.25 148.13 169.11 217.26
ENTERTAINMENT (7)
  045.27 142.34 160.02 269.12 270.03
  273.29 331.08

ENTERTAINMENTS (2)
  094.35 095.34
ENTERTAINS (1)
  269.07
ENTHUSIASM (1)
  016.13
ENTIRE (2)
  039.22 158.31
ENTIRELY (4)
  009.28 029.27 249.02 302.35
ENTIRENESS (1)
  291.03
ENTITLED (3)
  081.18 101.20 104.31
ENTITLES (1)
  031.02
ENTITY (1)
  135.07
ENTOMOLOGISTS (1)
  215.04
ENTRANCE (4)
  045.02 285.27 289.35 291.21
ENTRIES (1)
  132.29
ENTRY (4)
  132.31 203.10 279.24 292.05
ENUMERATING (1)
  076.24
ENVELOP (1)
  325.31
ENVIRON (1)
  134.26
EPAULET (1)
  276.06
EPIDERMIS (1)
  024.14
EPITAPH (1)
  258.02
EPITOME (1)
  301.08
EPOCHS (1)
  117.32
EQUABLE (2)
  044.32 102.13
EQUAL (13)
  025.15 047.36 056.32 057.29 072.01
  088.11 088.26 109.25 177.19 186.36
  224.12 282.29 284.10
EQUALLED (1)
  103.29
EQUALLY (12)
  033.01 034.14 047.28 059.31 166.13
  173.34 176.30 186.33 195.21 212.08
  251.23 257.13
EQUALS (1)
  251.06
EQUILIBRIUM (2)
  187.19 313.32
EQUIPAGE (1)
  023.06
EQUIVALENT (2)
  024.21 053.26
ER (3)
  115.10 193.27 254.31
ERA (1)
  107.36
ERAS (1)
  087.35
ERE (11)
  075.27 115.02 116.16 138.34 156.18
  208.33 277.18 278.03 309.16 313.26
  327.09
ERECT (9)
  105.23 163.36 165.09 178.12 178.14
  266.09 278.22 312.25 326.16
ERECTED (1)
  173.33

ERIT   (1)
  243.06
ERRAND   (2)
  207.32 251.14
ERRANDS   (1)
  116.29
ERRET   (1)
  322.01
ERROR   (4)
  020.31 091.18 091.18 173.15
ERUPTION   (1)
  160.12
ESCAPE   (4)
  063.07 163.38 168.27 204.10
ESCAPED   (4)
  168.36 169.16 182.19 189.25
ESCORT   (1)
  116.30
ESCULENTS   (1)
  015.35
ESOTERIC   (1)
  099.32
ESPECIALLY   (20)
  004.11 030.22 039.11 070.10 070.26
  084.35 131.26 133.07 137.01 162.22
  169.18 175.16 176.10 199.19 202.31
  234.17 246.17 306.23 318.15 318.34
ESQUIMAUX   (2)
  077.30 271.14
ESQUIRE   (1)
  257.05
ESSE   (1)
  163.14
ESSENCE   (1)
  224.28
ESSENTIAL   (7)
  012.05 063.05 090.33 092.14 131.32
  173.19 290.28
ESSENTIALLY   (4)
  214.11 214.23 293.18 329.06
ESSENTIALS   (1)
  243.34
ESTABLISH   (4)
  011.25 096.07 142.21 323.35
ESTABLISHED   (3)
  108.17 220.07 332.08
ESTABLISHMENT   (2)
  092.07 094.26
ESTATE   (2)
  074.35 081.19
ESTATES   (1)
  068.02
ESTEEM   (3)
  096.36 101.03 332.07
ESTEEMED   (3)
  076.21 095.29 221.10
ESTIMATE   (2)
  055.19 060.42
ESTIMATED   (1)
  296.24
ESTIMATES   (2)
  059.02 158.05
ESTIMATING   (1)
  031.20
ESTIMATION   (1)
  022.04
ESTIVATE   (1)
  296.15
ET   (7)
  005.35 243.05 243.05 243.06 310.35
  314.02 322.01
ETERNAL   (2)
  173.21 316.14
ETERNITIES   (1)
  017.04
ETERNITY   (5)
  008.06 097.02 098.22 137.24 311.15

ETESIAN   (1)
  167.32
ETHER   (5)
  167.33 282.20 314.16 317.04 325.32
ETHEREAL   (3)
  041.34 316.33 326.18
ETHICS   (1)
  291.05
ETIQUETTE   (1)
  136.15
EUGENIUS   (1)
  231.35
EULOGIES   (1)
  331.28
EUROPE   (2)
  101.28 109.12
EUROPEAN   (1)
  013.05
EURUS   (1)
  314.01
EV   (1)
  220.20
EVANGELIST   (1)
  052.35
EVAPORATE   (1)
  141.20
EVAPORATION   (2)
  175.35 292.09
EVAPORATIONS   (1)
  297.28
EVE   (2)
  028.04 179.19
EVELYN   (2)
  009.33 162.19
EVEN   (161)
  004.28 006.09 008.01 008.12 009.12
  010.02 010.03 011.36 014.36 015.13
  017.16 022.03 022.08 023.04 025.32
  028.12 029.06 031.19 032.36 033.09
  040.08 040.21 046.01 051.01 052.05
  052.07 053.24 055.24 057.16 061.16
  061.26 062.34 066.17 066.27 070.05
  072.33 073.15 077.22 078.23 081.13
  082.05 085.28 087.10 087.13 087.21
  090.27 092.03 093.24 099.08 100.11
  101.07 103.25 103.36 104.34 105.24
  106.01 106.05 106.06 106.25 106.34
  108.17 115.06 118.28 127.25 127.27
  127.32 127.36 128.07 130.03 131.05
  132.11 135.21 137.26 138.29 138.33
  141.08 150.26 153.05 156.06 157.10
  164.04 165.17 169.10 169.24 169.29
  170.25 170.35 172.03 172.06 176.21
  176.28 178.35 179.09 179.20 179.24
  179.36 187.23 190.15 193.25 195.33
  198.05 198.08 202.32 210.32 211.18
  213.26 213.31 214.08 216.15 217.13
  217.33 218.24 219.12 226.29 227.04
  230.12 239.25 240.17 242.01 245.04
  246.15 248.29 250.34 251.15 253.21
  253.22 253.34 256.06 262.25 265.02
  265.21 267.09 267.11 268.02 268.05
  274.04 279.19 282.19 283.08 284.23
  288.38 291.01 294.02 299.05 305.02
  306.27 307.01 309.30 309.31 315.01
  315.07 319.14 320.10 322.09 322.20
  324.30 325.35 328.08 328.10 329.34
  333.01
EVENING   (45)
  018.02 053.15 086.25 112.06 117.20
  123.22 123.35 124.05 126.03 129.03
  129.15 132.25 133.28 137.25 170.11
  202.27 206.34 208.27 217.01 217.12
  221.34 222.02 242.10 242.21 254.23
  267.17 271.18 272.06 276.14 276.25
  277.02 279.06 281.01 281.03 301.07
  301.10 301.26 301.33 302.31 312.07
  312.12 312.12 312.18 315.25 315.26

69

EXCLUSIVELY   (2)
  019.30 176.05
EXCLUSIVENESS   (1)
  108.12
EXCREMENT   (1)
  221.24
EXCREMENTITIOUS   (1)
  308.21
EXCREMENTS   (1)
  305.15
EXCURSION   (2)
  037.15 091.10
EXCURSIONS   (1)
  085.17
EXCUSE   (8)
  049.35 058.11 078.10 083.27 093.16
  150.30 211.36 221.26
EXCUSED   (1)
  192.10
EXECUTED   (1)
  134.11
EXECUTION   (1)
  235.01
EXEMPTED   (1)
  150.33
EXERCISE   (9)
  028.31 051.16 088.29 101.02 101.03
  104.15 151.05 161.04 223.06
EXERT   (1)
  103.05
EXERTION   (3)
  090.10 133.17 220.38
EXERTIONS   (1)
  012.09
EXERTS   (1)
  300.08
EXHALATIONS   (1)
  102.07
EXHAUSTED   (8)
  010.06 156.19 162.29 164.05 196.13
  196.14 302.21 314.37
EXHAUSTION   (1)
  136.29
EXHIBIT   (4)
  121.07 145.23 210.33 228.24
EXHIBITED   (1)
  149.17
EXHIBITING   (2)
  272.22 305.07
EXHIBITION   (1)
  135.04
EXHILARATING   (2)
  096.04 308.20
EXIST   (2)
  034.34 216.31
EXISTED   (1)
  292.28
EXISTENCE   (11)
  012.05 096.03 121.02 145.05 179.20
  222.17 254.12 254.36 298.08 306.06
  318.21
EXISTS   (2)
  108.01 217.32
EXOGENOUS   (1)
  024.13
EXORBITANT   (1)
  020.23
EXOTERIC   (1)
  325.17
EXPAND   (4)
  186.05 302.04 307.34 314.37
EXPANDED   (8)
  119.18 132.08 160.34 176.32 247.27
  270.06 323.36 327.13
EXPANSE   (2)
  188.03 234.34
EXPANSION   (3)
  024.07 197.10 289.31

EXPECT   (8)
  147.28 150.04 181.10 192.11 213.26
  243.08 301.34 330.03
EXPECTARE   (1)
  243.05
EXPECTATION   (2)
  090.16 210.33
EXPECTED   (6)
  089.12 168.35 198.34 270.17 281.25
  296.21
EXPECTER   (1)
  270.02
EXPECTING   (1)
  054.29
EXPECTS   (1)
  121.17
EXPEDIENCY   (1)
  150.03
EXPEDITION   (1)
  321.26
EXPEDITIONS   (2)
  020.27 102.19
EXPEDITIOUS   (1)
  318.29
EXPELLED   (2)
  096.14 219.12
EXPENSE   (7)
  019.26 049.33 050.15 059.01 092.09
  100.21 321.27
EXPENSES   (7)
  031.32 054.20 059.43 060.34 069.12
  069.15 205.28
EXPENSIVE   (5)
  051.12 055.35 071.23 162.34 242.23
EXPERIENCE   (36)
  003.31 006.36 009.05 009.09 009.16
  010.28 014.05 046.14 051.05 053.21
  055.29 061.14 069.26 070.33 081.18
  084.21 091.09 096.12 101.15 108.11
  108.15 133.24 135.11 135.13 161.12
  163.26 163.40 170.34 205.03 208.30
  211.07 214.19 214.32 227.08 290.07
  324.21
EXPERIENCED   (4)
  040.28 099.30 131.03 140.30
EXPERIENCES   (2)
  175.01 329.09
EXPERIENSQUE   (1)
  005.34
EXPERIMENT   (11)
  009.14 040.29 051.15 055.24 059.37
  064.07 084.19 134.27 246.09 300.26
  323.29
EXPERIMENTALISTS   (1)
  331.34
EXPERIMENTS   (5)
  059.14 065.06 065.10 119.17 162.34
EXPERT   (2)
  148.26 320.35
EXPIATING   (1)
  124.32
EXPIATORY   (1)
  250.29
EXPLAIN   (1)
  108.01
EXPLORE   (5)
  252.16 317.34 321.11 321.33 322.21
EXPLORING   (2)
  020.26 321.26
EXPORT   (2)
  020.08 092.15
EXPORTS   (1)
  035.26
EXPOSE   (1)
  272.21
EXPOSED   (11)
  004.19 027.15 065.30 079.12 163.32
  183.10 183.24 254.01 288.31 296.27

71

F				(1)
306.28				

FABLE				(8)
028.04	091.16	138.01	152.18	182.24
184.12	269.36	297.23		

FABLES				(2)
137.34	204.06			

FABULOUS				(6)
095.30	156.07	239.08	271.15	284.22
298.18				

FACE				(27)
004.20	017.33	019.30	021.15	033.08
074.01	090.14	098.11	098.11	107.35
193.18	194.31	195.33	204.25	206.20
206.20	206.32	226.07	247.05	254.22
262.10	274.19	282.08	308.07	308.08
311.30	327.27			

FACED		(2)
204.08	204.37	

FACITO	(1)
063.16	

FACT				(17)
011.23	011.24	045.28	046.33	058.06
077.26	090.18	098.11	120.14	134.08
138.01	187.20	215.03	288.16	290.24
299.32	321.27			

FACTITIOUS		(3)
006.11	038.19	211.29

FACTORIES	(1)
148.33	

FACTORY			(4)
026.32	089.17	136.23	287.15

FACTS			(4)
090.33	184.12	216.32	327.34

FACULTIES				(9)
021.03	035.10	098.30	104.18	104.29
105.32	215.01	222.13	254.04	

FACULTY		(2)
046.07	315.31	

FADE		(2)
067.15	138.11	

FAGINUS	(1)
172.27	

FAGOTS	(1)
249.23	

FAIL				(10)
027.04	033.01	033.11	038.23	094.35
096.11	112.34	143.35	166.27	264.06

FAILED				(9)
056.12	059.14	148.31	150.17	168.01
267.11	267.31	285.30	310.21	

FAILING	(1)
206.25	

FAILS	(1)
218.30	

FAILURE			(4)
056.06	069.20	078.29	096.12

FAILURES				(5)
009.07	010.10	033.04	033.04	033.05

FAIN				(8)
004.08	115.20	124.29	126.13	196.14
202.19	217.07	272.35		

FAINT				(17)
077.35	088.35	122.36	123.03	160.18
169.33	175.10	184.00	184.22	189.24
207.19	214.03	228.15	239.16	248.36
275.32	310.24			

FAINTEST		(2)
216.13	216.17	

FAINTLY			(4)
125.05	213.22	264.01	318.36

FAIR				(25)
035.11	080.12	097.13	133.30	163.38
171.36	173.09	185.09	188.22	197.10
197.13	201.22	203.04	206.34	208.35
224.21	248.31	264.02	272.15	278.11
279.17	299.16	303.28	315.05	327.16

FAIRER		(2)
199.32	327.18	

FAIREST			(3)
089.31	197.03	327.14	

FAIRLY				(5)
041.29	071.08	073.05	083.01	259.15

FAIRY	(1)
095.33	

FAITH				(16)
009.08	011.12	065.02	070.33	072.01
072.01	072.02	108.13	158.31	164.02
208.01	217.31	268.28	269.03	325.05
333.15				

FAITHFUL		(2)
018.19	216.17	

FAITHFULLY				(5)
018.13	018.29	018.34	062.31	330.26

FALCONRY	(1)
316.30	

FALL				(30)
010.01	018.02	045.16	064.27	074.28
097.18	113.36	114.15	132.22	166.17
172.06	179.23	179.25	181.07	181.19
185.02	187.34	188.07	194.28	217.13
227.14	233.24	236.31	275.02	277.24
293.10	301.10	316.38	323.14	327.24

FALLEN				(5)
124.30	141.02	156.02	180.09	323.19

FALLING				(6)
111.30	159.14	180.03	181.24	213.34
275.01				

FALLOW		(2)
082.02	294.27	

FALLS				(9)
137.20	170.08	180.17	181.10	188.17
211.01	291.19	314.23	332.28	

FALSE				(5)
024.10	024.15	033.29	202.04	327.30

FALSEHOOD		(2)
008.26	076.30	

FALSELY		(2)
080.19	221.25	

FAME				(9)
007.33	086.07	089.02	099.08	161.01
184.07	284.26	330.34	331.05	

FAMILIAR				(11)
106.25	113.18	130.11	210.15	225.31
228.21	271.04	272.04	275.36	276.07
280.25				

FAMILIAS	(1)
163.13	

FAMILIES				(9)
003.20	015.10	030.21	034.06	039.22
046.06	087.30	268.34	281.19	

FAMILY				(29)
027.22	030.13	030.15	031.20	037.31
037.32	039.24	044.01	064.26	072.26
099.08	103.17	109.31	174.32	204.21
204.30	206.11	232.23	243.03	250.32
258.17	258.30	259.10	260.20	261.09
263.30	265.03	265.07	333.24	

FAMINE		(2)
033.14	136.29	

FAMOUS				(5)
127.08	258.24	263.21	279.20	329.22

FAN	(1)
114.15	

FANCIED			(3)
085.01	132.06	313.25	

FANCIFUL		(2)
024.14	254.36	

FANCIFULLY	(1)
308.01	

FANCY				(8)
008.02	037.15	125.08	168.31	193.33
202.19	215.17	242.22		

FANTASTIC	(1)
119.16	

```
FAR                      ( 100)   FASTENED                        (  6)
012.36 015.34 022.30 023.09 026.36   172.04 198.32 229.14 231.11 261.05
029.23 030.08 031.30 040.06 050.23   284.11
058.25 059.34 063.31 064.22 072.33 FASTER                          (  2)
073.17 075.15 076.28 078.28 081.24   118.03 235.24
081.25 082.05 082.20 086.13 088.01 FASTING                         (  1)
088.05 090.22 102.03 105.08 107.05   143.19
109.18 111.34 116.34 117.25 117.35 FAT                             (  4)
119.16 120.04 121.21 125.06 125.20   215.35 252.05 252.10 306.24
130.03 131.17 133.09 135.17 137.11 FATAL                           (  3)
141.23 143.26 144.06 144.08 144.24   024.16 318.28 325.25
150.33 158.01 160.06 161.05 162.10 FATALLY                         (  2)
162.18 174.06 174.24 181.17 189.21   265.26 325.23
198.29 200.04 201.25 207.22 208.29 FATE                            ( 10)
212.17 213.08 214.34 217.28 223.22   005.26 007.36 020.33 111.18 118.14
232.18 232.25 236.16 236.30 236.33   118.23 164.16 215.15 230.22 263.16
239.03 245.02 245.03 259.20 259.29 FATES                           (  4)
260.03 260.25 267.23 271.27 272.01   008.05 025.05 191.34 320.16
277.08 277.13 278.11 278.21 283.34 FATHER                          ( 15)
284.36 288.14 289.20 290.31 293.15   032.12 051.36 052.10 067.31 071.12
294.11 324.20 326.11 326.19 333.03   096.17 101.16 145.07 199.07 204.09
                         (  8)         204.11 205.01 261.03 308.14 317.06
FARE                              FATHERLAND                      (  2)
034.21 053.09 053.14 054.01 070.11   039.31 160.28
203.05 211.26 214.33              FATHERS                         (  7)
FARINAM                   (  1)      015.08 032.08 076.22 164.12 213.13
063.17                               260.28 264.16
FARM                      ( 39)   FATHOM                          (  1)
018.21 022.25 032.25 032.25 032.33   285.32
039.12 055.03 055.11 056.02 056.09 FATHOMED                        (  2)
056.19 060.15 060.23 081.12 082.18   179.16 287.01
082.19 082.21 082.34 082.37 083.04 FATHOMS                         (  1)
084.06 084.10 093.15 108.09 115.32   287.29
145.08 195.29 196.20 196.24 196.31 FATIGUED                        (  1)
197.02 201.01 203.07 208.04 232.35   221.03
257.03 278.15 279.13 294.36       FATNESS                         (  1)
FARMER                    ( 39)      138.22
009.19 033.18 033.33 037.26 046.19 FATTED                          (  1)
054.26 055.26 056.08 057.10 063.35   239.18
064.25 064.27 064.29 081.10 082.35 FATTENED                        (  1)
083.03 100.25 115.02 115.24 116.27   224.11
135.31 136.07 157.30 158.22 165.28 FAULT                           (  3)
165.37 166.30 195.28 199.33 204.34   325.14 325.25 328.08
221.34 223.11 238.08 251.20 267.23 FAULTS                          (  3)
268.01 294.22 294.28 333.09         095.18 314.39 328.08
FARMERS                   ( 16)   FAUNS                           (  1)
017.24 032.15 033.02 095.22 109.15   220.11
117.35 121.12 153.05 156.23 162.07 FAUX                            (  1)
162.35 196.29 196.30 207.32 250.25   208.20
265.11                            FAVOR                           (  2)
FARMING                   (  4)      007.05 324.01
005.05 083.33 294.19 297.21       FAVORABLE                       (  6)
FARMS                     (  8)      099.20 123.03 144.02 160.14 160.22
005.04 032.19 032.30 081.08 082.06   210.30
165.25 267.25 320.15              FAVORED                         (  1)
FARTHER                   ( 19)      131.23
013.01 035.02 057.36 125.04 126.04 FAVORING                        (  2)
137.36 141.29 173.05 207.22 208.28   294.10 298.17
224.20 228.32 236.04 245.20 249.11 FEAR                            ( 21)
258.15 261.13 290.18 322.17         056.29 074.22 099.10 129.23 154.12
FARTHEST                  (  5)      219.14 220.10 224.29 226.34 255.09
097.01 216.30 235.13 267.35 322.24   256.27 276.02 277.28 281.04 283.18
FASHION                   ( 10)      285.23 310.18 316.01 316.04 323.18
025.21 039.14 039.27 075.11 103.09   324.18
118.10 120.11 206.20 254.19 294.15 FEARED                          (  3)
FASHIONABLE               (  4)      154.13 269.31 324.32
022.06 026.28 036.16 075.24       FEARING                         (  1)
FASHIONED                 (  1)      143.19
127.34                            FEARS                           (  3)
FASHIONS                  (  4)      007.31 078.24 096.03
026.08 036.33 134.10 283.14       FEAST                           (  4)
FAST                      ( 14)      068.09 068.29 142.35 165.31
006.32 052.28 068.21 092.13 095.27 FEATHER                         (  1)
097.11 097.19 097.19 113.05 137.20   045.11
229.11 294.09 313.13 320.08       FEATHERS                        (  3)
FASTED                    (  1)      149.17 266.10 306.32
068.20                            FEATURE                         (  2)
FASTEN                    (  1)      171.03 186.13
140.04
```

74

FEATURED   (2)
157.29 157.30
FEATURES   (3)
197.03 221.32 318.04
FEB   (1)
279.27
FEBRUARY   (1)
301.13
FED   (10)
015.14 034.29 138.22 164.25 214.23
215.21 218.07 223.25 276.27 279.14
FEEBLE   (2)
107.24 231.12
FEEBLER   (1)
127.17
FEEBLEST   (1)
106.11
FEED   (9)
006.21 039.05 074.26 088.20 147.21
215.21 239.17 248.36 276.14
FEEDER   (1)
215.15
FEEDING   (2)
215.06 318.10
FEEL   (25)
003.16 003.21 024.01 041.32 066.22
076.30 087.25 098.13 098.17 098.29
119.24 122.34 133.05 133.12 135.33
141.17 169.32 175.18 194.25 214.02
215.27 306.14 314.38 330.26 333.15
FEELER   (1)
231.01
FEELERS   (2)
229.17 231.13
FEELING   (6)
116.32 170.31 175.10 261.04 266.27
307.15
FEELINGS   (3)
211.30 211.34 231.24
FEELS   (2)
103.16 216.18
FEET   (82)
005.18 005.23 023.18 029.09 030.03
030.03 038.18 039.14 043.08 043.21
044.25 048.14 048.29 048.29 067.22
097.33 098.29 114.07 116.19 124.13
156.30 163.28 168.32 169.32 170.03
170.15 170.32 175.03 175.08 175.09
176.02 176.03 177.35 177.35 178.09
180.05 180.23 180.35 181.03 181.29
182.03 182.04 183.32 185.14 185.15
187.05 194.30 195.08 198.15 198.23
201.28 209.05 225.30 227.25 228.12
233.08 235.18 236.07 249.36 255.06
256.15 265.15 265.34 266.08 271.26
283.02 283.09 287.06 287.07 288.35
290.18 290.20 292.24 293.12 296.03
305.15 306.02 310.14 323.16 323.21
327.20 332.05
FELL   (18)
006.08 075.09 089.19 114.01 141.34
162.02 190.07 191.12 193.02 226.36
239.01 258.04 259.25 266.11 274.25
290.12 310.22 310.28
FELLED   (3)
146.18 315.19 316.07
FELLERS   (1)
146.34
FELLING   (1)
146.13
FELLOW   (16)
019.27 041.02 058.23 069.19 073.21
074.30 076.19 112.20 151.28 158.01
171.30 213.13 245.26 272.34 274.31
275.05
FELLOWS   (9)
072.36 078.06 084.03 109.02 131.26
133.16 135.29 213.36 295.02

FELT   (20)
022.36 131.28 142.11 160.27 161.01
169.34 170.03 190.20 210.06 211.31
231.23 233.13 240.17 250.25 254.21
259.35 261.07 266.11 276.04 301.19
FEMALE   (1)
233.03
FENCE   (7)
083.01 130.20 163.07 169.10 188.24
249.16 324.26
FENCED   (2)
130.12 208.10
FENCES   (5)
018.20 083.12 250.11 281.34 320.13
FENCING   (1)
151.15
FENDA   (1)
258.10
FERARUM   (1)
250.15
FERMENTATIONS   (1)
062.23
FEROCITY   (2)
231.05 231.25
FERTILE   (3)
100.17 184.13 194.22
FERTILITY   (4)
089.07 137.35 155.23 308.21
FERTILIZING   (1)
008.28
FERULE   (1)
327.09
FESTAL   (1)
126.14
FESTIVAL   (1)
165.26
FESTIVE   (1)
333.24
FESTOONS   (2)
157.18 201.12
FETCH   (2)
008.32 224.36
FETCHED   (1)
245.02
FETTERS   (2)
016.26 303.11
FEW   (72)
005.22 012.11 012.15 014.05 014.07
022.20 026.25 029.13 030.12 045.22
048.06 048.36 053.34 055.36 057.04
057.14 064.09 065.11 077.32 082.35
085.12 090.22 092.30 093.13 094.04
094.22 100.26 101.35 101.35 106.03
117.22 120.13 122.22 124.13 131.30
132.18 137.03 159.19 168.24 172.11
173.13 178.35 180.30 183.32 184.04
184.21 184.33 186.09 187.11 190.07
192.32 202.36 211.08 214.25 226.24
232.33 234.09 234.21 241.24 251.23
252.05 257.09 257.15 258.19 267.25
273.33 285.04 290.26 299.21 303.12
304.28 309.24
FEWER   (3)
049.01 144.03 188.21
FEWEST   (2)
019.36 269.15
FIBRE   (2)
161.32 307.30
FIBROUS   (1)
182.02
FICTILE   (1)
261.32
FICTION   (1)
135.16
FIDELITY   (3)
122.12 232.02 315.36
FIELD   (50)
005.08 018.23 028.23 041.08 057.35

FIRMLY   (CONTINUED)
293.04

FIRST (121)

```
003.24  003.27  003.32  009.11  012.10
012.27  021.26  025.28  027.34  028.06
028.35  030.11  038.20  038.34  038.36
039.05  039.12  039.26  040.01  040.09
043.05  048.26  052.31  053.08  054.07
055.04  062.01  062.17  062.19  062.28
066.35  068.09  072.12  078.33  084.15
084.26  086.11  098.24  099.25  099.35
101.31  107.26  111.20  114.07  120.01
123.24  130.27  137.18  145.28  148.06
149.28  150.35  151.32  163.28  163.30
164.15  166.36  168.10  168.23  171.20
176.08  177.02  179.32  179.34  182.27
185.18  191.11  191.14  191.20  192.34
195.19  201.30  208.14  211.27  212.14
213.01  214.04  230.34  236.05  239.36
242.24  246.16  246.35  248.16  249.02
258.29  260.02  260.26  262.29  264.21
268.23  272.08  273.30  274.20  275.22
281.04  282.21  282.34  291.30  296.08
297.21  299.15  302.18  303.01  304.15
306.08  307.12  309.25  310.23  310.32
312.15  313.03  314.35  315.34  317.17
319.02  319.18  328.03  332.27  333.10
333.20
```

FIRSTLY (1)
039.28

FISH (34)
```
059.33  098.22  114.30  120.15  120.18
120.29  130.29  178.03  180.31  184.07
184.09  184.13  184.24  185.24  187.04
187.16  188.07  194.22  206.09  206.27
206.30  207.21  210.04  211.26  213.04
213.17  213.34  214.22  224.13  235.15
239.05  283.36  285.02  311.34
```

FISHED (3)
130.30 211.26 214.03

FISHER (4)
173.31 213.01 214.10 297.32

FISHERIES (1)
120.17

FISHERMAN (9)
184.01 199.13 203.32 211.01 214.07
214.08 284.02 284.07 284.19

FISHERMEN (5)
154.16 173.33 210.27 271.12 301.31

FISHERS (2)
211.27 212.17

FISHES (18)
122.33 143.14 174.23 175.07 175.22
184.26 187.09 196.05 211.34 235.21
269.30 283.03 284.22 294.08 301.29
301.32 311.31 317.15

FISHHAWK (2)
114.28 185.07

FISHING (22)
098.19 170.17 173.26 174.34 181.01
190.30 203.04 205.05 210.20 211.12
211.16 211.30 213.14 213.19 213.23
213.25 223.03 224.02 224.25 283.11
283.23 316.19

FIST (1)
264.03

FIT (13)
018.08 023.22 023.31 026.16 061.05
064.18 085.06 095.23 102.34 177.32
198.35 201.09 232.12

FITCHBURG (4)
043.02 053.05 053.17 115.13

FITNESS (1)
046.02

FITS (4)
004.07 021.33 262.29 273.32

FITTED (1)
027.33

FITTEST (1)
269.23

FITTING (3)
050.34 125.36 148.23

FIVE (41)
005.17 024.30 030.36 038.18 043.08
043.30 043.31 069.09 091.36 093.03
109.23 114.06 124.03 124.07 132.36
133.22 140.15 161.18 163.17 177.34
178.08 178.09 180.23 180.28 180.35
183.13 184.09 189.30 228.12 232.10
248.09 252.15 284.09 287.06 289.28
296.03 296.16 297.13 302.34 321.32
323.17

FIX (2)
079.14 080.21

FIXED (2)
045.22 274.04

FIXTURE (1)
020.08

FLABBIEST (1)
126.32

FLAG (4)
127.27 178.34 199.15 199.15

FLAGS (1)
195.05

FLAKES (4)
029.34 189.03 247.30 310.27

FLAME (4)
068.28 252.38 254.29 311.03

FLAMES (3)
004.21 093.20 310.34

FLANNEL (1)
075.33

FLAP (1)
306.26

FLAPPED (1)
266.23

FLAPPING (2)
052.32 313.09

FLASH (2)
187.06 188.17

FLASHES (1)
203.32

FLAT (8)
040.22 145.13 194.33 226.26 263.10
285.20 305.29 305.31

FLATTED (1)
233.10

FLATTER (4)
108.25 131.27 131.28 305.27

FLATTERED (1)
108.26

FLATTERING (1)
007.06

FLATTISH (1)
248.04

FLATULENCY (1)
272.36

FLAVIATILIS (1)
246.08

FLAVOR (6)
059.39 062.05 077.06 126.16 173.11
173.14

FLAXEN (2)
119.26 175.06

FLEE (1)
207.34

FLEET (1)
115.10

FLEETING (2)
102.03 329.30

FLEETS (1)
201.04

FLESH (5)
005.23 214.12 215.35 221.31 318.24

FLESHED (1)
184.28

FLESHY (1)
307.30
FLEW (3)
226.20 272.14 275.26
FLICKERING (1)
242.20
FLIES (1)
117.13
FLIGHT (4)
189.36 237.05 252.30 316.33
FLIGHTS (1)
107.28
FLINT (13)
181.12 194.05 194.15 194.19 195.27
195.31 197.10 201.08 249.03 271.05
299.16 299.27 301.14
FLIT (2)
255.04 275.13
FLITTED (1)
111.29
FLITTING (2)
114.32 275.32
FLOAT (6)
087.13 159.22 188.32 191.12 269.33
332.29
FLOATED (4)
087.21 204.21 293.20 302.26
FLOATING (9)
117.12 164.29 173.27 187.09 189.34
191.06 191.29 297.32 298.20
FLOATS (1)
116.27
FLOCK (5)
128.05 190.01 248.34 275.30 295.11
FLOCKS (8)
070.02 088.19 088.23 121.33 238.34
269.34 275.24 313.22
FLOOD (4)
021.13 087.18 260.11 333.01
FLOOR (16)
038.08 039.18 042.19 043.15 043.19
112.36 113.03 128.02 142.01 225.28
241.25 262.23 280.30 283.05 311.27
332.11
FLOORING (1)
280.27
FLOUNDERED (1)
267.07
FLOUNDERING (1)
266.01
FLOUR (4)
059.16 062.05 063.36 295.29
FLOURISH (2)
080.12 239.29
FLOURISHES (2)
146.02 200.03
FLOURISHING (3)
079.13 110.10 280.17
FLOW (9)
079.16 194.11 305.03 306.25 307.08
307.33 307.35 308.13 308.14
FLOWED (2)
194.10 307.02
FLOWER (5)
077.04 079.03 114.18 130.02 238.32
FLOWERING (3)
016.03 220.01 239.21
FLOWERS (14)
112.20 113.35 129.26 153.04 155.17
196.07 196.25 199.19 200.02 216.26
263.25 284.30 309.05 316.16
FLOWERY (1)
308.28
FLOWING (4)
087.01 293.27 304.30 305.26
FLOWS (5)
220.03 292.11 305.09 307.25 309.11

FLUCTUATING (2)
063.30 092.02
FLUCTUATION (3)
181.07 181.32 293.01
FLUID (1)
307.17
FLURRIES (1)
041.12
FLUTE (4)
155.35 174.16 222.05 222.11
FLUTTER (2)
223.10 316.34
FLUTTERED (1)
228.19
FLUTTERING (2)
129.12 306.35
FLUVIATILE (1)
186.15
FLY (7)
124.11 137.14 165.13 215.11 226.07
283.34 313.29
FLYING (8)
053.01 114.26 228.08 233.17 248.30
312.30 313.21 324.15
FODDER (4)
007.27 117.05 157.28 157.28
FODDERING (1)
109.08
FOE (3)
042.31 229.27 230.03
FOES (4)
155.30 231.08 234.01 239.24
FOG (4)
042.05 119.05 302.32 302.33
FOGGY (2)
042.03 313.18
FOGS (2)
083.09 302.14
FOLDS (1)
201.19
FOLIACEOUS (2)
306.15 308.33
FOLIAGE (4)
305.18 306.03 306.05 306.08
FOLKS (4)
115.05 133.06 135.36 154.09
FOLLOW (11)
036.34 056.09 056.36 066.22 093.18
112.33 138.34 153.18 252.17 278.25
283.14
FOLLOWED (5)
019.09 050.29 216.20 279.04 302.32
FOLLOWING (9)
003.03 050.27 068.30 117.11 198.01
260.18 277.01 279.24 296.26
FOLLOWS (3)
026.08 048.35 176.08
FONDNESS (1)
016.12
FOOD (43)
009.20 012.14 012.18 012.21 012.25
013.08 013.18 013.20 013.26 013.35
014.01 015.21 037.20 039.29 046.05
059.01 060.16 060.42 061.16 064.23
065.01 143.20 143.30 205.14 214.20
214.28 214.31 215.02 215.03 215.29
217.33 218.02 218.10 218.11 218.15
218.20 238.06 238.17 251.24 252.06
265.02 274.23 330.35
FOOL (1)
005.29
FOOLISH (1)
020.03
FOOLISHLY (2)
069.33 330.24
FOOT (35)
004.26 029.02 053.12 136.29 143.03
143.09 162.02 180.22 185.16 192.23

78

FOOT   (CONTINUED)
  198.33 218.23 226.19 228.09 233.28
  248.14 256.27 262.11 280.18 281.16
  282.27 282.28 283.01 283.01 284.13
  288.33 290.19 299.29 300.10 302.24
  302.30 305.11 305.27 317.01 322.34
FOOTPATH   (1)
  113.29
FOOTSTEPS   (1)
  179.35
FOR   (885)
  003.35 004.03 004.06 004.23 004.25
  004.33 005.05 005.25 006.06 006.14
  006.15 006.28 006.30 006.31 006.35
  007.01 007.11 007.29 008.14 008.28
  008.30 008.31 009.01 009.01 009.07
  009.20 009.33 009.34 010.11 010.14
  010.24 010.25 011.29 012.03 012.19
  012.21 013.13 013.15 013.18 013.24
  014.06 014.11 015.28 015.32 015.33
  016.02 017.06 017.24 018.02 018.06
  018.09 018.12 018.28 019.14 019.29
  020.01 020.22 020.31 021.08 021.21
  021.24 022.04 022.13 022.14 022.18
  022.18 023.02 023.07 023.14 023.15
  024.08 024.27 024.30 024.31 024.32
  024.33 024.34 025.02 025.09 025.32
  026.20 027.08 027.10 027.26 028.10
  028.13 029.05 029.07 029.12 029.20
  029.25 030.16 030.25 031.15 031.21
  031.27 031.35 032.17 032.23 032.33
  033.24 033.30 033.34 034.02 034.07
  035.05 035.34 036.04 036.10 036.31
  036.36 037.09 037.27 037.28 037.31
  037.32 038.01 038.02 038.03 038.06
  038.06 038.15 038.30 038.30 038.36
  039.07 039.08 039.19 039.22 039.27
  040.03 040.04 040.23 040.36 041.13
  041.23 041.30 042.01 042.06 042.23
  042.29 042.36 042.38 043.02 043.12
  043.15 043.29 044.04 044.31 044.32
  045.05 045.11 045.17 045.32 045.35
  046.05 046.21 046.23 047.19 048.12
  048.16 048.20 048.33 049.06 049.32
  049.33 049.36 049.36 049.40 050.04
  050.20 050.22 050.23 050.34 050.34
  050.36 051.18 051.33 052.14 053.11
  053.20 053.31 054.25 054.27 054.32
  054.35 055.02 055.04 055.04 055.27
  055.34 056.08 056.28 056.28 056.29
  057.07 057.07 057.08 057.12 057.14
  058.05 058.08 058.11 058.12 058.12
  058.22 058.30 058.34 059.01 059.33
  059.37 060.07 060.08 060.23 060.36
  061.02 061.29 061.29 062.29 062.35
  063.05 063.27 063.31 063.34 064.03
  064.12 064.17 064.18 064.27 064.30
  064.32 065.02 065.05 065.07 065.08
  065.12 065.22 065.23 065.26 066.03
  066.28 067.12 067.12 067.26 068.05
  068.20 068.30 068.36 069.09 069.13
  069.16 069.19 069.20 069.26 069.30
  070.18 070.23 070.24 071.07 071.09
  071.18 071.21 071.22 071.25 072.27
  072.27 073.02 073.03 073.03 073.22
  073.24 074.13 074.17 074.19 074.22
  074.30 075.10 076.05 076.34 077.03
  077.22 077.34 078.10 078.17 079.15
  080.27 081.02 081.08 081.14 081.15
  081.22 081.26 082.02 082.19 082.21
  082.24 082.24 082.36 083.26 083.28
  083.29 084.04 084.20 084.29 085.25
  085.30 086.10 087.26 087.29 089.09
  090.08 090.10 091.11 091.19 091.30
  092.11 092.11 093.02 093.04 093.10
  093.13 093.29 093.30 094.03 094.10
  094.19 094.29 094.30 095.03 095.05
  095.23 095.29 097.12 097.26 097.30

FOR   (CONTINUED)
  098.31 099.05 099.07 099.35 100.09
  100.28 100.31 101.09 101.22 101.30
  102.31 103.15 103.21 103.27 104.09
  104.28 104.35 105.10 105.11 106.04
  106.04 106.09 106.14 106.14 106.21
  106.32 107.07 107.24 107.35 108.01
  108.24 108.26 108.29 108.32 109.17
  109.23 112.03 112.14 112.15 112.18
  112.18 112.19 112.26 114.33 114.36
  115.10 115.19 115.33 116.09 116.17
  116.25 116.36 117.13 117.17 118.08
  118.20 118.31 118.33 120.18 120.24
  120.29 121.01 121.06 121.12 121.15
  122.23 122.34 123.24 123.36 125.22
  125.26 126.12 126.21 126.36 127.03
  127.16 127.36 128.14 128.17 130.13
  130.14 130.21 130.29 131.05 131.16
  131.20 131.21 131.21 131.31 132.23
  134.06 135.24 136.01 136.12 136.21
  136.22 137.34 138.02 138.14 138.22
  138.30 140.05 140.09 140.10 140.10
  140.12 140.20 140.22 140.27 140.33
  141.25 141.33 142.09 142.23 142.29
  142.31 142.34 143.11 143.16 143.20
  143.21 143.24 143.26 143.35 144.08
  144.19 144.21 144.26 144.35 145.05
  145.17 145.28 145.36 147.13 147.20
  147.33 147.34 148.04 149.14 149.22
  149.31 149.32 150.12 150.30 150.31
  151.22 151.22 152.07 153.29 154.12
  154.18 154.21 155.05 155.23 155.26
  155.29 156.04 156.19 157.21 157.24
  157.25 157.27 157.28 157.35 158.18
  159.13 161.02 161.03 161.03 161.16
  161.23 162.09 162.11 162.13 162.18
  162.33 163.01 163.03 163.03 163.30
  163.31 163.32 164.05 164.05 164.17
  164.18 164.23 164.28 164.31 165.04
  166.22 167.05 167.08 167.29 168.23
  168.36 169.08 169.21 169.35 170.30
  171.11 171.27 172.02 173.10 173.12
  173.24 173.33 174.02 175.29 177.32
  178.27 180.28 180.34 181.09 181.13
  181.21 181.25 182.03 182.31 183.04
  183.06 183.30 185.19 185.21 185.35
  186.33 187.17 187.25 190.22 191.01
  191.13 191.13 191.28 192.02 192.07
  193.07 193.36 195.26 195.36 196.04
  196.18 196.23 196.23 196.27 196.32
  198.35 198.35 199.12 201.22 202.15
  202.35 203.26 203.33 204.03 204.34
  204.37 205.14 205.16 205.20 205.29
  205.35 206.09 206.12 206.35 207.16
  210.08 210.14 210.30 211.06 211.11
  211.22 211.26 211.31 211.35 212.05
  212.09 212.15 213.12 213.16 213.23
  213.29 213.30 213.36 214.18 214.27
  215.30 216.23 217.03 217.06 217.09
  218.20 218.21 218.22 218.23 218.33
  219.02 219.03 219.30 220.08 221.22
  222.13 222.18 223.16 223.20 223.22
  224.02 224.07 224.21 224.31 225.06
  225.14 225.18 226.08 226.24 226.30
  227.19 228.05 228.08 229.16 229.28
  229.33 230.05 230.16 230.17 230.18
  230.18 230.21 230.24 231.04 231.23
  232.20 232.24 233.18 233.21 233.22
  233.33 234.14 234.17 234.19 234.26
  235.16 235.19 235.27 235.29 236.31
  237.08 238.05 238.05 238.17 238.18
  238.20 238.24 238.25 238.28 239.04
  239.05 240.09 241.25 241.26 241.28
  241.29 242.25 242.32 243.08 243.35
  244.22 245.17 245.29 246.08 246.19
  246.20 246.27 246.29 246.31 247.26
  248.32 249.02 249.17 249.18 250.06
  251.05 251.16 251.18 251.36 252.06

```
FOR                          (CONTINUED)         FORESTAE                              ( 1)
253.22  254.01  254.13  254.16  254.37            250.15
255.03  256.07  256.11  256.15  256.16           FORESTER                              ( 1)
256.30  257.22  257.23  258.24  259.19            096.15
260.13  261.04  261.08  261.20  262.20           FORESTS                               ( 5)
262.32  264.20  264.35  265.01  265.09            166.09  190.27  249.24  263.29  317.27
265.20  265.27  266.31  266.33  267.33           FOREVER                               ( 19)
268.03  268.08  268.26  268.35  269.12            046.12  078.22  085.11  088.07  088.33
269.13  269.18  270.01  270.16  271.14            091.15  092.02  102.06  104.22  109.05
271.33  273.10  273.12  273.22  273.35            111.12  138.08  154.02  167.31  199.27
274.04  274.13  274.19  275.01  275.17            213.25  219.01  297.15  324.33
275.21  275.29  276.03  276.18  276.22           FORGE                                 ( 1)
277.04  277.24  277.25  277.28  277.29            092.19
277.29  278.01  278.15  278.23  279.07           FORGED                                ( 1)
279.08  279.13  279.18  279.29  279.30            016.25
279.31  280.10  280.14  280.14  280.22           FORGET                                ( 9)
282.32  283.23  283.24  283.31  285.14            025.34  103.32  149.25  166.08  193.37
285.20  285.30  285.33  287.08  287.12            201.20  216.31  268.17  312.17
287.16  287.21  287.22  288.10  288.35           FORGETTING                            ( 2)
289.25  290.05  291.22  292.02  292.04            103.31  111.06
292.06  292.08  292.11  293.13  293.17           FORGIVEN                              ( 1)
293.19  294.05  295.05  296.05  296.20            314.27
296.22  297.01  297.11  297.18  298.09           FORGIVING                             ( 1)
298.14  299.04  299.07  301.16  302.17            075.12
302.18  302.20  302.28  303.22  303.29           FORGOT                                ( 1)
303.35  306.03  306.07  306.14  307.20            062.33
308.18  311.10  312.16  312.17  313.07           FORGOTTEN                             ( 7)
313.17  314.24  314.32  315.02  315.03            037.29  037.36  147.29  239.20  254.17
316.32  317.26  318.18  319.07  320.09            314.40  328.04
320.25  321.01  321.14  323.04  323.10           FORKED                                ( 1)
323.13  323.15  323.26  324.29  325.19            203.32
326.14  326.27  326.29  326.30  327.20           FORKS                                 ( 1)
327.23  327.29  329.08  330.26  331.09            065.22
331.11  333.09  333.14  333.18  333.23           FORLORN                               ( 2)
FORBID                                ( 1)         207.15  271.34
194.10                                           FORM                                  ( 30)
FORBIDDEN                             ( 2)         007.19  011.08  015.14  025.02  059.09
089.06  201.22                                    063.34  086.35  104.25  121.05  136.09
FORC                                  ( 1)         141.05  157.12  191.25  195.26  219.32
080.18                                            221.17  242.28  248.08  252.33  261.20
FORCE                                 ( 3)         263.17  269.34  280.26  289.32  291.01
089.15  254.27  310.21                            291.25  297.33  305.29  305.31  307.26
FORCED                                ( 2)        FORMAL                                ( 2)
039.06  040.05                                    322.31  323.01
FORCES                                ( 1)        FORMED                                ( 10)
063.04                                            185.19  191.23  195.19  247.16  247.20
FORCIBLY                              ( 1)         248.01  267.06  295.30  295.34  307.12
171.31                                           FORMER                                ( 16)
FORE                                  ( 2)         030.02  034.20  056.16  064.03  118.05
098.32  230.03                                    148.26  166.11  167.29  178.01  211.13
FOREBODINGS                           ( 1)         256.01  256.17  283.33  299.22  326.19
124.30                                            327.21
FOREFATHERS                           ( 3)        FORMERLY                              ( 10)
040.06  064.12  110.06                            027.27  029.04  044.23  069.25  174.19
FOREGROUND                            ( 1)         191.17  198.07  227.27  252.10  279.36
185.36                                           FORMING                               ( 2)
FOREIGN                               ( 9)         233.11  252.14
007.19  094.24  095.10  119.22  127.22           FORMS                                 ( 15)
223.33  284.22  284.23  316.08                    004.28  035.07  113.23  177.02  220.26
FOREKNOWLEDGE                         ( 1)         242.21  293.23  304.29  305.10  305.17
263.17                                            305.33  305.35  307.20  309.11  310.03
FORELEG                               ( 1)        FORMULA                               ( 2)
230.35                                            033.19  290.05
FOREMOST                              ( 2)        FORSAKE                               ( 6)
104.25  259.19                                    073.08  078.09  090.17  093.18  170.08
FORENOON                              ( 6)         277.25
132.23  167.04  191.32  191.36  198.24           FORSAKEN                              ( 2)
274.32                                            142.10  201.06
FORESEE                               ( 3)        FORSAKING                             ( 1)
011.24  131.35  294.02                            112.03
FOREST                                ( 34)       FORSOOTH                              ( 6)
012.17  018.14  085.35  113.28  128.10            048.05  050.13  120.13  196.16  264.08
129.29  130.14  174.19  185.32  188.20            320.16
193.10  198.07  212.37  249.14  249.16           FORT                                  ( 1)
250.09  250.12  250.13  250.16  250.25            296.09
251.14  251.18  251.24  252.20  254.14           FORTH                                 ( 15)
256.23  273.09  274.05  281.13  281.28            039.04  182.02  186.06  187.31  195.16
312.28  315.18  326.27  332.11                    249.20  267.13  268.12  277.01  308.31
```

```
FORTH                    (CONTINUED)
309.26  311.02  311.15  331.19  333.25
FORTHWITH                        (   2)
077.23  219.27
FORTITUDE                        (   1)
080.19
FORTNIGHT                        (   4)
065.07  172.06  241.28  264.35
FORTUNE                          (   3)
054.07  109.20  112.08
FORTUNES                         (   2)
254.32  258.11
FORTY                            (  15)
005.18  032.18  070.27  143.16  175.02
175.08  176.01  197.12  198.23  247.06
247.18  252.11  275.07  290.10  306.01
FORUM                            (   2)
102.09  104.06
FORWARD                          (  10)
112.18  151.35  152.25  155.30  156.31
168.04  279.02  282.12  306.31  307.13
FOSSIL                           (   1)
309.05
FOUGHT                           (   4)
229.10  229.21  230.24  231.34
FOUND                            (  70)
014.36  023.13  024.09  025.01  030.04
032.26  034.22  044.33  045.35  049.32
058.07  062.06  064.07  069.10  069.15
069.21  070.25  071.09  076.13  082.24
085.30  098.06  102.09  112.22  131.05
133.17  133.24  135.23  141.09  142.18
143.25  147.36  151.08  159.20  172.18
185.22  190.31  195.12  203.28  204.06
210.10  210.15  213.33  217.17  222.08
224.21  225.24  227.01  235.27  239.05
239.15  247.18  265.06  266.29  267.19
277.35  279.26  287.15  288.24  289.16
290.17  292.11  292.28  296.21  303.28
304.11  322.38  325.26  325.26  327.01
FOUNDATION                       (  12)
021.11  038.11  038.30  045.13  045.33
046.31  051.01  256.34  270.01  285.14
324.30  330.12
FOUNDATIONS                      (   4)
050.32  096.09  245.14  324.08
FOUNDED                          (   2)
120.14  138.02
FOUNDER                          (   2)
091.31  103.17
FOUNDING                         (   2)
050.26  099.08
FOUNTAIN                         (   4)
138.29  179.30  188.09  262.18
FOUR                             (  31)
004.19  039.22  039.32  043.30  068.30
105.25  119.35  124.07  132.36  155.31
178.08  182.04  183.06  184.05  187.05
195.14  227.25  228.12  248.05  252.15
253.02  280.12  284.09  287.30  288.09
288.36  293.14  300.05  301.23  303.35
325.16
FOURTEEN                         (   2)
198.17  211.16
FOURTH                           (   7)
050.11  068.25  084.29  104.24  120.02
231.35  319.01
FOWL                             (   5)
190.29  196.06  236.09  304.10  317.32
FOWLING                          (   3)
211.15  211.31  211.35
FOWLS                            (   1)
024.04
FOX                              (  22)
066.10  117.31  122.15  128.06  129.21
152.18  232.15  233.09  263.14  276.35
277.05  277.07  277.15  277.24  278.03
278.12  278.17  278.26  278.33  279.04

FOX                     (CONTINUED)
279.20  279.25
FOXES                            (   3)
030.19  174.35  273.06
FRACTION                         (   1)
030.24
FRAGILE                          (   1)
310.09
FRAGMENT                         (   1)
309.01
FRAGRANCE                        (   6)
042.29  062.12  077.05  089.18  216.25
238.05
FRAGRANT                         (   1)
325.06
FRAME                            (   3)
045.06  085.22  224.24
FRAMED                           (   3)
042.38  043.27  332.33
FRANCE                           (   2)
202.28  322.12
FRANKINCENSE                     (   1)
325.06
FRANKLIN                         (   1)
321.07
FRANKNESS                        (   1)
151.33
FREE                             (  27)
006.09  029.16  032.30  034.10  037.14
037.33  057.15  057.15  066.11  066.24
069.13  070.24  070.29  078.19  079.07
079.19  084.04  113.17  165.34  167.08
196.24  207.25  214.16  227.22  237.06
281.13  316.37
FREEBORN                         (   1)
269.19
FREEDOM                          (   6)
012.23  029.05  029.15  070.11  154.18
244.17
FREELY                           (   9)
049.41  075.12  087.31  194.26  221.16
271.25  273.11  315.13  318.09
FREEMAN                          (   1)
257.34
FREER                            (   2)
056.16  266.34
FREEWILL                         (   1)
263.16
FREEZE                           (   7)
044.27  253.27  288.28  293.22  299.18
300.26  331.04
FREEZES                          (   1)
246.34
FREEZING                         (   5)
074.27  245.16  246.16  293.23  299.26
FREIGHT                          (   3)
020.18  115.16  119.19
FRENCH                           (   6)
095.10  106.14  120.10  146.15  148.02
279.28
FREQUENCY                        (   1)
136.22
FREQUENT                         (   7)
085.34  136.16  185.02  185.11  190.26
196.06  274.36
FREQUENTED                       (   1)
175.27
FREQUENTER                       (   2)
140.07  257.29
FREQUENTING                      (   1)
142.24
FREQUENTLY                       (  17)
026.16  061.10  061.29  082.33  130.05
133.04  145.24  167.24  169.30  174.15
228.36  234.08  265.28  276.19  287.25
300.24  309.30
FREQUENTS                        (   1)
197.34
```

FRESCO (1)
242.23
FRESH (29)
008.32 055.38 063.32 069.27 079.10
095.24 099.14 112.34 114.14 157.01
162.23 163.29 173.07 185.21 188.28
194.31 205.12 208.31 236.03 247.10
259.24 291.34 293.24 297.12 306.13
308.32 311.08 315.07 327.20
FRESHER (1)
158.32
FRESHET (3)
098.05 098.09 119.35
FRESHETS (2)
318.07 333.05
FRESHLY (4)
044.16 084.34 262.33 304.33
FRESHNESS (1)
085.26
FRETTED (1)
112.13
FRIDAY (1)
254.11
FRIDAYS (1)
254.10
FRIED (1)
217.04
FRIEND (9)
004.35 042.31 053.07 067.16 137.28
211.23 258.29 269.01 269.01
FRIENDLINESS (2)
132.04 165.03
FRIENDLY (3)
020.33 265.08 267.02
FRIENDS (10)
068.32 069.27 081.19 135.19 173.04
180.29 212.09 253.25 326.30 328.29
FRIENDSHIP (2)
131.12 140.10
FRIGHTENING (1)
250.15
FRINGE (2)
186.16 257.16
FRINGED (1)
137.23
FRISK (1)
274.16
FRITTERED (1)
091.21
FRIVOLOUS (2)
007.17 275.04
FRIZZLED (1)
152.31
FRO (1)
178.13
FROBISHER (1)
321.11
FROCK (1)
267.26
FROG (4)
114.31 260.02 260.10 313.28
FROGS (3)
126.12 167.14 184.32
FROM (474)
003.05 003.35 004.24 006.02 006.13
008.09 009.12 010.36 011.18 012.06
012.10 012.10 012.12 012.25 012.36
013.13 013.16 013.21 014.29 015.27
015.34 017.08 017.24 017.36 020.01
020.36 021.02 021.15 022.35 025.31
026.13 028.17 028.23 028.27 029.23
029.32 030.36 031.18 033.12 035.09
036.13 037.33 039.31 043.05 043.14
045.05 045.15 046.28 047.16 049.40
051.13 051.32 051.36 052.17 052.21
054.10 054.36 055.11 055.29 055.38
057.36 059.01 060.01 060.31 060.42
061.14 061.34 062.18 062.32 063.31

FROM (CONTINUED)
064.27 064.28 065.33 066.05 066.32
068.22 068.27 068.32 069.05 069.32
070.07 070.31 070.32 071.15 073.10
073.17 073.24 074.15 074.19 076.33
077.06 077.16 080.11 081.20 081.24
081.25 083.06 083.06 083.07 083.09
083.16 085.02 085.19 086.27 086.32
087.08 087.10 087.17 087.24 088.05
088.11 089.16 089.19 089.32 093.19
094.32 095.04 096.14 096.21 098.10
099.12 099.26 101.32 102.24 106.21
106.24 107.36 109.09 111.26 111.35
113.03 113.11 113.29 114.09 114.36
115.27 116.20 117.10 119.05 119.21
119.34 120.11 121.20 121.35 123.16
125.06 125.20 126.25 126.36 127.02
127.29 129.12 129.16 130.12 130.17
130.29 132.35 133.16 134.20 134.35
135.10 135.10 137.11 137.21 138.24
140.32 142.18 142.24 143.09 144.05
144.29 145.19 150.34 151.03 151.16
151.23 151.33 152.01 152.13 152.17
153.07 155.32 156.05 157.07 158.26
159.15 159.21 159.31 159.33 161.10
161.18 162.32 163.14 165.34 166.19
166.24 166.26 166.31 167.06 167.11
167.11 167.18 168.05 169.01 169.19
171.16 171.21 172.15 173.23 174.13
174.20 174.34 174.35 175.03 176.01
176.19 176.21 176.23 176.28 176.36
179.06 180.03 180.06 180.26 180.31
180.32 181.36 182.03 182.04 182.19
182.28 183.03 183.11 183.13 184.30
185.04 185.12 185.33 185.34 186.08
186.26 187.14 187.16 187.17 187.21
187.32 188.35 189.27 191.26 193.06
194.06 195.14 195.35 196.05 196.09
197.20 197.21 197.29 198.01 198.05
198.22 199.16 200.04 201.13 203.34
204.08 204.10 204.13 204.29 205.29
207.20 207.25 208.22 208.24 208.29
208.29 211.27 213.08 214.01 214.16
214.19 215.02 215.02 216.30 217.28
218.02 218.23 219.14 219.19 219.21
220.38 220.39 222.12 223.04 223.10
223.11 223.23 226.11 226.16 226.28
227.33 227.34 228.19 229.19 229.33
231.08 232.08 232.25 234.20 234.35
235.03 235.21 236.26 236.33 237.01
240.04 240.14 240.24 241.10 241.19
241.20 242.27 242.33 243.02 244.10
244.18 244.36 245.04 245.07 245.18
245.24 246.10 247.01 247.03 248.32
251.23 252.02 252.16 252.27 252.37
254.09 254.10 254.34 255.09 256.33
257.02 257.15 258.05 259.36 260.29
261.30 264.24 265.15 265.17 266.17
266.25 267.01 267.17 267.18 267.23
267.28 267.35 269.31 270.15 270.24
271.04 271.28 271.29 272.15 272.18
272.19 272.22 274.20 274.25 275.13
275.35 276.16 276.20 277.04 277.23
277.26 278.14 278.14 279.09 280.12
280.27 281.03 282.19 282.30 284.10
284.25 285.27 285.28 287.16 288.13
289.20 290.15 290.31 291.32 291.33
293.01 293.28 293.35 294.25 295.09
295.09 295.23 296.19 296.33 296.36
297.04 297.18 297.26 298.08 299.28
300.11 300.29 300.31 301.20 303.11
303.27 303.35 304.24 306.01 306.34
307.13 307.19 307.22 307.33 308.03
308.04 308.07 308.32 309.08 309.18
310.26 311.05 311.11 311.19
311.20 311.33 312.02 312.03 312.32
313.04 313.12 314.12 314.15 315.05
315.21 315.24 315.28 316.19 316.39

FROM   (CONTINUED)
317.12   317.18   317.18   318.12   322.14
323.16   327.23   328.11   328.12   328.31
328.32   329.13   329.20   329.31   330.03
331.02   332.12   332.14   333.11
FRONDS   (1)
307.03
FRONT   (13)
090.33   113.30   118.31   128.18   128.19
132.29   226.12   229.15   234.21   244.15
263.27   322.13   324.34
FRONTIER   (1)
011.33
FRONTING   (2)
098.11   168.18
FRONTS   (1)
117.16
FROST   (10)
098.06   222.03   238.25   266.34   273.02
283.11   305.02   308.26   309.17   311.06
FROSTBITTEN   (1)
239.14
FROSTS   (5)
083.09   163.38   189.09   189.25   239.29
FROSTY   (1)
041.35
FROZE   (3)
249.02   272.10   283.28
FROZEN   (12)
029.22   119.02   177.03   248.17   249.05
271.02   272.02   277.06   295.19   297.04
297.08   297.15
FRUGAL   (1)
142.04
FRUIT   (17)
014.31   015.33   062.11   077.05   079.08
089.19   173.19   182.07   201.11   203.11
238.16   238.34   239.08   258.01   262.32
268.26   309.05
FRUITFUL   (1)
051.06
FRUITS   (16)
006.12   006.24   014.01   037.25   062.13
068.10   068.29   155.17   166.36   173.10
196.26   196.27   196.27   201.22   215.23
220.02
FRY   (2)
076.30   225.07
FRYING   (1)
065.21
FUEGO   (2)
012.35   320.17
FUEL   (19)
008.32   012.21   012.31   013.09   013.13
013.19   013.20   013.35   043.35   054.32
055.01   064.24   064.29   128.17   198.35
249.21   251.05   251.18   251.35
FUERUNT   (1)
172.26
FUGITIVE   (2)
071.17   232.11
FUL   (2)
169.12   319.13
FULFIL   (1)
033.05
FULL   (24)
025.22   062.28   063.07   073.04   086.30
118.22   140.05   153.24   182.33   189.14
190.18   201.04   201.11   227.35   229.26
242.15   260.10   278.07   294.13   301.27
308.35   311.30   312.11   327.16
FULLEST   (1)
104.34
FULLY   (1)
187.35
FUMES   (1)
308.29

FUNCTION   (2)
219.32   221.20
FUNCTIONS   (2)
077.21   221.19
FUND   (1)
031.30
FUNERAL   (1)
031.31
FUNGI   (1)
201.15
FUNGUS   (1)
196.31
FUR   (1)
233.10
FURIOUS   (1)
259.26
FURNACE   (1)
308.35
FURNISH   (2)
038.02   258.20
FURNISHED   (6)
029.28   030.07   036.30   066.05   215.05
261.15
FURNISHES   (1)
009.20
FURNITURE   (24)
036.11   036.16   036.17   036.28   065.16
065.26   065.28   065.29   065.33   066.04
066.17   066.22   066.25   066.26   067.15
068.14   070.13   092.08   113.01   113.24
142.01   242.24   244.07   333.26
FURRING   (1)
330.26
FURROW   (5)
117.09   157.32   187.26   295.02   295.20
FURROWING   (2)
163.02   294.35
FURROWS   (3)
157.34   246.25   246.30
FURTHER   (6)
103.14   104.02   141.18   163.40   192.06
243.32
FUT   (1)
224.36
FUTURE   (10)
017.04   031.30   081.29   098.08   099.19
100.03   160.31   239.17   305.21   324.33
FUTURITY   (1)
111.19
FYNE   (3)
287.28   288.06   288.11

G (1)
306.31
GABARDINE (1)
208.15
GAIN (2)
056.31 205.22
GAINED (1)
163.40
GAINER (1)
056.30
GAINS (1)
216.29
GALA (1)
160.04
GALE (2)
047.33 128.16
GALES (2)
121.35 298.22
GALLERY (1)
240.07
GALLOWS (1)
328.01
GAME (9)
051.13 211.22 212.15 235.05 250.16
273.08 279.31 320.27 320.30
GAMES (3)
008.13 207.28 211.10
GANG (2)
093.02 295.02
GANGES (3)
192.18 298.12 298.17
GANTLET (2)
168.19 169.03
GAP (1)
169.09
GAPS (1)
168.25
GARDEN (10)
079.03 083.34 085.34 137.33 155.28
166.14 262.27 263.35 276.04 328.23
GARDENS (2)
256.22 264.26
GARLIC (2)
034.29 058.17
GARMENT (6)
024.12 024.12 024.27 025.02 030.25
299.08
GARMENTS (6)
021.35 024.17 075.24 075.30 085.07
134.23
GARRET (8)
023.15 045.33 048.30 054.09 067.33
085.18 244.03 328.28
GARRETS (2)
065.26 068.01
GASPING (1)
006.28
GATE (5)
017.10 019.05 024.26 128.18 128.19
GATED (1)
057.35
GATEWAY (1)
066.21
GATHER (4)
009.36 070.03 238.06 329.02
GATHERED (5)
061.20 098.10 117.30 120.11 144.35
GATHERING (2)
137.33 252.34
GATHERS (2)
036.31 227.19
GAUGE (1)
098.08
GAUGING (1)
021.05
GAUNT (1)
280.01

GAVE (20)
044.10 063.15 082.12 082.21 084.35
100.35 147.12 149.14 162.16 189.21
196.11 233.14 252.25 257.07 259.32
268.23 295.16 299.14 304.28 318.16
GAY (1)
066.26
GAZE (3)
096.35 099.13 326.18
GAZED (1)
260.28
GAZERS (1)
067.12
GAZETTE (1)
017.35
GAZETTES (1)
027.28
GEESE (7)
128.05 179.23 185.02 248.27 248.34
312.30 313.04
GEETA (2)
057.19 298.03
GELATINOUS (1)
125.17
GEM (3)
179.32 197.20 227.11
GEMS (1)
238.07
GENERAL (8)
068.23 105.31 148.16 180.21 215.07
246.16 288.29 328.32
GENERALLY (10)
014.02 106.19 129.35 130.35 140.12
153.02 153.19 288.34 301.04 325.34
GENERATED (1)
013.23
GENERATION (10)
011.01 026.07 026.22 034.07 035.12
164.13 164.24 191.13 263.23 331.22
GENERATIONS (2)
050.35 102.34
GENERATIVE (1)
219.34
GENEROSITY (4)
007.09 076.12 100.16 165.20
GENEROUS (3)
041.01 078.09 082.20
GENEROUSLY (1)
234.03
GENIAL (6)
073.36 166.20 169.26 254.03 307.35
308.13
GENIUS (20)
056.10 057.22 073.02 073.13 089.13
089.27 101.21 103.11 103.28 103.33
110.02 112.33 137.34 150.22 178.07
207.21 216.14 216.20 218.07 220.01
GENTLE (8)
086.23 131.14 131.36 175.09 179.21
188.10 309.20 314.18
GENTLEMAN (5)
022.16 066.31 206.06 257.05 294.28
GENTLEMEN (5)
162.35 170.30 214.18 215.31 329.22
GENTLENESS (1)
310.11
GENTLY (9)
097.19 178.13 188.04 189.19 189.28
222.14 269.29 283.32 304.15
GENUINE (6)
033.04 038.16 062.02 091.07 147.16
207.09
GENUS (1)
005.34
GEOLOGICAL (1)
194.09
GEOLOGIST (1)
288.15

GEOLOGISTS (2)
305.21 309.03
GEORGE (3)
146.24 149.21 150.01
GEORGIA (1)
329.29
GERBILLE (1)
232.23
GERENDO (1)
166.26
GERM (1)
264.05
GERMAN (2)
092.01 092.03
GERMS (2)
315.20 315.23
GESTURE (1)
245.32
GET (84)
005.14 005.30 006.37 006.37 007.05
016.25 023.14 025.06 025.29 026.04
026.33 029.04 029.12 029.13 033.20
038.13 050.26 053.08 053.12 053.16
060.23 062.05 064.24 066.04 069.21
070.24 072.05 072.17 074.22 090.29
091.07 092.19 092.22 093.05 105.06
105.11 109.06 113.13 115.28 117.07
118.08 118.12 120.04 122.16 140.34
143.23 145.22 145.33 145.35 149.08
150.01 163.09 168.26 170.21 170.24
171.21 171.36 172.24 196.22 198.34
205.12 205.22 206.36 207.34 209.06
221.29 224.01 228.14 234.07 234.30
240.16 241.26 252.01 265.11 274.29
275.05 283.27 294.01 295.23 295.32
302.16 322.11 327.33 328.24
GETS (5)
050.24 120.05 276.27 283.35 307.17
GETTING (14)
025.25 050.15 053.20 074.05 083.20
084.10 112.30 140.31 153.11 198.24
205.06 227.26 273.36 312.31
GEWGAWS (1)
038.09
GHASTLY (1)
231.10
GHOSTS (3)
086.17 255.09 285.05
GHOULS (1)
125.19
GIANT (2)
117.09 232.06
GIANTS (1)
271.16
GIFT (1)
078.26
GIFTS (1)
036.14
GIGS (2)
157.17 233.20
GILDED (1)
172.17
GILDING (1)
188.27
GILIAN (1)
232.36
GILL (1)
251.21
GILPIN (2)
250.09 287.26
GILT (2)
043.27 105.26
GINGER (1)
243.15
GINGERBREAD (1)
105.32
GINGHAMS (1)
120.10

GIRAFFE (1)
320.26
GIRAFFES (1)
320.28
GIRDED (1)
066.24
GIRDLED (1)
280.19
GIRDLING (1)
024.20
GIRL (2)
144.27 274.06
GIRLS (2)
136.23 153.02
GIRTH (1)
126.27
GIRTHS (1)
330.17
GIVE (30)
008.23 009.05 018.19 038.08 048.35
061.21 075.13 075.15 075.20 079.18
087.12 090.04 091.10 093.12 093.28
094.36 096.30 124.34 133.33 136.13
142.23 156.14 195.30 196.28 251.36
285.05 288.22 327.27 330.25 330.34
GIVEN (8)
055.05 058.10 060.41 211.13 226.27
279.31 290.02 327.04
GIVES (4)
063.35 114.28 162.25 315.12
GIVING (5)
190.06 206.20 231.31 245.28 263.28
GIZZARD (1)
105.24
GL (1)
125.15
GLABRA (2)
114.04 257.17
GLACIALIS (1)
233.24
GLAD (12)
029.03 063.07 065.06 093.02 113.13
153.03 158.21 205.31 217.05 243.33
276.27 295.16
GLADLY (3)
017.09 062.30 224.05
GLANCING (3)
168.04 307.21 313.29
GLASS (19)
043.27 044.02 049.10 065.19 094.26
099.30 150.31 159.04 177.18 177.20
186.35 187.10 187.12 231.16 246.23
248.18 264.11 283.05 326.17
GLASSES (3)
233.30 234.02 301.02
GLASSY (2)
114.29 186.21
GLAUCOUS (2)
197.31 199.20
GLE (1)
306.31
GLEAM (1)
255.01
GLEAMED (1)
316.20
GLEAMING (2)
041.15 186.24
GLEANING (1)
251.16
GLEE (1)
311.31
GLEES (1)
310.30
GLEN (1)
117.16
GLIDE (2)
187.28 187.31

GLIDING				(1)
203.13				
GLIMMER				(2)
098.12	189.24			
GLIMPSE				(3)
087.06	210.05	227.27		
GLISTENING				(1)
206.31				
GLOBE				(18)
008.34	014.10	077.27	077.35	093.33
097.35	119.24	139.09	254.12	285.20
306.14	306.22	306.26	306.31	306.35
308.23	320.23	332.04		
GLOBULE				(1)
302.07				
GLOBUS				(1)
306.26				
GLORIAE				(1)
243.06				
GLORIFY				(1)
091.14				
GLORIOUS				(8)
090.23	166.12	222.17	282.18	311.29
327.18	328.10	331.07		
GLORY				(3)
056.35	099.14	243.09		
GLOW				(1)
036.09				
GLOWING				(2)
240.29	253.06			
GLOWS				(1)
201.17				
GLUE				(1)
121.07				
GLUTTON				(1)
218.12				
GLUTTONOUS				(1)
215.10				
GNARLED				(2)
263.05	315.06			
GNAW				(2)
066.11	229.17			
GNAWED				(2)
083.14	280.13			
GNAWING				(4)
230.35	280.22	333.13	333.23	
GO				(100)
008.09	009.36	014.09	019.09	019.31
023.19	029.18	037.15	051.08	053.05
058.27	064.21	066.05	068.06	073.28
073.32	084.12	084.13	084.14	085.25
091.31	092.20	096.30	096.35	097.20
097.22	098.18	098.19	105.06	106.36
108.21	110.16	115.14	115.17	117.33
118.19	118.26	118.36	119.01	119.20
119.35	119.36	121.19	122.17	122.20
129.05	135.01	135.25	145.26	149.10
151.35	153.30	155.29	163.34	171.08
188.24	191.07	194.16	196.01	197.32
203.04	206.12	206.31	207.21	208.33
213.18	213.25	213.26	216.03	218.13
219.06	219.26	224.01	224.05	224.20
224.25	228.30	229.18	244.15	245.20
251.01	252.37	253.18	254.10	255.08
256.26	259.29	281.01	282.22	292.05
298.09	318.14	320.17	320.18	322.08
322.22	323.25	323.28	326.01	331.19
GOADED				(1)
108.27				
GOAL				(1)
169.02				
GOAT				(1)
220.20				
GOBBLE				(1)
318.22				
GOD				(36)
023.23	032.10	065.27	078.07	078.22
078.27	079.06	085.07	091.13	091.14

GOD				(CONTINUED)
097.05	137.11	153.12	193.24	194.02
194.10	196.04	196.22	196.23	219.30
220.03	221.28	230.21	236.24	236.28
239.26	249.19	250.29	250.30	268.25
269.04	315.12	322.06	328.27	330.04
330.31				
GODDESS				(2)
085.07	250.30			
GODLIKE				(1)
007.29				
GODS				(9)
044.20	131.23	139.06	169.05	201.14
203.31	220.10	252.38	298.04	
GOES				(26)
013.04	013.14	033.15	052.13	053.07
058.04	060.11	072.14	116.04	116.05
116.06	119.34	126.33	135.16	171.27
181.01	181.17	182.16	196.23	213.01
218.24	253.35	259.11	288.23	322.37
330.31				
GOFFE				(1)
137.29				
GOING				(29)
008.33	017.25	019.34	053.17	062.16
063.05	065.30	070.28	074.02	074.04
115.34	116.34	116.35	120.12	121.25
121.37	144.36	145.23	167.10	170.25
190.17	192.16	213.21	244.31	265.22
265.27	273.13	303.12	323.04	
GOINGS				(2)
268.04	283.16			
GOLD				(5)
057.23	250.36	252.18	285.02	322.12
GOLDEN				(17)
016.26	102.30	107.02	113.31	116.13
179.31	184.17	184.19	201.30	243.14
257.18	276.18	309.28	313.35	315.34
317.14	319.15			
GONDIBERT				(3)
259.08	260.13	260.13		
GONE				(34)
009.31	054.09	085.19	095.19	105.08
115.05	122.05	122.11	122.32	123.35
159.11	164.07	170.31	171.26	192.15
194.33	198.29	224.05	233.01	237.03
247.31	252.08	253.07	256.12	260.03
260.33	263.24	266.02	285.28	297.25
301.14	302.33	303.26	333.06	
GONG				(1)
301.16				
GOOD				(105)
004.06	004.15	010.30	010.32	011.03
018.19	020.11	021.07	021.10	021.10
021.11	024.28	030.01	030.16	034.32
036.21	043.10	043.22	043.22	043.23
045.05	049.19	050.04	051.10	054.12
054.13	054.26	057.31	059.40	061.30
062.24	064.08	069.19	069.24	072.36
073.03	073.09	073.20	073.23	073.28
073.30	074.03	074.05	074.18	074.23
074.25	075.01	078.28	084.01	084.13
089.20	094.36	103.14	104.27	106.02
106.04	107.25	107.26	112.08	114.01
127.26	131.16	131.20	131.21	131.21
135.01	144.34	146.10	147.35	148.35
149.23	151.01	152.35	153.20	161.02
165.17	183.08	183.28	185.32	195.03
196.04	198.34	206.28	207.21	208.40
210.19	213.07	213.08	217.04	219.28
224.30	225.11	239.04	241.09	242.27
246.10	248.24	253.03	256.28	295.32
297.13	314.40	323.10	330.23	331.29
GOODFELLOW				(1)
073.33				
GOODNESS				(6)
074.16	077.07	218.29	218.34	315.14
331.20				

GOODS   (2)
  168.31 261.17
GOODY   (1)
  251.21
GOOKIN   (1)
  029.28
GOOSE   (10)
  042.03 127.09 197.09 271.19 272.12
  272.21 313.18 320.07 329.27 329.27
GORGE   (1)
  289.08
GORGON   (1)
  080.14
GORRAPPIT   (1)
  147.04
GORRY   (1)
  149.27
GOSH   (1)
  145.35
GOSSAMER   (1)
  186.23
GOSSIP   (9)
  094.21 094.23 109.29 157.24 167.10
  167.23 168.10 173.04 256.20
GOSSIPS   (1)
  134.29
GOT   (68)
  003.16 005.06 005.13 018.09 018.34
  019.34 022.35 029.18 033.23 033.33
  033.35 047.04 048.21 054.30 055.07
  058.25 066.21 067.07 075.27 082.07
  082.35 083.02 088.28 105.07 105.09
  110.06 116.23 133.30 147.19 149.23
  149.35 152.10 155.12 156.13 156.22
  160.23 172.22 198.20 206.35 213.16
  225.04 228.30 237.07 238.34 242.26
  243.29 244.22 246.10 251.32 252.10
  252.23 257.12 272.27 273.24 279.30
  283.27 287.04 289.21 295.20 296.23
  299.07 310.13 313.10 317.14 325.15
  330.12 330.19 331.07
GOTHIC   (1)
  070.14
GOUGED   (1)
  093.35
GOURDS   (1)
  261.31
GOVERN   (1)
  172.32
GOVERNMENT   (3)
  321.32 323.08 332.32
GOVERNOR   (2)
  143.01 213.22
GOWN   (1)
  267.26
GRACE   (1)
  069.03
GRACEFUL   (6)
  114.11 159.20 191.10 281.12 309.29
  316.25
GRACEFULLY   (1)
  145.10
GRACEFULNESS   (1)
  169.09
GRACES   (1)
  025.21
GRADATIONS   (1)
  186.08
GRADES   (1)
  150.23
GRADING   (1)
  053.27
GRADUAL   (1)
  216.09
GRADUALLY   (17)
  035.34 047.16 062.20 063.22 114.19
  141.29 176.26 227.15 240.04 240.20
  291.27 301.21 302.14 304.06 305.29

GRADUALLY   (CONTINUED)
  326.30 333.21
GRADUATED   (1)
  293.03
GRAIN   (9)
  063.36 068.18 164.21 166.25 202.02
  239.18 269.28 294.24 300.18
GRAINS   (2)
  239.23 246.28
GRANADA   (1)
  094.32
GRANARIES   (1)
  309.34
GRANARY   (1)
  166.29
GRAND   (4)
  013.24 120.17 147.27 304.05
GRANDER   (1)
  141.29
GRANDEST   (1)
  134.11
GRANDEUR   (4)
  049.29 057.33 057.33 175.26
GRANDFATHER   (1)
  138.18
GRANDLY   (1)
  269.32
GRANDMOTHER   (2)
  138.19 209.03
GRANITE   (1)
  020.10
GRANTED   (2)
  034.11 056.33
GRANUM   (1)
  166.26
GRAPE   (2)
  018.26 191.22
GRAPES   (1)
  032.08
GRAPHICALLY   (1)
  119.31
GRAPING   (1)
  238.03
GRAPPLING   (1)
  295.27
GRASP   (1)
  274.25
GRASPING   (1)
  195.36
GRASS   (41)
  012.15 013.30 028.19 036.31 044.08
  055.21 113.01 113.09 129.35 130.02
  131.20 131.21 157.05 157.06 161.28
  163.19 164.21 172.36 172.36 176.17
  189.01 195.13 195.18 202.12 202.29
  224.19 238.08 238.15 263.09 267.12
  275.33 309.31 310.02 310.34 311.04
  311.11 314.18 314.22 316.21 319.17
  320.12
GRASSES   (1)
  309.29
GRASSHOPPERS   (1)
  094.16
GRASSY   (1)
  227.35
GRATE   (1)
  298.15
GRATEFUL   (1)
  157.30
GRATIFICATION   (1)
  068.22
GRATING   (1)
  304.15
GRATUITOUS   (1)
  274.02
GRATUITOUSLY   (1)
  006.21

GRAVE (3)
048.11 126.15 317.24
GRAVELLY (1)
156.32
GRAVELY (2)
025.03 036.07
GRAVES (5)
005.12 258.04 309.08 317.22 321.23
GRAVEYARD (1)
124.22
GRAVITATE (1)
330.05
GRAVITY (1)
108.12
GRAY (11)
083.10 125.03 145.13 148.34 157.29
228.04 233.07 247.25 284.28 305.25
312.10
GREASE (1)
196.34
GREASY (1)
204.25
GREAT (97)
009.15 013.02 013.33 015.05 020.35
020.36 022.05 022.20 028.23 029.33
032.01 032.25 033.03 035.15 038.21
047.32 050.16 050.18 052.20 056.23
064.28 066.31 066.34 067.30 074.10
076.29 077.27 091.33 095.12 096.01
104.08 104.09 105.22 119.03 121.28
128.18 137.01 137.12 138.18 138.19
140.14 144.06 144.34 145.01 145.15
153.06 157.21 160.04 161.09 161.10
167.25 176.11 181.20 183.36 184.36
188.03 190.34 196.34 199.21 216.01
220.30 231.32 231.33 232.03 239.25
245.15 247.33 248.07 249.17 250.12
252.05 254.10 260.06 262.09 265.05
265.10 270.02 270.02 272.34 275.18
282.19 285.02 296.35 297.01 299.32
301.26 303.08 303.31 309.06 311.18
311.22 313.09 320.24 328.18 331.28
331.30 331.32
GREATCOAT (1)
145.14
GREATER (30)
010.24 010.30 012.32 034.18 035.13
036.22 049.34 053.18 054.34 064.01
073.11 075.33 078.03 110.10 135.20
152.13 152.13 170.20 171.05 246.34
254.11 272.22 288.27 290.32 293.05
296.19 296.30 299.10 321.22 332.16
GREATEST (21)
038.15 069.30 076.29 123.08 154.01
181.16 194.19 211.23 216.29 223.32
232.02 234.35 244.24 287.05 289.14
289.17 289.17 289.18 290.12 290.16
293.01
GREATLY (5)
056.18 076.16 144.32 247.27 304.34
GREATNESS (1)
033.30
GRECIAN (3)
070.14 101.34 102.29
GREECE (2)
101.25 217.15
GREEDILY (2)
084.11 084.14
GREEDY (1)
094.22
GREEENER (1)
320.12
GREEK (8)
014.23 100.08 101.19 101.23 106.24
106.31 144.23 310.07
GREEKS (2)
088.28 192.26

GREEN (47)
008.05 029.35 039.20 041.23 042.27
059.04 061.25 077.26 077.27 087.03
114.11 121.11 121.22 122.10 156.32
156.35 161.31 166.21 175.30 176.13
176.16 176.21 176.26 176.27 176.29
176.30 177.13 177.21 177.24 179.08
179.17 189.31 197.30 201.06 247.24
252.21 253.01 284.27 296.32 297.04
297.26 308.27 311.03 311.05 311.12
311.15 333.20
GREENER (2)
312.25 314.19
GREENISH (5)
177.15 184.10 184.17 296.34 297.06
GREENNESS (1)
077.02
GREET (4)
146.13 154.19 216.25 311.02
GRENADIERS (1)
258.04
GREW (16)
024.12 111.33 113.30 114.04 173.18
195.09 198.14 226.09 233.10 238.30
274.22 276.07 302.25 312.29 326.30
326.31
GREY (1)
279.25
GRIEF (2)
074.13 250.21
GRIEFS (1)
077.12
GRIEVE (2)
138.14 144.32
GRIEVED (2)
250.21 250.23
GRIND (2)
064.05 197.15
GRINNELL (1)
321.09
GRIST (1)
197.16
GROCERIES (5)
007.11 012.03 064.17 115.30 167.26
GROCERY (2)
133.21 168.13
GROOVE (2)
132.35 132.37
GROOVES (1)
201.18
GROPED (1)
261.02
GROPING (4)
042.04 174.28 313.17 315.01
GROSS (7)
007.18 011.35 034.19 075.19 215.15
218.04 218.13
GROSSE (1)
261.12
GROSSEST (3)
012.03 064.17 219.33
GROTESQUE (3)
026.12 136.30 305.16
GROUND (64)
009.30 014.30 015.34 036.32 038.18
039.13 043.35 044.31 045.18 045.26
055.36 086.08 113.33 114.15 131.19
141.08 142.16 143.09 146.03 146.22
151.29 155.07 159.18 165.10 168.28
182.05 197.25 201.11 201.14 224.16
229.02 236.14 239.06 239.28 241.23
241.36 244.12 245.21 248.29 249.08
258.03 258.24 263.32 264.06 265.15
273.01 274.26 276.10 278.20 278.27
278.31 280.33 281.22 283.05 283.28
295.14 308.27 309.18 309.23 311.09
317.33 318.29 325.19 332.32

88

```
GROUNDS                              (  3)
  180.15  211.16  331.08
GROVE                                (  5)
  083.17  167.19  201.33  250.28  250.31
GROVELLING                           (  1)
  165.33
GROVES                               (  3)
  124.24  192.12  201.03
GROW                                 ( 16)
  064.03  114.13  164.03  166.22  179.03
  196.07  201.17  207.29  241.05  254.03
  257.11  257.35  266.20  280.24  320.05
  324.11
GROWING                              ( 10)
  054.24  064.11  096.15  114.06  122.25
  128.11  161.18  241.03  263.04  311.10
GROWL                                (  1)
  174.13
GROWN                                ( 15)
  047.16  067.04  155.06  164.30  174.03
  195.35  202.04  217.25  261.30  263.35
  264.02  280.18  283.24  296.12  302.15
GROWS                                ( 11)
  113.20  158.10  181.36  196.24  199.15
  216.16  218.36  227.25  257.18  263.23
  311.08
GROWTH                               (  4)
  006.20  156.03  249.26  303.18
GRUB                                 (  2)
  284.01  306.34
GRUBBING                             (  1)
  083.21
GRUEL                                (  2)
  207.07  268.14
GUARD                                (  1)
  229.36
GUARDED                              (  1)
  131.27
GUESS                                (  1)
  290.06
GUESSED                              (  2)
  031.28  295.07
GUEST                                (  5)
  036.10  140.32  142.03  244.17  270.21
GUESTS                               (  7)
  036.10  141.35  143.30  152.01  152.03
  152.11  245.10
GUIDANCE                             (  1)
  071.18
GUIDE                                (  2)
  232.19  256.16
GUIDED                               (  3)
  131.26  170.15  266.26
GUIDES                               (  1)
  291.06
GUILE                                (  1)
  193.15
GUILT                                (  1)
  059.30
GUILTY                               (  2)
  059.31  182.17
GUINEA                               (  1)
  257.09
GUISE                                (  1)
  258.29
GULF                                 (  2)
  110.18  298.21
GULISTAN                             (  1)
  079.03
GULL                                 (  1)
  185.08
GULPED                               (  1)
  126.27
GUM                                  (  1)
  085.01
GUN                                  ( 11)
  168.16  211.32  211.36  212.06  212.26
  213.04  251.03  277.36  301.26  303.23

GUN                       (CONTINUED)
  304.10
GUNNY                                (  1)
  119.28
GUNS                                 (  3)
  160.04  160.08  248.20
GURGLING                             (  3)
  125.14  257.31  310.16
GUSHED                               (  1)
  287.34
GUTTATUS                             (  1)
  184.24
GUTTURAL                             (  1)
  306.31
GUY                                  (  1)
  208.20
GYPSY                                (  1)
  113.10
GYRINUS                              (  1)
  187.24
```

```
HABET
  322.02  322.02                              (   2)
HABIT
  035.08  096.08  142.10  165.33  195.36      (   7)
  211.35  220.40
HABITAT
  064.30                                       (   1)
HABITATION
  068.27                                       (   1)
HABITS
  020.05  124.06  167.24  212.05               (   4)
HABITUALLY
  173.05                                       (   1)
HACK
  309.32                                       (   1)
HACKING
  075.35                                       (   1)
HAD                                            ( 512)
  003.05  003.11  004.33  005.06  008.19
  008.27  010.16  011.10  012.04  017.15
  017.18  017.33  018.17  018.20  019.07
  019.09  019.11  019.13  019.17  019.18
  019.33  022.35  027.05  027.16  027.31
  028.02  030.08  033.37  036.25  038.01
  041.21  041.22  041.22  041.24  041.29
  041.34  042.23  042.28  042.30  042.32
  042.35  042.38  043.15  043.24  043.29
  044.23  050.07  050.12  051.31  051.32
  051.34  051.35  052.02  052.03  052.27
  056.12  056.12  058.35  059.05  061.08
  062.12  065.26  067.04  067.06  067.20
  067.26  067.30  069.13  071.06  072.27
  073.31  074.06  075.25  075.30  078.24
  081.16  082.05  082.09  082.15  082.17
  082.17  082.19  082.23  082.24  082.35
  083.16  083.22  083.23  083.27  083.35
  083.35  085.05  085.15  085.21  085.26
  086.25  086.32  087.36  088.06  088.11
  088.15  090.06  090.34  090.35  093.27
  093.34  097.13  098.10  099.23  099.29
  099.35  101.24  101.28  104.32  105.03
  105.07  105.12  106.35  108.10  108.14
  108.35  112.09  112.10  112.21  112.25
  112.32  113.05  113.06  114.06  114.10
  114.18  115.04  116.23  120.31  123.13
  123.14  123.15  123.35  124.05  124.36
  125.03  129.33  131.25  132.26  136.11
  136.14  139.06  140.09  140.15  140.17
  143.14  143.17  143.18  143.19  143.23
  143.28  143.36  144.01  144.06  144.14
  145.06  145.25  146.18  146.21  146.29
  147.06  147.19  148.02  148.04  148.12
  148.17  148.32  148.33  148.36  149.15
  149.22  149.23  149.25  149.29  150.17
  151.01  151.05  151.14  151.21  151.24
  151.34  152.01  152.11  152.15  153.17
  153.17  154.14  154.21  154.21  155.05
  155.15  155.27  156.13  156.17  156.19
  156.21  156.22  156.36  157.02  157.07
  157.26  157.27  158.02  158.31  159.11
  160.08  160.10  160.17  160.22  160.23
  161.09  161.33  162.30  164.10  164.29
  167.07  167.21  168.19  169.13  169.25
  169.30  169.33  170.17  170.23  171.26
  172.02  172.08  172.13  173.03  173.25
  173.28  174.03  174.07  174.08  174.19
  174.24  174.30  174.32  175.07  175.17
  178.05  178.07  178.15  178.17  179.23
  179.24  179.25  183.12  183.29  185.01
  189.25  190.10  190.23  191.05  191.11
  191.16  191.22  191.27  191.34  193.07
  195.03  195.11  195.28  196.04  198.06
  198.07  198.24  198.24  198.29  198.33
  198.35  199.04  199.06  202.15  202.21
  202.24  203.26  203.35  204.20  204.28
  205.02  205.16  205.17  205.17  205.21
  206.15  206.35  207.16  208.31  208.32
  210.14  211.31  213.17  214.02  214.21

HAD                                 (CONTINUED)
  214.27  214.29  218.02  218.06  218.06
  219.25  222.03  223.03  225.26  225.27
  225.30  226.16  226.35  228.03  229.14
  229.20  229.27  229.27  229.28  229.29
  229.31  229.32  230.05  230.08  230.12
  231.02  231.08  231.23  231.23  232.20
  232.32  233.09  233.21  233.26  234.27
  235.13  235.16  236.10  237.03  238.19
  238.28  239.08  239.08  239.09  239.10
  239.10  239.36  240.30  241.14  241.30
  242.07  242.26  242.29  243.09  244.25
  245.20  246.04  246.06  246.11  246.14
  247.20  247.22  247.26  248.01  248.12
  248.16  248.18  248.25  248.26  248.26
  248.36  249.08  249.17  249.28  250.02
  250.19  251.29  251.32  252.08  252.09
  252.18  252.20  253.07  253.14  253.15
  254.01  254.21  256.12  257.24  258.06
  259.04  259.07  259.16  259.19  259.21
  260.25  260.26  261.03  261.05  261.25
  261.27  261.27  261.28  261.30  262.02
  262.02  262.20  262.21  262.28  262.28
  264.02  264.33  265.32  266.02  266.34
  267.07  269.17  269.21  270.04  270.09
  270.11  270.13  270.16  271.06  272.30
  273.02  273.24  274.28  275.21  275.25
  276.02  276.23  277.27  277.31  278.05
  279.08  279.13  279.19  279.20  280.08
  280.13  280.18  280.26  280.32  281.23
  282.03  282.04  283.26  284.07  284.15
  285.14  287.15  289.10  289.28  290.19
  293.15  294.23  294.26  294.27  295.12
  295.20  296.15  296.19  297.12  299.07
  300.01  300.28  301.17  301.28  302.23
  303.16  303.17  304.03  304.06  304.12
  304.14  306.11  307.02  309.24  309.27
  312.14  312.15  312.23  313.10  313.23
  316.07  316.33  317.01  317.21  319.04
  319.05  323.11  323.15  327.01  327.04
  327.07  327.09  327.10  327.15  327.17
  327.18  327.21  327.22  328.01  328.30
  330.15  330.15  330.18  331.07  331.14
  332.01  333.09
HADDOCK                                        (   1)
  284.26
HAGS                                           (   1)
  124.20
HAIR                                           (   6)
  033.22  049.13  145.12  168.32  253.24
  281.34
HALF                                           (  81)
  014.03  024.32  024.34  030.21  031.23
  047.13  054.21  067.32  083.06  086.04
  086.09  091.26  093.25  093.28  108.30
  113.28  114.33  118.31  123.34  123.36
  130.04  130.17  145.27  145.29  146.17
  151.03  151.12  156.11  157.34  158.14
  158.15  170.31  175.31  175.32  179.11
  185.15  187.23  190.14  195.14  195.21
  197.12  203.22  203.24  203.34  206.05
  210.11  213.12  227.33  228.28  229.36
  231.06  231.15  233.12  234.30  238.20
  238.27  247.09  249.34  257.14  264.01
  265.18  266.12  266.13  266.16  267.04
  273.23  274.01  274.21  282.28  284.17
  287.02  294.30  299.30  302.28  305.08
  305.09  322.33  325.12  325.13  330.19
  332.07
HALL                                           (   5)
  192.27  243.17  243.27  254.34  331.10
HALLS                                          (   3)
  023.20  057.14  140.20
HALO                                           (   2)
  202.18  202.21
HALVES                                         (   1)
  211.03
```

HAMLET   (1)
264.22
HAMLETS   (1)
252.32
HAMMER   (3)
245.23 309.21 330.26
HAMMERED   (3)
057.25 057.28 275.27
HAMMERING   (2)
057.26 221.29
HAMMERS   (1)
058.04
HAND   (51)
049.09 052.27 055.18 055.20 056.02
059.06 064.05 072.28 078.16 078.17
079.17 080.10 085.19 085.19 093.23
118.09 125.07 130.20 135.05 139.02
146.08 147.35 153.27 158.19 170.05
170.09 175.01 175.14 175.14 176.07
176.24 180.13 180.29 186.10 193.16
193.28 194.04 204.27 211.03 226.06
226.32 229.07 238.24 240.33 241.09
253.16 257.33 281.02 296.31 307.36
312.07
HANDED   (2)
024.26 025.35
HANDFUL   (2)
048.14 048.18
HANDKERCHIEF   (1)
203.25
HANDLE   (3)
178.15 178.21 206.23
HANDLES   (1)
070.07
HANDLING   (1)
006.25
HANDS   (33)
003.08 024.23 029.28 042.29 045.24
046.05 051.08 063.21 069.10 098.28
098.29 099.35 111.24 111.34 116.01
116.25 118.25 129.30 131.25 157.10
157.35 168.07 169.34 186.31 215.28
223.12 249.14 255.06 261.08 261.22
263.27 266.01 309.13
HANDSELLED   (1)
333.26
HANDSOME   (6)
039.33 114.01 133.29 201.28 246.01
311.22
HANDSOMELY   (2)
093.23 147.36
HANDSOMER   (1)
184.27
HANDWRITING   (1)
147.34
HANDY   (1)
257.34
HANG   (10)
021.34 025.20 038.04 078.34 086.20
120.24 200.21 223.31 326.01 330.07
HANGING   (3)
004.20 157.18 231.09
HANGS   (2)
201.12 244.01
HANNO   (2)
020.36 298.20
HAPPEN   (2)
095.09 203.21
HAPPENED   (2)
093.32 232.07
HAPPENS   (5)
022.16 022.17 026.27 031.06 328.20
HAPPILY   (1)
098.14
HAPPINESS   (1)
193.13
HAPPY   (4)
087.30 105.09 146.10 220.15

HARASSED   (1)
029.20
HARBOR   (6)
020.07 052.04 169.21 289.34 291.22
332.30
HARBORED   (1)
291.31
HARBORLESS   (1)
292.03
HARBORS   (1)
288.28
HARD   (38)
006.02 006.27 007.21 029.11 035.35
058.19 065.08 070.11 070.23 098.03
141.26 145.03 157.29 190.17 195.08
204.22 204.33 205.13 205.14 205.16
205.17 205.17 206.02 214.33 215.19
221.05 221.35 243.08 246.17 253.01
257.28 294.33 300.32 309.32 311.25
328.06 330.15 330.18
HARDER   (5)
241.03 241.05 241.11 265.14 287.04
HARDEST   (2)
161.16 201.19
HARDIER   (2)
027.17 267.14
HARDINESS   (1)
013.06
HARDLY   (25)
004.29 008.36 035.24 063.34 091.22
093.14 093.24 106.28 107.13 112.24
116.33 136.24 143.35 145.05 168.01
180.12 182.31 194.33 205.07 242.31
247.26 248.11 280.33 281.23 303.18
HARDNESS   (1)
016.10
HARDSHIP   (1)
070.35
HARDY   (1)
029.26
HARE   (3)
128.04 212.33 281.32
HAREM   (1)
037.09
HARES   (1)
280.25
HARIVANSA   (1)
085.28
HARK   (2)
121.30 223.24
HARLEQUIN   (1)
026.15
HARM   (1)
144.36
HARMLESS   (1)
133.04
HARMONIOUS   (1)
240.09
HARMONIZED   (2)
174.04 222.05
HARMONY   (6)
071.35 174.06 199.20 200.01 290.29
290.31
HARNESS   (1)
117.05
HARNESSED   (1)
066.19
HARP   (3)
123.07 218.31 218.32
HARPER   (1)
109.35
HARPY   (1)
195.36
HARRIERS   (2)
154.12 154.13
HARROWED   (1)
231.24

HARROWING (2)
163.02   294.34
HARRY (1)
251.21
HARSH (1)
272.18
HARVEST (5)
163.37   166.17   166.27   216.34   262.30
HARVESTED (2)
162.32   166.22
HARVESTING (1)
161.14
HAS (223)
003.33   004.01   006.15   006.18   006.20
006.36   009.01   009.02   009.03   009.05
010.02   010.09   011.23   012.09   012.10
012.24   013.30   014.23   015.23   015.28
015.30   016.09   018.07   021.25   023.13
023.15   023.18   026.02   031.08   031.12
032.32   032.35   033.21   033.33   033.35
034.13   034.14   034.15   036.32   043.04
044.35   047.07   047.16   052.33   056.32
057.36   061.36   066.12   066.20   066.32
066.33   067.18   069.31   070.31   071.04
071.08   072.01   072.02   074.04   074.32
077.26   079.06   079.09   079.17   082.13
082.37   083.01   085.19   089.23   089.23
091.19   091.22   091.31   093.32   093.34
094.01   095.35   099.16   099.17   100.18
100.26   103.07   103.22   103.24   106.21
106.28   106.29   106.31   107.12   107.23
107.35   108.06   108.06   108.10   109.18
115.09   118.06   120.17   121.16   121.22
125.11   125.16   125.31   126.16   126.27
126.28   129.31   131.08   133.29   137.06
137.07   137.34   138.20   142.36   144.19
144.21   144.34   149.24   149.25   149.35
155.35   157.12   162.23   162.34   164.05
171.02   171.14   172.18   175.27   179.30
180.01   180.09   180.27   180.34   181.06
181.29   182.20   185.32   186.03   186.07
192.22   192.23   192.35   193.03   193.37
194.03   194.13   195.25   195.30   196.20
197.25   199.12   199.34   201.31   203.08
211.08   211.09   212.26   212.27   213.02
214.36   215.01   217.30   217.34   218.01
218.21   220.08   225.15   226.18   232.27
239.13   239.13   244.22   246.26   249.20
252.13   252.23   254.05   258.25   260.07
262.07   264.23   266.33   268.31   269.15
277.33   279.27   279.34   282.14   283.35
285.34   287.07   288.18   289.35   290.10
290.36   291.36   292.27   296.32   297.29
300.03   300.18   302.02   303.14   303.18
308.12   308.25   310.06   311.18   315.07
315.18   315.30   318.24   322.14   323.31
324.31   330.18   331.35   332.36   333.06
333.06   333.18   333.21
HAST (2)
010.12   208.12
HASTE (18)
028.02   040.29   042.36   052.21   083.19
145.22   159.32   160.14   165.03   165.24
190.18   203.33   207.13   259.17   273.35
275.16   304.11   326.06
HASTENS (1)
320.26
HASTILY (1)
091.13
HASTY (6)
142.05   245.11   245.13   245.15   280.28
285.23
HAT (5)
007.10   022.24   023.22   024.33   035.34
HATCHED (5)
025.31   227.17   317.06   317.08   333.14
HATCHES (1)
169.23

HATCHING (1)
062.10
HATE (1)
208.18
HATH (2)
080.27   220.15
HATRED (1)
315.16
HAUGHTY (1)
156.26
HAUL (3)
249.17   267.28   295.06
HAULED (3)
198.28   249.30   295.26
HAUNT (1)
208.25
HAUNTED (1)
225.21
HAUNTS (2)
174.29   277.10
HAVE (604)
003.16   003.18   003.19   004.01   004.15
004.17   004.18   004.32   004.35   005.04
005.08   005.13   005.15   006.29   006.30
006.32   007.21   007.22   008.10   009.04
009.06   009.08   009.10   009.11   009.13
009.16   009.16   009.31   009.32   009.35
010.06   010.07   010.10   010.16   010.34
011.30   011.35   012.04   012.22   014.20
014.36   015.19   016.01   016.22   016.24
016.25   016.29   016.34   017.02   017.13
017.14   017.22   017.23   017.34   018.18
018.20   018.24   018.27   018.34   018.34
018.36   019.12   020.04   020.32   021.07
022.06   022.07   022.26   023.09   023.17
023.20   023.32   023.36   025.13   025.27
025.33   025.35   026.16   026.23   026.36
027.21   028.01   028.18   028.36   029.03
029.15   029.22   030.02   030.03   030.18
031.23   031.26   031.35   032.07   032.08
032.10   032.17   032.20   032.23   034.07
034.09   034.20   034.22   034.24   035.21
035.29   035.31   035.32   036.03   036.13
036.30   037.12   037.24   037.28   037.29
037.31   038.18   039.12   040.12   040.23
041.02   042.12   045.33   046.10   046.25
046.26   046.33   047.35   048.17   048.21
048.28   049.26   050.14   050.35   051.30
052.04   052.22   053.06   053.12   053.14
053.21   053.28   054.01   054.02   054.09
054.12   054.13   054.15   055.01   056.13
056.18   056.27   056.34   057.01   057.09
057.12   058.09   058.09   058.12   058.35
059.41   060.09   060.23   060.23   060.39
060.40   060.41   061.09   061.11   061.18
061.28   062.05   062.06   062.36   063.23
064.06   064.12   065.05   065.17   065.36
066.28   066.29   067.02   067.05   067.07
067.12   068.07   068.08   068.10   068.32
069.01   069.04   069.05   069.14   069.20
070.06   070.20   071.06   071.08   071.11
071.29   072.14   072.20   072.21   072.22
072.24   072.25   072.29   072.33   072.34
073.02   073.05   077.21   078.03   078.13
078.14   078.20   078.31   081.06   081.08
081.24   081.31   082.26   082.33   083.15
083.32   083.34   083.36   084.08   084.22
087.12   088.27   090.05   090.07   090.12
090.13   091.13   092.14   092.32   092.33
093.11   093.23   093.30   094.33   095.05
096.02   096.12   098.24   099.29   099.30
099.31   100.16   102.28   102.31   103.01
103.18   103.20   103.28   103.32   104.01
104.05   104.08   104.10   104.12   104.13
104.18   104.26   105.08   106.07   106.35
107.02   107.04   108.05   108.17   108.28
110.15   111.35   112.16   112.21   114.33
116.14   118.01   118.05   118.07   118.14

```
HAVE                         (CONTINUED)      HAVING                       (CONTINUED)
118.29  118.34  119.32  119.32  120.36        206.21  214.16  221.36  228.30  229.18
121.01  122.08  122.28  125.29  125.31        230.36  234.19  235.11  236.23  245.30
126.14  127.30  127.35  129.25  130.13        249.04  253.29  259.10  266.22  269.26
130.18  130.24  131.02  131.26  131.28        277.08  279.14  284.10  287.03  289.13
132.07  133.16  133.24  134.12  134.30        299.11  301.14  326.22
134.32  136.14  136.28  137.01  137.19        HAWK                              ( 6)
137.22  138.09  138.15  138.27  138.31        115.24  159.12  159.23  310.30  316.25
140.15  141.01  141.07  141.09  141.19        316.25
141.27  142.29  143.28  144.29  145.05        HAWKS                             ( 4)
146.34  148.14  148.15  151.23  151.28        114.25  125.33  159.27  316.35
152.09  152.35  155.20  155.25  156.02        HAY                               ( 9)
156.02  156.06  158.28  159.20  160.10        070.05  158.08  196.15  207.31  285.25
161.28  161.30  162.15  163.24  163.35        296.04  296.10  296.25  311.07
163.38  164.27  165.05  165.25  165.26        HAYING                            ( 1)
166.18  166.21  167.28  168.23  170.06        056.20
170.07  170.25  170.29  170.31  171.17        HAZE                              ( 2)
171.23  171.30  171.31  172.22  172.23        186.20  317.12
172.32  173.15  173.17  174.17  174.32        HAZEL                             ( 2)
176.06  176.14  176.29  177.10  177.20        182.28  263.03
177.24  178.14  179.07  179.10  179.15        HAZY                              ( 3)
179.34  179.35  181.09  181.12  181.22        041.15  188.30  224.35
181.31  182.06  182.09  182.10  182.26        HE                              ( 702)
182.34  183.34  184.08  184.08  184.14        003.33  003.34  004.01  006.16  006.18
185.06  185.18  185.28  186.04  186.21        006.19  007.29  007.30  007.30  007.31
187.03  189.09  191.18  191.28  191.36        009.21  009.23  010.08  012.16  015.14
192.06  192.30  192.32  192.33  192.35        015.19  015.23  015.31  019.03  019.05
192.36  193.35  194.03  194.10  195.06        019.09  019.11  019.12  019.13  021.28
195.12  195.18  196.14  196.17  197.18        022.18  022.25  023.19  024.23  024.24
197.33  199.03  199.28  201.06  201.28        024.25  024.35  027.13  027.16  027.17
201.35  202.04  202.16  202.30  205.12        027.32  027.34  028.02  028.14  028.32
205.13  210.13  210.23  210.27  211.13        030.05  030.32  030.33  031.07  031.19
211.26  212.06  212.10  212.11  213.09        031.22  032.27  033.20  033.21  033.23
213.33  213.34  213.35  214.01  214.02        033.24  033.33  034.18  034.20  036.01
214.23  214.25  216.07  216.10  216.28        036.10  037.01  037.02  037.19  037.20
217.02  217.05  217.17  217.25  218.03        037.21  037.25  037.26  038.08  038.35
218.05  220.36  220.38  223.08  223.15        039.03  041.03  041.26  041.29  043.04
223.23  223.32  223.35  224.01  224.03        043.31  043.33  043.35  044.18  044.10
224.14  224.21  224.33  225.04  225.17        046.22  046.31  047.11  047.15  048.08
225.18  225.22  226.30  226.31  228.14        048.15  048.17  049.34  050.24  050.31
229.04  230.07  230.23  230.30  231.28        051.10  051.27  051.32  052.09  052.10
231.30  232.05  233.19  233.20  235.17        052.25  052.35  052.36  053.07  054.08
236.34  239.27  239.32  242.09  243.03        054.09  055.32  055.33  055.35  056.01
243.21  243.29  243.29  244.26  244.27        056.03  056.28  056.36  057.08  058.25
244.28  244.31  245.19  246.10  246.29        058.25  058.25  058.28  061.31  061.35
251.17  251.27  253.13  254.24  257.32        061.36  065.24  066.07  066.10  066.12
258.28  261.20  261.35  262.03  262.12        066.15  066.16  066.18  066.18  066.19
262.19  264.14  264.15  264.17  265.01        066.33  067.06  067.16  068.03  068.12
265.19  267.06  267.24  267.32  267.33        070.29  071.03  071.05  071.06  071.06
268.11  269.13  270.05  271.11  272.27        071.08  071.15  071.15  072.01  072.02
274.08  275.15  276.05  276.06  279.30        072.02  072.03  072.08  072.15  073.30
283.22  284.08  284.12  284.29  285.12        073.36  074.08  074.26  075.18  075.20
285.17  285.18  285.20  285.24  285.28        075.27  075.29  075.30  075.31  075.36
285.29  287.31  287.34  288.07  288.13        076.03  076.19  076.20  076.28  077.09
289.29  290.04  290.33  291.04  292.08        077.20  077.21  077.22  077.24  077.25
297.02  297.08  298.04  300.04  300.25        077.34  078.07  078.09  079.08  082.03
300.35  301.30  302.01  302.11  302.15        082.14  082.21  082.35  083.26  089.23
302.32  303.24  304.07  304.19  304.34        091.23  091.31  091.33  093.25  093.26
306.20  307.03  308.14  310.05  312.01        093.33  093.36  095.18  096.17  096.19
314.31  315.23  317.02  317.16  317.21        096.20  096.30  096.31  099.14  099.15
318.02  319.12  321.21  321.23  322.06        100.09  100.26  103.09  103.14  103.16
322.35  322.38  323.03  323.19  324.06        103.17  105.11  106.14  106.14  106.15
324.22  325.16  325.24  327.34  328.09        106.17  106.17  106.18  106.23  106.24
328.15  330.12  330.19  331.13  331.30        106.26  106.28  108.11  108.15  112.11
332.01  332.02  332.04  332.08               115.04  115.32  117.16  117.17  117.21
HAVEN                             ( 14)       120.25  121.16  121.17  127.21  127.25
074.09  093.10  171.36  173.09  185.09        134.01  135.17  135.27  135.33  135.34
197.10  197.13  203.04  248.31  272.15        135.34  135.36  136.01  136.02  136.04
278.11  279.17  299.16  303.28                136.32  137.11  137.12  137.12  137.30
HAVENS                            ( 1)        137.30  142.03  143.07  143.14  144.14
187.31                                        144.18  144.21  144.25  144.34  144.34
HAVING                            ( 53)       144.37  145.02  145.05  145.09  145.13
015.27  019.06  022.04  027.10  028.13        145.15  145.17  145.20  145.20  145.23
029.12  042.08  042.32  044.28  048.09        145.23  145.24  145.24  145.28  145.29
064.23  068.12  068.20  082.33  085.31        145.31  145.31  146.01  146.02  146.06
085.32  096.18  098.05  104.21  105.09        146.09  146.09  146.13  146.15  146.16
111.25  136.11  144.32  159.02  169.22        146.18  146.20  146.21  146.21  146.24
170.05  170.28  173.03  183.14  191.30        146.26  146.28  146.29  146.29  146.30
```

93

```
HE                              (CONTINUED)
146.33  146.33  146.36  147.01  147.03
147.06  147.15  147.16  147.18  147.19
147.21  147.22  147.23  147.25  147.27
147.27  147.29  147.30  147.33  147.34
148.02  148.03  148.03  148.04  148.05
148.05  148.06  148.10  148.11  148.16
148.18  148.21  148.23  148.26  148.27
148.30  148.32  148.33  148.33  148.34
148.35  148.36  149.03  149.03  149.08
149.09  149.11  149.14  149.18  149.20
149.23  149.24  149.24  149.25  149.25
149.28  149.30  149.33  149.35  150.03
150.07  150.08  150.12  150.16  150.17
150.22  151.17  151.20  151.21  151.23
151.26  151.27  151.30  151.30  151.31
152.08  152.09  152.10  153.32  153.34
153.35  157.28  157.31  158.23  158.26
159.24  161.30  162.22  165.12  165.13
165.31  166.01  166.12  170.13  170.14
171.02  171.02  171.03  171.15  173.29
173.34  174.01  174.02  174.03  182.26
182.29  184.02  190.28  190.30  190.31
190.36  191.01  191.05  192.23  193.15
193.37  195.30  195.32  196.04  196.22
198.20  198.21  198.23  198.26  198.26
198.29  198.29  198.33  198.35  199.02
201.21  202.24  202.27  202.35  202.36
204.33  205.03  205.09  205.09  205.15
205.16  205.17  205.17  205.20  205.21
205.30  206.02  206.02  206.05  206.11
208.33  208.35  208.37  208.38  209.01
209.04  210.09  211.02  211.09  211.19
212.26  212.32  212.37  213.02  213.02
216.01  216.04  216.14  216.16  217.17
217.30  218.10  218.12  218.24  219.03
220.05  220.09  220.15  220.23  220.31
220.33  220.35  220.35  221.23  221.28
221.29  221.36  222.03  222.04  222.06
222.08  222.13  222.15  222.20  223.14
227.25  229.28  229.30  229.33  229.35
229.35  230.01  230.35  231.02  231.12
231.16  231.16  231.18  232.22  233.34
233.34  234.11  234.11  234.14  234.23
234.23  234.24  234.25  234.26  234.27
234.29  234.31  234.32  234.33  234.36
235.01  235.03  235.09  235.12  235.13
235.13  235.15  235.16  235.22  235.25
235.29  235.33  235.34  235.35  236.02
236.03  236.05  236.06  236.10  236.11
236.17  236.20  236.23  239.27  241.29
241.31  244.25  245.29  252.23  253.28
253.31  253.35  257.09  257.10  257.11
257.12  257.29  257.30  258.05  258.06
258.07  258.09  258.10  260.25  260.27
260.28  260.31  260.33  260.34  261.02
261.06  261.21  261.25  262.01  262.01
262.02  262.06  262.08  262.11  262.20
262.20  262.21  262.35  265.05  265.09
266.06  266.09  266.11  266.13  266.15
266.20  266.23  266.28  266.29  268.03
268.20  268.23  268.24  268.24  268.27
268.30  268.31  269.06  269.09  269.14
269.18  269.21  269.24  270.21  274.10
274.14  274.15  274.18  274.22  274.26
274.34  275.05  275.06  277.06  277.06
277.09  277.10  277.10  277.12  277.13
277.15  277.29  277.30  277.31  277.36
278.02  278.02  278.09  278.10  278.15
278.22  279.04  279.10  279.11  279.19
279.21  283.25  283.27  283.27  283.29
283.34  284.07  284.15  287.28  291.14
294.05  294.07  294.32  295.14  296.15
297.31  303.17  303.17  303.19  303.23
303.24  303.26  303.28  303.28  303.30
303.32  304.02  304.03  304.04  304.06
304.11  304.11  304.13  304.14  306.11
310.12  311.21  312.20  312.20  315.07


HE                              (CONTINUED)
315.13  315.30  320.07  320.27  320.28
321.09  322.32  323.06  323.09  323.31
323.32  323.33  324.02  324.03  324.32
326.02  326.03  326.05  326.09  326.10
326.11  326.12  326.24  326.26  326.29
326.31  326.34  326.36  327.01  327.02
327.03  327.06  327.07  327.09  327.15
327.19  328.01  328.02  330.17  330.21
331.10  332.29

HEAD                                ( 41)
005.01  005.01  025.23  025.31  027.13
093.26  095.02  098.29  098.31  111.23
121.13  122.01  138.29  141.04  151.25
168.21  178.12  178.27  186.22  202.27
203.25  210.35  222.07  228.20  234.31
235.26  240.13  242.20  243.19  259.16
265.36  280.29  287.28  293.30  301.16
301.18  308.02  313.11  322.19  327.10
332.13

HEADED                              (  3)
143.20  151.34  204.11

HEADEDNESS                          (  1)
268.15

HEADLANDS                           (  1)
171.08

HEADLONG                            (  2)
074.12  220.24

HEADS                               ( 18)
004.21  005.32  006.07  012.21  051.08
093.12  118.13  119.10  119.26  152.27
156.27  199.25  226.26  231.08  231.09
267.31  283.09  321.25

HEADWAY                             (  1)
066.19

HEALTH                              ( 13)
060.35  061.18  061.28  077.14  078.27
127.26  136.33  138.08  138.22  219.13
219.15  219.19  318.12

HEALTHY                             (  8)
008.22  125.18  127.21  131.10  131.32
139.08  216.18  264.09

HEAP                                (  9)
041.15  043.09  068.19  196.32  255.07
260.32  296.19  296.23  327.19

HEAPS                               (  4)
185.15  305.11  308.23  308.34

HEAR                                ( 57)
009.11  010.36  017.30  017.31  025.08
065.06  066.23  085.13  094.23  098.16
101.34  102.12  104.26  105.11  107.13
107.32  112.11  113.17  115.01  115.06
116.17  117.20  119.04  122.08  124.25
127.15  134.18  134.18  141.12  141.24
167.09  167.35  191.08  196.01  218.09
219.04  223.24  227.19  229.09  236.01
236.20  244.05  261.32  265.10  266.07
266.25  274.30  297.30  302.19  303.09
303.21  310.10  311.19  312.34  317.30
319.14  325.16

HEARD                               ( 97)
003.34  004.18  017.15  022.27  026.36
041.17  042.03  046.25  058.25  069.01
072.06  072.20  074.36  076.22  083.18
083.26  086.27  100.26  101.11  101.17
107.16  114.14  114.33  115.29  117.34
123.01  123.08  124.07  125.23  126.03
126.04  127.01  136.28  141.12  144.19
144.29  147.30  148.09  148.32  152.18
157.23  160.01  167.17  168.09  170.25
179.23  182.10  182.11  184.08  192.21
219.06  220.36  220.38  222.04  223.08
226.19  227.29  228.16  234.01  236.15
248.33  257.30  259.01  259.34  262.21
267.21  271.34  272.12  272.19  272.30
272.32  272.33  273.06  275.11  276.31
278.02  278.10  298.23  302.23  304.04
304.06  304.14  310.17  310.25  310.33
```

HEARD (CONTINUED)
312.15 312.15 313.17 313.22 316.22
319.02 319.04 320.06 324.31 333.06
333.13 333.22
HEARER   (1)
141.03
HEARING   (7)
141.26 149.16 174.35 260.18 272.06
287.15 333.16
HEARS   (2)
326.09 326.10
HEART   (9)
018.36 073.14 079.14 098.14 102.16
126.20 178.36 252.16 291.07
HEARTED   (1)
006.02
HEARTH   (10)
028.23 207.23 242.27 244.22 246.06
252.37 254.34 255.04 262.18 267.19
HEARTIEST   (1)
207.10
HEARTS   (3)
134.22 197.01 262.22
HEARTY   (2)
136.22 273.28
HEAT   (26)
012.31 012.32 013.11 015.14 013.18
013.23 013.25 015.17 021.27 073.36
117.06 141.19 166.15 176.36 247.27
251.36 259.35 294.02 295.16 300.10
300.25 300.35 307.16 308.13 311.02
333.14
HEATH   (1)
318.17
HEATHEN   (5)
023.09 077.18 112.12 221.08 266.35
HEATHENISH   (2)
058.02 221.10
HEAVE   (1)
309.08
HEAVED   (2)
206.13 288.02
HEAVEN   (33)
016.06 036.14 037.15 037.29 064.26
065.31 069.05 070.08 072.30 086.31
087.08 092.23 104.07 116.35 134.16
155.13 159.14 179.27 193.24 200.05
213.26 217.07 224.25 243.19 261.01
265.26 283.09 285.07 307.35 314.16
320.04 326.16 326.19
HEAVENLY   (3)
033.31 074.06 329.01
HEAVENS   (11)
004.22 015.32 116.14 158.34 159.16
159.22 176.22 182.14 242.01 269.20
317.07
HEAVIEST   (1)
282.28
HEAVING   (2)
188.10 304.16
HEAVY   (8)
115.36 132.32 170.23 232.13 250.04
261.05 275.01 318.15
HEBE   (1)
139.04
HEBREWS   (1)
106.35
HECTOR   (1)
162.01
HEEDLESS   (1)
092.09
HEEDLESSLY   (2)
114.13 238.10
HEEDLESSNESS   (1)
165.24
HEEL   (3)
018.17 115.04 302.13

HEELS   (2)
036.15 209.06
HEIGHT   (13)
176.01 181.16 181.21 181.32 182.01
182.04 185.16 187.36 237.01 248.08
289.25 291.11 304.17
HEIGHTS   (1)
009.32
HEIR   (1)
260.21
HELD   (12)
044.01 055.03 088.18 172.03 177.18
226.02 226.04 226.31 257.21 274.24
294.08 319.09
HELENA   (1)
262.05
HELL   (1)
016.06
HELM   (2)
169.24 169.25
HELP   (10)
022.18 025.26 044.19 045.03 074.34
152.07 164.34 205.03 287.05 330.31
HELPED   (9)
074.35 147.20 152.05 152.25 156.07
180.26 234.27 303.17 323.19
HELPING   (1)
311.22
HELPLESS   (1)
009.27
HELPS   (3)
030.27 078.29 193.39
HELVE   (2)
178.12 252.02
HEMLOCK   (2)
149.01 202.06
HEMP   (1)
119.27
HEN   (9)
152.26 154.12 159.27 185.17 212.20
226.13 226.14 227.17 317.29
HENCE   (5)
046.27 119.18 136.02 181.11 327.32
HENCEFORTH   (2)
192.10 320.15
HENRY   (1)
026.09
HENS   (9)
043.12 043.14 044.02 127.10 127.30
128.09 152.28 227.20 257.27
HER   (72)
022.34 025.15 036.23 043.21 052.26
061.31 076.24 076.26 076.32 082.13
085.07 095.05 102.30 110.12 125.10
137.34 137.35 138.05 138.21 138.22
173.18 179.32 182.19 199.35 204.26
210.31 210.32 218.25 226.11 226.13
226.20 226.21 226.21 228.08 228.11
228.14 232.27 232.28 233.01 233.02
233.04 233.08 233.10 233.12 233.15
233.16 257.21 257.23 257.25 257.26
257.30 257.30 257.31 268.23 278.07
278.34 278.36 280.26 280.28 280.29
280.30 281.08 282.08 282.14 295.12
303.16 303.17 308.31 317.32 319.07
322.19 324.26
HERALD   (1)
140.25
HERALDS   (1)
313.28
HERB   (5)
077.03 137.32 138.36 155.28 328.23
HERBA   (1)
311.01
HERBS   (3)
070.03 080.10 216.26
HERCULEAN   (1)
155.09

HIM   (CONTINUED)   HIS   (CONTINUED)
147.26 147.26 147.29 147.32 148.03   007.27 007.32 007.33 007.36 009.21
148.07 148.10 148.15 148.17 148.20   009.22 009.23 009.24 011.24 012.09
148.22 148.24 148.27 148.30 149.03   012.35 013.02 013.05 013.35 013.36
149.13 149.15 149.21 149.22 149.30   015.13 015.14 015.15 015.16 015.26
149.31 150.02 150.11 151.21 151.22   017.22 017.27 019.06 019.12 019.17
158.21 161.29 161.29 161.30 164.30   021.30 022.04 022.18 022.28 023.17
165.31 168.20 168.23 168.29 168.29   023.24 023.24 024.23 024.36 025.31
170.12 170.13 171.04 171.28 171.29   026.16 027.12 027.13 027.33 028.02
173.11 184.02 191.04 192.27 196.01   029.15 029.15 030.30 030.32 031.23
196.01 196.09 196.11 196.11 196.19   031.24 031.27 032.33 033.20 033.21
196.23 196.27 202.21 205.03 205.03   033.23 033.33 034.18 036.19 037.21
205.30 206.01 210.08 213.02 216.16   038.33 041.04 041.04 044.01 044.15
216.20 219.27 220.06 221.11 222.09   044.23 045.07 046.02 046.16 046.28
222.14 222.16 225.25 227.27 229.19   047.04 047.08 047.10 047.10 047.13
229.21 229.29 231.04 231.10 234.10   047.29 047.31 048.07 048.11 048.13
234.12 234.14 234.30 235.35 236.03   048.15 050.25 051.02 051.23 051.24
236.21 236.22 236.25 236.29 252.02   051.26 051.31 051.36 052.01 052.10
257.07 258.10 261.16 261.26 261.27   052.14 052.27 056.01 056.02 056.20
262.03 262.06 262.13 266.06 266.12   056.20 056.33 058.10 058.19 059.35
268.05 268.23 268.35 269.25 272.24   061.31 062.10 063.28 063.35 063.36
274.04 275.01 277.08 277.11 277.29   065.08 065.29 066.09 066.10 066.11
278.06 278.35 279.10 279.10 279.19   066.12 066.17 066.21 066.25 066.36
284.01 291.17 291.18 303.21 304.09   067.02 067.03 067.05 067.06 067.26
314.12 314.33 314.36 315.01 320.12   067.31 067.33 070.29 070.30 070.30
321.09 321.30 323.36 326.09 326.30   071.02 071.02 071.12 071.12 071.12
326.33 327.01 327.20 330.15 331.14   071.13 071.18 071.32 072.08 072.10
HIMSELF   (81)   073.13 073.14 073.31 073.36 074.03
007.33 007.35 015.30 019.09 024.23   074.06 074.06 074.13 074.23 074.32
028.03 028.32 031.33 037.01 037.33   074.32 075.19 075.19 076.02 076.27
051.05 051.27 057.01 065.11 070.29   077.01 077.07 077.12 077.21 077.21
076.20 077.24 077.34 094.02 096.16   077.26 077.29 077.35 078.06 078.06
096.20 097.05 106.15 108.20 110.01   078.07 078.09 078.09 081.10 081.11
112.23 120.22 136.01 137.28 143.07   081.12 081.14 081.14 082.12 082.37
145.23 146.26 146.28 147.28 147.35   083.23 084.24 087.32 088.18 088.19
148.23 149.30 150.12 150.17 151.16   088.22 088.23 089.25 089.27 090.19
151.31 161.31 164.18 172.09 172.10   090.26 090.27 091.22 091.23 091.32
185.01 205.06 205.10 212.37 216.00   092.34 093.14 093.16 093.26 093.27
220.21 220.33 221.26 222.08 222.23   093.34 093.34 093.35 094.10 095.14
229.14 231.14 234.22 235.33 250.20   095.18 096.14 096.17 096.19 096.32
253.31 259.11 260.24 262.10 265.08   097.14 099.33 102.13 102.19 103.02
266.23 274.14 274.19 274.33 277.28   103.08 103.12 103.13 103.14 103.15
285.31 297.31 303.33 320.09 321.09   105.26 106.18 107.01 107.14 107.17
322.38 323.05 323.06 323.06 326.02   107.17 107.36 108.07 108.07 108.08
326.24   108.10 108.12 108.16 110.02 112.22
HINDER   (1)   112.34 115.32 116.17 116.18 116.19
249.26   116.20 117.05 117.08 117.14 117.15
HINDERANCES   (1)   117.18 117.19 117.20 117.22 117.22
014.19   120.22 120.24 120.25 121.12 121.13
HINDERED   (2)   121.15 122.01 126.20 126.21 126.27
020.01 071.14   126.30 127.03 127.12 127.20 127.25
HINDOO   (6)   127.26 127.26 127.28 127.35 130.07
014.22 096.13 096.21 099.11 217.34   131.08 133.16 133.27 133.36 135.16
221.22   135.29 135.35 136.01 136.06 136.06
HINGES   (1)   136.07 136.26 136.31 140.25 141.04
049.16   143.04 143.08 143.10 144.17 144.18
HINT   (4)   144.23 144.24 144.26 144.35 145.01
016.34 142.27 289.23 315.12   145.06 145.09 145.16 145.16 145.19
HIPPOCRATES   (1)   145.22 145.24 145.25 145.25 146.02
010.02   146.02 146.06 146.11 146.11 146.12
HIRE   (7)   146.17 146.30 146.31 146.32 146.33
030.33 034.12 055.02 073.22 109.07   147.13 147.15 147.36 148.03 148.11
110.11 331.18   148.22 148.25 149.07 149.36 149.36
HIRED   (6)   150.06 150.13 150.18 150.19 150.29
032.21 108.09 134.12 157.07 258.29   151.21 151.27 157.24 157.30 158.27
295.12   158.27 159.24 161.25 161.29 162.02
HIRELING   (1)   164.20 164.21 164.21 165.07 165.12
230.23   165.29 166.10 166.12 166.13 166.14
HIRES   (1)   166.34 166.35 166.35 166.36 166.36
030.31   169.05 170.15 170.15 171.12 173.35
HIRING   (1)   174.03 174.12 182.27 183.32 186.14
030.29   191.02 192.23 192.25 193.16 193.17
HIRUNDO   (1)   193.17 193.37 195.30 195.33 195.34
185.03   196.17 196.18 196.20 196.20 196.22
HIS   (668)   196.23 196.26 198.25 198.29 199.01
003.33 003.35 005.11 005.37 006.17   199.07 199.33 201.20 202.23 202.25
006.19 006.19 006.20 007.10 007.10   202.26 204.07 204.09 204.09 204.09
007.10 007.11 007.11 007.26 007.27   204.23 204.33 204.37 205.01 205.08

97

98

HOMER				(7)
089.03	099.32	100.07	103.24	144.19
144.37	172.17			

HOMERIC (1)
144.14

HOMERS (2)
104.04 172.23

HOMESICK (1)
115.04

HOMESTEAD (2)
157.19 258.16

HOMESTEADS (1)
032.31

HOMEWARD (1)
190.19

HOMINY (1)
063.33

HOMOEOPATHIC (1)
167.12

HON (1)
329.29

HONEST				(9)
025.26	038.10	054.19	057.35	091.21
105.17	124.20	154.17	204.21	

HONESTLY				(6)
008.21	011.05	027.01	029.05	033.11
046.06				

HONESTY (1)
150.09

HONEY				(7)
053.01	160.25	215.12	300.16	300.20
302.13	302.29			

HONK (2)
249.01 313.12

HONKING (3)
272.11 272.16 312.30

HONOR (4)
010.35 143.26 192.33 322.34

HONORED (1)
045.07

II00				(14)
125.21	125.21	125.21	125.21	272.07
272.07	272.07	272.07	272.09	272.09
272.23	272.28	272.28	272.29	

HOOK				(7)
029.14	175.23	213.29	225.07	250.02
261.04	295.03			

HOOKED (1)
203.18

HOOKS (4)
130.31 213.28 213.29 235.19

HOOPER (1)
255.12

HOORER (2)
125.21 272.07

HOOTING (5)
125.07 125.26 127.09 256.07 272.01

HOP (1)
105.19

HOPE				(7)
104.07	125.12	166.24	166.25	204.16
310.24	312.11			

HOPEFUL (1)
206.32

HOPELESS (1)
120.34

HOPES (3)
121.01 217.11 254.31

HOPING (1)
206.36

HOPPERS (1)
168.12

HORIZON				(17)
020.20	086.10	087.04	087.31	115.27
123.07	123.23	130.09	130.18	160.11
161.07	167.20	209.01	252.25	272.24
288.17	312.14			

HORIZONTAL (1)
275.03

HORIZONTALLY (1)
289.31

HORN (3)
223.11 276.34 280.04

HORNBEAM (1)
202.03

HORNED (1)
175.14

HORNS (1)
279.32

HORNY (1)
195.35

HORRID (2)
287.34 288.13

HORRORS (1)
288.10

HORSE				(23)
017.11	017.16	028.13	038.26	052.34
056.04	056.27	056.29	056.36	116.18
116.21	117.03	137.14	163.08	163.09
192.21	192.24	220.20	233.23	261.24
281.34	318.13	330.16		

HORSES				(9)
007.27	021.34	057.13	157.07	157.36
196.32	295.28	295.36	297.20	

HOSE (1)
265.18

HOSMER (1)
230.23

HOSPITABLE (2)
258.11 269.06

HOSPITALALITY (1)
152.04

HOSPITALITY				(7)
142.12	152.04	207.10	244.23	270.22
331.02	331.11			

HOST (2)
204.33 244.21

HOT (4)
004.36 014.15 250.05 259.17

HOTEL (1)
231.19

HOTTER (1)
015.23

HOUND				(11)
017.11	017.15	210.11	223.25	277.07
277.21	277.25	277.27	278.07	278.30
279.20				

HOUNDING (3)
276.32 278.12 278.34

HOUNDS				(10)
152.18	276.31	277.15	277.18	278.03
278.11	278.28	279.07	279.12	280.06

HOUR				(37)
006.34	010.26	017.01	041.28	081.26
089.08	089.10	089.22	089.32	090.28
092.16	093.25	093.29	112.35	114.33
115.35	118.17	118.31	123.36	131.31
145.29	191.29	203.24	206.07	227.30
231.06	231.15	236.03	260.18	266.13
267.04	272.27	275.19	301.18	304.04
306.09	315.03			

HOURLY (2)
088.20 330.03

HOURS				(24)
030.13	044.30	045.23	056.02	100.10
100.22	104.20	112.04	112.13	117.23
132.21	163.08	174.34	192.02	223.09
236.31	247.18	253.05	268.05	274.19
301.23	312.03	323.33	328.10	

HOUSE				(200)
003.05	019.02	019.28	020.07	027.20
027.21	027.24	028.03	028.12	028.31
029.19	029.25	031.16	033.33	033.35
033.36	034.12	035.30	036.02	036.30
038.32	040.34	042.37	043.26	044.33

HOUSE (CONTINUED)
```
045.01  045.06  045.09  046.02  046.16
047.08  048.15  048.16  048.19  048.24
048.28  048.32  049.27  049.28  054.18
054.36  056.09  056.12  057.11  060.09
060.14  060.36  062.04  067.21  070.14
071.22  074.18  075.26  081.06  081.21
081.23  083.11  083.17  083.18  084.29
085.04  085.15  088.06  094.13  096.33
096.33  096.34  099.55  105.19  109.19
111.30  113.06  113.19  113.26  114.05
114.28  117.29  124.02  128.04  128.15
128.17  129.25  130.16  130.26  131.15
132.03  132.23  132.31  133.20  133.21
136.03  136.05  137.01  137.18  140.09
140.14  140.26  140.31  141.11  141.34
142.08  142.18  142.25  142.33  145.07
145.17  145.28  150.30  154.04  154.05
154.10  167.18  170.13  171.26  172.07
173.32  181.28  196.31  205.07  214.15
223.04  223.19  225.21  225.27  226.09
226.12  227.28  230.32  233.07  238.01
238.30  240.18  241.22  242.01  242.02
242.10  242.16  242.24  242.33  243.02
243.14  243.23  243.29  243.34  243.35
243.36  244.02  244.13  244.18  244.30
245.13  245.20  248.26  249.12  251.31
253.06  253.11  253.16  254.04  254.20
256.19  257.02  257.06  257.13  257.21
257.30  259.22  260.33  262.13  262.33
263.32  263.34  264.21  264.35  265.09
267.20  267.24  268.06  270.06  270.14
270.19  271.18  272.14  273.21  277.21
279.13  280.12  280.26  282.11  294.07
295.17  310.14  312.06  312.23  312.35
318.13  319.07  328.10  328.12  331.08
```
HOUSED   (2)
```
034.04  254.05
```
HOUSEHOLD   (4)
```
060.05  068.14  113.09  208.25
```
HOUSEHOLDS   (1)
```
092.10
```
HOUSEKEEPER   (4)
```
037.27  038.32  253.07  253.09
```
HOUSEKEEPERS   (2)
```
142.21  153.14
```
HOUSEKEEPING   (4)
```
038.29  066.33  067.19  223.17
```
HOUSES   (36)
```
005.04  012.24  015.21  029.31  030.05
032.22  034.02  034.08  034.14  036.20
036.35  038.02  038.05  038.27  039.03
039.12  039.21  039.27  039.34  040.09
048.36  057.09  057.12  068.16  074.08
081.30  132.28  140.18  168.17  168.35
169.11  232.35  244.29  250.11  265.13
297.12
```
HOUSEWIFE   (1)
```
036.21
```
HOUSEWIVES   (1)
```
063.01
```
HOUSEWORK   (2)
```
112.35  214.13
```
HOVERING   (2)
```
174.17  189.36
```
HOW   (143)
```
003.20  005.15  006.19  007.05  007.16
007.16  007.29  007.29  007.30  007.30
009.35  010.03  011.09  011.11  011.31
015.15  016.09  016.24  016.29  017.20
019.21  019.23  021.03  021.28  022.30
023.31  026.20  028.25  029.04  031.06
034.21  036.29  038.05  046.32  046.36
048.06  051.14  051.25  057.18
066.12  070.16  075.10  081.27  090.13
090.30  092.03  092.22  094.30  095.11
098.09  098.21  105.03  105.05  105.06
105.11  106.23  107.17  107.26  107.35
```

HOW (CONTINUED)
```
108.24  111.14  112.04  120.34  121.14
133.09  133.32  134.15  136.02  140.14
143.27  145.32  149.20  153.15  158.03
166.27  177.22  179.29  181.31  182.09
188.12  188.17  192.11  199.29  199.30
199.32  204.33  205.02  205.09  206.18
217.12  218.25  218.25  220.15  220.30
220.34  221.14  221.23  222.19  223.15
223.29  223.31  225.04  227.21  227.24
231.14  234.11  234.36  235.20  236.05
245.07  246.03  246.05  249.19  251.12
252.06  254.07  264.18  265.10  268.37
269.24  270.07  272.08  279.07  282.05
283.27  285.15  290.06  291.12  300.04
302.16  307.11  307.24  311.22  314.36
318.25  320.27  323.13  323.22  323.23
324.23  327.25  331.15
```
HOWARD   (2)
```
074.31  076.29
```
HOWARDS   (1)
```
074.33
```
HOWEVER   (39)
```
008.24  018.10  018.35  023.35  028.30
033.02  056.26  059.40  060.38  072.29
078.28  078.30  082.18  100.31  102.01
135.10  141.32  150.10  150.23  152.10
155.28  171.34  176.12  179.01  197.23
206.07  210.09  217.24  221.22  241.11
245.10  253.10  256.10  257.13  259.29
277.11  296.18  326.10  328.05
```
HOWL   (2)
```
236.12  248.25
```
HOWLINGS   (1)
```
125.19
```
HOWLS   (4)
```
125.12  137.20  236.14  236.24
```
HUBER   (1)
```
231.29
```
HUCKLEBERRIES   (5)
```
069.29  171.36  173.08  173.14  173.16
```
HUCKLEBERRY   (4)
```
018.24  116.02  173.16  173.22
```
HUCKLEBERRYING   (2)
```
153.30  206.12
```
HUDSON   (1)
```
272.22
```
HUDSONIUS   (1)
```
273.19
```
HUE   (6)
```
093.01  114.19  145.04  179.26  197.26
281.20
```
HUES   (1)
```
120.06
```
HUGE   (3)
```
115.37  140.20  199.10
```
HUGH   (1)
```
261.35
```
HUGS   (1)
```
117.02
```
HUM   (4)
```
088.36  123.06  160.16  160.22
```
HUMAN   (38)
```
009.30  010.21  012.11  014.29  028.09
035.04  038.16  040.05  065.10  074.16
080.11  102.24  103.21  124.31  125.10
125.12  130.35  132.06  135.07  148.28
173.03  199.34  211.07  216.08  221.19
227.26  229.09  231.25  254.07  256.16
263.16  264.19  269.01  307.31  307.34
311.14  331.35  332.17
```
HUMANE   (5)
```
073.02  211.24  211.33  212.26  212.30
```
HUMANELY   (1)
```
138.11
```
HUMANEST   (1)
```
132.13
```

HUMANITY (8)
049.36 211.06 211.21 211.28 212.07
214.07 308.26 310.19
HUMANIZED (1)
204.30
HUMBLE (12)
047.24 077.03 080.07 137.15 147.23
147.23 150.23 151.31 175.25 239.19
256.29 332.13
HUMBLER (2)
015.27 015.35
HUMBLY (1)
108.18
HUMILITY (4)
050.03 147.24 151.20 328.36
HUMMED (1)
174.04
HUMMING (2)
199.17 319.08
HUMMOCK (3)
317.18 317.18 321.20
HUMOR (1)
146.10
HUMOROUS (1)
137.27
HUNDRED (32)
005.19 030.02 031.01 031.17 033.01
037.07 052.11 057.35 074.33 090.10
091.25 091.36 109.22 109.22 115.14
152.29 176.03 176.03 190.14 194.21
251.08 251.10 287.05 287.07 288.35
289.12 290.17 294.16 295.22 297.19
297.33 321.32
HUNG (5)
125.33 131.01 168.28 252.04 271.30
HUNGER (1)
204.13
HUNGRY (7)
037.26 075.18 093.08 142.18 143.04
210.08 331.01
HUNT (6)
207.21 212.11 249.21 279.17 279.31
320.28
HUNTED (1)
211.23
HUNTER (19)
117.26 210.35 211.23 213.01 213.32
214.10 218.20 239.31 240.30 268.01
277.14 277.33 278.16 278.22 278.27
279.02 279.06 279.09 279.16
HUNTERS (14)
154.16 180.05 210.27 212.13 212.14
212.16 212.21 212.24 227.24 250.18
266.02 277.03 277.11 279.35
HUNTING (14)
145.34 158.35 210.24 211.12 211.16
213.06 233.01 276.34 277.19 277.28
278.07 279.08 279.30 280.04
HURLED (1)
074.11
HURRIED (1)
249.01
HURRY (2)
093.06 280.30
HURT (1)
145.23
HUSBANDMAN (3)
157.26 166.25 166.31
HUSBANDMEN (1)
297.19
HUSBANDRY (6)
055.31 081.11 157.08 162.08 165.23
165.36
HUSH (1)
324.16
HUSHED (2)
256.07 313.01

HUSKS (1)
119.27
HUSTLING (1)
121.37
HUT (5)
034.31 203.33 259.03 271.19 277.26
HUTS (1)
047.24
HYADES (1)
088.09
HYBRID (1)
305.08
HYBRIDS (1)
233.19
HYDE (1)
327.36
HYDRA (1)
004.36
HYGEIA (1)
138.36
HYMN (1)
078.21
HYMNS (1)
124.33
HYPOCRISY (1)
049.39

003.03	003.04	003.05	003.08	003.09
003.10	003.16	003.16	003.17	003.19
003.20	003.21	003.22	003.24	003.28
003.29	003.30	003.31	004.05	004.08
004.15	004.18	004.30	004.34	005.03
005.15	006.28	007.17	007.17	009.10
009.11	009.16	009.17	009.17	010.16
010.17	010.27	010.30	010.31	010.33
010.35	011.03	011.24	011.30	012.08
014.04	014.15	015.19	016.04	016.13
016.14	016.22	016.29	016.29	016.33
016.34	017.01	017.08	017.09	017.11
017.13	017.14	017.22	017.26	017.31
018.02	018.03	018.06	018.09	018.12
018.18	018.20	018.21	018.24	018.28
018.28	018.33	018.34	018.36	019.09
019.10	019.11	019.17	019.18	019.20
019.22	019.29	019.30	019.31	019.31
019.33	020.04	021.07	022.05	022.09
022.24	022.26	022.26	023.28	024.20
025.02	025.06	025.06	025.07	025.07
025.08	025.08	025.09	025.11	025.11
025.15	025.24	026.01	026.32	026.36
027.08	028.36	029.02	029.07	029.08
029.23	030.02	030.03	030.17	030.17
030.18	030.28	031.10	031.14	031.28
032.03	032.10	032.15	032.17	032.28
032.34	033.35	034.06	034.36	035.01
035.04	035.15	035.21	035.24	036.12
036.14	036.16	036.25	036.26	036.29
036.30	036.30	037.03	037.12	037.13
038.05	038.07	038.11	038.13	038.15
038.21	038.24	040.02	040.04	040.12
040.22	040.23	040.32	040.34	041.05
041.06	041.06	041.07	041.13	041.14
041.17	041.22	041.25	041.27	041.34
042.03	042.06	042.18	042.23	042.25
042.28	042.30	042.31	042.32	042.35
042.36	042.38	043.04	043.04	043.30
043.32	043.36	044.04	044.06	044.10
044.11	044.15	044.22	044.30	045.06
045.08	045.08	045.09	045.13	045.15
045.19	045.21	045.25	045.32	046.14
046.25	046.34	047.15	047.15	048.22
048.23	048.26	048.28	048.33	048.35
049.13	049.19	049.25	049.26	049.28
049.32	049.35	049.36	049.39	049.40
049.41	050.02	050.02	050.03	050.11
050.35	051.09	051.09	051.10	051.16
051.18	052.02	052.02	052.03	052.04
053.01	053.03	053.06	053.06	053.07
053.10	053.11	053.12	053.19	053.19
053.21	054.12	054.14	054.18	054.20
054.27	054.30	054.30	055.01	055.03
055.07	055.21	055.25	055.27	055.27
055.28	055.29	056.04	056.07	056.08
056.13	056.14	056.26	056.27	056.29
057.25	057.26	057.32	058.11	058.12
058.26	058.26	058.30	058.34	058.35
059.03	059.05	059.29	059.29	059.30
059.33	059.34	059.39	060.22	060.23
060.33	060.37	060.41	061.05	061.07
061.08	061.08	061.09	061.11	061.14
061.18	061.20	061.21	061.26	061.30
061.33	062.01	062.02	062.05	062.11
062.13	062.14	062.23	062.28	062.31
062.33	062.34	062.36	063.04	063.06
063.12	063.14	063.19	063.25	063.26
064.02	064.02	064.06	064.07	064.07
064.09	064.09	064.11	064.12	064.19
064.19	064.20	064.22	064.25	064.27
064.30	064.31	064.32	064.34	064.34
064.37	064.37	065.02	065.03	065.05
065.05	065.16	065.17	065.25	065.27
065.27	065.33	066.13	066.14	066.20
066.22	066.23	066.26	066.30	067.01
067.02	067.05	067.07	067.07	067.11

067.12	067.13	067.17	067.20	067.22
067.25	069.01	069.03	069.09	069.10
069.11	069.13	069.14	069.16	069.18
069.18	069.20	069.21	069.22	069.23
069.23	069.25	069.26	069.28	069.29
069.33	069.34	070.02	070.03	070.06
070.10	070.11	070.12	070.17	070.20
070.22	070.24	070.33	071.03	071.06
071.06	071.08	071.09	071.11	071.25
072.05	072.13	072.20	072.21	072.21
072.22	072.26	072.28	072.29	072.32
073.01	073.05	073.07	073.10	073.12
073.14	073.15	073.17	073.19	073.20
073.21	073.23	073.28	073.29	074.17
074.18	074.22	074.26	074.26	074.27
074.28	074.28	074.35	075.21	075.23
075.26	075.30	075.32	075.32	076.22
076.33	076.36	077.04	078.02	078.03
078.03	078.05	078.11	078.14	078.14
078.31	079.03	081.01	081.02	081.06
081.07	081.08	081.09	081.09	081.15
081.16	081.16	081.19	081.20	081.22
081.25	081.26	081.26	081.27	082.02
082.05	082.06	082.07	082.08	082.09
082.15	082.17	082.18	082.19	082.20
082.21	082.24	082.24	082.26	082.26
082.30	082.30	082.33	083.15	083.16
083.18	083.19	083.24	083.25	083.28
083.29	083.30	083.31	083.32	083.33
083.34	083.35	083.36	084.02	084.02
084.03	084.08	084.14	084.14	084.15
084.20	084.22	084.22	084.26	085.01
085.05	085.15	085.16	085.16	085.20
085.24	085.28	085.30	085.33	086.03
086.08	086.11	086.14	087.03	087.05
087.10	087.16	087.18	087.22	087.23
087.25	087.34	087.36	088.05	088.10
088.11	088.15	088.26	088.27	088.28
088.30	088.34	088.35	089.01	089.01
089.28	090.02	090.12	090.13	090.18
090.32	090.32	090.34	090.35	090.35
090.36	091.01	091.02	091.24	092.30
093.01	093.12	093.18	094.03	094.04
094.05	094.07	094.11	094.11	094.23
094.27	094.34	096.12	096.25	098.19
098.19	098.20	098.20	098.22	098.23
098.29	098.33	098.34	098.35	098.36
099.13	099.14	099.22	099.23	099.29
099.30	099.31	099.32	099.33	099.35
100.02	100.03	100.05	100.06	104.21
104.31	104.32	105.12	105.18	105.27
106.13	106.16	107.11	107.13	107.15
107.15	107.19	107.21	107.21	108.25
110.09	111.20	111.20	111.21	111.22
111.24	111.26	111.32	111.33	112.02
112.04	112.07	112.10	112.14	112.21
112.25	112.36	113.11	113.14	114.02
114.06	114.13	114.14	114.24	114.33
114.36	115.01	115.06	115.14	115.14
115.20	115.20	116.07	116.14	116.17
116.22	116.31	116.32	117.14	117.20
118.05	118.07	118.26	118.30	119.04
119.08	119.18	119.19	119.24	120.35
120.36	121.01	121.07	121.20	122.08
122.16	122.20	122.27	122.27	122.34
123.01	123.24	123.25	123.27	123.29
123.30	123.31	124.05	124.06	124.09
124.24	124.36	125.03	125.07	125.14
125.15	125.25	126.03	127.01	127.01
127.02	127.29	129.05	129.06	129.08
129.25	129.25	129.33	130.05	130.13
130.18	130.22	130.24	130.32	130.35
131.03	131.12	131.13	131.22	131.23
131.24	131.25	131.27	131.28	131.30
131.31	131.33	132.01	132.07	132.09
132.14	132.30	132.37	133.05	133.07

133.12	133.16	133.28	133.30	133.32	202.15	202.17	202.17	202.30	203.04
133.33	133.34	133.34	133.34	133.35	203.17	203.17	203.17	203.23	203.26
135.02	135.04	135.05	135.07	135.09	203.28	203.30	203.31	203.33	204.06
135.11	135.14	135.20	135.22	135.22	204.19	205.02	205.04	205.06	205.11
136.20	136.26	136.28	137.01	137.04	205.13	205.13	205.29	205.31	206.01
137.07	137.13	137.15	137.19	137.28	206.04	206.06	206.08	206.08	206.09
137.33	138.14	138.15	138.35	140.03	206.19	206.27	206.27	206.28	206.28
140.03	140.06	140.09	140.15	140.24	206.29	206.34	206.35	206.35	207.07
140.30	141.08	141.36	142.16	142.19	207.09	207.10	207.10	207.12	207.17
142.24	142.26	142.28	142.28	142.29	207.20	208.31	208.34	208.37	209.01
143.27	143.35	143.36	144.01	144.01	210.03	210.05	210.08	210.10	210.10
144.02	144.03	144.06	144.15	144.15	210.13	210.15	210.18	210.19	210.21
144.24	144.36	145.33	145.33	145.35	210.23	211.25	211.26	211.28	211.30
145.35	146.12	146.16	146.24	146.25	211.31	211.32	211.32	211.33	211.34
147.01	147.04	147.32	147.32	147.34	211.36	212.01	212.02	212.02	212.05
147.35	148.02	148.09	148.13	148.17	212.07	212.11	212.17	212.33	213.09
148.17	148.18	148.29	148.33	149.03	213.33	213.33	213.34	213.35	214.01
149.20	149.21	149.21	149.22	149.24	214.02	214.02	214.03	214.03	214.06
149.29	149.29	150.01	150.06	150.11	214.08	214.09	214.09	214.09	214.12
150.13	150.31	150.31	150.33	150.33	214.19	214.21	214.27	214.29	214.34
151.01	151.04	151.08	151.11	151.14	214.34	214.35	215.04	215.20	215.35
151.17	151.23	151.24	151.24	151.25	216.07	217.02	217.03	217.04	217.05
151.26	151.28	151.31	152.01	152.07	217.06	217.07	217.09	217.13	217.13
152.12	152.24	152.35	153.01	153.07	217.17	217.20	217.21	217.23	217.23
153.15	154.02	154.04	154.05	154.10	217.23	217.25	217.28	218.03	218.03
154.12	154.12	154.13	154.14	154.19	218.05	218.06	218.26	219.14	219.16
154.21	155.09	155.09	155.11	155.12	219.25	219.26	220.10	221.09	221.13
155.13	155.18	155.19	155.19	155.20	221.14	221.15	223.03	223.07	223.07
155.27	155.31	155.31	155.32	156.02	223.15	223.23	223.24	223.27	223.32
156.02	156.06	156.11	156.13	156.14	223.35	223.35	224.01	224.03	224.04
156.16	156.24	156.25	156.28	156.34	224.05	224.05	224.06	224.06	224.15
156.36	157.02	157.07	157.08	157.14	224.17	224.17	224.21	224.23	224.24
157.18	157.25	158.01	158.03	158.17	224.25	224.26	224.28	224.29	224.29
158.30	158.32	158.33	159.09	159.09	224.31	224.33	224.34	224.35	225.01
159.09	159.10	159.13	159.24	159.30	225.04	225.17	225.24	225.26	225.27
159.36	160.01	160.09	160.10	160.23	225.35	226.04	226.31	226.35	227.27
160.27	160.29	160.29	161.01	161.01	227.29	228.03	228.04	228.05	228.16
161.11	161.13	161.16	161.16	161.16	228.17	228.25	228.26	228.27	228.32
161.18	162.07	162.09	162.09	162.16	229.04	229.05	229.09	229.10	229.20
162.17	162.18	162.32	163.24	163.40	230.07	230.11	230.23	230.30	230.30
163.40	163.41	164.06	164.07	164.09	230.34	231.07	231.14	231.16	231.20
164.16	164.27	165.04	166.16	166.18	231.20	231.21	231.23	231.23	232.09
166.27	167.04	167.09	167.14	167.15	232.23	232.30	232.33	232.36	233.02
167.17	167.23	168.01	168.01	168.12	233.15	233.21	233.26	234.07	234.08
168.36	169.07	169.08	169.10	169.11	234.09	234.12	234.13	234.16	234.22
169.15	169.17	169.25	169.26	169.26	234.23	234.24	234.26	234.29	235.04
169.28	169.29	169.33	169.34	170.05	235.25	235.27	235.30	235.31	236.01
170.06	170.07	170.11	170.16	170.25	236.01	236.16	236.19	236.20	236.27
171.21	171.22	171.23	171.23	171.26	236.29	236.31	237.03	237.07	237.09
171.30	171.32	171.34	172.01	172.02	238.03	238.06	238.06	238.17	238.20
172.04	172.05	172.06	172.13	172.14	238.24	238.27	238.29	239.01	239.06
172.15	172.18	172.19	172.20	173.05	239.08	239.08	239.09	239.10	239.14
173.05	173.25	173.29	173.34	174.01	239.36	240.15	240.16	240.17	240.20
174.08	174.09	174.13	174.15	174.16	240.22	240.23	240.28	240.32	240.32
174.19	174.30	174.32	175.09	175.20	240.34	241.12	241.15	241.16	241.17
175.22	176.14	177.10	177.16	177.24	241.18	241.21	241.22	241.23	241.26
178.04	178.06	178.10	178.10	178.11	241.26	241.27	241.30	241.32	242.09
178.15	178.17	178.18	178.19	178.19	242.10	242.12	242.17	242.24	242.24
179.12	179.13	179.35	180.21	180.24	242.25	242.26	242.28	242.29	242.31
180.25	180.30	180.30	180.36	181.09	243.02	243.09	243.13	244.27	244.27
181.10	181.12	182.06	182.26	182.32	244.28	244.28	244.29	244.31	244.31
183.02	183.08	183.12	183.20	183.25	244.32	244.33	245.16	245.16	245.22
183.27	184.06	184.08	184.08	184.11	245.25	245.34	246.01	246.02	246.04
184.14	184.35	184.36	185.06	185.08	246.06	246.09	246.10	246.11	247.13
185.23	185.28	186.20	187.03	187.22	247.17	247.18	247.20	247.34	248.06
189.02	189.15	189.19	189.21	189.22	248.15	248.16	248.25	248.33	249.10
189.23	189.28	189.37	190.08	190.16	249.18	249.28	249.30	249.33	250.01
190.18	190.20	190.21	190.24	190.25	250.05	250.17	250.19	250.21	250.21
191.08	191.14	191.34	191.20	191.28	250.23	250.24	251.25	251.27	251.29
191.29	191.32	191.33	191.36	192.02	251.31	251.32	251.33	251.34	251.36
192.04	192.04	192.05	192.30	193.04	252.01	252.08	252.19	252.20	252.23
193.07	193.09	193.18	193.19	193.24	252.25	252.27	253.01	253.03	253.03
193.25	193.26	193.33	194.03	194.27	253.04	253.06	253.07	253.08	253.10
194.30	194.31	195.06	195.12	195.23	253.10	253.10	253.12	253.13	253.15
196.01	196.19	197.17	197.17	197.31	253.18	253.26	254.01	254.03	254.04
197.33	198.08	198.18	201.03	201.23	254.13	254.14	254.21	254.25	256.04
201.33	202.07	202.08	202.10	202.13	256.07	256.11	256.16	257.32	258.02

```
I                          (CONTINUED)    ICE                          (CONTINUED)
259.06  259.06  259.08  259.09  259.16    296.01  296.20  296.31  296.33  296.34
259.19  259.19  260.14  260.17  260.19    296.36  297.09  297.10  297.12  299.03
260.21  261.07  261.20  261.22  261.27    299.06  299.12  299.29  299.34  300.02
261.31  261.35  262.02  262.05  262.12    300.10  300.13  300.18  300.23  300.31
262.12  262.15  263.18  264.03  264.23    300.32  300.34  301.01  301.02  301.12
264.24  264.29  264.33  264.35  265.17    301.15  302.12  302.24  303.09  303.25
265.21  265.27  266.03  266.06  266.07    303.30  303.31  303.35  304.12  307.01
266.08  266.11  266.24  266.31  266.32    310.33  311.18  311.23  312.10  321.20
266.35  266.35  267.01  267.05  267.06    325.27  325.29  331.04
267.11  267.16  267.17  267.21  267.21    ICELAND                             ( 1)
268.17  268.27  269.09  269.16  269.24    294.25
270.05  270.06  270.11  270.13  270.16    ICES                                ( 2)
270.17  270.22  271.05  271.06  271.08    248.02  331.03
271.11  271.15  271.16  271.17  271.22    ICHTHYOLOGISTS                      ( 1)
271.25  271.29  271.34  272.04  272.05    184.30
272.11  272.19  272.26  272.27  272.29    ICICLES                             ( 3)
272.33  272.36  273.06  273.22  274.08    271.32  275.33  296.12
274.14  274.14  275.07  275.21  276.01    ICY                                 ( 2)
276.02  276.03  276.04  276.04  276.05    190.05  303.11
276.06  276.22  276.27  276.31  277.03    IDEA                                ( 7)
277.28  277.29  277.30  279.24  279.36    046.26  068.07  094.36  137.04  149.23
280.05  280.08  280.28  280.32  280.34    152.26  306.19
280.36  281.10  282.02  282.04  282.08    IDEALISTS                           ( 1)
282.21  282.34  283.03  283.36  284.05    259.33
284.06  284.18  284.20  285.02  285.09    IDEAS                               ( 3)
285.10  285.17  285.33  287.01  287.11    149.25  152.27  152.31
287.15  288.26  288.26  288.29  288.34    IDENTICAL                           ( 1)
289.10  289.12  289.15  289.22  290.06    311.09
290.09  290.14  290.18  291.04  292.08    IDENTIFIED                          ( 1)
292.25  292.25  292.34  293.12  293.29    134.18
294.13  294.15  294.23  294.25  294.26    IDIOTIC                             ( 1)
294.26  294.30  294.36  295.07  297.02    125.25
297.18  297.22  297.22  297.25  297.30    IDIOTS                              ( 1)
298.01  298.06  298.09  298.10  298.14    125.19
299.12  300.25  300.35  301.14  301.15    IDLE                                ( 5)
301.17  301.33  301.34  302.11  302.13    047.09  057.03  072.28  322.37  331.16
302.13  302.16  302.16  302.18  302.23    IDLENESS                            ( 3)
302.34  303.20  303.22  304.31  306.06    112.19  157.12  191.35
306.09  306.10  306.13  306.14  308.29    IDLY                                ( 1)
309.35  310.14  310.17  311.19  312.01    016.18
312.09  312.14  312.15  312.17  312.20    IF                                ( 492)
312.20  312.21  312.26  312.30  312.34    003.11  003.16  003.17  003.22  003.28
313.02  313.04  313.08  313.17  313.22    004.01  005.06  005.30  008.05  008.18
313.25  316.19  316.22  316.24  316.32    009.02  009.16  010.16  010.31  011.10
316.33  317.14  317.16  318.18  319.01    011.12  011.34  012.11  016.09  016.29
319.02  319.04  319.19  320.30  322.06    017.18  017.20  017.33  018.14  020.05
323.10  323.10  323.11  323.15  323.18    022.08  022.12  022.13  022.15  022.17
323.18  323.24  323.26  323.27  323.29    022.31  023.17  023.21  023.30  023.32
324.18  324.22  324.27  324.29  324.29    024.12  024.25  025.04  025.18  026.10
325.16  325.24  325.24  325.25  326.25    028.02  028.24  028.26  028.30  031.09
327.11  328.14  328.28  328.30  329.17    031.19  031.21  031.24  032.30  032.34
329.23  329.31  329.32  329.35  330.05    033.16  034.16  034.18  035.32  036.16
330.09  330.11  330.17  330.23  330.35    037.01  038.01  039.36  041.31  042.04
331.01  331.03  331.05  331.09  331.13    043.09  046.04  046.27  047.36  048.08
331.14  332.10  332.15  332.19  332.32    049.01  049.34  050.11  051.16  052.03
333.03  333.28                            052.27  053.01  053.16  053.18  053.28
IBEROS                              ( 1)  054.01  055.31  056.12  056.17  056.30
322.01                                    057.29  059.30  061.08  064.06  064.19
ICARIAN                             ( 2)  064.30  064.37  065.04  066.01  066.02
197.06  252.29                            066.06  066.13  066.28  067.07  067.16
ICE                               ( 123)  068.08  070.15  070.35  071.06  071.35
020.10  021.09  021.14  041.09  042.02    072.01  072.02  072.26  073.15  073.28
075.22  092.15  117.17  176.16  176.35    073.30  074.16  074.26  074.27  074.28
178.05  178.07  178.10  178.17  183.33    074.34  075.15  075.20  076.07  076.27
184.15  185.19  185.20  191.17  192.36    077.20  077.21  077.36  078.14  078.31
198.24  198.27  198.28  213.10  246.16    079.17  079.18  081.22  082.17  083.31
246.20  246.31  247.01  247.06  247.08    084.13  084.24  085.15  088.08  088.22
247.10  247.12  247.14  247.20  247.23    089.12  090.05  090.06  090.28  090.34
247.31  247.34  247.35  248.03  248.07    091.06  091.09  091.31  091.35  092.18
248.13  248.17  248.19  248.20  249.36    092.22  092.23  092.31  093.01  093.12
265.31  271.13  271.21  272.33  277.16    093.20  093.23  093.24  093.27  094.12
283.01  284.09  284.13  284.19  284.20    094.18  094.30  095.05  095.08  095.30
285.10  285.20  288.26  292.13  292.17    095.34  096.28  096.30  097.29  097.30
292.23  292.34  293.01  293.03  293.04    098.10  098.12  098.16  098.18  100.11
293.09  293.10  293.14  293.18  293.20    100.22  100.27  101.15  103.28  104.25
293.24  293.26  293.29  293.31  293.34    104.36  106.28  107.14  107.32  109.03
294.01  294.12  295.24  295.26  295.35    109.25  109.28  109.34  110.15  112.05
```

IF   (CONTINUED)
112.20 112.30 113.13 113.23 115.06
116.09 116.15 116.22 116.23 116.25
117.07 117.08 117.23 119.30 120.28
121.37 123.06 124.13 124.27 125.09
126.10 127.06 129.33 130.27 131.17
131.23 131.25 131.27 131.31 136.25
138.13 138.28 140.08 141.14 141.17
141.20 141.27 142.03 142.07 142.09
142.17 144.19 145.24 145.32 147.01
147.18 147.23 147.26 147.27 148.03
148.10 149.03 149.07 149.22 149.24
149.29 149.30 149.34 150.06 152.18
153.12 153.24 153.31 156.02 156.25
158.22 159.10 159.15 159.29 160.08
160.12 160.16 160.33 161.01 161.30
162.12 162.23 163.32 163.38 164.01
164.03 164.09 164.15 164.25 165.02
167.21 167.33 168.08 169.18 170.08
171.04 171.08 171.29 172.08 172.19
173.13 174.07 175.20 176.10 178.07
178.15 181.29 183.02 183.08 185.08
185.18 186.33 187.14 188.17 188.21
189.24 189.36 190.07 190.10 190.22
192.10 193.07 194.11 194.25 195.01
195.11 196.22 197.01 197.03 197.19
198.14 198.35 199.22 202.13 202.15
205.09 205.30 205.31 205.32 206.08
206.11 206.15 207.31 212.05 212.08
212.14 213.02 213.26 214.02 214.09
215.28 215.31 216.13 216.24 216.31
217.05 218.20 219.25 219.25 220.33
220.35 221.03 221.07 221.08 221.08
224.18 224.19 224.20 224.26 224.30
225.11 225.16 226.16 230.05 230.12
230.14 231.23 233.21 233.34 234.09
236.24 236.27 239.08 241.34 243.28
244.25 244.31 244.33 244.34 245.05
245.13 245.20 246.11 246.33 247.10
247.30 248.26 250.07 250.20 251.02
252.03 252.18 253.07 253.11 253.26
254.21 258.07 259.06 259.25 260.30
261.35 262.02 262.16 266.21 267.21
270.21 272.02 272.21 272.34 272.34
273.02 273.09 273.12 273.21 273.35
274.03 274.27 275.01 275.22 275.28
277.05 277.06 277.22 278.32 278.34
280.03 280.07 281.07 281.23 281.28
282.22 282.34 283.25 284.21 284.29
284.30 285.25 287.10 287.19 287.31
288.06 290.23 291.14 292.27 292.28
293.06 293.18 294.35 295.30 296.15
298.06 301.17 303.11 303.16 303.19
304.07 305.22 306.09 306.14 307.02
307.12 308.23 309.30 310.18 310.27
311.01 311.31 312.14 312.19 312.25
314.20 317.01 317.21 317.26 318.35
319.07 319.09 320.13 320.16 320.28
321.13 322.15 322.17 322.37 323.09
323.29 324.06 324.12 324.13 324.17
325.15 325.19 325.25 325.29 326.07
326.13 326.19 328.01 328.28 329.04
329.06 329.07 329.35 330.14 331.17
332.03 332.29

ICNOBLE   (1)
  051.04
IGNORANCE   (5)
  006.10 006.19 110.18 220.39 290.26
IGNORANT   (3)
  148.19 160.10 227.12
ILIAD   (4)
  045.28 089.03 099.32 102.18
ILL   (4)
  095.24 214.16 214.29 223.25
ILLE   (1)
  322.02
ILLITERATE   (4)
  103.06 106.26 107.20 150.24

ILLITERATENESS   (2)
  107.22 107.23
ILLUMINES   (1)
  010.15
ILLUSION   (3)
  052.12 325.17 327.21
ILLUSIVE   (1)
  285.21
ILLUSORY   (1)
  096.08
ILLUSTRATED   (1)
  308.15
ILLUSTRATES   (1)
  125.28
ILLUSTRIOUS   (1)
  331.23
IMAGE   (1)
  269.04
IMAGINABLE   (2)
  035.06 187.01
IMAGINARY   (1)
  274.12
IMAGINATION   (18)
  008.02 011.23 047.30 081.07 082.05
  085.02 087.26 135.17 136.31 202.34
  214.30 214.35 215.17 215.20 215.34
  242.22 287.10 288.22
IMAGINE   (4)
  028.08 088.02 127.10 195.02
IMAGINED   (2)
  096.16 323.32
IMAGING   (1)
  254.30
IMAGINING   (1)
  232.22
IMBIBES   (1)
  129.04
IMBODIMENT   (1)
  159.29
IMBRIBUS   (1)
  311.01
IMBRICATED   (1)
  305.13
IMBRUTE   (1)
  221.33
IMITATE   (1)
  125.16
IMITATED   (2)
  068.05 305.17
IMMEASURABLE   (2)
  159.08 285.32
IMMEDIATELY   (8)
  027.04 031.15 113.26 190.17 235.13
  236.25 287.32 293.16
IMMENSE   (1)
  251.07
IMMERSED   (1)
  150.19
IMMIGRANT   (1)
  067.02
IMMORTAL   (6)
  005.15 007.30 007.31 099.09 107.18
  216.27
IMMORTALITY   (3)
  269.02 317.23 333.16
IMPALING   (1)
  213.30
IMPART   (3)
  077.13 106.31 332.15
IMPARTED   (3)
  042.28 102.28 318.33
IMPARTIAL   (1)
  014.28
IMPARTIALLY   (1)
  056.05
IMPARTS   (2)
  123.12 177.27

IMPATIENT   (3)
155.05   173.25   266.21
IMPELLED   (1)
191.34
IMPERFECT   (4)
048.25   103.20   225.06   326.23
IMPERFECTION   (2)
103.12   186.02
IMPERFECTIONS   (1)
187.12
IMPERIALISTS   (1)
229.07
IMPERISHABLE   (1)
157.13
IMPERSONAL   (1)
025.05
IMPERTINENT   (3)
003.13   003.14   331.17
IMPERVIOUS   (2)
045.12   048.24
IMPLEMENTS   (5)
014.05   055.04   157.08   158.35   297.20
IMPLIED   (3)
014.15   072.14   260.35
IMPLIES   (1)
100.09
IMPLY   (2)
037.18   274.05
IMPORT   (1)
007.11
IMPORTANCE   (5)
011.09   017.27   055.22   239.30   242.03
IMPORTANT   (17)
009.04   012.11   021.29   031.33   050.22
052.23   052.35   086.31   087.16   094.04
095.11   133.14   136.22   149.19   230.27
324.12   326.11
IMPORTING   (1)
123.04
IMPORTS   (2)
020.16   121.12
IMPOSSIBLE   (6)
004.22   013.06   100.02   149.10   171.01
233.18
IMPOUNDED   (1)
083.02
IMPOVERISHED   (1)
016.23
IMPOVERISHING   (1)
016.08
IMPRESS   (1)
021.36
IMPRESSED   (5)
086.12   189.36   236.27   305.22   307.03
IMPRESSIBLE   (1)
323.20
IMPRESSION   (3)
194.33   282.03   318.26
IMPRESSIVE   (2)
195.26   304.05
IMPRESSIVELY   (1)
294.01
IMPRISONED   (2)
034.03   085.32
IMPROPERLY   (1)
172.17
IMPROPRIETY   (1)
038.22
IMPROVABLE   (1)
099.18
IMPROVE   (11)
016.19   017.02   031.11   045.04   048.20
083.36   092.21   099.18   204.26   208.38
246.32
IMPROVED   (9)
004.14   034.14   037.30   052.18   081.23
118.01   153.04   157.08   260.26

IMPROVEMENT   (6)
035.03   105.27   149.29   150.06   162.28
216.09
IMPROVEMENTS   (7)
012.03   020.27   031.02   034.12   052.12
083.23   092.05
IMPROVIDENCE   (1)
022.09
IMPROVING   (2)
034.13   190.04
IMPS   (2)
159.18   201.18
IMPUDENT   (1)
274.31
IMPULSE   (1)
208.31
IMPULSES   (2)
187.32   225.33
IMPUNITY   (1)
013.04
IMPURE   (2)
194.14   220.31
IMPURITY   (3)
188.29   220.05   221.16
IN   (1937)
003.04   003.05   003.06   003.09   003.22
003.23   003.23   003.24   003.25   004.01
004.05   004.10   004.12   004.12   004.15
004.16   004.18   004.20   004.31   005.06
005.09   005.27   005.37   006.09   006.17
007.14   007.14   007.15   007.24   008.01
008.05   008.14   008.25   008.35   009.25
009.26   009.27   009.28   010.17   010.19
010.26   010.26   010.26   010.31   011.33
012.13   012.19   013.05   013.10   013.10
013.13   013.25   013.34   014.04   014.11
014.15   014.24   014.24   014.31   015.08
015.12   015.13   015.14   015.31   015.31
015.34   016.03   016.06   016.11   016.14
016.15   016.22   016.30   017.01   017.06
017.07   017.25   017.26   017.30   017.32
017.33   017.35   018.04   018.10   018.23
018.27   018.28   019.02   019.20   019.28
019.34   020.07   020.10   020.12   020.28
021.01   021.05   021.14   021.24   021.27
022.04   022.04   022.21   022.31   022.34
023.03   023.04   023.06   023.14   023.15
023.23   023.23   023.32   024.01   024.02
024.03   024.04   024.23   024.24   024.36
025.09   025.14   025.24   025.26   025.30
025.31   026.02   027.03   027.10   027.12
027.12   027.14   027.15   027.19   027.23
027.24   027.26   027.27   027.28   027.33
027.35   028.02   028.08   028.10   028.12
028.17   028.21   028.22   028.28   028.29
028.32   028.36   029.01   029.09   029.13
029.15   029.15   029.22   029.30   030.04
030.10   030.11   030.11   030.12   030.14
030.15   030.20   030.21   030.33   031.10
031.16   031.16   031.30   031.36   032.01
032.02   032.11   032.29   032.35   033.01
033.09   033.10   033.20   033.25   034.04
034.06   034.08   034.19   034.22   034.23
034.33   035.03   035.04   035.05   035.14
035.25   035.28   036.15   036.18   036.25
036.29   036.31   037.03   037.14   037.15
037.17   037.19   037.21   037.21   037.36
038.13   038.33   038.36   039.08   039.08
039.10   039.11   039.13   039.17   039.21
039.25   039.25   039.27   039.28   039.28
039.29   039.31   039.31   039.35   040.08
040.10   040.15   040.18   040.21   040.35
041.02   041.08   041.09   041.15   041.16
041.19   041.24   041.25   041.30   041.35
041.35   042.02   042.24   042.26   042.33
042.36   043.14   043.21   043.26   043.29
044.04   044.09   044.12   044.22   044.27
044.30   044.31   044.33   045.01   045.03

045.07	045.15	045.16	045.17	045.18	119.13	119.16	119.35	120.05	120.09
045.19	045.24	045.24	045.27	045.34	121.02	121.18	121.32	121.33	122.03
046.02	046.03	046.09	046.14	046.14	122.11	122.13	122.27	122.33	123.06
046.15	046.24	046.30	046.33	046.34	123.12	123.19	123.22	123.34	124.07
047.04	047.23	047.27	047.31	047.36	124.11	124.12	124.24	124.30	124.33
048.01	048.08	048.13	049.22	049.29	125.06	125.08	125.10	125.17	125.20
049.29	049.41	050.11	050.12	050.15	126.03	126.07	126.07	126.10	126.26
050.22	050.30	051.26	051.29	051.35	126.30	127.08	127.14	127.14	127.36
052.08	052.10	052.15	052.20	052.23	128.01	128.06	128.09	128.16	128.18
052.34	053.14	053.16	053.30	054.05	129.05	129.07	129.10	129.18	129.27
054.07	054.11	054.15	054.20	054.31	129.34	130.12	130.28	130.30	131.05
055.26	055.30	056.03	056.06	056.08	131.08	131.15	131.18	131.19	131.28
056.20	056.22	057.02	057.05	057.13	131.34	131.35	132.02	132.02	132.03
057.15	057.25	057.33	058.06	058.10	132.11	132.18	132.22	132.25	132.25
058.24	058.30	058.34	059.32	060.11	132.27	132.29	132.30	132.32	133.09
060.20	060.29	061.01	061.12	061.16	133.13	133.23	133.25	134.02	134.08
061.21	061.23	061.24	062.04	062.07	134.21	134.22	134.33	135.02	135.03
062.09	062.13	062.14	062.20	062.28	135.03	135.21	135.25	135.29	135.31
062.30	063.06	063.08	063.17	063.24	135.32	135.35	136.03	136.05	136.06
063.29	063.32	063.33	063.33	064.05	136.06	136.07	136.07	136.19	136.23
064.25	064.27	064.29	065.10	065.12	136.24	136.26	136.28	137.01	137.02
065.19	065.25	065.30	066.10	066.27	137.05	137.08	137.08	137.09	137.14
066.29	067.08	067.14	067.31	067.33	137.18	137.19	137.21	137.31	137.32
068.21	068.26	068.27	068.32	068.35	138.03	138.13	138.21	138.30	138.32
069.11	069.15	069.22	069.26	069.27	138.33	139.02	139.02	140.06	140.09
070.01	070.07	070.12	070.14	070.27	140.11	140.28	140.30	140.33	141.06
070.33	071.10	071.18	071.21	071.23	141.10	141.21	141.24	141.30	141.35
071.32	072.04	072.10	072.13	072.22	142.02	142.06	142.07	142.07	142.15
072.26	072.30	072.31	072.36	073.23	142.22	143.16	143.17	143.34	143.36
073.29	073.33	074.01	074.02	074.03	144.04	144.17	144.23	144.24	144.27
074.08	074.24	074.30	074.32	074.34	144.36	145.07	145.09	145.09	145.17
074.36	075.22	075.23	076.03	076.07	145.19	145.25	145.27	145.29	145.31
076.09	076.12	076.18	077.21	077.26	145.36	146.01	146.02	146.13	146.15
077.33	078.06	079.03	079.08	080.06	146.27	146.29	146.30	146.33	146.35
080.09	080.21	081.07	081.08	081.13	146.35	147.04	147.05	147.06	147.07
081.29	082.03	082.16	082.37	083.09	147.07	147.24	148.01	148.11	148.16
083.19	083.22	083.22	083.28	084.10	148.17	148.22	148.24	148.26	148.31
084.15	084.23	084.26	084.35	085.17	149.01	149.02	149.04	149.13	150.06
085.18	085.21	085.24	085.28	086.05	150.08	150.11	150.19	150.22	151.06
086.08	086.18	086.22	086.23	086.35	151.13	151.15	151.20	151.25	151.30
087.01	087.04	087.07	087.09	087.12	152.09	152.15	152.18	152.29	152.30
087.18	087.19	087.20	087.25	087.31	152.31	152.33	153.03	153.04	153.08
087.36	088.03	088.06	088.08	088.13	153.11	153.20	153.33	154.05	154.10
088.29	089.03	089.09	089.28	089.29	154.16	154.17	155.06	155.23	156.06
090.03	090.09	090.10	090.13	090.17	156.09	156.15	156.16	156.26	156.27
090.27	091.10	091.11	091.23	091.28	156.29	156.29	156.33	156.34	156.35
091.36	092.10	092.11	092.23	092.34	157.04	157.04	157.17	157.18	157.23
092.35	093.03	093.08	093.15	093.23	157.32	158.03	158.04	158.06	158.09
093.36	094.06	094.10	094.12	094.17	158.10	158.15	158.30	158.34	159.13
094.30	094.32	095.01	095.02	095.10	159.14	159.14	159.22	159.22	159.27
095.15	096.12	096.14	096.16	096.22	160.01	160.07	160.11	160.28	160.31
096.32	096.35	096.36	097.02	097.05	161.06	161.11	161.18	161.22	161.23
097.06	097.12	097.23	097.25	098.03	161.30	161.32	162.03	162.05	162.06
098.17	098.17	098.19	098.22	098.30	162.07	162.12	162.18	162.19	162.23
099.03	099.07	099.09	099.14	099.15	163.11	163.22	163.26	163.28	164.03
099.29	100.02	100.04	100.07	100.09	164.16	164.19	164.24	164.30	165.03
100.11	100.12	100.19	100.25	100.30	165.20	166.12	166.13	166.17	166.23
100.34	101.01	101.18	101.20	101.22	166.35	167.04	167.04	167.12	167.13
101.22	101.23	102.09	102.10	102.16	167.14	167.15	167.17	167.19	167.20
102.19	102.25	103.04	103.19	103.19	167.31	168.07	168.09	168.10	168.18
103.25	104.06	104.13	104.14	104.16	168.24	168.25	169.09	169.17	169.22
104.22	104.23	104.29	104.30	104.30	169.27	169.28	169.29	169.31	169.36
105.21	105.27	105.29	105.34	106.03	170.01	170.02	170.12	170.14	170.17
106.05	106.15	106.17	106.25	106.28	170.23	170.26	170.28	170.29	170.34
106.33	107.18	107.20	107.28	107.36	170.35	171.03	171.04	171.05	171.09
108.05	108.09	108.30	109.11	109.11	171.12	171.17	171.35	172.06	172.21
109.22	109.24	109.25	109.25	109.28	172.30	173.20	173.31	173.34	173.35
109.30	109.32	110.12	111.06	111.25	174.03	174.15	174.15	174.20	174.24
111.26	111.27	111.28	111.30	111.33	174.28	174.31	175.02	175.05	175.09
111.33	112.23	112.25	113.07	113.14	175.16	175.17	175.17	175.33	176.09
113.19	113.25	113.27	113.30	113.35	176.09	176.11	176.14	176.27	176.27
113.36	114.02	114.09	114.12	114.17	176.31	176.35	177.04	177.15	177.17
114.18	115.02	115.07	115.09	115.21	177.27	178.04	178.05	178.14	178.18
116.13	116.14	117.06	117.10	117.12	178.25	178.31	178.32	179.03	179.05
117.16	117.17	117.17	117.20	117.27	179.09	179.11	179.20	179.20	179.28
117.29	117.30	117.33	118.01	118.03	179.29	179.31	179.32	180.02	180.08
118.03	118.04	118.14	118.31	118.34	180.11	180.12	180.14	180.20	180.20

IN				(CONTINUED)	IN				(CONTINUED)
180.31	180.35	181.01	181.04	182.03	249.14	249.20	249.23	249.27	250.09
182.05	182.12	182.24	182.34	183.05	250.17	250.27	250.34	250.34	251.05
183.07	183.09	183.12	183.13	183.13	251.07	251.10	251.14	251.21	251.30
183.17	183.20	183.22	183.24	183.25	252.07	252.07	252.19	252.21	252.23
183.26	183.28	183.30	183.32	183.34	252.23	252.30	253.04	253.11	253.15
184.11	184.13	184.17	184.28	184.33	253.18	253.20	253.28	253.30	253.31
184.36	185.01	185.02	185.12	185.14	253.33	254.06	254.18	254.19	254.22
185.15	185.16	185.17	185.22	185.28	254.32	256.08	256.10	256.11	256.15
185.35	185.36	186.03	186.06	186.19	256.23	256.24	256.32	257.07	257.24
187.01	187.04	187.05	187.11	187.12	258.02	258.05	258.16	258.25	258.26
187.16	187.23	187.30	187.34	188.08	258.29	258.32	259.12	259.12	259.17
188.08	188.13	188.15	188.19	188.19	259.25	259.34	260.06	260.09	260.14
188.28	188.33	188.34	188.36	189.08	260.19	260.22	260.25	261.08	261.11
189.10	189.10	189.12	189.30	189.33	261.13	261.17	261.19	261.20	261.22
189.35	190.03	190.11	190.28	191.22	261.28	261.32	262.09	262.11	262.26
191.32	192.02	192.02	192.04	192.18	262.27	263.01	263.04	263.17	263.27
192.25	193.02	193.15	193.17	193.17	263.28	263.32	263.32	263.34	264.03
193.28	193.31	194.09	194.12	194.16	264.22	265.02	265.03	265.03	265.07
194.19	194.22	194.28	194.31	195.09	265.14	265.17	265.24	266.05	266.29
195.10	195.12	195.15	195.16	195.18	267.08	267.11	267.30	268.09	268.32
195.32	195.34	196.02	196.05	196.17	269.04	269.19	270.01	270.14	270.15
196.30	196.32	197.02	197.15	197.22	270.19	271.10	271.14	271.17	271.17
197.23	197.27	198.04	198.08	198.10	271.18	271.19	271.20	271.30	271.33
198.12	198.14	198.17	198.18	198.19	271.33	272.06	272.09	272.13	272.23
198.23	198.24	198.25	198.27	198.29	272.31	272.33	272.34	272.35	273.03
198.32	198.33	199.01	199.11	199.13	273.03	273.07	273.07	273.11	273.20
199.16	199.18	199.19	199.33	200.01	273.22	273.26	274.03	274.05	274.07
201.07	201.12	201.19	201.24	201.25	274.10	274.16	274.18	274.30	274.32
201.26	201.29	201.32	201.34	202.07	275.08	275.12	275.16	275.19	275.24
202.10	202.14	202.23	202.25	202.27	275.28	275.33	275.34	276.01	276.03
202.31	202.33	203.20	203.28	203.28	276.15	276.17	276.22	276.30	276.30
204.02	204.12	204.13	204.24	204.27	276.34	277.05	277.07	277.34	277.35
204.31	205.06	205.09	205.22	205.32	278.01	278.07	278.08	278.09	278.09
206.07	206.12	206.22	207.11	207.14	278.35	279.02	279.03	279.15	279.18
207.14	207.15	207.24	208.15	208.36	279.22	279.26	279.29	279.33	279.34
208.39	209.04	210.15	210.20	210.26	280.06	280.12	280.23	280.30	280.34
210.28	210.29	210.30	210.31	211.11	281.01	282.01	282.04	282.04	282.06
212.16	212.23	212.33	213.02	213.05	282.07	282.22	282.31	282.34	283.06
213.06	213.31	213.34	214.05	214.09	283.07	283.10	283.16	283.18	283.19
214.10	214.20	214.33	215.01	215.04	283.20	283.27	283.29	283.32	283.36
215.05	215.08	215.08	215.15	215.16	284.03	284.05	284.09	284.19	284.19
216.01	216.09	216.11	216.23	217.21	284.27	284.33	284.35	285.03	285.11
217.26	217.31	217.33	218.02	218.30	285.15	285.18	285.18	285.24	285.31
219.09	219.10	219.12	219.21	219.29	287.13	287.19	287.22	287.26	287.28
219.32	220.06	220.39	221.19	221.20	287.30	287.34	288.08	288.17	288.28
222.07	222.13	222.14	222.15	223.03	288.29	288.32	288.34	288.35	288.38
223.12	223.27	223.33	223.33	224.10	289.05	289.12	289.14	289.35	290.02
224.15	224.19	224.24	224.29	225.19	290.06	290.07	290.11	290.18	290.21
225.24	225.34	226.06	226.08	226.09	290.28	290.29	291.02	291.04	291.06
226.10	226.12	226.13	226.19	226.24	291.07	291.16	291.17	291.18	291.23
226.31	227.01	227.07	227.22	227.23	291.30	291.30	292.12	292.13	292.14
227.27	227.30	228.01	228.06	228.09	292.20	292.31	293.05	293.07	293.17
228.22	228.23	229.02	229.08	229.11	293.20	293.21	294.03	294.05	294.06
229.11	229.24	229.28	230.14	230.15	294.16	294.22	294.31	294.33	294.35
230.17	230.33	231.17	231.19	231.35	295.07	295.13	295.17	295.18	295.20
231.35	232.04	232.09	232.13	232.13	295.32	295.34	296.02	296.02	296.14
232.18	232.28	232.31	232.34	232.35	296.18	296.23	297.03	297.06	297.12
232.35	233.01	233.01	233.06	233.09	297.25	297.28	297.32	297.33	298.01
233.13	233.24	233.25	233.28	234.08	298.02	298.04	298.12	298.15	298.21
234.10	234.10	234.15	234.19	234.21	298.22	299.05	299.09	299.12	299.17
235.03	235.04	235.14	235.17	235.18	299.21	299.27	299.28	299.31	299.34
236.17	236.31	236.34	237.02	237.07	299.35	300.01	300.03	300.07	300.11
238.03	238.10	238.24	238.32	238.34	300.17	300.25	300.26	300.30	301.04
238.35	239.09	239.18	239.26	239.29	301.25	301.27	301.35	302.04	302.07
240.06	240.11	240.23	241.14	241.24	302.10	302.12	302.12	302.13	302.27
242.13	242.19	242.31	242.34	243.02	302.28	302.35	303.01	303.02	303.02
243.03	243.09	243.11	243.14	243.25	303.03	303.03	303.04	303.07	303.12
243.26	243.33	244.15	244.19	244.20	303.15	303.33	303.34	304.10	304.11
244.23	244.27	244.30	244.30	244.33	304.13	304.30	305.02	305.02	305.03
245.03	245.08	245.09	245.18	245.20	305.11	305.17	305.32	305.33	305.36
245.22	245.26	245.34	246.04	246.14	306.09	306.10	306.17	306.19	306.22
246.14	246.25	246.30	247.04	247.06	306.31	306.34	307.01	307.07	307.09
247.15	247.21	247.27	248.03	248.05	307.18	307.21	307.24	307.27	307.29
248.08	248.09	248.11	248.12	248.14	308.12	308.22	308.31	308.35	309.13
248.17	248.18	248.24	248.24	248.28	309.17	309.20	309.22	309.30	310.04
248.28	248.30	248.35	249.01	249.05	310.05	310.19	310.33	310.34	311.10
249.05	249.06	249.07	249.07	249.14	311.23	311.28	311.30	312.13	312.15

IN   (CONTINUED)
312.31 312.32 313.02 313.02 313.03
313.04 313.05 313.13 313.15 313.18
313.20 313.21 313.22 313.26 313.27
313.33 313.34 314.20 314.24 314.26
314.26 315.14 315.16 315.19 315.19
316.28 316.36 317.02 317.07 317.09
317.10 317.20 317.22 317.23 317.29
318.13 318.15 318.23 318.31 318.34
319.01 319.06 319.14 319.18 320.05
320.08 320.08 320.09 320.33 320.35
321.25 321.28 321.32 322.09 322.18
322.31 322.31 322.33 322.35 323.01
323.05 323.06 323.30 323.32 324.01
324.01 324.03 324.06 324.18 324.24
324.26 324.28 324.28 324.33 324.34
325.18 325.33 326.06 326.07 326.20
326.23 326.25 326.26 326.30 327.01
327.06 327.15 327.17 327.29 327.32
327.33 328.03 328.08 328.10 328.13
328.16 328.32 329.07 329.17 329.19
329.24 329.24 329.33 329.33 329.35
330.16 330.28 330.32 330.36 331.10
331.12 331.12 331.15 331.19 331.24
331.26 331.36 332.02 332.21 332.24
332.30 332.32 332.33 332.35 332.35
333.09 333.10 333.10 333.11 333.15
333.19 333.20

INACCESSIBLE   (1)
  103.11
INADEQUACY   (1)
  325.02
INAUDIBLE   (1)
  071.35
INCAPACITATED   (2)
  065.11 331.11
INCASED   (1)
  117.17
INCENSE   (2)
  252.37 304.23
INCESSANT   (5)
  011.07 015.23 099.34 112.08 332.18
INCESSANTLY   (3)
  167.10 188.01 228.31
INCH   (21)
  114.12 132.35 178.01 195.14 195.22
  228.29 229.36 246.21 247.04 247.07
  247.09 247.19 248.05 248.11 248.11
  270.08 273.04 285.29 287.09 289.11
  293.04
INCHES   (24)
  012.15 042.18 065.19 132.36 163.28
  169.36 184.09 189.30 190.15 195.15
  198.17 233.11 241.25 246.23 248.05
  252.15 280.12 288.36 292.18 292.35
  293.14 299.35 300.06 302.31
INCIDENT   (1)
  303.05
INCIDENTAL   (1)
  050.43
INCIDENTS   (1)
  138.07
INCLINATION   (2)
  291.22 291.30
INCLINATIONS   (1)
  291.24
INCLINE   (1)
  220.23
INCLINED   (8)
  025.15 037.03 149.26 168.04 212.02
  215.02 290.19 325.11
INCLUDED   (1)
  248.02
INCLUDING   (1)
  260.07
INCOME   (5)
  003.18 055.10 069.16 076.09 163.13

INCONCEIVABLE   (1)
  273.34
INCONSIDERABLE   (2)
  219.22 288.25
INCONSISTENCIES   (1)
  049.37
INCONSOLABLE   (1)
  250.22
INCONSOLABLY   (1)
  016.20
INCONVENIENCE   (5)
  041.27 050.09 140.30 143.25 172.15
INCONVENIENT   (2)
  033.06 149.09
INCREASE   (2)
  013.21 224.21
INCREASED   (6)
  190.12 211.21 211.22 288.10 291.27
  300.09
INCREASES   (1)
  299.23
INCREASING   (6)
  067.36 073.35 190.20 222.23 301.22
  304.07
INCREDIBLE   (2)
  004.29 332.19
INCREDIBLY   (1)
  061.15
INCREDULITY   (1)
  180.29
INCURABLE   (2)
  011.08 120.34
INCURRED   (1)
  060.34
INDE   (1)
  005.34
INDEED   (26)
  016.09 018.34 065.36 078.31 087.05
  091.33 097.03 103.35 106.27 109.03
  112.30 122.02 125.22 148.28 151.08
  155.07 164.09 184.26 186.28 203.01
  205.19 235.35 241.22 281.31 295.05
  311.06
INDEFINITE   (1)
  195.26
INDEFINITELY   (2)
  203.20 272.01
INDENTATION   (1)
  086.34
INDENTED   (1)
  185.20
INDEPENDENCE   (7)
  015.02 033.22 060.35 063.31 084.28
  103.08 242.03
INDEPENDENT   (9)
  056.07 057.21 070.26 070.30 115.31
  183.33 241.36 289.32 328.17
INDEPENDENTLY   (1)
  037.25
INDEPENDENTS   (1)
  079.14
INDESCRIBABLE   (3)
  138.06 177.10 216.35
INDESCRIBABLY   (1)
  134.06
INDESTRUCTIBLE   (1)
  252.11
INDETERMINATE   (1)
  023.16
INDETERMINDABLE   (1)
  271.12
INDIA   (4)
  054.07 061.06 162.06 322.15
INDIAN   (36)
  008.01 019.01 019.05 027.28 030.27
  035.19 036.12 059.11 059.16 061.03
  062.01 062.07 063.29 064.03 077.31
  078.32 105.34 116.02 119.22 127.05

```
INDIAN                        (CONTINUED)        INERT                             (   2)
  159.02  169.21  182.24  191.09  195.09           306.07  307.19
  223.13  239.20  239.26  239.31  243.12         INEVITABLE                        (   2)
  247.22  254.19  265.05  265.08  267.02           057.04  095.35
  298.22                                          INEVITABLY                        (   2)
INDIANS                              (  13)         024.10  103.10
  028.36  029.29  030.08  064.21  068.11         INEXHAUSTIBLE                     (   2)
  075.03  112.15  143.27  164.14  182.12           160.02  318.03
  182.16  185.18  260.16                         INEXPRESSIBLE                     (   4)
INDICATE                             (   1)         146.14  160.30  218.01  310.08
  301.12                                          INFANCY                           (   5)
INDICATES                            (   4)         028.08  096.14  204.15  227.08  314.39
  007.36  181.31  291.19  299.18                 INFANT                            (   6)
INDICATING                           (   1)         043.26  147.06  156.04  156.08  204.11
  289.13                                           309.26
INDICATIVE                           (   1)       INFANTA                           (   1)
  175.11                                            094.31
INDIES                               (   1)       INFANTS                           (   1)
  329.29                                            108.29
INDIFFERENCE                         (   1)       INFER                             (   2)
  048.13                                            290.25  291.13
INDIFFERENT                          (   4)       INFERIOR                          (   2)
  134.04  217.25  218.36  219.01                   151.19  220.09
INDIFFERENTLY                        (   2)       INFERNAL                          (   4)
  030.01  268.11                                   124.24  165.32  285.27  320.18
INDIGENCE                            (   1)       INFERRED                          (   2)
  034.25                                            060.01  248.15
INDIGENOUS                           (   3)       INFEST                            (   1)
  127.25  239.30  281.18                           140.24
INDIGESTIONS                         (   1)       INFINITE                          (   7)
  308.30                                            090.16  132.04  171.19  217.08  248.15
INDIRECT                             (   2)         287.13  290.36
  258.09  321.27                                 INFINITELY                        (   4)
INDIRECTLY                           (   2)         033.07  073.11  171.05  317.36
  194.04  205.29                                 INFINITESIMAL                     (   1)
INDISPENSABLE                        (   8)         293.11
  014.18  020.05  021.20  030.25  062.15        INFIRM                            (   1)
  062.35  093.31  219.29                           153.21
INDISTINCT                           (   4)       INFIRMITY                         (   1)
  043.34  053.28  186.20  258.34                   327.30
INDISTINCTLY                         (   1)       INFLAME                           (   1)
  191.15                                            327.24
INDITO                               (   1)       INFLATED                          (   1)
  063.30                                            159.24
INDIVIDUAL                           (   5)       INFLEXIBLE                        (   1)
  031.30  032.01  212.23  291.31  291.35           041.36
INDIVIDUALIZE                        (   1)       INFLUENCE                         (  14)
  292.07                                            012.04  041.32  062.29  099.24  103.06
INDIVIDUALS                          (   1)         108.19  134.15  156.09  266.12  300.08
  141.06                                            301.19  301.25  314.23  314.38
INDOLENCE                            (   1)       INFLUENCES                        (   3)
  112.24                                            166.20  308.13  328.35
INDRA                                (   2)       INFLUX                            (   3)
  135.03  298.11                                   312.06  314.19  332.18
INDULGE                              (   1)       INFORM                            (   1)
  072.29                                            090.30
INDULGED                             (   2)       INFORMANT                         (   1)
  072.21  146.01                                   279.21
INDULGES                             (   1)       INFORMATION                       (   5)
  218.22                                            039.09  090.29  152.06  160.15  332.15
INDULGING                            (   1)       INFORMED                          (   3)
  312.32                                            020.23  044.11  052.02
INDUSTRIOUS                          (   2)       INFORMING                         (   3)
  019.06  070.18                                   010.29  115.24  258.09
INDUSTRY                             (   7)       INFRINGED                         (   1)
  024.07  040.17  103.08  164.01  191.36           192.35
  224.02  231.20                                 INGENUITY                         (   1)
INDWELLER                            (   2)         069.28
  046.36  047.17                                 INGENUUS                          (   1)
INEFFABLE                            (   1)         269.19
  164.31                                         INGRAHAM                          (   2)
INEFFECTUAL                          (   2)         257.05  257.05
  067.26  147.07                                 INGREDIENT                        (   2)
INEFFECTUALLY                        (   2)         063.05  326.23
  232.15  315.02                                 INHABIT                           (   6)
INEQUALITIES                         (   1)         034.15  116.23  118.33  133.08  184.27
  289.02                                            242.24
```

INSTRUCTOR (1)
  009.01
INSTRUMENTS (3)
  110.03 133.12 293.06
INSUFFICIENCY (1)
  103.13
INSUFFICIENT (1)
  055.34
INSULAR (1)
  087.15
INSULATED (1)
  087.21
INSULT (1)
  165.01
INSURANCE (2)
  218.33 259.28
INSURED (1)
  066.25
INTANGIBLE (1)
  216.35
INTEGRITY (1)
  006.15
INTEGUMENT (1)
  024.18
INTELLECT (8)
  098.26 102.15 103.11 151.20 269.06
  297.17 298.02 325.17
INTELLECTS (1)
  107.25
INTELLECTUAL (9)
  090.10 103.15 104.15 105.32 107.28
  147.04 152.32 222.01 325.34
INTELLECTUALLY (1)
  036.19
INTELLECTUALNESS (1)
  013.07
INTELLIGENCE (6)
  017.35 076.24 138.15 227.06 312.14
  332.16
INTELLIGENCES (2)
  089.30 134.24
INTELLIGENT (1)
  109.17
INTEMPERATE (1)
  077.19
INTEND (1)
  049.28
INTENDED (3)
  040.34 143.26 296.20
INTENSE (1)
  135.10
INTENTION (1)
  101.05
INTENTIONALLY (1)
  129.31
INTERCOURSE (4)
  077.07 151.34 151.36 174.05
INTEREST (9)
  003.22 008.05 021.04 028.14 041.02
  052.14 246.32 297.02 329.25
INTERESTED (8)
  056.06 065.10 146.09 211.04 225.25
  250.17 260.22 329.24
INTERESTING (16)
  022.29 047.22 047.28 072.13 099.06
  113.18 119.29 123.11 134.28 196.29
  246.17 249.19 252.06 297.10 303.07
  309.29
INTERESTS (1)
  007.28
INTERFERED (1)
  265.26
INTERFERES (1)
  118.18
INTERIOR (1)
  321.02
INTERLACE (1)
  305.07

INTERMEDIATE (2)
  181.14 188.36
INTERMITTING (1)
  179.17
INTERMIXED (1)
  184.21
INTERNAL (6)
  012.30 012.32 013.09 024.07 038.06
  092.05
INTERNALLY (2)
  293.24 306.22
INTERNECINE (1)
  229.06
INTERPRETATION (1)
  325.20
INTERPRETED (1)
  324.01
INTERRUPT (2)
  175.19 215.24
INTERRUPTED (4)
  122.36 266.19 271.24 277.30
INTERRUPTION (2)
  070.15 142.04
INTERSECT (1)
  291.10
INTERSECTED (1)
  289.17
INTERVAL (6)
  083.12 101.09 141.06 234.27 284.25
  315.20
INTERVALS (17)
  044.13 086.23 100.04 124.14 130.28
  136.11 146.28 181.19 186.36 210.31
  265.20 268.10 271.28 272.20 276.34
  284.16 313.13
INTERVENE (2)
  135.28 258.32
INTERVENING (3)
  087.22 123.10 307.05
INTERWOVEN (1)
  196.08
INTIMATE (4)
  102.21 141.20 157.09 161.20
INTIMATION (1)
  214.03
INTO (182)
  004.25 005.25 006.37 007.07 007.08
  008.09 009.36 015.32 017.32 018.31
  019.10 019.32 021.18 023.25 028.09
  029.14 029.33 033.24 034.08 036.22
  038.10 041.26 043.20 044.32 051.19
  052.27 052.31 063.13 063.21 067.10
  068.18 069.18 069.34 074.28 075.25
  078.15 078.35 081.32 084.21 086.18
  086.20 087.14 091.05 091.17 095.09
  098.27 102.23 102.32 103.22 105.13
  108.12 108.28 109.22 111.19 112.13
  114.11 116.03 116.21 116.36 119.30
  120.28 123.04 123.28 128.12 129.29
  129.32 140.28 140.34 141.02 141.13
  144.07 146.19 153.14 160.20 160.24
  168.11 168.27 169.11 169.18 170.11
  171.22 173.06 174.25 174.26 175.20
  175.21 176.19 178.08 178.26 179.04
  180.24 180.33 182.14 182.14 186.13
  190.24 191.07 191.12 191.14 194.29
  195.35 199.04 205.21 215.10 215.25
  218.15 219.33 222.22 223.22 224.28
  225.23 227.12 227.36 230.31 233.05
  233.06 235.01 240.20 240.22 241.31
  243.29 244.11 244.35 249.11 252.03
  254.23 254.26 256.13 260.11 260.28
  265.33 266.02 273.12 276.21 278.04
  278.31 279.01 279.05 281.12 282.20
  283.03 283.24 283.25 285.22 285.24
  289.21 291.10 291.35 292.05 292.11
  292.22 293.16 295.02 295.24 296.10
  296.36 299.24 305.27 305.34 306.06

052.07	052.07	052.08	052.09	052.12	151.19	153.24	153.31	153.31	153.32
052.13	052.23	052.35	053.07	053.09	153.34	154.04	154.05	155.20	155.21
053.09	053.23	053.25	053.25	053.26	155.23	155.24	155.34	156.03	156.09
053.33	054.01	054.11	054.13	055.22	156.25	157.11	158.08	159.22	159.23
056.10	056.19	056.21	056.22	056.24	162.25	162.33	163.26	163.32	164.02
056.26	056.31	056.31	057.04	057.10	164.07	164.13	165.23	165.29	165.30
057.12	057.13	057.22	057.23	057.25	165.34	165.36	165.36	166.13	166.26
057.34	058.05	058.13	058.16	058.20	167.10	167.29	168.10	168.11	169.02
062.21	062.26	062.30	063.09	063.10	169.28	170.27	170.33	171.03	171.05
063.24	063.32	063.36	064.26	064.29	171.30	172.22	173.12	173.15	173.19
064.36	065.02	065.10	065.23	065.24	173.20	175.25	175.28	175.30	176.13
065.25	065.32	066.02	066.03	066.06	176.20	176.24	176.28	176.30	176.34
066.13	066.20	066.25	066.27	066.31	176.35	177.06	177.15	177.19	177.19
067.16	067.23	068.21	068.23	068.28	177.25	177.28	177.33	178.23	178.25
069.01	069.24	070.15	070.29	070.34	178.29	178.30	179.04	179.05	179.08
071.01	071.18	071.18	071.21	071.21	179.17	179.31	180.07	180.12	180.19
071.22	071.33	071.33	071.34	071.34	180.24	180.35	181.04	181.07	181.17
072.04	072.16	072.20	073.04	073.11	181.27	181.27	181.34	182.01	182.16
073.16	073.17	073.22	073.22	073.36	182.22	182.24	182.36	183.01	183.07
074.15	074.16	074.16	074.30	074.30	183.07	183.08	183.09	183.10	183.20
075.17	075.18	075.19	075.29	075.36	183.22	183.24	184.07	184.12	184.18
076.02	076.03	076.12	076.13	076.15	184.29	185.08	185.13	185.17	185.27
076.15	076.16	076.17	076.34	077.09	185.32	185.35	186.02	186.12	186.13
077.09	077.19	077.22	077.24	077.25	186.34	187.06	187.08	187.08	187.10
077.27	077.27	077.29	078.01	078.05	187.19	187.20	187.29	187.33	187.35
078.07	078.11	078.12	078.17	078.25	188.03	188.04	188.05	188.06	188.08
079.08	079.10	079.12	079.15	079.17	188.19	188.25	188.31	188.34	188.35
081.21	082.02	082.31	084.07	084.13	188.36	189.02	189.04	189.11	192.10
084.27	085.12	085.13	085.17	085.29	192.21	192.23	192.26	193.01	193.02
086.27	087.11	087.14	087.15	087.15	193.04	193.08	193.10	193.12	193.13
089.07	089.08	089.09	089.11	089.23	193.14	193.18	193.19	193.22	194.04
089.36	090.02	090.02	090.03	090.04	194.05	194.08	194.21	194.22	194.23
090.09	090.12	090.20	090.22	090.25	195.04	195.27	195.36	196.08	196.23
090.26	090.36	091.12	091.14	091.18	197.02	197.09	197.11	197.12	197.13
091.21	092.01	092.03	092.06	092.11	197.20	197.23	198.03	198.13	198.16
092.14	092.18	092.27	092.31	092.34	199.13	199.17	201.21	202.01	202.31
093.04	093.04	093.13	093.14	093.23	202.33	203.10	205.24	205.35	205.36
093.31	094.08	094.10	094.18	094.20	207.32	208.07	208.40	210.16	210.33
094.21	095.12	095.16	095.23	095.30	210.34	211.02	211.03	211.06	211.20
095.34	096.04	096.08	096.12	096.22	211.23	212.03	212.23	212.25	212.36
096.23	096.27	096.34	097.03	097.07	213.06	213.08	213.27	214.03	214.05
097.12	097.26	097.29	098.04	098.19	214.11	214.31	214.32	215.03	215.14
098.21	098.23	098.26	098.28	098.29	215.15	215.19	215.21	215.26	215.30
098.31	098.34	099.15	099.18	099.19	215.31	215.33	215.35	215.36	215.36
100.21	100.25	100.36	101.01	101.01	216.02	216.08	216.26	216.27	216.28
101.07	101.09	101.11	101.14	101.15	216.34	217.01	217.09	217.10	217.24
101.16	102.04	102.09	102.09	102.13	217.27	217.28	217.32	217.32	217.33
102.20	102.20	102.22	103.09	103.11	217.34	218.16	218.16	218.18	218.18
103.16	103.21	104.16	104.22	104.29	218.25	218.28	218.28	218.30	218.31
104.29	105.30	105.33	106.03	106.15	218.32	218.35	219.03	219.03	219.06
106.19	106.28	107.17	107.24	107.30	219.17	219.22	219.32	219.36	220.04
108.11	108.13	108.17	108.34	109.01	220.05	220.06	220.08	220.08	220.09
109.10	109.13	109.16	109.24	110.08	220.20	220.21	220.22	220.26	220.27
110.14	110.15	111.08	111.09	111.11	220.27	220.31	220.32	220.34	220.35
111.13	111.17	111.18	112.06	112.06	221.25	221.27	221.31	222.18	223.07
112.15	112.23	112.23	114.31	115.07	223.22	223.25	223.26	223.29	224.02
115.11	115.31	116.32	117.02	117.08	224.11	224.12	224.13	224.32	225.02
117.24	117.30	118.04	118.10	118.11	225.04	226.10	226.25	226.34	227.06
118.12	118.22	118.22	118.24	119.03	227.10	227.17	227.21	227.28	230.13
119.10	119.14	119.15	119.29	121.07	231.29	232.03	232.22	233.15	233.18
121.08	121.08	121.09	121.18	121.36	235.08	235.17	235.20	236.15	239.20
122.07	122.11	122.15	123.17	123.18	239.27	240.26	241.03	241.11	241.27
123.18	124.19	124.20	124.35	125.26	241.35	242.02	242.09	243.06	243.30
126.35	127.05	127.22	127.25	127.26	244.09	244.12	244.14	244.17	244.23
127.28	129.03	129.04	129.07	129.11	244.24	245.03	245.04	245.09	246.02
129.14	129.17	129.20	130.08	130.09	246.16	246.19	246.24	246.27	246.31
130.10	130.10	130.16	130.16	130.22	247.01	247.02	247.10	249.20	249.32
130.23	131.15	131.17	133.09	133.12	250.28	250.29	250.31	250.33	250.33
133.15	133.27	133.29	134.05	134.09	251.01	251.09	251.12	251.12	251.17
134.12	134.15	134.24	134.27	135.12	252.06	252.07	257.16	258.05	259.12
135.14	135.14	135.15	135.21	135.26	259.23	260.25	262.06	263.08	263.15
135.27	135.30	135.33	136.05	136.10	263.20	264.26	265.10	267.27	268.03
136.26	137.09	137.10	137.11	137.11	269.14	269.23	270.19	275.17	276.18
137.12	137.22	137.30	137.30	138.02	276.19	276.20	276.28	279.31	280.20
138.04	138.17	139.01	140.13	141.21	280.23	281.17	281.22	281.23	281.23
141.25	142.20	142.35	143.24	147.05	281.28	282.11	282.30	283.09	283.20
147.09	147.11	149.26	150.05	151.01					

IS   (CONTINUED)
```
283.23  284.26  284.34  285.15  287.08
287.22  287.26  288.19  288.22  288.27
288.31  289.01  289.02  289.19  289.24
289.26  290.27  290.33  291.02  291.04
291.05  291.14  291.21  291.22  291.27
291.28  292.01  292.36  293.24  293.34
294.12  294.21  296.32  297.09  297.10
297.10  297.13  297.15  297.16  298.07
298.08  298.16  298.18  298.22  299.32
300.05  300.07  300.11  300.13  300.16
300.19  300.22  300.23  300.24  301.05
301.07  301.08  301.09  301.11  302.05
302.06  303.07  305.16  306.01  306.02
306.05  306.15  306.23  307.04  307.05
307.21  307.24  307.28  307.30  307.32
307.35  308.05  308.06  308.10  308.19
308.21  308.22  308.25  308.26  308.27
308.30  308.33  308.35  309.01  309.07
309.21  310.03  310.06  310.31  310.33
311.03  311.09  311.16  311.16  311.22
311.25  311.29  311.34  311.35  312.04
312.05  312.21  312.29  313.34  314.26
314.28  314.40  315.11  318.18  318.26
318.27  318.27  318.29  319.13  320.04
320.06  320.07  320.19  320.23  320.24
320.27  321.02  321.04  321.07  321.08
321.09  321.18  321.21  321.24  321.29
321.30  321.33  322.08  322.15  322.29
323.04  323.13  323.17  323.18  323.18
323.20  324.07  324.09  324.24  325.03
325.10  325.18  325.28  325.30  325.31
325.36  325.36  326.09  326.11  326.14
326.17  326.23  327.22  327.32  327.34
327.35  328.04  328.05  328.06  328.09
328.11  328.36  329.11  329.12  329.15
329.20  329.27  330.04  330.05  330.09
330.13  330.20  330.21  330.22  330.23
331.20  331.31  331.34  332.18  332.25
332.26  333.29  333.31  333.32  333.33
```
ISLAND   (4)
```
290.11  290.21  303.33  304.17
```
ISLANDER   (1)
```
035.19
```
ISLANDERS   (1)
```
004.09
```
ISLANDS   (2)
```
026.11  298.18
```
ISLE   (1)
```
245.08
```
ISLET   (2)
```
304.24  304.24
```
ISRAEL   (1)
```
032.11
```
ISSUE   (2)
```
133.24  230.33
```
ISTHMUS   (1)
```
321.29
```
IT   (1516)
```
003.24  003.27  004.01  004.06  004.07
004.13  004.13  004.14  004.14  004.14
004.22  005.04  005.17  005.21  005.27
005.29  005.30  005.30  005.37  006.27
006.28  006.34  007.21  007.22  007.35
008.14  008.18  008.20  008.22  009.01
009.02  009.08  009.15  009.16  009.20
010.01  010.16  010.32  011.12  011.19
011.31  011.32  012.01  012.13  012.15
012.27  012.28  013.06  013.16  014.25
014.34  014.34  015.03  015.12  015.28
015.28  015.29  016.12  016.25  016.25
016.30  016.32  016.33  017.03  017.09
017.26  017.27  017.28  017.31  017.32
017.33  017.33  017.34  017.34  018.29
018.30  019.10  019.12  019.14  019.14
019.16  019.17  019.19  019.20  019.21
021.03  021.05  021.09  021.09  021.10
021.13  021.19  021.25  022.13  022.13
```

IT   (CONTINUED)
```
022.18  022.29  023.14  023.25  023.26
023.32  024.02  024.05  024.22  025.06
025.11  025.16  025.20  026.01  026.10
026.12  026.14  026.27  026.30  026.30
026.35  027.10  027.15  027.27  028.12
028.13  026.15  028.21  028.24  028.31
029.03  029.07  029.10  029.13  029.14
029.14  029.24  030.30  030.31  030.32
031.06  031.09  031.11  031.12  031.12
031.15  031.28  032.14  032.23  032.26
032.27  032.33  033.06  033.24
033.34  033.34  033.35  033.37  034.02
034.09  034.14  034.15  034.15  034.21
034.29  034.32  035.10  035.20  036.01
036.17  036.21  036.33  037.05  037.12
037.21  038.03  038.14  039.18  039.22
040.11  040.16  040.24  040.36  041.01
041.04  041.04  041.05  041.05  041.05
041.11  041.23  041.29  042.01  042.27
042.33  042.37  043.04  043.06  043.09
043.14  043.15  043.26  043.33  044.07
044.29  045.10  045.12  045.21  045.31
046.01  046.17  046.18  046.21  046.22
046.27  046.32  046.34  047.11  047.14
047.25  048.05  048.07  048.09  048.10
048.16  048.19  049.30  049.39  050.01
050.34  050.35  051.01  051.11  051.13
051.25  052.04  052.19  052.22  053.25
053.25  053.33  053.35  054.06  054.21
054.26  054.30  055.34  055.36  055.38
056.02  056.21  056.26  056.36  057.04
057.13  057.15  058.04  058.09  058.12
058.13  058.15  058.16  058.18  058.21
058.22  059.37  059.40  060.37  060.42
061.02  061.04  061.09  061.14  062.04
062.08  062.21  063.01  063.04  063.05
063.09  063.10  063.13  063.14  063.22
063.23  063.23  063.23  063.27  064.10
064.19  064.21  064.24  064.33  064.35
065.34  066.01  066.06  066.19  066.25
066.35  067.08  067.09  067.10  067.11
067.17  067.22  067.22  067.23  068.08
068.19  068.36  069.02  069.21  069.32
070.06  070.15  070.20  070.26  071.01
071.08  071.16  071.26  071.35  072.06
072.10  072.16  073.05  073.05  073.06
073.12  073.15  073.16  073.20  073.22
074.03  074.16  074.16  074.36  075.06
075.14  075.15  075.16  075.19  075.21
075.29  075.32  075.36  076.03  076.10
076.13  076.16  076.17  076.17  076.27
077.01  077.13  077.24  077.25  077.29
077.36  078.12  078.17  078.28  078.30
078.31  079.10  079.18  081.12  081.13
081.14  081.15  081.17  081.17  081.25
082.02  082.11  082.12  082.14  082.16
082.20  082.21  082.27  082.36  083.02
083.02  083.02  083.09  083.16  083.19
083.24  083.28  083.29  083.29  083.31
083.31  084.05  084.10  084.11  084.12
084.12  084.13  084.13  084.15  084.15
084.16  084.33  084.35  085.02  085.13
085.23  085.26  086.05  086.11  086.14
086.29  087.11  087.14  087.16  088.08
088.33  089.02  089.05  089.12  089.27
089.36  090.04  090.22  090.34
091.01  091.06  091.06  091.08  091.09
091.09  091.10  091.11  091.12  091.12
091.14  091.18  091.35  092.03  092.11
092.13  092.14  092.25  093.01  093.02
093.04  093.21  093.21  093.21  093.22
093.22  093.23  093.24  093.33  093.33
094.05  094.20  094.35  094.35  095.19
095.32  096.11  096.22  096.23  096.24
097.15  097.22  097.26  097.29  097.29
098.12  098.15  098.20  098.21  098.26
098.30  098.32  099.14  099.15  100.06
```

100.09	100.21	100.25	101.03	101.07	189.32	189.33	190.07	190.17	190.27
101.13	101.36	102.20	102.22	102.23	190.28	190.30	190.32	190.34	190.35
103.16	103.21	103.32	105.01	105.05	190.36	191.01	191.05	191.06	191.07
106.23	106.27	107.17	107.30	108.13	191.07	191.12	191.20	191.27	192.15
108.15	108.34	109.01	109.12	109.13	192.23	192.32	192.35	193.01	193.01
109.13	109.14	109.16	109.20	109.35	193.03	193.04	193.06	193.07	193.12
110.15	112.05	112.06	112.15	112.23	193.14	193.14	193.17	193.17	193.18
112.29	112.34	113.03	113.04	113.08	193.19	193.22	193.33	193.35	193.39
113.16	113.22	115.15	116.10	116.22	194.02	194.04	194.09	194.11	194.13
116.23	116.24	117.08	117.24	118.06	194.15	194.20	194.23	194.25	195.01
118.10	118.18	118.20	118.25	119.15	195.02	195.03	195.30	195.34	195.36
120.05	120.09	120.19	120.23	120.24	196.02	196.02	196.03	196.03	196.04
120.26	120.27	120.28	121.01	121.05	196.05	196.05	196.06	196.06	196.10
121.05	121.18	121.25	122.07	122.21	196.13	196.14	196.15	196.16	196.18
122.22	122.24	122.27	123.03	123.07	196.18	196.19	196.19	196.23	197.23
123.12	123.12	123.18	123.18	123.24	197.25	197.33	197.34	197.34	197.35
123.27	123.31	124.14	124.20	124.27	198.03	198.05	198.14	198.14	198.20
125.08	125.16	125.18	125.22	125.26	198.21	198.23	198.28	198.30	198.32
127.02	127.07	127.18	127.18	128.05	198.34	199.01	199.02	199.08	199.13
129.07	129.17	129.32	129.33	130.19	199.17	202.01	202.10	202.14	202.15
130.22	130.23	130.24	130.28	131.09	202.16	202.22	202.28	202.33	202.34
131.16	131.17	131.17	131.19	131.21	202.36	203.19	203.22	203.31	204.15
131.23	131.27	132.37	133.30	133.34	204.19	204.28	205.14	205.18	205.19
134.24	134.32	135.04	135.12	135.14	205.19	205.20	205.21	206.16	206.17
135.14	135.15	135.16	135.20	136.08	206.20	206.22	206.23	207.32	207.35
136.09	136.24	137.07	137.08	137.23	208.26	208.35	208.38	208.40	210.04
137.23	138.30	138.32	139.09	140.13	210.16	210.21	211.29	212.04	212.12
141.03	141.03	141.09	142.04	142.19	212.30	213.04	213.25	213.27	213.27
142.20	142.21	143.09	143.24	143.32	213.35	213.35	213.36	214.02	214.03
143.32	144.16	144.19	145.02	145.27	214.23	214.24	214.32	215.03	215.04
145.27	145.29	146.07	146.19	146.19	215.07	215.19	215.26	215.26	215.33
147.25	147.33	148.06	148.13	148.14	215.35	215.36	216.08	216.15	216.20
148.29	149.01	149.09	149.18	149.18	217.01	217.05	217.17	217.24	217.30
150.08	150.14	150.14	150.21	151.10	217.33	217.34	218.16	218.16	218.31
151.25	151.29	151.32	151.32	152.10	219.03	219.04	219.10	219.14	219.14
153.09	153.11	153.18	153.20	153.31	219.23	219.24	220.03	220.26	220.27
155.21	155.34	156.12	156.14	156.15	220.36	220.37	221.05	221.07	221.12
156.24	157.12	157.13	157.20	157.22	221.13	221.23	222.01	222.08	222.09
157.27	157.33	157.35	158.02	158.12	222.09	222.22	223.06	223.25	223.28
158.24	158.24	158.24	158.24	158.24	223.29	223.33	223.33	224.02	224.07
158.25	158.25	158.26	158.29	158.30	224.20	224.30	224.32	224.32	224.34
159.08	159.14	160.16	160.25	160.32	224.34	225.01	225.04	225.25	225.30
160.35	161.11	161.11	161.12	161.22	225.31	225.32	225.34	225.35	226.04
162.14	162.18	162.23	162.24	162.24	226.05	226.06	226.25	226.36	227.10
162.25	162.26	162.33	163.32	163.35	227.17	227.21	228.05	228.33	229.04
164.05	164.16	164.32	165.17	165.17	229.23	229.30	230.13	230.17	230.18
165.23	165.30	166.05	166.20	166.21	230.24	230.27	230.31	230.32	233.03
166.26	166.29	167.26	167.32	167.33	233.17	234.35	235.03	235.05	235.17
167.34	168.08	168.11	169.17	169.18	235.27	236.05	236.28	238.20	238.31
169.25	169.28	170.09	170.11	170.27	239.10	239.12	239.13	239.13	239.15
170.33	171.01	171.03	171.03	171.03	239.27	239.33	240.06	240.26	241.06
171.04	171.30	171.33	172.08	172.36	241.26	241.29	241.34	241.34	242.02
173.13	173.15	174.07	175.11	175.15	242.04	242.08	242.09	242.09	242.17
175.20	175.23	175.27	175.28	175.30	242.18	242.25	242.27	242.31	242.31
176.22	176.24	176.24	176.28	176.30	242.34	243.02	243.07	243.08	244.19
176.32	177.06	177.06	177.15	177.16	244.34	245.03	245.13	245.14	245.16
177.19	177.26	177.27	177.35	178.08	245.24	246.04	246.05	246.11	246.19
178.08	178.14	178.16	178.16	178.20	246.27	246.29	246.33	246.33	246.34
178.20	178.21	178.27	178.29	178.29	246.36	247.03	247.31	247.35	248.01
178.30	178.31	178.34	179.07	179.16	248.02	248.19	248.26	249.14	249.18
179.24	179.31	179.31	180.12	180.13	249.18	249.22	250.21	250.23	250.29
180.13	180.19	180.22	180.23	180.24	250.33	251.01	251.01	251.03	251.03
180.25	180.27	180.36	181.07	181.12	251.12	251.13	251.17	252.01	252.03
181.21	181.21	181.22	181.34	181.36	252.03	252.03	252.03	252.05	253.05
182.12	182.20	182.22	183.01	183.04	253.07	253.08	253.12	253.15	253.15
183.07	183.08	183.11	183.20	183.22	254.08	254.14	254.17	254.20	254.23
183.26	183.28	183.29	184.23	184.33	256.09	256.21	256.23	256.27	256.30
184.34	184.35	185.02	185.04	185.08	256.33	257.16	258.08	259.04	259.04
185.09	185.11	185.35	186.02	186.04	259.05	259.15	259.20	259.22	259.23
186.11	186.13	186.16	186.22	186.27	259.31	260.03	260.03	260.03	260.17
186.28	186.29	186.34	187.02	187.04	260.30	261.06	261.07	261.07	261.08
187.04	187.06	187.07	187.10	187.10	261.28	262.14	262.15	262.21	262.30
187.11	187.15	187.18	187.19	187.28	262.30	263.09	263.34	264.06	265.06
187.28	187.30	187.33	188.04	188.04	265.10	265.15	266.28	266.33	266.35
188.08	188.09	188.24	188.25	188.25	266.36	269.08	269.19	269.20	270.05
188.29	188.31	188.35	188.36	189.03	270.08	270.20	271.06	271.07	271.07
189.04	189.07	189.16	189.17	189.19	271.22	271.24	272.05	272.05	272.06

272.29	272.31	272.34	273.26	273.35
274.26	274.28	274.29	274.34	274.34
274.36	275.01	275.03	275.05	275.06
275.18	275.19	275.28	276.19	276.20
276.21	276.28	279.11	279.21	280.02
280.20	280.23	280.23	281.07	281.10
281.22	281.23	281.23	282.23	282.24
282.28	282.29	282.30	282.32	284.14
284.34	285.03	285.10	285.14	285.17
285.26	287.01	287.07	287.09	287.11
287.16	287.32	287.33	287.34	288.09
288.14	288.19	288.22	288.22	290.11
290.36	291.02	291.05	291.29	292.01
292.12	292.24	292.24	292.36	293.05
293.15	293.20	293.24	293.34	294.05
294.11	294.12	295.05	295.06	295.10
295.24	296.06	296.08	296.08	296.12
296.23	296.26	296.26	296.28	296.33
297.13	297.15	297.35	298.15	298.18
299.11	299.12	299.14	299.18	299.18
299.32	299.33	300.07	300.13	300.13
300.14	300.15	300.16	300.23	301.06
301.07	301.16	301.19	301.20	301.20
301.23	301.28	301.30	301.35	302.02
302.03	302.03	302.13	302.25	302.27
302.30	302.32	302.35	303.12	303.26
303.30	304.02	304.07	304.18	305.05
305.09	305.09	305.16	305.22	306.19
306.21	306.23	306.30	306.30	307.02
307.24	307.25	308.12	308.12	308.14
308.15	308.21	308.27	308.30	309.12
309.12	309.24	310.02	310.06	311.08
311.09	311.13	311.22	311.24	311.28
311.29	311.31	311.32	311.33	312.01
312.05	312.08	312.14	312.26	312.29
313.23	313.24	314.23	314.26	315.11
316.08	316.31	316.32	316.33	316.34
316.35	316.37	317.01	317.01	317.04
317.04	317.05	317.06	317.07	317.26
317.28	318.16	318.24	318.26	318.29
319.19	320.19	320.30	321.03	321.04
321.30	321.33	322.08	322.15	322.29
322.37	323.04	323.11	323.13	323.17
323.18	323.18	323.18	323.19	323.20
324.09	324.22	325.18	325.29	326.08
326.11	326.17	326.21	326.25	326.27
327.04	327.13	327.31	327.32	328.05
328.05	328.06	328.06	328.06	328.07
328.09	328.20	328.32	328.36	329.11
329.12	329.20	329.27	330.01	330.10
330.15	330.18	330.20	330.20	330.21
330.27	331.25	331.28	332.06	332.12
332.25	332.30	332.35	332.36	333.03
333.13				

ITALY (1)
202.28
ITCH (1)
332.01
ITCHING (1)
160.11
ITEM (3)
050.22 060.02 067.19
ITEMS (1)
091.30
ITERATION (2)
161.22 161.23
ITS (354)

005.16	005.18	006.12	013.30	013.30
014.01	015.01	015.28	015.29	016.32
017.02	023.06	023.25	024.06	024.07
030.13	030.16	033.13	034.12	037.06
041.14	042.23	044.29	045.01	046.03
047.05	047.09	050.28	055.25	057.14
057.23	058.04	062.26	062.29	063.09
069.30	070.19	071.23	074.23	076.22
077.36	078.01	079.09	083.05	083.08
083.09	084.36	085.26	086.13	086.14

086.16	086.16	088.06	088.36	089.04
089.19	089.26	090.27	091.06	091.08
091.19	092.02	092.05	092.08	096.10
096.22	097.30	098.02	098.13	098.21
098.27	100.17	102.04	108.24	112.09
113.21	113.35	113.36	114.07	114.17
115.11	115.15	116.07	116.11	116.12
116.15	118.12	118.24	118.25	119.16
119.18	121.05	121.22	122.28	124.14
126.16	127.28	132.32	133.25	137.08
141.01	141.02	142.16	157.03	160.04
165.30	166.25	167.05	167.13	167.22
170.08	170.08	170.09	171.26	175.11
175.13	175.28	175.29	176.34	177.08
177.18	177.21	178.12	178.12	178.19
178.27	178.28	179.16	179.25	181.09
181.14	181.23	181.27	181.33	181.36
182.01	182.21	183.07	183.24	184.07
184.11	184.13	184.14	185.04	185.05
186.01	186.03	186.06	186.17	186.34
186.36	187.09	188.01	188.09	188.10
188.10	188.28	188.32	188.32	188.33
188.36	189.04	189.16	191.22	191.25
191.29	192.17	192.31	192.36	193.04
193.06	193.11	193.12	193.13	193.18
193.26	193.29	193.29	193.30	194.16
194.30	194.33	194.34	195.01	196.07
196.09	196.12	196.18	196.20	197.21
197.22	197.22	197.26	197.28	197.30
198.10	199.18	199.19	201.19	201.29
201.29	201.32	204.11	204.13	206.21
207.32	208.26	212.32	212.33	214.21
216.09	218.34	219.14	219.15	225.26
225.34	226.07	226.36	228.23	232.18
235.17	237.08	238.34	239.07	239.10
239.21	239.30	239.34	242.03	244.01
244.16	244.35	245.01	245.01	245.14
246.26	246.36	248.18	249.17	253.17
256.31	260.21	260.21	262.28	263.24
263.31	264.04	264.26	268.26	270.09
272.35	275.02	280.22	281.08	281.11
281.12	281.14	281.15	281.16	282.32
283.05	284.11	285.03	287.22	287.23
288.12	288.25	288.29	289.02	289.06
289.27	289.35	289.35	289.36	290.08
290.08	291.02	291.33	292.28	293.01
296.17	297.07	297.28	298.05	298.08
299.10	299.11	300.10	300.18	300.21
301.26	301.29	301.34	302.03	302.07
303.11	304.14	304.17	305.22	305.27
306.05	306.21	307.07	307.36	307.18
307.26	307.27	307.36	308.02	308.22
309.07	309.18	309.24	311.03	311.07
311.15	311.15	311.27	311.32	312.13
312.29	313.19	313.33	316.17	316.27
316.33	316.37	316.37	316.39	317.01
317.06	317.06	317.09	317.12	317.33
318.04	318.05	318.05	318.30	321.26
325.03	325.28	327.03	327.13	328.13
328.32	331.25	331.25	332.13	332.14
332.15	333.05	333.22	333.26	

ITSELF (49)

032.25	033.20	041.21	058.05	077.24
086.31	089.03	089.20	092.04	093.24
096.24	102.23	102.26	103.23	103.27
112.28	137.06	144.23	147.29	155.23
177.08	177.12	187.03	189.02	193.01
193.13	194.15	213.30	232.20	239.29
240.06	246.31	263.33	263.34	264.28
281.13	283.29	289.05	294.33	295.03
301.21	305.33	306.18	306.34	307.04
307.20	307.25	331.23	332.12	

IVY (1)
305.19

JACK
051.31 274.10   (2)
JACKET
023.22   (1)
JAIL
084.06 096.33 171.22   (3)
JAILER
315.08   (1)
JAMES
043.01 043.02 043.29   (3)
JAMMED
238.13   (1)
JAN
279.25   (1)
JANUARY
137.17 249.07 293.34 294.03   (4)
JAPAN
322.26   (1)
JAPANNED
065.23   (1)
JARRED
188.05   (1)
JARRING
276.16   (1)
JAW
219.17   (1)
JAWS
231.02   (1)
JAY
128.03   (1)
JAYS
238.27 238.33 275.10   (3)
JELLY
218.22   (1)
JERK
009.24 175.18 295.04   (3)
JERSEY
020.19   (1)
JEST
094.11 268.12 294.13 315.04   (4)
JESTING
029.23 124.21   (2)
JESUITS
075.03   (1)
JESUS
108.20   (1)
JEWELLER
168.31   (1)
JEWELS
317.16   (1)
JINGLE
271.29   (1)
JOB
053.16 058.20   (2)
JOBS
234.06   (1)
JOHN
121.10 204.07 204.17 204.22 206.13
206.25 206.31 206.32 208.32 208.37
221.34 279.25 333.28   (13)
JOHNSON
038.33   (1)

JOHNSWORT
113.31 155.16 155.27 156.05 224.17
309.32   (6)
JOINED
072.04 173.25   (2)

JOINT
053.29   (1)
JOINTS
033.16 114.14 165.18   (3)
JOKING   (1)

133.35
JONAS
018.22   (1)
JONATHAN
037.11 333.28   (2)

JONSONIAN
124.19   (1)
JOSTLED
260.04   (1)
JOURNAL
018.06   (1)
JOURNEY
037.21 143.13 143.19 243.32   (4)
JOVE
165.32   (1)
JOWL
141.16   (1)
JOY
080.18 165.21 188.11 193.13 216.25
311.31 314.38 315.08 332.22   (9)
JOYS
010.06   (1)
JUDGE
006.23 010.08 021.28 095.08 098.35
315.09 316.05   (7)
JUDGED
023.04 294.26   (2)
JUDGING
287.16   (1)
JUG
065.22 065.23 243.11 298.14   (4)
JUGA
314.02   (1)
JULY
045.10 059.02 084.29 294.03 296.26   (5)
JUMP
038.15 252.01   (2)
JUMPED
038.12 252.01   (2)
JUMPING
317.17   (1)
JUNE
163.28 199.18 226.10 233.01 311.10   (5)
JUNIPER
201.10   (1)
JUNK
119.27   (1)
JUNO
139.05   (1)
JUPITER
074.11 118.26 139.04   (3)
JUST   (39)
011.04 034.22 042.21 070.14 082.21
092.06 105.25 106.21 123.10 124.16
130.10 138.14 166.02 179.10 180.01
180.09 180.35 183.18 186.08 190.01
213.14 223.12 224.06 224.35 225.05
225.15 235.26 248.24 249.20 253.01
253.11 258.23 259.07 259.16 263.19
309.26 318.32 323.08 328.29
JUSTICE   (4)
076.14 076.34 164.31 173.22
)#
)#
)#
)#
)#
)#
)#
)#
)#
)#
)#

```
KNOW                        (CONTINUED)
016.02  016.16  016.24  016.33  017.09
018.22  021.02  021.32  022.20  028.21
032.30  034.06  035.01  037.11  040.13
042.11  047.16  051.17  058.29  058.30
059.30  061.30  070.16  070.21  078.04
078.16  080.31  082.36  090.18  091.09
093.02  094.30  095.11  095.14  095.33
098.09  098.24  104.15  106.11  106.13
106.35  109.18  109.34  116.22  135.07
136.36  144.20  145.02  148.16  148.18
151.32  152.11  153.16  154.07  158.03
160.27  161.17  173.13  179.14  180.19
183.20  185.23  190.36  192.15  201.33
207.20  211.05  213.25  213.28  218.10
220.30  220.35  220.35  220.36  221.09
225.01  231.14  231.20  235.23  237.08
240.21  247.32  260.21  261.27  262.06
269.16  271.15  277.13  283.21  288.20
289.26  290.26  291.12  294.23  308.29
321.09  332.06
KNOWING                             (    8)
016.08  078.17  107.26  148.12  170.32
204.15  205.01  239.12
KNOWLEDGE                           (    9)
006.20  011.22  021.06  103.20  117.28
148.28  213.11  232.14  326.33
KNOWN                               (   23)
019.02  019.31  052.04  086.07  093.22
104.01  107.13  169.33  170.36  171.07
173.18  177.20  181.12  182.06  192.30
239.20  257.15  281.19  283.23  292.36
295.25  314.31  332.36
KNOWS                               (   21)
025.32  042.16  046.04  047.23  080.18
080.26  096.24  116.09  155.13  157.16
166.01  171.02  179.29  180.18  219.24
289.22  293.06  307.34  330.21  332.30
333.17
KOHINOOR                            (    1)
199.28
KOUROO                              (    2)
326.20  327.02
```

```
L                                      (  1)
  306.30
LA                                     (  2)
  014.16  020.34
LABIUM                                 (  1)
  308.03
LABOR                                  ( 39)
  003.07  004.35  005.09  005.22  005.24
  006.17  018.09  021.03  025.33  031.21
  032.33  035.11  046.20  050.28  051.04
  056.24  058.33  060.27  069.10  070.18
  070.30  078.19  090.09  099.34  121.04
  155.09  155.14  157.10  159.07  160.31
  161.23  162.25  166.34  167.06  206.08
  221.36  275.18  306.25  308.03
LABORATORY                             (  1)
  306.10
LABORED                                (  2)
  259.09  297.34
LABORER                                (  3)
  070.25  070.28  254.22
LABORERS                               (  5)
  029.10  031.19  035.25  053.11  075.22
LABORING                               (  3)
  006.15  039.30  273.09
LABORIOSUS                             (  1)
  157.14
LABORIOUS                              (  1)
  157.18
LABORIOUSLY                            (  1)
  100.13
LABORS                                 (  8)
  004.31  006.12  090.01  103.30  196.20
  217.18  241.32  306.19
LABORUM                                (  1)
  005.34
LABYRINTH                              (  1)
  028.33
LACINIATED                             (  1)
  305.12
LADDER                                 (  2)
  168.03  244.04
LADEN                                  (  1)
  115.36
LADIES                                 (  5)
  000.03  037.09  170.30  215.32  329.22
LADING                                 (  1)
  120.22
LADY                                   (  3)
  067.19  139.08  218.22
LAETATION                              (  1)
  162.20
LAID                                   ( 17)
  038.30  045.13  092.28  092.31  097.12
  143.07  143.09  151.34  173.09  192.06
  192.34  195.30  225.27  226.35  238.20
  289.15  305.23
LAIN                                   (  6)
  023.15  041.21  232.27  285.20  294.27
  304.03
LAING                                  (  1)
  027.11
LAKE                                   ( 23)
  086.22  086.27  119.21  126.10  129.14
  137.07  181.35  185.34  186.12  186.22
  187.19  188.13  188.22  191.13  193.09
  194.19  197.13  197.35  197.35  202.14
  240.07  288.17  291.31
LAKES                                  (  9)
  086.14  179.24  197.05  197.19  199.22
  207.26  234.18  235.18  312.32
LAMBS                                  (  2)
  122.03  216.04
LAMP                                   (  6)
  043.18  065.23  098.07  250.08  253.35
  268.20
LAMPLIGHT                              (  1)
  014.07

LAMPREYS                               (  1)
  185.23
LANCE                                  (  1)
  192.28
LAND                                   ( 42)
  003.35  004.02  005.19  008.04  009.36
  039.09  054.11  054.28  055.28  062.31
  063.06  063.29  064.04  064.32  064.34
  081.32  087.23  092.11  132.18  156.12
  156.18  164.35  180.07  188.36  189.01
  196.13  204.36  207.35  234.32  261.18
  264.16  264.17  266.17  276.23  289.31
  291.23  293.02  294.26  317.36  320.18
  322.14  333.03
LANDED                                 (  1)
  298.22
LANDLORD                               (  2)
  029.19  293.35
LANDS                                  (  3)
  102.32  131.19  223.33
LANDSCAPE                              ( 14)
  081.20  082.26  156.07  165.36  176.15
  186.12  196.21  197.03  208.06  264.19
  269.22  271.05  304.22  318.34
LANDSCAPES                             (  2)
  082.28  287.27
LANES                                  (  1)
  168.18
LANGUAGE                               ( 14)
  100.12  100.23  100.30  101.08  101.10
  101.11  101.11  101.24  102.04  102.23
  103.19  106.29  111.07  244.34
LANGUAGES                              (  3)
  101.22  101.29  111.05
LAP                                    (  1)
  306.26
LAPLANDER                              (  1)
  027.12
LAPPED                                 (  1)
  045.12
LAPS                                   (  1)
  308.03
LAPSE                                  (  6)
  026.28  097.06  101.34  111.32  327.21
  333.30
LAPSES                                 (  1)
  308.04
LAPSING                                (  1)
  306.25
LAPSUS                                 (  1)
  306.25
LARD                                   (  1)
  059.20
LARDER                                 (  1)
  061.36
LARGE                                  ( 46)
  003.20  027.32  029.08  030.21  032.36
  034.34  044.01  048.30  071.22  083.34
  094.25  114.08  114.17  132.33  140.22
  163.17  165.25  165.25  177.20  177.23
  188.22  191.15  195.01  199.08  203.21
  212.15  225.08  228.27  233.09  238.31
  247.16  247.19  257.36  258.12  267.30
  277.27  280.15  281.08  296.06  299.03
  302.01  302.17  304.32  313.06  328.29
  332.26
LARGER                                 ( 18)
  015.21  029.21  050.06  056.19  087.33
  100.15  113.27  140.11  194.21  207.28
  227.36  228.28  242.32  243.13  308.06
  308.10  313.20  316.35
LARGEST                                (  4)
  057.12  076.01  248.14  302.05
LARK                                   (  4)
  041.17  128.07  252.31  297.23
LARVA                                  (  2)
  215.14  215.16
```

LARVAE				(1)
215.09				
LARYNX				(1)
272.28				
LASHES				(1)
186.15				
LAST				(101)
003.32	008.04	014.13	015.33	017.27
022.21	022.26	024.10	024.31	028.21
034.11	035.03	044.05	048.16	052.14
053.36	059.06	062.06	066.05	076.31
083.13	084.02	084.16	094.25	095.03
097.02	103.10	104.07	112.31	113.36
114.33	119.35	120.25	121.14	130.27
141.02	144.17	145.08	146.08	148.26
154.14	155.25	159.16	160.23	161.15
166.36	167.07	169.12	177.14	178.28
181.23	181.32	184.20	191.17	193.10
204.15	211.36	212.14	213.02	213.26
218.36	226.04	228.10	238.34	239.25
247.21	251.13	252.12	254.08	257.12
260.11	261.34	262.19	262.31	262.34
263.11	263.29	264.21	267.05	268.12
268.17	268.22	268.30	272.04	274.32
276.07	279.33	281.08	300.17	307.16
308.19	310.27	311.07	312.06	312.32
322.11	322.28	327.06	327.28	331.23
333.27				
LASTED				(3)
190.34	202.16	250.22		
LASTS				(1)
318.06				
LATCH				(3)
049.17	170.06	172.04		
LATE				(17)
008.23	029.18	055.10	114.09	126.03
150.08	155.19	157.25	157.25	169.17
170.02	190.15	213.33	247.31	263.10
278.09	312.31			
LATELY				(5)
043.25	072.06	120.02	297.33	314.14
LATER				(6)
086.20	103.27	156.29	174.03	180.30
299.16				
LATERAL				(1)
141.01				
LATEST				(1)
155.06				
LATH				(1)
330.24				
LATHING				(2)
245.22	245.32			
LATHS				(1)
049.08				
LATIN				(6)
061.22	100.26	101.20	101.23	106.24
166.23				
LATINS				(1)
006.38				
LATITUDE				(2)
061.16	324.24			
LATITUDES				(3)
044.31	077.17	321.12		
LATTER				(18)
026.28	064.04	136.08	140.23	181.17
189.09	198.13	205.02	226.03	229.28
234.13	278.23	283.31	290.15	293.10
299.31	307.19	330.19		
LATTERLY				(1)
108.31				
LAUGH				(7)
026.06	146.14	234.22	235.32	235.34
256.20	297.30			
LAUGHED				(3)
146.20	234.28	236.17		
LAUGHING				(1)
128.05				
LAUGHS				(2)
026.07	137.05			
LAUGHTER				(5)
026.14	146.22	233.26	236.08	268.11
LAUNCH				(1)
169.18				
LAUNCHED				(1)
266.23				
LAVA				(1)
305.04				
LAVATO				(1)
063.17				
LAVES				(1)
186.10				
LAVISHLY				(2)
016.07	192.03			
LAW				(12)
053.23	075.08	096.10	221.21	250.13
290.29	291.05	302.03	305.08	306.20
307.18	315.36			
LAWGIVER				(1)
221.22				
LAWS				(17)
012.05	134.11	210.01	218.34	218.36
268.33	290.23	290.26	290.33	290.34
322.32	323.02	323.03	323.07	323.35
323.36	324.03			
LAWYER				(3)
019.02	019.07	231.36		
LAWYERS				(1)
153.14				
LAXLY				(1)
324.34				
LAY				(32)
007.12	022.01	024.23	031.18	041.26
045.26	046.09	050.32	051.01	053.03
067.02	072.30	081.32	158.36	159.18
162.29	164.20	178.10	215.07	224.24
261.21	262.15	262.17	264.34	271.20
278.26	280.14	298.09	303.17	304.13
312.10	324.30			
LAYERS				(3)
296.04	333.13	333.19		
LAYING				(1)
005.27				
LAYS				(2)
283.33	294.05			
LAZY				(1)
080.08				
LB				(1)
306.29				
LE				(1)
261.12				
LEA				(1)
208.10				
LEACH				(2)
292.21	292.27			
LEACHED				(1)
158.29				
LEAD				(4)
008.07	052.20	216.15	250.04	
LEADEN				(1)
329.17				
LEADER				(2)
249.01	313.13			
LEADING				(1)
267.18				
LEADS				(3)
165.37	171.01	322.26		
LEAF				(25)
114.07	119.25	123.14	126.20	129.28
137.14	142.31	155.21	173.27	188.14
226.27	273.32	280.02	284.14	297.32
306.18	306.21	306.27	307.04	307.36
308.10	308.11	308.17	308.19	333.08
LEAGUE				(2)
122.14	153.29			

LEAK (3)
052.31 270.10 292.26
LEAKED (2)
204.18 292.22
LEAKIEST (1)
126.31
LEAN (4)
047.13 155.24 159.36 281.05
LEANED (1)
225.35
LEANING (3)
165.06 168.06 269.05
LEAP (6)
038.16 178.26 187.16 188.07 277.12
329.31
LEAPED (6)
190.13 203.18 259.20 278.03 278.04
332.05
LEAPING (2)
018.20 278.21
LEAPS (1)
324.26
LEARN (23)
003.18 011.34 032.28 051.14 051.24
051.25 064.20 090.15 090.34 094.24
100.22 101.13 107.04 108.08 155.18
169.31 171.14 216.04 244.12 244.33
263.19 317.34 322.16
LEARNED (29)
009.03 026.23 044.04 053.06 055.29
061.14 070.06 071.08 095.05 101.24
103.18 104.12 104.13 104.21 107.24
109.33 112.32 120.36 150.20 151.11
199.32 224.03 231.21 240.34 246.01
279.12 306.20 323.29 331.32
LEARNING (5)
076.23 101.31 103.33 110.02 169.12
LEARNS (1)
211.02
LEAST (51)
011.32 019.15 022.06 023.12 029.13
032.16 034.06 037.18 039.36 045.25
046.25 054.06 055.30 061.12 064.01
066.35 068.05 073.01 087.25 089.09
089.10 097.14 110.17 112.25 126.31
131.29 142.20 143.16 164.18 165.22
176.06 180.23 181.20 184.15 192.18
193.38 197.06 204.19 229.23 230.14
230.29 233.31 252.03 264.17 288.22
290.12 299.20 308.24 309.35 312.21
323.29
LEAVE (18)
036.22 057.29 066.06 107.06 108.35
109.35 129.30 145.25 145.27 184.33
187.31 213.20 216.09 224.07 228.11
287.20 287.24 315.08
LEAVEN (2)
062.25 063.25
LEAVENING (1)
062.22
LEAVES (51)
013.30 028.18 060.31 075.14 077.02
113.22 121.34 129.13 138.13 138.15
149.01 156.09 157.04 159.21 163.33
167.14 170.24 176.32 178.36 179.07
181.25 202.12 213.04 223.25 226.18
226.36 227.14 227.16 233.31 233.36
238.26 239.34 248.35 252.20 256.12
276.16 278.19 281.21 281.26 283.19
300.32 305.10 305.19 306.19 306.24
306.33 307.02 307.05 307.22 309.02
309.04
LEAVING (15)
035.34 042.20 052.02 081.17 146.05
159.28 163.24 169.24 189.32 207.12
230.03 238.09 248.09 278.20 296.07
LECTURE (5)
078.14 109.08 169.20 271.17 271.19

LECTURER (1)
076.23
LECTURES (1)
051.34
LECTURING (1)
078.11
LED (10)
021.23 113.29 166.05 203.06 226.11
228.07 232.16 235.01 257.28 259.18
LEDGER (1)
279.27
LEDGES (1)
279.18
LEEK (1)
161.31
LEFT (55)
008.21 009.08 010.02 010.12 029.05
037.19 044.27 049.27 054.32 055.16
056.02 066.10 078.16 080.27 081.34
082.24 083.03 088.11 125.11 129.26
130.02 130.33 133.35 134.25 145.06
154.19 166.06 172.12 179.35 190.02
191.17 192.05 194.34 201.34 205.32
216.10 224.33 232.06 236.29 237.06
240.30 253.03 253.07 253.22 258.15
260.34 261.10 261.16 263.15 266.15
277.08 287.03 319.20 321.20 323.10
LEG (6)
004.28 022.15 033.24 066.11 230.03
231.13
LEGALLY (1)
244.26
LEGGED (2)
113.10 281.23
LEGIBLE (1)
119.29
LEGION (1)
137.12
LEGIONS (1)
228.36
LEGISLATIVE (1)
023.20
LEGISLATURE (3)
196.11 213.26 213.30
LEGITIMATELY (1)
012.30
LEGS (8)
022.16 022.17 025.29 113.21 133.17
152.32 228.13 293.08
LEISURE (13)
006.15 048.17 051.03 051.05 051.06
060.35 070.22 103.08 109.02 146.26
246.22 269.13 302.11
LEND (3)
150.33 185.25 258.33
LENGTH (43)
011.25 023.13 045.03 053.30 062.32
074.11 084.20 100.28 115.17 123.32
155.03 156.07 160.13 175.13 189.06
190.12 203.26 216.18 225.34 231.15
236.23 246.20 248.21 257.24 265.22
266.19 274.15 274.22 275.10 275.36
278.30 279.05 281.12 289.17 289.21
289.36 290.02 290.16 291.08 302.12
304.16 304.19 305.33
LENGTHEN (1)
253.35
LENGTHWISE (1)
289.15
LENTICULAR (1)
248.04
LEOPARDS (1)
305.14
LEPUS (2)
280.25 281.16
LESS (44)
009.09 013.10 013.32 018.35 018.35
019.20 023.28 026.25 031.22 035.13

123

LESS			(CONTINUED)	
036.06	050.13	064.20	073.02	075.09
084.02	085.03	089.20	103.36	118.27
118.30	136.21	153.33	164.04	171.31
185.17	210.19	211.32	214.07	214.26
215.08	217.21	217.22	221.36	228.25
230.13	236.34	279.30	283.21	291.04
301.28	321.22	324.04	330.08	

LESSER (1)
197.23

LEST (3)
028.32 324.18 324.32

LET (73)
007.10	011.29	021.25	026.15	038.09
040.09	047.01	048.19	056.35	058.20
071.14	078.07	078.08	078.16	078.33
081.27	082.02	082.04	082.18	083.31
091.25	097.12	097.16	097.18	097.20
097.20	097.20	097.23	097.29	097.32
098.16	098.18	105.15	108.18	108.21
109.33	110.04	110.15	118.15	122.17
125.25	135.27	137.02	138.27	147.29
161.30	167.31	169.15	196.05	197.04
197.05	207.26	207.31	207.34	212.11
222.22	224.03	224.23	225.10	228.30
239.21	250.27	253.18	257.10	258.32
260.03	283.12	293.22	322.04	326.03
326.09	330.12	330.26		

LETHARGY (1)
259.09

LETTER (5)
020.14 020.15 094.36 098.24 100.19

LETTERS (4)
094.06 104.21 125.15 148.04

LETTING (2)
178.20 208.32

LETTRES (1)
048.04

LETTUCE (1)
139.05

LEUCISCUS (2)
184.04 311.33

LEUCOPUS (1)
225.24

LEVEL (21)
038.18	093.03	107.09	122.04	146.03
156.26	181.02	190.02	252.15	265.35
271.26	277.01	282.31	288.30	289.01
289.19	292.36	293.02	293.08	325.08
329.14				

LEVELLED (1)
278.25

LEVELLING (1)
161.26

LEVER (1)
181.30

LEVIPES (1)
281.16

LEVITY (1)
029.24

LEWIS (1)
321.10

LEXINGTON (1)
277.26

LIABILITY (1)
318.25

LIABLE (1)
246.02

LIBER (1)
024.18

LIBERAL (5)
079.17 109.03 109.06 323.35 324.01

LIBERALITY (1)
108.09

LIBERALIZING (1)
108.19

LIBERALLY (1)
106.07

LIBERTIES (1)
160.27

LIBERTY (4)
054.05 076.05 129.05 205.24

LIBRARY (4)
099.23 104.30 108.31 110.05

LICENSE (2)
288.22 324.02

LICHEN (4)
083.13 201.12 201.31 308.02

LICHENS (2)
125.33 305.13

LICK (1)
168.20

LICKS (1)
181.36

LID (1)
029.15

LIDS (3)
266.11 266.15 282.32

LIE (10)
026.26 068.01 082.02 107.18 146.17
164.18 246.20 287.17 292.16 308.34

LIEBIG (1)
013.08

LIES (7)
117.08 188.23 192.16 193.31 194.20
216.17 297.01

LIFE (200)
003.09	003.13	003.33	004.25	005.13
005.17	005.29	006.12	008.18	009.14
009.26	009.30	010.07	010.22	010.23
011.16	011.33	011.35	012.08	012.11
012.14	012.19	012.23	013.17	013.35
014.18	014.21	014.29	014.31	015.02
015.04	015.14	015.26	016.30	016.35
019.23	022.13	024.15	026.13	027.09
027.15	031.15	031.19	031.23	031.36
032.01	034.18	037.17	038.12	041.21
041.34	047.22	047.25	047.29	048.14
050.18	051.11	051.29	054.04	054.09
057.36	061.31	062.24	063.25	067.26
071.19	073.15	074.17	076.02	078.01
078.26	078.35	081.04	081.27	088.11
088.22	088.26	089.18	089.23	089.25
089.27	090.11	090.20	090.26	090.33
090.36	091.03	091.04	091.05	091.21
091.28	092.01	092.15	093.07	094.07
095.32	096.07	096.09	096.26	098.15
101.05	102.13	102.22	102.26	103.29
107.36	108.08	109.28	111.16	111.24
112.01	112.25	112.27	113.20	113.31
120.14	122.15	127.20	129.24	131.13
131.33	133.23	133.33	134.03	135.15
142.14	144.01	147.04	150.06	150.19
150.23	153.24	162.25	166.06	175.11
188.10	188.35	194.27	202.17	203.22
205.21	205.25	206.19	207.07	208.26
209.03	210.17	210.22	212.32	213.02
216.23	216.25	216.34	218.19	218.26
218.28	219.12	219.24	220.13	222.17
223.22	224.29	229.13	230.05	254.05
254.30	254.37	257.28	258.27	263.16
268.13	274.28	283.29	284.24	291.09
291.35	309.06	309.07	309.28	310.32
311.08	311.14	313.20	315.06	317.26
318.08	318.18	319.18	323.31	324.03
326.26	328.05	328.09	329.11	331.35
331.36	332.35	333.17	333.19	333.27

LIFETIME (1)
049.33

LIFT (1)
170.05

LIFTING (1)
311.07

LIGATURES (1)
121.04

```
LIGHT                          ( 55)
010.17 015.34 035.06 039.06 054.21
065.31 067.08 077.18 086.30 089.20
112.05 116.15 117.04 130.32 143.20
148.32 158.36 166.15 176.08 176.26
177.06 177.10 177.19 180.09 188.17
188.30 189.04 190.05 199.06 199.22
201.05 202.14 202.18 202.26 205.07
206.04 250.27 252.29 252.36 253.34
254.37 255.10 272.16 273.10 273.17
281.16 282.26 283.04 297.09 305.23
312.06 313.01 317.20 317.24 333.31
LIGHTED                        ( 2)
043.18 156.30
LIGHTING                       ( 1)
252.24
LIGHTNING                      ( 2)
132.33 307.22
LIGHTS                         ( 4)
020.29 176.28 308.23 329.01
LIKE                          (300)
003.17 004.27 006.24 010.15 011.02
015.06 015.15 015.23 015.35 024.01
024.03 024.04 024.12 024.25 026.04
026.34 040.10 041.30 042.05 042.08
046.09 047.22 047.34 051.10 058.30
061.13 062.12 062.27 065.25 067.04
068.32 069.35 071.15 072.03 073.10
073.32 075.02 079.19 080.14 083.25
085.29 086.09 086.12 086.17 086.27
087.20 087.21 089.33 091.03 091.16
091.17 092.01 092.18 092.18 095.33
097.28 097.32 101.14 102.08 104.33
108.27 110.04 111.33 112.07 112.14
113.10 114.02 114.15 114.23 115.23
115.34 116.08 116.11 116.12 116.13
116.18 117.11 119.12 119.24 121.23
121.34 122.02 122.03 122.27 124.10
124.18 125.12 129.14 132.05 135.01
136.34 140.04 141.06 144.27 148.13
150.09 151.24 152.18 152.26 152.28
155.12 155.16 156.28 159.14 159.20
160.05 163.37 164.03 165.09 166.13
167.32 168.07 169.04 171.07 171.25
172.35 172.35 174.25 177.03 177.16
177.26 170.24 179.03 179.10 179.14
180.02 184.10 184.16 184.20 184.22
185.09 186.23 187.10 187.12 190.02
194.12 195.20 195.36 196.10 196.31
199.10 199.24 201.04 201.04 201.15
201.18 201.30 202.06 202.15 202.34
204.11 204.30 205.05 205.06 206.06
207.30 208.03 210.11 210.21 211.13
211.17 212.33 213.11 213.35 214.26
216.25 219.12 220.02 221.25 223.29
223.32 223.33 225.33 226.07 226.13
227.02 229.15 231.10 232.19 232.32
233.09 233.12 233.13 233.31 234.18
235.15 236.09 236.12 237.02 239.14
239.16 240.22 240.29 246.21 246.23
247.11 247.22 248.18 259.33 261.31
262.07 263.14 264.15 265.02 266.13
267.01 268.26 269.32 271.15 271.23
272.08 272.13 273.09 273.32 274.35
275.32 275.34 276.18 278.36 281.27
282.31 284.27 284.28 284.28 284.30
285.05 287.21 288.08 288.38 290.10
292.35 293.21 293.25 294.09 294.11
295.10 296.01 296.09 296.12 296.31
297.01 297.07 297.19 297.24 297.32
301.14 301.21 304.09 305.04 305.34
307.14 307.14 307.22 308.34 309.02
309.04 309.11 309.13 309.18 310.01
310.35 311.04 311.26 312.31 313.07
313.34 314.22 315.03 315.19 315.29
316.23 316.25 316.26 316.28 316.29
316.34 316.35 316.38 317.15 318.22
318.33 319.07 319.10 320.21 320.22

LIKE                    (CONTINUED)
321.03 324.25 324.28 325.06 325.31
325.32 328.23 328.23 328.29 328.36
329.31 331.11 332.29 332.33 332.35
LIKED                          ( 2)
133.34 146.33
LIKELY                        ( 12)
010.32 019.27 052.01 056.25 073.16
081.23 084.02 138.04 162.31 169.14
224.27 304.02
LIKENED                        ( 1)
192.32
LIKEWISE                       ( 2)
238.16 248.17
LILAC                          ( 3)
261.11 263.23 264.04
LILY                           ( 2)
178.35 199.14
LIMBED                         ( 1)
027.32
LIMBS                          ( 7)
035.10 114.21 177.30 229.29 265.31
266.05 281.12
LIME                           ( 4)
040.19 049.12 120.04 246.07
LIMESTONE                      ( 2)
036.26 246.10
LIMITED                        ( 1)
211.17
LIMITS                         ( 4)
006.37 217.35 318.08 324.20
LIMPID                         ( 1)
227.12
LINCOLN                       ( 12)
086.06 123.01 125.06 157.15 194.19
232.35 238.22 256.27 258.03 261.12
271.09 271.17
LINE                          ( 34)
017.05 039.16 100.14 118.31 154.07
163.07 168.05 168.22 168.25 175.07
175.09 175.20 178.21 180.10 186.20
186.29 193.23 204.16 256.16 265.20
277.07 284.11 284.12 285.12 287.01
288.32 289.17 289.17 290.12 290.12
290.15 290.16 292.10 331.24
LINED                          ( 4)
030.06 040.09 040.13 317.11
LINEN                          ( 5)
028.19 099.27 120.07 257.22 264.13
LINES                          ( 8)
066.09 142.30 173.35 187.27 188.08
195.10 283.12 291.07
LINGERED                       ( 2)
241.21 256.31
LINGERING                      ( 1)
130.04
LINGUA                         ( 1)
272.03
LINK                           ( 4)
115.16 158.12 175.19 184.11
LINKS                          ( 1)
129.23
LINTEL                         ( 1)
263.24
LION                           ( 1)
326.01
LIP                            ( 1)
308.03
LIPS                           ( 4)
064.14 102.25 181.35 282.08
LIQUID                         ( 7)
176.18 193.13 199.26 215.12 282.24
306.30 316.08
LIQUIDS                        ( 1)
004.24
LIQUOR                         ( 4)
064.14 099.31 126.16 217.10
```

LISPING   (1)
275.32

LISPS   (1)
125.34

LIST   (2)
013.16   018.31

LISTEN   (4)
180.29   203.31   219.02   277.09

LISTENED   (4)
152.17   278.15   278.28   332.20

LISTENING   (3)
137.34   274.30   278.22

LISTENS   (2)
216.13   218.09

LIT   (1)
145.13

LITERAL   (1)
325.03

LITERALLY   (4)
047.32   153.28   186.34   295.22

LITERARY   (3)
076.24   103.30   172.10

LITERATURE   (9)
014.32   048.01   101.24   101.28   102.29
104.22   106.05   298.05   331.26

LITERATURES (2)
101.31   179.29

LITTLE   (110)
007.16   008.33   010.09   012.04   020.02
020.02   020.10   022.25   026.06   028.31
030.31   040.25   045.25   046.29   047.30
050.06   055.20   059.04   060.01   061.03
061.15   061.26   062.08   066.34   069.31
069.31   069.32   071.34   072.22   078.35
084.05   089.11   092.18   094.34   099.03
100.18   104.15   104.31   105.25   106.08
107.06   107.27   108.24   110.17   111.09
113.09   122.03   129.29   130.25   130.36
132.08   132.30   134.28   134.29   142.33
146.34   157.07   157.32   157.33   161.23
166.29   176.10   177.07   178.11   178.32
179.06   184.09   194.10   195.18   199.13
204.37   208.07   210.27   213.34   214.25
217.01   218.34   222.09   227.31   229.12
233.05   243.11   248.20   252.24   253.01
253.36   254.06   254.09   254.11   256.22
257.10   257.21   258.03   263.30   264.18
270.06   274.31   275.28   275.30   276.27
284.20   300.06   303.24   305.01   305.06
307.21   315.17   318.25   329.18   331.22

LIVE   (94)
004.10   005.13   006.28   006.35   009.19
010.26   011.12   011.15   011.32   014.12
014.35   015.01   015.07   016.09   019.35
019.35   024.24   027.18   028.21   030.28
032.05   032.10   039.21   040.15   051.13
051.14   054.08   055.32   061.05   065.01
065.03   065.08   070.35   071.06   072.03
078.02   081.07   081.20   081.26   081.26
084.04   084.15   088.17   090.32   090.36
091.02   091.03   091.16   091.31   092.17
093.06   096.11   096.25   109.25   114.36
118.20   130.22   136.19   136.26   147.15
151.17   157.28   170.28   172.19   193.25
206.11   208.38   214.09   214.33   215.27
216.01   218.26   222.17   223.16   227.21
227.25   243.25   257.07   282.06   302.10
303.07   303.19   317.23   323.12   323.31
324.02   324.34   328.05   328.14   328.16
329.17   329.35   332.04   332.32

LIVED   (47)
003.04   003.08   004.01   009.10   010.35
014.21   029.26   056.22   059.03   081.01
081.02   087.36   090.35   096.17   100.06
107.20   112.14   143.36   150.33   158.34
170.17   175.28   180.24   180.36   191.03
202.15   205.06   210.10   222.16   232.34
244.30   253.08   257.04   257.34   258.10

LIVED   (CONTINUED)
259.06   261.11   261.18   262.02   264.36
275.06   278.24   303.28   314.20   323.15
331.12   331.35

LIVELIHOOD (2)
033.19   069.20

LIVER   (3)
117.22   306.24   308.23

LIVERY   (1)
116.17

LIVES   (42)
003.34   006.35   008.07   009.06   010.13
011.25   015.13   020.35   024.05   028.22
035.31   038.02   038.28   040.07   058.08
067.28   076.35   092.13   092.21   093.36
097.12   104.25   104.28   107.34   109.04
112.31   131.08   144.30   144.31   154.05
154.10   165.37   198.19   199.30   208.02
210.28   219.08   244.36   276.28   320.15
323.12   328.17

LIVING   (40)
003.07   007.02   008.20   009.04   019.29
029.01   029.04   035.04   038.30   051.15
052.06   060.23   063.06   069.12   069.26
071.02   071.07   072.05   090.36   109.21
112.30   132.18   149.32   153.11   194.11
203.17   205.06   206.24   207.34   223.35
231.09   243.02   283.35   309.03   309.05
311.28   318.05   325.36   333.11   333.21

LL   (2)
161.30   320.32

LO   (7)
037.24   042.12   112.06   281.10   298.10
312.09   329.02

LOAD   (11)
005.16   036.15   065.34   066.01   066.22
119.28   122.03   261.23   267.28   285.25
285.29

LOADED   (2)
238.04   245.30

LOADS   (4)
070.05   197.32   259.27   294.18

LOAF   (3)
045.23   142.06   223.23

LOAFER   (1)
205.05

LOATH   (1)
080.29

LOAVES   (1)
062.09

LOBE   (5)
306.23   306.26   306.29   308.03   308.09

LOBED   (3)
305.13   306.29   306.30

LOBES   (3)
307.36   308.11   308.12

LOCALITY   (1)
183.03

LOCATION   (1)
258.22

LOCH   (3)
287.28   288.06   288.10

LOCK   (2)
031.05   172.02

LOCKED   (4)
029.10   229.11   283.26   291.23

LOCKS   (1)
230.06

LOCOMOTIVE (2)
115.22   295.09

LOCUST   (3)
223.08   332.02   332.31

LOCUSTS   (1)
052.36

LODGE   (5)
030.11   143.04   144.13   240.11   267.36

LODGED   (2)
030.03   256.13

```
LOUD                        (CONTINUED)      LUNCHEON                              (   2)
  238.26  257.24  272.11  303.10               283.18  320.08
LOUDER                               (   3)   LUNGS                                (   5)
  124.11  266.19  310.18                        013.10  127.26  272.27  305.15  306.24
LOUDLY                               (   1)   LURK                                 (   2)
  169.05                                        316.22  317.30
LOUISIANA                            (   1)   LUSTILY                              (   2)
  236.34                                        084.23  193.11
LOUNGE                               (   1)   LUSTY                                (   2)
  245.27                                        138.03  162.01
LOVE                                 (  38)   LUTHER                               (   1)
  015.01  021.23  029.15  053.04  057.32        230.20
  058.13  058.17  070.18  074.30  081.15      LUXURIANCE                           (   2)
  105.05  111.24  124.24  124.24  134.13        054.34  308.20
  135.22  137.28  137.33  140.03  149.20      LUXURIANT                            (   2)
  155.10  158.20  172.33  208.17  210.19        200.03  306.08
  237.08  241.04  253.23  268.03  283.36      LUXURIANTLY                          (   2)
  304.01  315.16  318.18  321.22  325.31        114.05  257.19
  328.08  330.05  330.34                      LUXURIES                             (   5)
LOVED                                (  10)     009.28  014.17  014.20  033.26  061.30
  061.05  070.04  075.11  105.03  105.04      LUXURIOUS                            (   7)
  148.29  153.08  195.31  196.03  251.27        029.21  036.02  036.33  040.03  055.34
LOVER                                (   1)     057.03  239.22
  310.11                                      LUXURIOUSLY                          (   2)
LOVERS                               (   3)     014.13  254.05
  016.13  124.23  238.13                      LUXURIOUSNESS                        (   1)
LOVES                                (   3)     100.08
  028.11  196.26  310.04                      LUXURY                               (  12)
LOVING                               (   1)     012.27  014.31  014.31  015.11  034.24
  145.30                                        037.04  049.30  057.20  092.09  104.17
LOW                                  (  29)     141.09  183.33
  037.35  041.31  080.20  086.08  087.27      LYCEUM                               (   2)
  107.09  107.20  120.14  124.29  131.19        108.30  109.24
  141.12  181.12  186.08  187.03  198.13      LYING                                (  13)
  214.33  217.13  248.31  253.18  254.32        007.06  067.32  176.22  184.14  191.16
  260.19  264.17  272.14  288.02  288.17        191.31  199.09  206.28  249.31  260.22
  291.17  304.04  310.31  312.30                260.30  282.10  284.18
LOWER                                (  14)   LYRE                                 (   2)
  022.04  074.08  086.31  180.20  180.22        123.10  169.05
  194.08  202.11  214.06  219.17  243.19
  248.03  260.06  266.04  329.13
LOWEST                               (   7)
  044.25  072.05  091.06  104.24  120.06
  150.23  181.27
LOWING                               (   2)
  123.22  126.06
LU                                   (   2)
  124.18  124.18
LUBEAT                               (   1)
  243.05
LUCID                                (   1)
  095.02
LUCK                                 (   3)
  151.01  208.35  208.36
LUCKY                                (   3)
  053.16  066.10  213.15
LUCUM                                (   1)
  250.28
LUDICROUS                            (   2)
  274.02  274.27
LULL                                 (   1)
  129.19
LULLED                               (   1)
  264.29
LULLS                                (   1)
  104.17
LUMBER                               (   1)
  119.34
LUMBERING                            (   3)
  009.25  115.37  248.28
LUMP                                 (   1)
  091.24
LUMPISH                              (   1)
  306.34
LUNATICS                             (   1)
  073.34
LUNCH                                (   3)
  225.29  227.31  283.12
```

MACHINE (3)
006.18 033.16 330.32
MACHINERY (1)
168.15
MACHINES (2)
104.36 105.01
MACULARIUS (1)
185.05
MAD (2)
094.16 310.19
MADAM (1)
022.34
MADE (131)
003.12 005.09 007.02 009.24 011.08
019.11 019.19 021.31 023.51 024.35
025.06 027.31 028.02 029.27 029.33
033.37 033.37 040.23 042.35 042.36
042.37 043.11 048.01 048.04 048.25
049.26 050.25 051.24 051.31 055.19
058.28 059.03 061.18 062.01 062.14
063.14 065.16 072.22 074.10 082.22
083.23 084.33 085.21 092.01 094.05
100.01 100.05 103.22 106.12 114.06
116.24 125.13 125.20 126.28 132.05
132.10 138.26 142.26 146.23 147.11
147.12 148.34 149.29 151.21 152.28
152.33 156.36 157.22 159.13 167.07
169.22 173.08 174.30 178.19 185.24
190.09 190.18 190.32 194.11 195.07
195.21 196.04 203.26 203.33 205.02
215.33 218.23 220.24 225.19 228.04
234.36 240.25 241.20 245.32 246.06
246.28 250.05 250.29 251.03 252.03
256.15 262.03 265.07 266.08 266.31
267.22 268.06 268.13 273.28 274.28
277.27 278.13 287.12 290.09 292.19
293.11 296.23 301.06 304.14 306.11
314.12 317.05 317.09 318.26 318.26
326.05 326.14 326.28 326.34 327.15
331.10
MADNESS (1)
277.22
MADRAS (1)
297.36
MAGGOT (3)
025.31 215.10 321.25
MAGIC (3)
019.08 114.11 123.18
MAGNANIMITY (5)
015.02 080.25 109.14 166.15 329.14
MAGNETIC (2)
052.21 078.32
MAGNETISM (1)
162.23
MAGNIFICENCE (1)
080.24
MAGNIFICENT (1)
140.23
MAGNIFICENTLY (1)
016.06
MAGNIFIED (1)
177.31
MAGNITUDE (1)
073.32
MAGNUS (1)
232.03
MAIDEN (1)
200.02
MAIDS (1)
132.28
MAIN (8)
003.26 042.18 049.29 052.27 073.24
120.33 180.27 311.19
MAINE (4)
052.21 052.22 119.34 172.07
MAINLY (7)
016.17 031.31 061.05 073.27 093.19
256.29 293.19

MAINSPRING (1)
058.16
MAINTAIN (6)
015.16 070.34 072.32 182.05 253.33
323.06
MAINTAINED (3)
005.20 026.01 069.09
MAINTAINING (1)
072.31
MAJESTIES (1)
021.32
MAJORITY (2)
032.36 034.11
MAKE (90)
007.10 007.29 009.20 015.07 018.52
019.14 019.15 019.16 019.21 023.19
025.03 025.17 026.03 029.36 037.35
039.02 040.27 040.28 044.19 051.06
053.25 054.07 059.40 063.20 064.08
064.14 072.33 073.18 075.16 077.03
077.25 078.29 082.11 088.25 089.27
090.22 090.26 091.32 092.36 097.21
100.28 107.21 116.18 121.07 125.09
131.13 134.08 135.18 136.16 140.35
144.17 151.04 151.05 152.36 155.14
163.34 166.11 166.21 168.17 169.10
175.13 184.31 191.01 197.32 201.20
206.18 212.13 212.35 213.07 215.06
215.23 224.31 225.09 225.15 226.28
234.02 244.20 246.31 248.20 251.03
290.04 290.21 320.21 323.15 324.10
326.22 327.36 328.02 331.16 333.30
MAKER (6)
021.32 048.12 144.16 162.14 193.14
308.16
MAKERS (1)
177.21
MAKES (23)
013.34 015.10 047.27 050.31 084.05
084.08 122.23 123.10 133.16 134.04
161.21 165.18 181.02 181.21 185.36
186.20 219.35 252.22 253.27 253.31
306.05 314.18 321.22
MAKING (44)
007.12 031.13 031.36 046.26 062.15
066.19 073.35 085.17 088.36 108.23
113.02 113.09 132.34 151.06 157.03
157.05 160.14 161.25 164.17 170.30
174.21 177.32 178.16 187.26 233.25
236.16 253.21 256.10 257.22 264.12
264.14 260.08 269.03 272.05 273.34
275.02 275.11 284.20 287.07 294.36
298.19 300.14 305.10 327.16
MALARIA (1)
037.16
MALE (1)
233.03
MALEFACTORS (1)
068.24
MAMELUKE (1)
329.32
MAMMOTH (1)
094.01
MAN (315)
005.10 005.13 005.25 006.15 007.24
007.35 008.17 009.03 010.07 010.34
011.23 012.05 012.09 012.19 012.24
013.07 013.08 013.31 013.34 015.16
015.18 015.30 019.13 020.05 021.04
022.03 023.13 023.21 023.31 024.20
024.22 026.12 027.18 027.31 028.05
029.11 029.20 030.31 030.35 031.08
031.10 031.21 031.32 031.34 032.26
032.32 034.17 035.21 036.03 036.08
036.14 036.25 036.32 037.17 037.25
037.33 038.19 040.27 041.20 045.06
045.34 046.02 046.15 046.18 047.02
047.07 047.12 048.05 048.13 049.41

MAN   (CONTINUED)
 051.04 052.24 052.33 053.23 055.02
 055.22 056.19 056.29 056.29 056.31
 056.35 057.06 057.35 061.16 061.23
 063.10 064.27 064.29 065.07 065.28
 065.34 066.07 066.12 066.15 066.20
 066.24 066.36 068.03 071.02 071.04
 072.01 072.14 073.13 074.17 074.25
 074.25 074.30 074.32 075.17 076.18
 076.23 076.36 077.05 077.19 077.20
 077.25 078.04 078.25 079.04 079.19
 082.02 082.13 082.17 082.22 082.25
 089.21 089.25 090.12 090.19 090.26
 091.14 091.21 091.30 092.27 092.27
 092.28 092.34 093.14 093.24 093.33
 093.34 094.09 094.12 095.13 096.28
 097.02 100.32 102.27 102.28 105.13
 106.36 106.36 107.35 108.09 112.22
 115.31 118.19 120.36 127.12 127.34
 130.27 131.06 131.11 131.32 133.15
 133.27 134.04 135.26 135.29 136.26
 136.28 138.14 140.05 142.25 144.14
 144.35 145.02 146.35 147.05 147.11
 148.09 148.17 149.16 149.18 149.24
 149.26 149.34 150.20 151.28 152.33
 153.26 153.31 153.34 154.05 154.09
 157.23 158.07 158.11 164.16 164.26
 165.06 165.20 168.19 169.24 171.11
 171.14 171.27 172.34 172.35 173.31
 180.04 186.10 188.13 190.26 191.03
 193.15 196.08 198.18 204.22 205.34
 208.12 208.33 209.02 212.36 213.31
 214.35 215.15 215.36 216.06 216.18
 216.19 216.34 216.34 217.10 218.15
 219.26 220.01 220.03 220.22 220.27
 220.35 221.27 221.32 222.01 225.15
 225.30 235.06 239.24 242.19 244.01
 244.26 245.09 249.20 250.36 251.26
 253.24 253.29 254.12 258.07 258.29
 261.23 262.06 263.35 264.23 268.25
 268.27 268.30 269.01 269.12 269.15
 269.23 270.24 276.34 277.26 277.32
 279.32 283.35 291.07 291.09 294.20
 295.12 295.16 296.14 296.36 297.29
 301.21 303.14 307.30 310.06 314.11
 315.18 315.28 315.29 315.32 318.27
 320.28 321.07 321.18 321.29 322.38
 323.04 324.11 324.28 325.19 326.01
 326.07 328.12 328.33 329.13 331.11
 331.12 331.18 332.28 332.36 333.24
MANAGE   (1)
 137.25
MANAGED   (1)
 038.07
MANAGEMENT   (1)
 050.19
MANAGER   (1)
 240.07
MANAGES   (1)
 227.24
MANGY   (1)
 152.31
MANIACAL   (1)
 125.26
MANIFEST   (3)
 166.32 244.14 308.05
MANIFESTATION   (1)
 023.06
MANIFESTED   (1)
 229.22
MANIFESTLY   (3)
 187.18 194.07 275.20
MANIKINS   (1)
 107.10
MANILLA   (1)
 119.27
MANKIND   (22)
 008.13 014.19 024.11 027.01 040.18

MANKIND   (CONTINUED)
 053.26 058.22 076.16 076.36 077.11
 078.32 093.27 102.16 103.06 104.09
 106.09 106.33 168.18 216.19 260.15
 321.07 331.22
MANLIER   (1)
 058.09
MANLIEST   (1)
 006.16
MANLY   (2)
 015.06 322.36
MANNA   (1)
 018.04
MANNER   (3)
 068.33 275.13 315.19
MANNERS   (7)
 057.30 078.20 152.17 207.11 262.06
 329.26 331.13
MANOEUVRE   (1)
 234.11
MANOEUVRED   (1)
 234.29
MANOEUVRES   (1)
 273.30
MANOEUVRING   (1)
 150.01
MANSION   (1)
 037.31
MANSIONS   (1)
 010.20
MANTEL   (1)
 038.09
MANTLE   (1)
 049.14
MANUFACTURERS   (1)
 026.23
MANURANCE   (1)
 164.04
MANURE   (9)
 054.28 056.01 156.14 157.31 162.16
 204.36 224.11 267.28 294.25
MANURED   (1)
 196.36
MANURES   (1)
 196.35
MANUS   (1)
 063.16
MANY   (162)
 003.20 005.15 006.35 007.05 007.20
 011.17 012.13 013.36 014.17 017.12
 017.20 017.23 017.29 018.12 020.17
 022.20 024.31 026.20 027.31 029.20
 031.06 042.08 042.11 050.10 055.30
 057.09 058.06 058.28 058.35 071.10
 072.36 073.18 075.31 079.05 081.22
 082.37 083.35 086.02 088.01 093.17
 106.23 107.35 112.29 114.18 115.25
 116.13 119.16 119.25 132.26 133.19
 133.33 138.21 140.14 140.18 141.26
 142.20 144.21 148.14 149.12 149.22
 150.15 150.29 153.35 155.10 162.01
 169.25 170.25 172.13 174.02 177.35
 178.04 178.25 179.07 179.29 180.12
 180.19 181.09 181.25 181.31 182.30
 184.30 190.03 190.30 190.34 191.15
 191.28 191.36 192.07 192.32 193.09
 197.31 198.05 201.23 202.07 203.21
 204.20 204.24 206.09 207.23 211.09
 213.36 214.26 214.27 214.33 219.06
 220.26 221.09 226.18 227.21 231.14
 232.12 239.04 240.04 241.06 241.08
 241.13 241.16 242.08 243.07 244.28
 245.15 246.05 246.25 248.11 249.24
 251.17 256.07 256.18 258.20 266.32
 267.32 268.13 270.07 271.03 273.36
 274.31 277.12 277.36 280.18 285.12
 285.18 288.11 294.04 294.18 295.29
 301.17 306.27 308.12 308.12 310.07

130

131

```
MAY                           (CONTINUED)          ME                           (CONTINUED)
158.26  163.39  165.16  176.32  177.05            281.04  281.13  282.03  287.05  292.20
177.35  180.16  185.12  187.04  187.13            292.23  294.14  295.10  295.32  297.11
192.10  193.04  193.14  194.09  198.13            303.20  304.28  305.22  306.11  308.20
199.08  203.21  205.25  207.29  211.10            308.30  309.10  313.25  316.30  316.32
213.04  215.22  215.33  216.04  216.07            318.14  318.16  323.11  328.16  328.29
216.15  217.14  217.31  218.13  219.13            328.30  329.21  329.28  330.07  330.10
219.15  219.15  221.23  224.08  224.14            330.10  330.25  330.25  330.26  330.34
224.17  224.36  225.08  226.29  228.24            331.04  331.09  331.10  332.14  332.17
239.24  239.34  241.11  242.21  242.25         MEADOW                                    ( 17)
243.07  243.25  243.31  247.06  254.07            180.33  181.01  196.16  203.06  204.35
254.29  255.08  268.02  273.12  281.33            238.08  238.09  264.36  278.14  287.25
287.06  288.16  291.35  292.11  294.05            292.23  292.28  292.31  296.10  309.32
299.22  300.20  301.06  301.35  308.01            310.31  317.29
308.18  309.09  312.27  314.29  314.31         MEADOWS                                   ( 13)
318.31  319.01  320.18  320.29  321.03            087.18  116.03  167.19  178.32  196.25
321.24  322.10  323.19  324.19  324.19            205.31  207.14  238.04  260.26  266.32
328.09  328.14  328.17  329.35  331.36            303.25  317.16  317.27
332.35  333.01  333.25                         MEADS                                     ( 1)
MAYBE                                  ( 1)        238.12
076.09                                         MEAGER                                    ( 1)
MAYFLOWER                              ( 1)        014.21
062.28                                         MEAL                                      ( 15)
ME                                   ( 310)       059.10  059.11  059.16  061.03  062.01
003.14  003.22  003.22  004.02  004.17            062.07  063.21  063.32  142.04  143.17
009.13  009.13  009.15  009.16  009.19            167.28  169.21  225.09  243.12  273.28
010.33  010.36  017.23  018.31  019.28         MEALS                                     ( 2)
025.03  025.13  025.14  025.18  029.06            091.34  136.12
029.11  038.24  041.30  043.13  043.18         MEAN                                      ( 40)
043.20  043.36  044.10  045.27  046.22            006.35  012.08  016.04  019.06  025.07
047.12  049.28  049.30  049.31  053.03            030.28  032.06  043.29  045.18  051.07
054.06  054.32  055.05  056.28  059.38            051.09  051.09  051.10  051.35  053.14
060.36  060.41  061.01  063.02  063.15            058.34  063.20  066.14  074.02  075.22
064.37  065.17  067.08  067.11  067.20            077.33  091.07  096.26  112.02  123.29
071.05  071.15  072.25  073.09  074.18            126.07  142.07  144.01  162.11  170.23
074.23  074.25  074.26  074.27  074.27            221.25  222.17  229.24  245.21  246.14
075.01  075.02  075.33  076.19  077.06            272.24  312.20  312.21  328.05  332.24
078.28  078.29  078.30  078.31  081.18         MEANDERING                                ( 2)
081.21  082.05  082.12  082.14  085.04            265.19  307.20
083.10  083.12  084.16  085.04  085.20         MEANER                                    ( 1)
085.23  086.12  087.11  087.36  090.03            029.35
091.11  093.32  098.30  099.15  100.05         MEANEST                                   ( 1)
106.34  112.21  113.07  115.18  115.18            165.37
115.19  115.24  118.24  119.19  119.22         MEANING                                   ( 8)
120.16  122.19  123.12  124.09  124.12            025.11  076.20  100.14  112.17  126.01
124.26  124.34  125.18  127.29  129.09            155.08  306.32  321.25
129.10  130.15  130.33  131.13  131.14         MEANLY                                    ( 1)
131.16  131.21  131.28  132.05  132.09            091.16
132.11  132.13  132.14  132.22  133.05         MEANNESS                                  ( 7)
133.14  133.32  134.28  135.06  135.12            091.08  091.08  165.02  199.32  219.07
135.13  137.02  137.24  137.36  138.27            221.33  329.02
140.08  140.22  142.19  142.26  144.04         MEANS                                     ( 20)
144.10  144.10  145.20  146.09  146.13            008.18  019.33  021.20  029.17  034.01
148.21  149.28  150.29  151.04  151.06            039.12  052.18  060.33  071.06  072.05
151.17  151.18  151.28  152.14  152.19            072.08  078.33  110.10  163.39  165.35
152.22  155.11  155.19  155.26  156.24            219.20  253.34  293.02  328.21  329.06
156.30  160.06  160.15  161.06  161.34         MEANT                                     ( 5)
164.05  166.19  166.19  166.22  167.21            125.09  147.34  157.24  165.13  294.26
167.25  170.20  171.33  174.17  175.02         MEANWHILE                                 ( 6)
182.11  183.02  189.36  190.28  191.34            043.32  155.03  204.32  207.03  224.09
193.02  193.06  193.14  196.01  196.28            275.24
196.30  198.19  202.13  202.20  203.24         MEASURE                                   ( 6)
204.33  205.14  206.10  207.16  210.14            025.19  050.16  060.34  100.09  216.01
210.21  212.10  214.05  214.23  217.19            258.32
219.26  223.23  224.07  224.23  224.30         MEASURED                                  ( 4)
228.10  228.11  232.33  233.04  233.14            010.08  057.10  135.27  326.10
233.21  234.21  235.01  235.10  235.27         MEASURES                                  ( 2)
235.32  236.10  236.29  240.19  240.19            186.14  198.17
241.28  241.31  242.27  245.11  245.20         MEASURING                                 ( 4)
249.09  249.17  250.32  251.28  251.33            004.26  025.18  238.10  289.21
254.27  254.29  256.10  258.08  258.10         MEAT                                      ( 9)
260.35  261.06  261.29  261.34  262.20            067.14  085.29  109.21  145.15  145.33
264.20  264.24  265.08  266.07  266.08            205.12  205.23  249.22  321.15
266.16  266.18  266.34  268.21  270.15         MEATS                                     ( 6)
271.10  272.04  272.18  272.26  273.14            062.18  073.34  104.35  145.18  321.13
273.18  273.20  273.29  274.18  277.05            321.15
277.14  277.21  277.31  277.36  277.36         MECHANICAL                                ( 2)
279.16  279.34  280.03  280.27  280.28            089.14  090.16
```

MECHANICS   (2)
  051.24 251.13
MEDICAL   (1)
  022.02
MEDICINE   (2)
  068.20 153.31
MEDICINES   (1)
  138.20
MEDIOCRITY   (1)
  080.21
MEDITATION   (2)
  224.06 224.26
MEDITATIONS   (2)
  113.07 122.35
MEDITERRANEAN   (1)
  223.35
MEDIUM   (2)
  090.24 285.21
MEEKNESS   (1)
  331.20
MEET   (20)
  023.02 054.20 060.23 061.06 066.15
  069.11 116.07 136.10 136.12 136.17
  155.30 165.03 165.04 192.27 298.10
  298.14 314.36 323.09 323.32 328.05
MEETING   (6)
  017.03 074.36 096.33 105.18 133.20
  136.16
MELANCHOLY   (6)
  053.36 124.30 125.08 131.06 131.07
  131.15
MELODIOUS   (5)
  078.22 123.23 125.21 271.34 280.03
MELODIOUSNESS   (1)
  125.14
MELODY   (2)
  123.04 123.13
MELT   (6)
  248.19 299.12 299.17 301.02 304.21
  309.09
MELTED   (8)
  042.02 185.20 248.07 256.14 276.12
  296.29 302.27 303.35
MELTING   (4)
  252.30 300.13 310.33 311.16
MELTS   (6)
  177.02 298.21 300.12 300.31 309.22
  328.13
MELVEN   (1)
  279.25
MEM   (1)
  225.02
MEMBER   (2)
  219.31 232.22
MEMBERS   (3)
  204.30 229.21 230.04
MEMBRANE   (1)
  233.16
MEMNON   (2)
  036.24 089.33
MEMOIRS   (1)
  202.23
MEMORABLE   (15)
  057.31 064.28 078.27 089.08 089.28
  089.31 094.11 101.09 112.06 170.33
  175.02 227.06 230.27 304.07 312.04
MEMORIES   (1)
  310.03
MEMORY   (9)
  057.28 126.18 137.35 152.35 155.34
  256.18 256.32 264.18 280.03
MEN   (204)
  003.34 004.34 005.03 005.24 005.31
  006.09 006.17 008.07 008.19 011.25
  012.01 015.09 015.09 015.17 016.17
  017.07 019.22 019.24 021.24 022.20
  022.30 022.33 023.33 024.02 025.01
  025.26 026.03 026.19 026.33 027.03

MEN   (CONTINUED)
  027.09 032.35 033.29 034.14 035.29
  037.24 039.25 041.02 041.30 042.11
  044.31 046.04 046.14 053.27 056.14
  056.15 056.16 057.02 058.07 061.28
  062.18 065.31 067.28 069.19 071.35
  072.06 073.25 076.31 077.28 080.14
  087.30 089.32 090.02 090.04 091.11
  091.17 092.13 092.18 093.02 093.08
  095.30 096.06 096.10 096.36 099.04
  100.27 101.19 104.12 104.25 105.17
  106.07 106.34 107.02 107.11 107.27
  108.06 108.18 108.36 109.18 110.12
  110.15 115.16 116.24 116.27 116.29
  117.12 118.01 118.16 118.26 118.32
  119.04 125.26 125.29 130.15 130.35
  131.22 133.04 133.19 133.22 134.21
  135.25 138.28 139.06 140.14 143.11
  143.35 147.20 147.25 149.33 150.05
  150.22 151.03 152.11 152.14 152.25
  152.27 152.31 153.05 153.10 153.17
  154.13 154.15 156.18 157.07 164.11
  164.24 165.04 167.16 167.21 170.17
  171.25 171.28 172.19 172.29 174.29
  192.25 192.32 192.36 193.36 196.32
  196.34 197.01 197.04 197.05 205.33
  208.01 208.24 210.17 211.05 211.10
  212.17 212.21 212.24 213.05 215.27
  215.32 219.21 219.23 223.13 230.12
  233.31 241.04 244.29 251.17 259.01
  259.19 264.10 267.25 267.29 268.29
  269.04 273.14 273.15 283.11 283.13
  285.15 287.11 287.13 292.13 294.17
  297.19 297.34 313.27 314.27 315.29
  321.33 323.21 324.28 325.10 325.30
  325.35 330.02 331.28 331.32
MENAGERIE   (1)
  174.12
MENCIUS   (1)
  219.22
MENDED   (3)
  022.08 022.17 171.35
MENDING   (1)
  060.08
MENOETIUS   (1)
  144.30
MENTAL   (3)
  108.34 136.33 218.04
MENTION   (3)
  184.11 202.08 327.12
MENTIONED   (2)
  182.26 230.34
MENTORS   (1)
  009.18
MERCENARY   (1)
  192.25
MERCHANDISE   (1)
  117.12
MERCHANT   (1)
  046.19
MERCHANTS   (5)
  012.01 020.36 032.36 033.02 115.25
MERCIES   (1)
  037.02
MERCURIAL   (1)
  203.14
MERCURY   (1)
  302.07
MERCY   (1)
  135.35
MERE   (12)
  006.10 008.27 050.05 126.18 144.05
  173.21 195.04 260.35 309.01 330.24
  332.03 333.30
MERELY   (48)
  003.33 009.28 014.36 015.07 017.19
  026.24 026.30 030.34 033.05 034.19
  037.30 037.34 047.04 047.27 051.11

MERELY   (CONTINUED)
```
MERELY                        (CONTINUED)
051.19  054.29  056.30  057.02  075.16
075.19  076.34  084.30  095.07  099.26
101.13  101.19  111.18  118.34  123.18
127.04  141.15  147.34  150.07  150.20
165.26  221.12  227.07  238.17  253.27
254.17  292.06  296.34  302.29  309.07
314.33  320.25  321.15
MERIDIAN                              (  1)
097.25
MERIT                                 (  1)
175.29
MERLIN                                (  1)
316.31
MERRY                                 (  4)
169.23  256.04  279.36  294.13
MESOPOTAMIA                           (  1)
241.08
MESS                                  (  3)
059.33  206.28  317.14
MESSAGES                              (  2)
052.35  070.07
MESSENGER                             (  6)
095.14  095.16  095.19  095.20  095.21
252.31
MESSENGERS                            (  1)
036.13
MET                                   ( 15)
005.15  017.14  017.23  067.02  090.12
144.02  148.22  151.28  164.25  224.10
232.30  256.08  269.21  280.06  329.23
METAL                                 (  1)
329.18
METALLURGY                            (  1)
051.34
METALS                                (  1)
309.09
METAMORPHOSE                          (  1)
105.12
METAPHOR                              (  1)
111.08
METAPHORS                             (  1)
245.01
METAPHYSICAL                          (  1)
151.27
METHINKS                              (  4)
051.15  122.08  150.35  224.23
METHOD                                (  3)
037.30  054.19  111.11
METHODS                               (  4)
011.35  015.17  119.16  295.24
METHOUGHT                             (  2)
204.31  312.16
METHUSELAH                            (  1)
303.20
METLING                               (  1)
302.15
MEWING                                (  1)
226.21
MEXICAN                               (  1)
161.02
MEXICANS                              (  1)
068.34
MEXICO                                (  1)
248.32
MICE                                  (  5)
119.12  225.21  275.30  280.10  280.13
MICHAEL                               (  1)
177.32
MICHAUX                               (  1)
251.04
MICROCOSM                             (  1)
077.24
MICROSCOPE                            (  2)
051.22  230.33
MID                                   (  7)
086.25  188.15  262.09  267.11  283.27
300.01  329.19
```

```
MIDDLE                                ( 30)
042.36  101.20  105.20  106.13  177.03
180.08  185.33  191.31  195.19  198.12
201.25  203.28  234.21  236.32  237.07
248.09  253.19  288.34  289.19  293.06
299.25  299.27  300.01  300.01  300.31
300.33  301.27  302.28  302.34  313.05
                                      (  3)
MIDDLESEX
033.15  140.26  160.24
MIDDLING                              (  1)
247.34
MIDNIGHT                              (  5)
117.15  124.20  174.34  252.34  280.05
MIDST                                 ( 17)
011.33  086.05  091.28  113.25  113.27
121.33  122.04  131.08  131.36  169.36
175.33  202.07  204.13  226.19  253.33
279.02  294.33
MIDSUMMER                             (  5)
138.13  228.06  261.22  280.17  317.12
MIDWINTER                             (  1)
179.09
MIGHT                                 ( 96)
005.07  010.13  016.19  018.03  018.27
029.12  034.01  035.33  040.14  040.25
046.33  046.36  051.10  053.04  054.08
054.13  056.28  058.03  058.11  059.40
063.03  063.28  064.18  064.31  068.04
069.24  069.30  070.03  070.22  072.28
081.20  081.24  081.26  083.28  085.07
090.30  093.18  094.28  098.06  098.09
100.35  112.11  123.26  127.03  140.07
142.09  143.22  146.04  146.05  147.15
150.04  150.22  151.35  153.27  161.16
162.15  165.15  168.20  171.30  171.31
175.20  178.14  179.01  183.04  186.28
189.25  197.35  199.02  202.16  205.09
206.05  206.11  210.13  211.28  213.07
213.18  224.01  232.17  234.33  235.15
239.05  244.26  244.29  246.10  249.21
264.12  265.19  266.29  268.11  269.11
285.25  292.29  293.07  316.08  316.32
332.14
MIGHTY                                (  1)
212.14
MIGRATE                               (  1)
222.20
MIGRATES                              (  1)
309.19
MIGRATING                             (  2)
152.15  324.23
MIGRATORIUS                           (  1)
312.22
MILD                                  (  2)
128.07  312.03
MILDEWY                               (  1)
125.17
MILDNESS                              (  1)
062.19
MILE                                  ( 31)
003.04  052.34  083.06  086.04  086.09
130.04  130.16  130.17  136.25  145.26
170.18  170.31  175.31  175.31  176.04
180.11  181.12  187.25  194.20  197.11
197.12  203.34  227.33  237.05  246.10
249.25  265.18  273.04  275.12  296.35
306.04
MILES                                 ( 20)
053.09  081.07  083.05  086.07  092.16
093.03  115.35  127.16  130.14  135.28
145.16  150.14  155.04  179.11  179.13
251.10  265.28  287.30  287.30  321.31
MILITARY                              (  1)
160.09
MILK                                  (  6)
067.14  083.03  205.11  205.16  270.20
270.23
```

MILKED   (1)
  083.02
MILKING   (1)
  324.27
MILKWEED   (1)
  234.18
MILKY   (1)
  133.13
MILL   (9)
  043.28 044.02 053.02 064.05 096.30
  137.16 196.18 218.24 233.27
MILLET   (1)
  157.05
MILLION   (5)
  054.10 090.09 091.26 092.10 294.30
MILLIONS   (2)
  090.08 090.11
MILLS   (2)
  065.12 168.10
MILTON   (1)
  076.26
MILWAUKIE   (1)
  120.09
MINCED   (1)
  112.13
MIND   (38)
  016.05 016.22 036.15 036.28 057.21
  069.28 080.11 081.13 082.13 084.10
  092.23 125.16 133.32 134.34 142.36
  149.27 151.24 166.35 175.13 185.28
  208.32 219.30 220.16 220.40 221.35
  222.22 224.24 226.27 234.36 269.14
  274.28 310.06 320.33 323.22 326.04
  326.22 328.14 332.30
MINDED   (4)
  112.04 151.13 170.04 196.10
MINDING   (1)
  018.29
MINDS   (6)
  051.16 080.22 133.18 160.25 171.09
  287.11
MINE   (14)
  017.23 032.12 032.13 054.14 067.15
  098.33 098.36 112.05 158.11 193.22
  235.05 251.27 252.17 259.05
MINERAL   (1)
  120.27
MINERVA   (2)
  033.37 239.32
MINGLE   (1)
  227.15
MINGLED   (5)
  074.23 159.01 183.22 194.15 298.16
MINISTERIAL   (1)
  157.26
MINISTERS   (2)
  096.18 153.11
MINK   (2)
  114.30 317.32
MINKS   (2)
  008.11 184.33
MINORITY   (1)
  034.21
MINSTRELS   (1)
  123.25
MINT   (1)
  087.08
MINUTE   (7)
  052.34 116.36 118.17 226.30 246.28
  247.10 248.15
MINUTES   (3)
  121.24 124.03 227.02
MIR   (1)
  099.27
MIRABEAU   (1)
  322.29
MIRACLE   (3)
  010.24 011.19 011.19

MIRACLES   (3)
  108.02 118.06 147.32
MIRACULOUSLY   (1)
  142.14
MIRAGE   (1)
  087.19
MIRROR   (5)
  188.20 188.25 188.28 240.06 307.04
MIRTH   (5)
  126.15 137.26 146.11 146.17 268.06
MISANTHROPE   (1)
  131.06
MISCALCULATED   (1)
  234.24
MISCHIEF   (2)
  070.20 260.12
MISCHIEVOUS   (1)
  259.05
MISCONCEPTION   (1)
  096.19
MISERABLE   (2)
  009.06 216.02
MISERY   (2)
  035.09 076.03
MISFORTUNE   (3)
  005.03 075.19 092.33
MISGIVING   (2)
  207.23 328.18
MISHAP   (1)
  245.31
MISLED   (1)
  216.20
MISSED   (1)
  172.16
MISSIONARIES   (1)
  075.07
MISSIONARY   (1)
  023.10
MISSISSIPPI   (2)
  321.04 322.25
MISSOURI   (1)
  210.35
MIST   (10)
  086.15 126.34 179.21 189.15 190.12
  190.18 284.16 304.20 304.22 313.05
MISTAKE   (10)
  005.24 006.10 034.32 098.04 123.24
  126.32 186.29 211.08 214.03 259.06
MISTAKES   (3)
  010.17 075.17 096.22
MISTRESS   (3)
  218.07 233.04 244.09
MISTS   (3)
  086.17 318.35 325.31
MISTY   (5)
  197.30 236.27 271.14 284.05 324.35
MITENS   (1)
  294.04
MITTENS   (1)
  262.55
MIX   (1)
  280.15
MIXED   (3)
  176.33 177.06 305.01
MIXTURE   (2)
  062.06 138.23
MOANING   (1)
  260.19
MOANS   (1)
  125.10
MOB   (2)
  102.12 118.14
MOCK   (1)
  137.10
MOCKING   (2)
  126.15 320.06
MODE   (14)
  003.12 008.19 014.16 026.33 045.19

```
MODE                    (CONTINUED)
050.25 071.07 076.02 112.25 112.32
150.06 205.25 208.39 284.06
MODEL                          ( 4)
194.34 196.31 197.02 294.36
MODERATE                       ( 2)
018.32 035.28
MODERN                        ( 16)
014.27 030.20 034.12 037.06 052.11
100.16 100.28 100.34 102.27 103.22
158.36 221.23 231.29 244.32 281.20
298.05
MODERNS                        ( 1)
325.34
MODES                          ( 3)
007.06 015.18 075.04
MODULATED                      ( 1)
123.16
MOILING                        ( 1)
222.17
MOIST                          ( 4)
202.29 305.30 306.23 310.25
MOISTURE                       ( 4)
141.19 158.08 246.04 307.17
MOLASSES                       ( 6)
059.09 061.04 064.08 065.23 121.09
243.11
MOLE                           ( 1)
013.29
MOLES                          ( 1)
253.20
MOLEST                         ( 1)
172.29
MOLESTED                       ( 2)
172.01 240.18
MOLTEN                         ( 2)
187.10 309.11
MOMENT                        ( 17)
010.21 011.29 017.05 025.09 056.11
092.04 097.05 111.23 117.28 121.15
153.27 230.15 235.34 276.03 278.23
324.28 326.31
MOMENTARILY                    ( 1)
216.28
MOMENTARY                      ( 1)
059.38
MOMENTS                        ( 4)
226.24 260.27 324.29 327.33
MOMUS                          ( 1)
033.36
MONARCH                        ( 1)
082.30
MONEY                         ( 22)
032.21 050.20 053.04 054.04 059.17
060.11 061.01 072.07 075.15 075.20
076.01 109.15 109.17 145.08 149.03
149.04 192.02 196.12 206.10 294.29
329.15 330.34
MONKEY                         ( 1)
025.23
MONKEYS                        ( 1)
025.24
MONOPOLY                       ( 1)
153.12
MONOTONOUS                     ( 1)
185.27
MONSTER                        ( 1)
004.35
MONSTERS                       ( 2)
051.28 051.29
MONSTROUS                      ( 1)
177.31
MONTH                          ( 6)
051.31 063.27 070.31 070.31 205.10
319.02
MONTHLY                        ( 1)
105.21

MONTHS                        ( 10)
003.08 059.01 060.16 060.17 060.18
149.22 183.06 249.32 282.33 331.36
MONUMENT                       ( 2)
057.31 325.03
MONUMENTS                      ( 5)
058.23 058.28 102.29 139.01 269.05
MOOD                           ( 5)
026.17 131.35 210.30 222.05 278.24
MOODS                          ( 1)
069.33
MOON                           ( 8)
057.32 067.13 067.14 073.31 130.24
174.17 280.05 322.28
MOONLESS                       ( 1)
088.13
MOONLIGHT                      ( 5)
174.34 175.06 202.32 273.07 323.27
MOORE                          ( 2)
192.26 192.27
MOOSE                          ( 3)
120.03 271.30 279.19
MOP                            ( 2)
132.29 204.27
MORAL                         ( 12)
033.06 050.01 090.03 105.29 145.04
157.13 195.03 206.01 218.28 219.05
267.27 321.28
MORALLY                        ( 2)
036.19 090.24
MORE                         ( 335)
004.02 004.29 005.05 007.15 011.03
012.18 013.10 014.02 014.02 014.21
014.27 015.20 015.20 015.21 015.22
015.22 016.06 016.07 017.06 018.30
018.30 019.30 021.35 022.25 025.16
026.25 026.34 027.22 028.22 028.24
029.06 029.21 030.20 031.13 031.22
031.23 032.11 033.19 036.02 036.05
036.18 037.04 039.10 040.01 040.02
040.20 040.25 040.28 041.28 041.34
042.31 045.07 045.20 045.31 047.07
049.13 049.31 049.35 050.12 050.14
050.23 052.04 055.07 055.20 055.33
055.34 056.07 057.01 057.18 057.31
057.34 058.15 059.03 059.16 060.10
061.23 063.10 063.11 063.27 064.01
064.10 065.36 066.29 069.09 070.22
071.01 071.22 073.27 075.21 075.23
075.24 076.21 078.01 083.23 084.13
084.16 084.20 085.03 085.20 085.35
086.31 087.07 087.24 088.03 089.22
090.18 090.23 091.22 092.12 093.20
094.06 095.11 096.10 097.06 098.28
099.03 099.20 099.23 100.01 100.28
101.02 102.13 102.21 102.21 103.05
103.36 105.29 105.33 107.33 108.33
109.17 109.18 110.10 113.18 116.33
117.19 118.27 118.28 119.16 119.24
119.29 122.34 125.13 125.36 127.25
130.27 130.30 131.17 131.23 132.35
133.02 135.07 135.14 135.24 136.09
136.35 137.04 137.13 137.15 137.28
142.09 143.10 143.36 144.02 145.02
146.04 147.17 150.20 152.15 154.14
155.11 157.09 157.23 160.13 162.33
164.27 165.09 166.20 168.12 168.34
169.35 171.31 172.07 172.22 173.06
174.06 175.22 176.07 176.08 177.06
177.12 177.30 181.21 184.25 191.10
192.04 192.08 193.07 194.05 194.22
194.33 199.30 199.30 201.15 202.05
203.30 205.07 210.22 210.30 211.11
211.18 211.30 212.26 213.25 214.07
214.24 214.32 216.06 216.12 216.16
216.26 216.26 216.27 217.25 221.08
221.09 221.36 222.10 227.03 229.22
230.12 231.16 232.29 233.03 233.05
```

MORE   (CONTINUED)   MOST   (188)
234.14   234.28   236.12   238.04   239.02   003.24   006.09   006.25   009.27   011.29
239.22   240.08   240.34   241.06   242.18   012.02   014.17   016.02   016.20   016.23
242.22   242.29   242.30   243.13   246.36   017.07   022.12   022.33   024.27   026.28
247.20   249.05   249.19   250.18   250.22   028.16   030.12   032.17   035.29   038.31
250.35   251.04   251.08   251.28   251.36   041.01   041.13   042.18   042.37   043.16
253.32   255.06   256.23   256.31   259.30   044.33   046.35   047.22   047.24   050.20
261.10   262.08   262.35   263.21   264.05   050.21   050.24   051.30   052.01   052.35
264.25   270.16   274.01   274.07   274.22   054.35   058.03   059.31   060.08   062.07
275.34   276.04   280.03   281.30   282.33   063.01   063.35   069.13   069.35   070.26
284.13   287.25   288.30   288.33   289.11   073.16   073.25   074.35   075.13   076.02
290.22   290.34   296.22   297.25   300.10   077.04   079.05   082.34   083.01   083.30
300.13   300.29   300.34   301.05   301.08   086.10   086.22   087.36   089.07   089.31
301.24   303.19   304.28   305.11   305.18   090.28   091.11   095.01   100.34   104.11
305.29   305.30   307.09   307.16   307.35   104.12   104.19   104.25   106.34   108.23
308.13   308.20   308.29   309.21   309.29   111.04   111.15   112.03   113.18   121.27
311.24   312.01   312.17   312.25   312.27   124.21   125.08   125.22   126.20   127.05
317.32   319.06   320.07   322.06   322.06   127.08   130.22   131.03   131.04   131.06
323.03   323.12   323.13   323.34   324.01   133.10   133.14   133.19   133.22   134.06
324.33   325.20   325.23   325.25   327.18   135.24   136.03   137.27   137.32   140.03
327.22   328.22   329.24   331.06   333.32   141.20   142.12   143.16   144.08   148.31
MOREOVER   (10)   149.05   150.05   153.22   155.23   155.25
003.31   071.26   073.05   108.08   162.28   157.22   160.19   160.22   164.28   165.04
182.36   183.22   195.23   211.25   329.06   168.17   168.22   168.36   169.29   171.06
MORNING   (90)   177.26   179.12   182.36   183.01   183.23
036.23   036.23   036.25   043.31   044.06   184.16   184.18   184.28   185.09   186.01
045.19   062.33   068.25   078.08   084.24   186.06   186.12   191.13   191.35   192.01
084.35   085.11   088.25   088.34   089.07   197.18   197.19   200.04   210.17   211.04
089.29   089.29   089.30   089.36   090.02   212.37   215.27   216.32   216.33   217.18
093.17   093.35   097.27   100.10   103.27   217.27   219.02   227.03   232.26   236.10
107.33   111.25   112.05   113.06   116.31   238.34   241.21   241.22   242.23   246.32
117.04   117.18   118.35   119.02   121.16   249.24   251.21   254.05   254.16   258.34
126.34   127.14   134.02   137.02   138.27   260.15   266.09   267.36   268.27   268.33
138.28   138.32   144.13   144.36   145.31   272.18   272.29   274.05   274.17   281.18
152.30   154.16   156.27   158.21   161.18   287.19   287.24   292.02   297.10   303.29
170.22   173.26   179.18   184.36   188.16   307.17   307.19   309.09   316.33   321.07
202.27   202.31   208.27   214.04   217.01   322.32   323.01   327.29   328.17   328.19
217.11   223.20   234.08   238.35   240.07   328.33   329.09   329.11   329.11   330.06
240.14   241.24   246.34   273.03   276.13   332.04   332.21   333.26
279.15   280.28   282.21   283.10   294.18   MOSTLY   (4)
298.01   301.04   301.08   301.09   301.13   029.26   049.04   054.24   191.18
307.09   313.04   314.07   314.27   314.35   MOTE   (2)
315.15   317.03   317.17   325.14   333.33   159.14   266.18
MORNINGS   (4)   MOTES   (4)
017.20   041.35   276.30   313.18   051.20   107.11   207.08   237.02
MORROW   (8)   MOTH   (1)
007.04   008.27   043.31   053.15   093.10   005.28
112.16   112.18   333.29   MOTHER   (14)
MORSEL   (1)   047.05   071.13   100.12   101.15   166.04
210.13   226.16   226.27   226.33   227.19   229.29
MORTAL   (8)   232.32   269.34   278.36   308.26
024.09   028.09   074.01   098.15   099.09   MOTHERS   (3)
201.22   285.06   327.24   076.22   101.14   212.34
MORTALITY   (2)   MOTION   (7)
125.11   269.02   116.08   141.02   161.07   162.21   188.16
MORTALS   (2)   188.35   199.11
282.13   316.10   MOTIONLESS   (2)
MORTAR   (3)   173.26   280.36
065.09   241.02   241.20   MOTIONS   (4)
MORTARIUM   (1)   187.01   225.34   273.25   274.04
063.17   MOTIVE   (2)
MORTARIUMQUE   (1)   083.27   149.32
063.16   MOTTLED   (1)
MORTGAGED   (1)   293.24
032.32   MOTTO   (1)
MORTGAGING   (2)   142.29
081.12   149.10   MOULD   (9)
MORTIFICATION   (1)   054.33   063.23   119.10   138.16   145.10
125.17   162.21   195.04   252.13   295.03
MORTISED   (1)   MOULDERING   (1)
042.22   194.32
MOSQUITO   (2)   MOULDS   (2)
088.36   097.17   307.02   309.10
MOSS   (3)   MOULT   (1)
283.32   283.34   296.12   233.25
MOSSY   (1)   MOULTING   (1)
203.11   024.03

137

MOUNDS (1)
327.03
MOUNTAIN (7)
012.17 037.23 085.04 086.13 087.07
121.34 290.35
MOUNTAINOUS (1)
291.14
MOUNTAINS (14)
085.09 086.21 117.05 117.10 121.11
121.22 121.35 122.02 122.10 152.35
287.31 289.25 316.07 323.27
MOUNTED (1)
261.04
MOUNTING (1)
316.36
MOUNTS (1)
088.19
MOURNING (3)
124.18 132.17 138.13
MOUSE (5)
140.28 225.16 264.36 267.10 280.21
MOUTH (11)
074.21 167.11 167.11 167.22 170.09
218.15 220.32 289.36 292.30 298.21
308.04
MOUTHS (2)
289.29 305.35
MOVABLE (1)
033.37
MOVE (9)
034.08 066.04 066.08 113.07 151.01
219.05 244.10 253.32 281.05
MOVED (2)
030.10 266.07
MOVING (2)
116.07 271.13
MOWER (1)
311.13
MOWING (1)
005.19
MR (7)
058.17 158.04 162.34 223.29 232.36
321.09 329.29
MRS (4)
043.13 076.30 153.15 255.12
MUCCLASSE (1)
068.11
MUCH (142)
003.10 003.28 004.08 006.06 006.14
007.16 009.02 011.04 011.10 011.31
013.15 014.25 014.26 018.03 020.09
021.28 026.10 028.27 033.12 042.21
043.08 045.25 045.27 046.18 048.02
048.05 049.30 049.38 051.16 051.33
054.30 055.20 056.14 056.16 056.19
057.18 057.25 058.06 058.13 064.26
065.05 066.16 071.30 074.29 078.30
080.05 085.27 086.31 088.35 093.20
095.11 102.01 106.19 109.21 111.08
112.01 113.18 124.03 130.23 130.30
133.18 135.06 137.28 140.03 151.12
151.22 151.24 152.20 153.20 157.09
157.09 159.10 163.02 163.39 163.41
164.20 164.23 169.08 169.15 175.27
177.04 182.15 184.22 184.27 190.13
194.21 195.24 197.24 199.29 199.30
199.32 203.34 206.05 211.34 212.04
214.14 214.28 215.02 215.08 217.24
223.06 223.08 223.15 225.07 225.25
227.16 228.28 230.25 231.21 235.24
235.33 239.14 240.16 240.26 242.16
244.25 245.20 249.19 250.19 251.12
252.06 256.23 258.27 266.36 268.07
270.10 273.29 274.06 275.21 281.25
283.21 287.04 288.10 290.21 299.22
299.33 300.04 300.24 315.28 322.34
325.23 328.24

MUCK (2)
196.32 199.29
MUD (10)
097.33 134.01 184.34 184.36 196.18
199.14 218.21 228.08 232.12 303.13
MUDDIED (1)
192.22
MUDDIER (1)
313.14
MUDDY (5)
150.27 177.15 178.30 304.01 325.29
MUFF (1)
233.12
MUFFLED (1)
119.04
MUGGY (1)
170.02
MULLEIN (1)
137.13
MULLEINS (1)
309.32
MULTA (1)
243.05
MULTIPLIED (1)
304.34
MULTITUDE (3)
077.10 101.34 104.10
MUMMY (1)
025.35
MUNGO (1)
321.10
MUNITIONS (1)
140.21
MUNITY (1)
153.28
MURDER (2)
187.21 212.31
MURDERED (1)
094.13
MURDERS (1)
258.30
MURMUR (1)
268.07
MUS (1)
225.23
MUSCLES (2)
038.16 184.33
MUSE (3)
192.10 204.06 330.30
MUSEUM (1)
028.33
MUSHROOM (1)
165.08
MUSIC (23)
036.24 085.11 089.17 089.34 095.35
097.31 110.03 123.28 123.31 124.26
124.28 127.04 131.10 159.06 160.06
217.13 218.30 219.07 278.16 304.25
309.19 324.32 326.10
MUSICAL (2)
124.16 230.08
MUSICIANS (1)
160.32
MUSING (1)
263.26
MUSKRAT (1)
066.11
MUSKRATS (8)
008.11 167.19 184.33 218.21 271.20
301.29 316.22 333.02
MUSKY (1)
059.39
MUSLINS (1)
120.10
MUSQUASH (2)
203.13 203.19
MUST (69)
004.01 009.07 019.29 021.12 023.20

```
MUST                          (CONTINUED)    MY                            (CONTINUED)
024.04  027.22  027.32  031.12  031.23       127.02  127.29  128.08  129.07  129.13
035.31  038.28  038.28  048.17  064.06       129.14  129.25  129.33  129.34  130.15
071.30  072.15  073.02  073.24  076.30       130.15  130.18  130.18  130.24  130.26
077.07  090.15  091.33  093.21  100.13       130.27  131.14  131.16  131.17  131.25
101.06  101.18  103.20  106.27  112.22       131.35  131.35  132.03  132.21  132.30
122.16  134.32  135.36  138.29  141.01       132.30  133.28  133.32  133.35  135.11
141.07  141.22  144.24  149.27  153.33       137.01  137.04  137.31  138.18  138.22
162.12  178.03  181.05  197.25  203.31       140.06  140.08  140.09  140.16  140.32
220.34  221.06  233.34  234.05  235.20       141.10  141.32  141.32  141.34  142.03
239.32  243.03  243.24  246.32  258.31       142.07  142.18  142.23  142.29  142.30
263.12  268.27  281.31  287.34  295.07       144.01  144.04  144.05  144.08  144.13
300.04  302.21  304.34  317.23  318.03       145.17  145.21  145.33  147.04  150.30
318.25  318.29  323.23  329.05                151.01  151.03  151.23  152.12  153.02
MUSTY                         (    2)        153.15  153.16  153.20  155.03  155.10
136.14  331.16                                155.10  155.13  155.20  155.21  155.24
MUTTERING                     (    2)        155.32  155.34  155.35  156.02  156.08
257.30  260.24                                156.08  156.26  156.30  157.06  157.10
MUTUAL                        (    4)        157.19  157.27  158.15  158.18  158.33
124.22  153.29  232.26  312.33                159.05  159.07  159.11  159.29  159.33
MUZZLE                        (    2)        159.36  160.07  160.29  160.30  161.04
236.13  278.31                                161.10  162.03  162.04  162.35  163.13
MY                            (  727)        163.26  164.16  167.06  167.18  169.04
003.07  003.07  003.10  003.11  003.12       169.08  169.21  169.21  169.24  169.31
003.12  003.18  003.21  003.31  003.31       169.32  169.34  170.03  170.03  170.05
004.04  004.32  005.03  006.35  009.12       170.07  170.07  171.35  171.36  172.03
009.18  010.11  010.14  010.30  010.31       172.04  172.04  172.07  172.10  172.11
017.03  017.06  017.10  017.23  017.31       172.11  172.12  173.04  173.08  173.24
017.32  018.08  018.09  018.09  018.10       173.32  173.34  174.05  174.10  174.30
018.13  018.24  018.29  018.30  018.32       175.20  178.06  178.19  180.29  181.17
018.33  018.36  019.02  019.20  019.20       181.28  182.10  183.06  183.25  184.12
019.22  019.27  019.30  019.34  022.04       184.35  185.28  187.21  188.21  189.20
022.09  023.22  023.22  025.02  025.19       190.01  190.19  190.21  190.23  191.30
025.19  029.04  029.05  032.15  035.04       191.31  191.34  192.10  193.02  193.28
036.15  036.26  036.28  038.14  040.29       193.31  194.24  194.30  194.31  197.09
040.34  041.14  041.22  041.35  042.07       197.13  197.14  202.16  202.18  203.05
042.24  042.25  042.28  042.29  042.34       203.06  203.25  203.25  203.27  204.31
042.36  042.37  043.14  044.22  045.04       204.32  204.33  205.03  205.04  205.06
045.06  045.09  045.15  045.16  045.17       205.14  206.34  207.01  207.08  207.13
045.21  045.23  045.24  045.26  046.15       207.13  207.18  207.19  207.21  210.03
046.23  048.21  048.24  048.32  049.20       210.04  210.06  210.22  210.24  211.14
049.31  049.35  049.37  049.38  049.40       211.26  211.29  211.30  211.32  211.33
050.06  052.01  053.07  054.18  054.20       211.36  212.09  212.12  212.28  212.34
054.36  055.01  055.03  055.10  055.24       213.11  213.13  213.36  214.17  214.20
056.10  056.12  056.12  058.27  058.30       214.22  214.27  214.30  214.35  216.07
058.32  059.30  059.31  059.34  059.35       216.34  217.03  217.27  217.28  218.07
060.22  060.42  061.03  061.10  061.14       221.14  221.16  223.03  223.04  223.28
061.21  061.35  062.02  062.04  062.12       223.35  224.04  224.29  224.29  224.32
062.20  062.33  062.35  063.08  063.09       225.21  225.29  225.32  225.32  225.35
063.13  063.26  064.02  064.22  065.05       226.01  226.01  226.02  226.05  226.06
065.16  066.26  066.26  067.07  067.15       226.08  226.11  226.12  226.31  227.20
067.16  067.22  067.23  069.10  069.12       227.28  227.31  227.34  228.13  228.20
069.13  069.15  069.16  069.18  069.19       228.26  228.27  229.02  230.32  230.32
069.23  069.28  069.28  069.30  069.32       231.23  231.26  234.09  235.28  235.30
069.33  070.01  070.11  070.12  071.04       236.17  238.17  238.23  238.24  238.30
071.07  071.25  072.20  072.28  072.35       240.11  240.12  240.18  240.32  240.33
073.06  073.08  073.17  073.18  073.20       241.14  241.20  241.25  241.27  241.32
073.22  073.24  074.17  074.19  074.24       242.10  242.16  242.24  242.24  242.30
075.23  075.26  078.10  081.13  081.19       243.09  243.11  244.29  245.10  245.20
081.25  082.05  082.07  082.16  082.16       245.24  246.04  246.09  247.33  248.35
082.23  082.25  082.31  083.16  083.25       249.11  249.12  249.12  249.12  249.14
083.29  083.35  084.03  084.07  084.11       249.14  249.16  249.36  250.32  251.27
084.25  084.26  084.27  084.29  085.02       251.28  251.32  251.32  252.19  252.21
085.08  085.18  085.30  086.10  087.24       252.27  252.37  253.02  253.06  253.09
087.26  088.06  088.13  088.26  088.37       253.14  253.16  253.16  253.20  253.25
091.10  094.03  094.06  095.17  098.28       254.02  254.04  254.04  254.05  254.31
098.29  098.29  098.30  098.31  098.33       254.32  256.05  256.08  256.13  256.15
099.20  099.32  099.34  099.35  099.35       256.16  256.18  256.19  256.24  257.04
100.04  105.11  107.14  107.15  107.22       257.20  258.02  259.14  259.16  259.16
108.25  111.24  111.25  111.26  111.30       260.35  261.08  261.24  261.32  262.32
112.01  112.01  112.08  112.10  112.10       264.21  264.34  265.18  265.24  265.27
112.11  112.11  112.19  112.25  112.27       265.27  265.36  266.01  266.08  266.20
112.28  112.36  113.01  113.06  113.07       267.17  267.18  267.19  267.24  267.35
113.08  113.10  113.15  113.26  113.30       268.17  268.20  271.06  271.19  271.20
114.13  114.24  114.25  114.26  114.28       271.25  272.06  272.14  272.16  272.34
114.30  115.22  116.36  118.07  121.20       273.02  273.17  273.17  273.23  274.17
122.28  122.28  122.35  123.29  124.01       274.18  275.31  275.32  276.03  276.08
                                              276.12  276.12  277.20  277.20  277.26
```

MY   (CONTINUED)
 279.21   280.03   280.06   280.07   280.10
 280.11   280.26   280.31   280.36   280.36
 281.02   281.03   282.05   282.07   282.11
 282.21   282.34   283.02   284.29   285.33
 289.16   293.08   293.26   295.02   295.17
 297.18   298.01   298.02   298.09   301.16
 302.13   302.17   304.31   310.14   310.14
 310.21   312.06   312.23   312.34   312.35
 313.01   313.03   313.11   313.23   318.13
 318.14   318.17   319.06   319.07   319.18
 323.16   323.16   323.29   324.18   324.20
 325.26   326.26   328.28   328.30   329.19
 329.19   329.21   329.21   329.32   331.12
 331.35   332.12
MYRIAD   (3)
 094.19   239.23   307.10
MYRIADS   (4)
 034.27   179.22   189.29   318.19
MYRMIDONS   (2)
 144.31   229.01
MYSELF   (65)
 003.05   003.28   016.14   019.29   025.10
 035.27   037.13   040.03   040.23   042.09
 046.23   048.34   049.36   049.41   055.03
 059.31   060.22   065.16   069.09   070.24
 071.09   072.29   072.32   075.32   078.04
 085.30   085.32   100.02   100.05   125.15
 130.19   130.25   131.22   131.27   135.07
 135.10   138.16   140.04   146.25   156.13
 163.41   164.06   169.18   189.29   197.17
 202.19   203.28   210.10   210.15   217.20
 217.29   230.11   238.04   240.16   240.28
 246.11   249.33   250.21   253.27   259.07
 264.29   266.03   289.22   293.30   332.12
MYSTERIOUS   (3)
 175.07   255.01   317.35
MYSTERY   (6)
 025.15   079.08   183.02   185.26   279.01
 279.03
MYTHOLOGICAL   (1)
 258.27
MYTHOLOGY   (7)
 010.27   116.22   137.36   165.22   258.25
 269.35   308.28

N (3)
125.01 125.04 125.05
NABATHAEAN (1)
314.05
NABATHAEAQUE (1)
314.01
NAIL (8)
038.03 091.27 172.03 206.20 245.23
330.24 330.27 330.31
NAILED (1)
043.28
NAILS (6)
010.03 044.07 044.14 049.15 065.04
119.28
NAKED (4)
013.01 013.04 022.29 274.21
NAKEDNESS (2)
021.28 037.17
NAME (19)
032.29 048.12 061.22 080.27 104.32
107.13 118.16 129.27 144.15 147.36
183.02 184.23 195.30 197.20 241.15
250.14 261.35 316.33 327.06
NAMED (10)
064.12 164.27 182.19 182.20 195.36
196.05 197.04 210.16 258.25 279.20
NAMELESS (1)
201.21
NAMELY (3)
059.01 064.32 290.19
NAMES (7)
037.11 094.33 107.12 152.34 197.06
298.23 328.06
NAP (1)
093.25
NAPE (1)
067.05
NAPKIN (1)
126.21
NAPOLEON (1)
262.04
NAPPING (1)
272.26
NARROW (12)
027.33 042.07 048.16 113.29 177.02
180.02 180.24 247.08 257.13 266.14
284.02 324.20
NARROWEST (1)
289.27
NARROWLY (1)
066.29
NARROWNESS (1)
003.30
NASAL (1)
332.23
NATI (1)
005.35
NATION (10)
056.21 056.22 056.25 058.04 092.04
092.14 101.08 106.35 108.23 156.17
NATIONAL (1)
230.09
NATIONS (18)
015.11 057.17 057.26 060.04 070.36
101.28 102.35 104.01 127.18 141.06
158.33 179.15 179.29 188.24 215.16
215.17 269.11 322.17
NATIVE (14)
020.09 020.10 096.14 127.15 127.23
144.24 145.09 147.36 155.32 157.19
225.23 232.29 272.23 317.09
NATIVES (4)
037.10 127.25 202.22 281.27
NATURAL (29)
003.15 004.23 028.16 046.16 051.23
074.25 078.33 103.04 112.23 119.15
121.05 123.03 123.28 131.05 136.35
141.07 145.02 159.01 186.01 186.07

NATURAL (CONTINUED)
203.22 217.06 232.18 264.07 281.25
283.19 292.06 303.19 315.32
NATURALIST (5)
012.34 213.03 225.25 283.30 283.31
NATURALISTS (1)
233.18
NATURALIZED (2)
127.06 322.18
NATURALLY (5)
102.36 140.06 142.10 147.22 210.34
NATURE (94)
006.04 006.23 010.21 011.05 012.29
015.10 017.08 017.20 029.27 037.19
045.34 067.18 078.34 079.13 080.13
088.27 097.16 099.06 100.36 114.03
116.28 123.33 124.35 125.08 125.29
126.02 128.10 129.05 129.23 130.13
131.08 132.02 135.02 138.07 138.10
138.19 147.12 158.06 159.23 162.09
165.20 166.01 171.14 175.19 186.07
186.14 188.27 188.36 193.37 199.34
200.03 207.30 210.25 210.29 216.27
219.10 219.14 220.09 221.05 221.19
238.13 239.16 239.21 245.06 264.20
269.25 276.28 281.07 281.14 281.16
281.21 282.06 282.09 282.12 283.30
283.36 287.33 288.23 290.23 290.28
303.14 303.21 308.16 308.25 308.35
309.35 313.32 315.17 315.28 315.29
318.02 318.17 318.18 324.13
NATURES (6)
008.22 016.05 130.31 133.26 325.07
327.30
NAUGHTS (1)
283.18
NAVIGATION (2)
020.28 052.03
NAVIGATORS (2)
020.35 292.01
NAY (10)
055.24 076.16 111.21 115.32 130.05
221.31 249.21 250.05 250.23 321.15
ND (1)
249.03
NE (1)
142.34
NEAR (52)
022.35 040.32 054.21 075.12 085.32
086.32 087.03 088.09 095.15 113.33
121.12 124.09 124.14 125.07 131.31
133.19 133.25 140.18 141.11 141.14
141.16 158.19 171.20 176.24 185.12
198.21 202.01 224.07 224.28 229.17
229.35 230.02 230.35 245.06 256.19
258.03 260.19 264.34 272.18 273.16
276.11 278.29 281.02 288.34 290.12
296.31 299.26 300.07 300.23 303.09
316.20 329.12
NEARER (20)
052.30 085.33 087.35 100.18 133.06
133.18 193.24 203.35 228.12 228.12
229.20 234.23 257.20 258.22 266.20
275.14 275.14 278.13 278.14 306.14
NEAREST (20)
040.33 082.08 083.06 088.13 102.22
130.15 132.12 134.09 168.21 182.35
198.19 203.33 205.04 228.21 232.36
235.08 261.14 275.26 276.08 281.21
NEARLY (24)
013.17 025.14 029.02 034.07 056.13
060.33 061.02 190.26 224.11 224.12
224.22 224.24 228.28 229.34 249.34
251.06 265.34 271.26 280.32 289.19
290.06 302.21 302.24 332.07
NEARNESS (1)
260.01

NEAT   (1)
  201.31
NEATLY   (2)
  029.31   245.25
NEBUCHADNEZZAR   (1)
  241.15
NEBULOSA   (1)
  266.04
NEC   (1)
  172.26
NECESSARIES   (7)
  008.18   009.26   011.35   012.19   014.08
  034.19   061.29
NECESSARILY   (3)
  060.11   245.01   246.24
NECESSARY   (34)
  004.13   011.31   012.08   012.14   015.24
  019.14   021.29   027.09   028.36   045.17
  051.04   051.33   056.01   056.17   061.16
  071.01   091.02   091.35   098.29   110.16
  152.36   168.14   217.05   221.19   244.03
  244.07   245.20   264.27   280.23   288.19
  302.18   321.13   322.30   329.16
NECESSITATED   (1)
  080.16
NECESSITIES   (2)
  046.01   047.17
NECESSITY   (12)
  005.26   012.28   013.24   019.23   023.01
  036.07   041.33   045.06   046.27   111.12
  134.32   211.27
NECK   (7)
  004.24   067.05   145.11   241.26   241.27
  266.09   266.10
NEED   (36)
  023.09   023.14   035.01   035.24   047.09
  055.35   065.24   075.14   085.25   091.22
  094.17   095.06   099.10   105.25   108.27
  119.33   136.17   142.22   172.32   205.34
  215.23   220.29   223.14   228.22   236.34
  254.06   257.11   290.23   291.12   292.25
  317.03   317.28   318.07   324.07   331.03
  332.19
NEEDED   (7)
  049.13   050.13   063.20   064.09   075.32
  265.09   282.23
NEEDLE   (2)
  123.14   132.08
NEEDLES   (3)
  123.06   149.08   332.11
NEEDLESSLY   (2)
  035.30   105.09
NEEDS   (6)
  142.14   144.08   171.11   183.31   188.24
  317.22
NEEDY   (2)
  076.02   080.05
NEGLECT   (1)
  314.24
NEGLECTED   (3)
  040.08   109.10   212.27
NEGRO   (3)
  007.19   257.09   257.34
NEIGH   (1)
  192.21
NEIGHBOR   (20)
  003.05   007.10   009.36   010.02   017.21
  032.34   044.12   071.13   071.31   083.06
  085.31   086.22   088.13   107.15   130.16
  147.18   167.23   196.10   262.13   314.32
NEIGHBORHOOD   (23)
  019.02   031.17   034.01   034.05   040.18
  051.19   087.12   130.35   131.31   132.06
  137.31   178.18   183.28   201.25   226.22
  227.23   233.05   238.33   261.33   266.27
  285.18   299.10   331.12
NEIGHBORING   (6)
  068.32   171.10   204.34   256.29   289.03

NEIGHBORING   (CONTINUED)
  292.22
NEIGHBORLINESS   (1)
  045.05
NEIGHBORS   (23)
  004.32   010.30   019.07   032.15   035.32
  050.10   067.36   073.20   083.15   084.25
  108.16   118.07   134.32   135.19   160.17
  198.26   205.04   222.02   223.01   225.16
  242.33   314.31   329.21
NEITHER   (14)
  010.04   038.26   063.12   079.12   099.19
  105.04   127.29   127.31   218.16   220.31
  229.22   251.24   261.17   324.11
NEPTUNE   (1)
  051.26
NERVE   (2)
  244.35   322.22
NERVES   (2)
  097.27   117.22
NERVII   (1)
  259.16
NERVOUS   (1)
  329.36
NEST   (7)
  046.03   112.11   225.26   244.14   252.32
  317.09   317.32
NESTED   (1)
  253.20
NESTS   (5)
  013.28   030.19   046.10   119.11   185.25
NETHERLAND   (2)
  039.08   039.11
NETTLE   (1)
  018.25
NEUTRAL   (2)
  109.31   141.08
NEVA   (2)
  021.11   021.14
NEVADA   (1)
  119.12
NEVER   (160)
  004.34   005.18   008.23   010.08   017.09
  017.26   018.03   018.07   018.34   023.12
  023.35   035.29   044.28   045.34   046.14
  050.21   050.29   051.23   055.06   056.24
  056.27   065.33   067.09   074.36   078.02
  078.03   078.04   078.11   082.07   085.25
  085.36   086.27   090.12   093.35   094.06
  094.11   094.17   095.06   095.12   097.06
  097.13   100.35   103.24   103.31   104.08
  105.08   107.14   107.15   107.16   107.19
  112.28   112.32   115.04   118.08   118.15
  122.20   124.36   125.03   126.17   127.27
  127.28   128.01   129.20   130.09   130.26
  130.34   131.09   131.28   132.07   133.30
  135.23   136.23   136.36   142.11   142.24
  142.27   142.28   147.04   147.09   147.21
  147.23   147.30   148.05   148.30   148.32
  150.01   151.24   152.07   157.12   164.35
  164.36   169.09   169.27   172.01   172.04
  172.16   173.16   173.17   177.24   182.17
  183.23   185.32   188.26   193.33   196.02
  196.02   196.02   196.03   196.03   199.31
  204.27   207.30   208.13   212.26   214.34
  216.33   217.03   218.11   218.28   218.30
  219.14   223.16   224.11   225.02   225.30
  227.19   228.30   229.10   229.16   231.21
  240.18   242.16   254.29   258.13   259.09
  261.01   261.28   262.19   262.21   262.28
  270.18   272.04   272.32   273.36   274.09
  283.20   285.02   296.05   296.23   299.09
  299.12   309.10   315.30   317.01   318.02
  318.09   322.35   323.08   331.31   333.30
NEVERTHELESS   (8)
  025.33   031.33   184.12   192.30   217.28
  232.26   245.14   320.18

142

```
NEW                              ( 124)
004.10  008.31  008.31  008.33  013.04
014.13  018.01  020.27  020.29  023.05
023.14  023.20  023.29  023.30  023.31
023.31  023.35  024.02  024.03  026.08
026.20  039.08  039.10  039.11  039.25
043.27  051.25  052.20  052.30  063.28
064.29  068.13  068.13  068.26  068.28
068.29  075.04  075.11  080.30  087.32
088.07  092.31  093.32  095.09  095.25
096.25  097.36  107.34  107.36  108.02
109.32  110.11  116.22  119.08  119.26
120.15  124.34  125.02  130.23  136.12
136.13  137.18  137.24  142.21  149.23
155.30  156.03  156.04  162.07  162.08
164.14  164.19  164.20  164.24  164.32
173.07  184.31  188.35  208.30  208.39
211.14  212.01  221.11  222.21  230.05
235.18  238.12  240.08  246.06  247.34
247.35  250.34  251.05  251.19  251.19
254.27  258.26  258.30  265.29  266.29
267.06  268.13  270.03  271.03  271.04
271.06  274.20  274.29  293.23  294.22
297.36  299.08  308.19  312.19  314.38
315.03  320.05  321.16  321.17  323.34
324.24  327.15  328.24  333.07
NEWER                            (   1)
331.06
NEWFOUNDLAND                     (   1)
074.29
NEWLY                            (   2)
066.05  089.15
NEWS                             (  16)
052.31  093.27  093.31  094.12  094.20
094.25  094.27  095.04  095.11  095.14
106.14  144.29  167.25  167.30  169.13
259.02
NEWSPAPER                        (   5)
042.26  094.12  109.30  167.11  167.12
NEWSPAPERS                       (   4)
095.02  095.09  109.29  329.08
NEWTON                           (   1)
076.26
NEXT                             (  45)
014.08  015.19  037.32  039.29  053.30
055.27  059.33  076.26  084.19  091.10
105.17  107.15  107.19  113.19  117.30
119.26  120.03  120.30  121.17  126.26
134.10  134.11  143.13  171.34  172.06
174.33  175.20  176.25  176.29  181.28
183.15  186.15  191.23  208.24  240.03
254.13  262.26  265.15  276.26  279.12
294.06  296.28  297.07  302.31  332.31
NIBBLE                           (   3)
077.29  163.32  280.31
NIBBLED                          (   3)
155.26  226.06  304.15
NIBBLING                         (   2)
253.20  274.20
NICHOLAS                         (   1)
231.36
NICK                             (   1)
017.02
NIGER                            (   1)
321.04
NIGH                             (   4)
005.16  011.07  017.31  239.13
NIGHT                            (  85)
007.25  011.13  013.28  017.01  020.16
027.13  027.14  027.28  029.10  029.14
034.31  037.28  043.31  053.12  084.33
089.11  093.31  111.33  117.27  124.15
124.31  125.23  126.05  128.06  129.10
130.25  130.34  135.34  136.03  136.19
143.06  147.02  155.35  159.12  169.18
170.01  170.02  170.11  170.16  170.21
170.30  171.05  172.05  174.25  175.10
183.26  185.01  193.37  197.15  207.27

NIGHT                       (CONTINUED)
208.24  216.24  227.29  241.25  243.34
248.27  248.27  248.33  249.03  252.35
254.32  256.15  258.13  259.06  260.18
262.25  270.03  272.09  272.25  273.27
279.12  279.14  282.02  282.17  282.23
301.09  301.13  301.24  303.10  313.03
316.25  318.15  320.09  322.27  330.28
NIGHTFALL                        (   1)
145.30
NIGHTLY                          (   2)
086.15  088.01
NIGHTS                           (  13)
028.25  084.27  088.14  092.20  095.34
133.07  143.17  169.29  174.21  175.16
271.33  273.07  330.25
NILE                             (   3)
058.10  159.35  321.04
NILOMETER                        (   1)
098.08
NIMBLY                           (   1)
232.17
NIMROD                           (   1)
280.01
NINE                             (  10)
076.10  093.08  093.09  105.02  163.16
163.18  179.11  272.11  313.11  316.20
NINETEENTH                       (   4)
108.22  109.25  109.27  329.36
NINETY                           (   4)
032.36  038.23  053.09  194.22
NINTH                            (   2)
046.18  295.15
NIP                              (   1)
067.08
NIPPED                           (   1)
028.02
NIPPING                          (   1)
266.33
NO                               ( 264)
003.21  004.08  004.35  005.21  006.18
006.29  007.15  007.16  008.13  008.21
008.23  008.36  009.04  010.28  013.32
015.08  017.10  017.23  018.06  019.04
021.11  021.33  022.03  022.18  031.35
034.17  035.21  036.31  037.06  037.27
037.36  038.03  038.32  038.32  039.12
042.36  045.06  046.01  046.21  047.07
047.36  049.31  050.25  053.23  053.30
053.36  054.28  055.33  056.21  056.21
056.22  058.12  059.32  062.08  066.12
067.12  067.20  069.04  069.05  070.15
070.31  073.18  074.01  074.15  074.24
074.31  077.34  079.07  080.26  080.27
083.27  083.36  089.20  090.18  093.29
098.04  099.10  099.16  099.17  102.18
103.01  103.21  105.25  106.04  106.08
108.32  111.10  111.11  111.14  112.20
118.12  118.13  118.19  119.33  120.08
121.01  122.33  124.20  124.32  125.27
126.12  126.32  127.11  128.08  128.09
128.18  128.18  128.19  128.19  130.16
131.07  132.14  133.17  135.13  135.14
137.04  137.13  137.15  138.35  140.06
142.04  143.26  143.33  144.36  146.25
147.16  147.24  148.05  148.13  154.12
157.31  159.08  160.23  161.11  161.23
162.16  162.19  165.26  166.32  169.32
172.02  172.15  178.31  181.36  182.07
182.23  183.01  183.29  185.23  186.02
187.29  188.03  188.24  188.25  188.27
188.27  188.31  189.17  192.07  193.15
193.22  194.03  196.10  196.19  196.24
196.25  196.25  197.03  197.03  199.29
199.34  202.21  203.30  204.27  207.28
207.28  208.09  208.12  210.13  211.19
212.26  212.30  213.06  213.25  214.08
215.06  216.08  216.19  216.21  217.22
```

NOTCH (1)
017.03
NOTCHED (1)
256.21
NOTE (12)
044.10 124.10 127.04 127.22 129.11
135.14 174.36 236.08 271.34 276.33
302.19 312.16
NOTES (8)
046.11 123.21 127.18 127.23 129.19
200.01 222.11 275.32
NOTHING (55)
004.24 009.13 009.18 009.20 016.33
028.01 052.22 052.27 053.31 054.27
058.05 060.40 065.17 067.11 070.20
072.27 077.09 079.18 083.10 095.09
104.16 104.35 112.06 120.19 127.13
129.08 131.10 131.13 142.08 143.05
143.28 143.31 147.28 148.16 183.35
188.21 189.11 196.16 196.24 213.28
221.21 223.32 223.33 225.16 243.35
255.05 260.32 261.21 268.02 271.09
277.22 308.29 308.33 326.26 331.09
NOTICE (4)
003.10 153.01 163.35 252.25
NOTICEABLE (1)
178.32
NOTICED (4)
202.33 289.13 297.02 301.15
NOTIFIED (1)
130.05
NOTION (1)
053.28
NOTIONS (2)
025.28 290.29
NOTWITHSTANDING (8)
049.38 055.23 059.38 093.15 119.07
212.06 267.16 289.18
NOURISH (1)
165.16
NOURISHED (1)
229.31
NOVEL (1)
112.29
NOVELDOM (1)
105.13
NOVELIST (2)
105.09 105.18
NOVELTY (2)
021.23 332.18
NOVEMBER (6)
189.10 189.12 189.18 240.23 242.04
249.09
NOW (118)
015.26 015.29 023.03 025.04 025.17
027.08 029.07 030.27 034.36 035.24
037.27 038.30 040.02 040.26 047.15
049.34 053.12 060.22 064.25 067.32
070.22 073.12 082.15 097.04 099.15
099.26 099.34 112.06 114.34 115.07
116.23 117.32 118.10 119.29 120.08
121.12 122.04 122.12 122.32 125.19
125.35 129.17 129.21 129.22 133.02
144.24 155.35 160.24 164.06 165.12
174.30 175.10 179.26 180.35 182.14
182.23 185.11 188.15 191.18 192.07
192.13 198.15 204.07 204.09 206.28
206.31 206.33 208.14 210.04 211.30
212.02 213.24 223.07 223.12 225.04
229.12 229.32 232.18 233.35 238.22
239.27 242.04 242.24 247.23 248.17
249.13 251.17 255.03 256.24 256.31
257.02 257.16 258.01 261.06 261.11
262.30 263.01 263.09 263.27 268.33
273.33 273.36 274.29 278.14 278.14
278.28 279.26 290.26 294.03 297.24
302.21 308.10 317.13 322.23 323.28
324.08 327.19 333.23

NOWADAYS (3)
014.33 066.36 244.21
NOWHERE (4)
078.25 178.30 217.27 266.33
NUCLEI (1)
284.31
NUDGINGS (1)
089.14
NUISANCES (1)
250.12
NUMB (1)
041.36
NUMBED (1)
240.15
NUMBER (13)
016.14 030.23 036.08 061.25 082.03
095.18 213.27 248.15 265.21 289.13
290.32 290.36 304.33
NUMBERS (4)
039.31 140.11 230.16 230.18
NUMBNESS (1)
167.34
NUMEROUS (8)
015.22 023.08 052.15 242.12 247.13
264.15 279.36 281.30
NUN (1)
212.18
NURSES (1)
080.08
NUT (6)
113.33 119.27 239.06 239.28 267.32
268.26
NUTS (10)
062.18 167.27 194.29 202.01 224.16
238.27 238.35 239.03 239.34 280.11
NUTSHELL (2)
007.07 097.17
NUTTING (3)
261.12 279.17 279.20
NYMPH (1)
123.21
NYMPHS (3)
126.11 179.31 187.15

```
O                            (  25)
  005.35  047.05  105.11  115.10  118.34
  124.36  124.36  124.36  124.36  143.13
  152.22  161.18  183.13  193.27  208.04
  223.17  223.21  248.33  269.34  272.11
  282.14  283.27  312.18  317.24  317.24
OAK                          (  13)
  043.28  087.27  144.34  156.34  175.33
  191.22  256.12  257.32  263.05  271.31
  283.18  284.14  326.12
OAKS                         (   8)
  081.33  113.32  125.03  156.22  201.07
  273.31  312.22  318.31
OAKUM                        (   2)
  270.11  320.22
OAR                          (   2)
  188.16  188.17
OARS                         (   3)
  190.19  190.23  235.28
OATS                         (   1)
  296.01
OBEDIENCE                    (   4)
  006.06  302.03  323.02  323.07
OBEDIENT                     (   1)
  226.33
OBEDIENTLY                   (   1)
  097.10
OBELISK                      (   1)
  295.31
OBESUS                       (   1)
  184.05
OBEY                         (   3)
  307.18  315.11  322.20
OBEYS                        (   1)
  305.08
OBJECT                       (  10)
  021.26  026.36  046.20  052.28  101.06
  131.05  165.25  246.31  266.18  297.02
OBJECTED                     (   1)
  325.27
OBJECTION                    (   5)
  033.36  212.07  214.20  216.17  217.18
OBJECTIONS                   (   1)
  061.06
OBJECTS                      (   6)
  038.27  090.22  113.18  152.10  213.03
  225.14
OBLATIONS                    (   1)
  134.23
OBLIGATION                   (   1)
  072.31
OBLIGED                      (  15)
  048.26  055.02  069.16  112.26  164.08
  170.12  170.29  182.34  186.31  217.23
  242.17  256.17  259.12  265.12  280.15
OBLITERATE                   (   1)
  267.04
OBLITERATED                  (   1)
  257.14
OBLONG                       (   1)
  247.08
OBSCENE                      (   1)
  221.14
OBSCURITIES                  (   1)
  017.06
OBSCURITY                    (   2)
  242.20  325.24
OBSEQUIOUS                   (   1)
  330.36
OBSERVANCE                   (   1)
  126.28
OBSERVATION                  (   1)
  181.17
OBSERVATORY                  (   1)
  017.36
OBSERVE                      (  10)
  012.28  067.11  095.31  102.07  150.14
  167.24  182.32  304.28  307.12  318.10

OBSERVED                     (  15)
  013.02  026.36  150.11  168.12  181.09
  189.15  202.31  217.34  228.27  289.12
  289.29  291.04  293.02  316.24  330.17
OBSERVER                     (   3)
  014.29  178.30  303.14
OBSERVERS                    (   1)
  099.05
OBSERVES                     (   1)
  287.31
OBSERVING                    (   3)
  210.31  289.06  290.07
OBSOLETELY                   (   1)
  166.24
OBSTACLE                     (   1)
  009.25
OBSTACLES                    (   1)
  019.36
OBSTINACY                    (   2)
  120.33  231.33
OBSTRUCTION                  (   2)
  028.25  303.27
OBTAIN                       (   9)
  011.36  015.25  023.07  036.05  049.33
  061.15  064.10  064.17  173.13
OBTAINED                     (  10)
  014.02  014.08  015.24  021.21  024.29
  032.04  040.20  171.34  179.27  241.09
OBTAINING                    (   1)
  034.19
OBTAINS                      (   2)
  012.09  051.04
OBTRUDE                      (   1)
  003.10
OBVIOUS                      (   5)
  153.09  180.11  213.10  247.13  309.29
OCCASION                     (   7)
  032.11  045.05  064.18  091.20  102.11
  102.13  224.27
OCCASIONAL                   (   4)
  027.25  102.01  137.19  192.09
OCCASIONALLY                 (  14)
  061.08  085.16  145.12  150.11  153.09
  160.06  173.24  174.03  184.34  236.09
  238.29  256.08  267.14  276.07
OCCASIONED                   (   2)
  181.13  287.33
OCCASIONS                    (   4)
  097.04  112.22  134.08  149.28
OCCIDENTALIS                 (   1)
  202.03
OCCUPANT                     (   2)
  050.09  083.13
OCCUPANTS                    (   3)
  047.14  180.07  256.17
OCCUPATION                   (   3)
  046.16  069.35  070.25
OCCUPIED                     (   6)
  006.10  038.14  055.23  247.33  253.16
  261.36
OCCUPIES                     (   3)
  257.13  263.05  288.12
OCCUPY                       (   5)
  045.09  060.37  119.13  219.13  264.24
OCCUPYING                    (   1)
  247.30
OCCUR                        (   3)
  134.05  168.26  281.28
OCCURRED                     (   3)
  108.05  138.02  261.29
OCCURS                       (   1)
  150.34
OCEAN                        (   7)
  134.24  144.06  194.17  288.24  289.23
  291.32  321.34
OCEANS                       (   2)
  119.23  321.11
```

OCTOBER
188.19	189.09	189.18	233.35	234.17
238.03	240.11			

ODD (2)
056.02	171.30

ODE (1)
084.22

ODOR (3)
074.15	130.04	267.20

ODOROUS (1)
137.32

ODORS (2)
119.20	214.16

ODYSSEY (1)
089.03

OF (3227)

003.04	003.06	003.07	003.11	003.12
003.18	003.21	003.23	003.31	003.32
003.33	003.34	004.04	004.19	004.20
004.24	004.26	004.27	004.28	004.29
004.31	004.36	005.06	005.09	005.11
005.17	005.19	005.23	005.24	005.30
006.04	006.12	006.23	006.23	006.27
006.29	006.34	006.35	006.38	007.01
007.02	007.07	007.08	007.19	007.23
007.23	007.24	007.32	007.33	007.35
008.01	008.03	008.03	008.07	008.07
008.11	008.13	008.15	008.16	008.17
008.18	008.19	008.23	008.27	008.35
009.03	009.11	009.21	009.22	009.25
009.26	009.30	009.34	010.04	010.06
010.08	010.15	010.18	010.20	010.26
010.27	010.28	010.28	010.30	010.31
010.35	011.01	011.04	011.07	011.08
011.09	011.16	011.23	011.29	011.33
011.35	012.01	012.04	012.05	012.07
012.08	012.09	012.14	012.15	012.15
012.16	012.17	012.19	012.21	012.23
012.24	012.26	012.26	012.27	012.31
012.31	012.34	012.34	013.06	013.07
013.11	013.13	013.14	013.21	013.28
013.30	013.30	013.33	013.35	013.36
014.10	014.16	014.17	014.17	014.18
014.19	014.26	014.27	014.28	014.29
014.30	014.30	014.31	014.33	015.02
015.03	015.03	015.05	015.09	015.09
015.11	015.12	015.13	015.14	015.20
016.12	016.13	016.17	016.18	016.18
016.19	016.21	016.23	016.25	016.31
016.34	017.01	017.02	017.03	017.16
017.23	017.27	017.33	017.34	017.36
018.06	018.08	018.12	018.14	018.14
018.18	018.19	018.21	018.23	018.31
019.02	019.18	019.18	019.21	019.23
019.26	020.02	020.16	020.17	020.22
020.22	020.23	020.24	020.24	020.25
020.26	020.26	020.29	020.31	020.33
020.35	021.02	021.03	021.04	021.04
021.04	021.05	021.08	021.12	021.15
021.22	021.23	021.24	021.26	021.27
021.28	021.29	021.33	021.36	022.18
022.25	022.27	022.31	022.32	022.32
023.01	023.04	023.05	023.11	023.26
023.29	023.30	024.04	024.11	024.15
024.33	024.36	025.02	025.11	025.12
025.18	025.18	025.19	025.25	025.26
025.28	026.03	026.06	026.09	026.10
026.11	026.15	026.19	026.19	026.24
026.25	026.28	026.34	026.35	027.09
027.09	027.14	027.15	027.21	027.22
027.25	027.29	027.29	027.30	027.34
028.01	028.03	028.05	028.06	028.07
028.08	028.16	028.16	028.18	028.18
028.19	028.19	028.20	028.20	028.24
029.01	029.21	029.24	029.25	029.26
029.27	029.29	029.30	029.32	029.34
029.36	029.36	030.09	030.18	030.23
030.24	030.25	030.27	030.29	030.36

OF (CONTINUED)

031.02	031.03	031.10	031.14	031.14
031.19	031.21	031.25	031.29	031.31
031.36	032.01	032.03	032.06	032.12
032.13	032.15	032.19	032.21	032.22
032.24	032.31	032.35	033.02	033.03
033.03	033.12	033.14	033.16	033.18
033.21	033.29	034.18	034.24	034.25
034.28	034.31	034.33	034.34	034.34
034.35	035.06	035.07	035.08	035.09
035.13	035.14	035.15	035.16	035.18
035.18	035.22	035.26	035.27	035.33
035.35	035.35	036.08	036.08	036.12
036.12	036.14	036.16	036.24	036.24
036.26	036.28	037.09	037.10	037.11
037.15	037.17	037.24	037.30	037.32
037.33	037.34	038.01	038.04	038.13
038.17	038.21	038.22	038.23	038.31
038.34	038.34	039.07	039.08	039.09
039.16	039.17	039.19	039.24	039.26
039.31	039.36	040.02	040.03	040.11
040.12	040.18	040.32	041.03	041.04
041.12	041.19	041.28	041.29	041.32
041.32	041.33	041.36	042.01	042.02
042.05	042.18	042.20	042.25	042.29
042.30	042.31	042.32	042.34	042.36
042.37	043.01	043.06	043.18	043.21
043.23	043.35	044.13	044.16	044.18
044.20	044.20	044.22	044.25	044.31
044.34	045.02	045.02	045.03	045.04
045.04	045.06	045.07	045.08	045.10
045.13	045.14	045.18	045.26	045.34
046.02	046.12	046.14	046.14	046.18
046.20	046.23	046.25	046.26	046.27
046.29	046.32	047.02	047.06	047.08
047.08	047.09	047.10	047.15	047.17
047.17	047.18	047.20	047.22	047.25
047.25	047.31	047.32	048.01	048.02
048.03	048.10	048.10	048.11	048.14
048.15	048.17	048.18	048.20	048.24
048.25	048.26	048.32	048.34	049.01
049.12	049.27	049.38	050.05	050.08
050.10	050.15	050.18	050.26	050.26
050.27	050.28	050.28	050.31	051.05
051.08	051.15	051.20	051.21	051.29
051.31	052.06	052.26	053.02	053.17
053.18	053.20	053.21	053.27	053.29
054.04	054.04	054.06	054.06	054.09
054.14	054.21	054.31	054.33	054.34
055.01	055.06	055.07	055.08	055.15
055.19	055.22	055.23	055.24	055.28
055.29	055.34	055.36	056.06	056.10
056.15	056.15	056.19	056.20	056.20
056.22	056.24	056.25	056.35	057.01
057.06	057.08	057.09	057.10	057.17
057.19	057.20	057.22	057.28	057.28
057.31	057.33	057.34	057.36	058.03
058.13	058.13	058.17	058.19	058.27
058.29	058.33	058.34	059.01	059.06
059.09	059.31	059.33	060.09	060.12
060.22	060.31	060.32	060.34	060.41
061.06	061.07	061.10	061.20	061.22
061.22	061.25	061.25	061.26	061.27
061.28	061.29	061.30	061.34	062.01
062.03	062.03	062.03	062.06	062.09
062.12	062.14	062.15	062.17	062.18
062.19	062.21	062.24	062.25	063.04
063.06	063.07	063.25	063.26	063.27
063.29	063.36	064.03	064.08	064.15
064.17	064.34	064.36	065.02	065.06
065.06	065.16	065.17	065.18	065.20
065.25	065.28	065.31	065.31	065.32
065.36	066.02	066.04	066.22	066.24
066.31	066.36	067.05	067.05	067.15
067.19	067.24	067.25	067.34	067.35
067.36	068.04	068.06	068.07	068.09
068.11	068.17	068.22	068.35	069.01
069.03	069.06	069.10	069.12	069.12

OF   (CONTINUED)

069.13	069.16	069.19	069.27	069.29
070.01	070.02	070.05	070.08	070.20
070.25	070.26	070.28	070.30	070.32
070.36	071.01	071.02	071.04	071.07
071.28	071.28	072.03	072.09	072.20
072.23	072.26	072.36	073.04	073.09
073.18	073.23	073.27	073.31	073.32
073.35	073.36	074.07	074.08	074.09
074.09	074.11	074.18	074.20	074.23
074.23	074.27	074.36	075.02	075.05
075.09	075.27	075.27	075.35	076.01
076.02	076.04	076.08	076.09	076.11
076.12	076.13	076.14	076.21	076.23
076.26	076.27	076.29	076.31	077.02
077.05	077.09	077.10	077.12	077.17
077.22	077.28	077.28	077.32	077.34
077.36	078.02	078.07	078.11	078.15
078.22	078.25	078.26	078.27	079.01
079.02	079.02	079.03	079.04	079.05
079.10	079.12	079.13	079.17	080.03
080.16	081.04	081.06	081.07	081.14
081.19	081.29	082.03	082.06	082.12
082.22	082.30	082.34	083.01	083.04
083.11	083.14	083.16	083.18	083.23
083.29	083.30	084.09	084.09	084.19
084.21	084.29	084.31	085.03	085.04
085.09	085.10	085.12	085.13	085.15
085.19	085.22	085.26	085.33	085.35
086.03	086.04	086.04	086.05	086.07
086.12	086.13	086.15	086.19	086.21
086.22	086.23	086.25	086.29	086.30
087.06	087.06	087.06	087.09	087.09
087.13	087.18	087.22	087.28	087.29
087.30	087.35	088.04	088.04	088.08
088.14	088.22	088.26	088.28	088.30
088.31	088.36	089.02	089.06	089.07
089.08	089.10	089.11	089.12	089.14
089.17	089.17	089.23	089.25	089.25
089.32	089.32	089.33	090.01	090.04
090.17	090.18	090.19	090.25	090.26
090.27	090.27	090.33	091.03	091.08
091.10	091.12	091.13	091.14	091.26
091.28	091.28	091.34	091.35	092.02
092.09	092.13	092.13	092.32	093.02
093.06	093.15	093.16	093.27	094.01
094.09	094.12	094.17	094.17	094.24
094.25	094.36	095.01	095.03	095.04
095.05	095.07	095.13	095.13	095.18
095.21	095.22	095.22	095.23	095.24
095.25	095.26	096.04	096.07	096.17
096.19	096.25	096.27	096.31	096.36
097.01	097.06	097.09	097.14	097.22
097.26	097.31	097.33	098.09	098.24
098.27	099.04	099.12	099.12	099.22
099.24	099.28	099.30	099.31	100.02
100.04	100.04	100.05	100.08	100.11
100.14	100.15	100.19	100.21	100.22
100.23	100.23	100.27	100.32	101.03
101.05	101.08	101.14	101.15	101.19
101.21	101.21	101.24	101.25	101.28
101.30	101.30	101.33	101.35	102.02
102.11	102.16	102.20	102.22	102.22
102.26	102.26	102.27	102.29	102.33
102.34	102.34	102.36	103.01	103.09
103.11	103.12	103.12	103.13	103.17
103.20	103.21	103.22	103.28	103.30
103.31	104.01	104.06	104.08	104.14
104.23	104.27	104.28	104.32	104.34
104.34	105.04	105.13	105.19	105.20
105.21	105.26	105.30	105.30	105.32
105.32	106.09	106.11	106.13	106.22
106.29	106.30	106.31	106.33	107.01
107.02	107.03	107.04	107.09	107.13
107.16	107.22	107.23	107.25	107.27
107.28	107.35	107.36	108.10	108.14
108.20	108.23	108.27	108.29	108.31
108.33	109.02	109.04	109.07	109.12

OF   (CONTINUED)

109.12	109.13	109.18	109.29	109.31
109.33	109.36	110.08	110.14	110.15
110.18	111.06	111.12	111.13	111.15
111.16	111.22	111.23	111.31	111.32
111.33	111.34	112.03	112.05	112.07
112.11	112.12	112.12	112.14	112.15
112.17	112.25	112.29	113.01	113.19
113.26	113.27	113.27	113.28	113.33
113.34	114.03	114.16	114.17	114.25
114.29	114.30	114.32	114.34	114.35
115.01	115.02	115.05	115.10	115.14
115.17	115.21	115.22	115.23	115.26
115.29	116.07	116.17	116.20	116.26
116.31	116.32	116.33	117.02	117.02
117.03	117.04	117.21	117.23	117.26
117.28	117.32	118.05	118.06	118.14
118.16	118.18	118.21	118.22	118.23
118.32	119.02	119.03	119.04	119.05
119.08	119.11	119.12	119.22	119.22
119.23	119.24	119.25	119.29	119.31
119.36	120.02	120.06	120.07	120.08
120.11	120.12	120.14	120.15	120.16
120.19	120.31	120.33	120.33	121.01
121.02	121.07	121.09	121.10	121.13
121.17	121.28	121.31	121.33	121.36
121.37	122.03	122.06	122.10	122.35
122.36	123.07	123.09	123.11	123.14
123.15	123.18	123.19	123.20	123.22
123.24	123.28	123.30	123.32	123.33
123.34	124.02	124.04	124.04	124.07
124.21	124.22	124.24	124.26	124.28
124.30	124.32	124.33	124.34	124.35
125.01	125.02	125.10	125.11	125.16
125.17	125.19	125.31	126.01	126.01
126.03	126.05	126.06	126.08	126.09
126.13	126.18	126.22	126.28	126.29
127.01	127.04	127.06	127.09	127.09
127.10	127.13	127.18	127.18	127.20
127.22	127.23	127.31	127.33	127.33
127.35	128.05	128.14	128.15	128.17
129.06	129.06	129.11	129.24	129.26
129.27	129.29	129.35	129.35	130.02
130.05	130.05	130.06	130.07	130.14
130.17	130.19	130.20	130.30	130.34
130.36	131.08	131.12	131.17	131.24
131.29	131.32	131.34	131.36	132.01
132.02	132.06	132.07	132.10	132.10
132.12	132.18	132.19	132.21	133.03
133.10	133.11	133.15	133.17	133.23
133.28	133.30	133.31	133.32	133.33
133.33	134.03	134.09	134.15	134.16
134.16	134.19	134.24	134.27	134.29
134.32	134.34	135.08	135.09	135.11
135.12	135.12	135.13	135.14	135.15
135.16	135.17	135.20	135.28	135.30
135.30	135.35	136.03	136.09	136.13
136.15	136.26	136.28	136.29	136.29
137.01	137.04	137.08	137.12	137.24
137.24	137.26	137.34	138.01	138.06
138.07	138.07	138.23	138.23	138.23
138.25	138.27	138.28	138.29	138.31
138.35	138.35	138.36	139.03	139.04
139.05	139.06	139.07	140.07	140.18
140.21	140.21	140.31	140.35	141.03
141.04	141.21	141.25	141.26	142.03
142.06	142.06	142.13	142.22	142.25
142.29	142.30	142.30	143.01	143.02
143.10	143.11	143.12	143.12	143.17
143.18	143.20	143.30	143.33	144.01
144.07	144.07	144.10	144.19	144.30
144.31	144.32	144.34	145.15	145.16
145.27	146.05	146.10	146.14	146.18
146.20	147.09	147.10	147.25	147.28
147.30	147.36	148.11	148.16	148.20
148.21	148.24	148.27	148.28	148.30
148.32	149.04	149.06	149.06	149.07
149.10	149.16	149.27	150.02	150.03

```
150.05  150.06  150.15  150.15  150.16
150.22  150.23  150.29  150.30  150.31
150.35  151.01  151.07  151.08  151.09
151.09  151.27  151.32  151.33  151.36
152.08  152.10  152.14  152.14  152.25
152.27  152.28  152.29  152.30  152.31
152.32  152.32  153.01  153.01  153.05
153.05  153.06  153.12  153.12  153.13
153.19  153.22  153.23  153.24  153.25
153.31  154.01  155.03  155.08  155.14
155.18  155.19  155.25  155.26  155.34
156.07  156.08  156.08  156.11  156.14
156.15  156.26  157.06  157.08  157.10
157.11  157.12  157.19  157.19  157.21
157.22  157.23  157.29  157.34  158.06
158.07  158.19  158.21  158.30  158.33
158.35  158.36  159.01  159.02  159.03
159.04  159.14  159.19  159.23  159.26
159.27  159.29  159.30  159.35  160.02
160.05  160.07  160.09  160.11  160.11
160.14  160.15  160.19  160.23  160.27
160.28  160.32  161.01  161.06  161.06
161.08  161.09  161.16  161.19  161.22
161.26  161.35  162.04  162.08  162.13
162.21  162.25  162.29  162.32  162.35
163.16  163.24  163.26  163.28  163.35
164.09  164.24  164.26  164.32  165.02
165.08  165.18  165.29  165.29  165.30
165.34  165.34  165.35  165.37  166.02
166.07  166.07  166.11  166.14  166.16
166.17  166.23  166.25  166.28  166.29
166.35  167.05  167.06  167.09  167.13
167.14  167.16  167.18  167.19  167.21
167.22  168.02  168.09  168.13  168.15
168.17  168.20  168.21  168.35  169.05
169.06  169.06  169.12  169.13  169.20
169.23  169.34  169.36  170.06  170.12
170.19  170.20  170.25  170.31  171.05
171.10  171.14  171.15  171.19  171.20
171.24  171.26  171.36  172.07  172.08
172.12  172.13  172.14  172.17  172.18
172.34  172.35  173.03  173.06  173.08
173.11  173.14  173.19  173.28  173.30
173.31  173.33  174.01  174.06  174.10
174.12  174.19  174.23  174.29  174.34
174.36  175.03  175.04  175.09  175.11
175.12  175.25  175.33  176.01  176.04
176.12  176.17  176.20  176.21  176.23
176.23  176.24  176.25  176.27  176.28
176.30  176.33  176.34  176.34  176.36
177.03  177.05  177.07  177.14  177.16
177.18  177.19  177.20  177.22  177.23
177.25  177.26  177.27  177.28  177.29
177.29  177.34  177.36  178.08  178.10
178.13  178.15  178.21  178.23  178.23
178.28  178.32  179.06  179.12  179.13
179.14  179.19  179.22  179.23  179.26
179.27  179.28  179.32  179.35  180.04
180.05  180.07  180.08  180.11  180.15
180.16  180.26  180.35  181.02  181.02
181.10  181.18  181.19  181.28  181.28
181.35  181.35  182.02  182.03  182.04
182.16  182.25  182.31  182.33  182.33
182.35  183.03  183.11  183.14  183.15
183.17  183.17  183.18  183.19  183.20
183.24  183.30  183.31  183.31  183.32
183.33  183.35  184.02  184.05  184.06
184.08  184.09  184.15  184.31  184.31
184.32  185.08  185.10  185.14  185.16
185.21  185.25  185.33  186.08  186.09
186.14  186.19  186.22  186.23  186.25
187.05  187.15  187.19  187.25  187.33
187.34  188.05  188.08  188.09  188.10
188.10  188.11  188.11  188.12  188.13
188.16  188.17  188.23  188.34  189.03
189.06  189.09  189.12  189.13  189.14
189.17  189.18  189.28  189.29  189.30
```

```
189.36  190.01  190.14  190.16  190.18
190.23  190.32  191.02  191.02  191.08
191.09  191.09  191.22  191.27  191.28
192.01  192.04  192.08  192.13  192.16
192.20  192.20  192.27  192.28  192.30
193.06  193.14  193.22  193.28  193.38
194.06  194.08  194.15  194.20  194.27
194.32  194.33  195.07  195.08  195.09
195.13  195.14  195.20  195.21  195.23
195.27  195.32  195.36  196.01  196.08
196.12  196.26  196.35  196.36  197.01
197.03  197.09  197.10  197.12  197.19
197.20  197.22  197.22  197.24  197.26
197.28  197.30  198.02  198.02  198.07
198.09  198.09  198.09  198.10  198.11
198.12  198.16  198.16  198.18  198.25
198.31  198.35  199.01  199.02  199.10
199.13  199.18  199.22  199.22  199.25
199.28  199.32  200.03  200.05  201.11
201.14  201.18  201.23  201.24  201.26
201.26  201.27  201.32  201.33  202.04
202.05  202.07  202.11  202.12  202.14
202.18  202.19  202.20  202.25  202.26
202.34  203.06  203.07  203.07  203.17
203.19  203.21  203.29  204.12  204.13
204.14  204.15  204.16  204.17  204.18
204.20  204.24  204.27  204.30  204.35
204.36  205.04  205.08  205.10  205.18
205.25  205.29  205.33  205.36  206.01
206.36  207.01  207.24  208.01  208.19
208.20  208.22  208.34  210.04  210.05
210.06  210.12  210.29  210.31  210.35
211.01  211.06  211.12  211.15  211.17
211.19  211.22  211.23  211.27  211.30
212.03  212.05  212.07  212.09  212.12
212.12  212.17  212.17  212.17  212.20
212.23  212.24  212.31  212.37  213.02
213.05  213.12  213.13  213.16  213.17
213.19  213.28  213.29  213.32  213.33
213.36  214.04  214.06  214.27  214.29
214.32  215.03  215.06  215.06  215.08
215.12  215.13  215.24  215.29  216.05
216.08  216.08  216.14  216.19  216.34
217.01  217.02  217.08  217.11  217.11
217.11  217.12  217.12  217.16  217.27
217.29  217.36  218.04  218.07  218.10
218.11  218.23  218.31  218.36  219.02
219.07  219.09  219.15  219.17  219.24
219.28  219.32  220.01  220.04  220.08
220.12  220.22  220.30  220.32  220.36
220.40  221.09  221.09  221.12  221.14
221.15  221.17  221.17  221.19  221.19
221.21  221.27  222.02  222.03  222.06
222.06  222.10  222.11  222.12  222.19
222.21  223.05  223.05  223.06  223.17
223.23  223.24  223.26  223.34  224.07
224.12  224.13  224.19  224.21  224.22
224.24  224.28  224.32  224.34  224.36
225.03  225.15  225.19  225.20  225.26
225.33  226.04  226.12  226.14  226.19
226.20  226.25  227.03  227.05  227.08
227.23  227.27  227.32  227.32  227.35
227.35  228.04  228.17  228.19  228.25
228.27  228.35  229.01  229.17  229.21
229.21  229.26  229.26  229.29  229.34
229.36  230.03  230.05  230.13  230.15
230.22  230.26  230.28  230.28  230.36
231.02  231.04  231.08  231.10  231.13
231.15  231.19  231.22  231.23  231.25
231.27  231.28  231.32  231.34  231.35
231.36  232.01  232.05  232.06  232.07
232.10  232.10  232.14  232.22  232.23
232.24  232.35  233.07  233.15  233.16
233.19  233.21  233.27  233.32  233.36
234.07  234.09  234.13  234.21  234.30
234.34  235.02  235.06  235.10  235.16
236.02  236.09  236.12  236.17  236.18
```

236.21	236.22	236.24	236.24	236.28
236.32	237.05	237.05	237.07	238.07
238.11	238.13	238.13	238.14	238.14
238.15	238.18	238.22	238.25	238.26
238.34	238.35	239.03	239.07	239.07
239.11	239.14	239.16	239.18	239.20
239.23	239.24	239.25	239.26	239.29
239.31	239.33	239.33	239.34	239.35
239.36	240.02	240.03	240.05	240.07
240.07	240.15	240.16	240.24	240.26
241.01	241.01	241.03	241.07	241.08
241.08	241.08	241.09	241.10	241.12
241.15	241.22	241.24	241.27	241.32
242.04	242.08	242.11	242.15	242.26
242.28	242.33	243.03	243.09	243.10
243.11	243.12	243.13	243.14	243.16
243.18	243.22	243.26	243.27	243.34
243.36	244.16	244.17	244.19	244.24
244.32	244.34	245.05	245.09	245.10
245.18	245.19	245.23	245.26	245.35
246.05	246.07	246.07	246.08	246.21
246.27	246.28	246.28	246.29	246.31
246.35	247.04	247.07	247.12	247.14
247.20	247.21	247.24	247.31	248.05
248.08	248.09	248.09	248.11	248.15
248.17	248.29	248.34	248.34	249.01
249.03	249.03	249.06	249.07	249.07
249.09	249.10	249.13	249.23	249.24
249.24	249.26	249.27	249.27	249.28
249.35	250.09	250.09	250.10	250.12
250.14	250.16	250.16	250.17	250.23
250.26	250.35	251.01	251.03	251.03
251.05	251.06	251.09	251.11	251.16
251.18	251.21	251.26	251.28	251.31
251.32	252.05	252.06	252.07	252.14
252.18	252.20	252.24	252.26	252.31
252.34	253.02	253.19	253.21	253.22
253.25	253.30	253.32	253.33	253.33
253.34	254.04	254.06	254.18	254.24
254.26	255.10	256.07	256.14	256.17
256.18	256.18	256.20	256.25	256.28
256.34	257.01	257.04	257.05	257.06
257.16	257.17	257.18	257.20	257.24
257.29	257.34	258.04	258.07	258.09
258.12	258.13	258.16	258.16	258.18
258.20	258.23	258.23	258.24	258.29
259.05	259.07	259.14	259.15	259.18
259.28	259.31	259.34	259.35	260.01
260.15	260.20	260.21	260.28	260.29
260.32	261.09	261.13	261.23	261.26
261.21	261.27	261.34	262.04	262.06
262.06	262.08	262.11	262.11	262.18
262.19	262.21	262.22	262.27	262.32
262.33	262.34	263.01	263.11	263.13
263.13	263.14	263.16	263.19	263.21
263.21	263.29	263.30	263.32	264.05
264.16	264.18	264.19	264.25	265.03
265.05	265.09	265.10	265.21	265.21
265.22	265.23	265.24	265.33	266.04
266.05	266.06	266.14	266.17	266.27
266.30	267.02	267.03	267.05	267.10
267.15	267.18	267.19	267.20	267.22
267.22	267.24	267.25	267.26	267.27
267.28	267.29	268.07	268.11	268.13
268.14	268.14	268.22	268.22	268.27
268.28	268.29	268.34	269.01	269.01
269.05	269.08	269.11	269.15	269.17
269.22	269.26	269.28	269.30	270.05
270.11	270.11	270.21	270.22	270.23
271.04	271.09	271.10	271.20	271.23
271.29	271.34	272.03	272.10	272.12
272.13	272.20	272.23	272.24	272.25
272.29	272.31	272.33	272.34	273.01
273.04	273.07	273.21	273.21	273.22
273.23	273.23	273.25	273.34	274.04
274.05	274.06	274.10	274.14	274.17
274.23	274.27	274.30	275.06	275.12

275.30	275.31	275.33	276.01	276.11
276.13	276.23	276.31	276.33	276.33
277.01	277.06	277.22	277.24	278.03
278.05	278.10	278.11	278.19	279.22
279.23	279.28	279.33	279.34	280.07
280.10	280.11	280.16	280.18	280.22
280.33	280.35	281.08	281.14	281.20
281.21	281.27	282.11	282.16	282.18
282.20	282.22	282.25	282.27	283.01
283.01	283.03	283.04	283.08	283.28
283.30	283.33	284.03	284.11	284.13
284.18	284.31	284.32	285.04	285.06
285.09	285.13	285.16	285.20	285.23
285.25	285.26	285.29	287.09	287.11
287.28	287.29	287.33	288.04	288.06
288.10	288.10	288.15	288.16	288.17
288.18	288.22	288.24	288.27	288.37
289.01	289.02	289.03	289.10	289.15
289.17	289.17	289.18	289.20	289.23
289.24	289.25	289.26	289.28	289.31
290.08	290.08	290.09	290.12	290.12
290.16	290.18	290.20	290.23	290.24
290.27	290.28	290.29	290.32	290.35
290.36	291.04	291.05	291.05	291.08
291.08	291.09	291.11	291.20	291.21
291.26	291.26	291.28	291.35	292.04
292.04	292.05	292.05	292.08	292.23
292.24	292.30	292.32	293.03	293.04
293.08	293.08	293.11	293.11	293.12
293.14	293.19	293.21	293.30	293.30
294.03	294.07	294.24	294.16	294.17
294.18	294.24	294.24	294.31	294.33
294.33	295.01	295.02	295.10	295.11
295.15	295.19	295.19	295.29	295.31
295.33	295.35	296.01	296.01	296.13
296.15	296.16	296.19	296.24	296.26
296.33	296.34	296.35	296.35	297.02
297.03	297.03	297.05	297.08	297.14
297.21	297.22	297.23	297.23	297.24
297.35	297.36	298.03	298.04	298.07
298.10	298.11	298.13	298.17	298.18
298.19	298.20	298.21	298.22	298.22
299.03	299.08	299.10	299.13	299.13
299.15	299.19	299.20	299.21	299.22
299.23	299.25	299.25	299.27	299.30
299.31	299.32	300.03	300.09	300.12
300.20	300.29	300.31	300.33	301.03
301.09	301.11	301.12	301.16	301.19
301.25	301.27	301.27	301.31	302.07
302.19	302.19	302.22	302.22	303.01
303.02	303.02	303.03	303.03	303.04
303.04	303.05	303.06	303.08	303.13
303.13	303.14	303.19	303.20	303.21
303.26	303.30	303.31	303.33	303.36
304.09	304.09	304.12	304.12	304.25
304.26	304.30	304.33	304.34	304.36
304.36	304.36	305.07	305.08	305.09
305.10	305.11	305.13	305.14	305.14
305.15	305.15	305.17	305.23	305.27
305.33	305.35	305.35	306.02	306.03
306.03	306.04	306.09	306.10	306.13
306.14	306.16	306.17	306.24	306.29
306.29	306.32	306.33	307.03	307.06
307.10	307.14	307.15	307.22	307.27
307.27	307.31	307.31	307.33	308.02
308.04	308.06	308.08	308.09	308.11
308.16	308.16	308.17	308.21	308.23
308.26	308.26	308.29	308.29	308.34
309.01	309.02	309.04	309.13	309.18
309.23	309.25	309.26	310.02	310.06
310.07	310.08	310.23	310.11	310.12
310.13	310.22	310.23	310.27	310.32
311.03	311.04	311.07	311.09	311.10
311.18	311.23	311.24	311.29	311.30
311.31	311.31	311.32	311.33	312.06
312.07	312.11	312.18	312.19	312.28

OF   (CONTINUED)
312.30   312.34   313.05   313.09   313.09
313.11   313.14   313.15   313.18   313.20
313.26   313.29   313.31   313.32   313.34
313.34   313.35   313.35   314.11   314.12
314.16   314.19   314.21   314.23   314.25
314.31   314.34   314.39   314.40   315.01
315.08   315.15   315.16   315.16   315.17
315.18   315.20   315.20   315.23   315.25
315.26   315.28   315.28   315.29   315.30
315.31   315.32   316.05   316.19   316.20
316.23   316.27   316.29   316.30   316.36
317.07   317.09   317.10   317.10   317.14
317.16   317.17   317.23   317.30   318.02
318.03   318.14   318.16   318.17   318.21
318.26   318.27   319.01   319.02   319.10
319.14   319.14   319.15   319.15   320.04
320.07   320.11   320.18   320.19   320.20
320.23   320.23   320.25   321.04   321.11
321.12   321.17   321.18   321.18   321.19
321.25   321.27   321.34   322.06   322.06
322.14   322.14   322.17   322.20   322.30
322.32   322.35   323.02   323.04   323.07
323.08   323.20   323.21   323.23   323.24
323.26   323.30   324.02   324.02   324.04
324.14   324.20   324.21   324.31   324.31
324.33   325.01   325.02   325.10   325.14
325.16   325.18   325.18   325.20   325.28
325.30   326.02   326.13   326.17   326.20
326.28   326.32   326.35   327.02   327.03
327.04   327.05   327.06   327.06   327.14
327.14   327.15   327.19   327.21   327.23
327.24   327.30   328.12   328.17   328.17
328.28   328.31   329.01   329.04   329.16
329.17   329.18   329.19   329.21   329.21
329.25   329.28   329.28   329.29   329.29
329.29   329.35   330.02   330.04   330.07
330.20   330.23   330.29   330.32   331.03
331.04   331.04   331.05   331.06   331.06
331.22   331.23   331.25   331.25   331.27
331.28   331.33   331.35   331.36   332.03
332.16   332.18   332.20   332.23   332.31
332.31   332.32   332.33   333.06   333.07
333.08   333.08   333.08   333.15   333.16
333.19   333.19   333.20   333.22   333.24
333.29   333.30
OFF   (110)
013.01   019.07   024.16   026.12   032.16
033.15   035.34   041.22   042.28   047.34
056.11   056.13   061.19   062.04   066.11
072.17   075.26   077.12   078.28   081.28
082.11   082.27   086.09   086.14   086.33
088.01   090.03   097.17   105.32   108.35
109.03   114.16   115.05   115.28   116.08
117.07   117.21   118.12   122.16   128.16
128.16   130.03   130.07   146.08   146.18
150.33   155.07   163.33   163.36   170.18
173.20   178.15   180.11   183.36   184.35
187.25   188.26   190.33   192.23   198.16
199.24   216.09   216.10   219.06   221.29
222.11   223.34   225.09   225.10   226.20
228.14   231.17   232.21   233.14   234.15
236.06   236.11   236.23   237.03   243.19
244.10   244.27   249.01   260.25   265.14
266.23   274.29   275.05   275.12   277.13
279.05   281.01   281.28   291.19   291.32
292.02   294.08   294.12   294.32   295.26
296.27   296.35   300.31   302.27   302.33
304.16   304.27   305.34   311.19   313.06
OFFENCE   (1)
142.12
OFFENCES   (1)
007.06
OFFEND   (1)
215.20
OFFENSIVE   (1)
221.22

OFFER   (8)
019.28   040.18   072.33   075.08   094.09
134.23   224.27   224.32
OFFERED   (8)
062.16   067.20   075.30   082.14   094.10
145.20   270.01   279.10
OFFERING   (2)
150.32   250.30
OFFERS   (6)
010.23   021.09   109.27   160.03   246.19
315.13
OFFICE   (6)
094.03   118.04   122.06   133.20   136.18
168.14
OFFICERS   (2)
018.32   076.14
OFFICES   (2)
004.16   094.24
OFTEN   (50)
006.20   009.35   016.01   020.18   020.32
022.15   023.21   024.14   030.03   034.03
035.06   066.12   069.28   075.17   077.11
094.10   111.21   115.19   118.11   124.10
140.16   142.14   145.18   151.14   167.35
170.35   171.15   187.13   193.35   194.24
210.30   226.26   227.12   227.13   234.07
239.10   252.08   256.28   261.18   265.25
270.22   271.07   271.33   288.16   297.04
297.22   322.38   328.16   329.03   329.19
OFTENER   (6)
021.23   084.12   211.19   247.10   320.20
328.20
OFTENEST   (1)
212.36
OH   (2)
124.36   206.27
OHIO   (1)
320.09
OIL   (4)
060.05   060.18   065.22   243.06
OLAUS   (1)
232.03
OLD   (109)
005.27   007.14   008.29   008.30   008.30
008.31   008.35   009.04   010.07   010.34
011.36   023.15   023.16   023.24   023.24
023.33   023.36   024.02   024.03   024.26
025.28   026.08   035.07   038.33   044.34
049.11   052.30   056.01   065.11   066.31
068.18   084.07   094.21   095.12   100.36
105.25   115.18   119.27   122.01   126.14
127.34   136.14   137.21   137.24   138.03
138.21   138.36   142.22   145.06   153.21
155.31   164.16   166.04   180.04   182.18
183.29   190.26   190.31   191.03   191.08
192.14   198.26   199.07   204.20   208.39
213.24   223.33   226.20   232.15   240.09
241.02   241.07   242.26   244.29   249.16
250.13   250.26   251.29   252.12   255.10
257.11   257.28   258.01   258.02   258.15
258.19   258.25   262.15   263.15   265.30
269.02   270.05   277.10   277.33   278.06
278.30   279.22   279.29   296.14   297.13
299.08   303.14   322.20   323.36   326.30
327.17   328.25   330.21   333.08
OLDER   (10)
023.18   103.36   156.01   173.30   241.11
241.27   243.22   310.07   326.31   331.06
OLDEST   (6)
099.11   102.35   120.25   155.34   182.11
264.22
OLEARIAM   (1)
243.04
OLERACEA   (1)
061.20
OLIT   (3)
311.20   311.20   311.20

```
OLIVE                        (    1)     ON                                    (CONTINUED)
  109.32                                    179.07   179.09   179.18   180.01   180.08
OLIVES                       (    1)       180.25   180.25   180.28   181.01   181.27
  047.36                                    181.35   182.32   182.34   183.16   183.24
OLYMPUS                      (    1)       183.33   184.14   184.20   185.07   185.19
  085.13                                    186.04   186.05   186.18   186.28   187.02
OMIT                         (    4)       187.09   187.15   187.30   187.33   187.35
  063.10   100.36   110.16   212.06         187.35   188.01   188.07   188.23   188.31
OMITTED                      (    3)       189.01   189.04   189.05   189.33   190.02
  003.24   063.01   108.06                  190.16   190.21   190.32   191.11   191.16
OMNIPRESENT                  (    2)       191.17   191.20   191.25   191.31   192.13
  217.31   233.34                           192.24   192.36   193.02   194.04   194.07
ON                           (  679)       194.26   194.28   195.03   195.06   195.16
  003.06   003.10   003.31   004.06   004.28   195.17   195.29   196.23   197.09   197.28
  004.28   005.14   006.24   006.36   007.25   198.28   199.02   199.03   199.09   199.21
  008.29   009.10   009.19   010.01   011.12   201.23   201.27   202.17   205.32   208.10
  011.25   012.04   015.26   017.03   017.03   210.22   210.34   210.35   211.20   212.07
  017.10   017.12   018.02   018.28   018.36   212.29   213.21   216.02   218.06   218.32
  020.07   021.08   021.12   021.34   022.24   219.01   219.07   220.08   221.02   221.36
  022.28   023.26   023.27   024.23   025.16   222.04   223.24   223.28   225.35   226.15
  025.20   025.23   026.01   026.05   026.05   226.30   226.30   226.35   226.36   227.18
  026.26   027.14   027.18   027.30   030.29   228.03   228.31   229.06   229.07   229.07
  031.27   031.35   032.09   032.27   032.33   229.16   229.20   229.25   229.35   230.09
  033.08   033.14   034.26   034.26   034.29   230.19   230.26   230.30   230.32   231.09
  035.17   036.26   036.31   037.04   037.04   231.33   232.22   232.27   233.08   233.28
  037.12   037.13   037.14   037.28   038.04   233.28   233.32   233.33   234.14   234.18
  038.13   038.16   038.18   039.34   040.23   235.05   235.10   235.24   235.28   236.24
  041.04   041.07   041.14   041.14   041.26   236.30   237.05   238.23   239.07   239.35
  042.01   042.06   042.19   042.20   042.20   240.12   240.13   241.02   241.10   241.16
  043.02   043.35   044.01   044.08   044.28   241.36   242.15   242.28   243.11   243.23
  045.10   045.18   045.26   047.10   048.30   243.26   243.28   244.28   245.21   246.20
  049.20   049.29   050.19   051.34   052.02   246.21   246.26   247.14   248.19   248.34
  052.13   053.11   053.12   054.27   054.28   249.03   249.14   249.29   249.30   249.36
  055.18   055.20   055.30   056.05   058.18   249.36   250.08   250.11   251.14   251.30
  058.21   059.06   060.32   060.34   061.05   251.35   252.18   253.12   253.13   253.26
  061.19   061.22   062.03   063.30   064.01   254.10   254.12   256.27   256.34   257.25
  064.04   064.35   065.01   065.03   065.08   257.26   257.33   257.33   258.03   258.13
  065.08   065.24   067.23   068.25   068.29   258.15   258.15   258.23   258.23   259.05
  069.22   070.34   071.07   075.09   075.22   259.07   259.16   259.33   260.02   260.22
  075.33   075.34   076.01   076.23   077.35   261.10   261.22   261.31   262.17   264.23
  079.15   081.06   081.11   081.13   081.17   264.24   265.35   265.35   266.01   266.04
  082.11   083.08   083.24   083.25   083.34   266.19   266.21   266.30   267.19   267.20
  084.24   084.28   085.04   085.23   086.11   267.25   267.32   269.10   269.11   269.32
  086.12   086.21   087.05   087.23   088.31   270.08   271.24   271.26   273.13   273.15
  091.27   092.25   092.28   092.32   093.14   273.24   274.01   274.04   275.15   275.36
  093.22   093.33   093.35   094.15   095.22   276.12   276.15   276.17   276.20   276.28
  096.08   097.18   098.12   099.16   099.25   277.01   277.15   278.07   278.12   278.26
  099.26   099.32   101.26   102.07   102.19   278.28   279.08   279.17   280.02   281.08
  102.25   102.36   103.06   104.19   104.24   282.08   282.10   282.11   282.33   283.18
  105.06   107.09   107.18   107.35   108.09   283.19   284.19   285.20   287.11   288.20
  108.33   108.34   109.15   109.19   109.21   288.32   289.15   289.34   290.16   291.18
  110.07   111.13   111.19   111.32   112.09   292.02   292.23   293.01   293.02   293.03
  113.01   113.02   113.03   113.09   113.16   293.09   293.09   293.31   293.13   293.18
  113.17   113.19   113.26   113.26   114.02   293.30   293.31   293.31   294.17   294.36
  114.08   114.27   115.16   115.32   116.29   295.06   295.26   295.28   295.35   296.03
  117.08   117.19   117.25   118.09   118.20   297.21   297.26   298.12   299.07   299.10
  118.23   119.02   119.36   120.13   120.14   299.17   299.25   300.06   300.33   301.04
  121.14   121.21   122.04   123.01   124.01   301.17   301.30   302.18   302.22   303.01
  125.01   125.03   125.04   125.13   125.31   303.25   303.32   303.34   304.15   304.22
  127.16   127.19   127.27   128.01   128.02   304.30   304.31   304.32   305.12   305.36
  128.06   129.11   129.27   129.33   130.20   306.04   306.07   306.07   306.08   306.12
  130.21   130.22   131.20   133.01   133.30   307.03   308.02   308.32   309.16   309.16
  134.25   134.25   134.26   135.04   135.05   310.34   311.07   311.20   311.32   312.12
  136.15   138.01   138.13   139.01   141.10   313.08   314.19   314.23   316.03   316.07
  141.33   142.23   142.31   143.02   143.03   316.19   316.21   317.01   317.17   318.10
  143.07   144.11   144.18   146.22   146.30   318.20   318.26   318.36   318.36   319.08
  146.32   147.14   147.29   148.30   149.10   319.16   320.14   321.02   322.13   322.23
  149.28   151.01   151.15   151.28   152.14   322.26   323.26   324.23   324.35   325.26
  152.19   153.27   155.21   155.34   156.23   326.16   327.03   327.09   327.24   327.36
  156.25   157.17   157.21   158.28   158.28   328.36   329.04   329.13   329.14   330.02
  159.18   159.19   159.19   159.36   160.04   330.10   330.27   330.33   331.09   331.14
  160.25   161.34   162.14   164.20   165.07   331.23   332.04   332.08   332.11
  165.10   166.08   166.09   167.10   167.25   ONCE                                   (   88)
  167.27   168.03   168.28   169.04   170.16     008.32   010.15   014.35   019.32   020.12
  171.36   172.11   173.09   173.18   173.26     021.22   021.31   029.26   032.29   051.14
  174.01   174.07   174.10   174.24   175.25     054.09   054.30   058.23   059.36   065.02
  176.02   176.08   177.08   177.13   177.26     067.20   076.22   078.01   084.03   084.12
  178.07   178.10   178.11   178.12   178.29     102.20   109.30   110.07   113.25   117.18
```

153

```
ONCE                          (CONTINUED)        ONE                          (CONTINUED)
117.26  118.07  120.24  124.07  124.30           220.32  221.01  221.01  221.17  221.34
126.23  127.05  131.29  132.04  140.16           222.04  224.13  224.18  225.02  225.09
147.01  149.22  162.17  165.23  167.26           225.24  225.26  225.35  226.36  228.26
169.01  171.12  173.35  178.04  182.23           228.28  228.29  228.36  229.07  229.17
188.04  190.15  191.04  193.01  193.38           229.19  230.23  231.32  232.35  233.31
193.39  201.35  202.10  210.09  220.03           234.16  234.20  235.03  235.31  236.23
221.32  226.35  228.30  232.23  232.30           238.31  239.05  241.03  242.34  243.16
235.01  235.24  239.19  239.22  244.02           243.19  243.27  243.36  244.22  244.33
245.27  251.31  252.23  256.12  256.25           245.10  245.28  247.11  247.17  247.28
256.30  257.35  258.17  258.34  261.10           247.35  249.33  249.35  253.09  256.08
263.08  263.15  263.26  276.02  277.15           257.17  257.28  257.30  258.03  258.28
277.34  294.34  301.24  304.09  307.09           259.01  259.06  259.23  260.05  260.11
313.08  319.06  325.12                           261.22  262.07  262.23  266.02  266.04
ONE                                              266.35  267.24  267.35  268.19  268.22
004.28  005.01  005.19  006.26  007.22           270.13  272.09  272.29  273.02  273.16
009.02  009.19  010.21  011.01  011.18           273.30  274.09  274.25  274.29  274.33
011.23  012.14  017.15  019.19  019.24           275.36  277.13  277.25  277.33  277.36
019.25  024.27  025.30  026.26  027.15           278.35  278.36  279.16  279.32  280.01
028.30  029.12  030.13  030.14  030.21           280.12  280.26  280.35  281.03  281.03
030.34  031.21  032.21  032.25  033.03           281.22  281.25  283.23  285.18  287.05
034.06  034.25  034.26  035.16  035.32           287.07  287.21  288.32  288.33  288.35
035.32  038.22  040.03  040.12  041.22           290.10  290.17  290.19  290.24  290.24
042.20  043.04  044.01  044.09  044.20           291.01  292.14  292.26  293.01  293.30
045.09  045.14  045.21  046.25  048.13           293.31  294.18  294.31  295.33  296.03
048.31  049.11  049.31  049.33  050.09           296.35  300.02  301.12  302.10  302.34
051.07  052.03  052.26  053.03  054.04           303.14  303.23  305.07  306.04  306.04
054.26  055.31  056.05  056.10  056.31           306.07  306.08  307.04  307.22  308.15
057.30  059.25  059.26  060.15  060.32           309.22  311.34  315.17  315.19  318.20
061.15  062.32  063.26  064.31  065.22           319.17  320.25  320.30  321.33  321.34
065.22  065.35  066.02  067.01  067.08           322.31  323.08  323.13  323.30  324.14
067.10  068.19  070.27  070.32  070.34           325.20  326.04  326.21  327.03  328.31
071.04  071.07  071.11  071.21  071.23           328.33  329.16  330.23  331.17  331.34
071.24  071.24  071.24  071.30  072.07           333.05
072.11  072.34  073.01  073.04  073.18           ONES                                   ( 16 )
074.07  074.28  074.30  075.24  075.25           024.28  042.22  042.25  075.31  087.04
075.35  076.18  076.30  077.35  078.23           108.02  184.22  217.29  225.05  225.22
079.02  084.22  085.32  087.13  088.30           228.36  232.04  238.29  240.33  312.04
090.09  090.10  091.30  091.35  092.27           327.18
094.06  094.12  094.13  094.14  094.14           ONLY                                   ( 248 )
094.15  094.16  094.16  094.18  094.24           003.08  004.33  005.11  006.24  007.06
095.08  095.25  095.25  096.17  097.16           009.09  011.17  011.34  012.24  013.20
098.24  100.03  101.02  101.11  104.23           013.22  013.26  014.18  015.04  015.36
104.27  106.21  106.22  108.06  109.05           016.33  017.28  018.09  019.07  022.11
109.05  109.22  110.16  110.17  112.16           022.25  023.19  025.19  026.12  026.25
113.02  115.10  115.27  117.36  120.02           027.03  031.11  034.10  035.23  042.19
120.12  123.09  123.32  123.34  124.08           043.16  043.24  043.36  046.29  046.32
124.12  125.01  125.20  127.34  129.04           047.18  050.06  050.12  052.05  055.32
129.31  130.20  132.32  133.18  133.28           055.36  056.17  057.06  058.04  061.32
133.28  135.30  136.20  136.21  136.25           064.09  064.24  070.27  071.14  071.16
137.03  137.10  138.01  138.23  139.02           071.32  076.11  076.15  076.32  080.23
140.09  140.18  140.30  142.03  142.26           080.28  082.36  083.03  083.31  084.08
142.30  143.08  143.13  143.18  143.35           084.24  085.10  085.15  085.33  086.07
144.21  145.36  147.26  149.17  149.29           088.13  090.09  090.10  090.33  092.11
149.33  149.34  151.13  152.07  152.24           093.12  095.31  095.34  096.01  096.29
152.25  152.26  152.29  152.33  155.34           097.08  098.16  099.20  099.34  100.22
156.08  156.33  158.04  158.28  159.29           100.33  101.35  102.24  102.26  102.30
161.09  161.21  161.26  162.14  162.29           103.12  103.31  104.09  104.10  104.16
165.01  167.05  167.17  167.26  168.18           107.05  107.09  107.24  108.30  109.14
168.35  170.15  170.19  170.35  171.20           111.04  112.16  117.14  117.18  117.26
172.16  173.12  173.22  173.30  174.01           119.01  120.13  121.06  122.36  124.09
174.06  175.23  175.27  175.32  176.03           124.11  125.22  126.16  126.34  128.01
176.03  176.06  176.15  176.20  177.25           134.07  135.07  135.17  139.07  140.24
177.27  178.08  178.11  178.24  179.10           141.22  143.09  143.17  144.09  145.24
180.08  180.15  180.25  181.10  182.16           147.07  147.10  148.25  153.05  155.13
182.18  182.24  183.04  183.16  183.17           155.15  156.12  157.20  157.35  158.11
183.34  184.05  184.14  184.16  185.09           161.10  162.13  164.11  166.25  166.36
186.25  187.06  187.33  189.12  189.28           167.33  169.24  170.32  171.11  172.21
190.10  190.16  191.09  193.03  194.01           172.30  178.01  178.35  179.27  180.32
194.04  194.21  194.30  195.02  195.22           182.18  183.31  184.07  184.08  185.35
196.34  197.34  198.07  198.09  201.33           189.01  194.25  195.22  196.11  196.15
202.04  202.19  202.20  202.33  203.04           198.35  202.22  205.23  208.24  208.34
203.19  203.20  203.27  204.26  204.27           211.02  211.30  212.01  212.05  212.14
204.37  205.04  205.31  206.23  207.06           213.09  217.09  217.26  218.30  220.10
208.09  210.18  212.12  213.07  213.14           220.22  220.29  223.21  224.03  226.27
216.03  216.13  216.18  216.21  217.29           226.32  227.24  228.22  229.04  229.05
218.08  218.08  218.09  218.09  218.09           231.05  231.13  231.29  232.12  238.11
218.10  220.26  220.27  220.29  220.30           239.20  243.16  245.05  245.05  245.10
```

ONE (476)

ONLY (CONTINUED)
246.20	246.22	250.05	251.11	253.12
253.24	254.20	256.14	259.03	260.20
263.01	263.31	265.06	266.14	268.26
269.01	271.03	271.24	272.09	274.23
280.27	281.02	281.25	288.08	289.31
290.19	290.24	290.26	291.06	291.12
292.03	294.32	296.07	298.23	300.05
300.08	302.34	309.12	309.16	310.18
314.40	317.31	320.12	320.24	321.07
322.22	325.13	326.35	327.34	329.15
330.04	330.09	330.21	330.31	332.20
332.22	332.25	333.31		

ONTO (1)
105.07

OONK (4)
126.24 126.24 126.24 126.30

OOZED (1)
263.08

OOZES (1)
311.09

OOZING (1)
227.33

OPAQUE (2)
247.24 311.27

OPEN (31)
005.07	018.15	028.21	035.05	036.31
041.08	041.10	089.01	136.17	157.20
220.04	226.32	227.05	238.24	244.14
254.15	256.32	261.11	266.10	266.13
267.02	276.22	277.01	283.02	283.33
296.02	299.12	303.01	305.23	315.09
323.20				

OPENED (4)
243.30 270.09 272.05 280.36

OPENING (6)
169.30 172.11 263.13 299.03 299.22
321.17

OPENS (1)
299.15

OPERATE (2)
072.14 301.01

OPERATED (1)
248.18

OPERATIONS (4)
230.02 303.16 303.21 308.16

OPERATIVE (1)
064.28

OPERATIVES (3)
026.34 035.14 050.32

OPINION (9)
007.32 007.34 007.35 008.27 024.11
097.33 150.13 212.17 217.28

OPINIONS (3)
021.24 147.21 153.13

OPIUM (1)
217.07

OPORTET (1)
163.14

OPPORTUNITIES (2)
061.09 314.25

OPPORTUNITY (7)
124.05 213.17 225.02 230.01 246.18
246.33 302.11

OPPOSED (1)
308.08

OPPOSITE (16)
048.32 086.09 086.36 087.27 141.10
141.30 177.13 178.29 186.20 186.27
235.10 245.18 289.07 289.26 290.13
290.14

OPPOSITION (3)
322.31 323.01 323.08

OPPRESSED (1)
131.29

OR (818)
003.03 003.24 003.32 004.12 004.20
004.21 004.25 004.26 004.27 004.34

OR (CONTINUED)
004.35	005.37	006.31	006.32	006.33
007.08	007.10	007.10	007.11	007.11
007.14	007.15	007.16	007.25	007.36
008.24	008.25	009.12	011.10	011.31
011.36	012.10	012.12	012.12	012.17
012.31	013.13	013.13	013.20	014.03
014.11	014.28	014.32	014.32	014.32
016.06	016.16	016.18	016.25	016.26
017.01	017.15	017.25	018.01	018.01
018.22	019.15	019.16	019.28	019.29
020.15	021.32	022.06	022.11	023.28
023.34	023.36	024.01	024.15	024.18
024.19	024.34	026.02	026.06	026.10
026.12	026.25	026.36	027.25	027.30
028.06	028.15	028.27	028.34	029.19
030.02	030.12	030.13	031.16	032.08
032.18	032.20	034.06	034.12	035.13
035.15	035.17	035.19	035.19	035.34
035.34	036.11	036.16	037.22	037.23
038.05	038.06	038.23	039.14	039.17
039.20	039.32	040.12	040.15	040.15
040.21	040.21	040.21	040.22	041.28
042.05	042.08	042.23	044.10	045.26
046.34	047.05	048.06	048.13	048.19
050.17	050.18	050.32	050.36	051.11
051.22	051.24	051.26	051.27	051.33
052.20	053.15	054.18	056.04	056.04
056.04	056.06	056.09	056.12	056.27
056.29	057.03	057.05	057.09	057.15
057.23	057.23	058.15	062.03	063.13
063.13	064.02	064.08	064.19	065.12
065.34	066.21	066.25	067.15	067.21
067.34	067.35	068.08	068.09	069.15
069.34	070.03	070.13	070.13	070.14
070.14	070.19	070.27	071.12	071.13
071.14	071.14	071.17	072.11	073.31
074.03	074.26	074.27	075.01	076.13
077.36	078.31	078.33	079.03	079.07
079.14	079.15	079.19	080.07	080.08
080.09	080.17	081.33	082.11	082.17
082.18	082.18	082.20	083.22	083.27
084.06	084.28	084.31	085.03	085.10
085.36	086.16	087.10	087.25	088.09
088.10	088.10	089.26	090.01	090.11
090.21	090.28	091.09	091.13	091.23
091.25	091.26	092.17	092.18	092.27
093.22	094.06	094.13	094.13	094.13
094.14	094.14	094.15	094.16	094.16
094.28	095.01	096.33	096.33	096.33
096.34	097.11	097.13	097.19	098.07
098.07	098.07	098.15	099.07	099.08
099.08	099.11	099.18	100.03	100.07
100.08	101.23	102.03	102.25	103.05
104.15	104.24	104.26	105.28	105.28
105.28	105.29	105.34	106.04	106.08
106.20	106.24	106.24	106.33	107.13
107.16	107.33	108.34	109.05	109.20
109.32	111.13	111.14	111.15	111.15
111.18	111.23	111.29	111.31	112.10
114.06	114.27	115.26	116.08	116.21
116.26	117.19	117.19	117.30	118.27
119.01	119.36	120.10	120.12	120.21
120.27	121.01	121.09	122.09	122.13
122.37	123.02	124.01	124.07	124.33
125.23	125.24	127.35	127.36	128.04
128.04	128.05	128.07	128.15	128.16
129.27	129.27	129.28	129.31	129.34
129.35	130.01	130.01	130.02	130.04
130.05	130.23	130.26	130.27	131.28
132.22	132.35	132.36	133.21	134.01
134.03	135.03	135.26	135.32	135.33
137.05	137.13	137.14	137.14	137.14
137.15	137.16	137.16	137.16	137.17
137.17	137.18	137.27	137.29	138.18
140.15	140.26	140.26	140.34	141.21
142.05	142.18	144.14	144.29	145.22
146.07	148.19	148.21	150.24	151.15

```
ORNAMENTAL                        (    1)      OUR                          (CONTINUED)
  038.25                                          037.34  038.02  038.02  038.05  038.27
ORNAMENTED                        (    1)         038.28  039.35  040.03  040.06  040.06
  180.14                                          040.09  040.10  040.27  046.01  048.02
ORNAMENTS                         (    9)         048.03  052.08  052.11  052.16  052.17
  046.26  046.32  047.01  047.03  047.32         064.14  066.04  066.04  066.08  071.19
  048.01  048.21  146.02  244.08                 071.19  072.05  074.34  076.17  077.06
ORNITHOLOGY                       (    2)         077.13  077.14  077.14  077.15  078.20
  212.01  212.03                                 078.21  078.35  078.35  081.04  086.07
ORPHAN                            (    1)         089.13  089.15  090.17  091.19  091.21
  134.32                                         092.01  092.21  092.24  093.12  096.26
ORPHEUS                           (    1)         097.10  097.12  097.32  098.17  098.18
  169.04                                         099.07  100.12  101.14  101.15  101.16
OSCILLATION                       (    1)         102.08  103.23  104.19  104.21  104.23
  313.31                                         104.25  104.30  106.02  106.28  107.08
OSTRICHES                         (    1)         107.08  107.12  107.28  107.31  107.34
  104.33                                         108.02  108.21  108.34  108.36  109.10
OTHER                             (  160)         109.28  109.36  110.06  110.08  110.09
  003.34  007.03  008.20  010.25  014.09         110.10  112.30  112.31  113.24  115.09
  015.17  017.36  019.15  022.23  023.01         115.11  123.11  124.35  127.08  130.08
  026.07  026.26  027.17  028.05  031.06         130.09  130.10  133.12  133.13  133.23
  032.16  033.09  034.26  035.20  037.08         133.23  134.06  134.08  134.09  134.25
  041.17  042.23  046.10  050.32  057.05         134.25  134.29  134.30  135.26  138.09
  058.34  060.35  062.13  063.11  063.13         138.18  140.18  141.05  141.29  143.12
  067.33  068.13  068.15  068.18  070.13         143.12  143.19  151.07  151.34  159.35
  070.32  071.31  072.09  072.16  073.01         160.28  164.23  164.33  165.01  165.18
  083.27  086.13  086.36  087.09  091.36         165.25  165.27  166.08  166.27  171.06
  093.29  094.24  094.35  095.25  101.14         171.08  171.09  171.19  172.18  174.05
  102.22  109.24  115.27  115.29  118.20         174.29  176.05  176.15  176.19  177.03
  119.11  121.19  124.17  126.05  127.18         177.25  194.19  195.27  197.05  197.19
  130.21  131.22  132.37  135.05  136.12         199.26  199.30  199.31  203.22  215.24
  136.13  136.19  139.03  140.21  141.14         218.19  218.19  218.28  218.34  219.07
  141.17  141.24  143.09  144.01  144.11         219.10  219.13  219.27  220.04  220.05
  149.15  151.25  153.07  156.34  157.36         220.12  220.13  221.30  221.31  225.20
  159.01  160.07  161.20  161.31  162.07         234.05  239.35  244.34  244.36  246.08
  162.27  164.16  164.22  164.28  167.20         249.24  250.24  250.36  251.02  251.03
  167.28  171.17  171.27  174.02  175.18         254.34  254.37  255.02  258.26  259.34
  179.10  180.29  184.28  185.14  185.31         260.01  260.04  260.05  260.09  267.31
  190.29  194.07  194.09  197.23  201.22         269.27  273.12  281.32  282.15  283.09
  202.32  205.28  207.26  215.12  216.02         283.09  284.23  284.27  290.26  290.28
  216.11  218.21  219.16  219.20  222.19         290.29  290.34  291.19  291.21  291.22
  223.05  228.28  229.07  229.11  229.18         292.02  293.06  294.17  298.05  298.08
  230.06  231.14  233.17  237.02  239.04         298.15  309.08  310.03  311.14  314.19
  239.11  242.23  245.03  249.04  249.36         314.24  314.25  314.30  314.31  317.26
  251.14  253.02  258.23  263.18  266.35         318.08  320.14  320.15  320.15  320.19
  267.31  268.29  270.13  273.08  278.05         320.20  320.23  320.24  321.02  324.35
  279.11  280.16  283.14  283.15  285.19         324.35  325.01  325.04  325.08  325.33
  290.14  293.31  293.31  294.24  296.22         327.30  329.03  329.05  329.05  331.15
  306.08  306.27  308.13  309.20  309.22         332.07  332.25  333.02  333.31
  309.33  318.32  319.04  320.22  327.26       OURS                              (    1)
OTHERS                            (   29)         010.15
  003.17  009.27  009.28  019.26  031.22       OURSELVES                         (   18)
  034.24  070.10  072.23  076.26  086.02         006.25  011.04  011.14  021.36  078.34
  092.32  104.30  151.14  157.26  158.14         090.15  097.32  099.07  108.32  134.33
  158.14  162.06  162.06  168.32  172.23         164.22  171.18  254.07  260.08  323.15
  181.24  202.07  210.28  211.33  215.30         326.17  327.31  332.07
  285.28  299.09  307.11  323.19               OUST                              (    1)
OTHERWISE                         (    6)         155.27
  024.09  167.34  188.02  210.26  215.31       OUT                               (  224)
  218.12                                         006.32  006.37  008.26  013.14  015.10
OTTER                             (    1)         019.05  023.24  024.26  025.12  025.28
  227.24                                         027.34  028.11  029.04  029.26  035.33
OTTOMANS                          (    1)         036.22  036.29  038.31  041.07  041.14
  037.07                                         041.29  043.24  045.18  047.11  047.16
OUGHT                             (    1)         047.18  048.10  054.31  058.20  058.27
  327.35                                         060.09  060.11  061.08  061.11  062.02
OUR                               (  294)         064.09  067.05  067.12  068.15  069.16
  006.02  006.04  006.22  006.23  007.34         070.19  071.09  071.11  073.23  074.07
  008.23  010.03  010.13  010.22  011.06         074.27  077.30  081.32  083.20  083.32
  011.06  011.13  011.15  012.05  012.07         085.25  086.11  087.01  091.02  092.19
  012.30  012.32  013.21  013.24  013.26         093.22  093.35  100.15  100.23  102.26
  013.27  013.27  013.33  015.12  021.01         106.36  112.11  113.01  113.09  113.13
  021.35  022.03  023.04  024.03  024.04         113.18  114.04  114.09  114.30  115.01
  024.08  024.11  024.13  024.14  024.15         115.02  115.05  119.05  119.35  119.36
  024.17  024.17  024.18  024.18  026.32         120.29  122.08  122.28  127.36  132.30
  027.24  027.26  028.16  028.22  028.25         133.03  133.25  138.25  138.34  139.03
  031.35  033.12  034.02  034.05  034.13         140.07  140.27  141.04  147.15  147.19
  035.03  035.25  036.11  036.17  036.20         150.29  153.15  154.18  156.13  157.19
```

OUT   (CONTINUED)

```
OUT
  158.22  160.12  162.29  163.30  163.31
  165.08  165.18  167.07  168.08  168.28
  169.06  169.15  170.13  170.31  170.36
  173.04  178.10  178.22  179.19  187.21
  190.14  190.33  194.01  197.15  198.20
  198.24  198.26  198.28  199.06  203.04
  203.05  204.12  205.35  206.04  207.06
  208.32  220.06  222.12  222.19  225.28
  225.28  228.03  228.26  229.14  233.10
  234.09  234.20  235.26  238.14  238.35
  240.05  240.16  241.14  241.16  243.21
  244.09  244.15  244.32  245.36  247.34
  248.13  249.13  251.32  251.36  252.10
  252.36  253.18  253.35  258.18  266.09
  266.17  267.27  268.05  272.24  273.21
  273.23  274.34  275.31  276.13  276.23
  277.15  278.01  278.05  280.07  280.32
  283.28  283.36  285.31  290.05  292.22
  292.23  293.22  295.19  295.21  295.23
  295.32  296.01  296.01  297.22  300.06
  302.22  303.12  303.13  303.26  305.02
  305.04  305.27  307.35  308.26  309.11
  309.18  311.09  312.09  313.35  314.29
  318.14  318.21  318.32  322.14  322.26
  323.04  326.35  327.33  332.31  333.02
  333.08  333.14  333.23  333.31
OUTER                                    ( 1)
  169.24
OUTGOES                                  ( 5)
  055.03  055.14  060.07  060.31  162.35
OUTGROW                                  ( 1)
  212.30
OUTLANDISH                               ( 2)
  159.34  322.04
OUTLET                                   ( 4)
  175.34  194.04  290.11  292.08
OUTLETS                                  ( 1)
  181.14
OUTLINE                                  ( 3)
  262.27  289.20  290.35
OUTLINES                                 ( 3)
  085.24  290.08  324.35
OUTLIVE                                  ( 2)
  138.04  263.33
OUTLIVED                                 ( 1)
  138.21
OUTLYING                                 ( 1)
  134.07
OUTMOST                                  ( 1)
  024.08
OUTRIGHT                                 ( 1)
  273.11
OUTSIDE                                  ( 9)
  017.29  024.13  030.25  043.05  085.13
  119.13  181.02  243.30  296.04
OUTSKIRTS                                ( 6)
  034.08  093.15  097.01  108.10  168.25
  170.28
OUTWARD                                  ( 9)
  004.12  011.34  014.24  015.14  034.23
  047.03  047.16  069.02  308.24
OUTWARDLY                                ( 1)
  306.18
OUTWEIGH                                 ( 1)
  032.24
OUTWIT                                   ( 1)
  053.24
OVA                                      ( 1)
  307.06
OVEN                                     ( 2)
  105.34  244.06
OVER                                   ( 186)
  004.21  004.22  005.32  006.07  009.31
  011.36  022.11  027.13  030.09  039.31
  042.04  042.35  045.22  047.13  048.06
  053.35  058.14  062.28  062.31  066.08
  072.07  077.06  078.09  078.35  081.10
```

OVER   (CONTINUED)

```
OVER
  085.08  085.09  087.03  087.10  092.29
  092.31  092.34  093.34  094.15  094.22
  110.16  110.17  112.01  112.26  113.15
  114.02  115.17  115.24  116.25  116.27
  117.13  118.13  120.03  120.32  121.13
  121.22  123.05  123.26  126.04  126.25
  127.17  129.12  135.16  136.20  140.27
  145.04  146.05  152.33  155.35  156.31
  159.24  160.14  161.15  164.35  167.23
  168.26  172.04  172.36  174.18  175.14
  177.35  178.16  178.20  178.26  179.31
  181.29  184.03  185.04  185.07  186.28
  186.30  186.36  187.25  187.28  188.03
  189.07  189.19  189.23  190.05  191.17
  191.23  191.29  198.28  199.04  202.26
  203.25  203.27  206.33  207.18  208.27
  216.19  218.23  219.27  219.28  222.18
  223.08  225.31  228.18  228.20  231.17
  234.19  235.30  236.36  240.13  242.20
  243.19  243.23  243.30  245.17  246.14
  247.29  248.31  249.02  252.08  257.31
  259.08  259.20  259.36  260.23  262.03
  262.23  262.30  266.31  268.13  271.07
  271.12  271.30  272.10  272.14  272.14
  272.35  273.06  273.20  273.31  274.24
  274.26  278.11  278.26  281.11  283.09
  284.08  284.12  284.32  288.29  290.01
  292.18  292.31  293.10  293.24  295.35
  296.28  300.23  301.20  308.19  310.25
  310.31  311.27  312.31  313.11  313.23
  316.27  316.27  316.38  316.38  318.23
  320.20  324.25  326.17  332.10  332.17
  332.34
OVERARCHING                              ( 1)
  269.23
OVERCAME                                 ( 1)
  259.16
OVERCAST                                 ( 3)
  086.25  189.14  236.19
OVERCOME                                 ( 5)
  090.07  141.01  221.06  221.06  326.36
OVERFLOW                                 ( 2)
  181.05  306.15
OVERFLOWED                               ( 2)
  146.11  178.33
OVERFLOWING                              ( 1)
  305.05
OVERGROWN                                ( 1)
  092.07
OVERHANG                                 ( 1)
  161.08
OVERHANGING                              ( 2)
  186.17  306.21
OVERHEAD                                 ( 7)
  039.19  043.22  112.18  159.12  242.15
  245.32  312.13
OVERHUNG                                 ( 1)
  312.08
OVERLAID                                 ( 2)
  040.11  306.02
OVERLAP                                  ( 2)
  185.30  305.06
OVERLAPPING                              ( 1)
  247.29
OVERLOOKED                               ( 1)
  238.19
OVERLOOKING                              ( 1)
  187.36
OVERRATED                                ( 1)
  076.17
OVERRATES                                ( 1)
  076.17
OVERSEE                                  ( 1)
  020.11
OVERSEER                                 ( 2)
  007.22  079.01
```

```
OVERSEERS                         (   2)
  151.09   295.23
OVERSHADOW                        (   1)
  291.16
OVERSHADOWED                      (   1)
  238.31
OVERSHADOWS                       (   1)
  057.11
OVERSIGHTS                        (   1)
  050.34
OVERTAKE                          (   3)
  207.27   234.10   277.08
OVERTOOK                          (   1)
  133.28
OVERWHELMED                       (   1)
  097.23
OVERWHELMING                      (   1)
  206.24
OWED                              (   2)
  210.23   218.03
OWING                             (  11)
  063.26   076.12   136.31   136.33   143.21
  177.21   183.15   199.09   211.21   262.29
  311.25
OWL                               (   8)
  117.31   125.07   127.10   128.04   128.05
  256.07   266.03   272.01
OWLS                              (   3)
  124.17   125.25   174.35
OWN                               ( 105)
  003.33   007.32   007.33   007.34   009.05
  012.09   012.30   012.32   012.35   014.05
  015.12   016.05   016.25   017.32   018.10
  020.19   021.13   024.11   024.36   030.21
  030.23   030.32   032.29   033.23   034.05
  034.12   040.29   043.21   046.02   046.03
  046.05   048.11   048.19   050.06   051.31
  063.29   063.36   065.12   070.19   071.12
  074.03   077.12   077.34   078.35   087.08
  089.04   089.15   092.08   096.22   101.30
  102.31   103.01   108.24   114.17   118.22
  118.23   130.18   130.24   130.31   134.30
  142.23   143.07   150.13   150.24   159.30
  170.21   186.14   188.32   195.33   196.09
  205.10   205.35   207.35   208.26   209.01
  214.17   215.28   216.07   219.15   221.29
  221.31   230.04   236.18   239.16   241.29
  254.14   256.24   260.27   265.24   265.26
  271.19   275.23   276.28   278.08   279.08
  291.33   297.07   314.30   316.10   318.08
  321.02   321.11   321.12   326.04   331.29
OWNED                             (   1)
  030.13
OWNER                             (  10)
  020.13   022.25   041.03   054.28   065.35
  082.12   082.36   083.08   085.15   287.15
OWNERS                            (   1)
  032.19
OWNING                            (   1)
  030.29
OWNS                              (   3)
  030.15   030.30   066.15
OX                                (   4)
  037.14   056.04   056.36   149.07
OXEN                              (  11)
  009.23   055.37   056.16   056.18   057.05
  057.12   108.28   120.32   121.37   196.32
  198.29
OXFORD                            (   1)
  109.05
```

PACE (6)
020.34 089.35 229.35 278.18 320.10
326.08
PACES (3)
273.33 273.36 281.03
PACIFIC (3)
127.27 321.34 322.25
PACING (1)
156.31
PACK (4)
113.10 276.31 277.02 277.19
PACKED (1)
065.30
PAD (2)
195.01 322.34
PADDLE (2)
174.10 234.22
PADDLED (3)
191.20 191.30 271.07
PADDLING (3)
177.35 189.28 234.16
PAGANINI (1)
158.27
PAGE (3)
006.33 099.34 297.21
PAGES (5)
003.03 004.02 004.10 100.10 325.26
PAGODA (1)
202.06
PAID (11)
018.35 032.23 032.33 038.06 038.06
147.20 162.18 168.23 168.27 201.23
213.16
PAIL (7)
132.29 145.18 183.31 234.07 282.22
283.24 324.25
PAILFUL (2)
183.25 228.05
PAILFULS (1)
246.05
PAIN (4)
006.03 077.21 167.34 188.11
PAINFUL (1)
167.35
PAINS (8)
013.25 018.10 018.10 057.29 084.11
097.30 103.14 326.16
PAINT (7)
017.09 031.03 047.10 048.15 048.18
090.21 090.23
PAINTED (2)
027.30 201.31
PAINTER (1)
047.23
PAINTERS (1)
221.30
PAINTINGS (3)
110.02 223.33 242.23
PAIR (6)
024.33 065.20 133.31 159.26 233.15
265.23
PAIRS (2)
075.27 075.27
PALACE (8)
030.35 031.27 034.26 034.31 205.10
244.32 311.26 328.16
PALACES (2)
034.15 204.12
PALATABLE (2)
012.15 114.04
PALATE (1)
218.05
PALAVER (1)
244.35
PALE (2)
047.12 048.19
PALESTINE (1)
161.05

PALM (3)
028.18 119.25 307.36
PALMLEAF (1)
035.34
PALTRY (2)
090.29 104.12
PAMPAS (1)
120.33
PAN (1)
065.21
PANACEA (1)
138.23
PANEM (1)
063.16
PANGS (1)
124.23
PANS (1)
068.13
PANTALOON (1)
022.15
PANTALOONS (3)
022.18 024.31 064.25
PANTING (1)
122.09
PANTRY (1)
244.02
PANTS (1)
075.27
PAP (1)
109.31
PAPER (12)
031.04 045.26 099.27 101.26 106.14
106.21 107.29 119.30 120.12 197.33
226.02 253.22
PAPERS (4)
070.24 094.34 109.31 172.03
PAPHLAGONIAN (1)
144.14
PAPILLAE (1)
302.05
PAR (1)
122.12
PARABLE (3)
162.14 245.05 297.24
PARADE (3)
142.26 321.26 329.33
PARADISE (1)
328.08
PARASITIC (1)
309.07
PARASOL (2)
027.26 043.26
PARCAE (1)
025.21
PARCHED (1)
333.01
PARCHING (2)
074.19 264.13
PARDON (5)
003.22 017.05 126.11 252.38 315.12
PARE (1)
146.07
PARENT (5)
226.23 227.13 228.17 243.01 317.06
PARINGS (1)
280.31
PARIS (5)
025.23 097.36 109.05 251.07 331.24
PARISH (5)
093.13 093.24 110.05 144.24 147.36
PARISIAN (1)
251.20
PARK (1)
321.10
PARLIAMENTARY (1)
245.09
PARLOR (6)
169.20 174.31 242.35 244.02 245.03

PARLOR   (CONTINUED)
283.03
PARLORS   (1)
244.34
PAROLE   (1)
257.26
PARRS   (1)
138.21
PARSNIPS   (1)
064.15
PARSON   (2)
110.05 213.06
PART   (103)
005.24 009.21 010.30 013.33 019.12
021.22 032.17 033.03 034.18 036.22
041.13 042.02 043.10 043.16 046.18
049.19 053.18 054.04 054.06 054.22
054.35 056.20 058.30 060.08 060.12
063.35 065.05 065.16 067.09 069.19
071.25 072.12 073.25 075.10 076.09
076.11 082.34 088.07 088.14 089.10
094.03 105.12 112.03 115.02 123.34
125.22 129.06 130.22 134.07 135.12
135.13 135.20 135.24 142.23 144.08
147.20 155.24 160.01 164.29 166.11
168.15 168.36 170.20 173.19 181.10
186.03 187.17 189.09 192.01 204.18
210.29 212.37 216.08 217.03 229.28
233.17 234.13 235.02 235.17 237.05
241.22 246.34 250.20 254.16 256.28
258.26 272.34 277.17 282.17 288.30
289.23 289.27 290.17 292.02 295.15
296.19 296.26 296.30 299.34 303.29
325.13 325.18 327.29
PARTAKES   (2)
024.15 176.23
PARTED   (1)
140.17
PARTIAL   (5)
009.06 027.23 071.33 077.07 089.25
PARTIALLY   (4)
165.08 291.23 309.23 310.25
PARTICLES   (1)
292.32
PARTICULAR   (26)
003.11 003.22 010.23 025.02 026.22
026.25 044.30 073.08 090.21 111.04
118.18 124.04 151.13 162.33 169.34
175.29 184.06 201.24 217.21 244.19
276.25 290.25 290.34 291.09 291.21
323.14
PARTICULARLY   (13)
004.02 039.10 147.30 166.02 180.07
202.28 215.01 228.21 230.30 242.11
253.13 303.07 310.01
PARTICULARS   (1)
279.34
PARTIES   (2)
017.34 223.20
PARTITION   (3)
071.29 248.10 248.12
PARTITIONS   (1)
039.23
PARTLY   (11)
055.24 059.37 075.10 107.26 123.20
138.15 166.23 174.33 183.16 203.12
249.30
PARTOOK   (1)
142.03
PARTRIDGE   (11)
114.35 125.35 143.18 173.15 226.10
273.08 276.15 276.27 281.24 281.26
281.33
PARTRIDGES   (3)
145.35 276.13 281.17
PARTS   (17)
020.17 085.10 087.35 088.09 095.10
105.21 119.22 124.07 173.06 179.05

PARTS   (CONTINUED)
185.14 212.12 224.10 251.21 283.16
285.28 299.17
PARTY   (3)
012.35 171.34 231.22
PASS   (11)
004.25 044.15 061.28 115.18 137.25
191.24 244.36 277.20 306.34 323.34
331.09
PASSABLE   (1)
018.16
PASSABLY   (1)
133.34
PASSAGE   (11)
043.12 084.09 116.31 130.06 159.30
232.10 260.14 295.35 296.06 321.05
323.25
PASSAGES   (1)
020.27
PASSED   (25)
025.27 026.13 043.24 043.36 045.23
085.08 130.26 132.37 148.02 158.03
174.02 178.20 179.16 189.19 207.05
235.11 242.13 257.30 271.14 272.14
280.09 284.12 304.31 313.03 327.18
PASSENGERS   (2)
193.35 320.21
PASSERS   (1)
297.02
PASSES   (7)
008.26 126.23 172.36 193.27 213.31
283.29 300.10
PASSING   (8)
020.20 022.23 085.18 112.19 169.35
190.01 271.18 299.11
PASSION   (1)
068.23
PASSIONS   (2)
080.11 219.27
PASSIVE   (1)
080.19
PASSWORD   (1)
126.26
PAST   (18)
016.30 017.04 099.19 119.19 122.15
123.34 126.18 145.17 212.30 226.11
249.18 249.33 255.09 259.26 298.18
310.18 312.29 314.25
PASTIME   (3)
070.35 072.28 112.35
PASTORAL   (2)
121.37 122.15
PASTURE   (9)
005.07 005.19 081.33 083.22 087.26
137.14 156.06 201.26 282.34
PASTURES   (8)
087.33 088.23 121.34 158.10 173.07
263.28 320.11 324.24
PASTURING   (1)
310.09
PATAGONIAN   (1)
077.30
PATCH   (3)
022.04 022.11 257.10
PATCHES   (1)
177.16
PATENT   (3)
043.27 179.27 233.29
PATENTED   (1)
308.17
PATH   (22)
041.35 044.11 073.24 113.34 118.22
118.23 122.27 128.18 128.19 169.31
169.32 170.03 170.12 180.02 210.06
224.34 256.10 265.17 280.06 318.13
323.16 330.09
PATHETICALLY   (1)
294.02

PATHS
018.15 168.27 323.21   (3)
PATIENCE
269.03   (1)
PATREM
163.13   (1)
PATREMFAMILIAS
243.03   (1)
PATRIARCH
126.34   (1)
PATRICK
044.12   (1)
PATRIOTIC
321.21   (1)
PATRIOTISM
230.17 321.24   (2)
PATRIOTS
230.20   (1)
PATROCLUS
144.26 144.27 229.33   (3)
PATRON
109.13   (1)
PATTERER
218.33   (1)
PATTERING
132.02   (1)
PATTERNS
026.20 026.24 080.28 120.08   (4)
PAULATIM
063.18   (1)
PAUNCHED
126.32   (1)
PAUNCHES
126.17   (1)
PAUPER
151.14 151.34   (2)
PAUSE
095.27 193.33 322.24   (3)
PAUSED
159.36   (1)
PAUSES
127.11 274.36   (2)
PAUSING
126.36 274.02   (2)
PAVE
120.21   (1)
PAVED
182.10   (1)
PAVEMENT
140.29   (1)
PAVER
183.02   (1)
PAVING
178.24   (1)
PAW
067.10 171.28 274.25   (3)
PAWS
098.32 226.07 281.06 305.14   (4)
PAY   (19)
006.30 007.03 007.04 029.20 030.24
031.25 036.04 043.30 050.35 070.23
078.13 083.28 093.29 115.33 171.23
205.16 218.35 244.05 251.15
PAYING
030.34 048.32 285.31   (3)
PAYS
049.34   (1)
PE
095.12   (1)
PEACE
020.24 140.21 169.14 266.29   (4)
PEACEFUL
061.24 115.11 188.12 228.25   (4)
PEAK
087.17   (1)
PEAKED
043.07   (1)

PEAKS
087.06 291.16   (2)
PEAR
231.34   (1)
PEARL
047.05 269.34   (2)
PEARLS
284.31   (1)
PEARLY
238.08 316.29   (2)
PEAS   (6)
054.23 055.09 059.05 157.25 163.05
243.10
PEASANT
251.22   (1)
PEAT
295.07   (1)
PEBBLE
195.20   (1)
PEBBLY
098.23   (1)
PECK
005.11 053.01 146.32 243.12   (4)
PECKED
204.32 276.01   (2)
PECULIAR   (7)
073.17 108.11 210.29 241.12 295.04
295.08 306.10
PECULIARITIES
153.01   (1)
PECULIARITY
047.26   (1)
PECULIARLY
313.25   (1)
PECUNIA
149.07   (1)
PECUNIARY   (6)
031.20 033.04 050.14 060.07 095.07
163.24
PEDAGOGUE
110.04   (1)
PEDANTIC
080.08   (1)
PEDDLED
268.23   (1)
PEDDLES
268.25   (1)
PEDESTAL
038.03   (1)
PEDRO
094.31   (1)
PEEL
327.03   (1)
PEELED
129.31   (1)
PEELING
146.18   (1)
PEEP
228.15 228.17   (2)
PEEPING
073.33 167.14 309.26   (3)
PEERING
026.13 119.10   (2)
PEETWEETS
185.05   (1)
PEG
025.20 244.01   (2)
PELEUS
144.31   (1)
PELLICLE
332.03   (1)
PELLUCID
179.17   (1)
PELTING
132.24   (1)
PEN
113.11   (1)

PENALTY (1)
078.12
PENANCE (2)
004.17 004.29
PENCIL (2)
058.19 129.27
PENDANTS (1)
238.07
PENETRATE (3)
096.27 160.06 283.30
PENETRATED (2)
117.26 317.16
PENETRATES (1)
115.22
PENINSULAR (1)
266.16
PENKNIFE (1)
051.36
PENN (1)
076.29
PENNY (3)
094.08 094.09 230.25
PENOBSCOT (1)
028.36
PEOPLE (15)
008.29 008.30 008.31 008.33 008.35
023.03 026.15 027.17 031.36 035.22
039.30 063.03 172.13 172.33 182.11
PEOPLING (1)
313.19
PEPPERED (1)
184.20
PER (2)
296.16 296.17
PERCEIVE (9)
038.11 061.33 096.01 096.25 134.17
179.02 211.33 301.35 310.21
PERCEIVED (3)
053.34 123.31 300.04
PERCEPTIBLE (1)
176.14
PERCEPTIBLY (1)
187.28
PERCEPTION (2)
218.04 325.08
PERCH (20)
125.03 174.16 175.04 177.36 184.02
184.26 186.28 187.22 189.29 190.13
190.23 206.28 206.30 208.40 266.21
266.29 283.13 283.24 284.01 284.02
PERCHANCE (35)
008.32 016.06 023.27 033.10 034.31
045.34 052.30 067.09 068.04 082.02
104.26 108.01 117.19 118.28 119.03
121.13 122.13 162.12 162.30 179.15
179.34 187.02 188.23 189.26 191.11
196.12 199.24 229.30 232.16 259.27
282.29 285.22 307.11 333.14 333.22
PERCHING (1)
114.27
PERENNIAL (8)
043.12 133.23 156.06 175.33 267.13
283.06 311.12 326.34
PERENNIALLY (1)
193.04
PERFECT (13)
032.02 159.24 188.20 201.32 202.06
215.05 226.34 246.17 247.19 289.04
326.24 326.25 333.27
PERFECTED (1)
016.01
PERFECTION (1)
326.21
PERFECTLY (7)
045.12 086.24 132.34 195.15 227.03
249.32 307.24
PERFORM (1)
077.21

PERFORMANCE (1)
221.12
PERFORMANCES (2)
147.31 158.27
PERFORMED (2)
090.07 270.22
PERFUMED (1)
201.30
PERHAPS (78)
004.02 021.23 022.08 023.34 028.01
028.24 031.17 031.32 034.21 038.24
041.01 041.28 046.28 050.10 070.19
075.20 076.32 087.19 098.07 099.04
103.06 106.22 122.35 144.20 145.09
149.34 150.16 157.11 167.03 170.07
172.17 178.01 178.36 179.18 185.24
187.08 189.05 190.35 192.31 195.14
197.18 197.35 210.23 211.22 215.22
216.21 216.32 217.26 219.11 220.07
227.26 236.15 239.05 239.28 244.09
246.28 248.04 263.07 264.20 269.14
275.06 277.02 280.23 284.08 291.11
291.33 292.10 297.08 297.30 302.31
305.20 307.28 315.02 322.10 323.11
326.08 328.09 332.14
PERILS (1)
208.29
PERIOD (9)
023.16 071.20 144.01 180.18 194.09
195.26 212.23 239.17 254.12
PERIODICAL (1)
181.08
PERIODS (2)
027.10 040.08
PERIPLUS (1)
298.19
PERMANENT (4)
096.02 125.10 193.03 250.35
PERMANENTLY (3)
035.08 150.23 199.22
PERMISSION (2)
248.26 257.07
PERMIT (1)
041.02
PERMITS (1)
100.15
PERMITTED (2)
064.30 260.36
PEROUSE (1)
020.34
PERPENDICULAR (2)
247.08 275.02
PERPETUAL (4)
089.36 097.08 100.24 311.04
PERPETUATE (1)
057.27
PERPLEXED (1)
208.13
PERPLEXITY (1)
171.05
PERSEVERANCE (1)
120.19
PERSEVERE (1)
073.15
PERSIAN (3)
014.23 298.21 314.06
PERSIDAQUE (1)
314.02
PERSON (9)
003.24 003.27 020.12 132.13 167.06
172.01 220.29 221.01 251.14
PERSONS (3)
071.10 072.31 137.32
PERSPIRATION (3)
013.03 116.26 324.36
PERSUADE (2)
007.09 072.25

PERSUASION (1)
309.20
PERSUASIVENESS (1)
075.09
PERTINACITY (1)
229.22
PERTINENT (2)
003.15 254.26
PERTINENTLY (1)
033.03
PERTURBATION (1)
097.19
PERVADE (1)
219.31
PERVADED (1)
283.04
PEST (1)
192.29
PETERBORO (1)
122.09
PETERSBURG (1)
021.14
PETTY (5)
092.02 096.03 096.03 117.01 321.19
PEWEE (2)
041.17 319.03
PFEIFFER (1)
022.34
PHAETON (1)
074.05
PHARAOHS (1)
034.28
PHE (1)
275.35
PHEASANT (1)
127.05
PHENOMENA (5)
188.12 301.03 304.28 310.08 329.30
PHENOMENON (5)
150.13 202.30 290.24 304.32 308.19
PHIL (1)
212.35
PHILADELPHIA (1)
251.05
PHILANTHROPHY (1)
074.29
PHILANTHROPIC (3)
072.22 074.36 077.32
PHILANTHROPIES (1)
078.15
PHILANTHROPIST (1)
077.10
PHILANTHROPISTS (1)
076.32
PHILANTHROPY (4)
074.34 076.15 076.34 077.30
PHILOSOPHER (16)
014.35 015.13 015.16 024.26 065.29
094.20 095.19 096.21 099.11 148.15
149.12 205.30 268.02 270.04 322.20
328.30
PHILOSOPHERS (9)
014.22 014.33 056.22 056.25 154.17
210.32 268.22 269.10 331.33
PHILOSOPHICAL (3)
110.03 149.05 331.27
PHILOSOPHY (14)
012.12 014.33 052.07 061.06 074.04
098.02 111.14 173.28 174.05 211.29
263.22 268.15 298.03 298.07
PHOEBE (2)
226.08 319.05
PHOENICIANS (1)
021.01
PHRASE (2)
008.36 027.20
PHTHIA (1)
144.29

PHYSICAL (8)
013.32 028.06 035.18 050.02 075.05
090.08 142.13 146.36
PIAZZA (1)
140.27
PICK (7)
069.36 107.01 133.36 193.05 225.29
275.14 275.31
PICKED (3)
219.16 241.16 270.12
PICKEREL (12)
178.06 183.34 184.13 184.15 187.17
203.27 207.14 283.13 283.23 284.01
284.03 284.18
PICKING (5)
069.29 161.15 238.35 275.25 320.22
PICKS (2)
187.17 304.24
PICTURE (7)
038.04 085.24 090.21 166.12 240.08
246.23 297.21
PICTURESQUE (1)
047.27
PIECE (9)
038.09 048.10 057.30 129.29 177.22
211.15 226.04 278.25 295.19
PIECEMEAL (1)
249.34
PIECES (4)
036.26 096.35 252.05 309.22
PIER (1)
020.33
PIERCE (2)
231.04 295.31
PIETY (2)
325.05 326.33
PIG (3)
056.04 127.30 223.26
PIGEONS (7)
114.26 145.32 145.34 159.31 201.35
223.09 313.21
PIGWEED (1)
161.28
PIKE (1)
294.21
PILE (15)
035.07 104.07 113.10 182.34 228.26
228.27 251.01 251.26 267.19 274.18
275.31 296.03 302.17 312.28 321.14
PILED (2)
267.03 320.14
PILES (1)
021.12
PILGRIM (1)
110.06
PILGRIMS (1)
154.17
PILING (1)
203.25
PILL (1)
138.17
PILLARS (1)
004.28
PILLOW (1)
241.25
PILOT (1)
020.12
PILOTS (1)
171.07
PILPAY (1)
225.17
PINE (50)
018.25 020.10 041.06 042.27 042.31
113.21 114.27 120.01 121.21 123.06
128.16 132.08 132.33 137.23 141.34
146.18 147.01 175.33 185.07 186.24
190.32 191.21 197.35 198.02 198.03
198.26 201.03 202.05 203.24 226.09

164

```
PINE                    (CONTINUED)
228.02  240.25  249.15  249.28  252.05
252.09  252.10  263.05  266.05  266.26
269.28  274.11  275.06  275.15  280.16
280.21  316.07  318.32  319.10  332.10
PINES                          ( 27)
040.35  041.08  054.24  081.33  111.27
113.12  113.28  128.13  156.01  167.17
169.35  181.23  181.28  208.26  227.36
228.19  256.25  257.16  258.19  265.31
265.33  266.24  271.31  280.11  282.10
284.28  312.22
PINIONS                         ( 3)
159.26  252.30  266.28
PINK                            ( 1)
201.16
PINNATE                         ( 1)
114.07
PINNED                          ( 2)
190.33  249.29
PINWEEDS                        ( 1)
309.28
PINY                            ( 1)
062.05
PIOUS                           ( 3)
076.04  166.02  166.06
PIPE                            ( 5)
130.05  130.07  192.18  262.17  267.20
PIPER                           ( 2)
157.05  161.28
PIPEWORT                        ( 1)
195.14
PIROUETTING                     ( 1)
310.16
PISCINE                         ( 1)
187.21
PISTOL                          ( 1)
146.27
PISTORIENSIS                    ( 1)
231.36
PIT                             ( 2)
039.13  294.15
PITCH                          ( 19)
042.30  113.28  128.13  132.33  181.23
181.28  198.02  227.36  240.25  249.28
250.07  252.09  258.19  263.05  274.11
275.15  280.11  312.22  319.10
PITIED                          ( 2)
067.05  314.33
PITIFUL                         ( 1)
026.12
PITTED                          ( 1)
228.35
PITY                            ( 6)
075.21  075.32  159.10  211.34  212.25
281.03
PIUS                            ( 1)
166.03
PLACE                          ( 57)
010.24  011.20  013.12  018.32  021.08
028.05  037.36  043.25  044.29  057.33
076.28  081.30  082.09  087.34  096.32
098.03  098.06  109.12  115.05  115.07
110.05  119.13  130.17  132.14  133.27
134.01  134.05  142.22  143.30  163.32
172.21  180.33  190.19  191.09  198.14
198.17  211.13  211.21  220.15  232.09
235.08  241.16  241.19  241.21  243.25
247.18  253.16  253.28  254.15  259.23
263.28  278.27  292.21  299.08  301.03
322.31  329.34
PLACED                         ( 10)
034.23  041.24  096.22  183.25  226.18
230.32  282.12  284.08  295.29  314.06
PLACES                         ( 13)
088.03  097.04  134.04  168.16  168.24
178.26  180.12  189.28  207.15  248.12
256.24  292.11  327.19

PLACID                          ( 1)
316.14
PLACING                         ( 1)
275.26
PLAIN                           ( 9)
115.11  169.25  208.15  269.04  271.10
282.33  288.18  289.08  309.17
PLAINLY                         ( 4)
130.30  185.21  204.22  266.08
PLAINS                          ( 5)
037.23  077.16  251.10  272.32  282.20
PLAN                            ( 2)
286.01  290.09
PLANE                           ( 1)
048.27
PLANED                          ( 1)
084.34
PLANET                          ( 3)
009.11  053.27  133.13
PLANETARY                       ( 1)
116.08
PLANK                           ( 4)
033.14  039.18  143.09  262.17
PLANNING                        ( 1)
222.08
PLANT                           ( 9)
055.07  071.14  084.02  157.25  163.27
163.41  164.13  238.16  315.07
PLANTATION                      ( 2)
128.07  152.17
PLANTED                        ( 10)
054.20  155.04  156.11  156.17  164.09
195.11  201.35  257.36  262.28  263.26
PLANTING                        ( 5)
158.23  158.29  161.13  163.31  227.31
PLANTS                          ( 9)
015.33  024.13  077.02  178.32  179.02
239.12  307.03  309.33  313.30
PLASH                           ( 2)
190.09  236.02
PLASTER                         ( 6)
157.33  158.30  245.16  245.24  246.02
246.04
PLASTERED                       ( 3)
048.28  242.10  242.17
PLASTERER                       ( 1)
245.30
PLASTERING                      ( 8)
007.14  031.04  084.31  243.17  245.35
248.25  253.22  330.24
PLASTIC                         ( 2)
156.28  309.13
PLATE                           ( 5)
094.26  177.20  231.03  287.24  288.09
PLATEAU                         ( 1)
087.27
PLATES                          ( 1)
065.22
PLATFORM                        ( 1)
295.27
PLATO                           ( 4)
107.13  107.14  149.16  149.18
PLAY                           ( 14)
008.14  051.11  056.21  096.09  129.30
135.15  147.19  211.10  211.20  242.21
266.34  280.02  316.24  330.12
PLAYED                          ( 8)
158.18  207.29  226.03  235.05  251.31
274.22  317.04  328.36
PLAYING                         ( 3)
174.15  222.04  230.09
PLAYS                           ( 1)
028.12
PLEAD                           ( 1)
103.01
PLEADINGS                       ( 1)
318.30
```

PLEASANT (18)
027.35 041.06 041.19 045.23 112.35
113.08 114.08 134.06 137.26 155.17
169.17 203.06 203.10 243.07 301.12
309.25 314.27 328.10
PLEASANTER (1)
240.26
PLEASANTEST (1)
132.21
PLEASANTLY (2)
042.35 258.11
PLEASE (3)
084.13 084.16 214.35
PLEASED (8)
029.18 173.32 173.34 191.08 241.32
242.16 245.22 261.31
PLEASES (2)
049.30 270.21
PLEASING (5)
086.33 125.22 174.06 185.25 251.29
PLEASURE (5)
044.30 046.12 072.24 092.32 099.31
PLEASURES (1)
096.03
PLECTRUM (1)
272.03
PLEDGED (1)
269.19
PLEIADES (1)
088.09
PLENTY (3)
065.25 079.17 143.33
PLODDING (1)
165.06
PLOTS (1)
263.27
PLOUGH (8)
009.25 055.03 055.37 072.09 118.33
141.04 288.32 295.20
PLOUGHED (1)
005.25
PLOUGHING (5)
054.31 055.02 163.02 251.33 294.34
PLOUGHMEN (1)
119.09
PLOUGHS (1)
294.19
PLOUGHSHARE (1)
295.19
PLOW (2)
117.09 117.09
PLUCKED (6)
006.12 037.25 130.03 149.18 173.16
263.25
PLUCKS (1)
238.09
PLUG (1)
192.20
PLUM (1)
046.33
PLUMAGE (2)
200.01 313.30
PLUMES (4)
047.34 187.02 297.31 320.09
PLUMP (1)
313.14
PLUMPER (1)
274.33
PLUNGES (1)
276.20
PLUS (2)
322.02 322.02
PLUTUS (1)
165.32
PLYMOUTH (1)
143.01
POCKET (4)
044.15 063.08 072.10 146.27

POCKETS (1)
168.07
PODS (1)
163.36
POEM (1)
085.12
POESY (1)
292.04
POET (18)
028.26 054.09 082.33 082.37 097.13
099.27 106.31 203.08 204.01 213.03
223.29 223.31 225.04 233.22 241.27
254.26 268.01 268.03
POETIC (6)
046.06 090.11 144.15 148.20 214.36
254.16
POETRY (13)
010.27 089.31 095.35 098.02 106.31
111.14 165.22 217.27 239.33 259.15
308.28 309.04 316.30
POETS (8)
089.33 104.08 104.09 124.21 127.22
154.17 210.32 224.02
POINT (20)
032.34 046.29 056.05 061.34 071.16
087.10 098.05 133.09 170.13 176.21
240.03 289.18 290.07 290.15 290.26
295.10 297.05 299.26 307.14 327.05
POINTED (3)
150.32 182.28 294.21
POINTING (2)
112.17 198.31
POINTS (8)
031.33 118.18 133.22 171.15 190.14
260.29 271.04 290.34
POISON (3)
215.26 244.28 318.27
POISONOUS (1)
318.28
POKED (1)
242.29
POLAR (1)
295.10
POLE (6)
124.02 128.03 210.04 213.04 243.24
327.09
POLES (1)
313.31
POLESTAR (1)
071.18
POLICY (2)
021.10 151.32
POLISH (1)
057.30
POLISHED (1)
327.08
POLITE (1)
142.27
POLITENESS (1)
136.15
POLITICAL (3)
017.34 052.06 076.25
POLITICS (1)
109.20
POLK (1)
232.10
POLLEN (1)
319.10
POMOTIS (1)
184.04
POMP (1)
329.33
POND (202)
003.06 019.34 021.07 040.33 041.07
041.09 041.24 042.04 044.07 045.15
055.01 075.22 086.03 086.11 086.34
087.17 087.20 088.29 113.03 113.29
114.29 115.13 122.33 125.01 126.35

POND   (CONTINUED)
128.06 129.07 130.10 130.20 130.30
132.33 137.05 137.06 137.22 141.10
145.29 150.26 150.32 153.04 155.33
158.09 159.21 167.04 170.17 172.14
173.26 174.01 174.20 174.26 175.09
175.28 176.27 178.13 179.10 179.10
179.19 179.28 179.36 180.08 180.17
180.34 181.06 181.12 181.18 181.28
181.33 182.14 182.20 182.23 182.35
183.05 183.06 183.12 183.31 184.12
184.27 185.15 186.19 186.30 187.36
188.07 189.15 190.04 190.26 191.01
191.03 192.16 194.05 194.15 194.19
195.05 195.07 195.27 197.09 197.12
197.20 198.06 198.19 199.04 199.12
199.21 201.08 203.35 207.13 208.31
210.10 211.25 213.12 213.18 213.23
213.30 218.24 228.07 232.24 232.36
233.25 233.33 234.02 234.19 235.02
235.06 235.14 235.17 236.19 236.33
236.36 240.01 240.26 241.19 242.08
245.18 246.14 248.35 249.27 249.34
260.02 260.10 261.14 264.08 268.18
271.06 271.20 272.10 272.14 272.33
277.01 282.01 282.25 283.25 284.05
284.17 285.10 285.13 285.16 286.01
287.12 289.06 289.10 289.20 289.24
289.33 290.07 290.09 290.21 291.04
292.12 292.22 292.25 293.12 293.19
294.07 294.18 294.33 296.30 297.05
297.12 299.04 299.09 299.16 299.27
299.31 300.03 300.27 301.04 301.14
301.18 301.26 301.31 301.32 302.06
302.12 303.28 303.33 311.30 312.11
313.02 313.05 313.07 318.33 319.01
319.11 323.17
PONDS   (24)
024.05 173.01 177.26 179.13 181.15
181.26 184.29 194.06 194.08 198.12
237.02 249.04 271.02 205.17 287.10
287.13 287.18 287.24 288.38 296.34
299.14 299.23 303.06 310.34
PONTIFICATE   (1)
231.35
POOL   (1)
199.33
POOLS   (1)
313.14
POOR   (64)
003.20 004.03 005.15 006.27 013.31
014.22 023.26 024.36 030.28 030.34
031.08 032.07 033.24 033.25 034.21
034.27 034.36 035.30 039.30 047.25
052.05 065.23 065.35 066.02 066.03
072.26 072.31 072.35 075.13 075.17
076.06 076.18 076.20 079.01 080.05
090.04 090.06 105.06 125.11 131.06
135.18 151.09 151.34 152.02 152.03
196.30 196.30 197.20 203.32 204.17
205.02 208.33 208.37 209.02 209.02
209.03 211.03 233.33 281.05 281.31
292.01 328.09 328.10 328.16
POORER   (4)
014.24 023.27 033.34 065.36
POOREST   (2)
064.04 328.07
POORLY   (1)
143.24
POP   (1)
063.08
POPE   (1)
172.23
POPGUNS   (1)
160.05
POPLAR   (1)
129.13

POPULOUS   (2)
077.31 243.13
PORCH   (1)
045.02
PORCIUS   (1)
063.15
PORE   (1)
129.05
PORES   (1)
079.01
PORK   (3)
059.12 061.04 064.06
PORRIDGE   (1)
162.11
PORT   (5)
021.10 071.19 091.32 140.35 206.18
PORTENTOUS   (1)
159.34
PORTICOES   (1)
331.15
PORTION   (13)
003.18 028.16 086.28 087.09 123.15
147.13 149.10 155.14 176.35 203.21
225.20 297.03 307.18
PORTIONLESS   (1)
005.20
PORTIONS   (2)
004.04 041.35
PORTS   (2)
292.05 298.22
PORTUGAL   (1)
322.12
PORTULACA   (1)
061.20
POSITION   (10)
004.23 020.29 092.35 153.21 153.26
227.01 247.32 253.17 300.21 327.30
POSITIVE   (3)
014.19 052.13 150.10
POSSESS   (2)
218.20 284.24
POSSESSED   (5)
010.33 046.25 057.27 278.32 315.30
POSSESSION   (7)
023.05 043.32 076.13 082.08 082.08
083.29 181.35
POSSESSOR   (1)
023.07
POSSIBILITY   (1)
011.16
POSSIBLE   (20)
013.34 017.20 036.01 062.13 071.10
071.33 081.05 084.04 123.08 131.27
153.20 156.25 163.37 180.28 189.20
212.14 222.18 284.29 288.28 324.33
POSSIBLY   (10)
012.25 032.05 040.15 053.15 058.11
093.12 107.34 140.07 141.24 219.13
POST   (7)
094.03 094.08 098.07 133.20 136.18
144.16 168.14
POSTAGE   (1)
094.08
POSTERITY   (5)
044.35 097.14 099.07 209.05 264.15
POSTS   (3)
048.29 144.17 243.20
POT   (6)
008.34 080.10 120.28 218.25 244.05
257.31
POTAMOGETONS   (1)
178.36
POTASH   (1)
158.09
POTATO   (8)
146.33 156.10 164.21 239.07 239.14
253.21 280.31 325.21

167

POTATOES (15)
044.26 054.22 055.08 059.04 059.23
061.03 131.19 163.04 163.17 197.02
214.25 243.10 254.18 259.12 331.18
POTS (3)
058.26 068.13 261.29
POTTER (5)
191.03 261.15 261.26 261.28 309.13
POTTERY (3)
159.03 261.23 264.13
POULTRY (1)
265.01
POUND (1)
287.02
POUNDS (5)
183.35 184.01 184.03 184.06 270.07
POURED (1)
329.18
POUT (1)
175.14
POUTS (4)
130.29 174.23 184.02 184.26
POVERTY (13)
012.12 014.30 065.35 080.03 082.25
120.12 195.27 196.28 209.03 324.05
324.05 329.02 329.07
POW (1)
182.13
POWDER (3)
260.15 260.16 292.30
POWDERY (1)
267.08
POWER (7)
057.17 118.12 134.10 139.06 162.24
330.10 332.27
POWERFUL (3)
025.27 309.21 312.18
POWERS (3)
066.36 077.33 134.16
PRACTICAL (4)
021.22 100.28 148.31 214.20
PRACTICALLY (8)
009.04 015.04 015.07 040.24 073.25
120.35 150.05 211.05
PRACTICE (5)
059.40 091.01 106.15 216.07 217.27
PRACTISE (4)
222.21 236.34 283.22 331.19
PRACTISED (4)
051.21 068.34 142.10 261.32
PRACTISING (2)
173.27 331.15
PRAETORS (1)
009.35
PRAIRIE (4)
012.15 167.22 210.34 238.15
PRAIRIES (3)
087.28 130.23 166.09
PRAISE (5)
019.24 076.33 078.27 147.30 325.09
PRAISED (1)
076.19
PRAISES (2)
106.25 169.05
PRANKS (3)
105.17 258.24 310.19
PRAY (8)
057.24 061.23 066.03 093.32 118.26
137.07 283.27 320.28
PRAYED (1)
250.30
PRAYER (2)
236.28 328.04
PRAYERS (1)
011.13
PREACH (1)
073.29

PREACHER (4)
046.19 095.21 147.31 315.10
PRECEDE (1)
309.04
PRECEDED (1)
047.21
PRECEDENTS (1)
010.09
PRECEDES (2)
308.27 308.28
PRECEDING (1)
054.25
PRECEPT (2)
036.07 322.20
PRECEPTS (1)
221.10
PRECIOUS (8)
062.27 102.19 188.21 199.25 238.05
251.01 284.30 327.10
PRECISE (1)
047.10
PRECISELY (5)
016.11 017.04 164.14 215.28 225.14
PRECISION (3)
117.34 124.03 265.23
PRECOCIOUS (1)
227.04
PRECURSORS (1)
313.28
PREDECESSORS (1)
009.31
PREDICAMENT (1)
052.24
PREDICT (1)
268.04
PREFACE (2)
152.05 260.14
PREFER (3)
158.29 217.06 217.16
PREFERRED (6)
008.20 070.10 071.26 072.34 171.32
325.29
PREFERRING (2)
067.22 192.01
PREGNANT (1)
306.21
PREJUDICE (1)
097.34
PREJUDICES (1)
008.23
PREMISES (6)
022.28 081.10 170.21 207.01 244.26
319.10
PREMIUM (1)
165.30
PREPARE (2)
013.20 013.29
PREPARED (4)
012.22 068.33 215.30 229.13
PREPAREDLY (1)
024.24
PREPARES (1)
217.33
PREPARING (3)
156.04 215.28 315.05
PRESCRIBE (2)
016.04 320.25
PRESCRIBED (1)
009.34
PRESENCE (6)
132.10 135.11 156.09 196.12 231.36
260.35
PRESENT (32)
003.09 012.27 014.04 016.11 017.05
017.28 026.03 032.04 036.20 041.31
049.31 056.04 056.06 067.25 070.20
082.22 084.19 097.05 099.19 108.02
111.23 165.02 180.06 182.22 214.08

```
PRESENT                    (CONTINUED)
  217.21  249.25  255.08  257.01  257.13
  268.32  314.21
PRESENTABLE                        (  1)
  150.18
PRESENTED                          (  3)
  052.26  188.29  244.17
PRESENTLY                          (  1)
  330.16
PRESERVATION                       (  1)
  250.17
PRESERVE                           ( 11)
  032.02  071.20  180.16  195.25  214.36
  218.25  219.23  313.32  315.26  315.27
  321.15
PRESERVED                          (  5)
  006.24  062.27  266.15  321.12  321.14
PRESERVES                          (  4)
  073.12  192.31  211.17  279.32
PRESERVING                         (  1)
  120.30
PRESIDED                           (  1)
  179.31
PRESIDENCY                         (  1)
  232.09
PRESIDENT                          (  1)
  330.04
PRESS                              (  3)
  025.27  093.16  100.17
PRESSED                            (  3)
  121.03  143.11  306.28
PRESSING                           (  3)
  040.01  040.02  306.30
PRESSURE                           (  4)
  029.34  094.27  195.08  270.08
PRESUME                            (  3)
  010.05  036.36  080.05
PRETEND                            (  3)
  150.25  180.19  325.15
PRETENDING                         (  1)
  228.12
PRETENDS                           (  1)
  066.16
PRETENSIONS                        (  1)
  080.03
PRETTY                             (  4)
  052.16  199.08  235.05  304.03
PREVAIL                            (  1)
  216.18
PREVAILED                          (  1)
  131.36
PREVAILING                         (  1)
  176.33
PREVAILS                           (  2)
  030.22  325.22
PREVALENCE                         (  1)
  149.14
PREVENT                            (  2)
  039.17  284.11
PREVENTED                          (  2)
  010.16  315.23
PREVENTS                           (  3)
  131.16  301.32  315.20
PREVIOUS                           (  5)
  232.07  240.06  252.08  280.13  298.07
PREVIOUSLY                         (  2)
  041.34  068.12
PREY                               (  4)
  129.21  227.14  232.06  318.20
PREYING                            (  1)
  216.02
PRICE                              ( 11)
  048.33  064.32  081.09  081.12  081.12
  081.13  121.15  196.21  251.05  251.11
  251.16
PRICELESS                          (  1)
  141.36

PRICES                             (  2)
  024.29  168.23
PRIDE                              (  2)
  159.10  331.21
PRIED                              (  1)
  153.14
PRIEST                             (  4)
  068.25  144.22  149.32  298.11
PRIESTS                            (  1)
  147.08
PRIME                              (  2)
  120.04  121.17
PRIMERS                            (  1)
  107.05
PRIMEVAL                           (  1)
  158.34
PRIMITIVE                          ( 17)
  011.33  023.25  028.16  037.18  041.31
  062.17  105.23  150.19  158.17  198.07
  208.39  210.18  211.11  243.17  284.06
  288.17  315.17
PRIMITUS                           (  1)
  310.35
PRIMORIBUS                         (  1)
  311.01
PRINCE                             (  5)
  057.22  096.20  148.24  251.22  282.14
PRINCES                            (  1)
  057.20
PRINCESS                           (  1)
  052.32
PRINCIPAL                          (  3)
  026.36  039.25  166.19
PRINCIPLE                          (  5)
  039.36  050.29  094.19  230.24  308.16
PRINCIPLES                         (  2)
  050.28  216.23
PRINT                              (  5)
  018.08  059.32  129.35  144.15  267.10
PRINTED                            (  6)
  100.11  100.20  103.25  111.09  119.30
  269.12
PRINTING                           (  1)
  026.31
PRINTS                             (  1)
  120.10
PRISON                             (  3)
  007.06  028.34  315.09
PRISONER                           (  1)
  007.32
PRISONERS                          (  1)
  257.26
PRIVACY                            (  1)
  130.15
PRIVATE                            (  7)
  007.35  009.07  019.36  078.07  140.19
  321.34  322.13
PRIVILEGE                          (  5)
  196.19  204.14  217.35  251.16  264.09
PRIVILEGED                         (  1)
  217.29
PRIVILEGES                         (  2)
  197.14  264.07
PRIZE                              (  1)
  164.27
PRIZED                             (  1)
  101.27
PROBABLY                           ( 29)
  009.13  012.06  016.30  027.18  033.08
  054.02  064.20  069.22  073.07  107.31
  109.20  124.14  139.07  179.06  180.04
  184.30  202.29  225.30  227.28  229.28
  236.12  239.23  241.11  248.13  288.23
  292.12  293.05  297.25  301.29
PROBE                              (  1)
  228.08
PROBLEM                            (  4)
  033.18  033.20  235.08  290.21
```

PROBLEMS   (4)
  012.23 015.03 021.04 321.06
PROCEED   (1)
  058.32
PROCEEDED   (2)
  241.34 326.26
PROCEEDING   (1)
  169.01
PROCEEDS   (1)
  076.04
PROCESS   (4)
  062.22 062.36 213.21 254.17
PROCESSION   (2)
  165.26 329.33
PROCLAIM   (1)
  312.05
PROCLAIMED   (1)
  068.23
PROCURE   (1)
  023.35
PROCURED   (1)
  062.32
PROCURING   (1)
  021.24
PRODUCE   (10)
  035.25 055.18 060.24 076.02 079.09
  155.17 166.35 182.07 187.01 306.04
PRODUCED   (9)
  031.12 047.21 107.12 189.20 190.22
  195.22 233.19 293.26 315.14
PRODUCES   (5)
  068.26 123.08 177.31 188.17 318.07
PRODUCING   (2)
  063.36 167.33
PRODUCT   (1)
  305.08
PRODUCTION   (1)
  035.27
PRODUCTIONS   (1)
  164.28
PRODUCTIVE   (1)
  191.35
PRODUCTS   (2)
  020.09 281.19
PROFANED   (5)
  089.23 130.34 185.08 197.18 199.12
PROFANITY   (1)
  182.15
PROFESS   (1)
  014.34
PROFESSED   (2)
  051.20 052.08
PROFESSION   (1)
  076.27
PROFESSIONS   (3)
  069.34 073.04 153.19
PROFESSOR   (3)
  051.20 106.28 267.26
PROFESSORS   (2)
  014.33 048.05
PROFILES   (1)
  291.01
PROFIT   (2)
  021.04 163.24
PROFITABLY   (1)
  068.05
PROFITED   (1)
  009.01
PROFITS   (2)
  069.30 166.02
PROFOUND   (1)
  134.15
PROGENITORS   (1)
  015.08
PROGRESS   (4)
  085.21 269.02 299.19 331.26
PROGRESSING   (1)
  187.24

PROJECTING   (2)
  198.04 291.19
PROLIFIC   (1)
  233.19
PROLONGED   (3)
  123.28 236.24 254.04
PROMINENT   (1)
  258.26
PROMISE   (1)
  239.16
PROMISED   (1)
  206.34
PROMISES   (1)
  184.25
PROMISING   (5)
  007.03 007.03 058.18 150.20 151.28
PROMONTORIES   (1)
  291.26
PROMONTORY   (2)
  240.03 289.04
PROMPT   (1)
  118.08
PROMPTING   (1)
  268.25
PRONOUN   (1)
  233.04
PRONOUNCE   (2)
  073.20 144.22
PRONOUNCED   (1)
  279.21
PRONUNCIATION   (1)
  105.28
PROOF   (4)
  008.25 119.33 264.17 317.23
PROP   (1)
  168.08
PROPER   (11)
  012.29 029.05 038.03 039.15 050.19
  142.12 148.01 176.07 191.13 213.03
  327.04
PROPERLY   (3)
  012.33 172.24 178.33
PROPERTY   (10)
  031.29 034.03 076.11 093.19 099.07
  133.30 149.08 165.35 165.35 328.22
PROPHESIED   (3)
  063.03 118.07 251.33
PROPHETS   (1)
  078.23
PROPITIOUS   (1)
  250.31
PROPORTION   (19)
  015.32 034.22 036.19 047.32 067.30
  069.15 069.16 071.23 082.03 091.36
  151.30 153.33 196.30 219.10 280.15
  287.19 289.35 299.32 324.03
PROPORTIONALLY   (2)
  106.29 124.11
PROPORTIONS   (3)
  094.33 288.07 327.16
PROPOSE   (2)
  084.22 109.16
PROPOSED   (3)
  072.06 075.01 152.33
PROPOSES   (2)
  194.02 197.34
PROPPED   (1)
  147.13
PROPRIETOR   (4)
  038.21 083.19 137.21 238.18
PROPRIETORS   (2)
  250.23 250.24
PROSPECT   (6)
  010.23 012.23 100.02 112.34 134.03
  172.13
PROSPECTING   (1)
  252.08

PROSPECTS (4)
020.24 022.12 169.13 314.19
PROSPERITY (1)
057.10
PROSTRATE (2)
221.02 243.22
PROTECT (1)
102.32
PROTECTED (3)
083.08 183.11 196.03
PROTECTION (2)
132.32 226.09
PROTOTYPE (1)
306.22
PROTRACTED (1)
117.24
PROUD (6)
142.29 160.27 203.31 219.07 316.35
325.25
PROVE (6)
071.31 074.06 089.20 151.26 239.29
321.03
PROVED (5)
091.06 170.11 177.24 253.09 292.29
PROVENDER (2)
105.01 173.21
PROVERB (1)
032.11
PROVES (4)
035.23 103.14 232.29 291.18
PROVIDE (3)
039.03 104.36 215.19
PROVIDED (4)
046.05 067.18 068.12 294.04
PROVIDENCE (1)
038.33
PROVIDING (1)
036.08
PROVINCE (1)
039.07
PROVINCES (1)
008.01
PROVINCIAL (3)
109.28 110.13 111.06
PROVING (2)
226.14 276.34
PROVISIONS (1)
068.18
PROVOCATIONS (1)
100.24
PROVOKE (1)
221.11
PROVOKED (1)
108.27
PROWLING (3)
175.11 227.15 280.06
PRUDENCE (2)
039.36 080.25
PRUDENT (2)
153.25 293.35
PSALM (2)
174.04 332.23
PUBLIC (11)
007.33 018.17 056.34 057.14 068.26
140.18 167.31 172.32 211.09 292.04
331.28
PUBLICANS (1)
036.36
PUBLISH (2)
059.30 091.08
PUBLISHED (1)
111.09
PUDDING (2)
142.05 245.11
PUDDINGS (1)
245.15
PUDDLE (1)
289.24

PUDDLES (3)
277.17 288.21 293.29
PUFF (2)
160.08 160.14
PULCHELLUS (1)
184.04
PULCHRE (1)
063.18
PULL (5)
074.27 158.24 158.25 158.25 287.04
PULLED (8)
178.22 212.20 262.14 263.20 269.29
284.12 284.14 320.14
PULLING (1)
175.14
PULLS (1)
093.13
PULP (2)
307.05 318.22
PULPY (2)
305.11 307.22
PULSE (2)
155.18 178.13
PULSING (1)
188.10
PUMILA (1)
113.34
PUMP (2)
031.05 183.30
PUMPKIN (4)
037.12 059.25 065.24 269.28
PUMPKINS (2)
064.08 064.15
PUNCTUALITY (1)
118.01
PUNISHED (1)
250.13
PUNISHMENT (1)
316.01
PUNISHMENTS (1)
172.33
PUNY (3)
108.31 263.31 298.06
PUPIL (1)
147.09
PUPS (2)
278.07 278.36
PURANA (1)
270.18
PURCHASE (1)
064.31
PURCHASER (1)
173.11
PURE (23)
062.01 068.28 105.33 120.27 176.17
179.04 179.14 179.24 183.07 187.12
188.22 194.24 199.16 199.28 213.20
219.16 268.03 287.12 297.26 298.16
317.20 327.25 327.25
PURELY (3)
020.09 096.08 221.28
PURER (3)
184.29 221.07 331.06
PURGATIVE (1)
308.29
PURI (1)
112.14
PURIFICATION (1)
068.34
PURIFIED (1)
068.33
PURIFIES (1)
254.23
PURIFY (1)
134.21
PURIFYING (1)
067.34

PURITAN   (1)
  218.12
PURITY   (18)
  175.29 177.28 192.32 193.38 194.13
  197.22 219.21 219.25 219.26 219.33
  220.04 220.04 220.27 220.31 220.39
  227.07 325.28 325.30
PURLINS   (1)
  243.18
PURPLE   (1)
  026.18
PURPOSE   (18)
  009.14 016.02 019.34 045.28 084.20
  092.13 093.29 106.21 175.12 185.19
  213.20 228.06 245.18 253.02 253.26
  273.22 325.36 326.32
PURPOSELY   (1)
  205.30
PURPOSES   (4)
  003.19 024.28 101.30 171.27
PURPRESTURES   (1)
  250.14
PURSE   (1)
  063.26
PURSLANE   (1)
  061.20
PURSUE   (6)
  051.18 071.12 109.03 170.14 171.28
  205.25
PURSUED   (5)
  157.11 160.30 165.23 234.22 277.15
PURSUERS   (2)
  277.08 278.20
PURSUING   (3)
  089.24 277.02 278.11
PURSUIT   (6)
  070.17 070.30 152.29 212.29 277.23
  278.07
PURSUITS   (7)
  029.05 034.17 070.36 073.02 099.04
  210.31 215.25
PUSHED   (3)
  029.11 184.35 195.06
PUSHES   (1)
  307.13
PUSHING   (6)
  005.13 005.17 114.05 114.09 292.23
  311.06
PUT   (60)
  008.33 026.05 030.12 038.21 046.32
  052.27 054.27 061.35 063.12 063.21
  067.10 081.13 082.37 083.12 091.04
  093.22 105.14 107.34 109.21 115.01
  116.21 117.06 120.28 121.09 122.28
  127.18 133.13 138.13 148.06 155.07
  170.29 171.22 172.03 181.30 215.25
  225.18 230.06 234.36 235.26 241.29
  244.09 250.33 254.11 267.13 269.11
  269.18 275.03 279.13 281.12 282.03
  289.11 302.30 303.16 323.05 323.33
  324.08 327.09 327.13 327.31 328.32
PUTRID   (1)
  297.14
PUTS   (7)
  025.23 027.13 033.07 236.13 282.12
  311.15 333.31
PUTTING   (8)
  004.06 084.21 120.19 157.01 252.02
  292.31 296.04 318.32
PUTTY   (1)
  330.27
PUZZLE   (3)
  108.04 151.27 305.21
PUZZLED   (1)
  182.09
PYGMIES   (4)
  091.18 107.10 271.16 326.02

PYGMY   (1)
  326.03
PYRAMIDS   (2)
  034.28 058.05
PYRRHA   (1)
  005.31
PYTHAGOREAN   (1)
  162.09

QUA (1)
005.35
QUACK (2)
138.23   249.01
QUACKS (1)
077.04
QUADRUPED (1)
309.18
QUADRUPEDS (2)
196.06   324.15
QUAESTUS (1)
166.03
QUAFFS (1)
126.22
QUAKING (1)
316.21
QUAKINGS (1)
303.13
QUALIFIED (1)
008.36
QUALITIES (5)
006.23   120.02   120.06   164.26   241.01
QUALITY (8)
090.25   120.02   121.17   130.01   147.24
164.31   218.17   241.09
QUANTITIES (2)
040.21   195.12
QUANTITY (4)
055.34   177.19   218.17   246.07
QUARTER (14)
024.33   041.28   095.04   155.26   176.04
180.11   187.25   194.06   207.20   237.05
248.05   273.04   296.35   306.03
QUARTERS (9)
118.33   120.11   175.31   232.13   240.12
240.23   266.02   293.04   302.22
QUARTS (2)
163.16   243.10
QUARTZ (1)
246.28
QUEEN (4)
026.10   026.11   243.20   244.30
QUEENS (1)
021.30
QUEER (1)
175.16
QUEEREST (1)
310.15
QUENCHED (1)
174.27
QUESTION (11)
021.22   022.30   029.06   038.20   133.14
148.12   251.12   282.03   282.08   282.09
282.13
QUESTIONABLE (1)
054.05
QUESTIONED (1)
095.15
QUESTIONS (7)
003.23   038.24   064.37   108.04   208.13
217.26   277.30
QUICK (2)
278.04   278.24
QUICKLY (1)
234.36
QUICKSANDS (3)
091.29   207.02   330.20
QUICKSILVER (1)
188.26
QUIET (6)
008.07   146.09   269.13   283.03   288.38
328.14
QUIETED (1)
022.29
QUIRKS (1)
285.05
QUITE (32)
025.25   054.30   075.03   090.13   091.02

QUITE (CONTINUED)
115.03   122.07   128.15   130.09   138.33
151.18   160.21   170.18   210.04   210.24
225.08   225.31   232.27   232.31   239.20
247.10   272.04   276.07   276.10   284.24
285.19   289.05   289.29   296.29   300.24
323.18   324.34
QUIVERING (1)
159.32
QUOIL (3)
261.35   262.01   262.05
QUOTE (1)
143.06
QUOTED (1)
025.05

R (18)
125.01 125.01 125.01 125.04 125.04
125.04 125.05 125.05 125.05 126.24
126.24 126.24 126.24 126.24 126.24
126.30 126.30 153.33
RABBIT (6)
125.35 129.22 267.09 281.24 281.26
281.34
RABBITS (5)
083.14 145.34 216.03 273.27 281.17
RACCOON (1)
227.27
RACE (35)
014.28 015.09 028.02 028.09 029.26
032.03 035.20 036.13 065.10 076.21
079.16 096.17 103.21 107.27 116.23
126.01 138.09 149.26 154.21 166.07
180.04 184.32 212.24 216.05 216.09
224.11 254.07 263.11 264.11 294.13
313.26 326.02 327.06 332.01 332.15
RACES (2)
024.21 228.35
RACKED (1)
270.06
RADIATED (1)
081.20
RADICALS (1)
306.28
RADICLE (1)
015.29
RADII (1)
011.18
RADIIS (1)
314.02
RAFT (1)
249.28
RAFTERS (7)
042.07 042.19 208.22 242.15 242.21
243.18 243.28
RAGE (1)
220.24
RAGGED (5)
023.36 075.18 075.23 075.28 281.05
RAGGEDLY (1)
273.08
RAGING (2)
119.03 229.06
RAGS (4)
026.18 075.21 120.05 159.16
RAIL (3)
092.32 208.10 320.13
RAILROAD (30)
021.08 029.09 037.03 041.14 043.02
053.18 053.24 053.25 054.11 092.25
092.26 094.15 114.34 115.10 115.13
118.02 118.10 122.19 130.04 130.19
154.15 176.31 182.35 192.35 197.17
202.17 238.23 249.29 266.32 304.31
RAILROADS (6)
035.03 052.19 092.21 092.22 092.24
304.35
RAILS (4)
041.16 092.19 092.28 097.18
RAIN (37)
008.28 018.13 045.13 048.25 084.30
086.23 120.23 131.14 131.36 132.22
138.07 138.12 161.33 179.21 189.13
190.07 190.17 190.20 204.10 204.29
207.12 223.27 234.15 236.27 243.20
268.20 292.09 293.23 300.18 300.30
302.32 304.20 312.09 312.26 312.27
314.18 318.06
RAINBOW (6)
202.11 202.14 206.33 207.18 217.02
317.10
RAINED (3)
029.14 042.02 318.24

RAINIEST (1)
085.28
RAINS (3)
132.27 155.22 302.14
RAINY (5)
027.25 027.36 133.06 144.20 144.22
RAISE (12)
039.19 054.27 055.21 055.33 063.28
064.02 155.13 164.22 170.05 174.09
175.14 197.01
RAISED (17)
043.08 055.33 059.05 099.11 099.13
100.23 109.25 129.15 159.21 231.16
241.24 250.11 262.17 264.21 271.21
293.20 295.27
RAISERS (1)
045.07
RAISES (2)
173.12 283.31
RAISING (4)
042.38 045.08 045.34 163.26
RAISINS (1)
167.27
RAKE (2)
238.09 238.14
RAKED (1)
116.03
RAKES (1)
294.20
RALEIGH (1)
005.37
RAMBLE (1)
153.08
RAMBLED (3)
168.01 173.05 201.03
RAMBLER (2)
042.33 172.09
RAMBLES (1)
319.17
RAMBLING (1)
192.08
RAMS (2)
115.34 122.02
RAN (8)
115.03 207.17 226.01 228.09 256.28
256.33 278.32 293.20
RANG (2)
118.09 126.08
RANGE (4)
099.22 130.13 289.03 329.07
RANGED (1)
273.06
RANGES (1)
087.07
RANGING (2)
069.36 210.10
RANK (7)
014.08 022.30 195.11 195.11 210.18
210.21 313.10
RANKS (4)
156.26 161.26 161.35 322.33
RANZ (1)
158.18
RAPID (4)
013.13 097.24 108.23 229.35
RAPIDLY (7)
190.20 245.25 295.26 301.06 301.08
303.12 307.24
RAPT (1)
111.27
RARE (12)
032.33 088.02 100.20 124.05 150.13
162.14 201.24 212.02 284.21 317.14
320.29 330.22
RAREFIES (1)
033.31
RARELY (15)
063.33 085.36 095.08 103.28 129.28

174

RECALL (1)
170.06
RECEDED (2)
288.13   290.14
RECEDING (1)
180.03
RECEIVE (8)
031.22   031.22   038.04   068.31   166.14
197.05   243.21   328.18
RECEIVED (9)
020.14   041.05   051.35   060.10   083.26
094.06   143.05   245.33   262.28
RECEIVING (2)
021.36   188.35
RECENT (4)
159.04   277.24   311.25   314.14
RECENTLY (5)
025.17   086.33   178.33   181.15   294.25
RECESS (1)
243.26
RECESSES (2)
204.24   274.05
RECESSIT (1)
314.01
RECIPE (1)
063.14
RECKLESS (1)
227.13
RECKON (1)
016.13
RECKONED (1)
152.01
RECKONING (2)
091.32   206.17
RECLAIMED (1)
130.12
RECLINES (1)
331.22
RECOGNITION (1)
321.27
RECOGNIZE (4)
096.32   165.19   171.03   171.24
RECOGNIZED (2)
022.24   125.29
RECOLLECT (1)
021.26
RECOLLECTION (2)
083.15   184.09
RECOMMEND (1)
320.03
RECOMMENDED (2)
169.02   210.20
RECOMMENDING (1)
218.34
RECOMMENDS (2)
118.24   157.32
RECONCILED (1)
215.34
RECONNOITRE (1)
235.26
RECORD (3)
038.16   069.06   333.05
RECORDED (6)
078.25   100.32   106.09   230.14   231.28
232.03
RECORDS (1)
331.27
RECOVER (2)
017.17   285.09
RECOVERED (4)
254.04   280.35   296.30   314.30
RECOVERING (1)
316.39
RECOVERS (1)
076.11
RECOVERY (1)
131.35

RECREATE (2)
135.36   222.01
RECREATION (3)
136.07   194.25   206.08
RECRUIT (1)
006.22
RECTITUDE (1)
315.37
RECURRED (1)
254.27
RED (25)
018.24   018.25   083.18   158.20   182.02
184.22   201.17   228.20   228.28   228.35
229.03   229.06   229.14   229.25   229.34
230.34   238.08   238.26   239.11   273.19
273.28   302.24   310.13   310.26   325.14
REDDENING (1)
207.18
REDDING (2)
109.35   167.26
REDDISH (1)
305.25
REDEEM (4)
077.20   196.16   205.33   222.22
REDEEMERS (1)
078.23
REDOLENT (1)
196.35
REDS (1)
228.36
REDUCE (3)
031.28   091.06   091.36
REDUCED (3)
011.23   275.29   286.01
REDUCES (1)
265.25
REED (1)
114.32
REEFS (2)
020.29   119.22
REEL (1)
183.36
REELS (1)
283.11
REFER (4)
013.33   034.36   035.16   035.24
REFERRED (10)
011.30   104.31   124.04   141.24   176.29
181.05   202.30   260.06   268.11   298.07
REFERS (1)
217.30
REFINE (1)
221.32
REFINED (2)
038.12   103.26
REFINEMENT (2)
062.19   109.14
REFIT (1)
292.06
REFLECT (4)
009.17   166.10   177.05   177.24
REFLECTED (18)
176.36   185.35   186.32   188.02   188.33
189.17   227.06   240.06   240.24   241.33
247.05   282.26   291.16   297.33   300.11
300.25   300.35   328.11
REFLECTING (6)
086.16   129.16   189.34   195.31   297.27
312.12
REFLECTION (5)
176.30   177.09   193.19   197.29   300.28
REFLECTIONS (4)
086.30   184.17   189.22   199.19
REFLECTS (3)
176.24   227.10   269.24
REFORM (1)
090.03

REFORMED (1)
078.12
REFORMER (3)
046.30 078.05 148.09
REFORMERS (2)
014.27 154.01
REFORMING (1)
077.23
REFORMS (1)
148.30
REFRESHED (4)
037.20 119.18 258.36 318.03
REFRESHING (1)
167.13
REFUGE (2)
190.11 295.17
REFUSAL (2)
082.06 082.06
REFUSE (3)
049.06 075.29 103.03
REFUSED (1)
090.28
REGAL (2)
080.24 331.13
REGARD (9)
019.24 021.24 032.21 033.02 053.24
247.33 259.10 303.15 327.33
REGARDED (8)
013.19 081.18 103.23 195.33 203.02
216.04 289.25 308.01
REGARDING (4)
165.34 217.28 240.17 277.21
REGARDLESS (1)
238.15
REGARDS (1)
213.27
REGION (3)
081.29 088.01 099.28
REGIONS (4)
014.10 285.27 295.10 320.33
REGNA (1)
314.01
REGRET (3)
150.07 192.04 194.14
REGRETS (1)
124.28
REGRETTED (3)
196.15 216.22 217.24
REGRETTING (1)
098.25
REGULAR (13)
116.33 132.34 146.28 185.21 232.30
268.10 272.17 272.20 284.16 289.20
308.28 311.24 313.12
REGULARITY (6)
117.33 247.28 248.07 288.29 289.02
301.26
REGULARLY (7)
062.31 123.34 180.17 182.10 225.29
273.27 276.25
REGULATE (2)
030.08 213.27
REGULATED (1)
221.21
REGULATES (1)
117.36
REGULATING (1)
112.31
REI (1)
243.05
REIGN (2)
239.21 239.33
REIGNS (2)
173.22 283.07
REINS (2)
157.17 157.30
REINVIGORATED (1)
089.26

REJECTED (2)
292.15 326.29
REJECTING (1)
259.33
REJOICE (3)
068.31 125.25 166.28
RELATED (6)
025.13 115.16 171.23 194.05 232.01
317.07
RELATES (1)
287.26
RELATION (3)
169.34 266.16 310.05
RELATIONS (3)
006.16 096.10 171.19
RELATIVE (1)
022.30
RELEASE (1)
082.15
RELEASED (2)
041.03 171.34
RELIANCE (2)
147.14 316.36
RELIC (1)
125.11
RELICS (2)
102.20 103.35
RELIEF (1)
050.01
RELIEVE (1)
076.03
RELIEVED (2)
136.30 265.07
RELIEVO (1)
180.14
RELIGION (6)
058.01 058.12 098.02 217.22 221.10
322.35
RELIGIOUS (4)
079.14 088.29 108.11 221.09
RELIGIOUSLY (3)
009.21 026.08 062.26
RELINQUISH (1)
070.17
RELINQUISHED (1)
239.01
RELINQUISHING (1)
166.34
RELISH (2)
161.02 217.04
REMAIN (6)
041.30 064.24 072.34 134.31 270.19
277.05
REMAINDER (2)
055.01 231.19
REMAINED (2)
159.17 183.26
REMAINING (5)
068.17 155.29 230.36 296.27 303.31
REMAINS (6)
098.22 099.13 257.14 276.21 297.15
325.04
REMARK (2)
045.01 261.07
REMARKABLE (18)
004.18 014.25 103.21 127.05 175.29
178.27 181.07 189.04 197.21 227.21
250.33 280.20 285.15 287.08 287.20
289.12 306.05 323.13
REMARKABLY (6)
147.35 182.33 184.18 189.15 194.23
227.04
REMARKED (2)
095.20 217.35
REMEMBER (26)
003.26 006.19 008.22 028.13 038.15
053.10 138.32 155.31 174.07 177.16
180.22 191.14 194.27 198.21 199.07

REMEMBER   (CONTINUED)
207.24   213.22   241.26   252.06   253.12
257.09   271.11   279.16   279.36   328.02
331.32
REMEMBERED   (7)
010.16   111.10   159.09   159.10   245.25
260.31   270.14
REMEMBERING   (2)
124.23   212.12
REMEMBERS   (3)
100.25   182.26   257.29
REMEMBRANCE   (2)
077.11   256.24
REMEMEMBERED   (1)
262.13
REMIND   (1)
251.28
REMINDED   (12)
070.04   087.23   111.32   125.18   148.23
161.06   165.29   297.23   305.14   316.29
329.03   332.16
REMINDING   (4)
085.04   119.21   120.16   124.26
REMINDS   (1)
054.06
REMINISCENCES   (1)
264.29
REMISSNESS   (1)
076.13
REMNANT   (1)
231.13
REMNANTS   (1)
256.34
REMOTE   (8)
088.03   096.36   117.16   129.16   135.10
242.32   298.08   312.14
REMOTENESS   (4)
088.11   101.32   152.13   244.36
REMOVAL   (2)
043.17   044.20
REMOVE   (1)
113.11
REMOVED   (4)
024.19   044.07   096.20   111.11
REMOVING   (1)
156.36
REMUNERATE   (1)
136.01
RENDERED   (2)
060.41   065.17
RENDING   (1)
192.21
RENEW   (1)
088.32
RENT   (11)
022.08   029.20   029.21   030.36   031.25
043.35   049.34   050.05   159.16   205.08
303.11
RENTS   (1)
119.32
REPAIR   (3)
071.32   142.14   205.18
REPAIRER   (1)
115.20
REPAIRS   (1)
188.27
REPAST   (1)
318.12
REPASTINATION   (1)
162.21
REPEAT   (1)
241.04
REPEATED   (3)
126.26   275.19   316.37
REPEATEDLY   (1)
213.33
REPEATING   (2)
104.23   123.19

REPEATS   (2)
100.26   126.30
REPENT   (1)
010.31
REPEOPLED   (1)
264.29
REPETITION   (1)
123.19
REPLIED   (2)
079.08   330.15
REPLY   (3)
019.04   126.36   133.08
REPORT   (1)
158.05
REPORTED   (4)
137.22   150.21   162.34   188.08
REPORTER   (2)
018.06   268.01
REPORTS   (3)
095.02   109.33   211.04
REPOSE   (3)
129.20   129.21   329.19
REPOSES   (1)
221.03
REPRESENT   (2)
044.18   125.29
REPRESENTATIVE   (1)
279.24
REPRESENTED   (6)
102.25   139.01   172.02   210.09   239.35
265.19
REPRESENTS   (1)
215.13
REPRINTS   (1)
180.13
REPROACH   (1)
215.36
REPROOF   (2)
144.26   219.03
REPROOFS   (1)
238.26
REPROVE   (1)
112.24
REPTILE   (2)
219.11   220.32
REPUBLICANS   (1)
229.06
REPUDIATION   (1)
033.11
REPUGNANCE   (1)
214.31
REPUTATION   (1)
142.23
REQUEST   (1)
172.30
REQUESTED   (1)
244.10
REQUIEM   (1)
089.03
REQUIRE   (10)
003.31   023.29   064.04   080.15   152.08
181.08   251.23   295.25   317.35   322.33
REQUIRED   (13)
031.15   031.32   036.27   055.28   069.32
070.26   076.27   087.32   177.23   206.02
240.33   327.22   329.15
REQUIRES   (10)
006.20   012.18   026.22   050.17   101.04
199.14   212.04   251.08   268.16   288.14
RESCUE   (4)
078.17   161.35   229.32   259.26
RESEMBLE   (2)
226.17   227.16
RESEMBLED   (1)
225.34
RESEMBLING   (1)
305.12

RESERVED (2)
101.16 194.12
RESERVEDLY (2)
101.06 141.17
RESIDE (2)
077.18 200.04
RESIDENCE (2)
050.10 099.20
RESIDUAL (1)
325.02
RESIGN (1)
046.12
RESIGNATION (2)
008.08 091.01
RESIGNED (1)
037.01
RESIST (3)
224.04 276.33 330.10
RESISTED (1)
171.31
RESISTLESS (1)
133.03
RESOLUTE (1)
216.16
RESOLUTELY (1)
229.10
RESOLUTION (4)
282.14 322.30 323.03 326.32
RESOLVE (2)
235.01 322.36
RESOLVED (6)
023.25 050.02 152.07 198.25 224.28
326.27
RESONANCE (1)
301.29
RESORT (2)
193.30 240.23
RESORTED (2)
183.27 251.17
RESOUND (4)
078.21 095.36 234.02 268.07
RESOUNDED (3)
256.19 278.29 301.16
RESOUNDING (1)
127.17
RESOUNDS (1)
197.07
RESOURCES (1)
236.18
RESPECT (27)
003.25 014.20 023.08 023.08 033.25
050.01 072.30 082.28 083.33 095.17
107.20 109.28 136.21 143.34 144.04
151.11 182.24 196.19 212.28 213.06
213.34 222.23 254.06 275.21 310.18
315.16 321.21
RESPECTABLE (6)
022.19 036.06 063.10 196.29 214.14
332.26
RESPECTED (4)
022.19 022.33 095.34 172.07
RESPECTING (1)
155.08
RESPECTIVE (1)
230.08
RESPECTIVELY (1)
176.03
RESPECTS (12)
024.24 045.19 050.12 056.22 072.32
109.11 197.23 214.33 217.21 244.05
326.25 327.01
RESPITE (1)
070.32
RESPLENDENT (1)
202.26
RESPONDED (1)
272.20

RESPONSES (1)
124.25
RESPONSIBILITY (1)
147.28
REST (42)
004.03 030.24 042.20 053.34 055.31
065.17 067.32 072.03 076.05 076.28
086.09 089.11 091.24 093.27 095.22
097.26 104.28 109.04 117.14 117.19
118.36 122.35 129.19 142.22 142.35
152.24 155.27 156.34 161.19 172.09
177.03 187.14 207.22 220.21 227.01
231.23 235.28 259.28 271.23 277.09
292.17 296.27
RESTED (2)
127.11 227.30
RESTING (3)
187.15 278.09 285.31
RESTLESS (7)
114.27 115.25 117.12 122.32 153.10
272.35 329.35
RESTLESSNESS (1)
125.02
RESTORE (1)
078.32
RESTORED (1)
312.26
RESTORING (1)
139.06
RESTRAIN (1)
026.14
RESTRAINED (1)
278.23
RESTRICTED (1)
329.06
RESULT (12)
013.11 105.30 120.07 151.32 157.14
163.26 176.33 205.29 216.21 219.25
290.26 327.26
RESULTS (6)
020.26 156.08 166.21 230.26 290.25
290.31
RESUME (2)
004.23 239.30
RESUMED (2)
312.23 327.07
RESURRECTION (1)
333.15
RETAIN (8)
012.30 013.22 021.26 022.30 024.02
061.17 121.05 277.14
RETAINED (4)
003.25 082.26 085.02 314.16
RETAINER (1)
057.22
RETAINS (1)
188.31
RETARD (1)
299.22
RETARDED (1)
142.15
RETICULATUS (1)
184.23
RETINUE (1)
036.15
RETIRED (4)
174.32 207.14 227.24 263.28
RETIREMENT (2)
051.03 083.05
RETIRES (1)
024.05
RETREAT (6)
067.17 203.07 229.23 234.05 245.13
258.05
RETREATED (4)
130.32 260.12 273.18 283.26
RETURN (10)
054.08 068.24 129.25 229.30 261.12

RIPENED
062.11 150.21   (2)
RIPENESS
077.06   (1)
RIPENS
010.14   (1)
RIPPED
283.17   (1)
RIPPLE
187.27 189.11 195.06 235.25 305.36   (6)
316.26
RIPPLED
129.14 189.02 236.26   (3)
RIPPLES
086.16 159.20 193.04   (3)
RIPPLING
129.11 187.28 190.09 201.05 233.36   (5)
RISE
015.31 041.33 078.09 097.18 127.19   (20)
127.19 175.35 179.25 181.10 181.19
181.23 181.32 185.34 207.25 209.04
234.04 235.29 236.35 293.10 332.36
RISEN
026.02 119.35 165.08 180.34 233.26   (7)
287.07 291.36
RISES
180.17 186.08 233.35 251.11 332.28   (5)
RISING
017.27 062.30 098.35 101.31 116.32   (17)
116.34 142.06 156.03 180.03 182.28
189.31 199.16 241.32 242.01 247.01
263.29 300.23
RISKS
153.35   (1)
RITES
221.12   (1)
RIVER
083.08 083.16 093.35 110.16 167.19   (24)
176.15 177.25 184.17 184.28 194.08
197.10 197.14 237.02 238.03 246.08
249.04 260.26 279.13 296.34 303.09
303.26 316.20 317.19 332.35
RIVERS
144.07 185.22 302.27 303.06 305.35   (7)
307.05 307.27
RIVET
330.32   (1)
RIVULETS
304.25   (1)
ROACH
184.03   (1)
ROAD
005.17 044.01 053.11 108.14 115.17   (34)
130.21 133.31 156.22 157.22 160.15
164.33 170.36 171.04 203.34 216.17
256.19 257.04 257.33 258.15 259.34
261.14 262.11 266.36 267.04 267.09
269.14 271.18 278.02 278.04 278.05
280.02 285.01 318.23 322.06
ROAM
129.22 238.21   (2)
ROAR
132.24 304.08   (2)
ROARS
129.18   (1)
ROAST
204.31 254.18   (2)
ROASTED
239.15   (1)
ROASTING
013.03   (1)
ROBBED
094.12   (1)
ROBBER
166.01   (1)
ROBBERY
172.20 322.29   (2)

ROBBING
006.33 013.28 253.31   (3)
ROBE
099.13 099.16   (2)
ROBED
269.22   (1)
ROBIN
073.33 226.08 312.15 312.19   (4)
ROBINHOOD
251.20   (1)
ROBINSON
274.10   (1)
ROBS
258.30   (1)
ROBUST
027.32 076.18 139.08   (3)
ROCK
020.32 028.10 110.07 147.01 278.21   (8)
278.26 278.33 300.22
ROCKS
028.15 083.20 098.03 159.19   (4)
ROD
057.34 098.35 113.31 179.04 182.27   (13)
257.18 266.06 274.01 282.24 293.01
300.34 302.28 316.26
RODGER
051.36   (1)
RODS
055.36 113.29 115.14 130.07 156.33   (29)
175.03 178.08 180.26 180.32 187.23
198.05 198.22 234.09 234.21 234.25
234.30 236.23 275.07 277.12 284.09
288.34 289.11 296.04 299.28 301.17
303.35 309.28 311.16 313.06
ROILING
228.05   (1)
ROLL
146.19 226.23   (2)
ROLLED
085.18 146.22 162.03 182.21 228.31   (6)
259.18
ROLLING
278.26 294.35 319.16   (3)
ROLLS
093.34 120.04   (2)
ROMAN
009.35 101.33 161.27 250.29 262.31   (5)
ROMANCE
105.20   (1)
ROMANS
166.04 250.26   (2)
ROME
101.25 162.05 217.15 331.25   (4)
ROOF
028.27 030.10 039.19 043.07 043.09   (19)
043.18 049.06 050.09 071.24 128.02
140.16 183.16 204.18 207.12 243.25
253.17 259.25 269.23 273.20
ROOFED
045.11   (1)
ROOFS
028.18   (1)
ROOM
019.28 037.06 050.07 067.20 087.20   (29)
128.14 133.20 135.35 140.08 140.13
140.33 141.05 141.31 141.32 141.32
143.11 167.25 168.13 169.20 183.12
186.05 204.30 225.33 241.29 242.34
242.35 243.16 254.20 271.19
ROOST
084.24 262.26   (2)
ROOSTS
223.10   (1)
ROOT
004.36 016.01 065.01 065.02 075.36   (16)
132.26 156.06 164.29 229.17 230.02
239.19 263.33 298.13 311.15 317.18
317.19

ROOTED (1)
015.30
ROOTS (14)
044.24 044.34 080.10 128.14 128.17
133.25 161.29 182.03 195.14 198.15
224.19 252.10 258.20 316.21
ROPE (4)
093.13 207.02 285.29 285.31
ROSE (10)
008.22 112.36 178.29 182.13 190.12
258.13 264.15 271.09 313.08 313.14
ROSETTES (1)
293.26
ROT (5)
131.18 248.19 300.19 325.21 325.22
ROTTED (1)
178.15
ROTTEN (5)
159.33 198.34 283.28 300.33 319.11
ROUGH (3)
066.08 084.32 242.14
ROUGHLY (1)
206.23
ROUND (49)
008.34 022.35 039.16 052.36 053.19
053.26 084.12 084.14 084.15 099.24
105.15 110.13 110.16 113.21 121.04
124.12 124.12 126.23 126.33 146.23
146.32 161.03 163.29 171.11 171.12
181.22 188.20 201.13 204.25 218.31
226.01 226.02 226.23 228.11 228.11
236.36 236.36 258.12 260.04 267.08
277.10 277.20 278.35 278.35 280.22
280.31 284.17 322.08 333.24
ROUNDABOUT (1)
142.27
ROUNDED (4)
178.23 193.16 248.04 308.09
ROUNDING (1)
269.36
ROUNDS (1)
333.06
ROUSED (1)
127.29
ROUT (3)
091.04 203.32 206.22
ROUTE (5)
169.31 170.19 256.29 313.15 323.14
ROUTES (2)
018.15 271.03
ROUTINE (3)
096.07 111.15 265.24
ROVING (1)
087.30
ROW (7)
027.29 160.01 168.02 181.28 190.19
295.30 295.30
ROWS (5)
155.04 155.10 156.33 158.32 163.28
RUB (1)
153.21
RUBBED (1)
173.20
RUBBING (2)
068.25 128.13
RUDDY (2)
138.03 203.12
RUDE (6)
029.25 047.14 101.29 243.16 267.29
310.10
RUDELY (1)
168.10
RUDER (1)
284.07
RUDEST (2)
040.08 254.02
RUDIMENT (1)
094.02

RUDIMENTAL (1)
273.14
RUFFLED (2)
129.15 245.34
RUG (1)
232.27
RUIN (5)
095.01 205.08 207.32 296.13 327.02
RUINED (2)
022.13 092.08
RUINOUS (1)
083.10
RUINS (3)
057.19 241.10 264.26
RULE (4)
215.07 289.15 289.24 291.05
RULER (1)
058.19
RULERS (3)
035.22 035.23 268.34
RULES (4)
016.04 062.33 126.13 136.15
RUM (2)
258.31 279.18
RUMBLE (2)
203.29 207.31
RUMBLING (2)
122.34 126.03
RUMFORD (1)
031.04
RUMOR (3)
220.37 233.27 262.01
RUN (43)
015.10 027.03 030.33 031.16 039.23
041.26 053.35 067.02 074.19 081.28
092.29 092.31 092.34 094.15 097.31
099.28 105.05 105.05 113.21 122.14
140.34 156.21 168.19 169.03 171.32
171.33 190.13 191.23 194.27 199.27
225.31 226.29 247.27 259.21 262.30
273.11 277.07 277.12 277.17 293.16
293.17 318.23 322.23
RUNAWAY (2)
152.16 152.24
RUNG (1)
259.17
RUNNING (10)
017.33 167.23 180.24 204.09 221.35
222.07 226.26 273.31 290.20 305.30
RUNS (6)
052.10 137.35 153.35 208.09 277.10
324.26
RUPTURE (1)
306.03
RUSH (4)
094.23 105.22 304.08 312.34
RUSHES (4)
053.31 194.34 195.05 195.09
RUSSET (2)
208.15 304.22
RUSSIA (1)
022.36
RUST (1)
005.28
RUSTIC (1)
243.04
RUSTICA (1)
084.07
RUSTLE (2)
167.13 278.19
RUSTLING (5)
223.24 233.30 233.35 238.25 281.25
RUSTY (2)
105.16 119.28
RUTHLESSLY (2)
161.24 195.30
RUTS (2)
295.34 323.24

RY
  220.20   (1)
RYE   (10)
  059.10   059.11   061.02   062.06   063.29
  064.03   105.34   169.20   243.12   294.24

S
(288)

003.34	004.36	005.13	005.29	007.01
007.03	009.36	010.07	010.25	010.28
012.05	012.17	013.08	017.07	019.13
019.15	019.19	019.22	021.36	022.16
022.28	023.12	025.23	026.07	027.29
030.36	031.19	031.21	032.09	034.17
034.18	035.22	036.08	036.11	036.12
036.18	036.23	036.25	037.17	037.33
039.04	039.05	041.20	046.02	046.03
047.28	049.25	050.03	050.05	051.36
053.10	054.04	055.22	056.21	056.31
056.32	057.35	059.37	061.15	064.25
065.32	066.07	066.27	066.30	067.10
067.26	067.31	070.28	070.34	071.12
071.13	071.13	074.07	074.30	076.05
076.31	076.36	081.10	087.08	088.05
088.22	089.03	093.25	093.26	093.31
096.13	096.17	097.17	099.32	102.01
102.27	102.28	110.11	111.31	113.10
115.24	115.33	115.33	115.35	116.27
118.19	119.04	120.29	120.36	121.03
122.19	124.11	127.06	127.22	129.23
136.02	136.19	138.10	138.18	138.19
141.14	141.17	141.24	142.25	144.34
144.36	145.07	149.16	149.18	150.20
151.26	152.02	152.03	152.30	153.27
154.18	155.15	155.20	158.05	158.22
159.14	160.17	160.18	161.27	161.27
161.28	161.28	166.30	167.23	167.26
168.31	171.21	172.23	173.23	174.22
174.33	180.04	181.12	185.17	185.28
185.34	186.10	186.12	186.13	188.30
192.05	192.26	194.01	194.02	194.05
194.15	194.19	195.27	197.10	199.33
201.08	202.11	202.34	204.11	204.17
205.01	205.33	206.29	207.12	209.03
212.18	212.36	213.08	217.07	218.23
218.29	218.33	219.30	220.15	220.23
221.32	221.35	223.11	223.18	223.31
223.32	223.34	224.02	224.03	224.13
225.10	225.11	226.27	227.19	227.33
229.11	229.15	230.15	230.21	231.05
232.10	232.36	233.22	238.16	239.26
243.19	244.14	244.26	244.29	245.30
249.03	249.20	252.22	254.12	254.37
256.30	257.03	257.14	257.33	258.18
258.22	258.36	259.03	259.08	259.22
259.22	260.08	260.15	261.20	261.26
261.28	261.36	262.11	262.21	263.27
263.35	264.08	265.03	265.06	265.26
267.01	267.09	267.26	269.04	269.10
270.03	271.05	271.09	272.22	276.28
278.16	278.23	279.06	291.09	293.26
296.36	299.16	299.27	301.14	301.19
302.20	303.21	304.19	311.07	314.27
315.06	317.10	319.18	320.30	321.34
322.31	325.19	328.04	328.12	328.16
330.16	333.09	333.25		

SABBATH (2)
162.30 259.13
SACCHARINE (1)
059.09
SACONTALA (1)
319.14
SACRAMENT (1)
069.01
SACRED (11)
089.22 106.33 165.23 165.30 192.18
250.29 250.31 298.17 322.32 323.02
323.03
SACREDNESS (1)
165.29
SACRIFICE (4)
032.03 050.18 111.22 321.21
SACRIFICED (3)
072.24 249.18 318.19

SACRIFICES (3)
072.23 134.23 165.31
SACRIFICING (1)
166.35
SAD (5)
020.03 069.26 078.29 132.17 144.26
SADDENS (2)
078.05 255.05
SADDLEBOW (1)
231.10
SADI (1)
079.04
SADLY (2)
109.10 212.27
SADNESS (1)
131.12
SAFE (7)
063.02 097.26 158.26 160.28 255.03
277.06 316.05
SAFELY (7)
007.15 011.03 094.10 098.07 145.30
160.24 184.01
SAFEST (2)
153.18 153.26
SAFETY (3)
037.04 237.06 324.18
SAFFRON (1)
183.03
SAGACITY (1)
122.12
SAGE (1)
328.23
SAGES (1)
151.36
SAHARA (1)
074.11
SAID (74)
004.10 005.31 009.18 011.20 012.33
019.09 021.13 025.35 031.07 032.35
035.28 038.17 041.04 043.33 044.18
050.33 054.26 057.12 058.25 076.19
081.26 083.08 083.32 084.22 087.32
108.17 112.15 127.30 142.08 143.05
143.31 146.33 148.03 148.34 149.24
149.33 151.23 151.30 153.08 153.19
163.21 163.40 164.06 176.13 187.03
194.03 194.21 197.11 206.31 208.35
222.16 223.26 225.22 227.17 232.04
235.17 239.27 241.02 262.01 265.01
276.20 283.22 289.22 294.28 297.15
301.01 312.01 322.29 326.24 328.02
328.31 330.18 330.22 332.25
SAIL (4)
071.14 097.27 169.19 321.30
SAILED (3)
024.01 169.26 236.06
SAILING (11)
024.09 115.24 140.34 169.25 206.17
234.09 234.20 237.07 310.31 313.05
320.24
SAILOR (2)
071.17 127.27
SAILORS (2)
026.04 320.22
SAILS (3)
119.29 159.24 190.02
SAINT (3)
028.27 038.05 093.11
SAINTS (2)
078.21 120.20
SAITH (2)
032.10 212.21
SAKE (8)
035.06 059.37 070.19 154.18 162.13
230.22 246.08 261.20
SAL (1)
063.12

184

SALAMANDER (1)
159.34
SALEABLE (1)
163.39
SALEM (1)
020.07
SALOONS (1)
117.27
SALT (13)
059.27 061.04 061.04 061.26 062.01
064.17 120.15 120.18 162.24 167.28
223.13 287.29 291.33
SALTED (1)
061.21
SALUTARY (1)
107.33
SALUTATION (1)
146.14
SALUTE (1)
022.23
SALUTED (1)
259.01
SALUTES (2)
146.28 268.10
SAM (1)
279.17
SAME (85)
010.14 010.21 010.21 012.29 014.27
015.20 015.32 020.17 025.24 044.06
045.28 046.02 058.13 060.01 064.32
065.09 066.06 100.01 108.04 108.14
108.15 116.32 123.09 123.20 126.26
126.31 131.34 134.05 136.07 148.08
156.05 156.05 161.10 166.04 176.21
177.22 181.06 181.16 181.17 182.33
183.19 188.22 191.10 193.01 193.08
193.11 193.13 193.19 197.26 197.26
202.30 211.27 212.32 215.22 217.06
220.27 222.18 227.01 237.08 239.12
241.20 247.18 258.35 260.18 265.21
265.22 269.16 274.13 274.16 274.35
277.18 283.05 295.36 297.04 297.26
298.16 299.27 300.13 310.05 312.18
313.14 317.33 327.32 329.05 329.06
SAMUEL (1)
027.11
SANCTIFY (1)
134.22
SAND (41)
018.25 041.15 044.26 044.29 049.25
092.29 113.03 113.32 113.33 122.24
156.29 159.19 176.26 176.31 176.34
178.25 179.05 180.24 185.18 191.33
193.29 195.18 197.32 197.33 241.20
245.17 246.25 287.17 295.04 304.29
304.36 305.03 305.05 305.23 305.31
306.05 307.08 307.14 307.24 307.25
327.07
SANDED (1)
283.05
SANDS (3)
197.22 306.17 311.32
SANDWICH (1)
004.09
SANDY (11)
054.21 098.20 185.13 186.18 194.19
195.07 195.16 198.32 288.38 306.03
306.15
SANE (2)
134.33 327.33
SANER (1)
322.38
SANEST (1)
269.15
SANG (5)
064.13 086.26 089.02 111.29 124.14
SANK (4)
182.18 185.20 190.36 330.16

SAP (1)
029.33
SAPLING (1)
043.28
SAPPY (2)
048.25 305.10
SAPWOOD (1)
252.13
SARDANAPALUS (1)
037.01
SARDINES (1)
218.23
SAT (27)
045.22 081.19 085.28 111.26 114.13
132.30 142.07 146.30 173.34 173.35
174.15 183.12 204.11 204.17 204.20
221.34 221.36 228.18 266.13 267.29
269.27 278.22 281.03 310.14 327.03
330.35 333.24
SATELLITE (1)
051.27
SATELLITES (1)
051.25
SATIN (1)
316.28
SATIRE (1)
219.07
SATIRICAL (1)
123.29
SATISFACTION (9)
078.26 126.30 146.14 218.02 242.30
243.01 330.11 330.29 331.26
SATISFACTIONS (1)
027.21
SATISFACTORY (2)
061.18 061.19
SATISFIED (10)
040.02 056.33 073.06 104.25 149.30
149.33 149.33 149.35 215.35 282.07
SATISFY (2)
040.01 238.13
SATURATED (3)
041.11 084.36 302.29
SATURATION (1)
126.19
SATURDAY (1)
120.29
SATURN (2)
166.07 243.22
SATYRS (1)
220.11
SAUCER (2)
105.23 248.08
SAUNTERING (1)
148.22
SAVAGE (26)
026.19 030.15 030.30 030.36 031.08
031.09 031.26 031.34 033.14 033.26
034.18 034.23 035.20 040.28 068.04
125.32 158.14 207.15 210.06 210.14
210.18 211.19 216.10 218.22 245.06
251.23
SAVAGENESS (1)
012.12
SAVAGES (5)
013.01 013.06 030.19 034.36 143.21
SAVE (5)
073.09 093.09 093.19 163.39 241.17
SAVES (3)
066.18 093.08 253.36
SAVING (1)
033.09
SAVOR (3)
218.10 218.11 315.01
SAVORINESS (1)
061.22
SAVORS (1)
218.18

185

```
SAW                              (  48)    SCATTERED                        (   3)
022.26  023.24  041.25  059.39  063.26     186.36  201.32  262.23
064.02  075.26  075.32  081.27  086.14   SCATTERING                        (   1)
094.34  107.15  146.12  148.17  160.01     304.16
161.11  161.34  164.16  174.16  178.11   SCENE                             (   1)
182.27  189.23  190.16  190.24  190.28     135.08
196.02  198.34  206.18  223.27  227.27   SCENERY                           (   5)
229.20  229.33  230.34  234.08  235.25     124.33  175.25  210.26  249.10  320.04
245.12  253.14  268.20  272.05  272.32   SCENES                            (   7)
274.09  277.15  293.29  294.14  294.25     004.30  112.29  132.11  142.28  155.34
297.18  319.01  327.19                      210.14  294.29
SAWDUST                          (   1)    SCENT                             (   5)
292.30                                       120.16  122.08  130.07  277.14  277.19
SAWED                            (   3)    SCENTED                           (   5)
042.22  062.04  198.27                       216.26  238.32  254.20  263.06  263.25
SAWS                             (   2)    SCHOLAR                           (   5)
294.07  294.20                               042.08  157.13  201.23  245.07  251.22
SAXON                            (   1)    SCHOLARS                          (   5)
251.02                                       015.05  101.32  101.35  101.35  269.07
SAY                              (  77)    SCHOOL                            (   9)
004.08  007.18  008.29  010.23  010.34     015.01  069.14  107.06  108.32  109.10
011.13  011.17  016.21  018.28  023.28     110.14  118.20  133.21  207.17
023.28  025.07  028.01  030.18  042.11   SCHOOLS                           (   8)
052.09  052.27  053.07  053.25  059.36     108.29  108.29  108.35  177.36  190.03
065.05  069.17  070.21  072.21  073.15     190.24  235.22  263.21
073.21  073.25  073.29  078.23  083.33   SCHOONER                          (   1)
084.03  088.26  088.30  089.28  089.30     138.25
090.01  091.24  093.08  093.18  096.34   SCIENCE                           (   5)
098.04  103.27  115.32  121.02  127.13     020.34  211.04  292.05  331.26  333.05
133.04  141.27  144.30  145.31  152.20   SCIENCES                          (   2)
157.06  164.08  177.21  178.31  183.35     042.13  051.18
193.19  195.19  197.25  207.21  216.22   SCIENTIFIC                        (   1)
221.13  223.19  224.32  231.29  231.31     076.24
242.25  249.21  257.08  269.02  270.07   SCINTILLATION                     (   1)
274.10  282.12  301.31  327.34  327.35     327.23
328.01  333.28                           SCIPIO                            (   1)
SAYING                           (   3)    258.06
032.07  079.04  170.27                   SCIURUS                           (   1)
SAYINGS                          (   2)    273.19
241.03  241.05                           SCOLLOPED                         (   1)
SAYS                             (  31)    185.30
005.27  009.19  012.34  022.36  027.11   SCORCHED                          (   1)
029.30  032.27  033.03  039.03  048.13     074.09
051.07  053.03  068.12  084.08  085.29   SCORE                             (   5)
099.27  106.14  106.18  134.31  144.34     043.35  152.29  212.07  253.13  325.26
144.37  162.19  166.01  217.30  218.08   SCORES                            (   1)
219.22  243.02  250.10  251.04  258.34     280.11
270.19                                   SCORNED                           (   1)
SCALDED                          (   1)    126.23
062.33                                   SCORNFUL                          (   1)
SCALE                            (   8)    103.07
083.34  104.07  175.25  284.03  289.10   SCOTLAND                          (   1)
301.04  304.33  330.07                     287.28
SCALES                           (   2)    SCOUR                             (   2)
252.14  311.33                             223.18  241.30
SCANT                            (   1)    SCRAP                             (   2)
281.06                                       095.03  119.28
SCANTY                           (   1)    SCRAPE                            (   1)
203.05                                       256.25
SCARCE                           (   1)    SCRAPS                            (   1)
121.24                                       045.25
SCARCELY                         (   4)    SCRATCHING                        (   1)
069.01  114.04  175.22  192.15             274.36
SCARCITY                         (   1)    SCREAM                            (   2)
211.22                                       115.23  124.19
SCARECROW                        (   2)    SCREAMING                         (   1)
022.21  022.23                             128.03
SCARED                           (   4)    SCREAMS                           (   2)
190.24  203.18  269.31  276.19             115.33  275.10
SCARES                           (   1)    SCREECH                           (   2)
301.32                                       124.17  128.04
SCARING                          (   1)    SCREWS                            (   1)
117.31                                       049.16
SCARLATINA                       (   1)    SCRIPTURE                         (   2)
160.13                                       106.36  261.28
SCARLET                          (   2)    SCRIPTURES                        (   2)
086.01  240.01                             104.01  106.33
```

SCRUBBED (1)
113.04
SCRUTETUR (1)
322.01
SCRUTINIZE (1)
322.04
SCRUTINY (2)
178.34 232.20
SCUD (1)
281.10
SCULLION (1)
214.17
SCULPTORS (1)
221.30
SCURF (1)
222.10
SCURVY (1)
034.05
SCUTTLE (1)
128.15
SCYPHUS (1)
172.27
SEA (21)
035.19 091.28 119.35 138.24 159.26
176.12 194.20 195.03 197.06 201.04
218.24 289.34 291.34 291.34 297.26
309.19 317.36 318.04 321.26 321.34
322.13
SEABOARD (1)
117.10
SEALERS (1)
271.14
SEAM (1)
247.21
SEAMLESS (1)
159.17
SEAMS (3)
004.05 022.11 270.09
SEARCH (3)
273.07 282.22 283.32
SEARCHED (1)
326.29
SEAS (2)
298.22 321.28
SEASHORE (1)
064.18
SEASON (28)
016.03 024.04 026.28 027.25 027.36
039.07 039.29 053.16 054.25 055.04
079.09 081.04 089.08 092.23 114.07
143.33 152.15 171.35 190.04 193.35
195.22 238.21 260.09 264.33 291.22
299.19 313.29 313.33
SEASONED (1)
333.22
SEASONING (1)
085.30
SEASONS (11)
018.16 018.27 024.21 029.33 111.33
131.12 138.04 144.22 270.13 319.16
320.11
SEAT (5)
077.22 081.21 081.22 113.15 115.36
SEATED (3)
086.03 095.15 099.28
SEATS (4)
080.21 191.31 208.36 208.36
SECLUDED (2)
180.31 228.01
SECOND (10)
012.29 049.09 108.10 120.01 211.03
225.27 232.08 240.33 241.09 319.19
SECONDLY (2)
021.27 039.29
SECRECY (1)
244.25
SECRET (3)
098.27 137.29 227.22

SECRETARY (1)
039.07
SECRETED (1)
185.01
SECRETS (3)
017.06 255.02 303.22
SECT (1)
173.30
SECTION (2)
287.23 288.08
SECURE (3)
032.05 103.15 253.25
SECURED (3)
012.22 060.36 199.26
SECURELY (1)
297.34
SECURES (3)
030.35 051.02 291.32
SEDES (1)
081.21
SEDGE (2)
114.31 317.31
SEDGES (1)
207.30
SEDGY (1)
194.31
SEDIMENT (3)
144.09 179.06 213.19
SEDULOUSLY (2)
105.33 161.26
SEE (130)
004.34 005.03 007.30 012.01 029.08
035.04 036.14 043.04 047.15 053.05
057.26 057.32 065.29 066.15 069.25
072.10 081.28 087.10 087.14 090.34
093.21 093.22 096.29 098.12 098.20
105.27 109.34 111.18 113.08 113.16
118.26 121.21 122.20 129.08 134.17
135.36 138.26 140.20 143.27 144.04
150.25 150.29 151.04 164.03 164.26
167.15 167.16 168.02 168.22 170.04
172.12 176.25 177.09 177.35 184.02
185.12 187.16 189.02 189.21 191.34
192.09 193.05 193.18 193.35 194.26
195.33 196.01 198.02 202.02 214.09
214.12 218.09 220.29 223.31 224.16
224.23 224.36 228.17 230.33 232.23
233.01 234.10 235.21 236.05 236.20
237.01 241.32 242.27 243.25 243.35
244.03 246.03 247.02 247.05 247.20
253.11 254.22 266.08 268.37 269.24
270.23 277.03 283.36 284.18 285.03
287.25 290.06 292.24 295.01 296.14
297.21 297.31 302.11 302.16 302.21
303.12 303.31 305.17 306.06 307.11
314.36 315.04 316.08 318.18 318.25
319.07 323.27 328.14 328.27 333.03
SEED (17)
015.28 046.34 055.04 055.05 062.31
117.13 158.23 163.06 163.30 295.01
164.01 164.23 166.16 239.25
314.13 316.16
SEEDS (12)
082.10 082.23 083.35 083.36 131.18
164.01 164.08 164.09 164.34 166.29
213.02 314.16
SEEING (10)
006.08 007.05 053.20 080.25 213.17
244.16 303.31 310.31 313.18 315.29
SEEK (11)
027.32 057.17 100.13 129.21 134.17
134.18 188.06 207.25 219.26 269.14
328.34
SEEKING (3)
210.12 273.10 277.04
SEEKS (5)
012.16 077.30 136.07 309.19 324.24

187

SEELEY   (1)
  044.12
SEEM   (12)
  049.35 059.40 063.14 066.28 073.06
  100.19 140.23 165.04 203.20 244.34
  298.06 328.16
SEEMED   (33)
  017.17 047.12 065.35 086.20 113.13
  114.10 131.35 142.14 145.04 151.33
  153.03 153.24 160.16 161.05 174.16
  175.20 189.34 190.20 207.21 214.23
  236.03 239.15 242.32 269.20 273.14
  282.12 295.10 304.08 308.15 313.23
  316.32 317.07 323.11
SEEMING   (2)
  005.26 095.27
SEEMINGLY   (9)
  016.22 044.19 066.24 189.33 207.04
  272.15 290.32 304.04 312.05
SEEMS   (9)
  009.30 056.30 116.22 116.24 131.23
  133.14 227.06 303.15 313.33
SEEN   (62)
  005.08 017.16 018.07 019.06 027.16
  028.36 030.02 041.34 043.08 056.18
  082.01 082.33 084.08 088.13 111.17
  115.04 116.14 120.17 148.18 149.22
  151.14 156.09 168.22 176.15 176.19
  177.17 178.28 184.14 185.33 186.10
  186.21 191.05 191.15 193.07 193.39
  198.13 199.09 223.32 225.30 226.21
  234.01 239.10 239.36 248.16 249.17
  257.32 261.10 262.07 262.21 267.10
  271.22 279.19 281.23 281.33 285.24
  287.32 288.08 296.31 305.06 307.21
  313.21 332.02
SEER   (2)
  066.14 111.18
SEES   (4)
  137.12 157.31 216.14 306.21
SEEST   (1)
  080.30
SEETHING   (1)
  087.19
SEGMENT   (1)
  217.02
SEIZE   (1)
  210.07
SEIZED   (2)
  171.22 245.29
SEIZES   (1)
  114.31
SEIZING   (2)
  274.32 304.10
SELDOM   (2)
  264.33 272.05
SELECT   (8)
  055.38 101.17 101.23 109.36 111.04
  153.26 163.29 230.03
SELECTED   (3)
  111.14 207.04 238.28
SELECTING   (1)
  274.15
SELECTMEN   (2)
  110.06 151.09
SELF   (10)
  008.01 018.12 070.34 153.35 155.08
  213.34 320.30 321.21 322.31 331.21
SELFISH   (1)
  072.20
SELFISHNESS   (2)
  076.17 165.33
SELL   (5)
  019.01 020.14 034.08 138.30 328.26
SELLING   (4)
  019.23 043.31 161.15 208.02
SELLS   (2)
  171.25 238.11

SELVAGE   (1)
  186.07
SELVES   (1)
  034.05
SEMBLANCE   (2)
  068.06 333.22
SEMI   (1)
  305.28
SENATE   (1)
  171.26
SEND   (8)
  003.35 015.29 051.19 077.18 152.22
  164.34 182.02 245.22
SENDING   (1)
  297.28
SENDS   (3)
  133.25 186.05 188.32
SENIORITY   (1)
  126.27
SENIORS   (1)
  009.12
SENSE   (31)
  012.14 015.08 020.02 033.10 048.08
  057.31 072.05 072.23 073.23 074.31
  080.13 100.15 103.03 103.14 104.16
  124.34 129.04 131.29 134.34 158.15
  160.10 165.29 210.29 218.04 225.19
  266.26 306.10 324.01 325.09 325.10
  325.10
SENSES   (8)
  028.22 062.12 127.35 131.08 134.06
  219.28 259.34 325.17
SENSIBLE   (4)
  057.34 103.12 132.01 135.09
SENSIBLY   (3)
  052.28 302.15 302.25
SENSITIVE   (5)
  219.02 266.28 282.25 302.02 302.06
SENSUAL   (2)
  218.17 219.11
SENSUALIST   (2)
  220.30 314.33
SENSUALITY   (6)
  219.33 220.26 220.39 220.40 221.17
  221.33
SENSUALLY   (1)
  220.28
SENSUOUS   (1)
  089.25
SENT   (9)
  015.28 020.15 023.10 095.13 207.16
  225.24 273.21 292.14 311.02
SENTENCE   (1)
  025.09
SENTENCES   (3)
  099.25 141.05 224.35
SENTIMENTAL   (2)
  046.30 119.17
SENTIMENTS   (2)
  260.05 315.32
SENTINELS   (1)
  093.27
SEPARATE   (4)
  049.01 049.39 071.25 305.28
SEPARATED   (4)
  083.07 134.20 187.14 280.26
SEPARATELY   (1)
  025.10
SEPARATES   (3)
  133.15 284.25 307.19
SEPARATING   (1)
  186.25
SEPHRONIA   (1)
  105.03
SEPTEMBER   (8)
  047.33 121.35 186.19 188.19 221.34
  239.36 296.29 319.20

SERENADE (1)
085.36
SERENADED (3)
123.25 125.07 174.35
SERENE (9)
027.35 102.31 119.14 131.32 138.17
227.05 282.07 312.02 314.36
SERENELY (2)
236.05 318.21
SERENITY (6)
086.25 129.14 193.38 268.37 269.24
283.06
SERFS (2)
005.09 208.03
SERGEANT (1)
279.29
SERIOUS (7)
026.12 052.17 099.21 147.03 172.15
217.18 224.06
SERIOUSLY (4)
069.29 094.09 094.27 240.19
SERMON (1)
095.26
SERMONS (1)
332.20
SERPENT (2)
139.02 139.03
SERVANT (3)
243.01 298.10 298.14
SERVANTS (1)
116.24
SERVE (9)
013.22 023.16 026.16 046.21 077.03
094.34 104.12 147.17 162.13
SERVED (3)
023.17 214.18 241.25
SERVES (4)
013.20 126.21 181.19 280.03
SERVICE (1)
004.06
SERVILE (1)
080.22
SERVING (1)
249.18
SERVITOR (1)
089.14
SERVITUDE (1)
007.19
SET (34)
018.36 032.09 033.21 034.10 036.33
044.04 045.06 064.09 066.13 066.14
066.20 073.29 078.19 093.22 098.07
117.35 136.15 169.19 184.01 188.20
190.02 203.04 224.15 234.21 235.19
248.24 257.25 259.05 259.32 274.34
295.20 302.13 317.01 320.15
SETS (2)
077.23 122.24
SETTING (6)
093.14 112.36 124.04 173.08 185.32
328.11
SETTLE (7)
088.08 097.32 207.07 234.18 237.04
304.10 330.05
SETTLED (7)
018.35 037.28 068.02 099.16 195.34
240.12 313.01
SETTLER (5)
137.21 182.25 264.21 265.03 270.05
SETTLERS (2)
038.34 164.15
SETTLES (1)
243.26
SETTLING (3)
085.21 272.15 303.06
SEVEN (14)
032.36 038.23 039.14 044.26 061.01
123.34 155.04 181.03 183.35 194.22

SEVEN (CONTINUED)
244.18 287.08 296.03 332.01
SEVENTEEN (2)
109.19 332.31
SEVENTEENTH (1)
332.02
SEVENTIETH (1)
164.18
SEVENTY (4)
005.17 010.35 197.11 287.29
SEVERAL (33)
010.22 012.20 015.18 039.34 054.31
061.19 062.08 071.25 074.08 082.06
094.25 101.28 104.30 144.02 160.32
170.10 170.23 172.05 173.10 182.03
189.13 199.08 204.07 225.05 229.21
248.32 250.01 288.30 293.12 299.35
312.24 323.11 333.14
SEVERE (5)
169.28 189.09 299.14 299.21 311.25
SEVERED (2)
230.36 231.08
SEVERELY (1)
250.13
SEVILLE (1)
094.32
SEWING (1)
023.11
SEX (2)
130.01 153.22
SEXTON (1)
110.05
SHADE (6)
117.01 156.34 161.30 183.32 227.30
265.13
SHADED (3)
228.01 263.34 305.32
SHADES (3)
120.13 305.23 314.18
SHADIEST (1)
246.15
SHADOW (8)
012.17 096.04 202.18 202.26 203.29
263.32 282.27 293.30
SHADOWS (6)
202.20 208.27 242.20 255.04 324.36
329.01
SHADOWY (1)
252.33
SHADY (2)
080.09 201.06
SHAFTS (1)
115.10
SHAKE (2)
067.22 245.13
SHAKING (4)
026.20 116.19 262.29 265.35
SHAKSPEARE (2)
076.25 148.19
SHAKSPEARES (1)
104.04
SHALL (54)
010.11 010.23 023.28 024.09 032.10
032.14 036.04 036.06 046.12 047.29
054.01 058.27 061.09 066.26 073.20
078.04 084.02 084.02 084.14 092.22
104.01 104.02 104.05 107.13 108.08
109.04 120.27 138.14 142.28 155.18
166.27 189.05 212.15 216.05 220.35
220.35 224.08 224.25 225.10 243.15
244.32 297.26 297.30 297.31 302.16
312.17 324.10 326.01 326.12 326.16
326.18 326.25 331.15 331.31
SHALLOW (23)
086.29 098.21 100.03 138.25 183.21
184.16 194.23 195.16 246.20 271.24
277.16 287.10 287.24 288.09 288.09
291.18 293.29 299.28 299.31 299.33

189

```
SHOESTRINGS                        (  1)     SHOULD                         (CONTINUED)
  033.20                                        165.03  165.15  166.14  166.24  170.08
SHONE                              (  4)        171.33  184.24  192.17  194.15  194.16
  041.16  044.28  125.31  231.05                205.31  206.09  206.23  208.28  210.27
SHOOK                              (  3)        212.11  214.09  215.21  224.26  230.07
  182.18  182.21  238.30                        233.22  242.18  244.01  257.11  262.03
SHOOT                              (  2)        268.17  269.09  269.12  270.06  276.05
  015.29  320.30                                280.21  290.23  292.27  299.33  302.03
SHOOTS                             (  2)        302.11  303.19  314.20  320.20  321.08
  227.13  315.05                                323.09  324.07  324.32  324.34  325.01
SHOP                               (  5)        325.25  326.06  326.11  326.26  326.28
  075.34  096.33  234.06  259.22  260.08        328.22  330.32  331.13  332.30
SHOPPING                           (  1)     SHOULDER                           (  5)
  170.29                                        169.21  207.18  238.23  249.36  276.03
SHOPS                              (  3)     SHOULDERED                         (  1)
  004.16  063.33  138.30                        211.15
SHORE                              ( 91)     SHOULDERS                          (  5)
  003.06  020.19  086.03  086.09  086.27        004.22  025.20  027.13  083.25  249.15
  086.27  086.35  087.27  114.31  126.07     SHOUT                              (  3)
  126.22  129.06  174.30  175.03  175.28        095.26  115.28  141.27
  176.25  176.29  178.23  180.01  180.27     SHOUTED                            (  1)
  180.32  181.25  181.27  181.33  181.34        259.25
  182.07  182.09  182.22  182.36  183.31     SHOUTS                             (  1)
  185.13  185.27  185.30  186.01  186.09        053.32
  186.10  186.15  186.20  187.32  188.06     SHOVED                             (  1)
  190.32  191.06  191.34  192.24  192.34        141.29
  193.11  193.26  194.31  195.03  195.05     SHOVEL                             (  1)
  195.17  196.13  197.07  197.26  198.05        252.16
  198.22  198.27  199.03  199.17  232.24     SHOW                               ( 10)
  234.16  234.20  240.25  241.19  245.18        032.03  033.15  039.36  043.18  076.06
  249.30  277.18  283.19  284.10  289.07        112.34  137.30  196.09  284.15  299.33
  290.04  291.15  291.18  291.26  291.30     SHOWED                             (  4)
  293.01  293.05  293.09  295.26  299.26        149.04  202.36  260.35  292.20
  299.28  300.05  302.28  303.35  304.14     SHOWER                             (  5)
  304.15  311.20  311.24  311.32  313.08        132.32  137.17  203.23  206.33  288.21
  319.12                                      SHOWERED                           (  1)
SHORES                             ( 14)        204.19
  126.29  185.06  191.25  192.06  195.29     SHOWERS                            (  2)
  196.07  288.17  289.03  290.09  291.12        170.23  319.13
  292.14  300.03  300.35  316.10             SHOWING                            (  5)
SHORN                              (  1)        083.14  247.23  289.33  308.35  316.27
  181.34                                      SHOWN                              (  1)
SHORT                              ( 18)        031.12
  018.28  055.23  070.33  083.23  110.04     SHOWS                              (  3)
  113.36  136.11  154.17  178.25  187.32        096.06  165.27  220.33
  190.04  202.15  225.33  276.30  278.24     SHREWDNESS                         (  1)
  290.15  301.23  315.03                        028.32
SHORTCOMINGS                       (  1)     SHRIEK                             (  1)
  049.37                                        295.09
SHORTER                            (  2)     SHRILL                             (  3)
  010.04  271.03                                127.16  127.28  257.23
SHORTEST                           (  1)     SHRINES                            (  1)
  288.06                                        202.08
SHORTLY                            (  1)     SHRINKING                          (  1)
  262.12                                        035.08
SHOT                               (  5)     SHRUB                              (  6)
  118.17  121.23  143.14  254.31  259.26        087.27  113.32  156.22  156.33  273.31
SHOULD                             (154)        312.22
  003.10  003.28  005.10  005.11  006.21     SHRUBS                             (  2)
  010.10  010.25  014.30  016.29  019.25        181.22  186.08
  020.32  022.13  023.35  027.04  034.20     SHUFFLED                           (  1)
  035.01  036.11  036.18  036.25  037.11        222.11
  041.32  046.22  050.29  051.07  051.11     SHUN                               (  1)
  052.04  053.19  053.21  054.09  056.13        328.06
  056.26  056.27  056.29  057.15  057.17     SHUT                               (  6)
  058.30  059.29  061.05  064.19  067.01        067.12  171.12  244.19  256.23  266.16
  067.13  069.22  071.02  071.05  072.06        313.02
  073.07  073.21  073.29  073.30  074.19     SHUTS                              (  1)
  074.22  074.26  074.27  074.28  076.10        245.36
  077.13  078.15  081.33  083.15  088.22     SHUTTER                            (  3)
  089.28  092.17  093.06  093.12  095.26        111.10  111.11  190.05
  096.28  096.30  096.31  097.22  097.30     SHUTTING                           (  1)
  104.21  107.25  109.11  109.12  109.26        207.08
  109.28  109.34  112.21  112.32  118.07     SHY                                (  2)
  119.30  131.17  133.05  133.12  136.27        226.11  275.22
  138.14  142.29  144.13  144.32  145.33     SIBERIA                            (  1)
  145.35  152.02  152.34  155.12  161.02        171.04
  164.19  164.25  164.33  164.35  164.36
```

SIBYL   (1)
 204.11
SIC   (1)
 063.16
SICK   (7)
 007.12 007.13 011.11 067.01 077.03
 144.35 320.03
SICKNESS   (1)
 153.23
SIDE   (87)
 003.31 014.09 034.26 039.03 042.20
 044.07 044.22 048.31 050.08 050.08
 060.32 071.32 081.07 086.12 113.26
 114.02 115.27 124.26 124.28 125.01
 125.04 141.04 141.10 144.12 147.14
 157.21 161.31 161.34 167.26 174.10
 174.14 178.12 178.29 180.02 180.25
 181.28 182.21 186.05 204.10 205.01
 218.06 219.01 223.05 226.36 229.08
 229.19 229.20 230.20 231.10 233.13
 233.32 235.10 240.24 240.26 245.22
 251.31 252.09 256.05 258.03 258.23
 275.35 276.12 276.14 277.13 280.02
 285.19 291.18 292.16 292.16 293.18
 295.02 295.29 295.30 296.03 299.17
 300.12 303.32 303.34 306.07 306.08
 308.02 308.24 308.32 315.04 320.22
 323.17 324.35
SIDES   (31)
 042.19 044.27 048.24 049.07 050.19
 086.21 086.36 113.34 134.26 168.29
 177.14 182.03 182.35 184.10 184.20
 194.32 207.23 225.33 233.10 234.04
 256.25 260.29 263.28 273.21 293.28
 300.28 304.30 306.04 308.04 311.17
 318.36
SIDEWALK   (1)
 170.32
SIERRA   (1)
 119.12
SIESTA   (1)
 301.23
SIEVE   (1)
 169.12
SIFTING   (1)
 276.17
SIGH   (2)
 138.11 206.13
SIGHED   (1)
 326.36
SIGHS   (2)
 124.28 125.01
SIGHT   (18)
 006.36 105.30 119.25 132.03 157.20
 193.36 206.36 208.14 213.07 266.22
 280.35 288.14 292.35 316.29 318.03
 320.32 322.14 332.12
SIGHTS   (3)
 160.01 214.16 293.09
SIGN   (5)
 069.02 093.04 120.24 269.11 321.14
SIGNAL   (2)
 226.15 313.09
SIGNIFICANT   (5)
 095.03 101.17 215.03 325.05 329.09
SIGNIFICANTLY   (1)
 204.32
SIGNIFIED   (2)
 027.21 027.30
SIGNIFY   (1)
 048.08
SIGNS   (3)
 168.28 302.19 309.25
SIGULARLY   (1)
 304.05
SILENCE   (5)
 008.25 106.27 278.35 279.01 279.03

SILENCES   (1)
 268.09
SILENT   (8)
 034.27 108.12 141.22 173.26 192.10
 221.17 262.25 280.08
SILENTLY   (1)
 112.07
SILICATES   (1)
 158.09
SILICIOUS   (1)
 307.28
SILK   (2)
 043.26 116.04
SILKS   (1)
 177.11
SILL   (5)
 043.11 230.33 231.17 243.23 263.24
SILLS   (1)
 128.10
SILLY   (1)
 236.01
SILVER   (6)
 016.26 057.23 107.01 116.13 202.02
 317.14
SILVERY   (5)
 184.10 187.08 307.21 310.24 311.32
SIMILAR   (8)
 022.17 033.25 068.34 073.18 185.22
 194.08 232.02 319.19
SIMMER   (1)
 167.32
SIMOOM   (1)
 074.20
SIMPLE   (21)
 003.32 010.13 014.21 025.25 036.11
 046.15 047.29 057.21 061.17 078.25
 078.33 131.11 145.02 148.31 150.03
 151.13 151.29 187.20 215.19 267.29
 281.18
SIMPLER   (3)
 030.17 063.09 070.36
SIMPLES   (1)
 137.33
SIMPLICITY   (10)
 015.02 037.17 063.31 088.26 091.24
 091.24 091.24 092.12 151.18 164.02
SIMPLIFIES   (1)
 324.03
SIMPLIFY   (2)
 091.34 091.34
SIMPLY   (19)
 014.14 024.22 025.06 046.06 055.32
 056.22 061.19 069.19 070.35 147.22
 148.19 172.20 176.33 206.11 221.18
 239.17 244.30 316.34 328.18
SIMUS   (1)
 005.35
SINCE   (40)
 019.01 026.35 063.01 067.25 070.06
 071.24 072.11 082.26 093.21 094.34
 099.14 099.17 116.11 118.02 132.07
 156.12 173.18 173.26 180.33 181.23
 181.32 192.05 197.17 197.31 197.34
 203.08 237.04 239.10 249.09 254.14
 258.02 258.14 258.18 267.33 269.21
 283.28 287.07 298.03 304.35 323.18
SINCERE   (5)
 003.32 026.13 088.27 147.03 151.29
SINCERELY   (5)
 004.01 011.15 052.07 075.01 118.11
SINCERITY   (4)
 125.05 164.02 164.36 330.36
SINECURE   (1)
 018.32
SINEWS   (1)
 119.02
SING   (8)
 028.28 046.08 068.30 124.02 126.10

SING   (CONTINUED)
143.22 192.11 310.30
SINGING   (12)
042.09 089.04 112.07 123.30 124.27
127.04 127.32 143.21 154.02 169.05
257.23 311.19
SINGLE   (16)
067.19 099.30 137.13 170.06 177.18
178.26 228.15 229.25 242.32 245.23
277.03 280.21 300.17 306.29 314.18
327.23
SINGLENESS   (1)
326.32
SINGS   (3)
033.27 158.20 161.01
SINGULAR   (7)
036.17 119.18 124.10 141.09 161.12
199.20 316.22
SINGULARLY   (2)
275.04 305.24
SINK   (2)
145.29 213.19
SINKING   (1)
310.32
SINKS   (2)
182.14 188.29
SINNER   (1)
314.29
SINNETH   (1)
032.13
SINS   (4)
077.10 124.32 221.04 314.27
SIPPIO   (1)
258.06
SIR   (2)
066.13 162.30
SIRENS   (1)
169.06
SIT   (25)
012.28 029.17 036.31 037.12 043.25
065.24 065.27 114.24 135.35 136.03
140.07 149.35 167.31 187.35 215.22
220.31 228.03 228.22 254.25 255.03
255.08 274.19 283.17 330.01 331.15
SITE   (6)
081.05 081.22 088.06 263.01 264.25
298.18
SITS   (5)
113.19 153.34 221.02 298.11 312.20
SITTING   (17)
004.19 012.36 042.27 089.01 104.24
112.09 124.01 151.15 157.16 163.36
167.22 168.03 185.07 226.06 266.04
275.15 280.35
SITUATED   (1)
097.25
SITUATION   (1)
137.04
SIX   (18)
029.09 039.14 042.18 043.33 043.36
044.25 056.20 069.11 114.07 180.26
181.03 249.31 285.29 285.30 296.03
302.30 323.17 332.04
SIXTEEN   (2)
292.34 297.18
SIXTH   (2)
073.32 183.14
SIXTY   (11)
005.10 024.34 030.02 053.10 130.06
175.08 175.32 190.27 287.29 290.20
333.09
SIZE   (8)
039.24 071.23 181.31 184.25 185.17
229.34 259.05 291.25
SIZEABLE   (1)
201.34
SIZED   (2)
114.01 247.35

SKATED   (2)
271.07 271.30
SKATER   (3)
186.35 189.24 246.21
SKATERS   (3)
187.27 187.29 189.08
SKATING   (1)
249.35
SKELETONS   (1)
012.05
SKEWER   (1)
225.09
SKIES   (2)
109.07 188.02
SKILFUL   (1)
146.01
SKILFULLY   (2)
207.09 274.34
SKILL   (5)
033.21 069.31 105.29 206.21 213.35
SKILLED   (1)
173.31
SKILLET   (1)
065.20
SKIM   (3)
185.03 186.28 294.26
SKIMMED   (4)
083.02 083.03 192.36 246.14
SKIMS   (1)
187.03
SKIN   (15)
024.15 026.31 027.12 027.12 035.35
047.04 075.28 136.26 195.31 222.10
262.32 279.10 279.28 294.32 320.25
SKINNED   (2)
279.04 302.02
SKINS   (4)
040.15 170.25 279.18 279.31
SKIP   (3)
105.19 109.29 122.02
SKIPPING   (1)
259.15
SKIRTS   (3)
130.21 168.32 252.34
SKULK   (2)
125.35 280.07
SKUNK   (3)
129.21 161.04 267.13
SKY   (32)
018.02 006.24 098.23 116.17 133.04
135.03 159.06 159.27 161.09 176.09
176.24 177.05 177.07 177.12 177.16
188.23 189.01 189.13 190.05 195.29
217.07 223.35 227.10 236.18 237.03
269.23 269.33 283.07 284.28 312.13
317.11 321.14
SKYROCKETS   (1)
174.26
SLACK   (1)
284.12
SLACKED   (1)
120.05
SLAG   (1)
308.34
SLANTED   (3)
048.06 048.09 301.20
SLANTING   (1)
237.04
SLATE   (1)
176.12
SLAUGHTER   (1)
059.34
SLAUGHTERING   (1)
216.04
SLAVE   (11)
007.23 007.32 071.17 076.04 076.05
152.24 232.11 257.05 257.06 257.34
322.13

SLAVERY (2)
  007.19 205.27
SLAVES (3)
  057.06 152.16 199.24
SLED (3)
  146.05 256.09 296.36
SLEDDED (1)
  295.25
SLEDGE (1)
  066.21
SLEDS (3)
  294.19 295.06 295.35
SLEEP (19)
  027.13 037.20 090.04 090.18 092.34
  093.31 104.18 119.01 143.20 171.16
  220.28 238.22 238.23 243.32 255.08
  259.11 260.13 268.05 282.05
SLEEPER (1)
  092.35
SLEEPERS (4)
  092.19 092.26 092.30 093.03
SLEEPS (1)
  119.01
SLEEPY (1)
  145.12
SLEETY (1)
  312.09
SLEEVE (1)
  226.01
SLEEVES (1)
  129.07
SLEIGH (2)
  271.29 277.04
SLEIGHS (1)
  285.01
SLENDER (7)
  019.33 146.07 159.20 186.15 275.29
  281.06 283.11
SLENDERNESS (1)
  281.15
SLEW (1)
  004.34
SLICE (1)
  048.26
SLID (2)
  178.08 271.29
SLIDE (2)
  146.05 308.07
SLIDES (3)
  098.21 245.02 311.27
SLIDING (1)
  249.34
SLIGHT (18)
  028.35 041.12 130.01 131.34 150.11
  159.31 161.07 168.27 175.10 186.20
  189.20 190.07 217.14 232.16 247.30
  296.07 313.31 316.25
SLIGHTEST (3)
  164.32 266.25 314.23
SLIGHTLY (3)
  085.22 187.26 248.04
SLIMY (2)
  218.26 310.32
SLINK (1)
  122.13
SLINKS (1)
  140.28
SLIP (3)
  178.19 263.31 306.25
SLIPPED (4)
  029.32 075.25 274.25 295.13
SLIPS (1)
  296.36
SLIT (1)
  266.15
SLOP (1)
  075.34

SLOPE (3)
  122.10 258.18 282.11
SLOPES (1)
  305.04
SLOPING (2)
  044.22 086.36
SLOTH (1)
  220.39
SLOTHFUL (1)
  221.01
SLOUGH (3)
  006.38 024.06 068.06
SLOUGHING (1)
  105.31
SLOUGHS (1)
  207.14
SLOW (6)
  013.11 095.28 097.11 175.13 230.10
  259.30
SLOWER (1)
  157.09
SLOWLY (5)
  156.31 175.13 241.34 271.13 307.15
SLUGGISH (4)
  145.10 159.33 220.40 312.03
SLUGGISHLY (1)
  266.21
SLUMBER (2)
  117.19 117.23
SLUMBERED (2)
  222.14 327.11
SLUMBERING (4)
  090.05 096.05 147.06 317.21
SLUMBEROUS (1)
  266.12
SLUMBERS (3)
  089.10 127.29 219.10
SLUSH (1)
  097.33
SLY (1)
  232.28
SMALL (59)
  020.06 030.24 041.08 043.07 044.07
  049.26 054.22 054.32 062.09 069.30
  071.23 086.03 086.22 087.22 125.33
  129.15 140.14 140.31 148.22 155.09
  158.35 159.17 163.18 163.27 166.11
  172.16 175.04 177.22 178.36 184.20
  185.16 185.34 189.29 194.06 197.09
  198.32 199.23 201.33 227.26 231.33
  232.03 232.04 232.19 238.07 238.17
  240.01 242.30 246.06 248.12 254.13
  264.05 267.10 268.06 284.33 287.08
  292.18 292.24 301.04 313.22
SMALLER (4)
  181.14 225.07 229.14 308.11
SMALLEST (2)
  087.14 195.21
SMEARED (1)
  160.26
SMELL (2)
  119.20 317.30
SMELLED (1)
  232.15
SMELLING (1)
  264.03
SMELLS (1)
  120.15
SMELTED (1)
  051.32
SMILED (1)
  112.08
SMILES (1)
  304.22
SMILING (1)
  288.11
SMITH (2)
  052.09 121.10

| SMITTEN | | | | (1) |
| 266.34 | | | | |

SMOKE				(6)
008.27	053.33	116.20	122.29	242.11
252.29				

| SMOKED | | | | (1) |
| 062.05 | | | | |

| SMOKING | | | | (1) |
| 304.23 | | | | |

| SMOKY | | | | (2) |
| 039.02 | 252.26 | | | |

SMOOTH				(22)
057.30	086.16	105.05	129.16	178.23
186.18	186.35	187.18	187.25	188.06
189.16	189.26	235.05	235.14	236.19
238.09	240.06	246.24	257.16	291.18
293.24	303.36			

| SMOOTHED | | | | (4) |
| 167.07 | 188.04 | 246.04 | 327.08 | |

| SMOOTHER | | | | (2) |
| 086.28 | 187.13 | | | |

| SMOOTHLY | | | | (2) |
| 092.29 | 269.30 | | | |

| SMOOTHNESS | | | | (1) |
| 236.22 | | | | |

| SMOTHERED | | | | (1) |
| 005.16 | | | | |

| SMOULDERING | | | | (1) |
| 260.24 | | | | |

| SNAKE | | | | (2) |
| 024.06 | 041.25 | | | |

| SNAKES | | | | (2) |
| 041.35 | 199.11 | | | |

| SNAPPED | | | | (1) |
| 128.16 | | | | |

| SNAPPING | | | | (1) |
| 278.31 | | | | |

| SNARES | | | | (1) |
| 281.35 | | | | |

| SNARING | | | | (1) |
| 216.03 | | | | |

| SNARL | | | | (1) |
| 238.10 | | | | |

| SNEAKING | | | | (2) |
| 006.35 | 275.13 | | | |

| SNEAKS | | | | (1) |
| 007.30 | | | | |

| SNIP | | | | (1) |
| 317.30 | | | | |

| SNIPES | | | | (1) |
| 320.29 | | | | |

| SNORING | | | | (1) |
| 325.11 | | | | |

| SNORT | | | | (2) |
| 116.18 | 117.15 | | | |

| SNOUT | | | | (1) |
| 098.32 | | | | |

SNOW				(67)
018.13	027.14	029.02	041.12	117.08
117.09	117.17	118.33	119.03	119.08
119.09	128.18	137.20	148.01	170.35
176.16	180.09	180.13	243.20	248.30
249.08	249.21	252.21	254.11	256.04
256.06	256.11	256.14	264.34	265.05
265.10	265.29	265.31	265.34	265.35
266.07	267.08	267.16	267.22	268.19
271.06	271.23	271.25	271.32	273.07
273.24	273.32	276.11	276.16	276.21
280.14	281.11	282.09	282.29	282.33
283.01	292.09	293.14	293.34	295.11
300.31	302.15	304.21	305.05	309.23
310.33	328.13			

| SNOWFLAKE | | | | (1) |
| 120.28 | | | | |

| SNOWS | | | | (3) |
| 254.10 | 265.17 | 267.36 | | |

| SNOWY | | | | (4) |
| 133.07 | 271.10 | 282.23 | 283.13 | |

| SNUG | | | | (3) |
| 169.21 | 253.21 | 264.36 | | |

SO				(436)
003.10	003.28	004.08	006.06	006.10
006.20	007.17	007.20	008.36	009.01
009.06	009.21	010.09	010.28	010.33
011.04	011.14	012.10	013.03	013.15
014.17	014.24	014.26	015.01	016.02
017.29	019.07	019.16	020.03	022.35
023.09	023.25	023.36	024.01	024.20
024.22	024.24	024.35	025.03	025.08
025.14	025.17	025.28	027.30	027.31
028.27	028.28	029.15	029.24	030.01
030.08	030.31	031.07	031.22	031.30
032.05	032.13	032.25	032.33	034.16
034.32	036.34	036.35	038.12	039.05
039.20	040.04	040.14	040.17	040.26
042.06	042.21	043.06	044.05	045.04
045.12	046.08	046.15	046.23	046.24
047.09	048.04	053.18	054.02	054.29
056.14	056.16	056.19	056.23	056.30
057.25	058.06	058.06	058.25	059.34
060.07	061.06	063.31	064.05	064.22
064.26	065.23	065.34	066.13	069.31
069.32	070.02	072.33	072.36	074.15
075.18	075.30	076.10	077.20	078.05
082.05	084.36	085.22	085.27	086.08
086.31	090.04	090.22	090.36	091.03
092.03	092.05	092.31	093.09	093.16
094.10	095.27	096.20	097.13	098.14
098.35	099.15	103.16	106.06	106.26
109.03	109.21	110.04	112.01	112.10
113.17	114.13	114.36	115.18	115.20
115.31	117.35	118.08	118.11	118.11
118.36	119.16	119.25	119.31	120.02
120.18	122.15	124.08	127.30	131.18
132.09	132.28	133.33	133.35	134.13
135.08	135.17	135.23	136.33	137.05
138.21	140.23	140.30	141.11	141.13
141.23	142.14	142.20	142.24	142.28
143.11	143.30	144.06	144.08	144.14
146.09	146.10	147.14	147.20	147.22
147.27	150.13	150.18	151.07	151.09
151.21	151.23	151.29	151.29	153.20
155.08	155.10	155.12	156.18	157.22
157.25	157.25	158.03	158.15	158.25
161.24	162.10	163.41	164.11	164.20
164.23	165.15	165.27	166.18	167.15
168.17	168.18	168.27	169.16	170.26
175.28	177.04	177.09	177.33	178.22
178.25	179.07	182.10	182.26	182.33
183.01	183.23	183.27	185.19	185.32
187.03	187.10	188.21	188.22	188.22
189.16	189.26	190.21	191.25	191.26
193.09	194.13	195.24	195.36	197.24
197.29	198.08	198.34	201.05	201.31
202.22	203.33	203.34	204.06	204.23
205.12	205.18	206.02	206.05	206.18
206.26	206.34	207.08	211.09	211.10
212.04	212.14	213.25	214.04	214.14
214.28	214.34	215.19	217.06	217.10
219.25	221.18	223.08	223.14	224.27
225.07	226.11	226.17	226.34	227.16
227.18	229.10	230.04	232.25	233.03
233.30	234.12	234.20	234.33	235.12
235.12	235.33	236.02	236.19	236.29
238.14	240.26	240.34	241.13	241.22
241.33	242.09	242.16	243.07	244.03
244.04	244.12	245.02	245.03	245.36
246.09	246.11	247.12	248.01	248.27
251.35	253.13	253.16	253.17	253.25
254.15	254.31	254.32	254.37	256.14
260.03	260.04	260.04	261.32	262.12
263.33	265.07	265.32	269.29	269.30
270.09	271.07	271.08	272.14	275.05
275.36	277.22	278.16	280.32	282.25
282.28	283.29	284.03	284.22	287.04
287.08	287.17	287.18	287.22	287.26

287.27   288.02   288.02   288.09   288.23
289.04   289.30   291.29   294.04   295.08
295.14   295.29   296.06   296.21   297.05
298.08   299.09   299.14   299.33   300.02
300.11   300.28   301.06   302.01   302.02
302.30   303.08   303.12   303.31   304.32
306.19   308.12   311.14   312.23   313.02
313.06   313.24   313.33   314.19   317.20
318.18   318.21   319.12   319.16   321.08
322.34   323.03   323.19   323.21   324.10
324.11   324.21   325.22   327.28   328.06
328.34   330.18   330.20   330.28   330.31
330.31
SOAK   (1)
041.24
SOAKED   (1)
149.01
SOAKING   (3)
190.21   249.31   250.06
SOAR   (2)
107.27   316.35
SOARING   (2)
159.28   316.26
SOARS   (1)
288.23
SOBER   (2)
217.08   268.07
SOBERED   (1)
279.01
SOBS   (1)
125.13
SOCIABLE   (1)
136.18
SOCIAL   (6)
013.32   056.07   117.30   137.26   223.06
267.24
SOCIETIES   (3)
109.33   331.28   331.32
SOCIETY   (38)
021.27   030.20   033.29   056.30   073.09
076.11   080.15   103.04   111.15   112.27
115.16   131.04   132.02   134.29   136.08
136.10   136.35   140.03   140.10   141.20
144.07   150.16   158.21   171.30   171.32
171.32   173.04   198.11   211.24   256.16
270.16   322.32   323.02   323.05   328.27
330.21   333.19   333.25
SOD   (3)
067.23   263.11   311.05
SODA   (1)
063.13
SODS   (2)
039.20   224.18
SOFT   (7)
086.16   201.05   228.19   276.21   306.29
317.11   323.20
SOFTENED   (2)
283.04   307.14
SOIL   (25)
005.09   005.25   015.28   039.01   054.21
107.12   155.22   155.23   156.19   157.01
157.03   157.19   158.32   159.05   164.04
165.34   224.10   264.16   264.26   281.27
294.27   295.05   295.19   307.29   321.22
SOILED   (2)
206.03   262.22
SOIREES   (1)
023.19
SOJOURNER   (2)
003.09   037.19
SOLD   (10)
026.26   054.25   060.24   063.33   064.32
082.20   163.16   196.17   211.31   279.32
SOLDERING   (1)
292.26
SOLDIER   (7)
026.17   047.09   172.18   231.08   262.02

268.01   322.33
SOLDIERS   (4)
172.09   229.10   232.05   257.25
SOLE   (1)
263.29
SOLELY   (4)
009.20   021.08   027.27   069.10
SOLEMN   (3)
124.21   271.31   278.17
SOLEMNITY   (1)
022.03
SOLEMNLY   (1)
126.15
SOLID   (13)
038.10   176.18   195.18   241.33   244.12
247.02   270.13   282.27   293.35   294.07
295.30   330.12   330.13
SOLIDAGO   (1)
257.18
SOLIDIFIED   (1)
294.11
SOLIDLY   (1)
103.26
SOLILOQUIZING   (1)
274.12
SOLITARY   (14)
024.05   071.26   100.19   108.09   130.22
133.16   135.31   146.09   211.12   244.20
274.05   297.30   313.18   317.32
SOLITUDE   (12)
111.28   129.01   131.29   135.24   135.27
136.02   140.09   144.07   153.06   297.28
324.04   324.05
SOLOMON   (2)
009.33   018.22
SOLVE   (2)
015.03   033.18
SOLVED   (1)
279.03
SOMBRE   (2)
145.04   189.18
SOME   (346)
003.13   003.16   003.19   003.23   003.34
006.27   006.29   007.01   008.27   009.08
009.10   009.26   009.26   009.30   010.17
011.07   011.32   013.13   013.34   014.09
015.03   016.13   016.20   016.34   017.06
017.36   019.08   019.36   020.06   020.07
020.31   021.31   022.02   023.26   023.27
024.01   024.21   025.30   025.34   028.09
028.11   030.02   031.22   034.22   038.10
038.36   040.35   041.10   041.12   042.06
042.29   042.32   045.04   045.19   045.23
046.01   047.18   051.20   052.30   053.15
054.19   055.08   056.19   056.34   058.08
058.11   059.05   059.43   060.05   060.41
061.07   062.25   062.27   064.06   066.23
066.29   067.17   068.04   069.26   070.10
070.18   071.05   072.20   072.23   072.26
072.28   074.22   074.23   076.05   077.05
077.06   078.19   080.08   081.16   081.23
083.20   083.21   085.01   085.21   085.33
086.19   087.04   087.06   087.09   087.12
088.03   089.10   089.14   092.32   093.28
094.07   096.23   097.14   098.31   100.09
100.22   105.06   105.25   109.07   109.11
111.31   112.05   115.24   117.16   117.29
118.06   121.11   121.17   121.21   121.28
123.17   123.22   125.02   125.11   125.32
126.06   126.25   129.19   129.29   130.01
130.12   130.14   130.29   132.21   134.02
136.21   137.03   138.30   140.25   140.28
144.01   144.22   144.29   146.01   149.10
149.32   149.33   149.34   151.02   151.08
152.01   152.15   153.01   156.02   156.19
158.13   158.20   159.01   159.03   160.05
160.11   160.12   160.13   161.22   162.04

```
SOME                      (CONTINUED)
162.12  164.26  167.09  167.28  168.29
168.30  169.11  169.19  169.28  170.28
171.10  172.22  173.25  174.36  175.11
175.14  176.17  176.28  176.29  178.07
178.29  179.35  180.16  180.26  182.09
183.03  183.15  184.02  184.09  184.31
185.14  185.15  185.21  189.24  190.16
191.22  191.28  194.09  195.31  196.07
197.11  197.28  198.06  198.35  201.23
201.26  201.28  201.34  202.05  202.21
203.11  207.19  208.31  208.38  210.12
212.09  213.06  215.05  215.12  218.06
219.02  220.12  221.20  222.02  222.04
222.21  223.19  223.25  225.19  227.15
227.18  228.22  229.31  230.09  231.19
232.16  232.19  232.22  233.16  233.17
233.32  233.33  239.17  239.31  240.08
240.15  241.35  242.13  242.20  243.25
243.26  243.26  243.27  243.27  243.28
244.16  245.17  246.15  246.25  246.29
248.30  248.30  249.25  250.25  250.29
252.09  253.21  253.25  253.29  256.04
256.05  256.24  257.08  258.04  258.06
258.16  258.32  260.30  263.05  263.10
263.17  266.19  267.11  267.14  268.21
269.08  269.26  273.02  273.09  274.32
278.06  281.16  281.35  282.03  283.35
284.07  285.20  287.13  288.37  292.29
292.32  294.24  295.09  295.18  296.22
296.34  297.12  302.19  304.02  305.13
305.20  308.25  312.14  313.18  314.16
314.36  315.04  317.08  317.11  317.13
317.22  317.31  318.08  320.10  321.20
322.10  323.33  325.14  325.33  328.09
332.15
SOMEBODY                               (  4)
050.18  066.30  160.17  330.03
SOMERSET                               (  1)
274.07
SOMERSETS                              (  1)
033.13
SOMETHING                              ( 31)
004.08  004.11  007.12  007.13  018.03
019.16  023.13  023.33  023.34  023.34
024.21  027.05  039.17  047.03  051.09
051.17  073.19  089.05  090.08  090.20
097.03  102.20  118.04  131.33  132.10
151.35  153.07  165.09  214.11  264.05
306.15
SOMETIME                               (  1)
093.04
SOMETIMES                              (111)
006.22  006.28  007.17  022.09  025.24
032.24  036.05  042.33  059.33  063.08
064.36  067.16  075.06  075.17  100.27
111.24  113.14  114.12  115.29  123.01
123.25  124.06  124.12  124.26  126.06
131.03  131.22  135.19  137.10  137.33
138.26  139.03  140.30  142.03  145.20
146.12  146.21  146.26  146.31  147.02
147.35  148.17  149.20  149.28  157.22
159.13  159.26  160.10  160.35  169.07
170.01  173.03  174.31  175.04  175.08
176.12  184.35  185.06  186.29  187.07
189.32  190.06  190.28  191.05  195.17
201.03  208.40  210.21  211.25  217.04
218.01  223.03  226.23  234.13  235.09
236.35  238.27  240.13  242.02  243.13
244.10  247.13  249.15  251.06  253.03
263.07  265.36  267.16  269.34  270.17
272.09  273.06  273.16  276.20  276.31
277.11  277.19  280.05  280.34  284.06
293.28  295.11  295.18  296.35  297.06
305.04  306.02  317.28  318.14  318.24
325.11
SOMEWHAT                               ( 24)
007.18  016.31  029.08  048.08  075.24

SOMEWHAT                   (CONTINUED)
085.24  086.05  091.13  118.01  130.10
184.10  216.35  217.21  230.11  236.09
257.28  272.08  293.21  293.25  297.07
308.21  309.24  311.24  316.23
SOMEWHERE                              (  8)
053.30  098.34  108.03  115.21  244.23
261.31  292.01  324.27
SOMNOLENCE                             (  1)
089.09
SON                                    (  7)
032.13  061.31  078.07  096.13  144.30
144.31  204.37
SONG                                   (  6)
252.31  302.23  310.26  311.19  312.18
313.29
SONGS                                  (  1)
331.30
SONGSTERS                              (  2)
085.35  127.24
SONOROUS                               (  2)
005.37  160.19
SONOROUSLY                             (  1)
272.07
SONS                                   (  2)
058.20  118.21
SOON                                   ( 43)
005.01  005.12  005.25  025.29  036.35
037.02  043.29  045.10  049.30  056.25
081.23  103.32  123.27  127.07  130.32
135.22  140.28  149.10  155.28  157.19
160.12  172.24  206.03  212.30  216.31
219.23  224.04  224.05  224.26  225.04
225.31  226.08  254.04  254.11  266.11
281.12  297.14  299.07  299.09  304.03
315.26  319.11  326.12
SOONER                                 (  1)
299.34
SOONEST                                (  1)
022.22
SOOT                                   (  2)
194.01  242.28
SOOTHED                                (  3)
132.24  260.34  316.16
SOOTHING                               (  2)
115.11  187.33
SORDID                                 (  1)
162.27
SORREL                                 (  2)
137.14  161.28
SORROW                                 (  2)
080.18  332.22
SORROWFUL                              (  1)
263.12
SORRY                                  (  2)
049.40  144.15
SORT                                   ( 23)
013.34  029.35  035.33  043.21  045.02
081.18  082.10  085.22  105.32  133.15
140.27  152.32  158.30  160.11  206.01
219.24  239.07  243.18  245.19  305.07
305.17  320.29  332.31
SORTING                                (  1)
306.12
SORTS                                  (  1)
104.34
SOUGHT                                 (  2)
212.01  267.24
SOUL                                   ( 15)
005.15  010.31  029.16  032.12  032.13
032.13  055.22  062.25  073.14  089.25
096.21  218.07  260.15  282.16  329.16
SOULS                                  (  5)
032.12  033.10  124.30  140.15  255.02
SOUND                                  ( 46)
022.07  042.34  092.30  093.19  101.12
115.11  121.20  123.05  123.08  123.15
123.17  124.10  125.08  125.26  126.04
```

```
SPEND                        (  21)        SPOILED                              (  1)
006.33  016.07  016.30  024.05  028.24     122.28
037.04  058.07  070.12  075.15  076.10     SPOILS                               (  1)
084.27  097.12  097.16  108.33  109.15     238.11
109.21  192.01  210.22  275.19  301.14     SPOKE                                (  6)
314.24                                     101.19  146.15  153.12  196.03  253.26
SPENDING                     (   6)        311.31
039.34  054.04  076.08  109.17  208.02     SPOKEN                               (  6)
210.28                                     017.13  101.10  102.04  141.22  221.21
SPENSER                      (   1)        270.05
142.30                                     SPONTANEOUSLY                        (  1)
SPENT                        (  16)        315.36
017.29  031.23  048.02  054.15  095.24     SPOON                                (  1)
109.19  109.24  161.19  172.06  174.33     065.22
190.25  191.28  192.03  203.22  231.18     SPORT                                (  7)
256.05                                     146.26  207.35  224.12  225.11  294.13
SPHERE                       (   4)        303.25  316.31
080.30  222.12  235.22  322.27             SPORTED                              (  2)
SPHERES                      (   1)        232.13  316.35
175.18                                     SPORTING                             (  2)
SPHERICAL                    (   2)        189.31  317.02
195.15  247.11                             SPORTS                               (  2)
SPHINX                       (   1)        071.01  212.08
322.19                                     SPORTSMAN                            (  2)
SPICA                        (   1)        227.13  236.33
166.23                                     SPORTSMEN                            (  3)
SPIDER                       (   5)        212.13  233.27  234.05
066.27  124.11  137.18  293.26  328.29     SPOT                                 (  8)
SPIDERS                      (   1)        055.38  081.05  196.34  228.01  228.23
243.28                                     233.08  260.19  264.24
SPIED                        (   1)        SPOTS                                (  2)
312.35                                     035.17  184.21
SPIKES                       (   1)        SPOTTED                              (  2)
044.14                                     047.04  159.34
SPIN                         (   1)        SPRANG                               (  1)
226.23                                     230.01
SPINNING                     (   2)        SPRAY                                (  2)
127.32  264.13                             158.19  194.31
SPINS                        (   1)        SPRAYS                               (  1)
025.22                                     305.11
SPIRAL                       (   1)        SPREAD                               (  2)
132.35                                     077.16  165.13
SPIRING                      (   1)        SPREADING                            (  5)
201.09                                     044.08  062.30  228.02  266.24  307.36
SPIRIT                       (   9)        SPREADS                              (  1)
042.05  048.09  101.01  110.08  188.34     305.27
189.07  219.30  321.23  325.17             SPRIGHTLY                            (  1)
SPIRITED                     (   1)        275.33
302.31                                     SPRING                               ( 81)
SPIRITS                      (   7)        005.01  031.05  033.12  033.22  041.16
124.29  124.29  126.08  127.26  146.21     041.19  041.32  044.17  074.10  078.08
162.31  332.09                             081.29  083.09  107.34  114.09  130.28
SPIRITUAL                    (   9)        132.22  139.10  175.33  176.32  176.35
040.06  069.03  076.22  099.28  147.05     179.18  179.18  179.21  183.19  183.28
150.02  210.17  218.19  219.19             185.02  188.13  188.16  189.27  192.22
SPIRITUS                     (   1)        198.18  223.23  227.32  228.03  228.18
062.26                                     233.14  262.21  263.08  263.25  264.03
SPIT                         (   1)        264.09  264.21  265.16  267.15  275.34
161.02                                     281.11  281.29  284.36  292.31  299.01
SPITE                        (   2)        300.08  300.18  301.10  302.04  302.12
009.25  239.29                             302.19  303.23  305.02  306.04  300.27
SPITTING                     (   1)        308.28  310.13  310.23  310.30  310.35
232.33                                     311.35  312.01  313.03  313.30  313.34
SPLENDID                     (   5)        314.26  314.27  314.35  314.38  315.21
015.21  028.34  044.33  058.02  120.09     316.14  317.17  326.13  328.14  330.11
SPLENDOR                     (   1)        331.36
073.31                                     SPRINGING                            (  3)
SPLINTER                     (   1)        041.09  193.11  306.06
146.07                                     SPRINGS                              (  6)
SPLIT                        (   5)        041.32  080.09  156.05  181.06  183.10
120.01  120.21  202.02  206.21  252.22     308.32
SPLITS                       (   1)        SPRINGY                              (  2)
020.32                                     267.12  295.05
SPLITTING                    (   2)        SPRINKLE                             (  2)
251.34  253.10                             008.28  117.11
SPOIL                        (   1)        SPRINKLED                            (  1)
120.19                                     113.03
```

SPROUT (1)
259.12
SPROUTS (3)
146.03 281.28 315.18
SPRUCE (3)
120.01 125.32 201.13
SPRUNG (2)
083.22 181.23
SPUN (1)
257.22
SPY (2)
233.30 234.02
SPYING (2)
228.10 278.33
SQUALIDNESS (1)
035.23
SQUARE (10)
039.13 042.18 044.25 068.27 130.14
136.25 190.33 241.33 247.07 296.04
SQUARES (4)
043.23 068.16 094.25 224.22
SQUASHED (1)
318.21
SQUAT (3)
064.31 226.26 226.34
SQUATTED (2)
088.15 261.15
SQUATTER (2)
049.25 054.29
SQUATTING (1)
064.35
SQUAW (2)
182.19 295.11
SQUEAK (1)
281.01
SQUEAKING (1)
175.15
SQUEAMISH (2)
207.11 217.03
SQUEEZE (1)
025.28
SQUINTING (1)
026.20
SQUIRE (3)
007.29 257.35 279.06
SQUIRMING (1)
175.15
SQUIRREL (10)
065.09 156.21 163.37 225.33 228.20
232.20 233.17 273.19 274.04 302.20
SQUIRRELS (14)
054.27 128.01 166.32 167.15 238.26
238.33 267.32 273.28 275.15 275.22
275.25 276.06 280.10 310.13
ST (9)
021.14 042.01 059.02 202.25 211.01
249.06 249.07 262.05 303.01
STABLE (4)
056.32 117.20 221.05 264.12
STABLER (1)
117.03
STABLES (2)
005.18 121.31
STACK (1)
295.28
STACKED (1)
296.02
STACKING (1)
292.15
STAFF (8)
062.24 063.25 165.07 293.03 294.21
326.22 327.08 327.16
STAGE (5)
118.04 125.17 213.32 301.25 307.22
STAGNANT (2)
183.21 331.21
STAGNATE (1)
317.26

STAGNATION (1)
105.30
STAID (2)
041.27 169.17
STAIN (1)
044.25
STAINED (1)
084.32
STAKE (3)
022.24 075.04 146.07
STAKES (1)
294.09
STALACTITE (1)
308.05
STALACTITES (1)
305.22
STALKED (1)
204.29
STALKS (1)
163.20
STALL (1)
117.18
STAMP (1)
112.12
STAMPED (2)
155.34 310.17
STAMPEDE (1)
122.07
STAMPING (1)
244.13
STAND (28)
017.03 021.03 038.02 065.27 073.12
081.34 098.11 102.36 104.18 134.34
135.09 141.16 156.01 161.03 164.36
169.08 193.04 201.10 203.24 220.31
243.21 280.08 292.02 304.18 321.01
330.01 332.10 332.17
STANDARD (4)
047.11 111.08 112.21 141.25
STANDING (31)
004.27 019.09 022.22 084.24 087.05
089.05 113.12 140.13 151.15 168.34
178.12 180.08 181.20 186.18 201.03
201.25 202.06 203.27 241.36 243.14
259.03 263.27 266.06 273.15 282.33
287.27 293.30 294.15 312.33 316.21
327.36
STANDS (8)
033.14 121.13 125.32 133.25 196.31
198.15 242.02 256.19
STAPLE (3)
035.26 035.27 261.04
STAPLES (1)
044.14
STAR (8)
073.32 097.01 117.18 133.11 217.01
252.35 327.09 333.33
STARCH (1)
329.11
STARED (1)
206.14
STARK (1)
125.30
STARRY (1)
216.27
STARS (8)
010.18 098.23 102.04 102.05 104.11
117.04 130.25 222.18
START (7)
053.12 068.02 072.14 117.18 276.22
307.09 322.23
STARTED (4)
060.33 203.23 304.11 304.13
STARTING (2)
017.24 054.10
STARTINGS (1)
117.32

STARTLED   (4)
235.31 272.11 280.27 312.30
STARTLING   (3)
010.28 258.08 303.10
STARTLINGLY   (1)
218.28
STARTS   (1)
273.32
STARVE   (2)
019.06 061.29
STARVED   (4)
093.07 108.30 127.36 210.11
STARVELING   (1)
204.17
STARVING   (2)
074.26 152.08
STATE   (39)
007.06 020.24 021.27 030.15 037.35
037.35 041.29 061.07 083.11 094.36
095.13 096.16 098.01 098.07 099.08
108.32 121.02 123.30 158.17 167.27
171.24 172.02 194.01 196.36 205.26
205.32 208.20 215.05 215.08 215.16
222.15 224.36 231.17 265.04 267.28
268.29 297.03 298.07 321.20
STATED   (2)
061.12 215.03
STATELY   (2)
234.08 309.26
STATEMENT   (3)
049.38 061.13 325.02
STATES   (8)
035.25 039.10 058.15 079.12 092.02
145.08 158.13 332.27
STATION   (3)
080.06 117.29 233.32
STATIONED   (2)
168.21 230.08
STATIONERY   (1)
014.07
STATISTICS   (2)
058.32 060.38
STATUARY   (1)
110.03
STATUE   (2)
090.21 099.12
STAY   (10)
028.11 079.01 092.23 121.09 135.25
170.11 211.20 222.16 245.11 327.11
STAYING   (2)
157.18 174.31
STEAD   (1)
327.27
STEADFASTNESS   (1)
073.11
STEADIER   (1)
118.20
STEADILY   (7)
073.35 095.30 180.34 182.29 251.11
311.08 312.01
STEADY   (6)
020.21 101.05 118.32 141.02 155.08
242.08
STEAL   (2)
005.29 249.21
STEALING   (1)
210.05
STEALS   (1)
114.30
STEALTHILY   (1)
086.17
STEALTHY   (2)
232.28 275.13
STEAM   (2)
116.12 122.29
STEAMBOAT   (1)
094.14

STEED   (4)
117.05 117.13 119.02 258.36
STEEL   (3)
184.16 241.13 295.19
STEEP   (4)
178.25 180.02 191.25 287.18
STEEPLE   (1)
105.07
STEER   (2)
169.33 292.04
STEERED   (1)
313.12
STEERING   (1)
171.07
STEERS   (1)
204.04
STEM   (1)
077.01
STEMMED   (1)
309.33
STEMS   (5)
113.36 157.02 182.03 239.11 240.02
STEP   (8)
043.20 170.06 253.36 265.36 267.22
281.10 290.36 326.09
STEPPED   (2)
178.06 276.08
STEPPES   (1)
087.29
STEPPING   (3)
243.23 265.23 272.12
STEPS   (4)
138.35 207.13 208.28 265.22
STEREOTYPE   (1)
125.09
STEREOTYPED   (2)
008.11 318.30
STERILE   (1)
264.16
STERN   (1)
092.12
STICK   (13)
017.03 042.22 062.03 121.09 132.37
238.24 274.17 274.24 284.11 326.29
326.29 327.03 327.06
STICKS   (7)
048.06 114.10 121.32 122.05 251.23
276.02 316.23
STIES   (2)
035.05 192.35
STIFF   (2)
241.26 241.27
STIFFNESS   (1)
165.17
STILL   (164)
007.02 009.28 017.12 018.35 018.35
021.27 023.27 028.17 032.26 034.02
036.02 036.28 037.19 040.05 040.35
041.36 044.13 044.29 044.33 045.01
045.19 045.31 049.01 055.27 057.10
062.30 063.06 063.34 064.10 064.27
064.31 067.17 070.36 071.22 082.23
085.18 086.24 087.06 087.24 091.16
093.12 096.08 099.13 101.36 103.10
103.36 104.01 119.03 120.30 121.05
122.05 124.17 126.09 129.17 129.18
130.36 131.08 131.20 136.06 147.29
156.01 158.06 158.32 168.34 171.09
173.05 177.02 177.30 179.16 179.23
180.05 180.16 182.30 188.33 189.06
189.14 192.06 197.06 199.05 199.09
204.25 206.19 210.15 210.35 213.05
215.13 221.35 222.05 226.04 226.26
226.32 227.22 227.29 228.22 231.09
231.11 232.17 233.15 240.29 241.03
241.11 242.02 243.16 247.19 250.33
251.23 252.07 252.12 253.05 257.01
257.14 257.20 257.35 258.01 258.20

201

STILL (CONTINUED)
260.24	261.07	262.26	263.23	264.04
267.01	267.13	268.09	268.25	273.15
274.22	278.11	278.15	278.20	278.27
278.28	279.32	280.34	281.26	282.02
290.16	290.18	290.33	296.18	298.11
302.24	303.25	304.03	304.18	305.31
306.12	306.33	307.05	307.29	308.06
308.30	311.15	311.18	312.08	313.19
314.37	321.24	323.18	326.18	327.20
329.05	329.27	332.20	333.12	

STILLNESS (2)
111.28 236.21

STING (1)
317.24

STINT (1)
167.05

STIR (6)
007.26 007.29 105.18 162.26 263.16
280.29

STIRP (1)
263.29

STIRRING (5)
017.22 114.16 142.05 167.31 174.12

STITCH (4)
093.08 283.16 328.02 328.03

STITCHES (1)
093.09

STOCK (4)
018.18 021.02 127.12 327.01

STOCKED (2)
061.36 196.34

STOCKING (1)
007.14

STOCKINGS (1)
075.27

STOCKS (5)
053.29 080.12 251.03 258.20 303.16

STOLE (1)
238.28

STOLEN (2)
006.33 191.36

STOMACH (2)
004.25 260.23

STONE (17)
041.24 057.09 057.25 057.26 057.29
057.34 058.03 080.14 145.19 188.14
188.25 263.07 263.11 287.01 287.03
320.14 322.19

STONECUTTERS (1)
058.20

STONED (2)
044.28 137.23

STONES (28)
005.32 006.07 028.20 040.22 045.14
049.25 057.32 141.13 159.01 159.05
178.24 178.24 179.03 182.21 182.30
182.33 182.36 185.16 188.20 199.25
241.19 247.14 260.31 263.02 284.28
284.30 319.11 327.10

STONY (8)
006.04 129.06 185.06 193.26 197.26
199.16 232.24 240.25

STOOD (32)
022.03 037.26 044.15 093.27 113.25
118.30 132.29 142.16 158.03 178.14
183.12 198.07 198.21 202.10 203.34
204.31 229.35 245.14 252.10 258.35
260.04 271.11 278.15 279.02 281.08
296.28 297.29 299.26 306.10 313.08
322.35 333.09

STOOLS (2)
201.13 324.11

STOP (7)
073.30 092.36 110.04 181.30 219.05
270.10 310.19

STOPPED (1)
261.24

STOPPING (3)
117.14 117.29 118.13

STOPPLES (1)
138.34

STOPS (2)
036.35 277.09

STORAGE (1)
140.20

STORE (11)
031.30 044.34 064.02 109.09 149.09
168.31 173.09 238.17 244.02 252.17
280.10

STORED (3)
012.02 066.29 252.20

STORES (3)
012.02 119.20 302.20

STORIES (2)
137.24 285.12

STORM (10)
086.23 119.01 119.08 129.16 131.09
170.35 189.13 265.35 312.02 321.31

STORMED (1)
045.21

STORMS (9)
018.13 018.13 091.29 119.32 132.22
169.28 188.27 256.04 291.27

STORMY (1)
176.11

STORY (7)
050.11 107.07 182.15 204.33 245.26
264.01 333.06

STOUT (3)
145.10 206.03 283.18

STOVE (7)
013.08 043.25 204.25 221.02 254.13
254.19 295.18

STOVES (1)
254.18

STRAGGLING (2)
168.24 259.18

STRAIGHT (4)
042.21 044.14 277.07 313.12

STRAIGHTEN (1)
048.27

STRAIGHTENING (1)
281.11

STRAIGHTWAY (3)
077.29 126.25 245.33

STRAIN (8)
011.07 073.29 124.18 125.20 160.36
280.02 310.22 324.31

STRAINED (1)
123.13

STRAINER (1)
292.31

STRAINING (2)
047.31 235.30

STRAINS (2)
085.10 161.05

STRANDED (1)
011.02

STRANDS (1)
305.27

STRANGE (10)
073.05 091.12 114.08 129.05 132.14
171.04 210.06 210.12 271.08 316.37

STRANGENESS (1)
171.14

STRANGER (3)
022.27 148.15 204.14

STRANGERS (1)
260.16

STRAP (1)
117.08

STRATTON (4)
257.02 258.17 279.27 279.29

STRATUM (4)
186.25 202.11 309.02 309.02

STRAW				(1)
028.20				
STRAWBERRIES				(1)
263.02				
STRAWBERRY				(2)
113.22	113.30			
STRAY				(2)
042.03	232.22			
STRAYING				(2)
123.26	151.16			
STREAKS				(2)
189.03	214.04			
STREAM				(14)
085.19	087.01	087.02	097.23	098.19
111.09	135.03	269.31	290.20	299.11
307.14	307.21	311.13	333.04	
STREAMER				(1)
252.27				
STREAMING				(2)
013.02	116.12			
STREAMS				(6)
293.17	305.06	305.28	307.09	311.05
321.11				
STREET				(8)
049.29	100.24	167.27	194.01	208.25
222.15	271.28	297.01		
STREETS				(10)
038.02	074.09	095.36	120.21	170.26
271.27	273.11	284.22	284.27	294.12
STRENGTH				(7)
011.06	061.18	136.34	143.23	155.12
247.14	318.12			
STRENGTHENED				(1)
333.16				
STRESS				(1)
164.20				
STRETCH				(6)
004.05	041.21	049.41	113.15	256.32
266.09				
STRETCHED				(6)
028.19	041.15	087.28	186.23	262.33
301.20				
STRETCHES				(1)
308.31				
STRETCHING				(2)
116.33	288.12			
STREWED				(1)
174.18				
STREWING				(1)
306.13				
STREWN				(4)
113.22	229.03	246.27	275.08	
STRICKEN				(1)
065.35				
STRICT				(1)
020.04				
STRICTA				(1)
257.18				
STRIDES				(1)
108.23				
STRIKE				(2)
065.01	122.14			
STRIKES				(1)
187.07				
STRIKING				(3)
075.36	174.09	280.29		
STRING				(12)
030.10	124.13	145.19	158.28	208.35
210.04	213.16	219.04	239.07	239.34
247.12	317.15			
STRINGS				(2)
078.18	123.07			
STRIP				(3)
047.33	075.26	300.33		
STRIPED				(2)
041.25	302.20			
STRIPPED				(4)
024.16	038.28	038.29	116.02	

STRIPS				(2)
191.02	233.11			
STRIVE				(1)
326.21				
STRIVES				(1)
076.03				
STRIX				(1)
266.04				
STROKE				(1)
327.12				
STROLL				(1)
137.33				
STROLLED				(2)
167.09	284.05			
STROLLING				(1)
019.01				
STRONG				(7)
016.04	120.15	147.12	255.03	309.33
318.16	333.07			
STRONGER				(4)
042.21	229.19	247.26	317.23	
STRONGEST				(1)
057.06				
STRONGLY				(2)
210.07	330.06			
STRUCK				(11)
132.33	133.01	190.07	190.10	193.06
241.12	252.18	272.02	278.34	301.15
301.17				
STRUCTURE				(1)
241.36				
STRUCTURES				(1)
045.09				
STRUGGLE				(3)
005.20	037.33	231.25		
STRUGGLED				(2)
228.31	231.06			
STRUGGLES				(1)
231.12				
STRUGGLING				(2)
230.31	273.10			
STRUNG				(1)
174.24				
STUCK				(2)
262.31	263.32			
STUDENT				(13)
049.32	050.05	050.17	050.21	051.02
052.05	100.07	100.29	111.17	135.29
136.02	136.05	220.40		
STUDENTS				(6)
004.03	050.33	050.36	051.07	099.05
109.05				
STUDIED				(5)
019.22	020.28	052.03	240.32	309.03
STUDIES				(6)
052.05	062.20	100.29	109.04	177.32
283.30				
STUDIOUS				(1)
014.06				
STUDS				(4)
042.07	042.19	084.34	296.07	
STUDY				(17)
036.04	051.11	051.23	062.14	069.14
080.31	100.01	100.27	100.30	100.36
102.10	187.07	187.36	205.34	246.22
246.33	247.32			
STUDYING				(4)
019.21	020.35	212.01	212.03	
STUFF				(3)
049.27	151.15	157.33		
STUMBLE				(2)
105.06	136.20			
STUMP				(4)
042.23	124.01	159.33	187.35	
STUMPS				(10)
054.31	146.05	156.03	156.14	198.31
201.15	228.27	251.31	252.11	258.19

STUNNED (1)
301.30
STUPENDOUS (1)
298.02
STUPID (2)
195.28 320.22
STUPIDITY (3)
080.17 148.21 324.18
STURDIEST (1)
140.07
STURDILY (1)
091.03
STURDY (2)
126.08 128.13
STYGIAN (1)
126.10
STYLE (8)
047.08 047.31 048.01 048.20 070.14
221.28 310.07 331.08
STYLED (2)
153.35 258.05
STYX (1)
285.27
SUANTERED (1)
269.17
SUB (1)
063.19
SUBDITA (1)
314.02
SUBDUE (1)
005.22
SUBEGERIS (1)
063.19
SUBIGITOQUE (1)
063.18
SUBJECT (11)
029.23 029.29 040.23 050.31 061.33
153.13 181.26 221.14 283.31 297.11
328.35
SUBJECTS (1)
134.27
SUBLIME (4)
091.09 096.05 097.03 097.07
SUBLIMITY (1)
298.08
SUBSCRIBED (1)
109.23
SUBSCRIPTION (2)
050.26 138.31
SUBSEQUENT (1)
288.18
SUBSIDED (1)
169.13
SUBSIDENCE (1)
291.28
SUBSISTENCE (1)
178.03
SUBSTANCE (2)
134.19 281.21
SUBSTANTIAL (3)
057.09 085.20 243.16
SUBSTANTIALS (1)
047.34
SUBSTITUTE (4)
149.31 239.04 245.28 326.15
SUBSTITUTED (2)
212.09 240.08
SUBSTITUTES (2)
064.11 239.04
SUBTILE (3)
134.15 134.24 164.30
SUBTLE (2)
007.07 014.36
SUBTLER (1)
189.06
SUBTRACT (1)
076.33

SUBTRACTED (2)
060.31 111.35
SUBURBAN (1)
047.29
SUCCEDANEOUS (1)
162.28
SUCCEED (6)
033.09 038.23 070.11 220.03 261.16
326.06
SUCCEEDED (2)
065.09 219.20
SUCCEEDING (2)
052.15 107.03
SUCCEEDS (2)
091.34 293.23
SUCCESS (8)
012.24 015.04 015.06 056.06 078.27
119.18 216.27 323.32
SUCCESSFUL (2)
019.24 234.07
SUCCESSFULLY (1)
236.10
SUCCESSION (3)
062.09 081.08 227.35
SUCCESSIVE (6)
050.34 127.20 179.07 179.14 185.30
204.24
SUCCESSIVELY (1)
104.05
SUCCESSORS (1)
199.27
SUCCINCT (1)
095.01
SUCH (191)
003.34 004.04 005.21 009.06 013.03
016.09 019.33 020.08 020.22 021.04
021.21 022.02 022.02 022.10 022.32
023.08 024.36 027.33 029.12 029.22
029.27 030.10 032.35 034.03 035.13
035.32 038.21 040.18 047.05 048.33
050.01 052.23 053.23 056.35 058.31
061.28 062.16 064.37 065.03 065.25
065.33 065.36 068.09 070.04 070.20
072.28 073.26 073.36 075.22 080.23
080.28 082.13 083.12 085.09 085.30
086.28 088.06 088.14 089.32 090.06
090.29 091.02 091.29 092.06 093.06
094.23 095.32 100.03 100.34 101.04
103.24 104.06 105.13 109.15 115.04
115.07 115.37 117.33 121.06 131.09
132.01 133.08 138.05 138.08 138.09
142.15 144.37 145.04 145.22 146.20
147.26 148.32 149.04 149.28 150.04
151.06 151.28 151.33 158.26 159.22
160.28 161.25 164.01 164.30 164.34
167.28 167.30 168.02 176.34 177.08
177.11 177.28 179.23 185.36 187.35
188.19 189.33 190.03 194.13 195.27
197.02 197.16 201.27 203.30 203.32
205.08 205.25 205.29 206.15 207.07
207.11 212.36 213.07 213.21 215.29
216.24 217.14 218.21 220.10 226.24
226.32 227.09 227.11 227.12 227.13
228.33 231.05 234.17 241.05 243.32
244.30 244.36 258.13 261.29 264.28
265.24 270.04 272.01 272.27 272.31
277.35 280.19 281.15 283.35 285.17
288.12 291.05 291.36 292.01 292.10
292.27 293.22 294.21 297.21 299.06
304.01 306.15 307.27 310.28 311.34
314.28 314.28 317.24 323.05 323.09
326.06 326.07 329.24 330.25 332.21
333.29
SUCKER (1)
140.04
SUCKERS (1)
185.23

SUCKING (1)
109.31
SUCKLED (1)
005.07
SUDBURY (3)
087.17 198.19 303.27
SUDDEN (2)
153.23 190.09
SUDDENLY (28)
085.31 092.36 114.09 114.15 132.01
169.07 174.27 182.18 190.22 203.28
226.15 234.19 235.06 235.31 249.09
272.17 274.01 274.09 278.16 278.33
295.02 295.15 300.17 306.06 312.06
312.23 312.35 327.13
SUENT (1)
033.17
SUFFER (3)
074.24 104.35 276.26
SUFFERANCE (1)
261.18
SUFFERED (3)
172.14 207.06 318.20
SUFFERER (1)
231.05
SUFFERING (3)
032.06 075.06 331.18
SUFFERS (2)
050.09 104.17
SUFFICE (4)
069.30 136.22 315.25 315.27
SUFFICED (4)
081.31 179.24 267.04 274.08
SUFFICIENT (10)
030.16 040.21 061.24 071.18 094.29
101.30 123.04 130.08 140.31 172.22
SUFFICIENTLY (4)
014.01 076.15 113.06 275.29
SUFFOCATED (1)
074.22
SUGAR (4)
046.33 046.35 059.19 329.11
SUGGEST (10)
032.04 137.03 149.05 149.31 165.22
177.12 185.31 227.07 291.17 332.20
SUGGESTED (12)
029.10 075.04 086.36 108.32 125.22
148.14 149.15 150.06 150.22 219.18
222.13 292.27
SUGGESTING (1)
125.28
SUGGESTIONS (2)
100.24 216.13
SUGGESTIVE (2)
085.24 310.08
SUGGESTS (3)
033.08 215.33 308.24
SUICIDE (1)
124.22
SUIT (6)
021.31 021.33 023.14 023.35 024.29
024.36
SUITABLE (7)
040.20 141.07 144.14 268.10 272.02
274.16 327.02
SUITED (2)
015.28 125.27
SULLEN (1)
304.08
SULPHUR (2)
319.10 319.13
SULTRY (1)
197.27
SUM (3)
031.18 060.31 109.25
SUMACH (3)
044.24 114.04 257.17

SUMACHS (4)
111.28 128.11 223.28 263.04
SUMMER (71)
013.33 017.21 024.33 027.27 030.26
054.34 056.03 069.36 081.27 085.17
099.33 111.20 111.25 114.24 115.23
119.26 123.35 125.23 138.07 141.35
145.17 149.23 155.14 156.15 157.03
162.04 164.01 164.07 171.20 174.21
176.09 180.12 180.20 180.35 181.06
183.21 183.22 183.30 185.06 191.32
192.03 202.08 206.12 240.29 242.04
247.22 249.27 253.33 262.09 283.06
283.25 283.25 292.12 294.01 294.06
294.11 296.28 300.03 301.11 309.30
310.02 310.12 311.06 312.12 312.12
312.19 319.16 320.17 322.27 326.13
333.27
SUMMERS (2)
069.13 102.28
SUMMERY (1)
275.35
SUMMONS (1)
140.25
SUMUS (1)
005.34
SUN (80)
004.20 008.22 010.14 013.36 017.26
018.05 028.01 041.16 042.01 043.11
044.09 044.28 067.13 067.15 070.29
073.30 074.07 074.13 086.14 089.36
098.12 111.30 113.06 113.16 116.32
116.36 120.22 124.05 125.31 126.34
130.24 137.09 137.10 138.07 138.10
141.33 156.22 156.30 156.30 159.03
161.29 161.33 166.08 173.07 176.36
183.16 183.24 186.33 187.01 187.34
188.30 221.02 223.21 229.13 240.24
240.27 252.36 256.14 288.31 291.06
296.27 300.08 300.29 301.19 301.24
304.19 304.21 306.07 307.07 307.17
311.02 311.30 314.28 314.34 316.28
318.35 322.28 325.01 328.11 333.33
SUNBEAMS (1)
276.17
SUNBURNT (1)
145.11
SUNDAY (5)
076.05 095.23 144.36 154.15 267.20
SUNDAYS (2)
123.01 259.12
SUNDERED (1)
314.14
SUNDOWN (1)
177.17
SUNG (5)
123.21 124.29 203.08 331.30 332.23
SUNK (7)
017.31 198.06 199.06 254.32 259.16
288.03 293.15
SUNNING (1)
168.03
SUNNY (8)
076.18 111.26 159.13 192.02 229.12
251.31 253.17 263.04
SUNRISE (4)
017.19 089.34 111.26 301.19
SUNS (1)
302.14
SUNSET (4)
116.17 208.33 276.24 317.11
SUNSHADES (1)
037.07
SUNSHINE (3)
080.09 208.07 318.33
SUPERFICIAL (2)
071.33 092.06

205

SUPERFLUITIES (2)
015.25 329.15
SUPERFLUITY (1)
077.08
SUPERFLUOUS (6)
031.29 036.09 091.20 117.21 205.28
329.14
SUPERFLUOUSLY (1)
006.11
SUPERINTEND (1)
020.15
SUPERINTENDENT (1)
029.29
SUPERIOR (6)
075.05 075.07 151.18 172.34 219.23
325.06
SUPERIORS (1)
036.20
SUPERNAL (1)
124.24
SUPERNUMERARY (1)
092.35
SUPERSEDE (1)
111.12
SUPERSTITION (1)
202.35
SUPERSTRUCTURE (2)
044.35 045.35
SUPPER (5)
144.18 156.02 172.13 173.08 249.20
SUPPLE (1)
165.18
SUPPLIANT (1)
316.03
SUPPLIED (3)
054.31 055.01 068.28
SUPPLY (4)
020.22 143.30 163.30 311.14
SUPPLYING (2)
009.22 274.19
SUPPORT (11)
038.19 070.27 072.26 146.06 167.26
206.10 249.24 281.32 282.28 321.13
324.14
SUPPORTED (2)
239.11 328.19
SUPPORTING (2)
243.18 328.21
SUPPORTS (2)
051.12 296.07
SUPPOSE (19)
031.24 034.32 053.08 062.28 106.24
144.36 151.26 153.29 169.29 173.15
183.04 206.19 268.29 287.19 291.36
317.22 325.24 327.31 330.08
SUPPOSED (7)
047.02 062.22 082.35 148.27 151.22
198.05 201.34
SUPPOSING (1)
073.17
SUPPRESSED (2)
112.10 146.17
SUPREME (1)
217.31
SURE (18)
009.17 015.12 022.05 033.01 038.19
075.13 081.30 094.11 127.01 133.34
164.13 164.26 233.02 238.28 251.15
259.30 281.27 326.18
SURELY (14)
015.20 022.32 069.29 120.26 133.19
164.05 193.15 216.10 219.03 235.23
295.28 301.34 302.04 320.27
SURER (1)
105.35
SURETY (1)
131.25

SURFACE (73)
053.27 074.09 086.13 086.16 096.27
114.29 125.31 129.17 155.15 175.05
177.04 177.08 177.36 183.21 186.22
186.34 187.09 187.18 187.25 187.29
188.02 188.23 188.28 188.33 189.05
189.06 189.11 189.16 189.23 189.26
189.32 190.06 190.15 190.17 191.29
193.06 193.12 195.31 198.04 198.16
199.10 199.22 233.36 234.14 234.26
234.31 235.06 235.15 235.19 235.24
235.25 235.31 236.07 236.20 236.26
236.30 246.21 246.36 248.16 282.25
290.08 291.29 291.36 293.19 300.07
300.22 300.23 309.24 311.28 311.28
323.20 332.05 332.08
SURFACES (3)
047.27 098.12 271.04
SURFEIT (1)
173.03
SURPASS (2)
049.28 066.35
SURPASSED (1)
082.16
SURPASSING (1)
127.08
SURPRISE (7)
013.02 016.30 148.11 232.25 289.16
301.15 304.12
SURPRISED (15)
032.28 140.24 179.35 189.24 198.30
213.09 228.32 232.23 235.20 246.02
248.06 284.21 288.29 303.20 303.30
SURPRISING (5)
140.13 170.33 234.36 236.05 284.34
SURROUND (1)
317.27
SURROUNDED (12)
033.26 087.11 136.32 172.08 175.04
189.29 191.21 242.14 249.09 251.09
287.31 291.14
SURROUNDING (10)
174.10 175.35 181.03 182.32 189.18
190.27 192.14 282.31 290.03 299.06
SURROUNDS (4)
077.11 097.09 110.01 110.18
SURVEY (4)
051.21 082.30 186.34 207.01
SURVEYED (4)
081.06 234.32 285.10 319.09
SURVEYING (3)
058.33 288.28 292.34
SURVEYOR (1)
018.14
SURVEYS (1)
159.24
SURVIVE (2)
054.01 253.24
SURVIVED (3)
028.17 231.18 265.01
SURVIVOR (2)
260.20 263.29
SUSPECT (6)
118.28 148.20 165.15 195.23 225.17
274.15
SUSPECTED (3)
157.27 227.23 302.01
SUSPECTING (2)
226.22 274.27
SUSPEND (1)
146.16
SUSPENDED (3)
004.20 030.09 316.03
SUSTAIN (9)
006.16 103.02 162.26 164.04 205.27
218.19 227.22 313.20 324.15
SUSTAINED (2)
038.07 100.02

206

T (11)
080.32 093.10 105.22 115.06 116.22
145.23 145.23 153.25 161.30 161.31
310.20

TABLE (12)
065.18 099.33 113.10 113.20 129.33
149.36 172.11 215.22 217.22 329.23
330.35 333.08

TABLECLOTH (1)
045.27

TABLES (5)
020.30 113.24 126.14 151.10 201.14

TACK (1)
236.32

TACKLE (1)
295.28

TADPOLES (1)
318.22

TAFFEREL (1)
320.20

TAIL (5)
066.10 095.25 121.03 233.09 281.06

TAILOR (4)
021.31 035.33 046.17 168.33

TAILORESS (1)
025.03

TAILORS (1)
328.02

TAILS (5)
120.30 121.07 175.05 190.10 309.31

TAINT (1)
067.14

TAINTED (1)
074.16

TAINTING (1)
073.34

TAKE (56)
010.24 013.12 013.26 024.25 031.18
039.09 043.32 047.01 048.14 048.18
053.04 063.20 066.36 067.07 069.21
077.15 078.18 078.35 083.25 085.25
093.09 106.20 109.12 109.30 113.15
115.19 116.16 124.17 129.29 132.26
147.28 150.02 150.24 152.28 172.21
173.13 190.19 198.26 206.19 207.33
210.21 234.25 241.06 253.03 268.34
273.12 282.21 283.13 295.17 299.08
301.03 323.25 328.03 328.31 328.33
330.08

TAKEN (22)
011.11 011.36 021.02 026.15 030.12
042.12 052.03 056.28 057.30 068.20
111.25 123.16 143.19 153.10 164.29
167.12 204.29 228.15 229.27 233.06
282.14 327.19

TAKES (12)
093.02 093.25 103.15 106.14 129.13
165.17 220.26 245.36 246.05 270.20
305.10 320.08

TAKING (10)
011.20 020.26 037.08 065.26 135.14
154.15 211.21 234.04 275.23 285.16

TALARIA (1)
209.06

TALE (4)
095.33 105.02 160.23 240.04

TALENT (1)
020.03

TALES (1)
120.14

TALK (14)
003.28 007.24 052.28 052.28 081.15
092.15 103.31 118.03 134.13 141.09
149.21 149.21 200.05 268.07

TALKED (7)
146.20 198.18 205.30 255.11 267.29
269.17 331.04

TALKERS (1)
141.15

TALKING (1)
274.12

TALKS (1)
009.23

TALL (2)
040.35 121.21

TALLER (1)
202.05

TALLOW (1)
252.18

TALONS (2)
195.35 319.09

TAME (2)
127.12 208.14

TAMELY (1)
208.24

TAN (1)
105.21

TANAGER (1)
086.01

TANGENT (1)
322.26

TANTIVY (2)
114.25 161.07

TAPEWORM (1)
067.32

TAPPING (1)
223.21

TARE (1)
021.05

TARGET (1)
179.01

TARN (1)
086.12

TARTAR (1)
059.36

TARTARUS (1)
295.14

TARTARY (1)
087.29

TARUS (1)
312.21

TASK (2)
021.03 101.02

TASKED (1)
090.26

TASTE (16)
026.19 026.23 038.30 075.19 106.04
110.01 136.13 161.16 183.29 201.22
218.05 218.21 218.22 221.23 239.14
258.02

TASTED (3)
081.10 114.02 173.16

TASTES (2)
238.13 325.30

TASTING (1)
274.23

TATTERS (1)
159.17

TATTOOING (1)
026.29

TAUGHT (4)
052.05 062.22 144.23 164.15

TAVERN (2)
168.30 258.35

TAX (7)
030.25 030.34 069.28 114.14 168.28
171.23 230.26

TAXES (1)
261.19

TCHING (1)
088.32

TEA (9)
077.03 094.22 148.35 205.11 205.15
205.23 214.28 217.12 230.26

TEACH (7)
036.07 069.19 090.34 110.12 147.08
216.05 219.26
TEACHER (2)
096.24 192.05
TEACHES (1)
221.23
TEAM (5)
055.02 122.37 256.30 273.02 295.13
TEAMS (4)
265.12 282.29 284.36 297.20
TEAMSTER (2)
007.24 120.22
TEARFUL (1)
124.27
TEARING (1)
080.11
TEARLESS (1)
263.09
TEARS (3)
138.12 144.27 263.14
TEDIUM (1)
010.05
TEEM (1)
281.32
TEETH (4)
032.09 065.08 219.17 267.32
TELEGRAPH (4)
018.01 020.19 052.21 092.15
TELESCOPE (1)
051.22
TELL (34)
009.13 016.29 017.09 022.32 048.36
065.33 082.17 092.03 093.30 093.32
106.34 118.21 120.26 129.33 137.36
148.06 160.08 171.01 182.09 182.11
217.20 231.27 245.09 258.31 263.35
277.05 283.21 287.02 296.33 301.33
312.27 328.02 329.21 329.28
TELLING (2)
121.15 205.03
TELLS (9)
025.03 038.35 071.15 091.17 098.30
137.24 190.28 202.23 202.36
TEMPERAMENT (1)
283.08
TEMPERANCE (2)
080.16 219.20
TEMPERATE (1)
220.34
TEMPERATELY (1)
215.23
TEMPERATURE (8)
044.32 183.11 183.18 299.20 299.23
299.30 300.09 301.12
TEMPERED (2)
040.22 258.35
TEMPERINGS (1)
162.27
TEMPEST (1)
272.13
TEMPESTS (1)
267.36
TEMPESTUOUS (2)
169.19 243.33
TEMPLE (3)
058.15 221.27 298.12
TEMPLES (3)
057.20 058.02 201.04
TEMPORAL (1)
046.01
TEMPT (2)
165.31 199.13
TEMPTED (8)
038.21 113.14 133.07 201.21 210.07
214.10 217.13 245.19
TEMPTS (1)
215.14

TEN (33)
014.11 031.18 048.29 050.18 054.18
069.21 082.14 082.15 082.17 082.18
082.19 082.22 082.23 091.22 091.23
121.24 147.15 150.14 185.14 198.20
204.35 211.15 227.02 233.11 233.31
248.33 249.05 265.15 265.28 289.10
292.24 296.24 299.15
TENANT (2)
048.10 317.07
TENDED (3)
257.36 263.26 289.30
TENDENCIES (1)
020.25
TENDER (11)
037.02 114.12 114.14 114.21 131.04
163.33 239.22 264.04 309.25 315.06
318.20
TENDERLY (1)
006.26
TENDERNESS (1)
310.09
TENDING (3)
062.09 109.09 250.14
TENDRILS (1)
163.34
TENDS (2)
281.35 308.12
TENEMENT (2)
040.11 261.36
TENONED (1)
042.23
TENT (2)
037.21 085.16
TENTH (3)
076.05 076.09 076.11
TENTHS (1)
076.10
TENTS (1)
029.01
TENURE (1)
212.32
TERM (1)
050.23
TERMINATED (1)
152.12
TERMINATING (1)
156.33
TERMINUS (1)
249.19
TERMS (3)
031.27 091.06 095.16
TERNATE (1)
298.20
TERRA (3)
295.06 295.35 317.01
TERRESTRIAL (2)
085.11 165.32
TERRIBLE (4)
097.24 168.34 202.24 262.29
TERRIBLY (1)
016.23
TERRIFIC (1)
133.03
TERRIFIED (1)
036.26
TERRITORY (1)
245.08
TERROR (1)
232.18
TERROREM (1)
250.14
TEST (1)
061.36
TESTAMENT (1)
144.23
TESTED (1)
323.03

TESTIFIED				(1)
018.17				
TESTS				(2)
010.13	022.10			
TESTU				(1)
063.19				
TETER				(1)
185.05				
TETHERED				(1)
124.13				
TETRAO				(1)
226.10				
TEXAS				(3)
052.22	052.22	329.28		
TEXT				(1)
212.20				
TEXTURE				(1)
019.18				
TH				(18)
045.10	059.02	249.05	249.06	249.07
249.09	279.25	279.27	299.25	301.13
302.22	303.02	303.02	303.03	303.03
303.04	316.19	319.20		
THALLUSES				(1)
305.13				
THAN				(291)
004.30	005.06	009.10	010.24	011.04
012.18	012.32	013.32	014.21	014.23
015.17	015.25	016.07	017.07	019.30
021.34	022.07	022.15	023.01	023.17
023.18	027.11	027.17	027.22	028.22
029.07	030.20	031.23	033.11	033.19
034.04	034.17	034.20	035.02	036.03
036.18	037.04	037.06	037.13	037.15
040.06	040.20	040.26	041.05	041.28
042.22	042.31	045.05	045.07	045.20
045.32	046.01	046.29	047.08	047.15
049.13	049.31	049.34	049.35	049.36
050.06	050.36	051.14	053.06	054.15
055.07	055.20	055.26	055.33	055.37
055.38	056.08	056.11	057.19	057.31
057.35	058.16	059.03	059.11	059.16
060.10	061.24	061.34	063.11	063.27
067.18	069.03	069.09	070.22	071.03
071.23	071.27	075.34	076.21	078.03
078.04	078.24	086.05	086.21	086.28
088.23	089.18	089.20	089.22	090.19
091.22	092.12	094.06	096.10	098.28
099.21	099.23	100.15	101.02	102.21
103.05	103.36	105.33	107.11	107.28
107.33	108.34	109.24	110.11	111.21
111.34	113.19	118.03	118.28	118.32
119.11	119.16	119.29	122.34	126.04
127.25	130.27	131.17	131.23	133.02
135.14	135.25	137.04	137.05	137.13
137.15	137.29	137.36	142.09	143.12
143.29	143.36	144.03	147.17	149.02
149.12	150.20	151.08	151.35	152.16
155.11	156.01	157.04	157.10	157.24
164.22	164.27	165.09	169.29	169.36
170.15	172.08	172.22	173.05	174.07
177.07	177.12	180.23	180.36	183.10
183.17	184.25	184.28	185.17	190.13
193.08	193.25	194.33	199.30	199.31
199.32	202.06	203.30	205.07	205.20
207.28	207.29	208.28	210.19	211.18
211.30	211.33	212.04	214.24	215.08
217.23	219.20	221.07	222.10	222.19
227.04	229.22	232.29	233.05	234.14
234.24	234.28	235.20	236.04	236.12
238.05	239.15	240.28	241.01	242.23
242.30	247.26	250.18	250.22	250.35
251.04	251.08	251.13	253.02	256.23
256.31	258.12	261.13	262.08	266.27
268.29	274.01	274.07	274.33	276.05
280.03	281.30	283.15	283.21	283.30
287.23	287.25	288.23	288.27	288.31
288.33	289.12	292.19	292.26	296.22

THAN			(CONTINUED)	
299.16	299.18	299.34	299.35	300.06
300.07	300.29	301.06	304.28	305.18
308.20	309.21	309.30	310.07	310.24
313.20	320.07	320.19	321.33	322.18
325.20	325.26	326.01	327.22	327.26
327.36	329.24	330.34	330.34	330.34
332.36				
THANG				(1)
088.32				
THANK				(5)
064.26	065.27	109.20	261.01	320.04
THANKED				(1)
196.04				
THANKFUL				(1)
287.11				
THANKSGIVINGS				(1)
165.28				
THAT				(1208)
003.25	003.26	003.27	004.05	004.13
004.34	005.07	005.31	006.04	006.12
006.14	006.29	007.09	007.12	007.17
007.20	007.35	008.03	008.22	008.28
008.30	009.08	009.09	009.16	009.17
010.02	010.03	010.14	010.33	011.01
011.03	011.21	011.21	011.22	011.25
011.26	011.31	012.01	012.03	012.09
012.11	012.31	012.35	013.16	013.20
013.31	014.12	014.12	014.26	015.12
015.26	015.31	016.02	016.22	017.05
017.09	018.02	018.04	018.23	018.30
018.36	019.07	019.11	019.14	019.16
019.27	020.32	021.07	021.13	021.20
021.25	021.26	021.33	022.05	022.12
022.26	022.27	022.36	023.15	023.25
023.29	024.01	024.02	024.04	024.11
024.20	024.22	024.23	024.24	024.25
024.36	025.07	025.08	025.10	025.11
025.28	025.34	026.01	026.02	026.10
026.16	026.21	026.23	026.27	026.32
026.34	027.01	027.02	027.08	027.11
027.30	027.32	028.16	029.03	029.11
029.26	030.05	030.17	030.18	030.30
031.06	031.09	031.11	031.12	031.22
031.28	032.02	032.04	032.07	032.08
032.13	032.17	032.18	032.22	032.25
032.28	032.33	032.36	033.03	033.06
033.07	033.08	033.35	033.35	033.37
034.03	034.11	034.22	034.33	034.35
035.03	035.11	035.18	035.21	035.21
035.31	036.03	036.17	036.27	037.03
037.18	037.35	038.07	038.11	038.15
038.17	038.20	038.35	039.06	039.10
039.20	039.23	040.07	040.14	041.04
041.13	041.21	041.30	042.15	042.16
042.21	043.19	043.24	044.12	045.12
045.24	046.03	046.22	046.33	046.34
047.03	047.04	047.09	048.15	049.12
049.32	049.36	050.02	050.11	050.33
050.35	051.07	051.09	051.10	051.11
051.28	052.02	052.06	052.08	052.31
052.32	053.03	053.06	053.06	053.07
053.09	053.13	053.19	053.21	053.28
053.34	054.01	054.03	054.08	054.13
054.14	054.26	055.22	055.25	055.25
055.26	055.31	055.36	055.37	056.14
056.21	056.22	056.26	056.31	056.32
056.33	056.36	057.02	057.04	057.17
057.34	057.36	058.06	058.25	058.26
059.30	059.32	059.39	059.40	060.07
060.42	061.05	061.08	061.14	061.16
061.28	061.31	061.33	062.12	062.21
062.34	063.02	063.14	063.24	063.32
064.02	064.07	064.09	064.17	064.20
064.28	064.34	064.37	065.03	065.04
065.05	065.07	065.24	065.24	065.32
066.10	066.15	066.16	066.20	067.06
067.06	067.08	067.11	067.13	067.28

			(CONTINUED)						(CONTINUED)
068.35	069.01	069.04	069.10	069.15	166.06	166.08	166.17	166.26	167.29
069.21	069.22	069.22	069.23	069.24	167.30	168.05	168.13	168.18	170.07
069.29	070.03	070.06	070.25	070.34	170.20	170.27	171.02	171.32	172.19
071.02	071.05	071.08	071.09	071.15	173.13	173.15	173.29	176.35	177.04
071.16	071.18	071.31	072.06	072.10	177.20	177.26	177.28	177.33	178.03
072.16	072.21	072.29	073.01	073.04	178.03	178.25	178.28	178.31	179.18
073.06	073.10	073.11	073.17	073.20	180.30	181.07	181.10	182.11	182.12
073.21	073.22	073.23	074.01	074.15	182.20	182.23	182.25	182.30	182.32
074.17	074.19	074.22	074.29	075.06	182.33	183.01	183.03	183.04	183.08
075.13	075.29	075.32	075.36	076.03	183.20	185.22	186.06	186.26	186.27
076.33	077.05	077.10	077.15	077.19	187.04	188.31	188.34	189.04	189.15
077.20	077.22	077.25	077.28	078.05	189.16	190.28	190.29	191.04	191.05
078.11	078.12	078.23	079.04	079.15	191.14	191.26	192.04	192.20	192.23
080.17	080.18	080.21	080.26	080.26	192.24	192.33	192.34	193.09	193.12
081.31	082.05	082.08	082.17	082.24	193.18	193.27	193.33	193.37	194.02
082.35	083.10	083.26	083.28	083.29	194.03	194.06	194.14	195.19	196.04
083.33	083.35	083.35	083.36	084.16	196.06	196.15	196.28	197.24	197.29
084.26	085.01	085.01	085.13	086.07	198.06	198.07	198.08	198.17	198.19
086.09	087.01	087.02	087.14	087.15	198.23	198.30	198.35	199.02	201.06
087.06	087.23	088.06	088.17	088.29	201.35	202.10	202.20	202.22	202.22
088.30	088.34	089.02	089.12	089.21	202.23	202.36	203.01	203.07	203.30
089.21	090.04	090.25	090.35	091.04	204.04	204.11	204.18	204.21	204.24
091.13	091.17	091.30	092.03	092.14	205.03	205.04	205.06	205.10	205.22
092.14	092.26	092.31	092.34	093.02	205.24	205.32	206.01	206.06	207.32
093.04	093.08	093.13	093.16	093.19	210.08	210.08	210.20	210.26	211.06
093.23	093.32	093.34	093.36	094.04	211.08	211.19	211.27	211.32	211.33
094.07	094.09	094.11	094.25	095.04	211.36	211.36	212.02	212.03	212.05
095.06	095.12	096.01	096.03	096.11	212.05	212.12	212.15	212.21	212.21
096.12	096.13	096.16	096.25	096.26	212.29	212.32	212.34	213.09	213.15
096.27	096.27	096.34	097.18	097.24	213.33	214.02	214.03	214.09	214.35
097.35	098.08	098.25	098.31	098.34	215.04	215.07	215.08	215.16	215.35
099.15	099.15	099.16	099.17	099.18	215.36	216.08	216.16	216.22	216.24
100.04	100.06	100.09	100.25	101.01	216.27	217.06	217.09	217.19	217.30
101.02	101.08	101.15	101.15	101.23	217.32	217.32	217.35	218.03	218.05
101.32	102.18	103.15	103.17	103.21	218.06	218.14	218.18	218.20	218.30
103.04	104.17	104.21	104.22	104.32	218.35	219.14	219.15	219.18	219.21
105.12	105.27	106.15	106.35	107.30	220.06	220.10	220.12	221.07	221.18
108.04	108.22	108.26	108.34	108.35	222.05	222.07	222.12	222.20	223.10
109.01	109.22	110.09	110.14	112.15	223.14	223.31	223.34	224.01	224.02
112.27	115.01	115.25	115.32	115.36	224.06	224.08	224.13	224.17	224.34
116.06	116.09	116.10	116.25	116.27	224.36	225.17	226.16	226.24	226.35
116.32	117.14	117.21	117.35	118.06	227.17	228.23	228.32	228.33	229.09
118.15	118.15	118.16	118.29	119.06	229.11	229.16	229.24	230.08	230.15
119.12	120.18	120.32	120.35	121.17	230.24	230.34	231.17	231.18	231.20
122.32	123.15	123.31	123.31	124.09	231.23	231.27	231.29	231.34	232.22
124.10	124.28	124.30	124.35	124.36	233.04	233.07	233.09	233.33	233.36
125.03	125.25	126.32	127.01	127.02	234.12	234.29	234.32	234.33	235.12
127.12	127.30	129.25	130.35	131.03	235.17	235.20	235.27	235.34	236.09
131.13	131.24	131.30	132.12	132.14	236.12	236.15	236.17	236.19	237.09
133.02	133.15	133.17	133.24	133.25	238.21	239.14	240.34	241.11	241.23
133.34	134.05	134.09	134.21	135.14	241.26	241.34	242.13	242.17	243.06
135.23	135.28	136.05	136.08	136.13	243.07	244.01	244.06	244.06	244.27
136.14	136.17	136.20	136.27	136.36	244.28	244.32	245.12	246.09	246.18
137.03	137.05	137.06	138.10	138.34	246.34	246.36	247.02	247.18	248.01
138.36	139.08	140.03	140.05	140.17	248.06	248.15	248.17	249.20	250.10
140.23	141.11	141.14	141.18	141.21	250.22	250.23	250.24	250.26	250.28
141.23	142.19	143.06	143.12	143.14	250.28	250.35	251.04	251.06	251.17
143.19	143.22	143.29	144.01	144.08	251.35	252.27	253.02	253.08	253.10
144.15	144.34	146.03	146.21	146.33	253.14	253.18	253.30	253.31	254.18
147.07	147.14	147.16	147.24	147.26	257.08	257.29	258.10	258.34	259.00
147.27	147.32	147.33	148.02	148.04	259.08	259.18	259.36	260.09	260.10
148.09	148.12	148.21	148.34	149.02	260.14	260.17	260.17	260.21	260.27
149.11	149.17	149.19	149.24	150.03	261.06	261.06	261.21	261.29	261.32
150.00	150.12	150.13	150.19	150.22	262.01	262.04	262.12	262.20	263.12
150.31	150.34	151.10	151.11	151.19	263.15	263.19	263.29	263.31	263.34
151.20	151.30	151.33	152.06	152.08	264.03	264.23	264.27	265.02	266.18
152.26	152.32	152.36	153.08	153.09	268.06	268.17	268.27	268.37	269.09
153.16	153.18	153.20	153.25	153.30	269.13	269.20	269.30	270.09	270.11
153.32	154.02	154.04	154.05	154.05	271.08	272.27	272.34	273.36	274.13
154.07	154.09	154.10	154.10	154.14	274.28	275.36	276.04	276.05	276.08
154.21	156.01	156.07	156.16	156.32	276.27	276.34	277.05	277.14	277.22
158.03	158.17	158.21	159.05	159.08	277.27	277.28	277.36	278.24	279.05
159.09	159.18	159.31	160.17	160.23	279.12	279.12	279.19	279.33	280.20
160.24	160.27	160.36	161.01	161.11	280.33	281.31	281.31	282.03	282.22
161.12	161.27	161.27	161.28	161.28	282.28	284.34	284.35	285.01	285.19
162.01	162.08	162.33	164.08	164.26	285.34	287.11	287.16	287.26	289.04
165.15	165.15	165.23	166.01	166.05	289.13	289.16	289.19	289.26	289.30

THAT   (CONTINUED)
290.02 290.25 291.18 291.29 291.29
291.36 292.02 292.17 292.19 292.25
292.26 292.27 292.36 294.05 294.26
294.28 295.07 295.17 295.32 296.14
296.16 296.17 296.28 297.02 297.12
297.14 297.16 297.29 297.35 298.06
299.07 299.13 299.32 300.13 300.19
300.25 301.15 301.31 302.11 302.30
303.22 303.23 303.24 304.02 304.12
305.09 306.18 307.12 307.21 308.15
308.18 308.25 308.30 308.35 310.06
310.17 310.22 310.32 311.10 312.26
313.06 313.24 313.24 313.25 313.26
314.11 314.22 314.23 315.16 315.28
315.29 315.30 316.08 316.23 316.31
317.34 317.35 317.36 318.18 318.19
318.20 318.23 318.27 319.12 320.13
320.27 321.06 321.08 321.25 321.28
321.30 322.23 322.24 322.29 322.32
322.34 323.11 323.13 323.19 323.29
324.07 324.10 324.10 324.12 324.29
324.31 324.35 325.09 325.16 325.24
325.33 325.36 326.03 326.11 326.22
326.27 327.06 327.20 327.22 327.34
328.19 328.20 328.27 329.04 330.06
330.09 330.09 330.14 330.15 330.18
330.21 330.28 331.03 331.31 332.17
332.24 332.25 332.26 332.28 332.33
333.28 333.29 333.32

THAW   (3)
042.01 137.17 309.20

THAWING   (6)
041.20 304.29 305.02 307.13 307.31
307.33

THE   (6830)
003.03 003.04 003.04 003.06 003.07
003.10 003.15 003.17 003.24 003.25
003.27 003.30 004.03 004.05 004.06
004.09 004.16 004.20 004.20 004.21
004.24 004.24 004.25 004.26 004.27
004.28 004.30 004.31 004.36 004.36
005.06 005.09 005.17 005.20 005.24
005.25 005.25 005.30 006.07 006.11
006.14 006.16 006.17 006.23 006.24
006.24 006.30 006.31 006.36 006.38
007.14 007.15 007.18 007.23 007.24
007.25 007.28 007.31 007.32 008.01
008.02 008.03 008.03 008.04 008.07
008.09 008.09 008.10 008.13 008.16
008.16 008.17 008.17 008.19 008.22
008.33 008.34 008.34 008.35 009.02
009.04 009.05 009.11 009.14 009.22
009.23 009.27 009.30 009.31 009.32
009.33 009.34 009.35 009.36 010.04
010.04 010.05 010.06 010.06 010.14
010.17 010.18 010.18 010.19 010.20
010.21 010.21 010.26 010.26 010.27
010.27 010.30 010.34 011.01 011.06
011.09 011.12 011.12 011.16 011.16
011.23 011.29 011.33 011.34 011.36
012.01 012.02 012.03 012.03 012.05
012.08 012.10 012.14 012.15 012.16
012.16 012.17 012.17 012.18 012.20
012.23 012.21 012.26 012.26 012.27
012.29 012.34 012.34 013.04 013.05
013.06 013.07 013.07 013.09 013.09
013.10 013.11 013.11 013.13 013.14
013.14 013.16 013.16 013.18 013.19
013.19 013.21 013.23 013.24 013.25
013.28 013.29 013.30 013.31 013.33
013.36 013.36 014.04 014.06 014.09
014.10 014.13 014.17 014.17 014.19
014.20 014.21 014.22 014.26 014.27
014.29 014.31 015.03 015.04 015.08
015.10 015.11 015.13 015.14 015.18
015.20 015.23 015.25 015.27 015.28
015.31 015.32 015.32 015.32 015.33

THE   (CONTINUED)
015.34 015.34 015.35 016.07 016.11
016.12 016.17 016.18 016.19 016.34
017.01 017.02 017.03 017.04 017.05
017.12 017.15 017.15 017.16 017.16
017.19 017.19 017.25 017.26 017.27
017.30 017.30 017.32 017.33 017.34
017.35 017.35 017.36 018.02 018.02
018.04 018.08 018.17 018.18 018.18
018.20 018.21 018.24 018.24 018.25
018.25 018.25 018.26 018.26 018.31
019.02 019.04 019.05 019.05 019.07
019.11 019.13 019.15 019.20 019.23
019.23 019.25 019.26 019.28 019.30
019.32 019.36 020.06 020.07 020.09
020.12 020.14 020.16 020.17 020.17
020.18 020.20 020.22 020.23 020.24
020.25 020.26 020.30 020.30 020.31
020.32 020.33 020.35 021.01 021.03
021.08 021.09 021.14 021.15 021.15
021.18 021.22 021.22 021.23 021.24
021.26 021.27 021.32 021.34 021.36
021.36 022.03 022.08 022.08 022.11
022.17 022.23 022.23 022.25 022.25
022.33 022.35 022.36 023.02 023.05
023.07 023.14 023.15 023.21 023.31
023.36 024.02 024.04 024.05 024.06
024.06 024.20 024.22 024.23 024.25
024.25 024.26 025.04 025.05 025.11
025.16 025.19 025.20 025.21 025.21
025.23 025.24 025.24 025.26 025.30
026.01 026.03 026.05 026.08 026.08
026.09 026.10 026.11 026.12 026.13
026.14 026.16 026.17 026.19 026.21
026.23 026.26 026.26 026.26 026.27
026.28 026.28 026.29 026.31 026.32
026.33 026.34 026.35 026.36 027.02
027.03 027.11 027.14 027.17 027.18
027.19 027.20 027.21 027.21 027.22
027.24 027.25 027.26 027.27 027.28
027.29 027.30 027.36 027.36 028.01
028.02 028.03 028.04 028.04 028.07
028.07 028.08 028.09 028.10 028.14
028.15 028.17 028.21 028.23 028.23
028.26 028.26 028.27 029.01 029.04
029.08 029.09 029.15 029.15 029.16
029.21 029.29 029.29 029.29 029.33
029.35 030.01 030.04 030.08 030.09
030.09 030.10 030.10 030.11 030.15
030.16 030.18 030.18 030.19 030.19
030.20 030.21 030.21 030.23 030.24
030.24 030.29 030.30 030.31 030.33
030.34 030.36 031.01 031.02 031.02
031.08 031.10 031.11 031.14 031.14
031.16 031.19 031.21 031.26 031.28
031.30 031.30 031.31 031.31 031.34
031.34 031.36 032.01 032.01 032.03
032.05 032.06 032.07 032.08 032.08
032.10 032.12 032.12 032.13 032.13
032.13 032.15 032.16 032.17 032.19
032.22 032.23 032.24 032.24 032.25
032.28 032.29 032.30 032.31 032.32
032.36 033.02 033.02 033.06 033.08
033.09 033.12 033.13 033.14 033.15
033.16 033.16 033.18 033.18 033.19
033.24 033.29 033.33 033.34 033.34
033.34 033.36 034.04 034.08 034.08
034.11 034.12 034.14 034.16 034.17
034.18 034.20 034.21 034.23 034.24
034.25 034.26 034.26 034.26 034.30
034.27 034.28 034.28 034.28 034.35
034.30 034.31 034.33 034.34 034.35
034.36 034.36 035.02 035.05 035.07
035.08 035.09 035.11 035.13 035.14
035.15 035.15 035.16 035.17 035.17
035.18 035.18 035.19 035.21 035.22
035.25 035.26 035.27 035.33 036.06
036.07 036.08 036.11 036.12 036.12

036.12	036.18	036.22	036.22	036.23
036.24	036.28	036.29	036.31	036.31
036.33	036.33	036.34	036.34	036.35
036.36	037.03	037.09	037.09	037.09
037.10	037.11	037.15	037.16	037.17
037.18	037.22	037.23	037.23	037.24
037.24	037.25	037.32	037.32	037.33
037.34	038.04	038.07	038.08	038.09
038.09	038.10	038.13	038.13	038.15
038.15	038.20	038.21	038.22	038.23
038.25	038.26	038.28	038.31	038.34
038.36	039.01	039.02	039.02	039.04
039.04	039.05	039.07	039.07	039.09
039.13	039.15	039.16	039.16	039.16
039.17	039.17	039.20	039.24	039.24
039.24	039.25	039.26	039.29	039.31
039.32	040.01	040.01	040.04	040.08
040.10	040.11	040.16	040.17	040.26
040.27	040.32	040.33	041.01	041.03
041.03	041.04	041.07	041.08	041.09
041.09	041.12	041.13	041.14	041.15
041.16	041.16	041.17	041.19	041.20
041.21	041.24	041.25	041.26	041.26
041.29	041.32	041.32	041.35	042.01
042.01	042.02	042.02	042.02	042.04
042.05	042.05	042.13	042.15	042.18
042.19	042.19	042.20	042.20	042.24
042.26	042.27	042.31	042.31	042.31
042.33	042.34	042.35	042.36	042.37
042.38	043.01	043.02	043.05	043.06
043.08	043.09	043.10	043.11	043.12
043.12	043.13	043.14	043.14	043.15
043.18	043.18	043.19	043.19	043.20
043.20	043.24	043.26	043.28	043.29
043.35	043.36	044.01	044.03	044.03
044.06	044.07	044.07	044.08	044.08
044.09	044.10	044.13	044.13	044.13
044.16	044.17	044.20	044.22	044.22
044.22	044.25	044.27	044.28	044.29
044.32	044.32	044.33	044.35	044.35
045.01	045.01	045.02	045.03	045.03
045.06	045.07	045.08	045.10	045.11
045.13	045.15	045.15	045.15	045.16
045.18	045.18	045.20	045.22	045.22
045.25	045.26	045.28	045.28	045.31
045.34	046.02	046.06	046.12	046.13
046.14	046.14	046.17	046.17	046.18
046.18	046.19	046.19	046.23	046.25
046.29	046.31	046.31	046.32	046.35
046.36	046.36	047.01	047.04	047.04
047.05	047.06	047.07	047.09	047.10
047.11	047.12	047.13	047.14	047.17
047.17	047.18	047.20	047.22	047.23
047.24	047.25	047.25	047.25	047.28
047.30	047.31	047.34	047.36	048.01
048.02	048.03	048.04	048.04	048.09
048.10	048.11	048.11	048.14	048.20
048.23	048.26	048.26	048.31	048.32
048.33	048.34	048.35	049.01	049.01
049.24	049.24	049.27	049.27	049.29
049.32	049.34	049.37	050.01	050.03
050.04	050.05	050.07	050.07	050.09
050.09	050.11	050.14	050.16	050.20
050.21	050.21	050.22	050.23	050.24
050.25	050.28	050.32	050.33	050.36
051.01	051.02	051.05	051.07	051.12
051.15	051.17	051.18	051.19	051.21
051.22	051.26	051.28	051.29	051.30
051.30	051.31	051.32	051.34	051.34
051.35	051.35	052.04	052.05	052.08
052.13	052.14	052.24	052.27	052.29
052.29	052.30	052.31	052.31	052.32
052.33	052.33	052.35	053.04	053.05
053.06	053.08	053.09	053.13	053.14
053.18	053.18	053.18	053.19	053.20
053.23	053.24	053.26	053.27	053.27
053.31	053.32	053.33	053.33	053.34

054.04	054.05	054.06	054.08	054.11
054.11	054.23	054.25	054.28	054.34
054.34	054.34	054.35	054.35	054.36
055.01	055.01	055.02	055.03	055.04
055.05	055.09	055.11	055.14	055.18
055.19	055.19	055.22	055.23	055.27
055.28	055.29	055.30	055.31	055.32
056.01	056.03	056.06	056.06	056.09
056.14	056.15	056.15	056.16	056.18
056.18	056.19	056.20	056.24	056.30
056.32	056.35	056.36	057.05	057.05
057.06	057.06	057.07	057.07	057.10
057.10	057.10	057.11	057.11	057.12
057.19	057.19	057.19	057.20	057.21
057.28	057.28	057.32	057.33	057.36
058.01	058.03	058.05	058.06	058.10
058.10	058.12	058.13	058.13	058.14
058.14	058.15	058.16	058.17	058.18
058.20	058.21	058.25	058.27	058.28
058.29	058.34	058.34	059.01	059.02
059.05	059.06	059.09	059.33	059.39
059.41	059.43	060.07	060.08	060.09
060.10	060.12	060.31	060.31	060.32
060.33	060.33	060.34	060.35	060.42
061.06	061.06	061.10	061.11	061.12
061.17	061.21	061.22	061.22	061.25
061.26	061.27	061.33	061.33	061.36
062.03	062.14	062.16	062.17	062.18
062.19	062.21	062.22	062.23	062.24
062.25	062.25	062.27	062.27	062.28
062.29	062.31	062.32	062.33	062.35
063.04	063.06	063.06	063.07	063.14
063.21	063.21	063.26	063.33	063.34
063.35	063.35	064.01	064.03	064.04
064.04	064.05	064.12	064.18	064.20
064.20	064.24	064.27	064.27	064.20
064.29	064.29	064.31	064.32	064.34
064.34	065.01	065.02	065.02	065.08
065.09	065.09	065.10	065.17	065.25
065.28	065.31	065.31	065.35	065.36
065.36	066.01	066.06	066.08	066.10
066.11	066.17	066.20	066.33	066.35
066.35	067.05	067.11	067.11	067.14
067.15	067.19	067.21	067.23	067.23
067.25	067.28	067.31	067.36	068.03
068.04	068.06	068.07	068.07	068.08
068.10	068.11	068.12	068.16	068.17
068.21	068.22	068.25	068.25	068.26
068.27	068.28	068.29	068.30	068.34
068.35	068.35	068.36	069.02	069.06
069.10	069.12	069.12	069.18	069.19
069.23	069.27	069.34	069.36	069.36
070.02	070.03	070.05	070.05	070.08
070.08	070.14	070.14	070.17	070.25
070.25	070.28	070.28	070.28	070.32
070.32	070.36	070.36	071.01	071.01
071.02	071.06	071.13	071.13	071.17
071.17	071.17	071.20	071.26	071.27
071.28	071.28	071.29	071.31	072.03
072.03	072.04	072.05	072.07	072.07
072.08	072.09	072.10	072.12	072.14
072.26	072.27	072.28	072.33	072.36
073.04	073.08	073.09	073.15	073.23
073.24	073.30	073.31	073.32	074.01
074.02	074.02	074.04	074.06	074.07
074.08	074.09	074.10	074.10	074.12
074.12	074.18	074.20	074.20	074.21
074.25	074.30	075.01	075.03	075.04
075.07	075.08	075.09	075.13	075.13
075.17	075.21	075.22	075.25	075.28
075.30	075.31	075.35	075.36	076.01
076.01	076.02	076.04	076.04	076.05
076.06	076.10	076.11	076.12	076.13
076.13	076.15	076.20	076.20	076.21
076.28	076.29	076.20	076.30	076.31
076.33	077.03	077.04	077.10	077.11
077.17	077.18	077.22	077.23	077.25

THE (CONTINUED)

077.25	077.26	077.28	077.30	077.30
077.31	077.33	077.33	077.35	078.05
078.07	078.08	078.08	078.11	078.18
078.21	078.23	078.24	078.24	078.26
078.34	079.01	079.02	079.02	079.03
079.05	079.05	079.07	079.10	079.12
079.13	079.15	079.16	079.18	079.19
080.03	080.06	080.09	080.11	080.15
080.20	080.30	081.05	081.06	081.08
081.20	081.24	081.25	081.27	081.28
081.28	081.29	081.32	081.34	082.01
082.03	082.06	082.06	082.08	082.09
082.12	082.15	082.16	082.19	082.19
082.21	082.26	082.34	082.34	082.36
083.01	083.02	083.03	083.03	083.04
083.04	083.06	083.06	083.07	083.08
083.08	083.09	083.10	083.11	083.11
083.13	083.13	083.15	083.16	083.17
083.18	083.19	083.20	083.22	083.25
083.29	083.30	083.30	084.01	084.01
084.06	084.08	084.09	084.12	084.13
084.16	084.19	084.21	084.24	084.26
084.28	084.30	084.31	084.33	084.35
085.03	085.05	085.08	085.09	085.10
085.11	085.12	085.13	085.13	085.14
085.15	085.15	085.17	085.18	085.19
085.21	085.23	085.25	085.25	085.28
085.28	085.31	085.34	085.34	085.35
085.36	086.01	086.01	086.01	086.02
086.03	086.04	086.05	086.06	086.08
086.09	086.09	086.11	086.11	086.12
086.13	086.14	086.17	086.18	086.19
086.19	086.20	086.20	086.21	086.23
086.24	086.25	086.26	086.28	086.29
086.30	086.31	086.32	086.34	086.35
086.35	087.03	087.04	087.06	087.06
087.07	087.09	087.11	087.13	087.13
087.17	087.17	087.20	087.20	087.24
087.25	087.26	087.27	087.28	087.28
087.29	087.30	087.31	087.35	088.04
088.04	088.08	088.08	088.09	088.09
088.11	088.14	088.19	088.22	088.28
088.29	088.30	088.31	088.35	088.35
089.04	089.06	089.07	089.07	089.07
089.08	089.08	089.11	089.11	089.14
089.16	089.18	089.19	089.20	089.25
089.29	089.30	089.31	089.32	089.33
089.36	089.36	090.01	090.01	090.03
090.08	090.13	090.17	090.19	090.23
090.25	090.25	090.25	090.27	090.30
090.32	090.33	091.03	091.07	091.08
091.12	091.14	091.16	091.24	091.28
091.29	091.31	092.04	092.05	092.10
092.10	092.11	092.14	092.20	092.25
092.26	092.28	092.29	092.32	092.33
092.35	092.36	093.03	093.11	093.13
093.14	093.15	093.19	093.20	093.24
093.26	093.27	093.31	093.31	093.35
093.36	093.36	094.02	094.03	094.07
094.08	094.15	094.17	094.18	094.23
094.24	094.24	094.25	094.26	094.27
094.31	094.32	094.33	094.34	094.35
094.36	095.01	095.02	095.03	095.04
095.05	095.09	095.13	095.14	095.16
095.18	095.19	095.19	095.21	095.22
095.23	095.23	095.23	095.24	095.33
095.36	096.04	096.04	096.05	096.16
096.19	096.21	096.21	096.23	096.27
096.29	096.30	096.31	096.32	097.01
097.01	097.01	097.02	097.05	097.06
097.06	097.08	097.09	097.09	097.11
097.13	097.13	097.17	097.18	097.20
097.21	097.23	097.25	097.26	097.26
097.28	097.29	097.30	097.33	097.35
098.12	098.14	098.17	098.17	098.19
098.20	098.22	098.24	098.24	098.25
098.26	098.27	098.34	098.35	099.03

THE (CONTINUED)

099.10	099.12	099.12	099.24	099.13
099.16	099.22	099.22	099.24	099.25
099.27	099.28	099.28	099.31	099.32
099.33	100.01	100.02	100.04	100.07
100.07	100.11	100.11	100.14	100.16
100.18	100.19	100.21	100.23	100.24
100.25	100.26	100.27	100.27	100.29
100.31	100.32	100.33	100.34	101.02
101.03	101.03	101.04	101.05	101.05
101.08	101.10	101.10	101.10	101.11
101.11	101.14	101.14	101.14	101.17
101.19	101.19	101.20	101.21	101.21
101.23	101.24	101.25	101.28	101.30
101.33	101.33	101.34	102.01	102.02
102.03	102.04	102.05	102.05	102.06
102.09	102.10	102.10	102.10	102.11
102.12	102.14	102.14	102.15	102.15
102.18	102.20	102.22	102.26	102.26
102.29	102.33	102.33	102.34	102.34
102.35	102.35	102.36	103.02	103.06
103.09	103.12	103.13	103.14	103.17
103.18	103.19	103.20	103.21	103.27
103.29	103.29	103.30	103.33	103.33
103.36	104.01	104.02	104.04	104.06
104.06	104.08	104.08	104.09	104.10
104.10	104.11	104.18	104.22	104.24
104.24	104.27	104.27	104.28	104.34
104.36	105.01	105.02	105.04	105.08
105.09	105.10	105.10	105.14	105.16
105.17	105.17	105.18	105.18	105.19
105.19	105.20	105.20	105.28	105.29
105.29	105.30	105.32	106.01	106.04
106.06	106.08	106.09	106.10	106.11
106.17	106.19	106.21	106.22	106.25
106.26	106.28	106.29	106.29	106.30
106.30	106.32	106.32	106.35	107.02
107.03	107.05	107.06	107.13	107.16
107.18	107.22	107.23	107.25	107.28
107.29	107.33	107.34	107.35	107.36
108.01	108.02	108.05	108.09	108.09
108.14	108.15	108.19	108.20	108.21
108.22	108.23	108.30	108.30	108.31
108.32	109.02	109.04	109.04	109.07
109.09	109.09	109.11	109.12	109.12
109.13	109.13	109.14	109.21	109.22
109.24	109.25	109.25	109.26	109.27
109.29	109.30	109.30	109.31	109.33
109.33	109.36	110.03	110.04	110.08
110.11	110.11	110.12	110.13	110.14
110.16	110.17	111.04	111.06	111.09
111.10	111.11	111.12	111.13	111.15
111.15	111.16	111.20	111.22	111.22
111.23	111.27	111.29	111.30	111.30
111.31	111.32	111.32	111.33	111.34
112.02	112.03	112.03	112.04	112.04
112.07	112.08	112.09	112.12	112.12
112.14	112.14	112.17	112.19	112.20
112.23	112.27	112.31	113.01	113.02
113.03	113.05	113.05	113.06	113.09
113.11	113.12	113.16	113.16	113.17
113.19	113.19	113.20	113.23	113.26
113.27	113.27	113.27	113.29	113.30
113.30	113.33	113.33	113.34	113.34
113.36	114.04	114.05	114.05	114.07
114.08	114.09	114.15	114.17	114.20
114.25	114.27	114.28	114.29	114.29
114.30	114.31	114.31	114.32	114.32
114.33	114.33	114.35	114.36	115.01
115.02	115.02	115.04	115.05	115.05
115.06	115.13	115.13	115.15	115.16
115.16	115.17	115.17	115.21	115.21
115.22	115.22	115.23	115.26	115.26
115.27	115.28	115.29	115.29	115.33
115.35	115.36	116.01	116.01	116.01
116.02	116.03	116.03	116.04	116.04
116.05	116.06	116.06	116.07	116.09
116.14	116.15	116.17	116.17	116.18

    (CONTINUED)   (CONTINUED)

116.18	116.19	116.21	116.22	116.24	131.03	131.04	131.06	131.08	131.12
116.25	116.25	116.26	116.28	116.31	131.12	131.14	131.15	131.18	131.18
116.31	116.31	116.32	116.32	116.35	131.19	131.19	131.20	131.20	131.21
116.36	117.01	117.01	117.02	117.02	131.23	131.28	131.30	131.31	131.34
117.03	117.03	117.03	117.04	117.04	131.35	132.02	132.02	132.05	132.10
117.04	117.06	117.07	117.08	117.09	132.12	132.17	132.18	132.18	132.21
117.10	117.10	117.10	117.11	117.12	132.22	132.23	132.23	132.23	132.28
117.13	117.13	117.16	117.16	117.18	132.28	132.30	132.32	132.33	132.37
117.21	117.21	117.23	117.25	117.26	133.04	133.10	133.11	133.13	133.14
117.27	117.28	117.30	117.31	117.31	133.19	133.20	133.20	133.20	133.21
117.31	117.32	117.32	117.33	117.35	133.21	133.22	133.23	133.24	133.25
118.02	118.03	118.03	118.04	118.05	133.27	133.31	133.33	133.36	133.36
118.06	118.09	118.10	118.11	118.13	134.02	134.04	134.05	134.06	134.08
118.13	118.14	118.15	118.18	118.19	134.10	134.12	134.13	134.15	134.15
118.20	118.20	118.21	118.23	118.31	134.19	134.21	134.27	134.28	134.34
118.32	118.32	118.33	118.34	118.34	135.02	135.03	135.03	135.05	135.07
118.35	119.01	119.01	119.03	119.04	135.11	135.15	135.15	135.16	135.17
119.05	119.06	119.07	119.09	119.10	135.20	135.21	135.21	135.23	135.24
119.11	119.12	119.13	119.19	119.20	135.28	135.29	135.30	135.31	135.31
119.21	119.23	119.24	119.24	119.25	135.32	135.32	135.35	135.36	136.02
119.25	119.26	119.26	119.27	119.31	136.03	136.04	136.04	136.05	136.05
119.32	119.34	119.35	119.36	120.03	136.07	136.07	136.08	136.17	136.18
120.05	120.06	120.07	120.15	120.16	136.18	136.23	136.26	136.28	136.29
120.17	120.19	120.20	120.20	120.21	136.30	137.02	137.05	137.05	137.07
120.21	120.23	120.30	120.31	120.32	137.08	137.08	137.09	137.11	137.15
120.32	120.33	121.01	121.02	121.06	137.16	137.16	137.18	137.19	137.20
121.11	121.12	121.13	121.14	121.14	137.20	137.21	137.36	138.02	138.06
121.17	121.18	121.20	121.22	121.23	138.10	138.11	138.12	138.12	138.15
121.24	121.27	121.30	121.30	121.32	138.17	138.24	138.28	138.29	138.30
121.33	121.33	121.35	121.35	121.35	138.30	138.33	138.34	138.35	138.36
121.36	121.37	122.01	122.01	122.02	139.02	139.03	139.05	139.06	139.06
122.02	122.04	122.08	122.09	122.09	139.07	139.09	140.05	140.07	140.07
122.10	122.11	122.14	122.14	122.16	140.12	140.13	140.20	140.23	140.25
122.16	122.17	122.19	122.23	122.24	140.27	140.29	140.31	140.32	140.35
122.25	122.27	122.32	122.32	122.33	141.03	141.03	141.04	141.06	141.09
122.33	122.35	122.35	122.36	122.37	141.10	141.20	141.25	141.28	141.30
123.01	123.01	123.02	123.04	123.05	141.33	141.34	141.36	142.01	142.01
123.06	123.06	123.07	123.08	123.09	142.05	142.06	142.07	142.12	142.13
123.09	123.10	123.11	123.13	123.14	142.15	142.22	142.23	142.26	142.29
123.15	123.15	123.17	123.18	123.19	142.33	142.36	142.36	143.01	143.03
123.20	123.20	123.20	123.22	123.22	143.05	143.06	143.07	143.08	143.08
123.23	123.24	123.28	123.28	123.31	143.09	143.13	143.16	143.21	143.27
123.32	123.34	123.35	123.35	124.01	143.30	143.36	144.06	144.07	144.08
124.02	124.04	124.05	124.07	124.09	144.09	144.11	144.22	144.23	144.25
124.13	124.15	124.17	124.18	124.21	144.31	145.04	145.07	145.09	145.25
124.22	124.23	124.23	124.24	124.26	145.26	145.27	145.27	145.29	145.31
124.27	124.28	124.29	124.29	124.31	145.32	145.33	146.03	146.03	146.05
124.31	125.01	125.02	125.03	125.04	146.13	146.17	146.19	146.22	146.24
125.06	125.08	125.10	125.13	125.15	146.27	146.29	146.31	146.32	146.34
125.17	125.17	125.22	125.25	125.30	146.35	147.01	147.01	147.04	147.08
125.31	125.31	125.32	125.34	125.34	147.08	147.09	147.09	147.10	147.28
125.35	126.01	126.03	126.03	126.05	147.30	147.31	147.31	147.34	147.36
126.06	126.07	126.07	126.08	126.08	148.01	148.01	148.01	148.08	148.10
126.11	126.11	126.13	126.15	126.18	148.12	148.22	148.26	148.30	148.30
126.18	126.19	126.22	126.23	126.24	148.31	148.34	149.04	149.05	149.06
126.25	126.26	126.26	126.28	126.29	149.06	149.07	149.09	149.11	149.14
126.29	126.31	126.31	126.33	126.33	149.19	149.19	149.25	149.26	149.31
126.34	126.34	126.35	127.01	127.03	149.36	149.36	150.02	150.02	150.15
127.04	127.05	127.08	127.09	127.09	150.15	150.23	150.30	150.32	150.35
127.09	127.09	127.10	127.10	127.11	151.01	151.03	151.05	151.06	151.08
127.13	127.15	127.16	127.17	127.17	151.09	151.09	151.10	151.12	151.12
127.19	127.22	127.23	127.25	127.27	151.15	151.18	151.21	151.22	151.25
127.27	127.31	127.32	127.32	127.33	151.25	151.26	151.32	151.34	151.35
127.33	127.33	127.36	128.01	128.02	152.02	152.03	152.06	152.09	152.09
128.02	128.03	128.04	128.06	128.06	152.15	152.18	152.18	152.18	152.24
128.09	128.14	128.15	128.16	128.17	152.25	152.34	153.01	153.03	153.04
128.18	128.18	128.19	129.03	129.06	153.04	153.06	153.08	153.12	153.18
129.07	129.09	129.10	129.10	129.11	153.19	153.21	153.21	153.22	153.26
129.11	129.11	129.12	129.12	129.14	153.28	153.31	153.32	153.35	154.01
129.15	129.16	129.17	129.18	129.18	154.04	154.05	154.05	154.07	154.09
129.19	129.19	129.20	129.21	129.22	154.09	154.10	154.12	154.13	154.14
129.24	129.29	129.29	129.30	129.34	154.18	154.19	155.01	155.03	155.05
129.35	130.03	130.04	130.06	130.06	155.06	155.06	155.08	155.11	155.15
130.07	130.09	130.10	130.17	130.19	155.16	155.22	155.23	155.23	155.25
130.20	130.20	130.20	130.21	130.21	155.27	155.28	155.33	155.34	155.35
130.21	130.22	130.27	130.28	130.29	156.01	156.05	156.05	156.08	156.12
130.30	130.33	130.34	130.36	130.36	156.15	156.15	156.15	156.18	156.19

THE   (CONTINUED)

```
156.22  156.22  156.23  156.23  156.25
156.26  156.27  156.29  156.29  156.30
156.30  156.32  156.33  156.34  156.34
156.35  156.36  157.01  157.01  157.03
157.05  157.10  157.11  157.12  157.13
157.18  157.19  157.20  157.22  157.22
157.23  157.23  157.26  157.29  157.29
157.29  157.32  158.02  158.03  158.05
158.05  158.06  158.06  158.07  158.08
158.09  158.09  158.10  158.12  158.18
158.19  158.20  158.21  158.23  158.32
158.33  158.36  159.02  159.03  159.04
159.04  159.05  159.06  159.06  159.11
159.12  159.12  159.13  159.14  159.16
159.18  159.18  159.19  159.21  159.21
159.22  159.23  159.23  159.25  159.26
159.27  159.29  159.30  159.35  160.01
160.02  160.02  160.04  160.07  160.07
160.08  160.10  160.11  160.14  160.15
160.16  160.16  160.17  160.19  160.20
160.21  160.22  160.22  160.23  160.24
160.25  160.27  160.31  160.33  160.34
160.36  161.07  161.08  161.08  161.09
161.09  161.10  161.15  161.15  161.18
161.19  161.19  161.20  161.22  161.23
161.29  161.30  161.34  161.35  161.36
162.03  162.05  162.07  162.13  162.14
162.18  162.21  162.22  162.22  162.24
162.25  162.25  162.27  162.32  162.34
163.26  163.27  163.27  163.33  163.34
164.01  164.03  164.08  164.09  164.14
164.15  164.16  164.17  164.17  164.19
164.26  164.27  164.29  164.32  164.33
164.35  165.02  165.08  165.10  165.28
165.29  165.30  165.30  165.32  165.32
165.34  165.35  165.36  165.37  165.37
166.01  166.04  166.04  166.07  166.08
166.09  166.11  166.11  166.13  166.14
166.16  166.17  166.17  166.19  166.23
166.24  166.25  166.28  166.28  166.29
166.29  166.30  166.30  166.31  166.32
166.32  166.35  167.01  167.04  167.04
167.06  167.07  167.08  167.09  167.09
167.13  167.14  167.14  167.15  167.16
167.16  167.16  167.17  167.17  167.19
167.19  167.20  167.22  167.24  167.29
167.29  167.32  167.35  168.02  168.05
168.09  168.10  168.13  168.13  168.13
168.13  168.14  168.14  168.15  168.16
168.17  168.19  168.21  168.21  168.23
168.23  168.24  168.25  168.25  168.26
168.29  168.30  168.30  168.31  168.31
168.32  168.32  168.32  168.32  168.33
168.33  168.36  169.02  169.03  169.05
169.05  169.06  169.06  169.12  169.13
169.14  169.15  169.16  169.18  169.22
169.24  169.25  169.26  169.28  169.30
169.30  169.31  169.32  169.33  169.36
169.36  170.01  170.03  170.04  170.05
170.09  170.09  170.11  170.12  170.12
170.13  170.13  170.17  170.18  170.19
170.20  170.20  170.23  170.24  170.26
170.26  170.27  170.28  170.30  170.32
170.34  171.01  171.05  171.09  171.13
171.14  171.17  171.19  171.20  171.20
171.21  171.21  171.24  171.24  171.25
171.26  171.33  171.34  171.35  172.02
172.03  172.06  172.06  172.09  172.10
172.10  172.11  172.14  172.23  172.33
172.34  172.35  172.35  172.36  172.36
172.36  173.01  173.06  173.07  173.10
173.11  173.12  173.14  173.14  173.14
173.18  173.19  173.20  173.20  173.23
173.24  173.26  173.26  173.30  173.33
174.01  174.01  174.01  174.08  174.09
174.10  174.10  174.12  174.15  174.16
174.16  174.17  174.18  174.19  174.19
```

THE   (CONTINUED)

```
174.22  174.23  174.24  174.31  174.25
174.26  174.29  174.30  174.31  174.32
174.33  174.34  174.36  175.03  175.05
175.06  175.09  175.09  175.15  175.21
175.25  175.33  175.35  175.35  176.01
176.01  176.02  176.08  176.08  176.08
176.12  176.14  176.15  176.17  176.21
176.22  176.22  176.23  176.24  176.24
176.25  176.26  176.27  176.27  176.29
176.30  176.30  176.31  176.31  176.32
176.33  176.33  176.34  176.34  176.34
176.35  176.35  176.36  176.36  177.01
177.01  177.02  177.03  177.04  177.05
177.05  177.05  177.07  177.09  177.12
177.13  177.13  177.14  177.16  177.17
177.18  177.21  177.22  177.24  177.27
177.29  177.29  177.30  177.33  177.33
177.34  177.36  177.36  178.01  178.04
178.05  178.07  178.09  178.09  178.10
178.11  178.11  178.13  178.13  178.15
178.15  178.17  178.18  178.20  178.21
178.21  178.22  178.23  178.28  178.29
178.32  179.03  179.03  179.04  179.04
179.05  179.06  179.06  179.12  179.23
179.26  179.27  179.28  179.30  179.31
179.32  179.34  179.36  180.01  180.02
180.04  180.04  180.05  180.06  180.07
180.08  180.08  180.13  180.14  180.17
180.20  180.20  180.21  180.27  180.27
180.28  180.31  180.32  180.34  180.35
181.01  181.02  181.03  181.03  181.05
181.06  181.11  181.13  181.14  181.16
181.16  181.17  181.19  181.20  181.22
181.23  181.27  181.27  181.28  181.32
181.33  181.34  181.34  181.35  181.35
182.01  182.01  182.04  182.04  182.05
182.05  182.06  182.06  182.09  182.11
182.11  182.12  182.14  182.14  182.14
182.15  182.16  182.18  182.19  182.21
182.22  182.25  182.28  182.28  182.30
182.31  182.31  182.32  182.33  182.35
182.35  182.36  183.02  183.02  183.06
183.07  183.08  183.09  183.09  183.10
183.11  183.11  183.12  183.13  183.13
183.14  183.14  183.15  183.16  183.16
183.17  183.17  183.18  183.18  183.18
183.19  183.19  183.20  183.24  183.24
183.26  183.27  183.28  183.29  183.30
183.31  183.32  183.33  183.35  184.06
184.08  184.14  184.17  184.18  184.20
184.20  184.22  184.25  185.01  185.01
184.29  184.36  185.01  185.01  185.02
185.03  185.04  185.07  185.08  185.10
185.13  185.13  185.14  185.18  185.19
185.20  185.20  185.25  185.25  185.26
185.27  185.28  185.29  185.29  185.32
185.33  185.34  185.35  185.36  186.01
186.03  186.04  186.05  186.07  186.08
186.08  186.09  186.10  186.10  186.12
186.14  186.14  186.14  186.15  186.15
186.16  186.18  186.18  186.19  186.20
186.21  186.21  186.24  186.24  186.25
186.27  186.27  186.29  186.30  186.32
186.32  186.34  186.35  187.01  187.01
187.04  187.05  187.07  187.07  187.09
187.11  187.12  187.14  187.15  187.18
187.19  187.22  187.25  187.26  187.27
187.28  187.32  187.34  187.34  187.34
187.36  187.36  188.02  188.05  188.06
188.07  188.09  188.10  188.10  188.11
188.12  188.12  188.13  188.13  188.18
188.22  188.23  188.23  188.30  188.30
188.34  188.34  189.01  189.02  189.02
189.03  189.03  189.05  189.08  189.08
189.09  189.11  189.12  189.12  189.13
189.14  189.15  189.17  189.18  189.18
189.20  189.22  189.23  189.25  189.26
```

189.27	189.30	189.32	189.34	189.35
190.02	190.03	190.04	190.06	190.10
190.11	190.12	190.12	190.12	190.13
190.15	190.16	190.17	190.18	190.19
190.20	190.22	190.23	190.23	190.24
190.32	190.34	190.36	191.01	191.03
191.03	191.05	191.06	191.08	191.09
191.10	191.11	191.12	191.13	191.13
191.16	191.17	191.17	191.23	191.23
191.24	191.25	191.26	191.27	191.30
191.31	191.31	191.33	191.33	191.35
192.01	192.01	192.04	192.05	192.06
192.08	192.08	192.09	192.11	192.13
192.13	192.13	192.14	192.15	192.16
192.18	192.18	192.20	192.22	192.22
192.24	192.26	192.27	192.27	192.28
192.28	192.30	192.33	192.34	192.35
192.36	193.01	193.02	193.08	193.11
193.13	193.14	193.18	193.27	193.28
193.33	193.34	193.36	193.36	193.39
194.01	194.04	194.07	194.12	194.14
194.16	194.24	194.25	194.25	194.26
194.27	194.28	194.29	194.29	194.31
194.32	194.32	194.33	194.34	195.03
195.06	195.07	195.07	195.08	195.08
195.08	195.09	195.09	195.11	195.17
195.18	195.20	195.20	195.20	195.23
195.23	195.27	195.28	195.31	195.33
195.35	196.05	196.06	196.06	196.08
196.10	196.13	196.13	196.14	196.18
196.21	196.26	196.28	196.31	196.36
197.02	197.03	197.03	197.04	197.06
197.06	197.17	197.17	197.18	197.19
197.19	197.20	197.21	197.22	197.25
197.26	197.28	197.29	197.29	197.32
198.01	198.02	198.02	198.04	198.05
198.06	198.07	198.09	198.10	198.10
198.11	198.12	198.12	198.13	198.14
198.15	198.15	198.16	198.16	198.18
198.18	198.19	198.22	198.22	198.23
198.24	198.25	198.25	198.26	198.27
198.27	198.28	198.31	198.31	198.31
198.32	198.33	199.02	199.03	199.04
199.04	199.05	199.05	199.09	199.10
199.14	199.14	199.15	199.16	199.16
199.17	199.18	199.21	199.21	199.22
199.25	199.28	199.32	199.33	199.34
199.35	200.02	200.03	200.04	201.06
201.07	201.08	201.10	201.11	201.12
201.13	201.14	201.14	201.15	201.16
201.17	201.18	201.19	201.19	201.20
201.25	201.26	201.27	201.29	201.30
201.30	201.34	201.35	202.01	202.02
202.03	202.03	202.03	202.07	202.07
202.08	202.10	202.11	202.12	202.12
202.17	202.18	202.19	202.20	202.25
202.26	202.29	202.30	202.31	202.33
203.05	203.07	203.18	203.18	203.18
203.19	203.23	203.27	203.28	203.29
203.31	203.33	203.35	203.35	204.02
204.06	204.08	204.10	204.10	204.10
204.12	204.13	204.14	204.14	204.15
204.16	204.16	204.18	204.18	204.20
204.24	204.26	204.28	204.29	204.29
204.30	204.35	204.36	204.36	205.01
205.02	205.08	205.18	205.21	205.23
205.26	205.27	205.29	205.31	205.32
205.33	205.35	206.07	206.12	206.30
206.33	206.33	206.36	207.01	207.03
207.06	207.08	207.10	207.12	207.12
207.13	207.17	207.18	207.18	207.20
207.24	207.25	207.26	207.27	207.31
207.33	207.35	208.06	208.14	208.19
208.20	208.22	208.22	208.24	208.31
208.36	210.03	210.10	210.11	210.14
210.19	210.19	210.19	210.22	210.28
210.31	210.34	210.34	210.35	210.35

211.01	211.03	211.08	211.11	211.12
211.13	211.15	211.17	211.20	211.22
211.23	211.23	211.24	211.25	211.27
211.27	211.32	211.34	211.35	211.36
212.04	212.05	212.06	212.07	212.07
212.12	212.17	212.20	212.23	212.23
212.24	212.24	212.24	212.25	212.25
212.30	212.32	212.33	212.35	212.36
212.37	212.37	213.02	213.04	213.05
213.08	213.09	213.11	213.13	213.17
213.17	213.18	213.19	213.20	213.21
213.22	213.23	213.26	213.27	213.29
213.29	213.30	213.31	213.32	214.04
214.06	214.13	214.15	214.18	214.18
214.20	214.31	214.31	215.01	215.09
215.10	215.12	215.13	215.13	215.14
215.14	215.15	215.15	215.20	215.21
215.22	215.23	215.24	215.26	215.34
216.08	216.08	216.10	216.11	216.13
216.17	216.19	216.21	216.22	216.24
216.24	216.29	216.32	216.32	216.34
216.35	217.02	217.06	217.06	217.09
217.11	217.17	217.18	217.20	217.22
217.30	217.31	217.35	217.35	218.04
218.05	218.07	218.10	218.11	218.15
218.16	218.17	218.17	218.17	218.20
218.20	218.22	218.23	218.24	218.25
218.30	218.30	218.31	218.31	218.31
218.32	218.32	218.33	218.35	218.35
218.36	218.36	219.01	219.02	219.05
219.07	219.12	219.16	219.16	219.19
219.23	219.28	219.28	219.29	219.29
219.30	219.31	219.32	219.33	219.33
219.36	220.02	220.03	220.06	220.07
220.09	220.11	220.11	220.21	220.22
220.27	220.31	220.32	220.37	220.39
221.02	221.04	221.08	221.10	221.12
221.14	221.19	221.22	221.24	221.27
221.28	222.03	222.06	222.10	222.11
222.11	222.15	222.15	222.15	223.04
223.04	223.05	223.05	223.05	223.06
223.07	223.08	223.09	223.11	223.12
223.16	223.17	223.18	223.21	223.23
223.24	223.24	223.25	223.26	223.26
223.27	223.30	223.31	223.34	224.02
224.02	224.07	224.09	224.10	224.11
224.12	224.12	224.13	224.15	224.16
224.16	224.19	224.19	224.21	224.22
224.22	224.24	224.28	224.33	225.01
225.06	225.07	225.09	225.10	225.11
225.21	225.21	225.23	225.24	225.27
225.27	225.28	225.29	225.33	225.33
225.35	226.02	226.03	226.09	226.10
226.12	226.12	226.12	226.14	226.14
226.14	226.16	226.17	226.19	226.19
226.20	226.22	226.25	226.35	227.01
227.01	227.02	227.04	227.07	227.09
227.10	227.10	227.11	227.12	227.13
227.16	227.19	227.22	227.23	227.24
227.27	227.27	227.30	227.32	227.34
227.36	228.03	228.07	228.07	228.08
228.09	228.16	228.16	228.17	228.17
228.18	228.18	228.19	228.20	228.20
228.23	228.28	228.28	228.31	228.33
228.35	228.35	228.36	229.01	229.02
229.03	229.04	229.05	229.05	229.06
229.06	229.07	229.07	229.12	229.13
229.14	229.16	229.17	229.18	229.18
229.19	229.23	229.24	229.25	229.28
229.28	229.34	229.34	229.34	229.36
230.01	230.02	230.03	230.10	230.10
230.10	230.12	230.13	230.13	230.14
230.15	230.16	230.17	230.20	230.22
230.26	230.28	230.30	230.30	230.33
230.34	230.35	231.02	231.02	231.04
231.04	231.07	231.07	231.08	231.09
231.13	231.16	231.17	231.19	231.22

231.22	231.23	231.24	231.25	231.27
231.28	231.29	231.33	231.35	231.35
231.35	232.01	232.01	232.01	232.04
232.05	232.06	232.07	232.07	232.08
232.08	232.09	232.10	232.14	232.14
232.17	232.21	232.22	232.23	232.24
232.24	232.25	232.26	232.28	232.29
232.31	232.34	232.35	232.36	233.02
233.03	233.05	233.09	233.10	233.12
233.13	233.13	233.19	233.20	233.21
233.24	233.24	233.25	233.25	233.27
233.28	233.30	233.32	233.33	233.35
233.35	233.36	233.36	234.02	234.02
234.03	234.08	234.13	234.13	234.14
234.16	234.18	234.18	234.19	234.20
234.20	234.24	234.26	234.27	234.31
234.32	234.32	234.34	234.35	234.35
235.01	235.02	235.05	235.06	235.07
235.08	235.10	235.11	235.14	235.14
235.16	235.16	235.18	235.19	235.20
235.24	235.25	235.30	235.34	236.02
236.02	236.06	236.07	236.13	236.15
236.16	236.18	236.19	236.20	236.21
236.21	236.22	236.22	236.24	236.26
236.26	236.26	236.28	236.28	236.30
236.31	236.32	236.32	236.33	236.36
237.02	237.02	237.07	237.08	238.03
238.07	238.07	238.08	238.09	238.10
238.11	238.11	238.11	238.13	238.14
238.15	238.15	238.16	238.18	238.21
238.23	238.25	238.25	238.26	238.26
238.27	238.28	238.30	238.32	238.33
238.33	238.34	238.35	238.35	238.35
239.02	239.06	239.07	239.07	239.11
239.12	239.19	239.22	239.24	239.24
239.25	239.25	239.26	239.26	239.27
239.31	239.31	239.32	239.33	239.36
240.01	240.02	240.03	240.03	240.05
240.06	240.07	240.07	240.09	240.10
240.11	240.13	240.22	240.23	240.24
240.25	240.25	240.25	240.26	240.27
240.29	240.29	241.01	241.01	241.08
241.10	241.10	241.12	241.12	241.15
241.18	241.18	241.18	241.19	241.20
241.20	241.21	241.21	241.22	241.23
241.24	241.25	241.31	241.31	241.35
241.36	242.01	242.01	242.02	242.04
242.07	242.07	242.10	242.12	242.12
242.14	242.15	242.21	242.22	242.23
242.27	242.27	242.28	242.28	242.28
242.29	242.33	243.02	243.10	243.20
243.22	243.23	243.25	243.25	243.26
243.27	243.28	243.30	243.30	243.31
243.34	243.36	243.36	244.05	244.06
244.06	244.07	244.08	244.08	244.09
244.09	244.11	244.11	244.11	244.12
244.15	244.15	244.17	244.17	244.21
244.22	244.23	244.24	244.25	244.34
245.03	245.04	245.04	245.05	245.06
245.07	245.08	245.08	245.09	245.13
245.18	245.18	245.21	245.21	245.23
245.24	245.25	245.25	245.26	245.27
245.31	245.34	245.35	245.36	246.01
246.02	246.03	246.04	246.06	246.07
246.07	246.08	246.08	246.14	246.14
246.15	246.16	246.16	246.18	246.19
246.21	246.21	246.22	246.24	246.25
246.27	246.30	246.31	246.31	246.32
246.33	246.34	246.35	247.01	247.01
247.03	247.06	247.08	247.09	247.10
247.12	247.14	247.14	247.17	247.21
247.21	247.21	247.23	247.23	247.24
247.24	247.26	247.30	247.31	247.32
247.33	247.35	248.01	248.02	248.03
248.03	248.07	248.07	248.08	248.08
248.09	248.10	248.10	248.12	248.14
248.15	248.16	248.17	248.19	248.19

248.20	248.24	248.25	248.26	248.27
248.28	248.29	248.31	248.32	248.33
248.34	248.35	248.36	249.02	249.03
249.03	249.04	249.05	249.06	249.06
249.07	249.07	249.08	249.08	249.09
249.10	249.13	249.14	249.18	249.20
249.21	249.23	249.26	249.26	249.27
249.27	249.27	249.27	249.28	249.29
249.29	249.34	249.36	249.36	250.03
250.06	250.07	250.07	250.09	250.10
250.11	250.11	250.12	250.13	250.14
250.15	250.16	250.16	250.16	250.17
250.17	250.18	250.18	250.19	250.23
250.24	250.26	250.27	250.29	251.04
251.06	251.09	251.10	251.11	251.13
251.14	251.15	251.16	251.16	251.18
251.18	251.18	251.19	251.19	251.19
251.20	251.20	251.21	251.22	251.22
251.22	251.23	251.24	251.28	251.28
251.30	251.31	251.31	251.35	251.36
252.01	252.02	252.07	252.07	252.10
252.12	252.13	252.14	252.14	252.15
252.16	252.17	252.19	252.20	252.20
252.21	252.22	252.23	252.24	252.25
252.25	252.32	252.36	252.36	252.38
253.11	253.11	253.12	253.18	253.18
253.20	253.22	253.24	253.26	253.27
253.33	253.34	253.35	254.01	254.02
254.03	254.05	254.07	254.09	254.12
254.13	254.14	254.15	254.16	254.19
254.19	254.19	254.20	254.21	254.22
254.22	254.24	254.25	254.26	254.26
255.08	255.09	255.09	255.10	255.10
256.06	256.06	256.07	256.09	256.09
256.11	256.11	256.12	256.12	256.14
256.14	256.14	256.16	256.17	256.18
256.19	256.20	256.20	256.23	256.25
256.28	256.30	256.30	256.33	256.33
256.34	257.01	257.02	257.02	257.03
257.04	257.10	257.15	257.16	257.17
257.20	257.22	257.24	257.32	257.33
257.33	257.35	258.02	258.03	258.05
258.12	258.15	258.15	258.15	258.16
258.16	258.17	258.20	258.23	258.23
258.23	258.23	258.24	258.29	258.30
258.31	258.33	258.35	258.35	258.36
259.01	259.05	259.07	259.07	259.09
259.13	259.13	259.17	259.17	259.19
259.20	259.21	259.23	259.24	259.25
259.26	259.28	259.28	259.28	259.30
259.32	259.32	259.33	259.34	259.35
259.35	259.36	260.01	260.01	260.06
260.18	260.19	260.20	260.20	260.21
260.23	260.23	260.26	260.26	260.27
260.28	260.31	260.30	260.34	260.36
260.36	261.02	261.03	261.04	261.05
261.08	261.10	261.10	261.11	261.11
261.13	261.13	261.14	261.14	261.17
261.19	261.19	261.25	261.27	261.29
261.34	262.07	262.10	262.10	262.11
262.11	262.12	262.18	262.18	262.19
262.19	262.23	262.24	262.26	262.27
262.27	262.32	262.33	262.33	263.01
263.01	263.04	263.06	263.07	263.08
263.11	263.11	263.11	263.12	263.13
263.16	263.21	263.23	263.24	263.24
263.26	263.29	263.30	263.30	263.31
263.32	263.32	263.32	263.34	264.01
264.08	264.12	264.14	264.15	264.16
264.16	264.18	264.19	264.19	264.21
264.22	264.23	264.25	264.26	264.28
264.29	264.33	265.03	265.04	265.06
265.06	265.07	265.07	265.09	265.09
265.10	265.11	265.11	265.13	265.14
265.14	265.14	265.15	265.15	265.17
265.17	265.18	265.20	265.21	265.22

			(CONTINUED)	
300.12	300.12	300.12	300.13	300.14
300.20	300.21	300.22	300.23	300.23
300.25	300.27	300.28	300.29	300.29
300.30	300.31	300.31	300.33	300.34
301.01	301.01	301.02	301.03	301.03
301.05	301.06	301.08	301.08	301.09
301.09	301.09	301.09	301.10	301.10
301.11	301.11	301.12	301.14	301.15
301.16	301.18	301.19	301.19	301.20
301.24	301.25	301.25	301.27	301.27
301.28	301.31	301.31	301.31	301.32
301.32	301.35	302.04	302.04	302.04
302.05	302.06	302.10	302.11	302.12
302.12	302.15	302.15	302.16	302.18
302.18	302.19	302.20	302.21	302.22
302.23	302.24	302.25	302.26	302.28
302.28	302.31	302.33	302.34	303.01
303.02	303.02	303.02	303.03	303.03
303.04	303.05	303.06	303.06	303.06
303.08	303.09	303.09	303.12	303.13
303.13	303.16	303.19	303.25	303.25
303.26	303.29	303.32	303.33	303.34
303.34	303.34	303.35	304.01	304.09
304.12	304.12	304.13	304.14	304.15
304.17	304.19	304.19	304.21	304.21
304.21	304.23	304.25	304.26	304.29
304.30	304.30	304.31	304.33	304.34
304.35	305.02	305.02	305.03	305.03
305.04	305.05	305.08	305.10	305.12
305.21	305.23	305.23	305.23	305.24
305.26	305.26	305.26	305.27	305.28
305.32	305.33	305.35	305.35	305.36
305.36	306.01	306.04	306.07	306.07
306.07	306.08	306.09	306.10	306.10
306.11	306.14	306.14	306.16	306.16
306.17	306.17	306.18	306.19	306.20
306.21	306.22	306.24	306.24	306.28
306.28	306.29	306.29	306.31	306.31
306.32	306.32	306.32	306.34	306.34
306.35	306.35	307.03	307.03	307.04
307.06	307.08	307.08	307.09	307.09
307.13	307.15	307.15	307.17	307.17
307.18	307.18	307.19	307.24	307.25
307.25	307.26	307.27	307.27	307.28
307.29	307.29	307.30	307.31	307.31
307.32	307.33	307.33	307.34	307.36
308.01	308.02	308.02	308.03	308.04
308.04	308.04	308.05	308.06	308.07
308.07	308.07	308.08	308.08	308.08
308.09	308.11	308.11	308.11	308.15
308.16	308.16	308.20	308.22	308.23
308.26	308.27	308.27	308.32	308.34
308.34	309.01	309.02	309.04	309.09
309.11	309.12	309.13	309.13	309.17
309.18	309.19	309.22	309.22	309.23
309.25	309.25	309.27	309.27	309.34
310.01	310.02	310.02	310.03	310.04
310.05	310.05	310.07	310.11	310.12
310.13	310.13	310.15	310.18	310.23
310.23	310.24	310.25	310.26	310.26
310.26	310.27	310.29	310.30	310.30
310.31	310.31	310.32	310.33	310.34
310.34	310.35	311.01	311.02	311.03
311.03	311.04	311.05	311.05	311.06
311.08	311.08	311.09	311.10	311.10
311.11	311.12	311.13	311.17	311.18
311.19	311.20	311.20	311.22	311.23
311.23	311.24	311.25	311.27	311.28
311.30	311.30	311.30	311.31	311.31
311.32	311.33	311.34	312.02	312.07
312.07	312.08	312.09	312.10	312.15
312.15	312.17	312.18	312.19	312.20
312.21	312.21	312.22	312.26	312.28
312.30	312.31	312.34	313.02	313.02
313.03	313.04	313.04	313.04	313.05
313.05	313.05	313.08	313.09	313.13
313.14	313.15	313.15	313.15	313.17

			(CONTINUED)	
313.18	313.19	313.19	313.21	313.22
313.24	313.26	313.27	313.28	313.28
313.31	313.32	313.34	313.34	313.35
313.35	314.04	314.04	314.06	314.06
314.07	314.12	314.13	314.14	314.15
314.18	314.19	314.21	314.22	314.23
314.23	314.24	314.29	314.30	314.34
314.34	314.35	314.38	314.38	314.39
315.03	315.07	315.08	315.08	315.09
315.10	315.11	315.12	315.14	315.15
315.16	315.16	315.17	315.18	315.18
315.19	315.19	315.20	315.23	315.25
315.26	315.27	315.28	315.29	315.30
315.30	315.31	315.34	316.03	316.05
316.07	316.08	316.16	316.19	316.19
316.20	316.20	316.21	316.22	316.23
316.27	316.28	316.29	316.31	316.33
316.35	316.36	317.02	317.03	317.04
317.05	317.05	317.07	317.07	317.07
317.08	317.09	317.10	317.10	317.11
317.17	317.19	317.19	317.21	317.27
317.28	317.29	317.29	317.30	317.30
317.31	317.32	317.33	317.33	318.03
318.04	318.05	318.06	318.06	318.10
318.10	318.12	318.13	318.13	318.15
318.15	318.16	318.16	318.23	318.24
318.26	318.31	318.32	318.33	318.34
318.35	318.36	318.36	319.01	319.02
319.02	319.02	319.03	319.03	319.03
319.04	319.04	319.05	319.09	319.10
319.10	319.10	319.11	319.11	319.12
319.13	319.15	319.15	319.16	319.18
319.19	319.19	320.03	320.03	320.05
320.06	320.07	320.08	320.09	320.10
320.11	320.11	320.11	320.13	320.18
320.19	320.20	320.21	320.22	320.23
320.23	320.24	320.25	320.26	320.27
321.01	321.02	321.03	321.04	321.04
321.04	321.04	321.06	321.07	321.10
321.10	321.14	321.18	321.19	321.19
321.20	321.21	321.22	321.22	321.23
321.25	321.27	321.28	321.33	321.34
322.04	322.06	322.08	322.08	322.09
322.11	322.15	322.17	322.19	322.20
322.20	322.21	322.22	322.22	322.22
322.25	322.25	322.32	322.33	322.35
322.36	323.01	323.07	323.10	323.17
323.20	323.20	323.21	323.21	323.22
323.23	323.23	323.23	323.25	323.26
323.26	323.27	323.27	323.30	323.31
323.36	324.02	324.03	324.04	324.06
324.08	324.17	324.20	324.21	324.23
324.25	324.25	324.26	324.30	324.33
324.36	325.01	325.02	325.02	325.04
325.09	325.10	325.12	325.14	325.16
325.17	325.18	325.18	325.21	325.22
325.27	325.28	325.29	325.30	325.31
325.31	325.32	325.35	325.35	325.36
326.03	326.10	326.13	326.18	326.19
326.20	326.27	327.02	327.03	327.04
327.04	327.04	327.05	327.05	327.06
327.06	327.06	327.07	327.08	327.09
327.09	327.10	327.12	327.13	327.14
327.14	327.14	327.17	327.19	327.21
327.23	327.24	327.25	327.26	327.28
327.29	327.32	327.34	327.34	327.36
328.01	328.02	328.03	328.08	328.11
328.11	328.12	328.12	328.13	328.13
328.16	328.17	328.20	328.25	328.29
328.30	328.32	328.33	329.01	329.01
329.04	329.05	329.06	329.09	329.10
329.11	329.11	329.12	329.16	329.17
329.19	329.20	329.23	329.24	329.25
329.25	329.25	329.28	329.29	329.31
329.34	329.35	330.04	330.04	330.07
330.07	330.08	330.09	330.14	330.14
330.14	330.15	330.16	330.16	330.17

222

THEREIN   (2)
123.18   204.06
THERMOMETER   (3)
183.14   292.10   299.24
THESE   (154)
003.23   004.02   004.10   004.28   004.34
005.05   005.14   012.22   012.31   013.01
013.06   020.11   025.32   027.22   031.01
031.07   031.27   032.31   036.05   037.05
038.24   039.21   040.25   049.24   050.12
050.34   059.02   060.10   060.38   064.10
065.10   066.07   067.33   070.16   078.15
083.24   095.16   097.03   098.33   101.22
108.04   110.07   113.16   113.23   117.27
118.17   118.26   119.32   120.05   121.06
121.19   127.14   129.15   131.36   134.29
143.15   145.30   151.20   153.19   154.09
155.33   156.09   158.34   159.36   160.05
160.36   161.05   164.05   164.22   164.34
166.16   166.21   168.09   168.35   168.36
169.01   172.15   172.21   175.01   179.02
181.35   182.08   182.21   182.32   184.07
184.24   185.10   185.25   189.28   191.14
195.10   195.15   197.14   197.23   202.08
205.26   207.28   207.30   212.09   216.23
217.21   217.26   220.30   221.13   221.26
222.19   223.09   223.27   224.10   224.35
225.14   225.15   225.26   227.14   227.20
229.01   233.14   239.01   239.03   239.18
242.21   246.29   247.03   247.12   248.19
254.18   256.17   257.29   261.13   261.34
263.02   263.14   264.10   264.10   264.18
268.24   272.32   275.30   280.16   280.24
283.27   284.15   285.27   288.07   289.01
291.24   293.16   294.12   295.25   308.33
309.16   321.06   327.12   331.36
THESEUS   (1)
080.29
THEY   (613)
003.13   004.04   004.33   004.35   005.06
005.07   005.08   005.10   005.12   005.12
005.13   005.14   005.26   005.29   005.30
006.08   008.20   008.20   009.07   009.08
009.09   009.10   009.12   009.16   012.02
014.12   014.15   015.06   015.33   015.36
015.36   016.09   016.16   016.16   016.19
016.21   016.21   017.14   017.17   017.18
020.05   021.33   022.12   022.13   022.16
022.31   023.08   023.09   023.17   023.19
023.23   023.23   025.03   025.04   025.12
025.13   025.16   025.17   025.17   025.26
025.29   026.04   026.05   026.05   026.21
027.03   027.04   027.05   027.17   027.31
029.03   029.34   029.36   030.05   030.28
031.35   032.17   032.18   032.19   032.23
032.28   032.32   033.11   035.31   035.31
036.27   037.19   038.35   039.01   039.03
039.06   039.15   039.21   039.30   039.33
040.10   040.13   041.18   041.31   041.33
042.11   042.12   042.21   043.22   044.34
045.08   046.08   047.26   047.35   050.19
051.11   052.17   053.28   053.36   054.01
054.02   056.11   057.29   060.39   060.39
061.28   062.11   062.12   065.04   065.04
067.13   068.02   068.05   068.07   068.07
068.14   068.18   068.22   068.29   068.31
069.04   069.05   070.22   070.23   070.23
072.10   072.12   072.17   072.34   073.16
075.06   075.10   075.12   075.13   075.28
076.07   076.07   076.29   079.04   079.06
081.30   081.31   088.30   090.05   090.05
090.06   090.07   092.17   092.28   092.30
092.34   092.36   093.04   093.09   093.30
093.30   094.21   094.33   096.11   096.35
097.31   100.19   100.20   100.30   100.31
100.33   101.07   101.09   101.23   101.24
101.26   101.27   102.05   102.07   102.31
103.01   103.02   103.19   103.30   104.10

THEY   (CONTINUED)
104.13   104.15   104.26   104.35   105.01
105.01   105.03   105.12   105.14   105.22
106.20   107.26   109.03   109.34   111.34
111.35   112.13   112.16   112.16   113.12
113.25   114.03   114.13   115.18   115.19
115.27   115.28   116.21   117.08   117.33
118.02   118.03   118.28   118.29   119.30
119.32   119.33   120.31   121.08   121.14
122.07   122.07   122.08   122.10   122.12
123.32   124.02   124.14   124.29   124.34
125.29   127.06   127.36   129.23   129.28
129.30   130.01   130.29   130.32   131.24
131.28   134.08   134.19   134.21   134.25
134.26   138.08   138.09   140.12   140.22
140.35   141.14   141.30   142.18   142.19
142.33   143.04   143.08   143.19   143.21
143.22   143.23   143.23   143.24   143.25
143.28   143.29   143.31   143.35   144.30
149.13   150.26   151.05   152.06   152.16
152.18   153.03   153.08   153.08   153.09
153.12   153.25   153.30   154.07   155.07
155.11   157.16   157.22   158.01   158.02
158.16   158.36   159.29   160.23   161.17
162.10   163.32   163.33   163.35   164.03
164.09   165.04   165.05   166.05   166.06
166.10   166.22   167.21   167.27   167.30
168.08   168.15   168.22   170.17   170.20
170.24   170.33   171.29   173.17   173.18
173.21   176.02   176.05   176.09   176.11
176.19   178.03   179.03   179.26   180.32
182.11   182.15   182.17   182.30   182.34
184.29   185.20   185.20   185.22   185.24
185.24   186.28   186.33   187.23   187.26
187.31   187.32   189.36   190.09   190.22
191.18   195.17   195.19   195.22   195.25
196.27   196.30   197.15   197.24   197.25
199.10   199.22   199.24   199.28   199.29
199.31   200.04   202.36   203.01   204.31
206.11   206.15   206.18   206.19   206.24
207.33   208.02   210.25   211.08   211.11
212.11   212.15   212.29   213.15   213.15
213.16   213.17   213.18   213.23   213.23
213.24   213.25   213.26   213.28   214.22
214.30   215.07   215.21   216.11   216.31
216.32   217.19   218.24   218.25   220.28
222.14   223.15   223.21   223.22   223.31
224.31   224.36   225.06   225.07   225.18
226.17   227.02   227.07   227.16   227.17
227.19   228.09   228.30   229.08   229.21
230.08   230.12   230.24   231.06   231.29
231.31   232.25   232.32   233.14   233.30
234.06   234.18   236.33   236.35   237.01
237.03   237.04   237.06   237.08   238.22
238.28   238.30   239.01   239.03   240.15
240.18   240.19   240.19   241.04   243.28
245.12   245.12   246.30   247.28   248.36
249.01   250.04   250.06   250.06   250.25
250.26   251.02   251.33   252.10   253.24
253.24   254.24   256.13   259.32   261.17
261.18   262.16   263.31   264.02   264.11
265.25   269.05   271.02   271.16   272.13
272.14   273.06   273.14   275.11   275.13
275.16   275.18   275.20   275.22   275.29
275.35   276.23   276.24   277.05   277.09
277.19   277.23   277.24   278.12   278.28
279.03   279.08   279.12   279.14   279.26
279.31   280.15   280.30   280.33   281.01
281.02   281.18   281.30   283.17   283.17
283.20   283.21   283.22   284.21   284.22
284.24   284.27   284.29   284.30   284.32
284.34   285.05   285.31   287.21   291.10
291.17   292.06   292.20   292.21   292.26
294.14   294.23   294.26   294.28   294.34
294.35   295.01   295.07   295.08   295.24
295.30   295.31   295.32   296.02   296.10
296.16   297.09   297.11   297.12   297.24
303.09   304.27   305.30   305.30   305.34

223

THEY (CONTINUED)
```
309.10   310.17   310.20   310.27   312.35
313.08   313.10   313.13   313.25   315.11
317.21   321.13   321.22   322.06   324.07
324.10   325.05   325.10   325.15   325.15
326.30   328.03   328.17   328.19   328.20
329.23   329.27   330.02   331.04   331.07
331.33   332.22   333.24
```

THICK (32)
```
024.27   024.30   024.31   042.30   130.09
136.19   137.09   145.11   145.32   170.26
180.01   191.21   206.02   231.03   233.10
246.21   247.25   248.11   252.14   278.10
292.16   292.35   293.35   294.03   299.08
299.29   300.10   302.02   302.24   302.31
306.23   308.10
```

THICKER (2)
```
024.17   300.34
```

THICKEST (1)
```
267.33
```

THIEF (2)
```
022.29   314.32
```

THIEVES (2)
```
005.28   275.21
```

THIEVING (1)
```
172.20
```

THIMBLES (1)
```
263.03
```

THIN (19)
```
007.08   024.14   024.28   029.01   039.07
071.30   087.21   098.21   098.35   143.10
161.35   182.27   206.04   247.30   248.09
250.27   268.13   285.06   306.27
```

THING (46)
```
006.18   009.03   009.14   010.32   010.34
019.10   025.25   031.14   038.12   051.20
054.12   055.05   055.10   068.07   070.06
073.03   075.31   076.33   077.20   081.14
093.32   095.06   096.34   106.17   109.34
144.37   146.22   147.27   149.34   150.21
151.19   152.07   172.16   196.20   196.22
219.22   223.32   235.03   244.01   244.03
244.04   277.25   281.05   302.02   304.06
328.01
```

THINGS (75)
```
005.14   008.15   009.26   009.32   015.24
016.12   025.33   031.06   031.07   036.05
037.08   042.11   050.20   050.21   052.17
055.21   055.35   065.36   067.34   068.15
070.10   070.16   078.13   082.03   083.27
088.30   091.36   095.01   095.32   096.02
096.27   098.27   107.35   108.03   109.15
109.17   111.07   113.17   118.10   121.19
121.19   134.09   134.19   135.01   137.26
141.32   142.01   142.35   148.14   148.16
148.32   150.02   169.04   205.29   211.02
220.30   221.13   221.26   224.29   268.29
283.10   283.22   294.04   312.05   314.11
317.23   317.35   317.35   323.33   324.16
326.13   327.12   328.24   328.25   329.24
```

THINK (88)
```
008.03   008.21   009.17   011.03   019.16
019.20   026.01   028.23   030.17   031.11
035.31   036.12   037.03   039.15   040.02
045.19   046.21   050.11   050.35   051.10
053.19   056.14   058.26   064.27   064.37
066.20   069.17   077.28   083.35   084.09
084.12   084.14   088.22   092.14   092.26
094.04   094.27   096.11   096.27   096.29
098.34   104.21   105.12   108.13   118.03
127.18   133.05   133.09   136.20   140.03
142.28   143.29   146.23   149.27   153.25
178.02   178.29   182.30   183.08   186.26
206.06   212.03   213.15   214.03   215.21
217.10   218.03   222.21   223.16   224.06
224.17   224.32   230.12   249.25   263.30
268.27   269.09   271.08   272.26   280.23
281.16   292.19   292.25   315.30   320.13
```

THINK (CONTINUED)
```
328.19   330.29   332.24
```

THINKERS (2)
```
015.05   332.09
```

THINKING (19)
```
008.24   019.11   046.23   048.15   107.09
134.33   135.26   150.12   150.18   190.17
192.17   204.26   206.22   208.38   224.34
235.03   274.29   294.27   331.25
```

THINKS (5)
```
007.35   061.31   121.13   136.01   162.31
```

THINLY (1)
```
199.15
```

THINNER (5)
```
040.06   292.18   299.35   300.24   306.33
```

THINNEST (1)
```
300.02
```

THIRD (13)
```
032.21   055.28   066.11   120.01   140.12
154.07   176.04   179.14   253.20   273.04
293.09   318.36   325.13
```

THIRDS (2)
```
027.25   065.12
```

THIRST (1)
```
294.03
```

THIRSTY (3)
```
207.06   246.03   264.11
```

THIRTEEN (1)
```
225.05
```

THIRTY (20)
```
009.10   030.03   032.18   050.06   050.08
053.09   058.21   070.27   092.16   140.15
175.03   177.34   180.36   198.23   247.06
251.04   252.11   288.34   296.03   297.25
```

THIS (506)
```
003.23   003.24   003.30   004.12   004.13
006.09   006.29   006.33   007.03   008.14
009.10   009.17   010.16   010.17   010.29
011.16   012.14   012.19   013.12   013.29
013.31   014.04   016.02   016.14   017.24
018.10   021.18   021.27   022.10   025.08
025.18   025.26   026.02   026.22   026.23
027.08   027.11   027.35   028.36   029.16
029.22   030.25   030.34   031.17   031.18
031.25   031.29   031.33   032.03   032.11
033.07   033.24   034.06   035.01   035.12
035.26   036.25   036.36   037.18   037.22
037.31   037.34   037.35   037.36   038.12
038.34   039.18   039.27   039.35   040.19
040.23   042.24   043.35   044.06   044.19
044.30   046.20   046.24   047.12   047.25
047.23   050.01   050.31   050.36   051.12
051.15   051.33   053.11   053.15   053.28
054.03   054.11   054.15   054.28   055.06
055.19   056.05   056.35   057.08   057.11
057.15   058.24   060.01   060.11   060.23
060.32   061.02   061.13   061.16   062.09
062.19   062.31   062.34   063.25   063.29
064.18   065.06   066.03   066.05   066.06
068.21   069.03   069.20   069.35   070.34
071.21   071.29   072.20   072.24   072.30
073.13   073.29   074.29   075.31   076.12
076.31   077.09   077.15   078.08   079.08
079.13   080.20   081.18   081.29   084.19
085.03   085.05   085.17   085.20   085.22
086.22   086.27   087.10   087.17   087.17
087.22   087.23   088.32   090.30   091.28
093.01   093.04   093.17   093.33   094.01
094.07   094.23   095.02   095.25   096.04
096.26   096.29   097.25   098.04   099.29
099.31   101.05   101.16   104.06   104.34
104.36   105.22   105.32   106.03   106.17
106.18   106.19   106.33   107.11   107.20
108.24   109.11   109.18   111.21   112.19
112.25   113.23   114.24   115.16   116.10
116.15   116.16   117.04   117.28   118.14
119.02   119.28   120.15   120.18   121.02
121.15   121.16   123.05   123.12   125.01
```

THIS (CONTINUED)
125.09 126.22 126.28 127.04 127.12
127.22 127.35 129.03 130.13 133.08
133.13 133.26 133.27 135.18 136.16
138.28 138.32 141.25 142.11 143.17
143.34 144.04 144.13 144.35 148.35
149.06 149.23 150.05 154.04 154.05
155.08 155.09 155.13 155.14 155.18
155.20 155.22 155.32 155.33 156.06
156.19 157.02 157.06 158.04 158.25
158.36 159.31 161.09 162.20 162.28
162.28 163.26 163.39 163.40 164.04
164.06 164.12 166.17 166.33 168.05
171.12 172.14 172.18 172.18 174.20
174.28 175.18 175.21 175.28 176.29
176.35 177.28 179.10 179.13 179.14
179.30 179.34 180.07 180.16 181.02
181.04 181.06 181.07 181.20 181.20
181.32 181.32 182.16 182.24 184.12
184.23 184.27 187.18 187.20 187.21
187.36 188.03 188.30 190.26 192.34
193.16 193.38 195.04 195.07 195.29
197.13 198.06 198.16 198.20 199.12
201.25 202.02 202.29 204.21 206.13
208.33 208.37 208.39 209.04 210.23
211.35 212.04 212.16 212.28 212.29
213.05 214.05 214.12 215.08 215.14
215.20 215.22 215.31 215.32 216.02
217.35 218.26 218.32 219.19 220.36
222.07 222.17 222.19 223.18 224.14
224.24 224.25 224.26 225.17 226.35
227.34 228.06 229.26 229.33 230.07
230.16 230.26 231.34 232.07 233.20
233.32 234.08 234.24 234.31 235.21
236.08 236.14 236.18 239.15 239.19
240.07 241.03 242.03 245.17 247.27
248.12 249.30 249.34 250.31 250.34
250.34 251.07 251.10 251.12 252.06
252.16 252.24 252.37 252.38 253.13
254.06 256.27 257.10 259.17 260.19
260.22 263.19 264.33 265.03 270.22
271.16 272.14 272.25 273.22 273.33
276.18 277.25 279.16 279.23 279.33
282.17 282.18 282.19 284.35 285.02
285.13 285.18 287.08 287.12 287.21
288.16 288.38 289.12 289.22 289.24
290.06 290.10 290.18 291.27 291.35
292.06 293.20 294.05 294.36 296.11
296.16 296.19 296.23 297.05 297.16
299.09 299.10 299.29 299.35 300.25
300.30 300.35 306.02 306.05 306.08
306.12 306.15 306.20 308.15 308.17
308.18 308.19 308.24 308.26 308.27
309.11 310.10 311.12 311.29 312.01
312.21 313.29 313.31 314.35 315.29
316.29 317.14 318.18 319.13 320.17
321.05 322.09 322.13 322.27 322.36
323.29 325.18 325.26 327.28 329.35
330.18 331.22 332.36 333.01 333.16
333.29
THISTLE   (2)
187.09 206.23
THITHER   (13)
114.33 140.08 141.35 150.32 173.23
194.11 194.24 213.01 222.20 228.05
228.07 237.03 266.01
THITHERWARD   (1)
245.32
THOMASTON   (1)
120.04
THOR   (1)
309.21
THOROUGH   (1)
190.21
THOROUGHLY   (8)
011.14 063.22 069.14 120.18 132.31
139.07 150.08 303.15

THOSE   (114)
003.21 004.32 012.06 015.24 016.10
016.14 016.31 016.33 021.20 027.23
029.32 030.23 035.28 039.09 039.10
039.23 045.24 050.16 050.20 050.36
058.30 060.22 064.12 066.27 070.21
072.24 075.03 075.09 077.02 080.11
080.31 083.27 085.33 085.35 087.08
087.35 087.35 088.09 092.26 099.24
101.22 102.12 103.10 103.18 103.35
104.33 106.01 111.33 112.26 115.10
120.09 123.30 128.07 132.27 138.23
138.25 138.31 141.26 142.28 142.30
148.04 152.01 152.28 159.24 161.33
162.04 162.29 164.10 164.28 168.21
169.03 172.01 177.16 184.16 184.28
185.22 187.33 190.28 192.05 193.34
203.19 211.05 211.18 212.28 217.29
220.23 222.18 223.31 225.08 230.27
230.28 232.06 236.24 241.03 241.28
247.13 247.15 247.19 256.08 261.30
262.29 267.33 274.06 290.30 292.15
296.35 305.34 309.33 311.24 315.31
317.16 325.12 330.23 332.13
THOU   (8)
010.12 080.05 080.30 208.12 250.31
252.37 254.34 254.35
THOUGH   (179)
011.33 015.35 018.03 018.21 021.12
021.31 026.27 027.04 027.09 027.22
027.34 030.18 031.11 033.26 035.30
038.11 040.14 040.17 041.10 042.32
043.10 046.34 050.07 053.31 055.03
057.08 059.03 059.37 060.01 063.01
065.11 069.05 070.07 075.14 075.28
099.22 099.33 101.29 111.03 114.03
114.08 115.29 126.12 126.14 129.07
129.17 130.36 131.16 133.30 136.05
136.08 137.29 142.08 142.20 143.25
144.20 145.01 145.21 146.15 150.16
150.20 150.26 151.02 152.09 152.12
153.08 153.32 155.10 156.23 158.15
161.09 162.16 164.32 166.16 169.27
171.02 171.06 172.05 172.13 175.26
176.02 179.12 180.18 180.20 181.21
182.16 183.20 183.27 184.13 189.17
189.19 190.20 192.33 193.39 198.03
202.32 203.22 206.05 212.13 213.17
214.07 214.34 215.05 216.20 218.05
218.35 220.26 221.12 222.07 227.22
230.35 231.29 234.01 235.19 236.18
238.06 240.19 241.15 241.23 241.30
242.08 242.17 246.30 246.32 247.19
247.25 249.32 250.03 250.19 250.20
251.07 252.12 253.01 253.06 254.01
256.22 256.28 257.14 259.04 262.20
266.32 267.06 268.32 269.30 271.06
271.22 272.04 275.22 278.25 280.18
285.35 288.14 291.01 292.10 293.04
294.09 296.05 296.06 296.25 300.27
300.33 301.06 301.34 302.27 304.33
312.07 312.13 313.23 321.03 322.15
323.17 326.17 326.25 327.17
THOUGHT   (83)
003.13 021.07 025.09 029.03 047.19
057.17 069.28 069.33 071.05 072.29
081.24 089.35 099.21 102.27 104.31
109.16 118.35 125.18 127.02 132.07
132.14 137.30 141.01 147.27 147.33
149.02 149.09 149.18 150.14 150.26
151.10 153.05 153.22 153.25 154.01
157.03 157.20 166.05 169.26 170.07
174.22 193.12 193.17 193.31 196.11
199.02 203.17 203.31 207.07 221.05
222.06 222.06 223.35 231.20 233.16
235.04 236.01 237.03 250.06 253.10
259.20 260.02 260.09 262.30 269.08

225

THOUGHT (CONTINUED)
269.26 278.04 278.25 287.14 287.16
291.20 291.31 291.32 292.21 303.22
303.24 304.02 321.18 328.34 330.17
330.22 331.03 331.05

THOUGHTFULLY (2)
141.18 330.01

THOUGHTLESS (1)
212.30

THOUGHTS (33)
014.36 027.24 042.09 044.17 088.18
088.24 094.10 100.32 125.30 131.36
132.26 134.30 135.08 135.35 140.33
140.34 148.03 148.05 159.30 169.04
169.23 175.16 222.04 224.29 224.33
225.20 254.23 292.02 314.20 328.15
328.27 328.30 332.13

THOUSAND (28)
004.18 010.13 033.25 042.14 049.11
071.22 075.35 091.26 091.30 093.09
102.28 109.19 119.36 121.31 142.16
152.27 171.02 186.11 192.25 213.18
251.08 295.33 296.24 304.25 312.16
312.17 320.33 321.31

THOUSANDS (5)
039.34 108.13 175.04 230.22 240.11

THOUSANDTH (1)
105.02

THRASHER (2)
158.20 319.03

THREAD (5)
149.08 174.24 186.23 196.08 328.03

THREADED (1)
232.17

THREADING (3)
037.22 276.31 278.17

THREADS (2)
026.25 254.08

THREATEN (1)
207.32

THREATENED (1)
260.10

THREATENING (1)
316.01

THREATENS (1)
037.05

THREE (62)
024.28 029.09 032.35 033.09 036.26
038.23 039.22 039.32 065.18 065.19
065.22 066.35 068.20 068.30 075.26
091.25 091.34 110.05 113.10 118.34
136.12 140.09 140.10 156.13 163.08
163.23 173.14 175.31 182.04 184.15
187.05 190.14 223.09 224.18 224.35
230.04 230.23 230.30 233.29 233.29
240.01 240.02 246.23 251.08 251.09
253.05 270.05 272.08 278.07 282.32
288.36 289.28 292.18 293.03 293.13
296.17 299.30 300.05 301.22 303.35
318.07 328.31

THREES (1)
114.26

THREESCORE (1)
147.15

THRENODIES (1)
124.33

THRESHING (1)
161.14

THREW (3)
036.29 174.25 273.23

THRICE (1)
143.14

THRIFTY (1)
258.20

THRILL (2)
210.06 218.32

THRILLED (1)
218.03

THRILLING (3)
085.35 272.29 328.10

THRILLS (2)
188.11 188.11

THRIVE (1)
281.27

THRIVED (1)
264.14

THROAT (2)
233.08 306.32

THROATS (3)
098.17 275.17 275.30

THROES (1)
309.08

THROUGH (138)
005.29 006.10 010.25 025.27 026.21
038.10 039.23 041.07 044.24 050.03
051.22 052.31 054.33 058.24 062.20
062.22 066.21 068.06 074.13 079.16
081.28 083.18 086.34 087.01 088.37
090.24 092.15 094.05 094.09 096.28
097.33 097.36 097.36 098.01 098.02
098.14 098.33 099.28 099.33 105.18
108.19 110.07 111.10 111.30 114.05
117.25 121.23 128.12 129.04 133.36
141.04 143.03 144.21 148.22 155.33
157.15 167.32 168.02 169.15 170.18
174.28 177.01 177.17 178.05 178.11
189.35 192.08 192.09 194.09 194.24
195.05 197.28 202.13 203.05 203.06
206.17 207.20 208.01 210.03 213.32
223.04 227.34 228.16 229.15 233.30
242.01 245.02 245.14 247.03 247.06
247.15 256.11 256.12 256.33 260.05
265.28 266.23 267.23 267.36 268.19
268.19 268.20 269.33 273.31 275.04
278.29 283.01 283.04 283.12 284.12
284.16 284.33 285.19 285.21 287.23
288.26 290.20 291.02 291.08 292.21
292.33 294.12 295.13 299.11 300.08
300.10 302.16 302.30 304.23 304.31
305.04 313.05 314.29 318.35 321.31
323.02 323.07 327.30

THROUGHOUT (3)
085.03 124.15 192.22

THROW (7)
066.34 090.03 094.30 110.17 141.13
156.27 260.02

THROWING (4)
005.32 006.07 086.14 274.21

THROWN (4)
097.17 122.07 130.03 280.32

THRUSH (4)
044.10 086.01 086.26 319.04

THRUST (2)
192.28 299.24

THRUSTING (1)
241.31

THSENG (1)
218.08

THUMB (2)
091.27 226.05

THUMP (3)
280.29 280.29 280.29

THUNDER (6)
116.19 132.32 203.29 207.31 301.33
318.06

THUNDERBOLT (1)
074.12

THUNDERED (1)
204.19

THUNDERING (3)
095.26 301.31 301.34

THUNDERS (1)
302.03

THUS (72)
006.26 013.23 015.31 016.25 018.28
024.06 027.16 036.06 041.02 048.28

THUS (CONTINUED)
049.32 056.03 057.06 059.29 060.36
063.20 064.22 069.05 069.09 077.32
081.06 082.24 084.10 089.19 103.16
117.06 117.36 118.21 136.21 142.16
160.06 162.07 165.03 165.06 170.02
170.16 174.05 175.22 181.08 181.30
181.33 182.17 184.06 180.04 188.08
189.05 192.01 194.12 212.17 213.30
240.28 250.11 253.35 259.32 266.13
266.16 266.25 276.26 277.23 280.21
292.17 293.15 296.02 296.29 297.18
297.35 306.06 306.16 306.33 308.15
315.23 319.18

THY (25)
010.10 079.14 079.17 080.07 080.07
080.10 080.29 138.18 203.10 207.24
207.24 207.29 207.34 207.35 208.10
208.15 252.30 252.32 252.32 252.34
254.30 254.36 255.01 317.24 317.25

THYSELF (2)
088.32 322.21

TICKET (2)
138.31 193.35

TICKING (1)
112.14

TICKLED (1)
146.23

TICKS (1)
262.31

TID (2)
215.14 218.22

TIDE (3)
021.13 181.26 332.28

TIDES (1)
291.28

TIDORE (1)
298.20

TIDY (2)
075.23 214.14

TIE (1)
078.18

TIED (5)
056.03 097.28 191.02 250.01 284.14

TIERRA (2)
012.34 320.17

TIGER (1)
274.35

TIGHT (7)
029.31 030.01 048.28 169.22 205.06
285.34 301.17

TIGHTER (1)
143.31

TIGRIS (1)
079.15

TILES (1)
028.20

TILL (60)
012.21 015.36 018.30 039.04 062.23
062.32 068.02 070.23 072.15 073.36
074.11 074.22 075.24 089.06 097.29
098.02 100.04 105.15 111.26 127.20
138.33 141.30 145.30 161.19 170.22
171.10 171.16 171.17 174.31 178.14
178.29 183.13 187.32 196.27 209.05
215.30 216.20 228.12 229.13 229.35
234.13 245.16 248.27 257.11 263.10
268.20 274.22 274.32 275.29 277.09
280.08 292.26 296.29 305.30 305.33
309.31 311.28 320.12 322.09 329.30

TILLAGE (1)
005.19

TIMBER (8)
020.10 029.34 039.01 040.36 042.07
049.24 062.03 115.34

TIMBERS (4)
042.18 042.20 084.36 280.30

TIME (164)
006.18 006.33 008.06 017.02 018.06
018.28 020.18 021.02 021.02 026.06
028.08 039.28 042.24 044.16 048.02
053.15 053.30 054.03 054.15 054.32
055.18 055.23 055.38 055.38 058.12
059.02 063.26 067.21 068.36 069.18
069.24 070.12 072.16 076.01 078.19
083.36 085.20 086.28 087.18 087.34
089.29 093.08 094.32 094.32 098.10
099.26 100.01 102.33 105.17 108.34
109.01 111.33 111.35 113.05 124.04
126.36 126.36 131.34 132.26 134.02
135.21 136.11 137.24 138.32 140.05
143.32 147.33 148.08 149.11 149.16
151.10 152.17 152.17 153.05 153.10
156.36 159.15 159.15 164.18 165.05
168.05 168.05 170.22 170.35 172.19
173.29 174.20 174.20 174.36 174.36
176.20 177.08 178.15 180.06 180.06
181.16 181.36 182.01 183.15 184.14
188.22 195.04 213.16 214.01 214.01
217.36 219.31 225.29 226.32 227.14
230.07 234.26 234.30 235.16 236.19
241.35 249.02 253.12 253.36 254.02
254.09 258.32 262.30 264.35 265.02
268.19 270.15 270.15 272.25 274.01
274.07 274.13 274.20 274.20 277.29
278.15 285.06 285.21 299.35 300.13
310.14 310.28 313.15 313.22 314.24
317.08 317.34 323.13 324.27 326.23
326.24 326.35 326.35 327.07 327.21
327.22 327.32 332.07 333.30

TIMES (32)
016.19 017.36 027.31 035.35 050.18
061.24 066.03 093.17 097.04 100.13
111.21 121.16 121.18 134.04 136.13
168.36 170.10 171.03 183.07 202.32
204.20 213.19 241.28 243.08 248.32
267.29 277.35 281.20 288.09 315.24
327.11 329.25

TIMID (2)
153.22 164.12

TIMIDLY (1)
047.13

TIN (1)
145.17

TINDER (1)
327.24

TINGE (1)
177.28

TINGED (2)
087.04 202.16

TINGES (1)
197.30

TINGING (1)
202.12

TINKER (1)
327.36

TINKERING (1)
092.20

TINKLED (3)
159.05 259.30 310.27

TINKLING (4)
207.19 275.33 285.01 304.25

TINT (8)
102.31 123.12 137.08 176.25 177.21
177.24 258.33 296.32

TINTED (1)
296.13

TINTINNABULUM (2)
160.18 329.20

TINTS (4)
047.05 156.36 189.17 216.35

TIP (1)
105.19

TIPPED				
181.29				(1)
TIPTOE				
087.05	104.19			(2)
TIRED				
143.04	147.02	147.04	172.09	(4)
TISSUE				
062.28	307.30			(2)
TIT				
107.27	275.30			(2)
TITANIC				
318.04				(1)
TITLE				
181.33	184.07	196.10	258.06	(4)
TITLES				
106.34				(1)
TITTLE				
105.21				(1)
TO				(2774)

003.14	003.16	003.18	003.19	003.22
003.23	003.25	003.30	003.35	004.02
004.03	004.05	004.06	004.10	004.17
004.17	004.19	004.23	004.36	005.04
005.09	005.11	005.13	005.22	005.30
006.06	006.16	006.17	006.18	006.20
006.27	006.30	006.32	006.33	006.37
006.37	007.03	007.04	007.04	007.04
007.05	007.05	007.10	007.13	007.18
007.18	007.21	007.22	007.25	007.26
007.27	008.03	008.05	008.10	008.15
008.16	008.20	008.23	008.26	008.26
008.27	008.32	008.32	008.35	009.05
009.11	009.14	009.15	009.17	009.19
009.20	009.22	009.30	009.30	009.32
009.33	009.36	010.02	010.06	010.08
010.11	010.23	010.24	010.31	010.32
011.06	011.06	011.08	011.11	011.14
011.15	011.19	011.20	011.24	011.24
011.30	011.32	011.34	011.36	011.36
012.01	012.06	012.11	012.13	012.13
012.14	012.16	012.22	012.28	012.33
012.36	013.02	013.02	013.06	013.08
013.15	013.20	013.20	013.22	013.24
013.25	013.29	013.31	013.32	013.34
014.11	014.19	014.20	014.34	014.35
014.35	014.36	014.36	015.01	015.01
015.01	015.03	015.07	015.24	015.25
015.26	015.28	016.04	016.04	016.10
016.13	016.14	016.17	016.24	016.29
016.29	017.02	017.03	017.05	017.14
017.17	017.19	017.25	017.28	017.30
017.31	018.01	018.02	018.06	018.08
018.17	018.20	018.23	018.33	019.01
019.03	019.06	019.08	019.09	019.13
019.14	019.15	019.16	019.17	019.19
019.20	019.21	019.22	019.23	019.27
019.30	019.31	019.32	019.34	019.35
019.35	019.35	020.01	020.04	020.05
020.11	020.12	020.13	020.14	020.15
020.16	020.21	020.21	020.23	020.28
020.29	020.31	020.34	021.01	021.02
021.02	021.02	021.03	021.10	021.11
021.18	021.19	021.20	021.21	021.22
021.22	021.25	021.26	021.28	021.30
021.32	021.34	021.35	022.01	022.06
022.07	022.14	022.14	022.16	022.17
022.33	022.35	023.02	023.09	023.10
023.13	023.14	023.14	023.19	023.20
023.22	023.26	023.27	023.31	023.33
023.34	023.34	024.02	024.05	024.05
024.21	024.29	025.01	025.06	025.10
025.13	025.15	025.20	025.27	025.28
025.35	025.35	026.03	026.04	026.16
027.15	027.32	028.01	028.03	028.04
028.11	028.11	028.15	028.18	028.21
028.23	028.24	028.30	028.31	029.03
029.03	029.04	029.08	029.11	029.13

029.20	029.20	029.22	029.28	029.29
030.08	030.27	030.28	030.32	030.33
030.33	031.01	031.02	031.07	031.15
031.18	031.18	031.25	031.26	031.31
031.32	031.33	032.01	032.02	032.03
032.04	032.05	032.11	032.26	032.28
032.34	032.34	033.01	033.02	033.05
033.18	033.20	033.22	033.25	033.31
034.05	034.07	034.09	034.11	034.15
034.16	034.28	034.31	034.32	034.36
034.36	035.01	035.01	035.02	035.11
035.13	035.16	035.25	035.27	035.28
035.28	035.29	035.32	036.01	036.02
036.04	036.04	036.05	036.05	036.14
036.16	036.27	036.27	036.36	037.01
037.04	037.05	037.11	037.12	037.15
037.33	037.34	037.36	038.01	038.02
038.03	038.04	038.10	038.16	038.17
038.19	038.19	038.21	038.21	039.05
039.06	039.09	039.12	039.13	039.17
039.24	039.28	039.29	039.30	039.33
040.01	040.04	040.05	040.05	040.08
040.16	040.26	040.28	040.29	040.33
040.34	040.34	040.35	040.36	041.02
041.02	041.14	041.18	041.21	041.24
041.25	041.30	041.33	042.01	042.09
042.28	043.04	043.08	043.13	043.13
043.18	043.20	043.25	043.28	043.30
043.31	043.31	043.31	043.32	043.32
043.33	044.03	044.07	044.08	044.14
044.15	044.18	044.22	044.26	044.33
045.04	045.08	045.09	045.12	045.23
045.31	046.13	046.13	046.17	046.20
046.23	046.28	046.32	047.07	047.09
047.10	047.12	047.12	047.14	047.21
047.30	047.34	048.14	048.20	048.25
048.26	048.36	049.28	049.35	049.39
050.01	050.04	050.26	050.28	050.30
050.32	050.33	050.33	050.35	051.01
051.01	051.04	051.08	051.13	051.14
051.17	051.19	051.21	051.23	051.25
051.26	051.27	051.27	052.01	052.01
052.14	052.16	052.18	052.19	052.20
052.21	052.22	052.23	052.24	052.25
052.27	052.28	052.28	052.29	052.30
053.02	053.03	053.04	053.05	053.05
053.07	053.15	053.16	053.17	053.21
053.24	053.25	053.26	053.27	053.30
053.31	054.03	054.05	054.07	054.07
054.08	054.18	054.20	054.24	054.27
054.29	055.02	055.06	055.10	055.10
055.23	055.35	055.37	055.37	055.37
055.38	055.38	056.01	056.03	056.05
056.09	056.14	056.18	056.23	056.25
056.28	056.30	056.33	057.02	057.11
057.12	057.18	057.22	057.24	057.24
057.27	057.30	057.32	058.05	058.07
058.09	058.10	058.16	058.20	058.21
058.22	058.24	058.24	058.27	058.29
058.30	058.32	059.02	059.34	059.40
060.02	060.22	060.23	060.23	060.34
060.37	061.06	061.09	061.10	061.15
061.27	061.28	061.31	061.35	061.36
062.04	062.05	062.08	062.12	062.16
062.23	063.04	063.07	063.09	063.10
063.11	063.14	063.20	063.26	063.35
064.09	064.10	064.14	064.17	064.18
064.21	064.24	064.27	064.29	064.31
065.01	065.03	065.05	065.06	065.07
065.26	065.29	065.31	065.34	066.04
066.05	066.05	066.06	066.07	066.11
066.16	066.17	066.19	066.19	066.28
066.30	066.33	066.36	067.01	067.07
067.07	067.09	067.12	067.17	067.18
067.19	067.20	067.21	067.22	067.22
067.23	067.31	067.37	068.01	068.01
068.09	068.10	068.24	068.36	068.36

TO (CONTINUED)

069.05	069.16	069.16	069.17	069.21
069.23	069.25	069.27	069.28	069.31
069.36	070.02	070.04	070.04	070.05
070.08	070.10	070.12	070.15	070.15
070.16	070.17	070.18	070.20	070.21
070.21	070.22	070.27	070.29	070.29
070.31	070.32	070.34	071.11	071.15
071.23	071.27	071.27	071.30	071.35
072.02	072.04	072.04	072.05	072.10
072.23	072.25	072.25	072.27	072.29
072.33	072.34	072.36	073.01	073.08
073.09	073.13	073.21	073.21	073.22
073.27	073.29	073.31	074.05	074.12
074.17	074.23	074.25	074.34	074.35
075.01	075.01	075.05	075.05	075.07
075.21	075.16	075.21	075.26	075.26
075.28	075.29	075.32	075.33	075.35
076.02	076.03	076.05	076.06	076.12
076.13	076.19	076.20	076.28	076.34
076.35	077.06	077.18	077.25	077.26
077.28	077.36	078.02	078.08	078.13
078.29	079.01	079.02	079.12	079.16
079.18	080.06	080.14	080.29	080.31
081.05	081.09	081.12	081.15	081.16
081.17	081.18	081.23	081.24	081.32
081.33	081.34	082.01	082.03	082.04
082.08	082.10	082.11	082.11	082.14
082.15	082.15	082.16	082.20	082.25
082.28	082.31	083.04	083.10	083.19
083.23	083.24	083.25	083.31	083.33
084.02	084.03	084.06	084.10	084.11
084.12	084.20	084.22	084.23	084.23
084.24	084.27	085.02	085.06	085.19
085.25	085.25	085.31	085.33	085.34
086.07	086.20	086.27	087.03	087.11
087.12	087.13	087.27	087.35	087.35
088.02	088.08	088.09	088.09	088.12
088.13	088.23	088.25	088.32	089.11
089.12	089.18	089.20	089.34	090.03
090.11	090.11	090.12	090.15	090.19
090.20	090.21	090.21	090.22	090.23
090.25	090.26	090.32	090.32	090.33
090.34	090.35	090.36	091.01	091.02
091.03	091.04	091.04	091.04	091.05
091.06	091.07	091.07	091.08	091.09
091.10	091.11	091.14	091.22	091.30
091.31	091.31	092.20	092.20	092.21
092.22	092.33	093.02	093.03	093.07
093.09	093.09	093.10	093.19	093.21
093.22	093.28	093.29	093.33	094.05
094.20	094.24	094.26	094.30	094.32
094.35	095.06	095.11	095.13	095.14
095.15	095.17	095.31	095.32	095.35
096.06	096.11	096.15	096.16	096.16
096.18	096.20	096.23	096.24	096.28
096.30	096.35	097.07	097.10	097.21
097.28	098.03	098.10	098.11	098.11
098.28	098.36	099.06	099.20	099.21
099.26	099.26	099.28	099.29	099.35
100.01	100.10	100.13	100.18	100.18
100.24	100.34	100.36	100.36	101.01
101.05	101.07	101.08	101.17	101.18
101.21	101.27	101.32	102.10	102.10
102.11	102.12	102.15	102.16	102.22
102.29	102.29	102.32	103.01	103.09
103.10	103.15	103.18	103.32	103.33
103.34	104.05	104.07	104.12	104.12
104.13	104.13	104.18	104.18	104.19
104.20	104.31	104.32	104.35	104.36
105.01	105.10	105.14	105.16	105.21
106.03	106.11	106.12	106.15	106.18
106.18	106.20	106.26	106.26	106.27
106.31	106.32	107.01	107.04	107.11
107.16	107.24	107.31	107.34	108.05
108.07	108.15	108.17	108.22	108.25
108.26	108.27	108.36	109.03	109.05
109.08	109.08	109.16	109.18	109.21

TO (CONTINUED)

109.33	109.35	109.36	110.01	110.08
110.08	110.12	111.03	111.17	111.22
111.23	111.24	112.05	112.15	112.16
112.18	112.19	112.26	112.27	112.29
112.31	112.34	113.06	113.07	113.08
113.13	113.14	113.14	113.16	113.23
113.24	113.24	113.29	114.03	114.08
114.10	114.15	114.28	114.36	115.02
115.14	115.16	115.18	115.18	115.20
115.28	115.28	115.36	116.01	116.15
116.23	116.27	116.34	116.35	117.05
117.06	117.10	117.18	118.08	118.09
118.11	118.12	118.13	118.19	118.21
118.24	118.26	118.36	119.01	119.21
119.35	120.02	120.07	120.12	120.20
121.07	121.10	121.27	122.05	122.07
122.13	122.19	122.20	123.11	123.12
123.12	123.16	123.17	123.29	123.29
123.31	124.02	124.04	124.05	124.24
125.02	125.09	125.15	125.27	126.01
126.10	126.16	126.18	126.21	126.27
126.31	126.36	127.03	127.10	127.12
127.13	127.13	127.19	127.34	128.06
128.08	128.09	128.10	128.18	128.19
129.08	129.10	129.10	129.25	129.29
129.30	130.15	130.18	130.25	130.29
130.33	130.33	131.07	131.10	131.11
131.13	131.15	131.18	131.18	131.30
131.32	131.33	131.35	132.10	132.11
132.12	132.14	132.23	132.26	132.29
132.35	133.05	133.06	133.06	133.07
133.08	133.14	133.14	133.18	133.19
133.19	133.19	133.23	133.24	133.31
133.32	133.35	133.36	134.01	134.03
134.03	134.06	134.08	134.09	134.10
134.12	134.13	134.17	134.18	134.23
134.23	134.28	134.30	135.06	135.08
135.20	135.21	135.22	136.11	136.14
136.16	136.17	136.25	136.31	136.32
136.33	136.35	137.10	137.22	137.25
137.30	137.32	137.33	137.34	138.04
138.26	138.31	139.04	139.06	140.04
140.05	140.18	140.21	140.23	140.26
140.31	140.32	140.34	141.05	141.09
141.10	141.11	141.12	141.16	141.18
141.19	141.22	141.25	141.27	141.28
142.04	142.05	142.11	142.21	142.26
142.27	142.29	143.03	143.06	143.21
143.22	143.23	143.28	143.29	143.30
144.04	144.10	144.13	144.20	144.23
144.25	144.26	144.37	144.37	145.03
145.04	145.07	145.08	145.16	145.22
145.22	145.23	145.27	145.30	146.03
146.06	146.07	146.28	146.31	146.33
147.01	147.09	147.10	147.17	147.18
147.19	147.21	147.26	148.03	148.05
148.06	148.07	148.07	148.10	148.14
148.15	148.16	148.16	148.20	148.23
148.27	148.28	148.29	148.29	148.31
149.04	149.08	149.10	149.11	149.15
149.20	149.24	149.26	149.31	149.35
149.36	149.36	150.02	150.03	150.04
150.11	150.14	150.15	150.17	150.21
150.25	150.26	150.29	150.32	151.04
151.04	151.06	151.08	151.11	151.16
151.17	151.19	151.26	151.27	151.31
151.35	152.04	152.04	152.05	152.07
152.36	153.03	153.16	153.17	153.18
153.20	153.23	153.28	153.33	153.34
154.18	154.19	155.05	155.07	155.10
155.11	155.14	155.20	155.21	155.27
155.30	155.32	155.33	155.35	156.07
156.18	156.19	156.24	156.26	156.30
157.11	157.13	157.14	157.16	157.25
157.26	157.30	157.35	157.36	158.03
158.17	158.21	158.28	158.29	158.36

			(CONTINUED)	
159.06	159.07	159.11	159.11	159.15
159.16	159.22	159.25	159.31	159.36
160.05	160.06	160.18	160.20	160.27
160.29	161.04	161.17	161.18	161.29
161.34	162.05	162.06	162.06	162.08
162.09	162.13	162.20	162.26	162.28
162.33	163.09	163.29	163.40	164.06
164.08	164.08	164.13	164.15	164.16
164.18	164.26	164.34	164.35	165.04
165.13	165.19	165.20	165.25	165.31
165.32	166.03	166.08	166.19	166.20
166.20	166.34	167.09	167.09	167.11
167.11	167.15	167.16	167.21	167.23
167.23	167.24	167.25	167.26	167.34
167.35	168.02	168.05	168.08	168.17
168.19	168.21	168.25	168.29	168.29
168.34	169.02	169.03	169.05	169.10
169.14	169.16	169.17	169.30	169.31
169.32	170.05	170.05	170.06	170.09
170.10	170.12	170.12	170.13	170.14
170.14	170.19	170.24	170.28	170.29
170.34	171.01	171.01	171.04	171.12
171.13	171.14	171.18	171.21	171.21
171.23	171.26	171.29	171.29	171.35
171.36	172.03	172.05	172.14	172.19
172.33	173.07	173.11	173.11	173.12
173.15	173.29	173.32	173.35	174.07
174.08	174.09	174.16	174.19	174.20
174.22	174.29	174.32	174.33	174.36
175.02	175.13	175.15	175.17	175.18
175.18	175.19	175.26	175.29	176.01
176.01	176.02	176.13	176.17	176.19
176.27	176.30	177.09	177.18	177.21
177.23	177.25	177.27	178.05	178.07
178.13	178.19	178.28	178.33	179.07
179.25	179.27	179.34	179.36	180.06
180.07	180.19	180.21	180.28	180.29
180.31	181.05	181.07	181.08	181.22
181.26	181.30	181.32	181.33	181.36
182.04	182.05	182.09	182.29	182.31
182.34	183.02	183.10	183.15	183.16
183.24	183.27	183.32	183.35	184.07
184.11	184.12	184.23	185.20	185.22
185.26	185.27	186.02	186.05	186.09
186.10	186.27	186.31	186.31	187.04
187.35	188.21	188.29	188.32	189.11
189.16	189.22	189.28	189.29	189.31
189.34	190.06	190.13	190.17	190.18
190.26	190.36	191.01	191.01	191.06
191.08	191.12	191.15	191.31	191.33
191.34	192.01	192.11	192.16	192.16
192.17	192.18	192.19	192.19	192.27
192.32	193.05	193.12	193.13	193.14
193.18	193.23	193.24	193.25	193.33
193.39	194.05	194.07	194.11	194.16
194.21	194.25	194.30	195.06	195.08
195.10	195.14	195.30	195.30	196.01
196.01	196.10	196.16	196.19	196.19
196.22	196.23	196.28	196.30	196.34
197.01	197.04	197.09	197.11	197.16
197.31	197.32	197.32	197.33	197.34
198.28	198.30	198.34	198.35	199.09
199.13	199.23	199.25	199.26	199.28
201.03	201.07	201.07	201.10	201.11
201.24	201.35	202.02	202.18	202.30
202.36	203.04	203.04	203.05	203.12
203.17	203.24	203.27	203.29	203.31
203.32	203.33	203.35	204.04	204.10
204.10	204.21	204.23	204.26	204.31
205.02	205.09	205.12	205.12	205.14
205.16	205.16	205.17	205.18	205.22
205.25	205.26	205.27	205.27	205.30
205.31	205.33	205.34	205.34	205.36
206.10	206.14	206.15	206.16	206.17
206.18	206.20	206.21	206.23	206.36
206.36	207.06	207.06	207.07	207.09
207.13	207.13	207.16	207.16	207.19

			(CONTINUED)	
207.21	207.29	207.32	207.33	207.34
207.34	208.09	208.38	208.39	209.02
209.04	209.06	210.07	210.21	210.21
210.23	210.23	210.25	210.33	210.33
211.13	211.20	211.21	211.22	211.25
211.26	211.32	212.02	212.04	212.06
212.08	212.28	212.36	213.09	213.11
213.19	213.24	213.26	213.26	213.27
213.28	213.29	214.01	214.06	214.09
214.10	214.12	214.14	214.15	214.20
214.23	214.25	214.29	214.30	214.31
214.33	214.34	214.36	215.02	215.19
215.21	215.27	215.33	215.34	215.35
216.03	216.06	216.06	216.09	216.13
216.15	216.22	216.23	216.29	216.31
216.34	217.05	217.07	217.16	217.18
217.18	217.19	217.20	217.22	217.23
217.24	217.29	217.32	217.34	217.35
218.03	218.04	218.13	218.14	218.17
218.19	218.24	218.25	219.02	219.25
219.26	219.29	219.30	220.03	220.09
220.11	220.12	220.16	220.21	220.24
220.29	220.30	220.37	221.05	221.11
221.12	221.13	221.23	221.23	221.28
221.32	221.33	222.01	222.03	222.12
222.16	222.19	222.21	222.21	223.04
223.12	223.17	223.25	223.26	223.30
223.32	224.01	224.01	224.10	224.12
224.14	224.15	224.26	224.20	224.22
224.25	225.18	225.19	224.30	224.32
225.10	226.12	226.19	225.22	225.24
226.12	226.12	226.19	226.33	226.33
227.14	227.14	227.24	227.25	227.34
228.03	228.08	228.13	228.19	228.24
228.25	228.26	228.32	228.36	229.13
229.15	229.17	229.18	229.19	229.23
229.29	229.32	230.03	230.06	230.07
230.10	230.25	230.27	230.33	230.34
231.02	231.04	231.14	231.30	232.05
232.06	232.07	232.12	232.23	233.01
233.18	233.21	233.25	233.31	234.05
234.07	234.10	234.18	234.26	234.26
234.27	234.31	235.01	235.04	235.08
235.08	235.16	235.21	235.23	235.26
235.28	235.28	235.29	236.05	236.06
236.13	236.25	236.34	236.35	237.01
237.05	238.03	238.12	238.12	238.13
238.21	238.24	238.29	239.01	239.08
239.12	239.16	240.05	239.27	240.05
240.11	240.12	240.16	240.23	240.23
240.27	240.32	240.34	241.02	241.04
241.07	241.17	241.27	241.29	241.29
241.30	241.32	241.34	241.35	242.01
242.07	242.09	242.09	242.17	242.19
242.22	242.24	242.25	242.26	242.27
243.07	243.19	243.21	243.22	243.24
243.33	244.06	244.10	244.16	244.17
244.18	244.19	244.21	244.22	244.28
244.33	245.06	245.06	245.11	245.14
245.20	245.21	245.22	245.22	245.24
245.25	245.27	245.28	245.28	245.33
246.02	246.03	246.05	246.11	246.31
246.33	246.35	247.04	247.07	247.14
247.14	247.17	247.31	247.32	247.33
248.06	248.08	248.19	248.20	248.25
248.26	248.30	248.36	249.11	249.13
249.16	249.18	249.21	249.21	249.24
250.15	250.27	250.27	250.29	250.31
250.32	251.01	251.02	251.09	251.12
251.14	251.15	251.18	251.24	251.27
251.28	251.36	252.01	252.06	252.19
252.25	252.38	253.03	253.12	253.18
253.25	253.26	253.26	254.01	254.03
254.06	254.07	254.08	254.12	254.18
254.27	254.29	255.06	255.08	256.09
256.09	256.17	256.26	256.27	256.29
256.33	257.07	257.15	257.20	257.31

TO   (CONTINUED)

```
258.01  258.07  258.22  258.22  258.28
258.32  258.33  259.10  259.11  259.12
259.13  259.14  259.21  259.26  259.29
260.02  260.02  260.03  260.06  260.13
260.16  260.16  260.24  260.27  260.30
261.02  261.05  261.06  261.06  261.12
261.14  261.16  261.19  261.23  261.26
261.29  261.31  262.05  262.05  262.08
262.12  262.20  262.26  262.29  262.32
263.10  263.19  263.25  263.28  264.01
264.09  264.10  264.14  264.15  264.21
265.01  265.10  265.11  265.12  265.18
265.24  265.29  265.32  265.33  266.05
266.11  266.16  266.18  266.24  266.35
267.01  267.04  267.10  267.11  267.21
267.24  267.27  267.28  267.35  268.08
268.12  268.23  268.30  268.35  269.08
269.16  269.19  270.02  270.07  270.09
270.10  270.14  270.15  270.19  270.20
270.21  270.23  271.03  271.11  271.17
271.27  272.04  272.12  272.20  272.21
272.26  273.11  273.14  273.14  273.16
273.24  274.08  274.12  274.17  274.20
274.26  274.28  274.30  274.34  275.03
275.05  275.06  275.13  275.16  275.19
275.22  275.26  275.30  276.07  276.14
276.18  276.22  276.24  276.25  276.33
277.01  277.09  277.10  277.13  277.13
277.16  277.17  277.26  277.26  277.30
277.33  277.34  278.15  278.16  278.22
278.28  278.31  278.32  279.06  279.07
279.17  279.22  280.12  280.15  280.23
280.24  280.29  280.30  280.31  281.04
281.20  281.20  281.21  281.21  281.22
281.25  281.27  282.03  282.04  282.08
282.09  282.12  282.16  282.18  282.18
282.21  282.24  282.26  282.27  282.29
282.30  283.02  283.08  283.13  283.23
283.33  283.36  283.36  284.11  284.11
284.14  284.20  284.22  284.23  284.23
284.29  285.03  285.06  285.09  285.16
285.19  285.23  285.26  285.27  285.30
285.32  287.03  287.05  287.06  287.14
287.19  287.27  288.07  288.15  288.19
288.20  288.31  288.37  289.01  289.03
289.11  289.16  289.22  289.23  289.29
289.30  289.32  290.04  290.06  290.14
290.17  290.18  290.25  290.30  290.35
291.12  291.13  291.19  291.29  291.33
291.36  292.07  292.14  292.16  292.23
292.25  292.30  293.05  293.13  293.16
293.17  293.19  293.22  293.28  294.01
294.01  294.02  294.10  294.10  294.14
294.14  294.17  294.23  294.26  294.29
294.30  294.31  294.34  295.01  295.03
295.04  295.09  295.10  295.17  295.20
295.22  295.23  295.25  295.26  295.26
295.28  295.31  296.05  296.10  296.15
296.21  296.23  296.24  296.27  297.02
297.09  298.07  298.07  298.09  298.14
299.04  299.08  299.11  299.12  299.16
299.18  300.05  300.15  300.19  300.23
300.26  300.28  301.02  301.14  301.14
301.18  301.34  302.02  302.03  302.06
302.10  302.10  302.11  302.13  302.17
302.19  303.07  303.11  303.15  303.17
303.18  303.19  303.21  303.28  303.31
303.34  304.09  304.10  304.11  304.13
304.17  304.18  304.24  304.28  304.31
305.03  305.05  305.20  305.21  305.23
306.01  306.11  306.14  306.24  306.25
306.31  306.34  307.08  307.18  307.18
307.23  307.26  307.33  307.35  308.13
308.14  308.20  308.22  309.02  309.19
309.25  310.02  310.04  310.05  310.19
310.21  310.21  310.30  311.02  311.12
311.14  311.15  311.22  311.24  311.25
```

TO   (CONTINUED)

```
311.29  312.02  312.03  313.12  313.13
313.15  313.31  313.33  314.04  314.28
314.29  315.04  315.05  315.13  315.14
315.16  315.21  315.25  315.27  316.08
316.32  317.02  317.03  317.08  317.16
317.18  317.18  317.28  317.30  317.33
317.34  318.07  318.13  318.14  318.18
318.19  318.20  318.25  318.26  318.30
318.34  319.06  319.19  320.03  320.10
320.15  320.17  320.18  320.26  320.26
320.30  321.08  321.13  321.15  321.16
321.22  321.29  321.30  321.33  321.33
322.08  322.08  322.11  322.15  322.16
322.16  322.19  322.22  322.27  322.29
322.30  322.31  322.31  323.01  323.02
323.04  323.05  323.05  323.07  323.08
323.09  323.11  323.12  323.17  323.19
323.24  323.25  323.31  323.35
324.12  324.21  324.21  324.27  324.28
324.30  325.06  325.08  325.11  325.21
325.22  325.24  325.27  325.36  326.02
326.04  326.06  326.10  326.18  326.21
326.22  326.24  326.27  327.03  327.12
327.14  327.24  327.27  327.33  327.35
328.01  328.02  328.02  328.16  328.16
328.18  328.24  328.25  328.28  328.29
328.34  328.35  328.35  328.35  329.03
329.09  329.10  329.15  329.31  329.32
329.32  329.34  329.35  330.05  330.05
330.05  330.08  330.09  330.11  330.11
330.16  330.17  330.20  330.30  331.04
331.04  331.17  331.18  331.19  331.23
332.11  332.15  332.21  333.05  333.26
333.30  333.31  333.32  333.33
```

```
TOAD                                    (  2)
  201.13  324.11
TOADS                                   (  1)
  318.23
TOBACCO                                 (  2)
  078.11  078.12
TODAY                                   (  4)
  026.22  040.15  072.14  224.14
TOE                                     (  2)
  017.05  105.19
TOES                                    (  3)
  091.23  281.08  307.32
TOGETHER                                ( 25)
  053.13  068.18  068.26  072.05  072.07
  002.10  105.10  105.22  141.16  155.04
  169.14  173.35  190.33  191.02  204.17
  247.27  249.29  250.01  257.27  259.22
  269.21  269.29  283.16  298.15  305.30
TOIL                                    (  5)
  006.13  015.27  032.22  057.21  164.04
TOILET                                  (  1)
  008.04
TOILING                                 (  1)
  032.17
TOL                                     (  1)
  105.21
TOLD                                    ( 38)
  009.13  013.04  043.28  059.29  071.05
  121.16  147.26  147.32  148.21  150.31
  151.17  160.23  170.19  180.30  191.04
  198.19  204.33  206.01  233.04  239.09
  240.04  244.19  258.08  258.11  259.01
  277.14  277.29  277.36  279.07  279.09
  279.16  279.19  279.34  285.12  295.32
  297.11  300.25  303.20
TOLERABLE                               (  2)
  044.13  136.16
TOLERATE                                (  1)
  332.19
TOLERATES                               (  1)
  185.09
TOM                                     (  1)
  327.36
```

TOMB
037.32 058.04 058.08 333.22 (4)
TOMBS
034.28 (1)
TOMORROW
269.16 (1)
TONE
119.04 141.29 260.06 (3)
TONGS
065.20 (1)
TONGUE (6)
100.12 101.12 101.16 101.16 103.23
277.33
TONGUES
101.20 238.14 322.16 (3)
TONIC
317.28 (1)
TONIGHT
193.06 (1)
TONS
295.33 296.24 (2)
TOO (75)
006.13 006.14 008.05 008.23 012.36
013.12 017.03 018.08 019.17 026.17
035.13 052.19 055.10 067.16 074.02
077.11 080.05 081.16 081.24 081.25
082.19 092.13 101.17 109.10 115.20
117.05 122.03 122.11 131.16 136.10
137.31 144.18 150.08 152.35 155.29
162.15 163.02 185.21 185.21 199.28
201.22 204.23 204.30 205.04 208.36
210.14 213.24 220.23 221.22 223.22
223.22 224.14 225.04 225.08 225.12
228.07 228.18 231.03 234.06 238.06
247.31 252.25 254.36 255.02 257.12
266.11 270.17 275.01 275.17 288.24
295.24 308.10 310.10 311.22 322.28
TOOK (32)
039.35 044.03 044.06 044.30 061.31
081.11 081.13 081.14 084.26 141.36
142.26 174.29 190.11 191.09 206.34
230.30 232.09 241.27 242.08 254.20
265.21 271.16 277.36 279.14 281.10
294.32 295.19 301.23 303.23 313.15
314.21 322.29
TOOLS (6)
005.05 029.10 037.24 037.24 042.24
294.19
TOOTH (1)
206.20
TOP (15)
016.01 086.32 132.35 158.30 176.23
176.28 187.16 198.02 198.16 199.04
201.27 274.10 274.17 275.06 310.02
TOPMOST (1)
158.19
TOPOGRAPHICAL (1)
198.08
TOPPLE (1)
296.08
TOPS (8)
004.28 018.02 037.23 130.17 159.19
161.08 265.32 265.33
TORCH (1)
243.24
TORMENTORS (1)
075.05
TORN (5)
119.29 128.16 159.16 231.01 238.15
TORPID (3)
041.21 041.29 254.03
TORRENT (1)
135.01
TORRID (1)
028.01
TORTOISE (3)
047.04 047.08 313.27

TORTOISES (2)
184.32 318.23
TORTURE (1)
075.05
TOSCAR (1)
132.19
TOSS (1)
048.16
TOSSED (1)
178.06
TOTAL (1)
174.28
TOTANUS (1)
185.05
TOTEM (1)
239.19
TOTTERING (1)
067.03
TOUCH (3)
136.27 187.04 219.04
TOUCHED (2)
141.30 278.06
TOUCHES (2)
115.13 130.19
TOUCHING (1)
191.33
TOUGH (2)
155.29 208.22
TOUGHNESS (1)
241.12
TOUR (1)
088.37
TOWARD (28)
085.21 086.36 087.17 087.28 118.17
152.25 170.22 191.07 198.27 207.17
210.16 210.17 232.19 234.20 242.04
245.31 248.31 261.12 272.15 278.11
291.06 293.03 295.14 301.24 312.35
322.25 324.36 330.06
TOWARDS (1)
058.04
TOWERED (1)
162.01
TOWERS (2)
057.20 058.22
TOWN (55)
004.13 017.30 018.18 018.31 022.14
024.25 029.01 032.29 034.06 038.34
057.12 058.24 068.11 068.17 068.21
068.24 068.27 072.26 086.06 096.29
104.32 106.03 106.34 109.18 109.19
109.25 115.02 115.26 117.29 134.01
144.06 151.10 152.02 155.32 160.04
160.08 169.17 170.28 173.06 183.09
192.22 198.09 213.14 223.05 234.05
251.10 257.21 258.22 265.03 267.01
270.24 279.23 320.16 328.16 328.20
TOWNCLERK (1)
279.23
TOWNS (10)
023.05 030.22 068.32 115.30 117.26
200.04 227.23 249.24 283.16 307.06
TOWNSFOLK (1)
257.22
TOWNSHIP (3)
121.24 201.34 313.24
TOWNSMAN (4)
076.19 107.14 107.22 148.21
TOWNSMEN (13)
003.12 005.03 017.23 018.30 072.21
072.35 108.25 112.20 133.28 182.10
256.18 261.15 283.15
TOYS (1)
052.16
TR (4)
126.24 126.24 126.24 126.30
TRACE (5)
130.02 159.35 179.35 180.16 305.32

TRACED   (1)
214.29
TRACES   (3)
184.34   186.09   297.29
TRACK   (18)
074.08   097.11   097.17   115.20   115.28
118.12   118.20   118.23   122.16   152.19
153.19   169.33   224.33   232.22   267.09
277.27   295.36   323.15
TRACKS   (7)
017.14   223.27   246.26   256.13   265.24
267.05   267.18
TRACTS   (1)
299.03
TRADE   (18)
014.11   017.07   020.06   020.25   021.09
064.22   069.20   069.34   070.06   070.07
070.08   104.14   145.33   162.06   207.35
224.03   262.04   321.17
TRADER   (5)
103.07   120.23   120.24   121.11   279.23
TRADERS   (2)
109.16   115.26
TRADES   (1)
058.35
TRADESMEN   (1)
251.13
TRADITION   (4)
097.34   182.11   258.34   323.24
TRADITIONS   (1)
310.29
TRAGEDIES   (1)
258.31
TRAGEDY   (1)
135.15
TRAGIC   (1)
262.06
TRAIL   (4)
017.12   085.07   226.21   277.24
TRAILING   (3)
210.04   249.15   277.03
TRAIN   (12)
037.16   069.17   116.07   116.17   116.33
117.01   117.02   119.19   121.17   121.30
123.35   222.03
TRAINERS   (1)
160.16
TRAINING   (1)
101.04
TRAINS   (1)
115.17
TRAMP   (2)
017.15   117.15
TRAMPED   (1)
265.28
TRANQUIL   (1)
315.15
TRANSACT   (1)
019.36
TRANSCENDENT   (1)
284.24
TRANSCENDS   (1)
306.36
TRANSCRIPT   (2)
103.21   103.24
TRANSFER   (1)
245.24
TRANSFERRED   (2)
044.13   113.24
TRANSFIXES   (1)
219.05
TRANSFORMATION   (1)
273.16
TRANSFORMED   (1)
215.09
TRANSGRESSED   (1)
318.08

TRANSGRESSIONS   (1)
124.34
TRANSIENT   (6)
055.25   102.11   134.07   299.20   311.26
329.30
TRANSITORY   (3)
077.08   079.15   101.12
TRANSLATE   (1)
144.25
TRANSLATED   (3)
102.23   285.06   325.03
TRANSLATES   (1)
306.36
TRANSLATION   (1)
084.08
TRANSLATIONS   (1)
100.17
TRANSMIGRATION   (1)
059.36
TRANSMIT   (1)
282.15
TRANSMITTED   (1)
177.01
TRANSMUTE   (1)
219.32
TRANSPARENCY   (1)
178.27
TRANSPARENT   (8)
177.33   189.33   199.30   246.18   247.23
297.10   300.32   312.11
TRANSPIRE   (1)
089.28
TRANSPORTATION   (1)
049.20
TRANSPORTED   (2)
067.37   173.23
TRANSVERSE   (1)
178.02
TRAP   (7)
033.22   044.04   048.31   066.10   066.10
067.07   244.11
TRAPPER   (1)
211.01
TRAPPINGS   (1)
026.16
TRAPS   (2)
066.07   092.08
TRAVEL   (10)
053.04   054.03   072.07   097.11   100.04
143.23   285.01   320.34   322.17   330.09
TRAVELLED   (5)
004.15   053.13   108.14   171.02   246.26
TRAVELLER   (24)
025.23   036.34   046.11   053.07   111.31
130.06   130.26   150.29   168.19   168.26
210.34   211.02   226.18   227.11   243.31
256.30   257.15   258.36   263.26   267.05
290.35   304.24   330.14   330.16
TRAVELLERS   (8)
017.12   114.35   157.15   157.23   158.01
238.19   312.31   322.18
TRAVELLING   (9)
023.01   062.20   066.31   085.06   116.15
174.18   184.34   218.33   271.18
TRAVELS   (4)
022.34   072.15   117.19   323.22
TREACHEROUSLY   (1)
044.11
TREAD   (2)
226.29   248.34
TREASURE   (2)
252.05   260.30
TREASURED   (1)
102.33
TREASURES   (4)
005.27   101.33   243.36   294.05
TREAT   (2)
006.25   222.23

233

TREATED				(3)
015.35	029.24	108.16		

TREATING		(1)
061.33		

TREE				(40)
004.26	018.01	018.25	027.30	037.27
042.31	049.14	064.15	079.18	082.01
128.16	136.29	146.06	161.08	191.11
198.14	198.16	198.20	199.03	202.05
223.20	231.34	238.31	240.05	249.15
258.21	265.29	275.07	275.13	275.14
280.22	293.12	298.13	307.04	309.04
326.12	331.13	333.08	333.11	333.21

TREED		(1)
232.20		

TREES				(48)
009.34	029.32	039.17	079.05	083.14
083.21	086.20	127.16	146.02	146.13
146.24	169.31	169.34	181.22	181.34
186.04	186.09	186.15	188.03	189.01
191.23	192.13	196.25	201.08	201.13
201.24	201.34	203.11	208.22	238.30
239.01	257.36	258.01	261.31	265.13
265.14	265.33	268.21	276.24	276.25
280.17	280.24	283.35	293.31	297.28
313.26	318.06	318.32		

TREMBLE		(2)
006.14	223.29	

TREMBLES		(1)
218.31		

TREMBLING				(6)
099.13	188.06	226.34	262.10	281.04
282.25				

TREMENDOUS		(1)
272.19		

TREMONT		(1)
140.25		

TREMULOUS		(2)
125.05	161.07	

TRENCHES		(1)
161.36		

TREND		(1)
291.12		

TRESPASS		(1)
010.01		

TRESPASSERS		(2)
195.34	250.10	

TRESSES		(1)
310.12		

TRET		(1)
021.05		

TRIAL		(2)
047.12	299.14	

TRIANGLES		(1)
010.19		

TRIBE			(3)
065.09	239.20	239.31	

TRIBES		(1)
216.10		

TRICKS		(1)
236.33		

TRIED				(16)
009.16	010.09	062.05	065.07	065.07
065.09	069.14	069.20	073.05	112.21
132.28	148.05	183.20	205.02	213.35
267.31				

TRIES		(1)
089.27		

TRIFLE		(1)
205.14		

TRIFLER		(1)
329.13		

TRIFLES		(2)
161.03	221.26	

TRIFLING				(4)
004.31	014.09	057.24	058.31	

TRIG		(1)
066.23		

TRIGONOMETRICAL		(1)
274.17		

TRILL		(1)
112.09		

TRILLED		(1)
124.25		

TRIM		(1)
140.34		

TRIMMINGS		(1)
317.10		

TRINITY		(1)
047.06		

TRIPPED		(1)
092.08		

TRIVIAL				(10)
061.22	123.20	144.04	171.06	204.03
207.16	221.22	298.06	329.36	333.26

TRIVIALNESS		(2)
063.07	100.23	

TROD			(3)
044.04	229.05	323.18	

TRODDEN		(2)
180.06	271.30	

TROJAN		(1)
192.24		

TROJANS		(1)
161.33		

TROONK		(1)
126.36		

TROOP		(2)
228.10	259.18	

TROPE		(1)
245.07		

TROPES		(2)
162.13	245.01	

TROPHIES		(2)
104.06	231.10	

TROPHY		(2)
262.34	277.04	

TROPIC		(1)
298.21		

TROPICAL		(2)
114.07	119.23	

TROT		(1)
108.28		

TROTS		(1)
052.34		

TROTTERS		(1)
273.35		

TROTTING		(1)
209.05		

TROUBLE				(10)
011.30	018.19	059.17	061.15	142.29
214.26	240.16	254.06	285.16	328.23

TROUBLED				(4)
011.31	064.21	112.33	272.36	

TROUGH		(2)
063.21	063.21	

TROUSERS		(1)
023.22		

TROUT				(4)
184.22	203.14	203.19	235.19	

TROWEL			(3)
240.34	241.07	245.30	

TROWELS		(1)
241.01		

TROY		(1)
044.21		

TRUCE		(2)
218.29	314.28	

TRUE				(70)
006.15	008.18	008.26	011.22	012.23
014.27	017.26	021.25	024.19	025.16
032.23	033.01	046.24	050.12	056.24
057.36	071.20	071.21	071.34	075.29
076.22	077.24	087.08	091.10	094.35
096.10	096.35	097.03	101.01	101.01
105.04	108.13	109.21	112.23	143.24

TRUE
144.14 149.14 150.05 151.29 151.30
166.31 171.30 173.10 181.17 186.33
196.29 197.05 205.24 211.06 215.32
216.01 216.14 216.34 217.31 218.11
223.35 224.02 241.04 252.04 259.33
269.01 281.27 287.16 291.04 292.01
308.21 315.31 323.18 324.31 326.18
(3)
TRUER
069.01 071.22 074.04
TRULY (9)
022.19 047.01 078.32 124.19 134.31
285.32 305.16 331.13 332.09
TRUMP (2)
126.08 129.10
TRUMPERY (3)
066.17 066.32 067.30
TRUMPET (3)
052.26 089.02 161.01
TRUMPETED (1)
284.27
TRUMPETS (1)
260.06
TRUNK (5)
066.34 066.34 146.18 231.33 266.05
TRUNKS (2)
191.15 192.13
TRUST (15)
004.05 011.03 015.03 045.08 061.09
073.01 081.16 131.13 147.10 160.31
166.15 172.18 208.37 283.14 320.30
(2)
TRUSTED
008.24 008.28
TRUSTING (2)
212.29 313.13
TRUSTWORTHY (1)
253.09
TRUTH (26)
046.27 046.32 047.14 049.38 050.04
082.15 096.23 096.36 099.09
115.09 151.18 151.27 151.33 162.19
164.02 164.31 217.20 245.06 324.21
325.01 325.03 327.28 327.35 330.35
331.01
TRUTHFULNESS (1)
047.18
TRUTHS (1)
095.30
TRY (14)
008.30 010.13 022.09 023.32 047.10
053.08 072.28 125.15 164.19 224.35
247.14 264.20 315.06 330.08
TRYING (6)
006.37 006.37 017.30 051.15 126.10
269.27
TSEU (3)
095.13 095.14 218.08
TU (2)
124.20 124.21
TUB (3)
080.07 088.31 260.09
TUBE (1)
302.07
TUBER (1)
239.15
TUBEROSA (1)
239.06
TUBS (1)
223.18
TUCK (1)
296.10
TUCKED (1)
007.13
TUITION (1)
050.22
TUMBLED (1)
146.21

TUMBLER (2)
230.32 231.07
TUMBLING (2)
316.26 316.39
TUMBLINGS (1)
229.16
TUMID (1)
288.02
TUMULT (1)
301.22
TUMULTUOUS (2)
236.30 313.06
TUNE (1)
174.29
TUNNEL (1)
052.29
TURF (1)
294.20
TURN (21)
008.26 047.11 048.19 052.03 084.10
108.05 126.30 136.07 161.29 161.31
168.26 196.18 224.18 259.34 260.10
266.21 272.35 308.19 313.33 326.12
328.25
TURNED (18)
019.30 033.23 083.32 151.11 156.16
159.33 160.29 170.33 171.11 171.12
196.28 240.01 245.29 247.35 266.35
269.20 279.05 308.24
TURNING (7)
062.09 119.11 162.21 192.20 204.34
234.31 316.38
TURNIP (1)
163.06
TURNIPS (2)
054.23 055.09
TURNOUT (1)
160.09
TURNS (8)
033.13 080.14 103.10 118.15 220.04
228.24 260.29 263.18
TURTLE (5)
184.34 184.36 218.14 228.18 232.12
TURTLEDOVE (1)
017.11
TURTLES (1)
218.21
TUSKS (1)
219.18
TWANG (1)
332.23
TWELVE (10)
004.31 004.33 054.19 055.07 094.28
121.04 162.32 163.16 198.21 233.11
TWELVEMONTH (1)
094.28
TWENTY (22)
014.11 030.36 032.18 038.18 043.30
061.01 109.23 115.34 121.16 140.15
142.07 142.17 145.06 158.28 175.03
177.34 178.09 180.28 193.08 296.16
306.01 313.11
TWICE (6)
070.23 210.09 229.34 235.25 247.25
251.34
TWIG (6)
188.14 275.26 284.13 312.20 312.21
312.28
TWIGGY (1)
281.34
TWIGS (4)
129.34 180.11 226.18 276.17
TWILIGHT (8)
017.25 125.27 125.30 132.25 266.27
273.26 280.34 283.07
TWIN (1)
197.23

235

```
TWINKLE                                            (    1)
   222.18
TWINKLING                                          (    1)
   088.12
TWIST                                              (    2)
   004.24   120.31
TWITTERING                                         (    1)
   313.23
TWO                                                (  118)
   003.08   003.08   005.01   017.04   017.15
   022.11   024.32   024.34   026.24   027.25
   030.12   034.06   039.22   039.27   040.12
   042.19   043.21   043.23   044.10   044.29
   045.14   048.31   049.09   049.12   050.08
   054.21   059.03   061.02   061.14   063.15
   064.03   065.21   068.35   072.06   075.27
   083.05   084.21   086.06   091.25   094.06
   100.03   102.28   105.26   115.29   133.10
   133.17   137.10   140.10   140.35   141.13
   142.09   143.10   143.14   143.17   156.11
   156.13   157.34   157.35   161.32   167.09
   169.35   170.16   170.19   175.22   176.06
   178.24   179.01   179.04   179.11   180.22
   180.34   181.10   184.03   186.34   187.27
   190.32   201.28   205.10   206.07   206.09
   215.12   227.30   228.27   228.34   228.36
   230.19   233.11   233.28   233.28   239.36
   241.30   243.10   245.10   246.11   246.22
   247.21   248.02   249.31   253.36   263.31
   265.34   271.26   276.22   281.03   285.17
   287.06   289.33   290.13   290.14   291.06
   292.18   293.08   293.17   296.17   310.14
   311.16   316.27   327.32
TWOS                                               (    1)
   114.26
TYING                                              (    1)
   169.24
TYPE                                               (    3)
   120.33   180.14   267.10
TYPES                                              (    1)
   310.05
TYPICAL                                            (    1)
   305.18
TYRANT                                             (    3)
   007.34   232.08   310.11
```

236

U
```
U
124.18  299.26  299.27  299.28  (  5)
                                299.29
UBI                             (  1)
063.18
UDDIN                           (  1)
099.27
UGLY                            (  1)
238.09
ULYSSES                         (  1)
097.29
UMBELLUS                        (  1)
226.10
UMBELS                          (  1)
113.35
UMBILICARIA                     (  1)
308.02
UMBRAGEOUS                      (  1)
079.06
UMBRELLAS                       (  1)
036.09
UNABLE                          (  2)
006.30  276.32
UNACCOUNTABLE                   (  1)
132.04
UNACCOUNTABLY                   (  1)
210.15
UNALTERABLE                     (  1)
026.31
UNARMED                         (  1)
203.32
UNBELIEVERS                     (  1)
064.36
UNBLUSHINGLY                    (  1)
059.30
UNBROKEN                        (  2)
174.06  261.30
UNCERTAIN                       (  3)
092.18  175.12  274.16
UNCERTAINTIES                   (  1)
011.14
UNCERTAINTY                     (  2)
091.12  274.27
UNCHANGED                       (  1)
193.01
UNCHRONICLED                    (  1)
158.33
UNCLE                           (  2)
259.11  279.35
UNCLEAN                         (  4)
195.28  214.11  219.35  221.01
UNCLEANNESS                     (  2)
214.21  221.04
UNCLEANSED                      (  1)
196.33
UNCLES                          (  1)
076.21
UNCOMMITTED                     (  1)
084.04
UNCOMMON                        (  3)
108.35  110.14  213.07
UNCOMMONLY                      (  1)
043.03
UNCONCERNED                     (  1)
044.16
UNCONSCIOUS                     (  4)
008.11  047.18  047.22  077.09
UNCONSCIOUSLY                   (  2)
101.13  171.06
UNCULTIVATED                    (  1)
144.11
UNDECEIVED                      (  1)
186.30
UNDEFINED                       (  1)
324.34
UNDER                           ( 91)
005.16  005.24  008.12  008.33  012.20
024.09  028.27  037.27  038.08  038.36
043.12  043.20  044.32  045.22  048.06

UNDER                              (CONTINUED)
050.08  052.29  063.23  067.03  069.21
072.30  077.17  095.02  097.22  109.06
113.20  114.32  115.27  126.21  126.35
128.02  128.04  128.11  128.15  134.29
140.16  144.02  144.35  158.34  159.33
167.19  169.23  182.08  185.01  186.27
191.24  196.35  197.25  203.24  204.18
207.09  207.33  215.13  226.26  227.33
228.02  230.32  231.06  233.12  233.13
235.11  235.23  238.23  246.36  247.27
248.01  248.07  248.14  248.16  249.16
250.13  263.11  275.27  280.26  280.36
283.02  283.09  289.01  292.22  292.24
292.35  293.14  299.29  300.12  305.20
307.35  310.13  310.14  314.06  324.08
333.18
UNDERBRED                       (  1)
107.19
UNDERGOING                      (  1)
013.03
UNDERLIE                        (  4)
071.24  092.26  257.01  294.10
UNDERNEATH                      (  4)
225.26  287.04  294.15  300.27
UNDERSIDE                       (  1)
316.27
UNDERSIZED                      (  1)
225.06
UNDERSTAND                      (  9)
033.35  065.04  065.05  088.34  102.16
107.32  324.10  324.13  324.17
UNDERSTANDING                   (  1)
011.24
UNDERSTANDINGLY                 (  1)
040.22
UNDERSTANDINGS                  (  1)
324.14
UNDERSTOOD                      (  2)
039.23  294.30
UNDERTAKE                       (  2)
003.22  072.25
UNDERTAKEN                      (  2)
004.32  205.36
UNDERTAKING                     (  1)
021.21
UNDERTOOK                       (  2)
058.24  203.13
UNDERWENT                       (  1)
101.04
UNDERWRITER                     (  1)
020.13
UNDEVELOPED                     (  1)
125.28
UNDILUTED                       (  1)
138.27
UNDISCOVERED                    (  1)
320.34
UNDISTINGUISHABLE               (  2)
188.11  195.04
UNDISTURBED                     (  1)
111.28
UNDONE                          (  2)
010.12  036.23
UNDOUBTED                       (  1)
285.26
UNDOUBTEDLY                     (  2)
010.05  071.21
UNDULATED                       (  1)
292.35
UNDULATING                      (  1)
180.10
UNDULATION                      (  2)
199.10  293.07
UNDULATIONS                     (  4)
089.16  141.14  187.22  189.20
UNDUSTED                        (  1)
036.28
```

UNEARTHLY (2)
235.32 236.11
UNEASY (2)
153.14 266.20
UNELASTIC (1)
033.14
UNEQUAL (2)
229.33 255.10
UNEQUALLED (1)
137.35
UNEVEN (1)
300.14
UNEXHAUSTED (1)
309.33
UNEXPECTED (3)
140.11 266.24 323.32
UNEXPECTEDLY (5)
119.14 235.10 271.08 303.29 333.25
UNEXPLORABLE (1)
317.36
UNEXPLORED (4)
144.10 185.31 317.27 321.30
UNFATHOMABLE (1)
318.01
UNFATHOMED (2)
093.36 318.01
UNFENCED (1)
128.09
UNFINISHED (1)
234.06
UNFLEDGED (1)
159.25
UNFOLD (2)
132.26 141.05
UNFOLDING (2)
116.15 263.24
UNFORTUNATE (2)
105.07 219.03
UNFORTUNATELY (3)
003.29 029.07 183.01
UNFREQUENTED (4)
018.20 117.25 130.14 173.06
UNGAINLY (2)
235.21 294.18
UNHEALTHY (2)
014.10 281.09
UNHESITATINGLY (2)
069.34 072.34
UNHURRIED (1)
095.36
UNIFORM (1)
176.27
UNIMAGINABLE (1)
088.36
UNIMPROVED (3)
052.18 158.07 264.10
UNINHABITED (1)
203.35
UNINSTRUCTIVE (1)
060.39
UNINTENDED (1)
073.25
UNINTERRUPTED (2)
085.12 113.08
UNINTERRUPTEDLY (1)
299.24
UNIO (1)
246.07
UNION (1)
233.19
UNITED (3)
058.15 230.04 332.27
UNIVERSAL (14)
020.34 021.06 023.07 053.23 102.21
105.13 108.16 123.09 138.19 250.35
260.11 304.07 318.27 323.34
UNIVERSALLY (4)
046.07 046.07 221.01 264.11

UNIVERSE (17)
010.20 073.09 087.35 088.08 097.10
119.13 134.21 218.33 218.36 274.03
274.13 282.17 317.02 320.19 324.04
329.35 330.33
UNIVERSITIES (2)
109.01 109.02
UNIVERSITY (1)
099.21
UNJUST (1)
043.34
UNKEMPT (1)
152.27
UNKNOWN (3)
009.29 172.21 174.36
UNLEAVENED (1)
062.17
UNLESS (14)
012.16 036.32 055.06 061.36 071.03
091.01 095.07 103.23 120.09 130.28
208.37 213.16 223.34 237.08
UNLIKE (2)
181.25 304.05
UNLUCKY (1)
262.15
UNMARKED (1)
258.04
UNMERCHANTABLE (1)
054.35
UNMISTAKABLE (1)
272.17
UNMIXED (2)
163.29 165.20
UNMOLESTED (1)
083.28
UNMUSICAL (1)
046.11
UNNATURAL (2)
080.17 177.30
UNNATURALLY (1)
014.15
UNNECESSARY (6)
005.21 013.36 014.03 027.26 057.03
214.24
UNOBSCURED (1)
180.10
UNOBSERVED (1)
043.05
UNOBSTRUCTED (1)
181.25
UNOCCUPIED (1)
259.04
UNPATCHED (1)
022.07
UNPLASTERED (1)
085.06
UNPLEASANT (1)
131.33
UNPLEASANTLY (1)
123.27
UNPRETENDING (1)
047.24
UNPROFANED (1)
088.07
UNPROFITABLE (1)
051.05
UNQUESTIONABLE (1)
090.19
UNQUESTIONABLY (2)
027.02 214.05
UNREAPED (1)
158.11
UNREASONABLE (1)
285.35
UNRELAXED (1)
097.27
UNREMEMBERED (1)
179.29

UNREPENTANT				(1)
126.09				
UNRESTRAINED				(1)
312.32				
UNROOFED				(1)
296.26				
UNROOFS				(1)
294.07				
UNRUFFLED				(1)
236.06				
UNSATISFIED				(1)
125.30				
UNSOPHISTICATED				(1)
147.16				
UNSPEAKABLE				(1)
240.21				
UNSPEAKABLY				(1)
127.21				
UNSUITABLE				(1)
326.28				
UNSURVEYED				(1)
318.01				
UNSUSPECTED				(1)
268.33				
UNSUSPECTING				(1)
288.15				
UNTENABLE				(1)
318.29				
UNTIL				(19)
004.22	022.01	023.36	045.35	096.23
111.30	120.25	126.33	160.13	170.04
174.13	178.11	191.32	213.01	259.34
277.24	300.16	301.08	307.16	
UNTIMELY				(1)
132.17				
UNTOLD				(1)
020.33				
UNTRIED				(1)
009.15				
UNUSALLY				(1)
311.25				
UNUSUAL				(2)
054.20	285.35			
UNUSUALLY				(5)
129.09	162.17	214.19	217.03	287.22
UNUTTERABLE				(1)
108.03				
UNWEARIABLE				(1)
235.12				
UNWEARIED				(4)
105.24	117.24	119.15	269.03	
UNWEARIEDLY				(1)
020.19				
UNWIELDY				(2)
034.03	092.06			
UNWILLING				(2)
113.13	281.04			
UNWILLINGLY				(1)
011.13				
UNWISE				(1)
224.21				
UNWITTINGLY				(1)
180.06				
UP				(215)
005.02	005.27	007.12	008.23	013.09
013.19	020.21	029.10	029.17	029.18
029.33	030.12	031.18	039.09	039.19
041.09	044.16	045.06	045.15	048.14
048.16	048.18	050.26	053.03	053.28
054.09	054.10	054.24	055.27	055.37
058.22	065.30	066.36	073.31	074.10
077.17	078.35	083.16	083.21	083.22
084.25	084.26	085.18	086.12	086.19
088.28	090.29	092.02	092.08	092.36
093.05	093.26	094.15	094.34	096.15
096.15	105.06	105.07	105.08	105.09
106.18	107.01	114.05	114.29	116.03
116.04	116.05	117.03	118.31	120.01

UP			(CONTINUED)	
120.08	120.24	121.19	121.20	122.09
123.16	124.17	126.13	128.10	128.11
128.17	133.01	133.33	138.30	140.13
145.13	146.04	146.19	153.11	155.28
156.16	157.30	158.24	158.24	158.24
158.25	158.25	159.21	159.33	160.15
161.29	161.31	161.36	164.11	168.08
168.11	169.25	169.30	170.30	173.09
174.12	175.13	177.18	179.08	179.20
181.23	182.34	183.15	188.09	189.27
191.06	193.11	193.12	195.06	199.06
203.23	203.27	204.34	211.28	214.18
219.16	224.18	225.07	225.29	225.32
226.01	228.05	228.15	230.30	232.32
233.34	234.21	234.23	234.34	234.36
235.10	235.34	236.02	236.11	236.23
238.20	243.24	244.19	245.29	246.03
248.36	249.30	252.21	252.34	253.29
254.20	256.17	257.11	257.27	259.24
261.01	262.16	263.13	264.02	267.03
269.11	271.09	273.20	274.11	274.28
275.14	275.25	276.19	277.09	279.13
280.01	280.22	280.24	281.29	283.26
285.05	285.11	292.15	294.05	295.03
295.16	296.02	297.28	299.04	299.09
299.33	301.22	302.26	303.05	304.11
304.16	304.20	307.24	310.15	310.34
312.01	313.08	315.21	316.24	317.12
318.22	320.14	325.15	330.16	330.28
UPLAND				(2)
156.11	156.32			
UPLANDS				(2)
131.20	333.01			
UPON				(61)
017.34	020.17	020.19	020.32	025.29
038.09	039.01	048.07	066.30	080.12
086.20	091.18	091.19	092.02	092.25
092.33	099.14	121.05	124.01	126.20
142.19	143.10	143.11	144.04	145.30
146.23	156.27	158.19	160.19	161.04
164.36	169.21	170.36	173.32	182.13
194.32	204.11	204.14	223.10	229.30
230.01	240.09	243.24	244.01	250.33
262.17	262.33	270.15	276.02	276.08
277.12	277.24	277.35	278.21	292.03
295.30	301.20	303.16	309.02	309.12
312.20				
UPPER				(3)
175.15	233.12	248.03		
UPRIGHT				(1)
084.33				
UPRIGHTNESS				(1)
076.36				
UPSET				(1)
097.23				
UPWARD				(10)
015.29	161.29	175.20	198.30	247.10
247.35	252.30	252.37	254.31	300.15
URGED				(2)
033.36	034.02			
URINE				(1)
221.24				
URN				(2)
127.33	333.15			
US				(106)
010.24	011.10	011.29	013.20	013.25
019.06	025.35	028.17	028.26	031.35
037.09	038.02	038.35	041.18	068.05
074.34	074.34	078.33	089.09	089.10
090.17	090.30	091.17	092.25	094.36
096.30	097.09	097.12	097.12	097.16
097.18	097.23	097.32	098.16	098.18
100.18	102.21	103.33	104.17	107.04
107.35	108.01	108.05	108.27	109.08
109.33	110.15	110.18	130.08	130.11
134.10	134.12	134.25	134.26	134.30
135.01	135.18	137.25	138.17	141.21

```
US                          (CONTINUED)
 143.07  143.11  143.18  162.26  165.17
 165.17  165.18  165.19  165.24  165.34
 165.37  174.02  199.26  202.23  202.36
 210.25  210.25  215.24  218.20  218.32
 219.05  219.09  219.35  219.36  220.05
 224.31  231.27  251.01  255.10  265.25
 269.18  282.19  291.06  296.15  303.07
 308.18  313.33  314.22  318.01  318.11
 327.28  329.02  329.04  330.12  332.35
 333.31
USE                                 (  31)
 006.20  008.16  012.10  012.27  016.25
 025.18  032.11  040.25  055.37  056.23
 059.39  061.17  063.25  064.11  070.16
 077.03  078.11  098.32  100.15  181.20
 204.36  205.11  205.29  215.06  220.20
 225.18  233.03  242.25  244.01  261.29
 262.16
USED                                (  36)
 029.08  048.33  061.26  063.34  072.25
 085.16  090.29  105.14  143.22  151.14
 161.18  170.19  174.09  180.29  182.15
 190.26  190.31  191.01  195.06  197.31
 202.18  213.28  214.28  240.23  241.30
 247.14  253.01  254.13  254.18  265.17
 276.22  277.33  279.17  279.22  280.30
 292.36
USEFUL                              (   3)
 038.26  166.06  243.19
USELESS                             (   1)
 122.05
USHER                               (   1)
 129.10
USHERED                             (   1)
 132.25
USING                               (   6)
 019.33  020.27  065.08  077.33  288.06
 307.25
USNEA                               (   2)
 125.33  201.12
USUAL                               (  18)
 019.33  021.19  034.33  045.20  048.33
 067.30  086.21  112.01  157.10  171.09
 180.19  202.06  212.35  233.25  236.08
 241.01  242.30  296.22
USUALLY                             (  13)
 042.25  115.14  121.08  130.32  145.15
 167.04  179.05  183.25  189.10  271.23
 273.19  287.27  291.24
UTENSILS                            (   5)
 030.08  060.05  068.14  160.20  244.08
UTI                                 (   1)
 243.05
UTICENSIS                           (   1)
 257.08
UTILITARIAN                         (   1)
 255.07
UTILITY                             (   2)
 018.17  021.25
UTMOST                              (   1)
 151.18
UTOPIAN                             (   1)
 109.16
UTTER                               (   1)
 140.32
UTTERED                             (   5)
 107.03  108.03  236.11  236.23  268.12
```

V   (1)
 306.28
VACANCIES   (1)
 163.31
VACATE   (1)
 043.31
VACATION   (1)
 015.27
VACHES   (1)
 158.18
VAGABOND   (1)
 051.27
VAGANCE   (1)
 324.22
VAGANT   (1)
 324.19
VAGUE   (2)
 160.10 266.18
VAGUELY   (1)
 007.31
VAIN   (9)
 076.03 100.25 215.34 234.19 261.19
 282.04 285.32 311.28 326.16
VAINLY   (1)
 126.35
VALE   (5)
 123.16 123.16 174.14 252.26 268.08
VALES   (1)
 229.02
VALET   (2)
 023.17 023.18
VALHALLA   (2)
 201.10 296.09
VALIANT   (1)
 016.04
VALID   (1)
 033.36
VALLEY   (11)
 087.02 087.19 121.37 125.13 186.24
 229.12 229.26 288.11 289.08 308.08
 317.19
VALLEYS   (4)
 009.32 037.22 287.20 289.26
VALOR   (2)
 100.16 118.32
VALUABLE   (8)
 009.11 009.17 050.23 054.06 082.34
 170.34 175.02 212.08
VALUE   (19)
 009.03 031.21 032.24 055.19 059.06
 060.40 064.34 076.36 086.22 087.13
 109.16 136.12 136.26 158.06 166.16
 196.12 199.29 250.33 250.35
VALUED   (3)
 015.33 070.11 192.01
VALUES   (1)
 216.30
VANISH   (1)
 050.16
VANITY   (2)
 058.16 103.13
VANTAGE   (1)
 014.29
VAPOR   (2)
 053.33 182.28
VAPOROUS   (2)
 007.09 102.08
VAPORS   (1)
 098.35
VARIATION   (1)
 288.35
VARIED   (1)
 282.16
VARIES   (1)
 290.35
VARIETIES   (1)
 184.31

VARIETY   (7)
 010.06 061.26 112.17 124.34 164.32
 211.26 256.31
VARIOUS   (19)
 010.20 010.22 014.02 030.07 049.01
 058.33 062.23 064.11 148.30 158.11
 161.21 173.28 220.02 246.01 252.26
 273.26 275.08 304.36 305.23
VARIOUSLY   (1)
 305.31
VARRO   (1)
 166.03
VARY   (2)
 133.26 288.33
VASE   (1)
 188.05
VAST   (16)
 004.27 087.31 125.28 130.13 134.15
 140.23 160.33 167.29 175.17 215.18
 243.16 271.30 285.24 296.09 304.09
 318.04
VASTER   (1)
 307.05
VASTNESS   (1)
 171.13
VATICANS   (1)
 104.02
VAULTS   (1)
 033.13
VED   (2)
 217.30 219.29
VEDANT   (1)
 217.35
VEDAS   (4)
 089.29 104.03 298.12 325.18
VEER   (1)
 236.32
VEERY   (2)
 086.01 319.03
VEGETABLE   (16)
 009.19 009.24 065.01 120.27 138.16
 138.19 195.04 201.16 212.16 215.29
 252.13 305.19 306.17 308.09 309.07
 310.04
VEGETABLES   (2)
 104.35 203.06
VEGETATE   (1)
 104.28
VEGETATION   (6)
 044.25 305.09 305.16 305.33 305.35
 309.27
VEIL   (1)
 099.12
VEILING   (1)
 252.35
VEILS   (1)
 282.17
VEIN   (2)
 098.34 252.18
VEINS   (4)
 195.02 304.26 308.01 314.37
VELOCITY   (2)
 116.09 183.36
VELVET   (1)
 037.13
VELVETY   (2)
 114.19 239.11
VENDACEM   (1)
 163.13
VENERABLE   (2)
 281.19 296.12
VENETIAN   (1)
 031.04
VENISON   (3)
 210.12 250.17 281.13
VENTURE   (3)
 061.35 268.31 302.22

VIRGIL (2)
103.25 160.18
VIRGIN (2)
054.33 295.03
VIRID (1)
197.34
VIRTUE (16)
047.10 064.26 076.15 080.08 080.26
091.19 134.31 162.24 172.33 218.29
220.36 243.09 295.18 315.16 315.23
331.29
VIRTUES (9)
080.12 080.23 150.09 164.10 172.34
172.35 260.21 315.20 331.16
VIRTUOUS (1)
172.34
VIRTUTI (1)
243.06
VIRUS (1)
074.23
VISHNU (2)
270.18 298.11
VISIBLE (11)
035.06 069.02 073.35 088.36 130.16
175.34 194.03 204.28 263.08 290.11
312.13
VISION (6)
096.26 099.16 177.09 193.38 202.24
252.34
VISIONS (2)
136.30 266.19
VISIT (8)
064.18 143.02 152.11 197.33 201.24
235.16 244.29 260.27
VISITATION (1)
150.34
VISITED (11)
085.05 128.08 143.32 151.16 193.18
199.17 202.08 202.20 239.02 262.15
285.17
VISITOR (7)
038.08 152.08 170.10 235.21 264.33
268.18 270.18
VISITORS (12)
129.25 129.33 140.01 140.10 142.30
143.36 151.03 152.34 153.02 154.14
240.14 256.02
VISITS (3)
068.31 137.19 184.35
VISTA (2)
086.33 118.31
VISTAS (2)
177.17 192.09
VITAE (1)
322.02
VITAL (12)
013.14 013.25 015.17 021.27 063.04
067.09 105.30 117.06 142.15 162.31
241.22 329.09
VITALITY (1)
164.10
VITALS (4)
168.13 231.02 306.14 306.16
VITIATED (1)
290.27
VITREOUS (1)
177.15
VITRUVIUS (1)
058.19
VITUS (1)
093.11
VIVACIOUS (1)
263.23
VIVID (1)
176.29
VOCAL (1)
310.16

VOCATION (3)
122.04 122.11 267.25
VOICE (12)
010.36 077.17 095.26 114.28 123.20
127.28 141.24 222.16 257.24 272.19
272.23 278.10
VOICES (3)
123.24 126.14 169.06
VOID (1)
221.24
VOLATILE (1)
325.01
VOLUME (2)
172.16 272.23
VOLUMES (1)
104.30
VOLUNTARILY (1)
017.07
VOLUNTARY (1)
014.30
VOLUPTUOUS (1)
168.06
VORACIOUS (1)
215.09
VORACIOUSLY (1)
274.21
VOTING (2)
007.07 162.11
VOYAGE (1)
320.21
VOYAGES (1)
083.16
VOYAGING (1)
320.24
VULCAN (1)
249.18
VULGAR (5)
057.33 131.11 173.15 315.04 328.33
VULPINE (1)
273.17
VULTURE (1)
318.10

```
WACHITO                               (   1)
 093.35
WADE                                  (   1)
 317.28
WADED                                 (   2)
 269.29  300.03
WADER                                 (   1)
 195.08
WADING                                (   3)
 207.14  209.05  265.33
WAFTED                                (   4)
 077.05  144.10  179.07  298.18
WAGER                                 (   1)
 273.35
WAGES                                 (   3)
 053.10  053.10  147.20
WAGON                                 (   2)
 111.31  285.29
WAGONS                                (   4)
 126.04  138.26  170.29  259.26
WAIFS                                 (   1)
 160.05
WAILING                               (   3)
 077.17  124.25  124.33
WAINSCOT                              (   1)
 039.18
WAIT                                  (   5)
 019.32  072.15  235.28  238.25  331.10
WAITED                                (   2)
 270.22  279.03
WAITERS                               (   1)
 245.02
WAITING                               (   2)
 018.01  041.36
WAIVE                                 (   1)
 011.04
WAKE                                  (   4)
 084.24  092.36  313.15  330.28
WAKED                                 (   5)
 093.28  155.35  273.01  273.19  317.21
WAKEFUL                               (   1)
 104.19
WAKES                                 (   1)
 093.26
WAKING                                (   3)
 301.21  324.28  324.29
WALDEN                                (  83)
 003.06  019.34  021.07  040.33  126.11
 130.30  133.31  137.06  137.22  150.26
 175.25  176.20  177.23  179.19  179.27
 181.15  181.19  182.19  183.04  183.23
 183.34  188.19  191.20  192.19  192.24
 192.31  193.08  193.19  193.25  194.03
 194.20  197.18  197.24  197.27  198.11
 199.21  203.17  213.12  235.20  237.07
 240.24  248.30  249.02  252.26  257.07
 257.23  262.05  264.08  267.04  268.08
 271.23  272.03  277.16  277.34  278.01
 278.10  284.18  284.32  284.32  285.01
 285.10  285.19  285.34  286.01  288.07
 292.08  294.33  295.12  296.31  297.03
 297.27  298.16  299.07  299.23  299.25
 299.34  300.32  302.35  311.16  311.35
 313.06  319.20  325.27
WALDENS                               (   1)
 284.33
WALDENSES                             (   1)
 284.34
WALK                                  (  23)
 024.26  067.01  096.28  111.19  127.13
 129.06  150.14  154.16  170.07  181.22
 186.26  194.24  253.04  267.17  271.25
 274.08  274.09  276.14  281.34  285.18
 302.14  329.33  329.34
WALKED                                (  15)
 043.05  081.10  124.31  139.09  146.28
 167.14  167.15  202.17  226.07  255.09
 260.17  266.31  278.02  278.35  284.16

WALKING                               (   6)
 009.23  092.34  132.37  165.10  232.24
 295.12
WALKS                                 (   6)
 035.04  046.15  171.06  256.08  261.08
 265.27
WALL                                  (  18)
 027.33  039.16  057.34  071.25  071.29
 098.06  127.36  141.30  245.25  259.36
 260.23  261.02  261.11  263.28  277.12
 278.04  278.05  329.17
WALLED                                (   1)
 183.05
WALLS                                 (  10)
 038.28  043.19  084.31  115.35  168.26
 182.34  240.10  240.13  267.03  320.14
WALNUT                                (   3)
 064.15  129.28  142.31
WALNUTS                               (   1)
 257.10
WAND                                  (   1)
 129.32
WANDER                                (   4)
 232.25  318.09  322.04  324.20
WANDERED                              (   4)
 057.36  088.23  170.20  175.17
WANDERER                              (   2)
 264.01  264.34
WANDERING                             (   1)
 038.17
WANDERINGS                            (   1)
 089.04
WANT                                  (  30)
 013.13  015.19  019.04  020.02  023.33
 025.06  039.29  061.29  061.30  069.31
 077.04  092.09  092.24  103.16  110.14
 128.14  133.06  133.18  140.33  141.18
 143.11  143.20  145.34  145.35  146.25
 148.10  206.09  208.01  262.35  328.27
WANTED                                (   8)
 028.05  082.07  083.31  091.02  141.05
 155.11  162.09  294.29
WANTING                               (   1)
 112.22
WANTONLY                              (   1)
 212.31
WANTS                                 (   5)
 030.17  040.01  040.02  050.21  109.14
WAR                                   (  12)
 020.24  136.17  158.35  161.32  169.13
 205.28  228.34  229.06  231.05  231.22
 257.24  279.29
WARBLE                                (   1)
 112.10
WARBLINGS                             (   1)
 310.24
WARDEN                                (   1)
 250.20
WARDROBE                              (   1)
 021.30
WARE                                  (   1)
 261.16
WAREHOUSE                             (   1)
 065.28
WARES                                 (   1)
 268.23
WARILY                                (   2)
 273.31  275.11
WARM                                  (  33)
 013.01  013.10  013.25  014.13  014.14
 027.35  029.31  030.01  030.04  039.21
 067.16  074.27  075.26  149.02  172.09
 174.15  183.23  217.11  223.22  247.22
 249.25  251.24  262.34  267.12  300.30
 301.07  302.32  303.30  303.36  304.20
 309.24  314.35  316.15
WARMED                                (   9)
 015.15  015.18  121.03  146.30  176.36
```

```
WARMED                (CONTINUED)          WAS                      (CONTINUED)
240.27  240.28  251.33  301.05             133.01  133.34  133.34  135.16  135.17
WARMER                          (   4)     135.23  136.30  138.02  138.36  139.05
300.04  302.14  302.25  303.08             139.07  139.09  140.11  141.31  141.34
WARMEST                         (   6)     142.04  142.08  142.11  142.24  142.34
183.19  183.25  228.07  277.35  292.13     143.05  143.26  143.27  143.33  144.05
300.01                                     144.09  145.01  145.01  145.05  145.09
WARMING                         (   1)     145.15  146.01  146.09  146.12  146.35
238.01                                     146.36  147.01  147.04  147.16  147.22
WARMS                           (   4)     147.24  147.26  147.33  148.07  148.18
253.28  253.30  255.06  300.12             148.26  148.27  148.34  149.02  149.30
WARMTH                          (  10)     150.03  150.08  150.10  150.12  150.18
012.26  013.21  015.20  028.06  028.06     150.26  150.33  151.07  151.10  151.11
028.07  045.17  187.34  242.25  253.23     151.20  151.24  151.25  151.26  151.27
WARN                            (   1)     151.29  151.31  151.32  153.09  153.10
212.34                                     153.15  153.18  153.20  153.21  153.28
WARNED                          (   3)     154.02  154.07  154.19  155.04  155.08
118.11  121.20  156.24                     155.13  155.31  155.32  156.12  156.13
WARNING                         (   3)     156.23  157.06  157.08  157.14  157.19
043.20  115.28  153.27                     157.20  157.24  158.04  158.11  158.15
WARP                            (   1)     158.25  158.26  158.30  159.06  159.08
044.09                                     159.30  160.09  160.09  160.25  160.29
WARPED                          (   1)     160.33  160.35  161.09  161.12  161.15
043.10                                     161.17  161.23  162.14  162.18  163.13
WARRANT                         (   3)     165.23  167.08  167.13  167.18  167.20
131.25  224.17  292.25                     168.09  168.33  169.10  169.11  169.14
WARRIOR                         (   2)     169.15  169.17  169.18  169.25  169.26
230.02  231.03                             169.32  170.05  170.11  170.14  170.14
WARS                            (   2)     170.26  171.22  171.34  172.01  172.05
172.29  322.23                             172.07  172.12  172.17  173.08  173.24
WAS                             ( 833)     173.30  173.32  173.34  174.05  174.08
003.17  010.17  012.01  014.34  017.22     174.18  175.15  175.22  178.09  179.19
017.27  017.30  018.06  018.12  018.23     180.22  180.23  180.30  180.33  180.36
019.04  019.14  019.16  019.31  019.34     182.20  182.23  183.02  183.04  183.06
021.18  022.25  022.29  023.02  023.25     183.16  183.19  183.28  183.29  189.14
026.10  027.27  027.29  027.31  027.34     189.14  189.15  189.16  189.22  189.28
027.35  028.15  029.02  029.06  029.11     190.17  190.27  190.32  190.33  190.34
029.26  029.28  030.11  033.35  034.15     190.36  191.04  191.08  191.18  191.20
035.20  036.26  036.28  037.20  037.22     191.29  191.32  191.35  192.02  193.10
037.26  038.35  039.05  039.35  041.04     193.12  193.15  194.24  194.25  194.34
041.05  041.09  041.11  041.20  042.03     195.02  196.15  196.16  196.19  198.05
042.22  042.27  042.28  042.31  042.34     198.06  198.20  198.22  198.23  198.29
042.37  043.03  043.06  043.06  043.09     198.30  198.32  198.34  199.03  199.05
043.11  043.15  043.25  043.26  043.29     199.08  202.14  202.22  202.27  202.28
043.36  044.11  044.18  044.29  045.06     202.29  202.29  203.19  203.22  204.15
045.10  045.12  045.21  046.32  048.26     204.20  204.22  204.23  205.03  205.05
048.34  048.35  049.12  049.27  052.02     205.19  205.19  205.19  205.20  205.20
052.19  052.24  052.26  052.26  054.25     206.06  206.07  206.17  206.33  207.04
054.26  055.02  055.05  055.11  055.19     207.04  207.12  208.34  208.35  210.07
055.25  056.07  056.08  056.24  057.25     210.08  211.29  211.35  211.36  212.01
057.33  058.23  059.06  059.06  060.40     212.12  212.28  213.14  214.21  214.23
061.02  061.05  061.10  061.27  062.04     217.03  217.23  219.18  221.20  221.22
062.08  062.34  064.23  064.32  064.33     222.01  222.07  222.09  222.10  222.21
066.10  067.06  067.25  067.30  067.32     223.06  223.10  224.10  224.23  224.24
067.35  068.36  069.16  069.20  069.23     224.28  224.29  224.34  224.34  224.35
069.25  070.25  072.10  074.17  074.31     225.01  225.26  226.33  227.01  227.09
075.01  075.21  075.31  076.20  081.25     227.09  227.32  227.34  228.02  228.07
082.06  082.09  082.17  082.22  083.10     228.21  228.25  228.32  228.34  229.02
083.17  083.19  083.24  083.35  084.19     229.04  229.05  229.23  229.24  229.31
084.28  084.29  084.30  085.05  085.16     230.11  230.18  230.21  230.23  230.24
085.22  085.23  085.27  085.30  085.33     230.35  231.01  231.03  231.12  231.22
086.03  086.08  086.10  086.17  086.22     231.34  232.23  232.26  232.34  232.34
086.26  086.33  087.02  087.22  087.23     233.01  233.02  233.03  233.06  233.07
007.24  087.26  088.01  088.10  088.14     233.17  234.13  234.16  234.23  234.34
088.17  088.25  088.29  088.35  089.01     234.35  235.03  235.04  235.05  235.12
089.03  089.05  090.12  090.36  091.01     235.27  235.30  235.35  236.05  236.08
091.04  093.16  094.23  095.04  095.12     236.14  236.18  236.19  236.27  236.29
096.13  096.14  096.19  096.20  098.25     237.06  238.16  238.20  238.32  239.19
098.26  099.14  099.15  099.17  099.20     241.02  241.02  241.12  241.32  241.34
099.22  100.06  107.18  111.32  112.05     242.04  242.04  242.17  242.17  242.18
112.19  112.28  112.29  112.35  112.36     242.30  242.34  245.16  245.22  245.24
113.08  113.14  113.16  113.23  113.26     245.27  246.02  247.23  247.25  247.31
114.08  114.16  115.01  117.03  117.06     247.31  248.02  248.02  248.03  248.06
118.02  118.35  120.01  123.03  123.19     248.07  248.13  248.28  249.13  249.17
123.25  123.27  123.27  123.31  124.14     249.18  249.26  249.30  249.32  250.17
125.07  127.31  130.26  130.34  130.34     250.20  250.22  250.23  251.02  251.13
131.09  131.09  131.30  131.32  131.33     251.33  251.34  251.36  252.03  252.03
131.34  132.01  132.09  132.13  132.31     252.27  253.06  253.06  253.07  253.08
```

WAS (CONTINUED)

253.10	253.12	253.12	253.17	253.26
254.16	254.36	256.07	256.16	256.16
256.23	257.09	257.25	257.26	258.09
258.18	259.03	259.04	259.05	259.20
259.29	259.31	260.03	260.22	260.30
260.32	260.34	260.34	261.01	261.07
261.22	261.23	261.31	261.32	261.34
262.01	262.04	262.06	262.07	262.10
262.14	262.27	262.30	262.30	262.33
263.05	263.07	263.09	265.04	265.05
265.09	265.14	265.34	266.14	266.35
266.36	267.10	268.01	268.09	268.18
269.18	270.03	270.07	270.13	271.06
271.07	271.24	271.26	272.05	272.11
272.29	273.01	273.25	274.14	274.24
274.30	275.23	276.01	276.03	276.04
276.08	276.10	276.11	276.34	277.16
277.29	277.35	278.09	278.18	278.24
278.25	279.03	279.23	279.29	279.33
279.35	280.05	281.15	281.15	282.05
282.25	284.06	285.09	285.30	287.05
287.12	288.29	289.14	289.36	290.01
290.17	290.19	291.30	291.31	292.18
292.20	292.21	292.24	292.34	292.34
293.03	293.05	293.20	293.29	294.20
294.27	294.29	294.36	295.05	295.06
295.14	295.16	295.18	295.33	296.20
296.20	296.21	296.25	296.26	296.29
297.03	297.13	297.22	299.06	299.35
300.22	301.22	301.24	302.10	302.24
302.25	302.27	302.29	303.01	303.17
303.20	303.25	303.26	303.30	303.30
303.35	303.36	304.14	304.36	305.05
306.12	309.23	309.25	309.31	310.22
311.35	312.07	312.10	312.13	312.30
314.11	315.34	316.14	316.19	316.33
317.04	317.05	317.09	317.24	317.25
318.12	318.15	318.17	319.07	319.18
319.19	321.25	322.30	322.36	322.37
325.26	326.05	326.20	326.20	327.02
327.05	327.08	327.13	327.25	327.25
328.01	329.18	331.02	331.03	331.12
332.33	333.03	333.13		

WASH (6)
063.20 065.21 192.19 194.01 195.16
243.31

WASHED (3)
167.06 194.30 333.04

WASHING (2)
060.07 244.08

WASN (1)
145.23

WASPS (2)
240.11 240.22

WASSAILERS (1)
126.09

WAST (1)
279.22

WASTE (13)
039.28 093.06 101.26 142.13 157.33
192.04 192.07 194.16 205.18 241.17
249.23 273.34 274.31

WASTED (3)
104.36 205.20 296.18

WASTING (1)
274.06

WATCH (2)
045.23 116.31

WATCHED (4)
159.26 229.10 236.31 313.04

WATCHING (6)
017.36 142.05 230.01 266.03 266.12
273.25

WATCHMEN (1)
129.23

WATER (177)
007.27 012.16 041.11 041.26 061.04

WATER (CONTINUED)

061.32	063.22	064.20	075.25	086.24
086.30	087.12	087.22	113.02	126.23
126.25	129.12	133.25	141.13	148.36
149.01	149.02	150.31	155.22	156.01
166.20	174.22	175.03	176.01	176.16
176.18	177.18	177.23	177.24	177.28
177.33	178.09	178.26	179.01	179.04
179.16	179.32	180.04	180.25	181.03
181.11	181.20	181.27	182.01	182.04
183.07	183.09	183.12	183.17	183.20
183.22	183.23	183.32	184.29	185.07
185.13	185.34	185.35	186.05	186.10
187.07	187.14	187.15	187.24	187.26
187.30	188.05	188.24	188.34	189.02
189.08	189.31	189.34	190.10	190.14
190.29	190.35	191.08	191.12	191.23
192.09	192.17	193.01	193.16	193.29
194.29	195.09	195.16	195.29	197.14
198.05	198.13	198.16	198.22	199.10
199.16	199.20	203.28	207.04	217.05
217.09	223.23	225.11	228.04	233.36
234.07	234.32	234.34	235.23	236.02
236.09	236.22	237.08	240.03	246.05
246.22	246.24	247.03	247.24	248.10
250.07	264.07	277.13	277.35	282.22
284.20	284.32	287.04	287.29	289.01
289.08	289.30	289.31	290.01	292.11
292.24	292.36	293.14	293.15	293.20
293.22	293.27	295.05	296.31	297.03
297.07	297.08	297.14	297.27	298.10
298.13	298.14	298.16	298.17	299.05
299.19	299.29	299.31	300.04	300.11
300.12	300.22	300.26	301.05	302.26
302.29	303.36	305.33	307.03	307.28
311.29	332.35			

WATERED (4)
018.24 177.11 263.33 311.26

WATERFOWL (1)
234.04

WATERLOGGED (3)
199.05 249.32 250.04

WATERLOGGEDNESS (1)
126.19

WATERLOO (2)
262.02 262.34

WATERMELON (1)
059.26

WATERS (17)
131.14 137.08 176.05 176.19 177.03
179.25 181.26 194.14 196.14 197.22
197.26 197.30 210.35 287.34 288.04
288.13 291.29

WATERY (3)
285.05 285.22 307.04

WAVE (4)
120.03 159.23 189.01 194.17

WAVED (1)
311.26

WAVELESS (1)
283.06

WAVES (15)
129.15 129.18 177.05 177.14 182.31
190.12 194.26 195.11 195.20 195.23
234.03 263.07 291.09 297.33 316.08

WAVING (4)
162.01 195.10 224.17 239.18

WAVY (1)
201.05

WAXED (1)
126.14

WAXEN (1)
238.07

WAXWORK (1)
201.18

WAY (101)
005.37 008.23 008.35 011.17 024.01
037.16 038.08 041.14 043.24 045.24

WEATHERS   (1)
  138.04
WEAVE   (3)
  019.08 019.10 019.21
WEAVES   (1)
  025.22
WEAVING   (1)
  008.04
WEB   (3)
  066.27 124.11 293.26
WEBBED   (2)
  209.05 236.07
WEBSTER   (2)
  232.10 330.04
WEDGE   (3)
  041.23 097.32 206.22
WEE   (1)
  281.05
WEED   (3)
  157.02 179.08 203.27
WEEDING   (1)
  224.20
WEEDS   (11)
  126.12 149.27 156.26 157.01 161.22
  161.33 166.28 178.31 180.10 309.35
  325.30
WEEDY   (1)
  161.36
WEEK   (21)
  053.13 061.02 086.11 095.23 095.24
  112.12 145.36 183.29 183.30 206.10
  240.05 240.05 264.35 265.20 277.28
  279.08 297.01 299.15 313.17 319.02
  323.16
WEEKS   (9)
  052.30 056.20 069.11 131.30 242.08
  246.16 256.07 318.07 333.14
WEEVIL   (1)
  243.10
WEI   (1)
  095.13
WEIGH   (3)
  184.25 330.05 330.08
WEIGHED   (2)
  113.36 158.08
WEIGHING   (4)
  183.35 184.03 184.05 287.01
WEIGHT   (6)
  114.17 114.20 114.32 184.06 232.21
  270.07
WEIGHTY   (1)
  029.34
WELCOME   (3)
  154.20 154.20 268.18
WELCOMED   (1)
  254.35
WELL   (128)
  003.29 004.14 005.14 005.15 006.19
  008.36 010.33 011.06 011.07 012.35
  016.15 016.16 017.31 019.02 019.07
  024.11 027.01 028.12 028.24 030.06
  032.16 032.27 040.22 041.20 043.33
  046.28 048.17 053.11 056.13 061.06
  061.07 061.36 063.21 063.23 066.36
  068.08 069.13 070.12 072.04 073.03
  078.33 081.25 084.27 087.11 087.14
  100.36 101.01 109.03 111.14 117.36
  129.07 132.23 133.34 134.13 138.17
  142.17 143.05 146.10 146.16 146.25
  148.13 149.25 155.31 162.18 169.11
  170.34 170.36 171.07 174.04 175.21
  175.30 177.20 179.14 179.34 182.26
  182.29 183.06 186.32 202.04 204.31
  206.36 212.16 213.15 214.17 214.26
  219.16 224.19 225.10 227.12 228.04
  233.23 235.27 239.13 242.11 242.25
  253.23 254.15 255.03 258.35 260.36
  260.36 261.03 261.10 262.08 263.08

WELL   (CONTINUED)
  269.26 271.30 272.28 273.13 278.14
  279.14 280.01 283.09 284.19 289.24
  292.36 295.24 296.21 298.01 298.09
  298.16 300.18 322.35 324.15 324.15
  327.28 327.28 333.22
WELLED   (1)
  189.27
WELLING   (2)
  188.09 193.12
WELLS   (4)
  183.10 183.17 263.13 263.14
WEN   (1)
  067.04
WENDING   (1)
  007.25
WENT   (54)
  018.28 019.01 019.05 023.02 040.33
  042.06 054.07 059.34 069.34 072.08
  090.32 112.04 133.35 142.17 143.02
  145.31 152.12 162.18 167.24 171.21
  191.07 194.27 203.17 211.32 213.23
  214.34 228.05 228.26 229.13 229.13
  231.17 234.07 234.15 238.03 239.03
  240.22 253.03 253.15 259.02 259.24
  262.04 262.26 269.32 271.17 273.29
  275.22 278.01 294.14 294.34 295.08
  302.34 319.16 323.10 331.01
WERE   (379)
  003.29 004.31 004.33 005.08 006.28
  007.02 009.10 012.35 012.36 013.01
  013.01 014.23 018.10 019.27 021.21
  022.31 025.20 028.24 030.05 030.07
  033.17 034.29 034.29 035.32 036.16
  037.21 039.06 039.36 041.09 041.10
  041.12 041.19 042.21 042.24 042.29
  043.09 043.14 043.22 043.33 044.27
  045.11 045.24 046.27 047.03 048.01
  048.24 052.28 053.10 055.04 055.10
  056.02 057.29 058.31 059.03 059.31
  060.08 060.12 062.11 062.35 064.11
  064.25 064.30 066.07 067.34 068.09
  069.04 069.15 071.35 073.28 075.03
  075.06 075.10 075.28 076.29 076.31
  077.01 077.36 080.31 081.09 083.05
  084.36 085.09 086.17 087.34 088.08
  088.19 088.31 091.09 091.17 093.01
  093.24 094.07 094.26 098.13 098.18
  099.25 101.07 101.20 101.22 101.26
  101.26 101.32 103.19 107.14 107.27
  109.01 111.21 111.34 111.35 112.11
  112.13 112.26 112.30 113.07 114.03
  115.05 115.15 116.23 116.26 117.07
  117.23 118.09 120.32 121.37 123.03
  123.07 123.32 124.15 124.27 127.36
  128.01 130.01 130.24 130.27 130.28
  131.23 131.26 132.21 135.12 136.25
  141.11 142.10 143.04 143.12 143.15
  143.24 143.29 144.08 144.10 144.19
  145.12 145.33 147.06 147.25 147.32
  148.25 149.07 151.02 151.10 151.21
  153.16 153.35 155.05 155.06 155.07
  157.34 158.12 158.16 158.22 158.35
  159.16 159.29 160.20 160.25 160.28
  160.32 161.17 162.35 164.09 164.10
  164.12 164.15 164.26 165.02 166.06
  168.13 168.17 168.21 168.28 170.18
  170.24 170.24 171.04 172.19 172.30
  174.26 174.27 175.01 175.23 176.16
  178.27 178.31 179.19 180.14 182.12
  182.17 182.17 186.29 188.09 190.01
  190.03 190.22 190.30 191.12 191.15
  191.26 194.29 194.29 195.01 195.19
  197.01 199.01 199.22 201.35 202.08
  202.22 205.30 205.32 205.32 206.03
  211.17 211.18 211.34 212.29 213.15
  213.24 214.09 214.18 214.30 216.21
  216.22 216.23 217.05 222.02 223.34

248

WERE   (CONTINUED)
```
224.19  225.21  227.20  228.33  229.08
229.11  229.34  230.04  230.31  231.09
232.33  234.06  234.25  236.22  236.28
238.19  238.28  239.03  240.15  242.34
244.31  245.03  245.10  246.03  247.19
247.23  248.14  248.17  250.12  250.13
251.35  252.05  252.24  256.21  256.26
257.27  258.07  259.36  260.09  261.17
261.29  262.16  262.23  263.16  263.18
264.06  264.11  265.12  265.25  266.28
267.03  268.10  269.30  271.02  271.16
271.27  272.31  272.35  272.36  273.26
273.35  274.03  275.01  275.11  275.11
275.20  275.23  275.28  275.29  275.35
279.01  279.32  279.35  280.11  280.15
280.17  280.20  280.25  280.32  284.09
284.21  284.30  285.25  287.10  289.04
289.21  289.29  292.13  292.14  292.15
293.06  293.08  293.10  293.13  294.14
294.35  295.26  295.34  298.15  303.11
303.22  304.35  305.22  306.14  308.23
310.17  310.20  311.33  312.08  313.21
313.25  316.01  316.01  316.05  317.20
317.26  318.35  321.14  324.07  324.12
324.12  324.17  324.17  325.25  325.29
326.14  326.14  326.19  328.28  329.04
330.35  331.01  331.13  331.17
```
WEST   (15)
```
008.01  022.35  037.08  058.29  087.07
087.28  111.31  177.17  191.27  207.18
239.26  245.08  267.07  321.01  321.05
```
WESTERLY   (3)
```
021.13  179.11  311.17
```
WESTERN   (5)
```
094.15  122.10  185.28  269.33  322.24
```
WESTON   (2)
```
279.06  279.09
```
WESTWARD   (4)
```
138.34  157.15  173.05  186.30
```
WET   (4)
```
028.12  170.24  180.21  204.13
```
WETHER   (1)
```
122.01
```
WHALLEY   (1)
```
137.29
```
WHANG   (1)
```
278.26
```
WHARF   (1)
```
119.21
```
WHAT   (252)
```
003.16  003.18  003.33  004.13  004.18
005.08  006.34  007.27  007.35  008.02
008.08  008.12  008.16  008.17  008.25
008.29  010.01  010.08  010.11  010.18
010.19  010.23  010.30  010.32  011.09
011.10  011.21  011.29  011.29  011.34
011.35  012.01  012.02  012.03  013.25
014.30  015.10  015.10  015.19  017.14
017.30  019.04  022.19  022.19  025.06
025.07  025.12  025.13  025.18  026.04
026.05  027.03  028.21  031.14  032.03
032.06  032.35  035.23  035.29  036.16
036.24  040.13  045.32  046.13  046.20
047.02  047.15  047.36  048.07  048.17
048.36  051.27  054.10  056.31  057.24
057.29  058.02  059.06  061.23  065.28
066.03  066.13  066.19  066.26  069.24
069.26  070.21  071.21  071.34  073.22
073.23  074.33  077.16  077.17  078.05
078.16  079.08  080.31  081.02  081.21
081.33  082.21  082.27  083.14  083.26
088.22  089.27  090.01  090.34  090.36
092.26  093.24  093.30  094.19  095.11
095.12  095.16  095.20  095.20  095.34
096.19  096.34  097.07  097.31  100.15
100.31  101.33  102.08  103.28  104.18
104.29  106.02  106.16  107.18  107.24
```
WHAT   (CONTINUED)
```
109.08  111.13  111.17  111.18  112.02
116.20  118.24  119.36  121.08  122.19
123.19  130.01  130.13  133.15  133.18
133.29  137.06  138.01  138.17  143.25
144.20  145.01  147.05  148.06  152.16
153.24  155.08  155.18  155.23  155.26
157.31  158.27  161.13  165.19  166.16
169.13  172.12  172.12  172.32  179.30
180.18  185.24  187.20  191.34  195.28
200.02  205.35  206.29  207.20  207.31
211.04  215.33  216.15  217.32  219.24
219.32  220.01  220.34  220.37  221.06
221.25  223.07  224.34  226.25  231.02
232.34  237.06  240.20  245.09  247.32
250.33  254.31  254.32  260.33  261.27
263.05  263.12  272.24  274.30  275.23
277.13  277.31  279.01  281.17  282.05
287.10  287.15  287.34  291.04  292.21
293.26  295.01  296.20  300.22  306.05
307.30  307.34  308.17  310.28  316.30
321.01  321.01  321.25  322.30  323.01
325.36  326.05  326.14  327.34  327.35
329.23  330.01  330.22  331.33  332.20
332.30  333.17
```
WHATEVER   (19)
```
010.10  012.08  016.15  047.20  068.23
072.03  100.30  110.01  142.25  153.22
168.09  211.28  216.07  242.35  250.30
281.27  287.32  300.20  323.06
```
WHATSOEVER   (1)
```
162.20
```
WHEAT   (4)
```
025.34  049.40  105.34  166.23
```
WHEATEN   (1)
```
040.07
```
WHEEL   (3)
```
127.32  261.26  261.28
```
WHEELBARROW   (4)
```
014.06  082.11  082.24  082.27
```
WHEELED   (1)
```
313.01
```
WHEN   (394)
```
003.03  005.10  005.30  007.23  008.16
011.23  013.12  015.18  015.23  016.19
019.11  022.26  022.34  023.02  025.02
025.08  025.32  026.17  028.08  028.14
029.04  029.14  029.33  029.34  030.18
032.15  033.33  036.12  036.28  037.19
037.25  038.05  039.32  040.02  041.13
041.22  043.04  044.15  045.21  045.24
046.08  047.12  047.29  048.21  052.25
053.10  053.32  057.02  057.25  058.21
059.02  062.18  063.22  066.25  067.02
068.02  068.03  068.11  069.25  070.17
071.29  072.29  073.30  074.05  074.35
080.30  081.16  082.09  082.37  083.17
084.02  084.09  084.26  084.36  085.17
086.23  087.14  087.16  087.32  089.01
090.02  090.35  092.33  093.25  094.35
095.36  099.31  101.28  103.06  103.32
103.35  104.02  106.16  107.06  108.36
111.11  111.22  112.36  114.15  114.18
116.07  116.17  117.16  118.09  119.01
119.19  120.25  120.31  120.36  122.01
123.02  123.27  123.30  124.14  124.17
126.28  127.11  129.03  129.25  130.28
131.22  131.31  132.25  132.28  135.15
135.25  135.25  135.34  137.02  137.09
137.20  138.02  140.10  140.24  140.32
141.13  141.35  142.18  143.01  143.06
143.32  145.25  146.16  146.26  147.12
147.32  148.21  149.03  149.22  150.35
152.11  153.15  155.31  157.11  157.26
159.05  159.36  160.09  160.21  160.32
161.17  163.34  164.25  165.19  169.17
169.25  170.03  170.10  170.26  170.33
171.21  172.06  172.30  172.36  173.34
```

083.18 083.22 083.27 084.20 084.28
084.33 085.05 085.08 085.16 085.33
085.36 086.35 087.11 087.18 087.23
087.27 087.36 088.11 088.30 089.07
089.10 089.13 090.17 090.24 090.24
092.05 093.16 094.09 094.10 094.27
095.12 096.08 096.17 096.22 096.28
097.09 097.35 098.03 099.18 099.18
099.24 100.20 100.23 100.26 100.33
101.03 101.08 101.18 101.23 101.26
102.15 103.14 103.19 103.33 103.35
104.17 104.31 104.32 106.10 107.02
107.07 107.18 107.32 108.01 109.17
109.27 110.18 111.05 111.07 111.08
111.09 112.11 113.11 113.29 113.36
114.06 114.10 114.18 116.14 116.27
116.32 117.01 117.02 117.10 118.35
119.03 119.06 119.10 119.20 119.25
119.33 119.34 120.04 120.07 120.08
120.13 120.20 121.07 121.22 123.07
123.13 123.13 123.15 124.35 125.16
125.27 125.29 125.30 126.21 129.23
129.30 130.20 131.14 131.25 132.11
132.22 132.26 132.28 132.31 133.08
133.13 133.15 134.01 134.10 134.27
135.06 135.09 135.12 136.31 136.32
138.17 138.20 138.24 138.26 139.03
140.24 140.28 141.21 141.27 142.14
142.26 142.30 144.07 144.18 145.03
145.12 145.19 146.03 146.07 146.11
146.18 146.22 146.29 147.08 147.09
147.34 148.26 148.27 150.21 150.34
152.28 152.34 153.07 155.15 155.22
155.23 156.16 157.02 158.02 158.06
158.30 159.01 159.07 159.23 160.02
160.04 160.09 160.25 161.08 161.13
162.04 162.15 162.23 162.25 162.30
164.09 164.27 164.27 164.28 165.28
165.31 165.34 166.12 166.18 166.20
166.21 167.07 167.10 167.12 168.01
168.10 169.33 169.34 170.03 170.14
170.20 171.01 171.24 172.03 172.17
173.20 174.04 174.16 174.18 174.22
174.74 175.07 175.18 175.21 176.26
177.14 177.30 178.17 178.18 178.19
178.33 179.01 179.07 179.23 179.32
180.15 180.25 180.27 180.33 181.05
181.22 181.26 181.36 182.07 182.13
182.16 183.09 183.11 183.12 183.23
183.36 183.36 184.11 184.18 184.26
184.36 185.10 185.34 185.35 186.13
186.16 186.28 187.09 188.01 188.25
188.28 188.31 189.25 190.23 190.31
191.09 191.11 191.16 191.24 191.24
192.09 192.17 193.01 194.05 194.08
194.09 194.10 195.05 195.09 195.25
195.32 195.34 196.06 196.07 196.10
197.28 198.14 199.14 199.33 201.24
201.28 201.30 201.32 202.04 202.11
202.14 202.24 202.30 202.31 203.07
203.11 203.20 203.21 203.23 203.34
204.18 204.28 205.07 205.28 206.03
206.05 206.06 207.30 210.09 210.13
210.26 212.32 213.11 213.29 213.36
214.05 214.14 214.29 215.14 216.14
216.18 217.02 218.02 218.06 218.15
218.16 218.18 218.31 218.32 219.09
219.12 219.18 219.21 219.34 220.03
220.09 220.23 220.37 222.10 222.14
222.15 223.11 223.26 225.05 225.14
225.21 225.22 225.34 226.02 226.09
226.10 227.16 227.19 227.32 229.04
230.06 230.30 231.15 231.22 232.04
232.09 232.16 232.20 232.27 233.15
233.18 236.33 237.01 237.06 238.08
238.18 238.28 238.31 238.32 239.08
239.19 240.24 240.29 241.04 241.13

241.28 242.19 242.28 243.15 243.29
245.19 245.36 246.02 246.03 246.08
246.35 247.15 247.16 248.14 248.16
248.20 249.17 249.25 250.02 250.26
251.29 251.30 251.32 252.20 253.28
253.31 254.24 256.19 256.21 257.01
257.10 257.36 258.09 258.35 259.09
260.07 260.30 260.35 261.01 261.03
261.04 262.24 262.28 262.31 263.20
263.31 264.24 265.01 265.06 265.17
266.15 267.06 267.32 267.33 268.11
268.14 268.15 269.23 269.33 269.34
270.01 271.11 271.20 273.23 273.26
274.24 275.14 275.17 275.25 276.01
276.17 276.28 278.13 279.21 279.35
280.07 280.12 280.24 280.32 281.29
281.35 282.04 282.11 282.13 282.19
282.25 283.22 284.07 284.09 284.14
284.19 284.25 285.14 285.25 287.06
287.07 287.22 287.28 288.07 288.13
288.28 288.31 289.28 290.09 290.18
290.30 290.31 290.33 291.23 291.29
291.30 292.19 292.22 292.32 292.34
293.15 293.17 294.06 294.30 295.33
297.03 297.13 298.05 298.23 299.14
300.15 301.22 302.03 303.28 304.08
304.23 304.26 304.29 304.31 305.08
305.32 306.01 307.02 307.18 307.21
307.28 309.04 309.11 309.27 309.34
309.35 310.03 310.04 312.04 312.23
314.22 314.25 315.12 315.13 315.18
315.19 315.20 315.34 316.23 316.28
317.04 317.06 317.15 317.27 318.06
318.11 318.14 318.22 321.06 321.19
321.22 321.24 321.29 322.11 322.24
323.07 323.22 323.31 324.09 324.16
324.22 324.24 324.25 325.04 325.10
325.22 325.28 325.30 325.31 326.10
326.13 326.15 327.17 327.27 328.22
329.10 330.06 330.10 330.30 331.07
331.16 331.31 332.04 332.29 333.02
333.04 333.06 333.07 333.09 333.13
333.21 333.29 333.31 333.32   (2)

WHICHEVER
269.20 276.14

WHILE   (122)
004.23 009.23 012.35 013.05 013.18
014.01 019.15 019.17 019.19 019.20
019.22 024.27 024.30 029.01 030.31
031.08 034.13 038.08 043.29 045.18
045.31 050.23 050.33 051.12 051.29
051.35 052.06 052.09 053.14 058.34
064.10 066.28 069.33 072.35 074.02
075.23 077.33 082.34 083.29 086.17
088.08 093.36 095.30 098.20 103.02
104.18 110.13 111.03 111.29 113.16
116.35 118.11 121.19 126.07 127.03
131.12 131.36 134.29 142.07 143.23
143.36 144.25 146.19 156.23 156.25
158.23 170.23 172.22 173.07 173.35
182.17 194.25 199.05 202.01 202.15
204.19 205.01 207.33 208.34 210.10
212.27 213.18 213.22 215.26 224.08
226.02 228.09 229.05 229.19 229.25
230.10 235.03 240.27 245.21 246.14
247.01 251.34 252.23 256.05 261.18
264.06 272.05 272.16 275.02 276.03
279.03 279.04 283.10 285.30 287.12
292.34 293.34 299.23 304.13 314.26
314.28 319.09 322.08 325.20 328.30
330.01 332.23   (3)

WHIMSICAL
026.24 275.05 291.24   (1)

WHINNERING
227.29   (4)

WHIPPOORWILL
086.02 128.02 129.11 319.02

```
WINDOW                  (CONTINUED)
073.33  084.34  111.31  114.13  114.24
128.03  168.28  230.33  231.17  243.26
251.27  253.11  273.17  274.18  280.36
283.02  283.04  297.18  297.26  312.09
319.06
WINDOWS                          (  9)
049.09  089.01  128.11  172.04  226.11
240.12  253.34  282.07  328.11
WINDS                            (  6)
085.08  138.11  167.33  298.18  304.20
313.30
WINDY                            (  2)
129.08  194.28
WINE                             ( 10)
024.03  099.30  126.09  126.16  217.10
243.06  330.35  331.05  331.06  332.34
WINES                            (  2)
047.36  140.21
WING                             (  5)
097.18  185.08  276.21  302.24  310.26
WINGED                           (  9)
116.21  121.22  232.35  233.22  252.29
266.14  281.22  307.01  333.17
WINGS                            ( 16)
042.12  159.25  165.12  215.13  226.21
228.13  233.15  248.29  266.24  272.13
276.16  306.33  312.34  313.09  316.28
319.08
WINKLES                          (  1)
201.16
WINNOWED                         (  1)
144.05
WINNOWING                        (  1)
159.32
WINSLOW                          (  2)
143.01  143.32
WINTER                           (105)
017.21  017.29  024.34  027.25  027.36
030.26  035.05  041.19  044.27  048.23
081.27  081.28  084.30  094.17  108.31
109.24  110.07  115.23  117.04  118.33
125.24  127.14  137.19  138.08  146.29
149.29  177.16  178.04  180.08  180.20
183.09  190.05  193.10  198.23  202.09
233.09  238.20  240.12  240.21  240.22
246.06  248.24  249.10  249.33  251.30
253.04  253.19  253.24  253.33  254.13
256.02  256.05  259.08  265.25  266.02
267.11  268.17  268.21  271.01  271.33
271.33  272.06  272.10  273.22  276.11
276.19  276.30  276.30  280.13  280.14
280.19  280.26  282.01  282.02  282.24
283.27  292.13  294.10  294.16  294.24
294.33  296.14  296.23  296.28  297.06
299.13  300.01  300.31  301.09  302.16
302.22  304.26  305.03  308.29  309.28
310.03  310.08  310.27  311.14  311.34
312.02  312.08  312.29  314.26  322.27
WINTERS                          (  1)
069.12
WINTRY                           (  1)
294.10
WIPE                             (  1)
067.22
WIRY                             (  2)
228.15  275.35
WIS                              (  2)
311.21  311.21
WISDOM                           ( 11)
008.15  015.01  050.12  100.16  104.27
106.09  107.16  108.08  214.08  220.38
227.08
WISE                             ( 33)
009.33  014.09  014.29  018.04  025.01
031.11  031.26  035.22  071.17  079.04
096.01  098.25  107.03  108.06  108.15
110.12  124.19  127.21  133.27  137.27

WISE                    (CONTINUED)
148.09  148.19  151.32  217.10  219.25
224.32  267.32  277.25  283.19  294.02
303.15  318.26  332.08
WISEACRE                         (  1)
241.07
WISELY                           (  2)
070.36  320.03
WISER                            ( 10)
040.28  053.06  058.09  096.12  107.11
143.29  147.25  151.08  217.23  277.29
WISEST                           (  5)
009.03  010.34  014.20  067.09  107.02
WISH                             ( 12)
019.03  032.03  054.14  070.12  090.36
091.01  098.28  108.25  151.17  152.05
323.24  323.27
WISHED                           (  9)
039.09  051.17  082.14  090.32  148.03
149.08  206.09  211.25  261.26
WISHES                           (  3)
039.13  049.32  069.27
WISHING                          (  4)
034.07  054.18  074.05  149.31
WISS                             (  1)
311.21
WIT                              ( 13)
040.25  094.28  106.30  109.21  110.02
116.06  151.05  151.06  151.11  152.14
260.14  260.16  325.14
WITCHES                          (  1)
131.01
WITH                             (817)
004.20  004.26  004.32  004.36  005.08
005.20  006.11  006.22  007.28  007.34
008.10  008.34  009.21  009.22  009.24
010.04  012.16  012.23  012.31  012.32
013.02  013.04  013.07  013.15  013.17
013.26  013.27  014.20  015.30  016.12
016.32  017.35  018.09  018.32  019.36
020.06  020.34  021.13  022.14  022.15
022.28  023.28  023.33  025.15  025.22
025.30  026.15  027.24  028.03  028.14
029.05  029.24  029.32  029.34  029.35
030.06  030.07  030.29  030.36  031.20
032.07  032.20  032.21  032.27  032.33
033.02  033.15  033.21  033.22  034.12
035.05  035.18  035.21  035.24  036.06
036.21  037.06  037.08  037.14  037.20
038.15  038.27  038.34  039.15  039.16
039.18  039.20  039.21  040.09  040.10
040.11  040.13  040.24  040.25  041.06
041.11  041.18  041.23  041.35  042.07
042.30  042.33  043.07  044.17  044.20
045.03  046.04  046.11  046.25  047.07
047.08  048.10  048.25  048.27  048.30
049.10  050.19  050.24  050.30  051.08
051.23  052.07  052.11  052.11  053.24
054.22  054.22  054.32  056.02  056.33
056.36  057.04  057.05  057.27  058.19
058.32  059.31  060.33  061.25  066.26
066.31  068.13  068.17  068.19  068.28
068.31  070.21  070.28  072.01  072.15
073.06  073.14  073.27  074.12  074.18
074.21  074.24  075.09  075.15  075.21
076.10  077.11  078.06  078.21  078.21
078.26  078.31  078.31  080.10  081.11
082.10  082.12  082.28  083.33  083.36
084.32  084.36  085.20  086.10  087.05
088.12  088.27  089.01  089.30  089.35
090.07  091.18  092.02  092.04  092.07
092.29  093.06  094.18  094.29  095.17
095.25  095.26  095.32  096.17  097.22
097.27  097.27  098.23  098.28  098.32
099.03  099.09  099.34  100.17  102.04
102.18  102.21  104.03  104.03  105.17
105.23  105.24  106.03  106.08  106.12
106.23  107.11  108.08  108.18  108.20
```

WOOL   (3)
  145.14 263.20 310.02
WOOLLEN   (2)
  027.16 116.05
WORD   (12)
  025.10 050.04 063.24 073.24 081.14
  100.14 102.20 112.16 118.10 149.07
  196.04 306.23
WORDS   (31)
  008.16 012.08 043.21 057.05 100.22
  100.26 102.02 104.23 106.05 107.02
  107.17 107.31 108.07 123.21 140.33
  143.07 151.21 171.17 174.02
  221.14 245.03 245.29 254.26 268.28
  306.27 316.02 316.05 325.01 325.04
  332.22
WORE   (7)
  028.04 120.32 145.13 206.04 262.09
  293.17 323.16
WORK   (87)
  008.14 011.09 017.26 021.25 021.29
  023.11 036.23 036.23 036.25 038.01
  042.37 044.18 044.30 048.34 051.08
  055.05 056.02 056.17 056.17 056.20
  056.28 057.03 057.05 070.23 070.23
  073.13 092.20 093.10 097.32 100.04
  102.22 102.22 104.30 111.23 111.34
  112.05 134.14 135.17 135.32 136.06
  145.07 145.16 145.22 146.12 146.17
  147.20 149.24 155.20 156.25 157.06
  162.12 165.07 193.14 198.29 204.09
  205.12 205.13 205.16 221.04 221.35
  222.06 222.13 223.15 236.07 241.17
  241.32 243.15 251.29 275.22 282.19
  282.21 288.20 292.13 294.34 297.19
  306.12 314.36 324.07 326.23 326.24
  327.07 327.13 327.21 330.29 330.29
  330.33 331.16
WORKED   (13)
  018.23 041.06 041.13 043.02 156.28
  204.33 204.37 205.17 206.02 222.13
  241.22 269.35 295.28
WORKHOUSE   (2)
  028.32 035.15
WORKING   (8)
  038.33 053.17 069.11 135.26 145.32
  147.02 204.22 260.25
WORKMAN   (2)
  134.12 134.13
WORKMEN   (1)
  245.28
WORKS   (15)
  035.11 037.32 055.30 056.34 057.01
  057.07 057.08 076.35 101.21 103.25
  104.03 112.03 188.13 239.35 326.31
WORKSHOP   (2)
  192.05 245.04
WORLD   (93)
  004.12 010.26 013.32 022.35 025.26
  027.33 028.11 035.15 036.25 037.22
  037.31 051.22 052.30 053.19 053.26
  058.14 060.12 066.05 068.36 071.10
  072.03 072.07 073.15 074.03 074.04
  077.23 077.25 079.02 082.16 083.25
  085.21 087.31 089.07 091.09 094.01
  099.25 099.29 102.34 104.06 105.10
  106.17 109.04 109.30 110.12 115.01
  119.24 120.33 122.33 128.20 130.25
  130.33 138.32 145.04 148.10 152.03
  152.10 158.04 169.14 171.13 171.18
  179.28 204.16 209.04 218.31 223.07
  223.30 224.24 225.15 251.22 260.07
  262.07 268.23 269.10 269.18 292.06
  294.06 298.05 306.11 314.12 314.34
  314.35 316.09 320.05 321.29 322.08
  322.37 323.23 323.26 325.18 327.16
  328.29 332.19 332.32

WORLDLY   (1)
  261.17
WORLDS   (2)
  010.27 321.16
WORM   (2)
  224.18 284.01
WORMEATEN   (1)
  164.10
WORMS   (13)
  155.24 163.30 174.23 206.30 211.35
  218.20 219.12 224.09 225.08 228.08
  239.05 246.28 283.28
WORMWOOD   (3)
  157.04 161.27 262.31
WORMY   (1)
  024.07
WORN   (18)
  006.32 023.24 024.17 068.15 130.11
  148.33 162.29 169.33 173.04 180.05
  206.04 241.14 276.06 293.27 295.34
  302.26 322.26 323.22
WORRY   (2)
  154.09 223.14
WORSE   (10)
  007.22 033.07 033.10 054.13 070.20
  078.04 121.02 143.12 220.24 292.26
WORSHIP   (5)
  023.23 025.21 057.15 108.18 201.07
WORSHIPPER   (2)
  088.27 138.35
WORSHIPS   (1)
  221.28
WORST   (4)
  007.23 022.08 029.16 157.12
WORTH   (25)
  019.14 019.17 019.19 019.20 019.22
  045.31 073.27 078.17 088.08 094.07
  100.21 107.03 109.18 113.16 110.11
  123.04 123.19 127.03 131.17 165.02
  194.25 202.01 215.26 231.21 322.08
WORTHIER   (2)
  034.17 207.28
WORTHIES   (6)
  076.25 079.02 080.31 107.25 108.20
  168.02
WORTHIEST   (2)
  197.05 215.24
WORTHILY   (1)
  096.11
WORTHLESS   (1)
  260.04
WORTHY   (11)
  057.01 074.32 074.35 090.27 092.10
  095.20 095.21 096.02 107.09 116.23
  270.01
WOULD   (307)
  003.13 003.35 004.08 006.17 008.28
  010.16 010.29 011.32 016.02 016.30
  016.32 017.08 017.34 018.04 018.31
  019.12 019.12 019.17 021.07 021.14
  022.13 022.13 022.22 022.30 024.02
  025.27 025.29 025.30 025.33 027.15
  028.01 028.24 029.03 029.22 030.26
  031.26 032.30 036.03 036.16 036.21
  036.30 037.02 037.12 037.13 041.33
  043.17 044.26 045.31 046.07 047.33
  048.08 050.13 050.14 050.15 050.19
  050.35 051.15 051.18 051.30 051.33
  051.36 055.32 055.35 055.36 056.03
  056.23 056.34 057.31 058.09 059.32
  059.36 059.39 061.15 063.08 063.13
  064.24 065.29 066.35 067.09 067.11
  068.08 069.21 070.21 071.06 071.11
  071.15 071.20 072.12 072.12 073.12
  073.15 073.18 074.24 075.08 075.33
  076.07 076.33 077.18 077.20 078.07
  078.31 083.30 084.03 085.01 090.07
  090.30 091.31 093.18 095.30 095.33

WOULD

			(CONTINUED)	
095.36	096.30	096.35	098.22	098.33
099.04	100.28	102.14	107.33	111.35
115.20	116.16	116.29	118.08	123.24
124.02	124.12	124.28	126.13	127.07
127.18	127.19	127.30	127.34	131.20
131.21	132.36	133.05	134.02	136.22
136.24	138.10	138.11	141.20	143.20
144.20	145.03	145.24	145.31	146.06
146.13	146.16	146.24	146.31	147.17
147.19	147.28	148.06	148.14	149.09
149.20	149.28	150.14	153.26	153.29
153.30	156.24	158.22	160.12	163.38
165.06	165.12	167.35	170.08	172.20
172.23	173.13	177.23	178.28	178.31
184.23	184.31	186.26	190.05	191.06
191.07	194.14	195.19	196.14	196.17
196.21	196.21	197.24	198.26	199.24
201.06	202.19	202.35	206.11	212.29
213.19	213.21	214.02	214.25	215.27
217.07	219.24	219.26	220.33	221.03
223.16	224.15	224.27	224.30	224.31
225.28	225.31	228.10	228.14	231.21
233.20	234.11	234.11	234.25	235.09
235.13	235.29	235.31	236.35	237.04
241.06	243.33	244.11	244.34	244.35
245.13	245.19	250.24	250.28	253.05
253.11	254.08	254.11	256.25	260.14
262.35	263.33	264.16	266.09	266.20
267.06	272.02	272.35	273.03	273.30
274.08	274.10	274.15	274.26	274.31
274.34	275.05	275.07	277.05	277.06
277.07	277.20	279.30	280.01	280.07
281.01	283.17	284.07	284.15	285.03
287.10	287.17	287.20	287.24	289.23
290.21	292.32	296.17	296.18	302.01
302.32	303.24	304.02	304.07	307.34
308.14	312.27	317.20	317.26	320.27
320.28	320.30	321.06	322.16	322.17
322.38	325.14	328.29	330.23	330.25
330.30	331.16			

WOUNDED (1)
230.20
WOUNDS (2)
231.14 318.28
WOVEN (7)
019.17 028.19 064.25 116.04 129.32
186.07 317.10
WOW (1)
182.13
WRAPPED (1)
042.27
WRAPPING (1)
062.14
WRATH (2)
089.04 229.31
WREATH (1)
129.27
WREATHS (3)
114.02 116.13 201.11
WRECK (2)
194.32 195.02
WRECKED (1)
094.14
WRECKS (4)
174.19 246.27 304.17 318.05
WRESTLED (1)
228.31
WRETCH (1)
080.05
WRETCHEDNESS (1)
091.20
WRINKLE (2)
167.07 193.03
WRINKLED (1)
204.10
WRITE (8)
020.15 084.22 094.28 119.31 147.35

WRITE (CONTINUED)
148.03 148.05 152.34
WRITER (4)
003.32 102.13 145.01 147.31
WRITERS (3)
018.09 100.18 103.27
WRITES (1)
116.06
WRITING (5)
029.30 039.08 145.01 167.03 310.15
WRITINGS (1)
325.19
WRITTEN (18)
099.25 100.30 101.07 101.09 101.10
101.21 101.22 101.26 101.29 102.02
102.19 103.19 111.05 120.13 147.36
148.04 258.28 310.29
WRONG (5)
092.35 149.19 198.30 199.06 308.24
WROTE (4)
003.03 094.07 147.32 327.06
WROUGHT (3)
030.06 118.06 119.30
WYMAN (3)
261.14 261.25 261.36

258

```
YANKEE
  028.31  092.27  211.08  295.22  (  4)
YANKEES
  145.22                          (  1)
YARD                             ( 16)
  113.30  115.24  126.07  128.09  128.09
  128.18  128.19  197.02  229.02  263.27
  267.28  270.20  271.25  271.30  324.26
  329.31
YARDED                           (  1)
  324.23
YAVE                             (  1)
  212.20
YAWNED                           (  1)
  301.21
YE                               (  8)
  032.07  032.07  032.10  200.05  208.17
  208.18  257.31  269.13
YEAR                             ( 48)
  027.26  039.05  041.18  050.07  055.26
  055.27  059.33  060.15  063.06  069.11
  070.27  070.32  074.14  085.05  095.06
  105.25  164.14  166.17  166.33  180.27
  181.21  183.07  190.16  192.07  195.23
  197.15  197.15  204.37  214.06  233.05
  251.12  277.34  299.07  301.03  301.09
  302.34  309.26  310.23  311.07  311.12
  311.12  315.06  319.18  319.19  332.02
  332.31  332.36  333.02
YEARNING                         (  1)
  028.16
YEARS                            ( 76)
  003.08  009.10  010.35  014.11  016.30
  018.12  024.31  031.19  032.18  039.22
  039.32  055.29  059.04  061.02  061.14
  068.35  069.09  069.21  077.32  081.28
  082.37  084.21  092.31  094.07  094.29
  108.14  109.22  121.04  133.04  145.06
  145.07  147.15  155.31  156.12  158.34
  174.03  178.04  180.28  180.30  180.34
  181.01  181.09  181.11  181.31  186.11
  190.27  190.35  193.08  193.09  197.31
  198.01  198.20  199.07  204.02  211.36
  213.33  214.27  217.25  232.10  232.33
  241.02  249.31  251.04  251.17  252.08
  252.11  259.03  277.36  297.13  290.04
  312.16  323.17  332.01  333.10  333.12
  333.23
YEAST                            (  3)
  061.01  062.33  063.03
YELLOW                           ( 17)
  018.26  041.15  055.09  129.28  142.31
  156.32  157.03  176.34  178.35  197.35
  198.03  198.26  201.29  252.17  265.30
  311.03  319.15
YELLOWISH                        (  4)
  176.25  177.27  269.28  305.25
YELLOWSTONE                      (  1)
  320.13
YELP                             (  2)
  276.32  277.21
YES                              (  6)
  054.12  059.29  093.23  206.27  212.11
  331.29
YESTERDAY                        (  5)
  112.15  112.18  269.16  312.10  314.32
YET                              (138)
  006.25  008.20  009.11  011.09  014.09
  014.34  017.07  017.21  018.07  019.19
  022.05  027.16  032.23  033.14  035.21
  036.03  040.04  041.10  041.29  042.25
  057.01  060.09  061.17  061.28  063.04
  063.31  070.11  070.15  089.23  090.12
  094.22  097.13  100.02  103.10  103.24
  104.08  104.16  105.25  107.04  107.19
  118.18  120.27  124.24  125.12  129.14
  131.03  131.09  137.07  138.05  140.16
  144.30  145.10  148.17  150.01  150.08

YET                              (CONTINUED)
  150.18  151.21  156.21  158.29  159.17
  159.35  170.36  172.07  172.13  173.06
  173.13  175.28  177.18  178.01  179.34
  181.03  187.13  193.33  194.34  195.20
  204.27  205.21  206.03  207.06  207.07
  209.01  211.13  212.06  213.25  214.04
  214.06  215.22  215.30  216.16  216.21
  217.03  219.16  219.30  222.09  227.05
  228.02  229.08  229.27  235.22  236.04
  236.09  241.26  242.12  247.02  249.10
  258.11  258.22  258.31  265.25  267.11
  272.30  276.10  276.35  281.04  283.23
  284.29  285.29  287.09  293.34  302.02
  307.24  308.14  316.07  320.13  320.20
  320.34  321.20  321.30  322.09  322.37
  323.02  325.05  326.14  330.20  331.35
  332.02  332.07  332.19
YIELD                            (  7)
  023.08  083.30  173.10  203.11  227.11
  272.02  295.33
YIELDED                          (  3)
  082.27  155.15  159.07
YIELDING                         (  2)
  061.27  223.25
YIELDS                           (  5)
  102.10  157.13  158.06  307.19  329.11
YONDER                           (  2)
  133.10  224.16
YORE                             (  3)
  193.06  269.17  312.18
YORK                             (  6)
  052.20  097.36  162.07  235.18  238.12
  251.05
YOU                              (298)
  004.09  006.27  006.29  006.30  006.35
  007.09  007.10  007.12  007.23  008.05
  008.10  008.29  008.29  008.30  009.19
  009.35  010.33  010.34  010.34  017.05
  019.03  019.05  020.08  021.03  021.12
  022.22  022.31  023.11  023.32  023.32
  025.33  029.17  029.18  029.18  029.20
  032.07  032.30  035.16  038.22  038.22
  048.18  048.20  048.21  051.07  053.03
  053.04  053.04  053.13  053.16  053.17
  053.20  054.13  054.14  054.14  055.06
  058.02  063.23  065.36  066.01  066.13
  066.14  066.15  066.15  066.28  066.29
  070.07  071.29  073.02  073.26  073.26
  074.22  074.28  075.08  075.13  075.15
  075.20  076.08  076.09  078.14  084.05
  084.09  084.13  084.13  087.14  087.14
  092.03  092.25  092.30  094.09  094.18
  094.19  094.30  095.05  095.06  096.29
  097.26  098.06  098.10  098.11  098.13
  098.14  100.22  111.17  111.19  112.34
  115.06  120.20  125.08  127.30  132.36
  133.05  133.09  133.13  135.15  140.33
  141.13  142.22  142.23  144.27  144.29
  146.07  147.18  147.19  147.26  149.26
  149.27  150.04  152.22  152.33  153.24
  153.29  156.24  157.31  158.23  158.26
  161.30  163.38  163.39  164.08  170.27
  172.32  172.32  173.13  173.15  175.13
  175.19  176.25  177.35  178.02  178.26
  185.12  185.18  186.22  186.26  186.26
  186.30  186.31  186.34  187.13  187.16
  187.23  191.07  191.26  192.09  192.11
  193.20  195.19  197.01  197.24  198.02
  202.02  205.22  205.24  205.25  205.27
  206.27  206.30  212.34  215.26  216.24
  216.28  218.25  220.33  220.34  221.03
  221.07  221.07  221.08  221.08  222.16
  222.18  223.29  223.29  224.05  224.08
  224.14  224.15  224.16  224.17  224.18
  224.18  224.19  224.20  226.23  226.24
  226.29  228.22  228.24  230.12  240.27
  243.21  243.24  243.29  243.29  243.33
```

```
YOU                        (CONTINUED)
243.35  244.03  244.10  244.13  244.15
244.21  244.24  244.28  246.20  246.29
246.32  246.33  246.34  247.02  247.05
249.21  252.16  252.18  254.22  258.22
262.08  272.24  272.26  272.30  274.09
276.14  277.31  281.23  283.24  284.16
290.04  293.26  296.33  302.30  305.12
305.14  305.32  306.16  306.34  307.11
307.12  307.12  309.08  309.10  310.20
312.27  314.31  314.36  315.04  319.12
320.16  320.17  320.18  320.32  321.13
321.17  322.09  322.10  322.16  322.17
324.06  324.10  324.11  324.13  324.23
327.34  327.35  328.07  328.07  328.09
328.27  329.06  329.07  329.08  329.10
329.12  329.27  330.17  330.19  330.28
330.30  330.31  330.33
YOUNG                                ( 41)
005.03  009.05  009.09  028.14  035.07
036.08  044.12  055.31  058.18  065.07
071.04  072.06  083.21  113.27  128.10
138.03  138.20  139.08  144.27  153.02
153.17  153.17  163.34  163.36  170.16
193.04  210.24  212.36  213.05  226.15
226.25  227.03  227.36  228.11  228.14
228.17  232.31  249.26  274.11  281.09
282.10
YOUNGER                              (  4)
191.29  257.12  261.25  310.24
YOUNGEST                             (  1)
315.07
YOUR                                 (106)
004.11  004.11  006.34  007.09  009.36
020.05  020.19  021.12  022.21  023.32
025.33  038.25  041.02  041.03  048.14
048.15  048.19  048.19  053.14  053.22
054.15  058.22  059.41  063.20  075.14
076.09  078.16  078.16  078.18  078.18
080.16  080.18  080.22  084.10  084.11
087.12  091.25  091.27  091.27  095.07
095.16  096.36  098.15  111.18  112.33
115.30  115.30  115.33  118.16  118.22
118.23  120.21  122.15  128.10  128.11
128.12  128.17  140.33  140.35  142.22
146.08  147.18  149.27  152.04  152.04
156.25  158.21  158.29  175.16  175.19
178.27  186.22  186.31  186.32  194.26
197.01  206.29  215.25  216.27  216.28
226.15  226.28  226.30  235.07  243.21
244.05  244.06  244.07  246.20  246.22
247.05  302.30  309.09  312.28  314.31
320.32  320.33  321.11  321.12  324.07
328.05  328.09  328.26  328.26  329.07
330.29
YOURS                                (  2)
158.22  235.08
YOURSELF                             ( 14)
007.23  008.10  020.12  020.23  071.27
075.15  216.29  221.08  224.14  244.20
244.22  272.28  328.23  328.35
YOURSELVES                           (  2)
007.07  007.12
YOUTH                                ( 13)
009.01  040.36  071.13  139.07  182.12
200.02  207.25  217.26  218.36  260.28
311.04  311.31  326.34
YOUTHFUL                             (  3)
100.21  193.02  331.33
YOUTHS                               (  3)
051.14  123.30  212.28
YU                                   (  1)
095.12
```

260

```
ZAG                              (   1)
  274.35
ZANZIBAR                         (   1)
  322.09
ZEBULON                          (   1)
  105.02
ZENDAVESTAS                      (   1)
  104.03
ZEPHYR                           (   2)
  191.30   219.02
ZEPHYRS                          (   1)
  316.14
ZIG                              (   1)
  274.35
ZILPHA                           (   1)
  257.21
ZOROASTER
  108.13   108.19
```

Appendix A:
Word Frequency List
of Words Appearing
100 or More Times

Word	Count	Word	Count
A	2810	NOT	912
ABOUT	154	NOW	118
ALL	447	OF	3227
AN	356	OFF	110
AND	4250	OLD	109
ANY	227	ON	679
ARE	594	ONE	476
AS	1103	ONLY	248
AT	607	OR	818
BE	647	OTHER	160
BEEN	159	OUR	294
BEFORE	125	OUT	224
BUT	715	OVER	186
BY	647	OWN	105
CAN	156	PART	103
COULD	168	POND	202
DAY	203	S	288
DID	125	SEE	130
DO	184	SHOULD	154
DOWN	112	SO	436
EVEN	161	SOME	346
EVERY	139	SOMETIMES	111
FAR	100	STILL	164
FIRST	121	SUCH	191
FOR	885	THAN	291
FROM	474	THAT	1208
GO	100	THE	6830
GOOD	105	THEIR	453
HAD	512	THEM	307
HAS	223	THEN	117
HAVE	604	THERE	375
HE	702	THESE	154
HIM	250	THEY	613
HIS	668	THIS	506
HOUSE	200	THOSE	114
HOW	143	THOUGH	179
I	1817	THROUGH	138
ICE	123	TIME	164
IF	492	TO	2774
IN	1937	TWO	118
INTO	182	UP	215
IS	1180	US	106
IT	1516	VERY	119
ITS	354	WAS	833
KNOW	107	WATER	177
LAST	101	WAY	101
LIFE	200	WE	447
LIKE	300	WELL	128
LITTLE	110	WERE	379
LONG	140	WHAT	252
MADE	131	WHEN	394
MAN	315	WHERE	209
MANY	162	WHICH	794
MAY	198	WHILE	122
ME	310	WHO	343
MEN	204	WILL	241
MORE	335	WINTER	105
MOST	188	WITH	817
MUCH	142	WITHOUT	145
MY	727	WOODS	151
NEVER	160	WOULD	307
NEW	124	YET	138
NO	264	YOU	298
NOR	104	YOUR	106

Appendix B
Histograms (for Each Chapter)
of Word Lengths

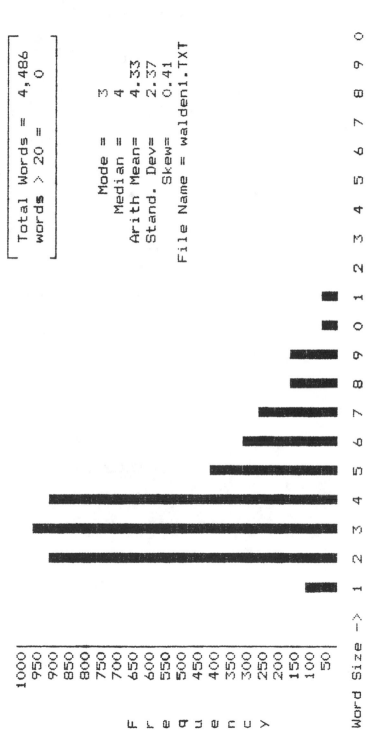

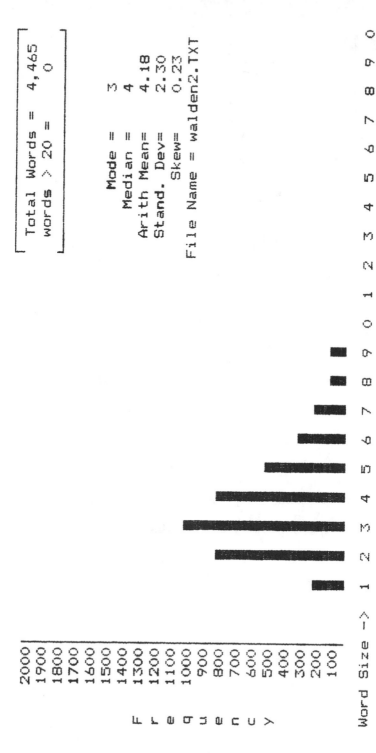

Total Words = 4,465
words > 20 = 0

Mode = 3
Median = 4
Arith Mean= 4.18
Stand. Dev= 2.30
Skew= 0.23
File Name = walden2.TXT

Word Size -> 1 2 3 4 5 6 7 8 9 0 1 2 3 4 5 6 7 8 9 0

hit any key to continue

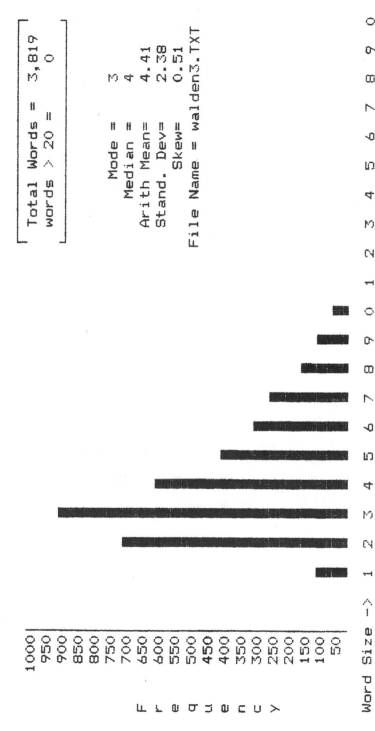

Total Words = 3,819
words > 20 = 0

Mode = 3
Median = 4
Arith Mean= 4.41
Stand. Dev= 2.38
Skew= 0.51

File Name = walden3.TXT

Frequency

Word Size -> 1 2 3 4 5 6 7 8 9 0 1 2 3 4 5 6 7 8 9 0

hit any key to continue

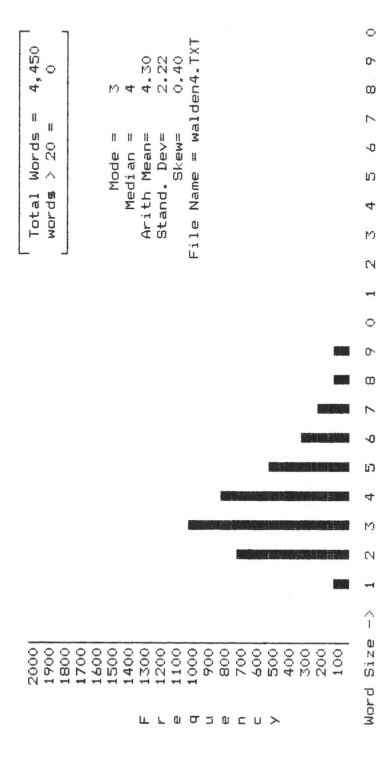

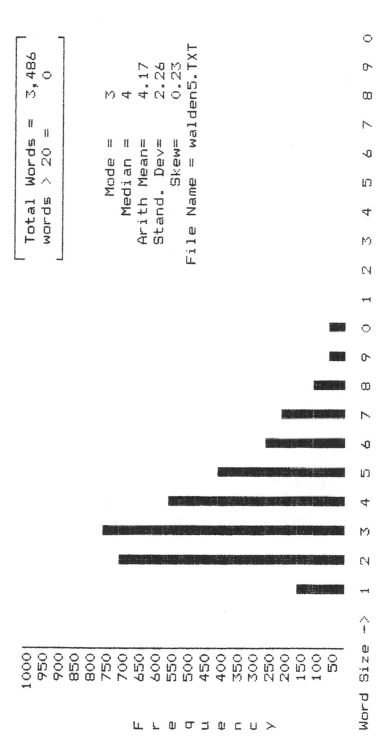

Total Words = 3,486
words > 20 = 0

Mode = 3
Median = 4
Arith Mean= 4.17
Stand. Dev= 2.26
Skew= 0.23

File Name = walden5.TXT

Word Size -> 1 2 3 4 5 6 7 8 9 0 1 2 3 4 5 6 7 8 9 0

hit any key to continue

Frequency

1000
950
900
850
800
750
700
650
600
550
500
450
400
350
300
250
200
150
100
50

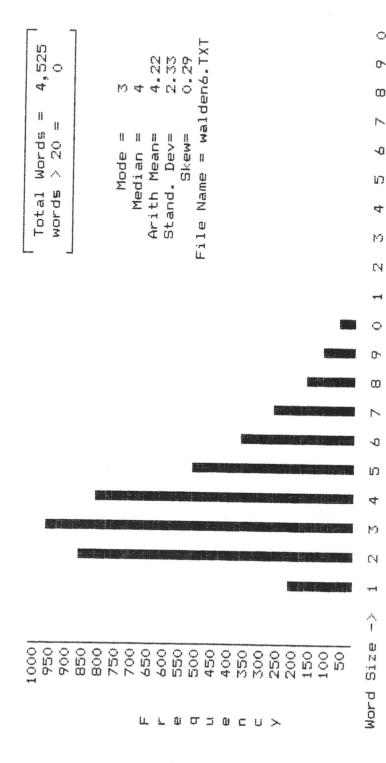

Total Words = 4,525
words > 20 = 0

Mode = 3
Median = 4
Arith Mean= 4.22
Stand. Dev= 2.33
Skew= 0.29

File Name = walden6.TXT

Word Size ->   1 2 3 4 5 6 7 8 9 0   1 2 3 4 5 6 7 8 9 0

hit any key to continue

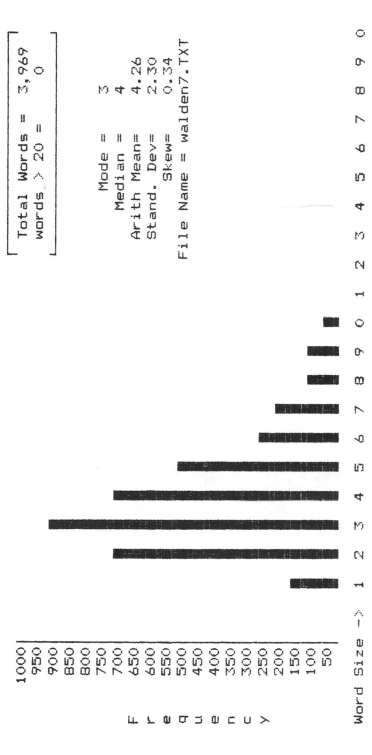

Total Words = 3,969
words > 20 = 0

Mode = 3
Median = 4
Arith Mean= 4.26
Stand. Dev= 2.30
Skew= 0.34

File Name = walden7.TXT

Word Size -> 1 2 3 4 5 6 7 8 9 0

hit any key to continue

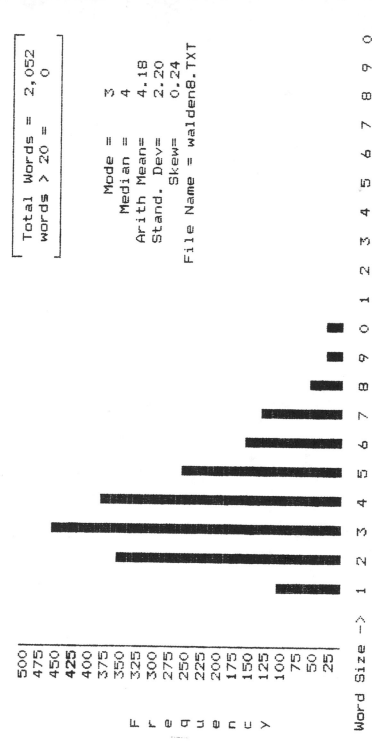

Total Words = 2,052
words > 20 = 0

Mode = 3
Median = 4
Arith Mean= 4.18
Stand. Dev= 2.20
Skew= 0.24

File Name = walden8.TXT

Word Size -> 1 2 3 4 5 6 7 8 9 0

hit any key to continue

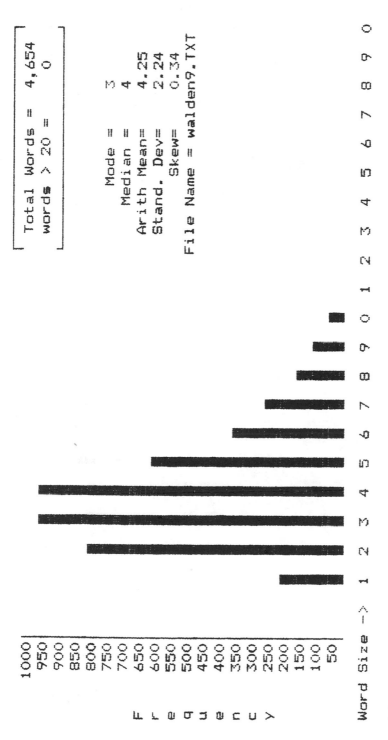

Total Words = 4,654
words > 20 = 0

Mode = 3
Median = 4
Arith Mean= 4.25
Stand. Dev= 2.24
Skew= 0.34
File Name = walden9.TXT

Word Size ->

hit any key to continue

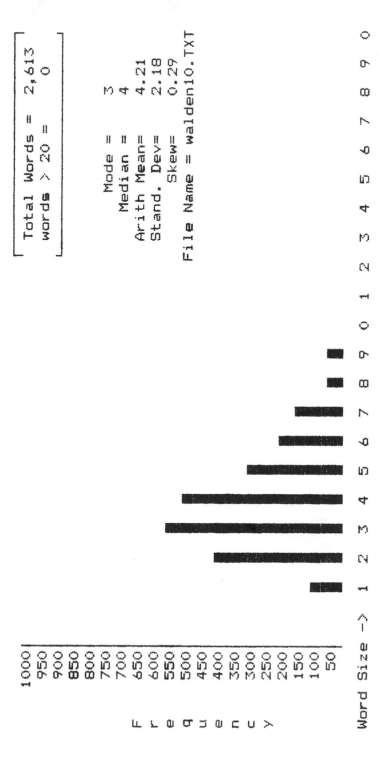

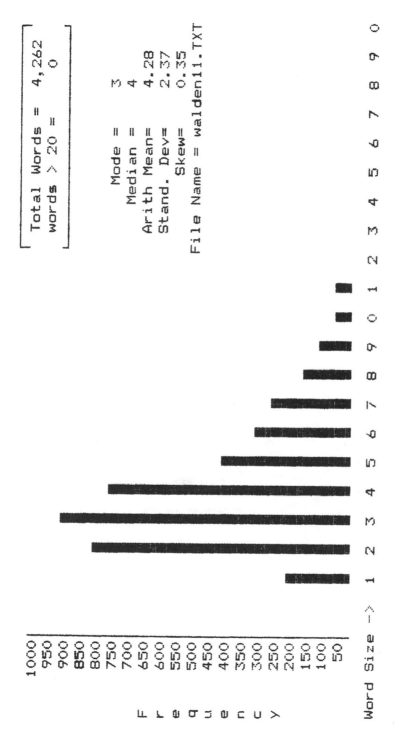

Total Words = 4,262
words > 20 = 0

Mode = 3
Median = 4
Arith Mean= 4.28
Stand. Dev= 2.37
Skew= 0.35
File Name = walden11.TXT

Word Size -->

hit any key to continue

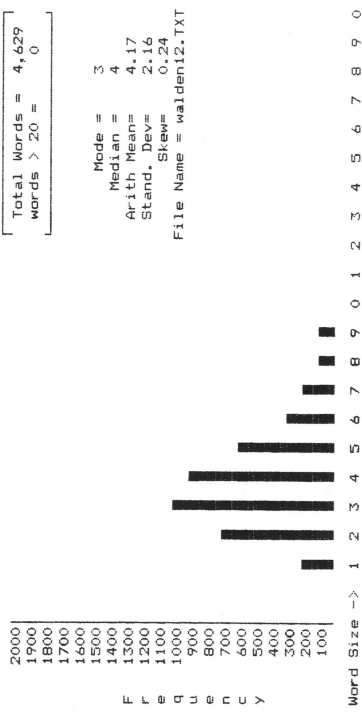

```
Total Words =   4,629
words > 20 =        0


      Mode =   3
    Median =   4
Arith Mean=   4.17
Stand. Dev=   2.16
     Skew=   0.24
File Name = walden12.TXT
```

```
2000
1900
1800
1700
1600
1500
1400
1300
1200
1100
1000
 900
 800
 700
 600
 500
 400
 300
 200
 100
     1  2  3  4  5  6  7  8  9  0  1  2  3  4  5  6  7  8  9  0

Word Size ->  1  2  3  4  5  6  7  8  9

hit any key to continue
```

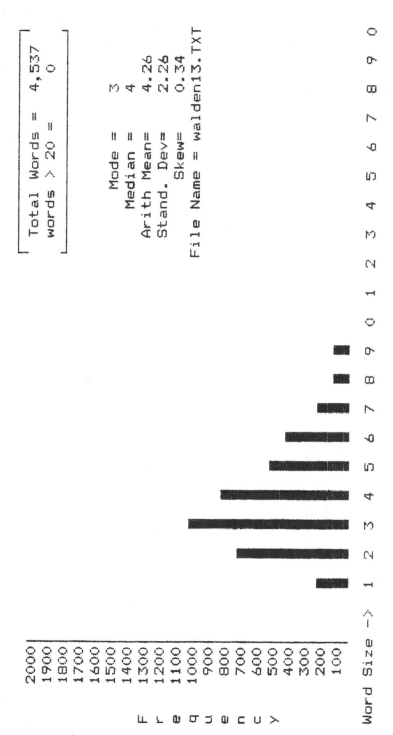

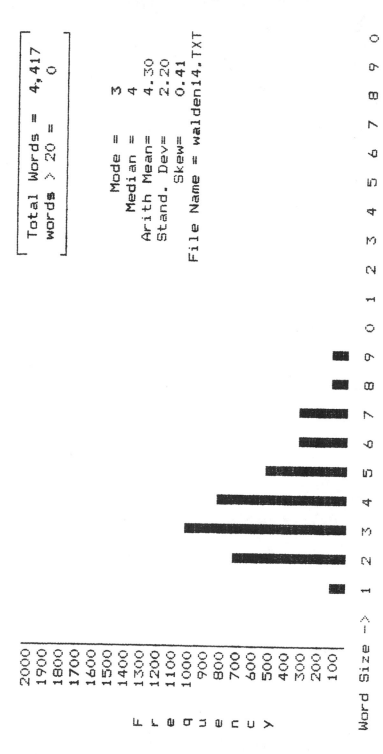

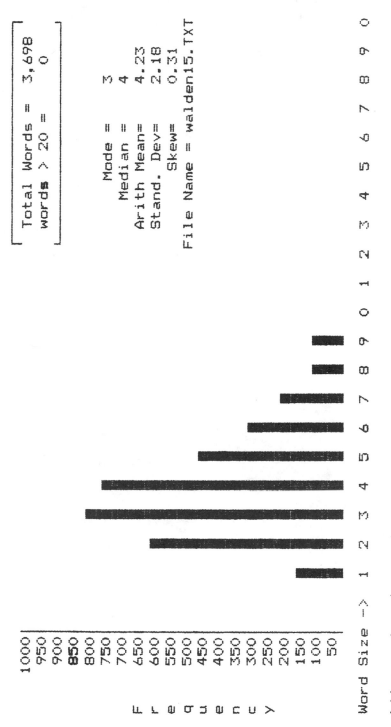

Total Words = 3,698
words > 20 = 0

Mode = 3
Median = 4
Arith Mean= 4.23
Stand. Dev= 2.18
Skew= 0.31

File Name = walden15.TXT

Word Size -> 1 2 3 4 5 6 7 8 9 0 1 2 3 4 5 6 7 8 9 0

hit any key to continue

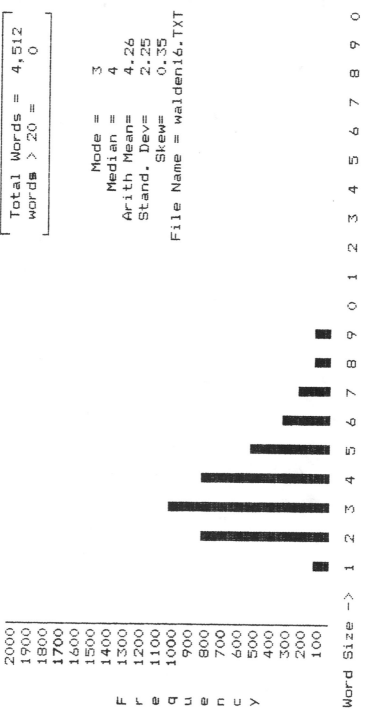

Total Words = 4,512
words > 20 = 0

Mode = 3
Median = 4
Arith Mean= 4.26
Stand. Dev= 2.25
Skew= 0.35

File Name = walden16.TXT

Word Size -> 1 2 3 4 5 6 7 8 9 0 1 2 3 4 5 6 7 8 9 0

hit any key to continue

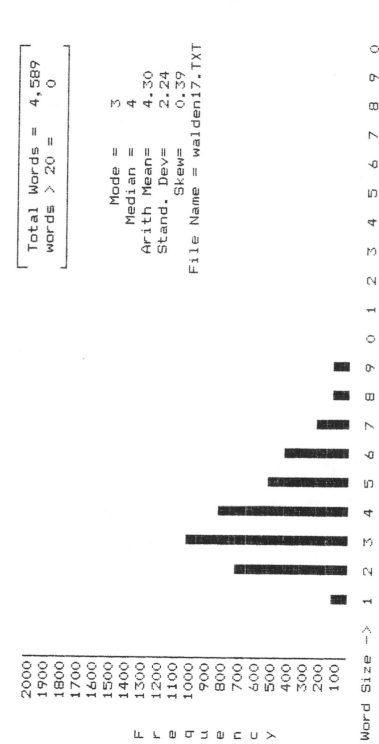

Total Words = 4,589
words > 20 = 0

Mode = 3
Median = 4
Arith Mean= 4.30
Stand. Dev= 2.24
Skew= 0.39

File Name = walden17.TXT

Word Size —>

hit any key to continue

Total Words = 4,566
words > 20 = 0

Mode = 3
Median = 4
Arith Mean= 4.24
Stand. Dev= 2.30
Skew= 0.31

File Name = walden18.TXT

Frequency

2000
1900
1800
1700
1600
1500
1400
1300
1200
1100
1000
900
800
700
600
500
400
300
200
100

Word Size -> 1 2 3 4 5 6 7 8 9 0 1 2 3 4 5 6 7 8 9 0

hit any key to continue

Appendix C
BASIC Simple
Word Search Program

```
10 '   SEARCH WALDEN            By CLIFTON A. KELLER and KIRBY G. GUILD
20 CLS                         'Clear Screen
30 FILES                       'Display List Of Files To Choose From
40 PRINT :PRINT :GOTO 60
50 PRINT "*** File error ***", ERR
60 INPUT "File name to access: ";F$
70 ON ERROR GOTO 50            'Display Error Code And Input Another File Name
80 OPEN F$ FOR INPUT AS #1:GOTO 100      'Open File for Acces
90 ON ERROR GOTO 0             'Clear `on error' so Regular Error Handling occurs
100 PRINT:PRINT:PRINT:LINE INPUT "Word or phrase to find: ";W$
110 PRINT " "
120 ON ERROR GOTO 0
130 INPUT "Enter the number of lines before and after the target line ",N
135 INPUT "Do you desire full printout (Y/N)";Y$        'On Printer
136 IF INSTR("Yy",Y$)>0 THEN PAPER=1 ELSE PAPER=0
140 N=2*N+1                    'Dimention Array to Two Times The Number Of Lines
150 DIM A$(N+2)                Either Side of Target Word / Phrase
210 C=N
220 '                          SEARCH AND FIND LOOP
225 CLS
230 L=C MOD N
240 LINE INPUT #1,A$(L)        'Input A Line From The Selected File
245 IF EOF(1) THEN 320         'If The End Of The File Has Been Reached Then End
250 C=C+1                      'Increment Counter Of Lines
260 A$(L)=" "+A$(L)+" "        'Add A Space At Both Ends Of The Selected Line
270 IF INSTR(A$(L),"*") > 0 THEN A$(N+1)=A$(L)   '*=Character Preceding Page No.
280 M=(L+(N-1)/2+1) MOD N      'Calculates Storage Location In The Array A$(x)
290 X=INSTR(A$(M),W$)          'Check If The Word or Phrase Is In The Current Line
300 IF X > 0 THEN GOSUB 330        'Print Region Around Target Word/Phrase
310 GOTO 220                   'Return To The Beginning Of The Search And Find Loop
320 END
325 '
330 '                          PRINT REGION AROUND TARGET WORD / PHRASE
340 CLS                        'Clear Screen
350 LOCATE 3                   'Vertical Tab To Third Line
360 FOR I=1 TO N               'Start Display/Print Loop
370 X=(L+I) MOD N: GOSUB 440       'Print routine With emphasized Target
380 NEXT I                     'Continue With Loop
382 PRINT
383 PRINT "Page ";A$(N+1)"     Line ";C;"     Count to this point ";OC
385 PRINT                      'OC= No. Of Occurrences Of Target Word/Phrase
387 IF PAPER THEN LPRINT CHR$(13);"Page ";A$(N+1)"     Line ";C;"     Count t
o this point ";OC
388 IF PAPER THEN LPRINT CHR$(13);CHR$(13)
390 PRINT:COLOR 0,7:PRINT"Press any key to continue"
400 COLOR 7,0
405 IF PAPER THEN 430
410 IF INKEY$="" THEN 410          'Wait For A Keystroke
430 RETURN                     'End Of Subroutine
432 '
440 '                          PRINT SUBROUTINE WITH EMPHASIZED TARGET
450 IF I=(N+1)/2 THEN COLOR 0,7 'Inverse Color if Target Line
460 PRINT I;                   'Print Line Number
461 IF PAPER THEN LPRINT I;
470 COLOR 7,0                  'Reset Color
475 PRINT TAB(6) ". . . ";
476 IF PAPER THEN LPRINT TAB(6) ". . . ";
480 B$=A$(X)
490 LL=INSTR(B$,W$)
508 IF PAPER AND LL<1 THEN LPRINT B$
510 IF LL<1 THEN PRINT B$:GOTO 590         'Print Line Without Target Word/Phrase
515 IF I=(N+1)/2 THEN OC=OC+1
520 PRINT LEFT$(B$,LL-1);          'Print Line Upto Target
521 IF PAPER THEN LPRINT LEFT$(B$,LL-1);
530 COLOR 0,7                  'Inverse Color
540 PRINT W$;                  'Print Target
541 IF PAPER THEN LPRINT CHR$(14);CHR$(15);W$;CHR$(18);CHR$(20);
550 COLOR 7,0                  'Reset Color
560 LL=LL+LEN(W$)              '
570 B$=MID$(B$,LL)             'Truncate Line
580 GOTO 490                   'Look For More Occurances Of Target Word/Phrase
590 RETURN
```